Organizational Communication and Sustainable Development:
ICTs for Mobility

Anette Hallin
Royal Institute of Technology, Sweden

Tina Karrbom Gustavsson
Royal Institute of Technology, Sweden

T0338752

INFORMATION SCIENCE REFERENCE

Hershey · New York

Director of Editorial Content: Kristin Klinger
Senior Managing Editor: Jamie Snavely
Assistant Managing Editor: Michael Brehm
Publishing Assistant: Sean Woznicki
Typesetter: Kurt Smith, Michael Brehm
Cover Design: Lisa Tosheff
Printed at: Yurchak Printing Inc.

Published in the United States of America by
Information Science Reference (an imprint of IGI Global)
701 E. Chocolate Avenue
Hershey PA 17033
Tel: 717-533-8845
Fax: 717-533-8661
E-mail: cust@igi-global.com
Web site: http://www.igi-global.com/reference

Library of Congress Cataloging-in-Publication Data

Organizational communication and sustainable development : ICTs for mobility /
Anette Hallin and Tina Karrbom Gustavsson, editors.
   p. cm.
  Includes bibliographical references and index.
  Summary: "This book covers the use, effects, potentials and limitations of
new technology for information and communication in social settings and aims
to develop an understanding of different perspectives of sustainable
development"--Provided by publisher.
  ISBN 978-1-60566-822-2 (hardcover) -- ISBN 978-1-60566-823-9 (ebook) 1.
Communication in organizations. 2. Corporate governance. 3. Management
information systems. 4. Sustainable development. I. Hallin, Anette, 1969-
II. Gustavsson, Tina Karrbom, 1973-
  HD30.3.O724 2010
  658.4'5--dc22
                 2009026086

British Cataloguing in Publication Data
A Cataloguing in Publication record for this book is available from the British Library.

Table of Contents

Section 1
Sustainable Development

Section 2
Communicating Sustainability

Section 3
Sustainable Communication

Section 4
Critical Perspectives

Detailed Table of Contents

Section 1
Sustainable Development

Chapter 1

ICTs for Business Enterprise Mobility: Mobile Communications, Mobility and the Creation
of Sustainable Value 1

Per Andersson, Centre for Information and Communication Research (CIC), Stockholm School of Economics, Sweden

Susanne Sweet, Centre for Information and Communication Research (CIC), Stockholm School of Economics, Sweden

Christopher Rosenqvist, Centre for Information and Communication Research (CIC), Stockholm School of Economics, Sweden

This chapter puts focus on and relates to three central concepts "sustainability", "mobility", and "customer value". The results from two long-term lines of research and two research programs are combined in the chapter. The first focuses on the effects of the use of new wireless communication and information on organizations in terms of changed "mobility" of people and artifacts within and between organizations. The second research area addressed is that of social and environmental enterprise and business. The chapter has the aim and ambition to contribute to a conceptual discussion on sustainability, mobility, and value. Based on the discussion, the chapter presents a set of propositions to help advance research in this relatively new research field. Short empirical examples are presented, followed by a concluding discussion and a set of propositions for further research.

Chapter 2

ICT Instruments as Possible Support for the Equal Distribution of Population 19

Aleksandra Djukic, Faculty of Architecture, University of Belgrade, Serbia

Vesna Tomic, Ski resorts of Serbia, Belgrade, Serbia

Unequal city development, namely the faster development of large centers and concentration of power, globalization and local specificities in certain locations, have caused a lack of balance between large city centers and smaller settlements and villages. In Serbia, there are major differences in the level of development, as well as in cultural features of settlements. There are significant economic differences between settlements in the north, the east, and the south of the country, since settlements developed in valleys and hence had better traffic communication, and could therefore be competitive and stay abreast of transformations. Smaller settlements and villages (especially those along the borders, in National parks and in difficult to access rural regions), are marginalized, and face many problems, most often caused by lack of infrastructure, decrease of the number of inhabitants, the dissolution of the secondary and tertiary sector. Today, a quarter of the total population lives in the capital city of Belgrade, while a considerable number of settlements are completely shutting down. These settlements once had their identity and a harmonious balance of all elements constituting the life of the community and the individual. A distinctive social aspect contributed to a rich cultural heritage, but over time this was gradually lost and begins to disappear. The question is if any of the processes (globalization, technological revolution), which contribute to the demographic and economic decline of rural regions, could form a basis for renewal. A classical planner's approach would imply the networking of settlements and providing equal population distribution by investing in infrastructure and providing conditions for settlements through the development of central functions, requiring considerable investments. The other possibility relies on the development of information and communication technologies (ICT), which could provide for many necessities: access to and exchange of information, paying bills and ordering products from a distance, working from home, meetings via internet conferences, etc. The use of internet technologies in order to develop settlements, by converting traditional into "net" technologies, can make up for disadvantages of life in smaller settlements and enable their revitalization, by networking them into a global net of settlements, without geographical borders and limits.

Chapter 3

Information and Communication Technology (ICT) changes the concept of place and social life. Researchers should find some solutions about how to combine ICT with sustainable construction to revitalize an existing neighborhood and to create a new model for growing areas especially in small cities. The objectives of this study are to search for new ways to create sustainable communities with the sustainable use of ICTs, to discuss the advantages and disadvantages and the use of ICTs in cities, to put a new approach as 'eco-tech' city, and to explore the potential ways of creating sustainability in practice. The study summarizes the advantages and disadvantages of the use of ICTs in cities and describes smart city and eco-tech city concepts. The following part, which is consisted of a discussion of urban planning and design, incorporating ICT for the construction of sustainable communities, explores the prospect that dehumanized communication can be ameliorated through progressive, innovative and green urban planning and design strategies.

Martin Kreeb, Potsdam University of Management and Communication, Germany
Georg Dold, Potsdam University of Management and Communication, Germany
Hans-Dietrich Haasis, Bremen University, Institute for Production and Logistics, ISL, Germany

This chapter describes concept, design and future implementation of a knowledge based Internet portal - ECORadar Shakti India - aimed at small and medium sized enterprises of the Indian megacity Hyderabad. The portal sets out to use the simplest and most persuasive means to motivate and enable sustainability management in those enterprises that have so far taken little or no interest in this aspect of management. Hyderabad, a prime example of an emerging mega city, is a laboratory where the goal of becoming a sustainable mega city faces of difficult challenges. The intention to work towards a sustainable future will be difficult to achieve without adequate data, tools and implementation strategies. The research idea of this approach in Hyderabad was set up in a research program funded by the German Federal Ministry of Education and Research (BMBF).

Section 2
Communicating Sustainability

Arun Sahay, Strategic Management, Management Development Institute, Gurgaon, India

Despite business's business being business, the business owners have been doing acts of benevolence depending upon the owner's religion, faith, values and beliefs. Establishment of temples, mosques, churches, schools, hospitals etc. has been usual practice through which firms have shown their concern about the society and made contribution to the social cause. However, of late, it is observed that progressive businesses, after understanding the nuances of sustainable development and its reporting, have moved from philanthropic mode of contributing to society to the concept of Corporate Social Responsibity (CSR). Some of them have gone beyond CSR and have entered the domain of Strategic CSR. In the process, a new concept of Corporate Sustainability, which is based on Triple Bottom-line concept, has emerged in strategic management literature. Thus, today CSR activities are being aligned with the business strategy of the firm. In the developed countries, firms are increasingly integrating CSR with the core business activities e.g. innovation, marketing, finance etc. This article attempts to look into firm's CSR and corporate sustainability with special reference to a developing country - India.

Cecilia Mark-Herbert, Department of Economics, The Swedish University of Agriculture
Sciences, Uppsala, Sweden
Jonas Rorarius, Department of Economics, The Swedish University of Agriculture Sciences,
Uppsala, Sweden

Corporate needs to assess, evaluate and communicate sustainability efforts are evident in the increasing use of management tools. A selected set of commonly used sustainability management tools are compared in this study with a key question in mind: how well does each of them provide grounds for assessing and communicating corporate sustainability ambitions? Each of the tools reflects different aspects of responsible conduct; expressed in economic, environmental, social and temporal & spatial terms. They represent a partial foundation for ex ante assessment and ex post evaluation and, as such, grounds for providing information and communicating. Selecting suitable tools for making sustainability management assessments presupposes an awareness of a need to integrate the perspectives on sustainability as well as finding a suitable marketing tool mix.

Elke Perl-Vorbach, Institute of Systems Sciences, Innovation and Sustainability
Research Karl Franzens University Graz, Austria

The collection, managing and communication of environmental information are nowadays seen as an essential prerequisite for sustainable development. However, ways of generating and exchanging environmental information differ within and between companies. Moreover, the use of highly sophisticated environmental information systems can still be seen at in its infancy. The aim of this chapter is thus to assess ways of the application of environmental information systems for sustainable development, both within and between organizations, can be supported. An empirical analysis of those barriers and obstacles, which inhibit the implementation of environmental information systems, is also carried out. Additionally, we also pay attention to forms of industry wide environmental protection, and take existing cooperation and relationships, sustainable supply chains, and recycling networks into account. For this purpose, basic conditions for the inter-organizational exchange of environmental information are investigated. This provides the basis for identifying means to strengthen the position of environmental protection in connection with inter-organizational exchange of environmental information. Improved methods of implementing environmental information systems within and between companies are developed, thus promoting greater cooperation for sustainable development.

Section 3
Sustainable Communication

Jakob Lauring, Department of Management, Aarhus School of Business, Aarhus University,
Denmark
Anders Klitmøller, Department of Management, Aarhus School of Business, Aarhus University,
Denmark

Based on a qualitative study of 14 knowledge intensive companies, this chapter suggests that multi-cultural and multilingual firms are faced with certain challenges in the attempt to fruitfully utilize the diverse background of their workforce. Firstly, through informal settings, the employees to create social boundaries within the firm use native languages strategically. Secondly, even though the introduction of English as cooperate language might solve some communication issues, it tends to render the communication less nuanced, thereby reducing the use of human resources within the firm. Thirdly, ICT does not necessarily solve communication problems within a given company. It can even be used as a social 'tool' to uphold social boundaries or social fragmentation. It is suggested that in order to address these challenges, the management should seek to reward not only individual employees, but also expand the notion of performance to include the collectivity of the workplace.

Chapter 9

Maria Adenfelt, Department of Business Studies, Uppsala University, Sweden
Katarina Lagerström, Department of Business Administration, School of Business,
Economics and Law, University of Gothenburgn Sweden

Globalization trends make the task of revisiting the nature of the organization of global development projects (GDPs) within MNCs imperative. In this study, GDPs are viewed as contemporary ventures that seek scale economies in response to opportunities and threats posed by globalization trends. Our focus is to obtain a better understanding of how communication is managed and organized in GDPs. The study is of a GDP with the aim of developing a common global product to be used by all subsidiaries in an MNC, but with openings for local market adaptations. The empirical findings show that: (1) the management had two goals with the project, which were conveyed and understood differently depending on organizational level and organizational belonging, (2) the administrative heritage of the MNC influenced the use of information communication technology for sharing information and knowledge, and (3) the impact of frequency and structure of communication for information processing.

Chapter 10

Mattias Jacobsson, Umeå School of Business, Umeå University, Sweden
Anneli Linde, Umeå School of Business, Umeå University, Sweden
Henrik Linderoth, University of Skövde, Sweden

The aim of this chapter is to draw attention to the use of ICT in the building and construction industry with a special interest in the day-to-day activities of those companies that are working to develop more environmentally friendly and sustainable production processes. The chapter is based on a comprehensive survey of ICT use and attitudes to environmental related issues in middle and large sized construction companies in Sweden and two case studies: One of ICT use in a larger Swedish building and construction company and one of communication, coordination, and decision making processes in a construction project. Based on the empirical data we argue that in order to enhance a more environmentally friendly building and construction industry there is a need for a more genuine cooperation and knowledge sharing between different actors both in crossing project boundaries as well as overriding contractual limitations.

Decisions in a construction project must be taken earlier in the process and construction companies need to focus more on those processes over which they actually do have power.

This chapter deals with the challenge of ensuring and sustaining cultural competitiveness in a globalised world where control and management tend to be made at a distance. The authors illustrate this by arguing that family-run businesses have a special culture that makes them good at creating and taking part in innovative networks. Today this culture is however threatened. Implementation of technologies for controlling and governing at a distance destroy this special family-run business culture. As a solution to this problem the authors suggest that new technologies of communication have the potential to strengthen the ability to create innovative networks. New technologies of communication do this when they give rise to alternative forms of communication and thus complement management based on "controlling and acting at a distance".

This chapter is based on the assumption that keeping the number and length of business and commuting trips at reasonable levels could contribute to reaching targets of environmental sustainability. The authors highlight a couple of options for reducing or avoiding business trips and commuting through workplace location or improved use of communications. They present case studies concerning travel and communications, carried out by using diaries and interviews. They also present relevant literature on social practices and sustainability goals in relation to use of ICT. The aim is to shed light on variation in the use of travel and communications on an individual level in work life. The case studies illustrate that such variation is mainly due to the concrete practices involved in execution of professional duties and roles. Duties that involve a clearly defined end result or product being delivered regularly by the member of staff are correlated to clearly defined needs for communications. Less clearly defined end results of the work duties seem to make it harder for the individual to plan and perform communication and travel in a more energy saving way. The difference in professional duties can thus be expressed in terms of clarity and maturity. Another factor that affect who can replace travel with ICTs is relations of power, e.g., when a purchaser dictates the terms for a subcontractor concerning how and where to "deliver" his working time, service or product. The importance of clarity, maturity and power aspects means that professional practices need to be studied at a detailed level to find out who could substitute ICTs for travel and how this could be done.

Section 4
Critical Perspectives

This chapter, recognizing that the main communication concepts are deeply geographical in their inner nature, has the intent of introducing an analysis of the connection there should be between geography, communication, organization and sustainability. The author will use the geography of information as the main framework to detect these links and to present the analysis of a regional communication infrastructure to understand how the Internet can be pivotal to communication and local development strategies. The analysis will present regional communication policies, projects and practices to understand if these are positive or negative forces for a regional sustainable development.

In Africa, family structures are today committed or involved in the dynamics of social transformation which jeopardize their mode of constitution their future, the sustenance of intergenerational and individual relationships as well as the traditional systems of social relationships based on direct and personal communication. This chapter is a sociological analysis of the future of the family through its relationship with NICT notably the Internet and the cellular telephone. The analyses lay emphasizes on the consequences of NICTs on the modalities for the constitution of marriage covenants, family relationships and intergenerational transfers.

In this chapter the mutual shaping of the technology and gender is analyzed in relation to the phenomenon of gender digital divide. The discussion starts with the re-construction of the theoretical background, shedding light on different analytical approaches to technological development. The gender blind perspective of mainstream technology studies is uncovered; looking at theoretical contributes of feminist and gender studies. This positioning is aimed to consider the cultural and material aspects involved in the digital gender gap. The chapter leads to a general conclusion: it is of utmost importance that researchers, decision-makers and professionals in Information Technology field take into account that all spheres inhabited by human beings are inevitably gendered. The gender mainstreaming approach may inform the construction of a gender-aware research agenda and the identification of the following transformative actions. The synergy among researchers, practitioners and decision-makers at political and business level is crucial for a gender-sensitive and sustainable development.

Foreword

SUSTAINABLE DEVELOPMENT AND ORGANIZATIONAL COMMUNICATION: ICTS FOR MOBILITY – SOME REFLECTIONS FOR GLOBAL RESILIENCE

Since the presentation of the World Commission on Environment and Development report *Our Common Future*, 'sustainable development' has become an area of practical, theoretical and political importance (WCED - World Commission on Environment and Development, 1987). How we should live in order not to endanger the possibilities of future generations is a crucial question, not only important for economic and environmental reasons, but also for ethical reasons. And even though there are many different political opinions regarding the implications, there seems to be a broad agreement about the importance of the question.

So far, most of the attention to 'sustainable development' has been given to issues regarding economy and the natural environment, which of course is good. Social or cultural aspects of 'sustainable development' that have been studied concern many different aspects such as the distribution of economic and material resources (i.e. welfare issues from a global perspective); the way we interact on a workplace or between suppliers on a global supply-chain; how crucial studies and knowledge in language and culture are to a sustainable development (Packalén, 2010); or public health issues, both regionally and globally (Rosling *et al*, 2006). To me, an important way of approaching social aspects of 'sustainable development' is to talk about values, confronting yourself and others with what is important in life, for humanity and for you personally. To me as a privileged citizen of a materially wealthy Western country, a good and respectful dialogue is an important cornerstone for understanding the culture and life circumstances of people in other parts of the world than the privileged West and thereby become and stay connected with those in less materially wealthy countries.

The question raised in this book, how organizational communication can be understood from a sustainability perspective when ICTs are involved, is new and interesting. What does the good conversation of two people sitting in the same room have to do with ICTs? We know that ICTs have involved great possibilities and led to improvements in organizational life, for instance the added possibility of staying connected in real time with people around the world without having to travel so much physically. We know today that we travel more despite such ICT advances, that such technologies still promise more than they can deliver, and that they have had not only positive effects. Instead, ICTs seem to have increased our exchange with people, making us travel even more. It has also affected our communication patterns – today we seem quite careless with what we write, how much we write and to whom we send our e-mail messages, which is a huge difference compared to the 'art' of writing letters by hand, only fifteen years ago.

And even though technology is constantly improving, the 'killer application' is yet to come, because there always seem to be a bug in the technologies we use, turning our hopes to despair when not having enough knowledge of how to fix it. The greening of the ICT-industry has only begun, and there is still a long way to go before we have solutions to problems regarding energy and the scarcity of raw material used in for example computers.

Google is maybe the most prominent and largest service provider on the Internet and I think it may serve as a good illustration of why the topic of this book, how organizational communication can be understood from a sustainability perspective when ICTs are involved, is important. (Google has company, however, by Microsoft, Apple, Yahoo!, the search engine of Ask and many more.)

As one of the dominant factories of the information age, the server and computing halls of Google consume much more electricity than the industrial brick-and-mortar factories of the early 20th century. In The Dalles, a city at the Columbia River in the north of the US state of Oregon, there used to be an aluminium plant that was heavy on its electricity consumption. This plant is shut down, but just next doors two factory halls, as big as soccer fields, have recently been raised for Google. In each hall, several thousands of servers work 24/7 to provide us with YouTube videos, weather forecasts, daily news or photos of friends and family, but also to enable business transactions of money transfers, contacts throughout value chains, or the route planning of planes in the air. Each server hosts many processors that use as much energy as a fast hot plate. (Another astonishing figure is that a 'life' on Second Life is said to use as much energy as an average person in real life in Brazil…). Estimations name about 3 million server halls in use worldwide that is increasing exponentially through the social networking of people. Early 2008, 65 million users were part of the digital meeting point of Facebook, more than 200 million traded on eBay, and 280 million had e-mail accounts in Hotmail alone (Rohwetter, 2008).

Processors, servers and server halls need to be cooled, and air-conditioning work hard to keep them at low working temperature. When planes are flying into or leaving Silicon Valley airports, around the headquarters of Google in Mountain View, Yahoo! in Sunnyvale and Apple in Cupertino, it is well known that they feel bumps when flying over the hot air of the air-conditioning parts of server halls of these corporations.

The effect of this increase of digital transactions through ICTs is an electricity use that equals the emission of greenhouse gases by the global air traffic; that also equals the electricity production of Vattenfall, one of the dominant electricity producing companies in the world. This has made the ICT industry aware of their environmental burden and initiatives for sustainable development appear; one example is that Green IT has become an important aspect of the yearly CeBit, the world's largest trade fair showcase for ICT solutions for home and work environments; another example is the Climate Savers Computing Initiative that by 2010 wants to half the electricity use of computers.[1]

So far, the illustration of electricity-consuming server halls of Google and the like has linked the ICT industry to sustainable development, but what about organizational communication? Well, many of these corporations are stuck in managerial incentives programmes that focus on economic dimensions only. While Chief Information Officers (CIO) are developing server halls, their electricity costs are more often than not identified as indirect costs of building or maintenance managers. CIOs thus prefer cheaper rather than green servers low on electricity use. Also, green thinking has yet to become part of the agenda of CIOs. Internet business cases have to rethink their environmental burden and take more responsibility for sustainable development and the way ICT can help reducing the environmental load and reaching global resilience[2]. Thus, the agenda of sustainable development and corporate social responsibility (Dobers, 2009a; Dobers, 2009b) should clearly become part of management and organizational communication.

In order to find answers to these pressing questions, the international community of academia, business, politics, administrations and the big volunteer corps must work together, taking shared responsibility in thinking, communicating and acting. Areas of 'sustainable development', 'organizational communication' and 'ICTs' have an advantage since they all are transdisciplinary in character. This means that they build not only on interdisciplinary theoretical grounds and on many different knowledge interests (Dobers *et al*, 2001), but that they encompass a number of practical fields, having the possibilities of drawing from all of these. In fact, the responsibility for solving the problems within each area – as well as within the area at their intersection – is a common responsibility.

So is ICT the answer to a more sustainable world? Does ICTs improve organizational communication from a social, cultural, environmental and economic perspective? The three areas that this book aims at bringing together – 'Sustainable development', 'Organizational communication' and 'ICTs' – are three interesting and rapidly expanding fields of scientific inquiry, and their intersection provides several challenging questions, both for scholars and practitioners. The three fields share a common interest for normative claims, which can be explained with the fact that they more or less are driven by the common vision to solve problems; globally as well as locally. Since the three areas draw from a wide range of fields, scholars sometimes find it difficult to find room in the established scientific community. This is why publications like this book are important; they bring together scholars and practitioners from various fields, building a common ground that is necessary if we are to succeed in creating a fair, just and sustainable development.

Peter Dobers
School of Sustainable Development of Society and Technology
Mälardalen University, Sweden

Peter Dobers *has an interest in how ideas of corporate (social) responsibility, guided tours, broadband, city images or sustainable development travel the world, and are enabled or disabled. He holds a chair in management and sustainable development at Mälardalen University and is currently associate dean of the Faculty for Humanities, Social and Caring Sciences. He has also been visiting professor at Umeå School of Business and Economics in the years of 2006-2008. Dobers has published widely in areas such as corporate (social) responsibility, sustainable development, urban studies and modern information and communication technology and is frequently commissioned as guest speaker by industry and municipalities.*

REFERENCES

Dobers, P (ed.) 2009a. *Corporate social responsibility. Challenges and practices.* Santérus Academic Press Sweden: Stockholm.

Dobers, P. 2009b. Corporate social responsibility. Management and methods. *Corporate Social Responsibility and Environmental Management 16*(4).

Dobers, P, Strannegård, L and Wolff, R. 2001. Knowledge interests in corporate environmental management. *Business Strategy and the Environment 10*(6): pp. 335-343.

Packalén, S. 2010. Culture and sustainability. *Corporate Social Responsibility and Environmental Management 17*(2).

Rohwetter, M, "Digitaler Hunger", *Die Zeit,* No. 10, 2008, pp. 21.

Rosling, H, Lindstrand, A, Bergström, S, Rubenson, B and Stenson, B. 2006. *Global health. An introductory textbook.* Studentlitteratur: Lund.

WCED - World Commission on Environment and Development. 1987. *Our common future.* Oxford University Press: Oxford.

ENDNOTES

[1]   http://www.climatesaverscomputing.org
[2]   For the concept of 'resilience', see for instance the Stockholm Resilience Center at www.stockholmresilience.org

Preface

In this book, three different but converging processes are investigated; sustainable development, globalization and technical development. Each process is complicated and multi-faceted, but here, their mutual interaction, effects and possibilities have gained attention and interest.

"Sustainable development" are words of honor in many settings today, due to the world-wide debate on how we shall lead our lives and form our societies so that the generations to come have good possibilities of leading their lives. According to the classic definition in the so called "Brundtland-report", sustainable development involves economic, environmental as well as social consideration, and in the report, social sustainability is defined as the building of long term, stable and dynamic societies where basic human needs are fulfilled, but where local and regional values, traditions and actions are acknowledged and respected at the same time[1]. And in a time that has witnessed and to a large extent embraced a rapid development of technologies that in some cases seem to threaten these very basic ideas of social and cultural society, there is a pressing need to dig deeper into how technology – or rather ICTs - is related to social and cultural sustainability. Moreover, due to the process of globalization, where the mobility of people, goods and ideas is a general feature, this is a relevant issue world-wide and therefore this book will explore this question by, as previously described, going into the heart of human activities: communication.

This book is thus about the use, effects, potentials and limitations of new technology for information and communication in social settings such as private corporations, organizations, the web, societies and families. The overall aim of the book is to develop an understanding of how the different perspectives of sustainable development, globalization and technical development interact, through managerial as well as general human actions, and which measures can be taken to secure sustainable development. This means that this book, rather than answering the overall question of how mobility can meet sustainability in contemporary organizational communication, discusses and highlights different aspects of the issue.

As will become obvious to the reader, the book contains a variety of perspectives, from different parts of the world, different theoretical fields as well as different approaches. Thus, the book is to be seen as a patch work in the word's most positive sense, which rather than being the ultimate collection building a coherent theory, brings together a collage of texts on the theme. In this book, different perspectives on organizational communication and sustainable development are displayed, indicating how the central concepts of "organizational communication", "sustainable development" and "ICTs for mobility" can and are interpreted in a variety of ways.

THEMES AND CHALLENGES

Reading the chapters, it becomes clear that there is a realm of concepts associated with "sustainable development", such as "Corporate Social Responsibility", "sustainable construction", "green strategies", "sustainability tools" and "philanthropy" which reflect the wide spread of the sustainability idea into different theoretical and practical settings. It is clear that "sustainable development" as a concept is political, in the sense that there are several related concepts, framing the basic concept differently. At the same time, the chapters in this book also show that sustainable development is not merely a question of rhetoric – the book contains several examples of actions undertaken, aiming at creating a better world for future generations.

Also, it becomes clear that there are more similarities than differences in the usage of ICTs independent of the social setting. Most organizations and corporations use Internet, E-mail, Intranet, digital communities, mobile phones etc – ICTs is a global phenomenon. The variety of information and communication tools and strategies is limited and the arguments for using ICTs are often similar independent on the setting – often cost- and time efficiency as well as environmental-arguments are used. However, several authors in the book also draws our attention to the down sides of using ICTs, such as information overload and the problems of decisions being made from a distance, with little or no knowledge and awareness of local effects. Is that sustainable communication?

STRUCTURE OF THE BOOK

There are of course several ways of structuring a book with chapters of such broad scope. We have chosen a thematic structure including four themes: Sustainable Development, Communicating Sustainability, Sustainable Communication and Critical Perspectives. In each section there are chapters ranging from basic research to case descriptions and more visionary texts. Our hope is that by putting the texts together this way, the reading will evoke new insights as well as new, fruitful questions.

The first theme, *Sustainable Development*, contains chapters about how ICTs can contribute to the work with and for sustainable development in organizations on local, regional, national and international levels. Here, Per Andersson, Susanne Sweet and Christopher Rosenqvist have contributed with a chapter about how the spread and use of mobile phones and wireless services impact the business and development in developing countries. The authors introduce the concept of value, a concept they argue is of increasing importance but difficult to define or measure. They elaborate on a conceptual framework that addresses some contemporary issues of the new emerging, wireless world such as: the 'value' created by new wireless applications. The chapter provides an interesting discussion of the value of mobility for economic sustainability.

In the following chapter, Aleksandra Djukic and Vesna Tomic discuss how ICTs can be used in the development of a country that has an unequal distribution of population which, the authors argue, is a sustainability issue since the rapid urbanization leads to the emptying of certain regions, and thus the overthrow and challenge of local values and traditions which instead might help build the country. The case they explore is Serbia, but according to the authors all SEE-countries (South Eastern Europe) share the same challenge today.

The next chapter takes us from the national level to the city level. Here, Özge Yalciner Ercoskun provides a thorough overview of the 'eco-tech city' concept and an evaluation of the use of ICTs in cities with the aim of exploring the potential ways of creating sustainable cities. The chapter argues that in this development, urban planners as well as policy makers must take an active role in incorporating ICTs for the construction of sustainable communities, in order to avoid dehumanized communication.

Ercoskun's chapter is followed by a chapter which illustrates how the work with creating the sustainable city can be carried out in practice. Written by Martin Kreeb, Georg Dold and Hans-Dietrich Haasis, the chapter reports on the ECORadar-Shakti, which is an interactive internet portal aimed at helping and motivating managers of small- and middle sized companies in Hyperbad, India, to work more with sustainability issues. This chapter, being an in-depth description of the project, highlights the problems and success factors of these kinds of initiatives.

Communicating Sustainability is the theme for the second section, which includes chapters that all deals with the possibilities and problems of communicating sustainability, with or without ICTs. The section begins with the chapter by Arun Sahay who sketches the development of how businesses have gone from being philanthropic to corporate social responsible as the CSR-activities of the firm have been aligned with the business strategies of the firm. This way, Sahay shows how sustainability are much older than the concepts we use to denote these kinds of activities today, but how "CSR" and similar concepts have forced companies to adopt these ideas into their ordinary activities and into their strategies in order to be able to communicate them externally.

The chapter written by Cecilia Mark-Herbert and Jonas Rorarius looks at different tools that are used for assessing organizational sustainability. By evaluating the tools according to the framework proposed here, the authors conclude that the different tools are geared differently – some put larger emphasis on economic sustainability, or environmental sustainability, for example – an insight which is important, not only for those interested in selecting evaluation tools for organizational sustainability, but for organizations' possibilities of communicating sustainability to external audiences.

Elke Perl-Vorbach's chapter takes an interorganizational approach to the communication of sustainability. Based on an empirical survey of 138 Austrian companies, she draws the conclusion that companies are surprisingly unaware of the advantages of interorganizational cooperation regarding reaching sustainability. This indicates a need both of more research, as well as the dissemination of this knowledge from academia to practitioners.

Sustainable communication is the book's third theme. Here, the chapters discuss communication from a social and cultural sustainability, departing from case studies in companies, projects as well as businesses of various kinds.

Anders Klitmøller and Jakob Lauring depart from a qualitative study of a number of knowledge intensive companies and suggest that multi-cultural and multilingual firms are faced with certain challenges in the attempt to fruitfully utilize the diverse background of their workforce. They argue that native languages are used strategically by the employees to create social boundaries within the firm and that even though the introduction of English as cooperate language might solve some communication issues, it tends to render the communication less nuanced, thereby reducing the innovative potential within the firm. According to Klitmøller and Lauring ICT does not necessarily solve communication problems within a given company but may instead be used as a social 'tool' to uphold social boundaries and fragmentation. It is suggested that it is necessary to expand the notion of performance to include the collectivity of the workplace.

In their chapter Maria Adenfelt and Katarina Hamberg Lagerström provides a better understanding of the management and organization of global development projects (GDP) with focus on communication and coordination. The study is based on a GDP developing and implementing a common IT-system open for local market adaptations. The authors elaborate on the duality of what was actually communicated to the project members and what actually were the intentions from management. Adenfelt and Hamberg Lagerström show that the duality had negative effects on the project outcome. Thus, communication was not to be understood as contributing to social sustainability.

In the next chapter Mattias Jacobsson, Anneli Linde and Henrik Linderoth elaborate on challenges in the construction sector in Sweden. Based on several empirical studies of the construction sector the authors discuss challenges that relate to the construction sector becoming more sustainable. The focus of this chapter is the area of environmental management and its relations to communication and information practise in construction companies.

The authors Per Forsberg and Mikael Lind focus on family-run businesses when illustrating the challenges of ensuring and sustaining cultural competitiveness in family-run businesses in a globalised world where control and management tend to be made at a distance. The authors argue that family-run businesses have a special culture that makes them good at creating and taking part in innovative networks – a culture that is threatened by the implementation of ICTs for controlling and governing at a distance. As a solution to this problem the authors suggest that new technologies of communication have the potential to strengthen the ability to create innovative networks.

Greger Henriksson and Minna Räsänen take a sustainability perspective on travelling. They base their chapter on the assumption that keeping the number and length of business and commuting trips at reasonable levels could contribute to reaching targets of environmental sustainability. The chapter shed light on variation in the use of travel and communications on an individual level in work life and provide some examples of ways in which ICTs may lead to improvements.

The section called *Critical perspectives* gathers chapters of various kinds raising issues stemming from neglect of all dimensions of the communication process; cultural specificities as well as gender problems when it comes to implementing and using ICTs.

In his chapter, Marco Tortora uses geography of communication as a theoretical framework to understand the issue of organizational communication. After illustrating the framework with an example from Tuscany, Italy, Tortora provides a brief empirical example – also from Tuscany – which points to the difficulties that can arise in the geography of communication due to a mismatch between the local and the regional level. If organizational communication is to be sustainable, argues Tortora, all aspects of the geography of communication must be taken into account; i.e. it is not sufficient only to build infrastructure, for example for ICTs, those that are to use it must become involved so that the infrastructure is filled with relevant content.

Honoré Mimche and Norbert Tohnain Lengha's chapter takes us to Africa, and discusses the impact of new information and communication technologies (NICTs) on the organization of the family. Despite its advantages, Mimche and Lengha points to the problems of NICTs when it comes to upholding cultural traditions regarding family matters, which can be discussed from a cultural sustainability-perspective. To what extent should we allow the new technologies change our societies is the overall question that this chapter evokes.

The final chapter in this section, written by Michaela Cozza looks at technology from a gender perspective. There is, argues Cozza, a gender digital divide, which is understudied, due to "gender blindness". This affects the way we perceive new technology, and Cozza's conclusion is that even though there have been attempts to deal with it, the big question still remains: "how is technology gendered"?

TARGET AUDIENCE

As should be clear from the brief description of the different chapters above, this book encompasses chapters discussing the issue of organizational communication, sustainable development and ICTs both theoretically and practically, and our hope is that this book will be beneficial to a range of different readers; scholars and practitioners, managers and others working in organizations interested in a deeper understanding of the area of sustainable development, as well as politicians and government authorities.

FINALLY...

The world is always changing – that is what we call development. During the one year long process of editing this book, the word has changed immensely. Financial systems have broken down, there is a worldwide depression and many people have lost their savings and their jobs. This has of course an impact on the three processes we set out studying in the book: sustainable development, globalization and technical development. The conditions for corporations, organizations and individuals to fulfill their goals and dreams and to develop new and more sustainable ways to communicate have changed. However, the question of how how mobility can meet sustainability in contemporary organizational communication is still highly pressing. What are the advantages of ICTs? Which are its negative aspects? Which problems are solved and which are created?

This book is a timely contribution to researchers, politicians, students and decision makers with a fresh and thought provoking discussion on ICTs in relation to sustainable development and communication, an area of growing importance. This way, our hope is that the book will not only provide answers, but stimulate new questions and studies regarding the cross roads of sustainable development, globalization and technical development.

ENDNOTE

[1]   WCED - World Commission on Environment and Development. 1987. *Our common future*. Oxford University Press: Oxford.

Acknowledgment

We have both been working as ass. Professors at the Department of Industrial Management at The Royal Institute of Technology in Stockholm, Sweden for several years. Our research has focused on the areas of organization studies, industrial management, project management and communication as well as the managing and organizing of cities. During the last couple of years, our interest in the area of sustainable development has grown and we have attended interesting national and international conferences linking organizational research with sustainable development research. This book can be understood as our way of further establishing such a linkage. We have also written texts on CSR and organizations, for example "Managing Death – Corporate Social Responsibility and Tragedy" in *Corporate Social Responsibility and Environmental Management* (2009; 16:4).

Apparently, we are not the only ones who finds the connection between organizational studies and sustainable development interesting, in fact, the response to our call for chapters to this book was overwhelming, not only in number of submitted abstracts, but in the variety of fields and perspectives which were and are represented by the authors of the call. The cross-section of "Organizational communication", "Sustainable Development" and "ICTs for mobility" is obviously interested for many, both theoretically and practically. This means that the task of editing this book has involved several challenges. However, we have had great help by all the reviewers in the double-blind review process. Our deepest gratitude to all of you:

Sven Antvik, Tech. Lic.
Henrikke Bauman, Ph.D.
Fredrik Barcheus, Ph.D.
Henrik Blomgren, Ph.D.
Pär Blomkvist, Ph.D.
Mats Engwall, Professor
Claes Gustafsson, Professor
Anna Jerbrant, Tech. Lic.
Nina Kivinen, Ph.D.
Fredrik Lagergren, Ph.D.

Joakim Lilliesköld, Ph.D.
Monica Lindgren, Ph.D.
Kent Thoren, Ph.D.
Kristina Palm, Ph.D.
Thomas Westin, Ph.D.
Nina Wormbs, Ph.D.
Adrian Ratkic, Ph.D.
David Sköld, Ph.D.
May-Britt Öhman, Ph.D.

Anette Hallin & Tina Karrbom Gustavsson
Stockholm, May 2009

Section 1
Sustainable Development

Chapter 1
ICTs for Business Enterprise Mobility:
Mobile Communications, Mobility and the Creation of Sustainable Value

Per Andersson
Centre for Information and Communication Research (CIC), Stockholm School of Economics, Sweden

Susanne Sweet
Centre for Information and Communication Research (CIC), Stockholm School of Economics, Sweden

Christopher Rosenqvist
Centre for Information and Communication Research (CIC), Stockholm School of Economics, Sweden

ABSTRACT

This chapter puts focus on and relates to three central concepts "sustainability", "mobility", and "customer value". The results from two long-term lines of research and two research programs are combined in the chapter. The first focuses on the effects of the use of new wireless communication and information on organizations in terms of changed "mobility" of people and artifacts within and between organizations. The second research area addressed is that of social and environmental enterprise and business. The chapter has the aim and ambition to contribute to a conceptual discussion on sustainability, mobility, and value. Based on the discussion, the chapter presents a set of propositions to help advance research in this relatively new research field. Short empirical examples are presented, followed by a concluding discussion and a set of propositions for further research.

THE VALUE OF MOBILITY FOR SUSTAINABILITY?

How can the spread and use of mobile phones and wireless services impact business and development in poor and developing countries? Is there a link between increased *mobility* of business enterprises and citizens in developing countries and economic development of these countries? In addition, if we extend the scope, how can enterprise mobility support issues of environmental sustainability and corporate social responsibility? The problem can also be phrased in theoretical terms: what relation, if any, is there between *mobility*, including the

DOI: 10.4018/978-1-60566-822-2.ch001

value of mobility, and *sustainability* (in broad terms)? The business magazine Forbes (11 Aug 2008) reports a London Business School study that states that every time 10 more people out of 100 start using mobiles, GDP growth rises a half percentage point (p.75).

In this chapter, we approach this and similar observations, but from a business (and user/consumer) perspective, looking at the way business processes supported by wireless information and communication technologies (ICTs) can affect and support sustainability and corporate social responsibility. In "business processes" we include both the entrepreneurial SME, Small and Medium size enterprise, type of business that we can find in developing countries, and the activities of foreign multinational corporations, MNCs in such regions. When talking about environmental sustainability we also extend the geographical scope outside of the developing regions of the world.

This chapter puts focus on and relates to three central concepts "sustainability", "mobility", and (customer) "value". The results from two long-term lines of research and two research programs are combined in the chapter. The first focuses on the effects of the use of new wireless (in combination with wire line) communications and information on organizations in terms of changed work operations, changed modes of organizing, and changed business development. – or decreased – "mobility" of people and artifacts within and between organizations. The second research area addressed is that of social and environmental enterprise and business. This research is focusing on sustainability and Corporate Social Responsibility (CSR) and addresses the move towards more ethical, environmental and social sustainability in production and consumption. The discussion in this chapter connects both to the general research studies on sustainability and corporate responsibility conducted at SuRe[1] and to the recently started project that address sustainability and innovation in poor and emerging markets. The latter research project connects to an emerging line of research

on business at the "base of the pyramid", BoP (c.f. Prahalad & Hart, 2002; Prahalad, 2005, Kandachar & Halme, 2008).

Aim and Structure of the Chapter

The chapter has the aim and ambition to contribute to a conceptual discussion. Following the background we elaborate on three central concepts: sustainability, mobility, and value. Based on this discussion, the aim is also to present a set of propositions to help advance research in this relatively new research field. Short empirical examples are presented, followed in the concluding discussion by a set of propositions for further research.

Two Basic Assumptions

This chapter advances two propositions. *Firstly*, the conceptual framework presented assumes that 'value' created by wireless technologies and applications that enhance 'mobility' can be connected to 'sustainability'. Organizations' and consumers' 'mobility problems', i.e. basically information and communication needs that can be partly solved by the use of wireless solutions, vary. Individual consumers in the same segment and enterprise customers in the same industry or 'user environment' will value different solutions to their problems differently. The extent to which a mobile solution solves a customer's communication and information problem(s) is partly a measure of its value to the customer. The chapter attempts to link user value associated with wireless technology to various aspects of sustainability.

Secondly, linking user value of wireless solutions requires understanding that individual suppliers cannot (and most often do not) create mobile solutions and value in isolation. Value from mobility solutions can only be created in constellations of cooperating actors, in various 'value constellations' using terms of Normann and Ramirez (1993). To make this linkage clear we adopt a systemic perspective, connecting to the systems theory tradition by Churchman (1968) and others, later developed into more *network like*, systemic approaches (e.g. Håkansson 1982, Axelsson and Easton 1992, Håkansson and Snehota 1995). The systemic, network approach assumes that both suppliers and customers – for example users of mobile solutions – are interconnected in both stable and changing constellations and we link these dynamic constellations to sustainability.

SUSTAINABILITY AND MOBILITY: INTRODUCTORY EXAMPLES

Empirical examples of how mobility affects sustainability often focus on transportation and climate issues connected to mobility: communication via phones, web, web cameras, etc. are more often discussed as a way of reducing the need for mobility and thus actual travel, in connection to both business activity and commuting. Additionally, connectivity offered by ICT solutions can lift awareness and impact opinion formation, information sharing and action regarding social and environmental problems.

Widespread globalization of production and consumption brings into focus the need and benefits to monitoring and sharing information regarding the affects of global production and consumption, and via technologies of connectivity significant networks of civil society organizations have been built and continue to increase in their influence regarding sustainability agenda-building and action. Mobile phones, satellite connections and Internet all play a role in diffusing knowledge fast about abuses of human rights, working conditions, environmental damage etc. Similar examples often form the empirical foundations when mobility and (environmental) sustainability are discussed.

A short empirical illustration on Nike can serve as introduction. In the mid- and late 1990s Nike was reported on in media as supporting poor and unethical working conditions in its Vietnamese and Indonesian suppliers' factories. Several human rights and labor organizations protested and focused on getting Nike to take-on increased responsibility in their supply chain. Nike responded to the pressure and in a speech in 1998 Nike CEO Mr. Knight specified Nike's policy on working conditions in its supplier factories, including health and safety standards, introducing a minimum age for workers, inclusion of NGOs to help monitoring factories and make the information publicly available. In an attempt to regain public trust, Nike also installed on-line real time cameras in selected factories that were accessible from Nike's web site making it possible for anyone to view the conditions in the factories. Nike used connectivity technology to both monitor and make transparent its actions regarding social issues of importance to its stakeholders. The Nike example made available information, in real-time, while reducing the need for stakeholders and others to travel and monitor for themselves. This type of 'mobility solution' can be extended to the monitoring of environmental problems or habitats that could be difficult or expensive for humans to reach and monitor. For example, using a combination of ICT monitoring technology to prevent poachers of endangered species or to measure and send important health data of remote eco-systems.

When the link between mobile communications and sustainability are discussed we see a dominance of empirical examples taking the perspective of companies of the Western developed world marketing mobile systems and services to developing countries. Infrastructure system suppliers and mobile network operators are typically in focus. The underlying idea is that developing countries often will take the leap directly into wireless communications, jumping over the step of wire line telephone communications. The fact that this business also can have effects on small-scale business, on business communications, and business entrepreneurship are most often treated as *indirect*. For the global, mobile telephony suppliers and operators it is primarily a question of market expansion, while the effects on e.g. business communications and development in the local countries are secondary, mainly treated as long-term effects and marketing arguments.

However, there are exceptions where Western based firms see the diffusion of mobile communications and the emergence of sustainable development as the primary business. In two of our empirical illustrations we will give examples of this. Furthermore, we believe that we also need to direct our focus primarily on *the ways in which mobile communications affect aspects of sustainability within and between small business firms in developing countries*, starting in the economic sustainability effects, but including also the socio-political and environmental sustainability effects. One of the empirical examples is a case of a locally developed ICT solution in and for the people in a developing country. New systems and services for intra- and inter-organizational communication in local small business contexts in developing countries will have varying effects on different dimensions of sustainability. Our chapter suggests a framework for studying such interdependencies and causalities.

BACKGROUND STUDIES AND NOTES ON METHOD

Methodologically, this study draws both on secondary sources, building on results from previous studies, and on a set of new, preliminary studies of mobile systems in complex enterprise contexts, described below. Important input to this study comes from two previous studies. Our discussion builds on a set of long-term research projects and programs. The chapter combines 1) conceptual and empirical studies on mobile communications (mainly in developed business-world settings), with 2) previous and ongoing sustainability research.

The first set of background studies includes a research project, entitled Organizations Imple-

ment and Use Mobile Solutions – Studies of the Enterprise Market for Wireless Services and Applications, which was organized as a broad, long-term research program of user oriented, business development studies. In total, enterprise users in 20 industrial sectors were covered in the program, with one or several cases in each sector. The aim in all cases was to start with the "user environment", i.e. to select a wide variety of enterprise settings to be able to compare different organizational circumstances and settings in which the new wireless technologies were implemented. General differences and similarities concerning user settings and logics, communication patterns, implementation problems, purchasing and procurement procedures, and more were studied. The project applied a number of different methods to study product development, implementation and use processes. Qualitative, ethnographic approaches were in focus of data collections. Other studies in the overall research program built on a broad set of secondary sources. Andersson et al (2007), reported on a three-year project focusing primarily on enterprise users of wireless information and communication applications. The overall research question guiding the project and studies of mobility-in-use in organizations was: How are new mobile technologies implemented and used in different types of enterprise contexts? The focus on "How"-questions signals an explorative focus with the aim to develop knowledge on how different types of organizations adopt, integrate, and use new wireless solutions. Focus was on the effects on enterprise organization internal and external communication patterns, work practices, organizing processes, knowledge processes, and processes of business development, when implementing new mobile solutions.

The second set of studies relates to a new line of research in the field of business administration that suggests market-based activities and solutions aiming at poverty alleviation and market development by addressing and serving the needs of the poor, conceptualized as the Base of the Pyramid,

BoP[2]. Base of the Pyramid refers to the 4 billion people who live on less than $ 2/day (Kandachar & Halme, 2008) and whose needs go largely unmet. Some of the interest in this approach stems from a recognition that aid and charity based solutions have failed to alleviate poverty and that the income gap between the rich and the poor has continued to widen in spite of international governmental developing efforts and corporate social responsibility programs.

The basic idea behind the approach is that the private sector can contribute to poverty alleviation through entrepreneurial activities that address needs of the people that live at the BoP, by 1) viewing these groups as groups of people making-up viable markets and therefore creating offerings that are based on their needs, and 2) by enhancing innovation at the BoP that will contribute to increased economic activity. Since Prahalad and Hart (2002) introduced the BoP-concept the research field has advanced and several researchers are now also addressing issues of ecological sustainability in relation to BoP-strategies. Potential problems of increased energy consumption and resource depletion, in the wake of increased consumption of 4 billion people, as well as the relation between poverty, dependence and vulnerability with respect to eco-systems and natural resources, are emerging areas of interest to researchers. In particular the relation between BoP-strategies and social and environmental impacts is not well investigated which calls for increased research.

The empirical examples that we have used in this chapter to illustrate our conceptual discussion, are cases collected from different studies of CSR and BoP in connection to the diffusion of information and communication technologies. We have used examples that are using ICT technologies to solve challenges at the Base of the Pyramid and that illustrate mobility and sustainability issues, connecting social with economic development. The three illustrative examples we use are *Digicel* – a mobile telephone operator who creates value

to small business in developing countries; *MyC4* that via a web-platform service connects investors with small entrepreneurs in Africa; and *WIZZIT* – a mobile banking service for the un-banked in South Africa.

Next, we elaborate on each of our three central concepts in focus: sustainability, mobility and value, followed by combining them in a discussion.

SUSTAINABILITY

Sustainability

What do we mean by sustainability in this context? The field of sustainable development can be conceptually broken into three constituent parts: environmental, economic and socio-political sustainability:

There are many definitions of the concept. One of the most cited stems from the UN Commission (UN, 1987): "Sustainable development is development that meets the needs of the present without compromising the ability of future generations to meet their own needs". It contains two key concepts:

- The concept of 'needs', in particular the essential needs of the world's poor, to which overriding priority should be given; and
- The idea of limitations imposed by the state of technology and social organization on the environment's ability to meet present and future needs.

United Nations Division for Sustainable Development lists a very large number of areas as coming within the scope of sustainable development.[3] Some research activities start from this definition to argue that the environment is a combination of nature and culture. The Network of Excellence "Sustainable Development in a Diverse World", sponsored by the European

Figure 1. The concept of sustainable development (retrieved from Wikipedia, 2009)

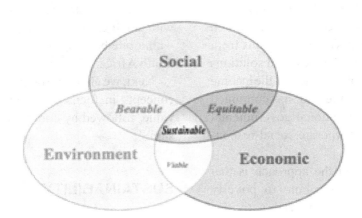

Union, integrates multidisciplinary capacities and interprets cultural diversity as a key element of a new strategy for sustainable development. Still other researchers view environmental and social challenges as opportunities for development action. This is particularly true in the concept of sustainable enterprise that frames these global needs as "opportunities for private enterprise to provide innovative and entrepreneurial solutions." The Universal Declaration on Cultural Diversity (UNESCO, 2001) further elaborates the concept by stating that "...cultural diversity is as necessary for humankind as biodiversity is for nature"; it becomes "one of the roots of development understood not simply in terms of economic growth, but also as a means to achieve a more satisfactory intellectual, emotional, moral and spiritual existence". As argued, in this vision, cultural diversity is the fourth policy area of sustainable development.

Dimensions of Economic Sustainability

Central to the focus of this chapter is one of the three dimensions described, i.e. economic sustainability. In connection to this, Agenda 21 identified *information, integration*, and *partici-*

pation as key, interdependent building blocks to help countries achieve development. It has been argued, "in sustainable development everyone is a user and provider of information. It stresses the need to change from old sector-centered ways of doing business to new approaches that involve cross-sectoral co-ordination and the integration of environmental and social concerns into all development processes. Furthermore, Agenda 21 emphasizes that broad public participation in decision making is a fundamental prerequisite for achieving sustainable development" (UN 2008).

In addition to the governmental sector, new approaches in the field of business has also emerged that stress the importance of the role of the market and the consumer to solve poverty and other global challenges. One of the fastest growing fields of research and practice approaches is called BoP, Base of the Pyramid. BoP refers to the approximately 4 billion lowest income people who earn less than $2.5/day (Hart & Prahalad, 2002). Prahalad and Hart argue that this vast market is highly ignored, both in terms of their needs but also as a potential profitable market. In the process of entering and tapping poor or emerging markets, innovations of products and services emerge as well as new partnerships between different sectors that allegedly improve the economic, social and environmental status of such market (c.f. Prahalad, 2004). A number of business cases and anecdotal data exist that show promise on such approach. For example the Danish company MyC4 (described below) which offers an online Web-based credit system linking investors with small business enterprises in BoP-markets, connecting the North with the South.

As these multiple dimensions of development have been taken into account by governments, agencies and other organizations, we have seen a different language emerging in development papers and reports. The World Bank defines participation as 'a process through which stakeholders influence and share control over development initiatives and the decisions and resources which affect them', and talks about the need to 'empower' the poor - helping them move from being 'beneficiaries' to 'clients' (World Bank 1996). The United Nations Development Program (UNDP) used the term 'sustainable human development' to describe a human-centeredness of sustainable development (UNDP 1996). The ability of people to exercise meaningful choices for their own benefit and that of society is said to be at the heart of the initiatives to strengthen community resilience and community adaptation in the face of global environmental change and other sustainability issues.[4]

In this chapter we will include all three sustainability dimensions described above: environmental sustainability, economic sustainability and socio-political sustainability. As we focus on aspects of economic sustainability, information, integration, and participation will be adopted as important, interdependent building blocks.

MOBILITY[5] IN GENERAL AND ENTERPRISE MOBILITY

Next we address our second area of focus, mobility. Behind developed world companies'

and organizations' strategic decision to increase organizational mobility with the help of new information and communication technologies there are often several different objectives. Among the most important effects and points forwarded by companies are[6]:

- Increased work flexibility through increased mobility
- Improved internal coordination and communication through mobile communications
- Improved and changed customer services through use of mobile solutions
- Changes in the internal organizational structures and processes through new solutions
- Changes in the inter-personal communication within organizations
- Changes in security and control through new mobile solutions
- General improved operational efficiency and productivity with the new mobile solution

In most companies, several of these factors are mentioned when asked about the content of mobility, which suggests a multidimensional view of the concept. When asked about the purpose of mobility, three parts of the organizational systems are generally referred to:

- Increased mobility as a way to increase *the internal efficiency* of the buyer organization
- Increased mobility as a way to increase *efficiency in the buyer's exchanges with customers*
- Increased mobility as a way to increase the value creation towards and *effectiveness in relation to the users' own customers*

Being able to access a user organizations' information system in an efficient way e.g. through mobile phones or terminals is important when considering mobility solutions. From an empirical point of view, it is difficult to separate *mobility* from *connectivity* and *accessibility*. It is often argued that the major aim when implementing new integrated mobile systems is increased connectivity in the first place, and mobility would be a consequence of this. For example, field representatives in both manufacturing and service companies who were equipped with new systems that linked them via mobile telephony to the company's information data bases and fixed telephony system, saw it as a major advantage to be connected. In other words, they could be connected to information sources if they should need it, wherever they were situated. Successively, when learning to use this connectivity, it could also affect the representatives' mode of using and changing their mobility, in the way they moved in time and space. Hence, increased mobility, via increased connectivity and accessibility, as a way to increase the internal efficiency of an organization, would successively lead to increased mobility. This would be a way to increase efficiency in the users' exchanges with their customers, and subsequently, to mobility as a way to increase the value creation and effectiveness in relation to their customers.

The concept "mobility" entails other complications. Implementation of "mobility" solutions could mean that certain organizational functions in fact would become more "stationary", when other functions were made more mobile, and vice versa. Studies pointed to several issues that made the concept sometimes misleading. Concerning the interdependence between "mobile" and "stationary" aspects of "mobility solutions", mobility in use could not be discussed and analyzed without including its opposite. In fact, in many customer studies, the increased mobility of some parts of the user organization was based on the fact that other parts could be made more stationary. One of the changes anticipated or actually seen in organizations when new wireless technologies have been implemented is a shift in the "mobility" of work

forces, in their movements in space and time. The mobility concept is not easy to catch and is closely related to the philosophical discussion on time and space and configured in place and space (See for example Casey 1993, 1997, Tuan 1977).

The grand question about mobility and time and space has also been discussed and scrutinized by social scientists on a concrete level, frequently for more pragmatic ambitions. One such strategy to highlight the concept of mobility is to discuss it in terms of where different communication solutions are used. Kristoffersen and Ljungberg (1999; 2000), for example, distinguish between different work forces using IT in different situations: while *wandering, visiting or traveling*. In their studies of mobile workers, Kakihara and Sörensen (2004) argued mobility could be understood better when analyzed along three dimensions: *locational mobility* (concerned with workers' geographical movement), *operational mobility* (concerned with workers' capability for flexible operation), and *interactional mobility* (associated with mobile workers' intensive and fluid interaction with a wide range of people). Another mobility distinction is made by Luff & Heath (1998). Their often quoted paper makes a distinction between micro-mobility, local mobility and remote mobility, where the last denotes the situation when geographically separated people interact through the use of technology. Weilenmann (2003) distinguishes between the mobility of individuals, mobility of the setting, mobility of technologies/artifacts, and mobility of information.

In line with e.g. Weilenmann, several authors criticize the narrow use of the mobility concept when looking at work forces as "only" dealing with aspects of remoteness from a specific geographical location (aspects of "space") or dependency issues (power). Instead they propose to highlight the dynamism of work as such. Kakihara and Sörensen (2004) argue along this line:

For example, the concept is typically used in such forms as 'mobile technology', 'mobile office', and 'mobile work'.... All of these usages of 'mobile' refer to some sense of geographical movement or remoteness from a certain fixed point or location. ...However, such usage of the concept ignores another important aspect of the original meaning, referring to transformation or motion of objects, states, conditions, or structures. (p. 183-84)

Summing up, there is a growing literature on "mobility" in social science, focusing on the dimensions of the concept as such, focusing on its relevance in economic, enterprise contexts where different work processes are in focus, and focusing on shifts and changes in mobility as an effect of the introduction of wireless technologies and applications. Some of this will be connected to our sustainability focus and developing country contexts as we present the three cases. But first, we comment on the customer value concept and the value of mobility.

THE VALUE OF MOBILITY

Mobile devices and services can create *new value* for users, e.g. for enterprise users. Researchers and practitioners have increasingly discussed the notion of value.[7] However, there is little agreement in the literature on what constitutes "value" and "customer value" (Payne and Holt 2001). Value and value creation processes have been viewed from the perspective of the individual consumer, from the perspective of organizations' internal value creation processes and value creation toward customers, and, increasingly, also from an interactive perspective including both organizations and customers. And as stated by Lindgreen and Wynstra (2005), although value is an increasingly relevant concept, many enterprises cannot define value or measure it.

Relatively little is known about what new value that is created from mobile offerings, and how it

is created and changed over time.[8] It is possible to distinguish between two forms of value: value of the products/offerings and value of the actual relationship between the buyer and the seller (e.g. of a mobile solution). Following different suggestions for value analyses[9,] three important areas for understanding value are, for example, how value analysis is realized by customers, how value analysis can be brought into the development of offerings, and how value actually is delivered in various value constellations to customers. Hence, the creation and consumption of value involves more than only a single supplier and a single customer, but most often several "stakeholders".[10] In addition, when offerings are seen in the context of long-term supplier-customer relations, customer value becomes dynamic. Value is created and exchanged over time in a series of transactions.

What does the concept of value mean in the context of wireless offerings for enterprise users, and dimensions of sustainability? It is proposed that we need a *"wider"* perspective on value. Firstly, this wider perspective includes a stronger emphasis on the fact that groups of actors together create value for users/customers, and others. Normann and Ramirez (1993) describe such networks of connected, value creating actors as *value constellations*. Secondly, when analyzing value creation from mobile offerings, we need a *dynamic* perspective on value and value creation.

Much literature on customer value has focused on the *value of use*, i.e. it is directly related to the consumption event (Payne and Holt 2001). Some scholars have emphasized the situation of use as the context during which parties interact (Chen and Nath 2004). Woodruff and Gardial (1996) suggested that consumers could gain value just by owning a product. Research on customer value can contribute an understanding for how individuals experience e.g. benefits and sacrifices of mobile offerings in different user contexts. Important for mobile services and applications is that *technical, temporal and spatial value dimensions* can be perceived as important parts of

Table 1. Mobility dimensions

"Locational mobility"	"Operational mobility"	"Interactional mobility"

customers' perceived value of services (Heinonen 2004). It can be assumed that an important part of the "new" customer value created in the use of new wireless applications concern aspects of time and location.

As stated by Lindgreen and Wynstra (2004), although value is an increasingly relevant concept, many enterprises cannot define value or measure it, for example what value that is associated with various aspects of "sustainability". (See also Paavilainen 2001). Relatively little is known about what new value in terms of sustainability that is created by wireless information and communication technologies, mobile offerings, how it is created and how it changes over time. Next, we combine some of our conceptual discussion above on sustainability, mobility and value.

DISCUSSION: THE VALUE OF MOBILITY FOR ECONOMIC SUSTAINABILITY

So, how can we approach the connections and interdependencies between sustainability, mobility and value? Building on the introductory conceptual overview above, we can choose to take the starting point in the three generally accepted dimensions of sustainability: sociopolitical, environmental and economic sustainability. With our empirical focus on "mobile solutions" (i.e. wireless ICTs) used in "enterprise contexts", our starting point

here is the economic sustainability and the three dimensions described identified in Agenda 21: *information, integration,* and *participation* as important, interdependent building blocks to help countries achieve economic development and sustainability (Figure 2).

Information implies that everyone is a user and provider of information. Integration implies the presence of cross-sectoral coordination and the integration of social and environmental concerns. Participation, lastly, implies public participation in decision-making. Although all three are important, it can be anticipated that in a commercial enterprise context, economic sustainability is more openly connected to the first two (information and integration) while the third, participation, is more strongly connected to sociopolitical sustainability. However, we can also anticipate that "participation in decision making" can also be transferred to the more private, enterprise sphere: taking part in the daily "decision making" that is part of enterprise life, will be strongly connected to aspects of information exchange and integration within and between enterprises.

In line with the discussion on sustainability, we can choose to delimit the mobility aspects to three dimensions (Kakihara and Sörensen, 2004) (Table 1).

The value of changes in mobility (affecting sustainability) can in general terms be technical, spatial and temporal (Heinonen 2004) and effect

Table 2. Value dimensions and economic effects

Value dimensions	"Technical value"	"Spatial value"	"Temporal value"
Economic effects	"Efficiency"	"Effectiveness"	"Innovation"

three central economic aspects: efficiency, effectiveness and innovation (Table 2).

This gives us a conceptual framework to discuss empirical examples linked to the area of wireless communications and their links to aspects of sustainability. The starting point being that like the three central concepts (sustainability, mobility, value) this is multifaceted area, and understanding some of the interdependencies between our main variables is part of the aim of this chapter.

How can we anticipate these dimensions to be connected to dimensions of *organizational communication*, here in a developing country setting?

- Firstly, based on our previous studies of intra- and inter-organizational effects of increased use of mobile communications, we can anticipate also in developing countries, important effects on economic sustainability, mainly as a direct effect of *changed integration*. Changed opportunities for inter-organizational communication e.g. between more or less local "buyers" and "sellers", less dependent on time and space (i.e. increased *spatial and temporal value)* could lead to more frequent and regular communication leading to increased integrations, and hence more stable and *efficient* business interaction.

- Secondly, it can be anticipated that the increased use of mobile communications between small business firms – where the boundaries between private and business communication can be expected to be less clear – will through the increased opportunities for *information* exchange – spill over on participation in connected societal (private) processes, increasing the opportunities for *participation* and changed *sociopolitical sustainability*. In short, people have the opportunity to keep better informed both on business and private/social matters.

Next, we bring up three empirical illustrations. Our starting point in the conceptual framework is the creation of economic sustainability, with a particular focus on the use of mobile solutions in business enterprises. In our final discussion, we extend it to the other dimensions and concepts described.

EMPIRICAL ILLUSTRATIONS

Example 1. Digicel and the Creation of New Temporal and Spatial Values[11]

Mobile operator Digicel has built a powerful position as supplier of wireless services and phones in the poverty stricken part of the world. During a few years time the company has built a position in over 27 countries (2008), dominating the position in a dozen of these, mainly poverty stricken, developing countries. In addition, the operator is targeting seventeen more countries in the developing world. Forbes describes some of the effects of Digicel's operations: "In a speech, the treasury minister (of Papua New Guinea) noted that 0.7 percentage points of 6.2% GDP growth had come from cell phone "competition". The country's biggest paper ran a story about the boost, with Digicel in the headline. Perhaps letting people peddle phones is one of the best things a poor country can do to spur growth. One reason: Entrepreneurs use mobiles to work around the long delays, crumbling infrastructure and countless little Third World frustrations that cut into opportunities. Haitian merchant Jean Maurice Buteau exports 150.000 more mangoes a year now because his truck drivers can call when stranded on a rutted road with a broken axle or shot spring, and fruit rotting in the back. Samoan fisherman Finau Afitu earns 80 dollars a week, four times his pre-Digicel pay, because he can check which markets want his fish by phone instead of walking to each one while they go bad. 'My kids can buy lunch at school now', he says. According to a London Business School study, every time 10 more people out of 100 start using mobiles GDP growth rises a half percentage point – something Digicel is helping a dozen countries achieve two or three times over (p.75). The article argues, "…indeed, it's hard to overstate the impact cell phones are having on poor citizens. Fittler Larsen, an impoverished betel nut seller in a PNG squatter settlement of 20.000, is making more money now that he can call wholesalers to check if new shipments have arrived. 'I used to spend half a day getting supplies' says the 19-year-old…now I can stay here and sell more'…"

The introductory case on the telecom operator Digicel indicates three short examples of how their introduction of mobile communications has changed the business operations of three small enterprises in developing countries. Firstly, the Haitian merchant Jean Maurice Buteau exports 150.000 more mangoes a year now because his truck drivers can call when stranded on a rutted road with a broken axle or shot spring, and fruit rotting in the back. Secondly, the Samoan fisherman Finau Afitu earns 80 dollars a week, four times his pre-Digicel pay, because he can now check which markets want his fish by phone instead of walking to each one while they go bad. Thirdly, Fittler Larsen, the impoverished betel nut seller in a PNG squatter settlement, is making more money now that he can call wholesalers to check if new shipments have arrived, staying where he is and still sell instead of spending half a day getting supplies. The first and the third example indicate an increased (logistical) efficiency from the use of mobile communications. The third example also shows that a *decreased* spatial, locational mobility – the betel nut seller can actually stay in the same place – thereby increasing the possibility to re-distribute his use of the time send on various business activities. The three examples also indicate some potential effects on economic sustainability in terms of both information exchange and integration (between business sectors). The three entrepreneurs in the examples become both users and providers of information.

The presence of cross-sectoral coordination is also indicated, for example in case example two.

Example 2. MyC4. Internet Platform for Investments to Promote Entrepreneurship and Fight Poverty

Mads Kjaer, former CEO of Kjaer Group A/S and with extensive experience from the African continent, and Tim Vang, a Danish entrepreneur, started MyC4 in May 2006, inspired by the Grameen Bank in Bangladesh. Building on their capabilities and visions they set out to create a web based investment platform that linked individual small business and entrepreneurship in Africa with individual investors, primarily from the North. The formation of the company and the design of the idea linked Tim's capabilities as an IT-platform builder and a successful entrepreneur with Mads' African knowledge and insights about the needs of capital for the poor. The vision is that MyC4 via the Internet could be an important tool to raise and give access to capital for African entrepreneurs and in so doing creating sustainable prosperity fighting to end extreme poverty. MyC4 has also received grants from the Danish Aid Agency for developing the platform. The platform is a meeting arena for individual investors and individual entrepreneurs. The entrepreneurs are screened for economic sustainability and have to fulfill several criteria to be included on the web platform. Most importantly they have to show a history of economic sustainability, which excludes new companies/entrepreneurs from this service. As an investor you can screen the entrepreneurs and, if you find a business you want to invest in, you offer to loan a specified amount to a, of you specified, interest rate. As an entrepreneur you specify your capital need and by the end of the "bid" period you can review the offers and make a decision on which one to accept or not.

This case shows how an innovation has increased and simplified connections between borrowers of small loans, small business, and investors, thus creating both technical and spatial value. This solution also overcomes the so-called poverty penalty, the phenomenon that the poor often have to pay more for product and services than the affluent. This is commonly connected to the informality of the economy in poor regions. If there is no access to banking services for the poor, moneylenders in the informal sector offering loans to very large interest might be the only option available, i.e., the availability of affordable capital to develop small business is influencing social-political sustainability as well as overcoming spatial and social distances. The informational value for both the investor in finding attractive investment objects, and for the lending entrepreneur in comparing offerings from investors is one of MyC4 platform's great advantages. In addition, the effectiveness and efficiency in overcoming relational transaction costs is prevalent in this case. The decreased spatial mobility also creates environmental sustainable value since it diminishes transportation, as well as social value connecting investments to the underserved.

Example 3. WIZZIT: Mobile Banking for the Poor in South Africa[12]

Access to banking services is a global concern, with only 1 out of 6.5 billion people of the world population having a bank account (Richardson & Callegari, 2008), with the majority of people located in developing countries. This lack of access will have large implications for their ability to transact effectively as economic citizens, workers and consumers.

In South Africa about 50% of the adult population lack access to banking services, in spite of post-apartheid reforms to give the previous marginalized black majority access and benefit from all parts of the economy. After the fall of apartheid the banks continued offering services to the more affluent part of the population as well as not offering services in all parts of the country. The high costs associated with providing physi-

cal bank branches covering the country as well offering services to the less attractive lower end of the market called for new models for offering services to the un- and under-banked people in South Africa. Associated to the lack of geographical access to banking services in South Africa, was the issue that a majority of the employed population are migrant workers who to a large extent transfer money by informal and expensive means to family and friends back to their home community. Usually they have no other means than using taxi or bus drivers, that could cost up to 25% of the value of the money transferred (Richardson & Callegari, 2008).

One of the additional challenges to not having a bank account in South Africa was that salary payments had to be administered in cash. With a high crime rate and an increasing problem with armed robberies and muggings, carrying cash became an everyday risk for people.

To solve these challenges a group consisting of two entrepreneurs and a leading South African politician were looking for other methods than cash payments for the unbanked in South Africa. In 2005 they formed WIZZIT that offered a full-service mobile phone based banking facility, unrestricted by various networks, type of SIM cards or age of mobile phone. WIZZIT have arrangements with three business partners, a division of the South African Bank of Athens Ltd, one of the major banks in South Africa, and the post office to enable deposits for their customers. WIZZIT also is an accredited issuer of MasterCard's Maestro debit cards that use mobile phone technology as a payment channel. This solution offers a new, affordable and an easy access way of cash-less transactional account using no fixed fees but use a 'pay-as-you-use' model. The fee is per transaction ranging from US$0.13 to max US$0.67 and requires no minimum balance to open. The banking services can be performed 24 hours a day and all days of the week using the mobile telephone. The transactions are done over the mobile phone, but the account holders do not even have to own their phone, it is sufficient with the SIM card, available to very low cost, that can be inserted in any mobile telephone. Common is to have one shared handset for a household.

In addition to the un- and under-banked customers, a key strategy is to offer a growing sector of small- and medium sized business affordable banking services, also connecting it to safer payment practices for employees, reducing the risks of robbery. This payroll system service is called iWIZZ. This have created less risks and over time it has also changed the workers habits from carrying and spending all of the salary to saving some on the account.

The WIZZIT can also be used in selected stores for payments (at POS, Point of Sales). WIZZIT do not have branches but use independent field agents, WIZZkids, who promote the product and help unbanked customers open accounts. WIZ-Zkids are recruited among WIZZIT's clients and are trained and certified by WIZZIT, in 2007 more than 3000 had been certified. WIZZkids are earning a commission on each sale and are working in their local area that creates closeness to the customers. It is required by South African law to be able to identify the customer, why WIZZkids become a key doing so and connect to proof of income and residential address.

The WIZZkid forms a relational link between WIZZIT and the customer that complements the mobile phone service that perform the actual transactions. This system also creates jobs and provides education and financial literacy for a large proportion of the South African people previously ignored or excluded from banking services. The value model is based on bringing affordable services and social value to a previously neglected part of the market and slowly building business value through adding more customers and services to the established ones.

This case shows how connecting communication technologies with standard services that address needs that previously were ignored, can create innovation that has yet to be introduced in developed world. By increasing connectivity

between people and banking services, several benefits can be seen. The previously un-bankable are given access to banking services without long travel as well a decreasing transaction costs in transferring money to relatives, thus creating spatial and economic value. Using the services makes it possible to have savings that can be the starting point for credit, and further development. It also gives employment opportunities for entrepreneurs in distributing the solutions on the local level, thus helping to establish economic sustainability to individuals and households. In addition, similar to the MyC4 case, WIZZIT gives availability to capital as well as to services that can help small business, influencing the social-political sustainability as well as overcoming spatial and social distances.

Lastly, the effectiveness and efficiency in overcoming transportation and transaction costs is prevalent in this case. The decreased spatial mobility creates environmental sustainable value since it diminishes transportation as well as social value connecting banking services to the un-banked and the underserved.

PROPOSITIONS AND IMPLICATIONS FOR SUSTAINABILITY AND CHANGED COMMUNICATION

To summarize the conceptual discussion and ideas from the short empirical illustrations above, we end the paper with a set of propositional statements. Our standpoint is that the research area we are approaching in this chapter is fairly new and still undeveloped and is in need of both conceptual work and deeper empirical investigations. The aim of our concluding discussion and propositions is to indicate potentially productive avenues for future research. Our empirical illustrations are short; we will rely also on our conceptual framework and explorative thinking, and also prior empirical experiences, when we elaborate on 3 final propositions. The three propositions take the three dimensions of sustainability (economic, sociopolitical and environmental) as starting point, connecting them to the other dimensions of the conceptual framework:

Proposition 1. The opportunities and willingness to explore effectiveness effects and innovativeness in the use of wireless communications is high in developing countries, leading to positive effects on economic sustainability. Several empirical examples of the use of wireless communications in various developing world contexts (e.g. in connection with small enterprise business operations) seem to indicate a high degree of (business) innovativeness in the actual use and employment of the new technologies. This increased economic sustainability is in several cases connected to processes of improved and radically new patterns of information exchange, sometimes leading to increased integration between actors, i.e., new interactional mobility. In economic terms, this innovativeness in the use processes of new technologies seems to be linked to the exploration of new patterns of business interactions. Hence, the technical value for the users of the new wireless technologies and applications is often high, having effects on business development and subsequently on economic sustainability. There are also indications that in certain areas (e.g. mobile banking) this innovativeness in the developing world could benefit the advancement of similar technologies and applications in the developed world.

Proposition 2. The opportunities to explore economic sustainability through wireless communications can be an important starting point and driver for improved information exchange and integration between professional and private lives among users, in turn leading to effects on sociopolitical sustainability. Several empirical examples indicate that the introduction of mobile communications among small business users in developing countries have important spillover and integration effects on other parts of the users' private and sociopolitical lives. The boundary between the private and public spheres in the actual use of mobile communications is very weak

or diffuse, leading to important spillover effects. Hence, through changes in interactional mobility based on shifts in information and integration, there will be important links between economic and sociopolitical sustainability enabled by the new mobile communications.

Proposition 3. *The opportunities to explore economic sustainability through wireless communications can contribute to balance the direct and indirect effects on the use of natural resources and on the impact on the natural environment in developing countries, leading to effects on the environmental sustainability.* In general increased economic development will increase consumption that will have a negative effect on environment. Also increased production and innovation will have a negative effect on the use of natural resources and will create environmental pollution. The use of wireless communications can have an influence on both consumption and production and therefore lead to negative effects on environmental sustainability. On the other hand our examples show that wireless communication through its capacity to create spatial value can contribute to replacing or reducing transportation needs as well as be used to monitor the health of natural habitats and eco-systems in remote areas. The use of ICTs can also lead to increased information exchange that can support promotion and diffusion of knowledge of protection of the natural environment.

Hence, the increased use of wireless communications can contribute to a negative effect on environmental sustainability, but also mediate or balance the general negative impact on environment with increased economic development.

CONCLUDING WORDS

We set out to explore, mainly conceptually the link between dimensions of (organizational) mobile communications and dimensions of economic sustainability. However, we can anticipate – both from a theoretical and an empirical point of view – that intra-and inter-organizational effects of changed potential for communication will be linked also to other aspects of sustainability, to socio-political sustainability in the first step, but also to various dimensions of environmental sustainability. We have explored mainly the use of ICTs in the setting of developing countries where currently several ICT solutions are explored to increase mobility and contribute to reduction of economic poverty. We can see opportunities of economic and socio-political value-creation on the organizational and individual level using ICT solutions developed with the needs of the poor in focus.

However, on the societal level we can also anticipate possible negative environmental impact that must be considered when introducing mobile communication solutions. We therefore believe it is of importance to further research on the connection between mobility and sustainability that can offer insights and models for how business approaches and technological solutions can offer solutions to societal problems such as poverty and environmental degradation.

REFERENCES

Andersson, P., Essler, U., & Thorngren, B. (2007). *Beyond Mobility*. Lund: Studentlitteratur

Axelsson, B., & Easton, G. (Eds.). (1992). *Industrial Networks - A New View of Reality*. London: Routledge.

Casey, E. (1993). *Getting back into place: toward a renewed understanding of the place-world*. Bloomington, IN: Indiana University Press

Casey, E. (1997). *The fate of place: a philosophical history*. Berkeley, CA: University of California Press.

Chen, L., & Nath, R. (2004). A framework for mobile business applications. *International Journal of Mobile Communications*, 2(4), 368–381. doi:10.1504/IJMC.2004.005857

Håkansson, H. (Ed.). (1982). *International Marketing and Purchasing of Industrial Goods - An Interaction Approach*. Chichester, UK: Wiley.

Håkansson, H., & Snehota, I. (1995). *Developing Relationships in Business Networks*. London: Routledge.

Heinonen, K. (2004). Reconceptualizing customer perceived value – the value of time and place. *Managing Service Quality*, 14(2/3), 205–215. doi:10.1108/09604520410528626

Kakihara, M., & Sörensen, C. (2004). Mobile Urban Professionals in Tokyo. *Info*, 6.

Kandachar, P., & Halme, M. (Eds.). (2008). *Sustainability Challenges and Solutions at the Base of the Pyramid. Business, Technology and the Poor*. London: Greenleaf Publishing Ltd.

Kristoffersen, S., & Ljungberg, F. (1999). Mobile use of IT. In *Proceedings of the 22nd Information Systems Research Seminar in Scandinavia, IRIS 22*.

Kristoffersen, S., & Ljungberg, F. (2000). Mobility: From Stationary to Mobile Work. In K. Braa, C. Sorenssen, & B. Dahlbom (eds.) *Planet Internet*. Lund, Sweden: Studentlitteratur.

Lindgreen, A., & Wynstra, F. (2005). Value in business markets: What do we know? Where are we going? *Industrial Marketing Management*, 34(7), 732–748. doi:10.1016/j.indmarman.2005.01.001

Luff, P., & Heath, C. (1998). Mobility in collaboration. In *Proceedings of the 1998 ACM conference on Computer supported cooperative work*. Seattle, Washington.

Norman, R., & Ramirez, R. (1993). From Value Chain to Value Constellation: Designing Interactive Strategy. *Harvard Business Review*, 65–77.

Paavilainen, J. (2001). Mobile Business Strategies. *Understanding the technologies and opportunities*. London: Addison-Wesley.

Payne, A., & Holt, S. (2001). Diagnosing Customer Value: Integrating the Value Process and Relationship Marketing. *British Journal of Management, 12*(2), 159–182. doi:10.1111/1467-8551.00192

Prahalad, C. K. (2005). *The Fortune at the Bottom of the Pyramid, eradicating poverty through profits*. Boston: Wharton School Publishing.

Prahalad, C.K. & Hart, S. (2002). The Fortune at the Bottom of the Pyramid. *Strategy + Business*, (January).

Richardson, B., & Callegari, N. (2008). WIZZIT. Mobile banking for the poor in South Africa. In Kandachar, P. & M. Halme (Eds) *Sustainability Challenges and Solutions at the Base of the Pyramid: business, technology and the poor*. London: Greenleaf Publishing Ltd.

Tuan, Y.-F. (1977). *Space and place: the perspective of experience*. Minneapolis, MN: University of Minnesota Press.

UN (1987). *Report of the World Commission on Environment and Development: Our Common Future*. Transmitted to the General Assembly as an Annex to document A/42/427 - Development and International Co-operation: Environment.

UN (2008). Overview of progress towards sustainable development: a review of the implementation of Agenda 21. *Programme for the Further Implementation of Agenda 21 and the Johannesburg Plan of Implementation*. Report of the Secretary-General E/CN.17/2008/2

Weilenmann, A. (2003). *Doing Mobility*. PhD Thesis, Gothenburg Studies in Informatics, Report 28, Gothenburg, Sweden: Gothenburg University.

Wikipedia (2009). *Sustainable Development*. Retrieved April 30, 2009 from http://en.wikipedia.org/wiki/Sustainable_development

Woodruff, R. B., & Gardial, S. F. (1996). *Know Your Customer: New Approaches to Understanding Customer Value and Satisfaction*. Cambridge, MA: Blackwell Publishers.

ENDNOTES

[1] Sustainability Research Group

[2] Base of the Pyramid was initially called Bottom of the Pyramid (e.g. Prahalad & Hart, 2002).

[3] Agriculture, Atmosphere, Biodiversity, Biotechnology, Capacity-building, Climate Change, Consumption and Production Patterns, Demographics, Desertification and Drought, Disaster Reduction and Management, Education and Awareness, Energy, Finance, Forests, Fresh Water, Health, Human Settlements, Indicators, Industry, Information for Decision Making and Participation, Integrated Decision Making, International Law, International Cooperation for Enabling Environment, Institutional Arrangements, Land management, Major Groups, Mountains, National Sustainable Development Strategies, Oceans and Seas, Poverty, Sanitation, Science, SIDS, Sustainable tourism, Technology, Toxic Chemicals, Trade and Environment, Transport, Waste (Hazardous), Waste (Radioactive), Waste (Solid), Water

[4] http://translate.google.com/translate?hl=sv&sl=en&u=http://www.wikipedia.org/&sa=X&oi=translate&resnum=3&ct=result&prev=/search%3Fq%3Dwikipedia%26hl%3Dsv%26client%3Dsafari%26rls%3Dsv-se

[5] This and the next section on value builds on two existing texts: 1) Andersson et al (eds),

Beyond Mobility, Lund: Studentlitteratur, 2007, and 2) a chapter text in a manuscript: Andersson et al, "Mobile Organizations" (forthcoming EFI, Stockholm School of Economics)

[6] Building on the research project "Mobile Organizations"

[7] For reviews of the concept see Payne and Holt, 2001; Khalifa, 2004.

[8] A promising framework for discussing such values is presented by Chen & Nath (2004).

[9] Lindgreen & Wynstra (2005)

[10] Payne and Holt, 2001

[11] Fortune 11 Aug 2008, pp. 72-77

[12] Based on the case WIZZIT described in Richardson and Callegari (2008).

Chapter 2
ICT Instruments as Possible Support for the Equal Distribution of Population

Aleksandra Djukic
Faculty of Architecture, University of Belgrade, Serbia

Vesna Tomic
Ski resorts of Serbia, Belgrade, Serbia

ABSTRACT

Unequal city development, namely the faster development of large centers and concentration of power, globalization and local specificities in certain locations, have caused a lack of balance between large city centers and smaller settlements and villages. In Serbia, there are major differences in the level of development, as well as in cultural features of settlements. There are significant economic differences between settlements in the north, the east, and the south of the country, since settlements developed in valleys and hence had better traffic communication, and could therefore be competitive and stay abreast of transformations. Smaller settlements and villages (especially those along the borders, in National parks and in difficult to access rural regions), are marginalized, and face many problems, most often caused by lack of infrastructure, decrease of the number of inhabitants, the dissolution of the secondary and tertiary sector. Today, a quarter of the total population lives in the capital city of Belgrade, while a considerable number of settlements are completely shutting down. These settlements once had their identity and a harmonious balance of all elements constituting the life of the community and the individual. A distinctive social aspect contributed to a rich cultural heritage, but over time this was gradually lost and begins to disappear. The question is if any of the processes (globalization, technological revolution), which contribute to the demographic and economic decline of rural regions, could form a basis for renewal. A classical planner's approach would imply the networking of settlements and providing equal population distribution by investing in infrastructure and providing conditions for settlements through

DOI: 10.4018/978-1-60566-822-2.ch002

the development of central functions, requiring considerable investments. The other possibility relies on the development of information and communication technologies (ICT), which could provide for many necessities: access to and exchange of information, paying bills and ordering products from a distance, working from home, meetings via Internet conferences, etc. The use of Internet technologies in order to develop settlements, by converting traditional into "net" technologies, can make up for disadvantages of life in smaller settlements and enable their revitalization, by networking them into a global net of settlements, without geographical borders and limits.

INTRODUCTION

Technologies of the industrial, super industrial and postindustrial society, or the ''third wave'' have caused and are still causing simultaneous opposing assumptions for the future. Technologies that we are developing are both a tool for progress and a disintegrator for the foundations of living and of values that have until now formed the human community.

Utilization of information and communication technologies (ICT), especially the Internet, is becoming an ever more important factor for the development of cities and regions. This development and utilization is a global phenomenon, which surpasses and neutralizes many cultural, regional and economic differences between geographically distant areas. It contributes to bring closer spatially distant areas, to a change of spatial formulas, and to generating new forms of settlements. Accepted and adopted notions about the nature of space, time, distances and lifestyles are questioned – subjected to our revision (Graham, Marvin, 1999).

Processes of globalization are changing economies, the organization of the society, and the life of each and every individual. People are losing their jobs, and becoming asocial. However, new and numerous possibilities for work and different social relationships are also opening up for them.

During the last 20 - 30 years, which have generated rapid development of important new

scientific theories and insights about life on our planet and our own life, from consciousness about the impact on the environment and theories of sustainability, to the discovery of links between our emotions and neurobiological processes, attempts to scientifically foresee the future development of economy, settlements and the society have become almost indispensable.

According to certain theoreticians (Mitchel, 1996; Castels, 1997; Grapham, 1996; Batty, 1996), development and creation of ICT infrastructures is regarded as the basic means to support the community in order to upgrade its social and economic development. According to Mitchel, (1996), today, the overall success of cities can be measured by the refinement and spread of implementation of state of the art ICT means, while in modern business many strategies and business decisions are preconditioned by new technologies and the need to be integrated into a global information society. ICT implementation may permit a higher level of democratization and citizen participation, but will also influence perception and a mixture of the real and the simulated, the public and the private (Grapham and Marvin, 1996). Virillio (2000) interprets changes pessimistically, claiming that humanity is facing a "housebound paranoid culture".

Relevant to global trends, present everywhere to different degrees, local changes have also encompassed the social system, economic and demographic development, which requires a completely different approach and answers differing from those we are accustomed to.

This chapter will investigate the potential for taking the additional ''step'' in solving the problem of unequal distribution of population by applying new technologies in the spirit of local traditions and values. In our opinion, problems of sustainable development must today be approached pragmatically, but with a high level of innovation and creativity when reinterpreting known structures, concepts, values and processes. The case used here, as a starting point for the discussion, is Serbia, a country that has quite a different position today compared to 20 years ago.

DEVELOPMENT PROBLEMS IN SERBIA

Demographic Trends in Serbia

The process of rural depopulation in Serbia is significant in recent decades and presents one of the very serious problems requiring solutions by implementing strategies at the highest state level. Economy and sociology experts warn that if nothing is done, in a few years Serbia will be an agricultural country without villages and peasants. Almost 2,000 villages in Serbia have no inhabitants, while 200 villages have no inhabitants less than 20 years of age. Some 260,000 men around 50 years of age who have not formed families live in villages, while approximately a quarter of the total population lives in the capital city – Belgrade (The Statistical Office of the Republic of Serbia, 2002).

Census data, which will be presented, does not contain data for Kosovo and Metohia, since the 2002 census was not performed in this territory. Due to the boycott by the Albanian population, the 1991 census was also not fully implemented in the municipalities of Bujanovac and Preshevo, therefore for most settlements in the territory of these municipalities the population was determined by an estimate.

The Republic of Serbia has a population of approximately 7.5 million. According to the OECD definition it is a predominantly rural country (population density below 150 per km^2). Today, over 50% of the Serbian population lives in cities, while only some 10% works in agriculture. Data from 1948 shows that at that time 18% of the population lived in cities, and approximately 75% worked in agriculture.

This significant change of the manufacturing and at the same time also of the demographic structure, is a consequence of the centralized state administration from after World War II, until the end of the 20th century, based on ideas of social justice, development of self management, and the working class as the promoter of political ideas. For this reason, means at the disposal of the state were channeled into developing specific branches of the economy, primarily industry, and into pronounced construction of socially owned apartments for workers. The population moved to cities, where factories were established, and conditions for economic progress were better.

The state intensively built apartments in urban centers, especially in Belgrade. In the 1970s, 44,000 apartments were built annually in Serbia, in the 1980s approximately 64,000, and in the 1990s approximately 18,000. In Belgrade, annual construction in 1978 was 12,000 apartments, in 1080s the average was 10,000 apartments annually, in 1999, there was 1,000 apartments, and in the period from 2000 to 2003 the average was 2,000-3,000 apartments annually.

The end of the 20th century brought changes that would lead to the development of the free market, when the consequences of the neglected development of rural areas, especially in eastern parts of central Serbia will begin to be felt. These parts of the country remained far from developed centers, without adequate traffic links, with underdeveloped technical and social infrastructure. Many companies were closed in the process of transition, reducing potentials for employment.

Figure 1. Municipalities, according to population density (Books of Census 2002. Belgrade, Serbia: The Statistical Office of the Republic of Serbia. Used with permission.)

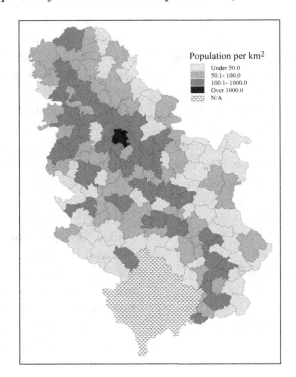

According to comparative data of the 1991 and the 2002 census, it can be concluded that the process of population reduction was most pronounced in the eastern part of Central Serbia (Figure 1). In Eastern Serbia, in certain municipalities as much as 25% of the population are temporarily employed abroad, mostly due to economic reasons. Population growth is present in the north of the country, in Vojvodina, where there is a registered negative natural population growth, but there is an overall population growth due to migrations in the territory of the former Yugoslavia (Figure 2).

The majority of the population lives in urban centers. Zones with the highest growth of population at the beginning of this century are the gravitational areas of Belgrade and Novi Sad. Population has decreased in 75% of municipalities, and in 32 municipalities, i.e. 20%, this decrease was over 10%.

Until 1981 the migration balance (ratio between emigrants and immigrants) in the territory of Serbia (Central Serbia and Vojvodina) was positive. Between two censuses (1981-1991) the migration balance in Serbia was negative, because there was less immigration from other parts of ex-Yugoslavia and more pronounced emigration of the population ''due to the economic and social crisis and the intimation of tragic events that will take place in this area at the beginning of the 1990s'' (Stevanovic, 2006, pg 71).

According to the census of 2002, the share of migrants in the overall population in Serbia (Kosovo and Metohia excluded) was 45.8%, in Central Serbia 45.4%, in Vojvodina 46.9%. Also, migrants represented over one half (50.9%) of the population in urban and 39.2% of the population in other settlements. The process of depopulation of parts of Serbia is very pronounced in certain areas, mostly in East Serbia. For example, in the

Figure 2. Municipalities, according to average annual level of net migration, Period 1991- 2002, (Books of Census 2002. Belgrade, Serbia: The Statistical Office of the Republic of Serbia. Used with permission.)

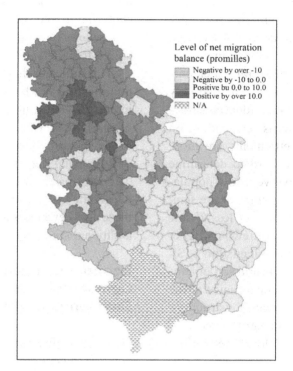

municipality of Crna Trava, in the 1991-2002 period, population decreased by almost a third.

It is not only that villages are left devoid of population, but also the age and educational structure of the remaining population does not offer sufficient internal potentials to oppose such processes.

Over 20% of the population of extraurban parts of Serbia is older than 60 years, i.e. 44.32% of agricultural households are over 50 years of age.

These underdeveloped areas have a higher share of less educated population, since approximately 90% of the highly educated population, and approximately 70% of the population with high school education lives in cities, while only 28% of the population with high school and university education lives outside urban centers. In some villages elementary schools are being shut down, and there are registered schools with

only one pupil. Incomplete schools (only four grades), and schools with combined classes are present in rural, underdeveloped parts of the country. Incomplete schools in Central Serbia on the average have 1.8 classrooms, 25.3 pupils and 1.8 teachers. In addition, conditions are not much more favorable relevant to basic healthcare and social welfare.

Spatial Determinants of Rural Settlements in Serbia

It is very hard to differentiate village settlements from small towns, due to the fact that in both types of settlements a certain percentage of the population is active in agricultural production.

From the aspect of relations between man and the environment, relations are artificial (without integration between man and his environment), static and local (no attention is devoted to the broader, but only to the immediate environment), with a very low level of environmental awareness. Waters, especially streams, are insufficiently regulated, most often used to deposit waste, and are in most cases without any protection.

The majority of undeveloped rural settlements (Central Serbia) have preserved the authenticity of morphological patterns, of individual constructions as well as urban patterns. Depending on natural conditions, these settlements are more or less dispersed, making it hard to determine the building region, and have very low population densities (1- 3 inhabitants/km²), or are semi compact and compact, with more or less visible building regions, and with somewhat higher population densities (5-25 inhabitants/km²) (Simonovic, 1976). These types if rural settlements are harmonized with the environment and with the existing authentic manner of ethnic constructions (characteristic appearance of constructions, utilization of natural materials with local specificities in finishing details).

The status of constructed physical structures (built during the last fifty years) is chaotic. Most frequently, building is carried out without approvals and without adequate planning documentation, with numerous individual housing constructions that are not fully completed. In municipalities with considerable numbers of the population temporarily working abroad, this population constructs buildings for when they return, most frequently oversized, which remain unoccupied for years. Buildings designated to provide social standards are in poor condition, are not maintained, and their functionality and offer often do not fulfill the needs of the population.

It can be said that from the aspect of infrastructural equipment they are at a very low level. Numerous villages do not have an adequate traffic structure (they are even cut off from large centers during the winter), and there are still many buildings without waterworks and sewage (without indoor toilets).

A comparison of the 1991 and the 2002 census shows that the presence of utilities in rural households (%), has somewhat, but not significantly improved, i.e. the level of availability of waterworks, sewage and electricity went from 64.2% to 66.8%.

This indicates that the state and the local communities did not have economic potentials and interest to invest in infrastructural development of rural areas, which is a result simultaneously of the specific morphology of these settlements (low housing density), and of the complex and deteriorating economic situation that Serbia faced during the last decade of 20th century. This made these areas even less attractive, and presented an additional stimulus for migrations.

Economic Aspects of Negative Demographic and Spatial Development Trends

Geographically, and in a certain sense also according to economic development, the territory is divided into developed flatlands and valleys (plains in the north – Vojvodina; in the south the broad river valleys of Central Serbia), and the less developed areas (the hills of Central Serbia, the difficult to access rural regions, zones of national parks, and zones along the state borders).

The lack of balance in development was particularly deleterious for the economy of Serbia during the last 20 years, because with the decline of power of urban centers, a phenomenon unavoidable at the beginning of economic restructuring, "support" from diversified development of agriculture and tourism was lacking. In recent years, private initiative has partially, even though slowly, made up for this (in agriculture, Serbia has highest revenues from sugar, raspberries and corn; and efforts are being made to expand production of strawberry type fruits, to develop production of herbs, flower seedlings, etc.).

Global political changes, processes of globalization, on one hand and the inefficient economy of the country on the other influenced the economic and social crisis of the 1980s. Subsequent events in ex-Yugoslavia caused additional economic deterioration of the then republic, and now the independent state of Serbia.

1993 saw the second largest inflation in history of $2.35 \cdot 10^{23}$ percent, or 64% daily on the average.

According to data of the Ministry of Finance, Serbian GDP is now approximately five times higher than in 2000, or one third of the European average. Previous data shows how devastating the events in the 1990s were for the economy and the potential of the country, since it is expected that it will take until 2008 for the average salary to once more reach 375 euro (which was its value in 1991). The highest GDP is realized in the City of Belgrade, with the regions in Central Serbia lagging two- to three-fold (The Statistical Office of the Republic of Serbia, 2002).

These differently developed regions also differ culturally and socially, with the highest frequency of (the still present) local differences and cultural clashes during the two most pronounced waves of migration – after World War II, and during the disintegration of Yugoslavia.

Principles of Equal Development

Today, one of the adopted principles of town planning is the planning of equal regional development, grounded in good reasons of efficiency, economic and social stability, and optimum control of development. Pronounced differences in development of parts of Serbia, resulting in depopulation and unequal economic development, require targeted national and local policies and initiatives.

Those European countries that had uniform development after World War II, today mostly have a well developed network of connected settlements, with good infrastructure and links, good working conditions, satisfying social, healthcare and other needs regarded as a standard for quality

of life, and with their own necessary autonomy, i.e. responsibilities and initiatives.

Even after World War II, the development of settlements in Serbia was not sufficiently channeled toward the autonomy of individual parts – municipalities and regions, nor was there sufficient investments in equal development of settlements. In fact, compared to the level of traffic communications in developed European countries, certain parts of the country can be regarded as cut off from other parts of its territory.

Sustainable Development: Comparative Advantages, Development of Tourism and Agriculture

All stated data on economic, demographic and spatial development indicate that the overall development of Serbia since the last decade of the 20th century is unsustainable. The 2001-2007 period brought an accelerated revival of the economy. Compared to the preceding period, when the structure of generation and utilization of GDP was disrupted, with a growing domination of the primary sector, the neglecting and decline of industry and stagnation of the services sector, the state set new goals in the National Strategy for Sustainable Development (2008). This document is harmonized with local strategies for sustainable development (2005), social welfare (2005), poverty reduction (2003), development of small and medium sized enterprises (2003), agriculture (2005), tourism (2006), stimulating foreign investments (2006), development of information society (2006), and other relevant documents.

One of the more significant priorities of the National Strategy is balanced regional development, implying a reduction of regional inequalities, rising of regional competitiveness, stimulating balanced regional development, and sustainable rural development.

Today, the period of economic stagnation appears as an advantage for Serbia - infrastructure was not developed; industrial production was reduced or was not developed. In underdeveloped rural areas, this contributed to preservation and protection of the environment, as well as of the cultural heritage, opening up the possibility for future development in line with principles of sustainability.

According to market demands and their potentials, local communities in Serbia can offer the following as their unique comparative advantage, as a starting point for sustainable development of those regions:

- Space/ nature, with autochthon values of preserved natural entities, with the potential for producing healthy food and other natural products, the potential to use renewable sources of energy, to develop offers for active vacations, etc.
- Social aspects – individuals and communities with a local way of life as the basis for vitality, joint work, fulfillment of all social needs, development of individual and collective creativity/identity; communities sharing tasks, exchanging experiences and emotions, and unselfishly offering assistance;
- Cultural heritage – accessibility of cultural monuments, archeological and other sights, authentic architecture, and traditional local customs.

Today, underdeveloped, rural regions of Central Serbia, hilly and mountainous regions, national parks and natural reservations can develop tourism, agriculture, local crafts, and can make an attempt to use this to become competitive on the domestic and the foreign market.

For developing countries, tourism offers good opportunities, as a branch of the economy that still has a good outlook, especially since most individuals taking recreational trips come from economically developed countries and go to less developed ones, and because today, in addition to the usual vacation services, other products and values can also be offered as part of an extended tourist service, additionally increasing the expected income.

The economic branch of tourism in Serbia has significant growth. Foreign currency income from tourism in 2007 was 30% higher than in 2006, amounting to 531.3 million US dollars, with a surplus of 44 million US dollars.

The share of foreign guests has grown to approximately 30%. In 2007 foreign guests realized 23% more overnight stays than in 2006, with highest numbers in the cities of Belgrade and Novi Sad, and in the mountain resorts of Kopaonik and Zlatibor.

Tourist centers have a better offer of original domestic food products and products of home made crafts, more and more with adequate certificates, however this form of offer of ecologically high quality is still only starting. In addition ''ethno villages'' are also appearing, as specific catering facilities offering authentic Serbian rural environments with characteristics reminiscent of the 19th and the beginning of the 20th century (Figure3, Figure 4).

Tourism and accompanying activities have better potentials for development if they are also technologically competitive, if they apply modern technologies, especially the utilization of global distribution systems and the Internet, as important factors for promotion and sales of tourist products. Their utilization would be especially important for smaller tourist destinations in rural areas of Serbia, because this would enable them to have a broad access to the tourism market at a lower cost. Researches show that younger generations in such areas are interested in new technologies and that they accept the principles of sustainability (Stupar, 2003).

Figure 3. Rural settlement, Stara planina, eastern part of Serbia (photo by arch. Ana Graovac, 2008. Used with permission).

ICT

Global ICT Development Trends

Today, information and communication technologies are in the development phase, offering tremendous possibilities to the society and the individual, with the outlook of becoming a part of our daily life that will fully transform the conducting of business, manufacturing, cultural development, and many other routine relations.

State of the art ICT are recognized as an important development factor, and are the focus of interest and activity of many international institutions, with themes relevant to their development and implementation present in many international documents: Agenda 21, Aarhus Convention, Lisbon Strategy 2000 and 2005, and eEurope Action Plan. In its documents, the EU initiates and supports projects prompting experimentation of cities relevant to ICT (eEurope 2002, eEurope 2005).

There is practically no country without its own policy for ICT development, and results of the already realized and of projects in realization offer significant experiences from the aspect of access, techniques, and potential results.

Benefits and advantages of ICT, especially the Internet, for the development of settlements, are enormous. This pertains to the quality of regulations, i.e. the "comfort" offered by the legal framework controlling utilization of the Internet, and influences the attractiveness of the state for potential investors in IT, telecommunications and other multimedia technologies. The manner whereby the use of ICT supplements existing components of cities reflects the existing social conditions of a country (Narushige, 2000).

ICT development projects differ, primarily relevant to their base, the level of development of the telecommunication system, the presence of ICT users, and the level of development of the information network. The basic goal is to

Figure 4. Traditional household, Stara planina, eastern part of Serbia Serbia (photo by arch. Ana Grao-vac, 2008. Used with permission).

utilize technological potentials in accordance with principles of sustainable development. The EU has its vision of sustainable development within a knowledge-based society (knowledge society), operationalized in the Policy of Sustainable Development until 2030.

Today, ICT is developing in several directions that can roughly be divided into two basic ones: development of ICT foundation – infrastructure (introduction of ICT as an integral part of all public services and of the economy, better accessibility of ICT, development of active data bases), and scientific research work – future ICT (development of next generation ICT, development of ICT as a "constitutive technology" (ISTAG, 2006)).

Developed countries are investing in ICT development. USA and Japan are channeling 30% of the funds for scientific research into ICT development, and Europe 18% (ISTAG, 2006). Serbia, on the other hand has no designated funds for ICT development in the budget for scientific research, however in the 2006-2008 period the National Investment Plan (NIP) will invest 42.8 million euro for the development of e-Government (SCORE project, 2007). Within the NIP, in addition to regular funds, additional investments for science in the 2006- 2011 period, a total of 30 million euro, are envisaged, and funds for co financing technical designing of project proposals for FP7 are also planned in the Budget. However, compared to funds invested in developed countries these are not large funds.

To understand and define potentials for applying ICT for development of rural regions, one should keep in mind the multifunctional character of agriculture, and the diverse range of activities in rural areas. ICT can in fact offer the required scope of response and assistance, and additionally speed up development by offering very diverse services - eGovernance, eCommunities, eCulture, eHealth, eBusiness, food safety, knowledge and education – distance learning (Serge, Vittuari, Ricci, 2005).

Figure 5. Household devices (Adapted from Dr. Dragan Vukmirovic, Kristina Pavlovic, Vladimir Sutic (edit). (2008). Upotreba informaciono-komunikacionih tehnologija u Republici Srbiji, 2008. Beograd, Republika Srbija: Republicki zavod za statistiku Srbije).

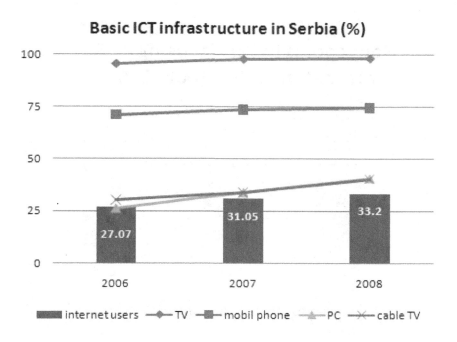

ICT Development Trends in Serbia

The infrastructural basis for ICT development in Serbia is constantly improving in recent years. Presently, there are three large providers of mobile telephone services and one provider of fixed telephone services. In the last five years, investments in this sector were over 1 billion euro. Optic infrastructure was set up, and all large cities were covered. Today, 74.5% of the Serbian population has mobile phones, and 98.4% of households have TV sets (Figure 5). iDVT is a completely new offer and good market response is expected.

In 2006 the Republic Agency for Telecommunications was formed, and it is expected to contribute to the development and regulation of this sector (Score project, Strengthening of Strategic Cooperation between the EU and the West Balkan Region in ICT Research, Review of Research Activities for ICT in Serbia).

According to data from 2008, 40.8% of Serbian households have PCs (in 2006 this was 26.5%). As for other phenomena analyzed in this assay, the presence of PCs in the urban and in rural regions in Serbia is 47.5% and 31.2%. Even though this difference is considerable, it is encouraging that this gap has decreased relevant to 2007, and that the level of growth has almost doubled (Figure 6).

The number of Internet users is also growing parallel to the growth of the number of PC users, however Internet is used to a larger extent by higher income households (Figure 7).

Relevant to the educational structure, according to data from 2008, among PC users individuals with university and higher education dominate (57%), followed by high school education (23.7%), with lowest numbers among individuals with lower than high school education (19.3%). In recent years there is a trend of growth for users with high school, higher and university educa-

Figure 6. Internet use in households, according to the type of settlement (2006 – 2008). (Adapted from Dr. Dragan Vukmirovic, Kristina Pavlovic, Vladimir Sutic (edit). (2008). Upotreba informaciono-komunikacionih tehnologija u Republici Srbiji, 2008. Beograd, Republika Srbija: Republicki zavod za statistiku Srbije).

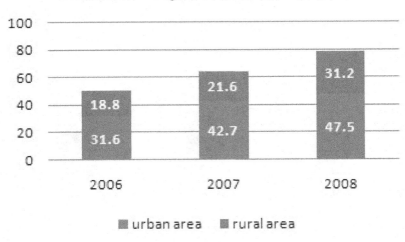

Figure 7. Internet use in households, according to the level of income (2008). (Adapted from Dr. Dragan Vukmirovic, Kristina Pavlovic, Vladimir Sutic (edit). (2008). Upotreba informaciono-komunikacionih tehnologija u Republici Srbiji, 2008. Beograd, Republika Srbija: Republicki zavod za statistiku Srbije).

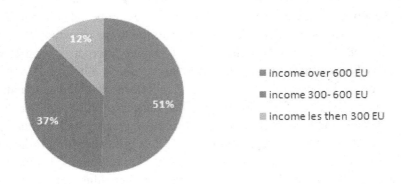

Figure 8. PC users according to educational structure (2006-2008). (Adapted from Dr. Dragan Vukmirovic, Kristina Pavlovic, Vladimir Sutic (edit) (2008). Upotreba informaciono-komunikacionih tehnologija u Republici Srbiji, 2008. Beograd, Republika Srbija: Republicki zavod za statistiku Srbije).

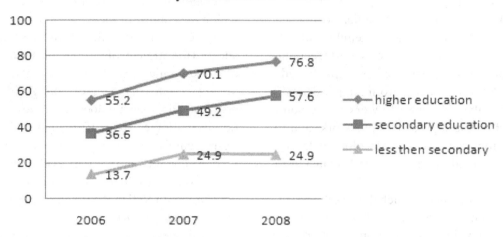

tion, while the percentage of users with lower levels of education is stagnating. Introduction of PC literacy in the educational system is in its infancy, although the number of PCs in schools has significantly grown in recent years. In 2003, about 14% of Serbian eighth grade students had the opportunity to use computers in science teaching (Antonijevic, 2003)(Figure 8).

Approximately 1.25 million inhabitants of Serbia use the Internet on a daily basis, and approximately 7% shop via the Internet. Projections for e-Commerce for 2010 are 346 million euro. The majority of users (60.4%) use the Internet as a source of information about goods and services, and 27% as a source of tourism information. Presently only 12.7% of investigation participants use Internet services for regular administrative services, even though this field has had the highest investments.

It is clear that rural regions in Central Serbia have less possibility to develop ICT, due to the fact that they have lower income, a lower level of education structure, and more modest conditions for education. Regardless, 2008 has seen a positive trend of growth of the number of Internet users in extra urban environments, as high as 44%.

Research of PC use in Serbia implemented by the Republic Statistical Bureau in 2008 indicates that approximately 98% of companies use computers in their operations, and that there have been no significant changes in the last three years. Approximately 92% of companies have Internet access, and of these approximately 69% have websites. In a survey in ICT users and their influence on operations, 22.5% of companies states that ICT use significantly contributed to the organization of the work process, 10.7% that this has significantly helped the development of new products and services, and 9.8% that this has significantly contributed to higher company income.

State Strategies and Programs for ICT Development

Together with other SEE countries, in 2002 Serbia signed eEurope projects, undertaking specific international obligations relevant to ICT development and implementation.

In 2002, SEE countries (Albania, Bosnia and Herzegovina, Croatia, Federal Republic of Yugoslavia (Serbia and Montenegro), Macedonia, and Moldova), signed the "eSEEurope Agenda for the Development of Information Society", undertaking the obligation to work in the coming period on the legislative framework, and to form environments for ICT development, as a basis for regional cooperation and inclusion in European trends.

The main document, which defines the policy of the Government of Serbia relative to ICT, is the Strategy of Development of Information Society in the Republic of Serbia, adopted in 2006. Its basic goals were to upgrade the status in ICT, to establish basic relations for participation of all most important partners, to direct certain funds for ICT utilization into priority national projects, to enable local initiatives, to promote social change, to indicate shortcomings, to research the effects of network communication, and to secure ICT development as the infrastructure which enables and offers required services.

The Strategy for the Development of Information Society is in its initial phase of implementation, and additional initiatives are needed to speed up its implementation and to assist the development of information society in Serbia (SCOREproject, 2007). To date, Serbia participated in FP 5 and FP 6 programs, within which some 60 projects were realized. The problem is that the regulation of the legislative framework which should support and ensure ICT development is lagging relevant to the planned dynamics, and that the means accessible within EU funds from 2007 to 2013 are still insufficiently used. To a certain extent, this is also due to the insufficient level of preparation for implementing the system of applying for such funds.

The Strategy for the Development of Information Society in the Republic of Serbia places considerable emphasis on the development of national research capacities, which is well positioned within the context of EU development plans, as well as within the context of local potentials and needs.

The Government of the Republic of Serbia has adopted the Strategy of Sustainable Development of the Republic of Serbia for 2008, and Serbia is the first country in the region, along with Montenegro, to adopt such a document. New information technologies are confirmed as an important instrument for the development of a competitive market economy and for the development or human resources as the main support for economic development (National Strategy for Sustainable Development, 2008).

Serbia needs to invest in human resources, especially in view of the fact that at the end of the 20th century 320 thousand educated individuals, mostly under 40 years of age, left the country (Penev, 2006). Regardless of this, the scientific research system in Serbia is much more developed and of better quality than could be presumed based on the level of economic development, which results from the constant influx of new educated human resources (SCOREproject, 2007).

The focus of development policies in Serbia is development of human resources, i.e. of scientific research work, which represents an apparent potential and a comparative advantage. Main areas of research supported by state investment are software, computer hardware, and telecommunication systems. Regardless of the visible benefit of such investments the fact remains that most projects under development will not contribute to the development of underdeveloped, rural areas, but will further strengthen the already existing lack of balance. There is the danger that implemented policies and strategies will not contribute to, or at least will not stop the process of depopulation of underdeveloped rural areas.

The strategy of AR Vojvodina adopted in 2007 – ''Basic Directions of Technological Development of the Autonomous Region of Vojvodina'', a region which has owing to migration trends annulled negative population growth, is aimed at providing means to retain and employ human resources. Central Serbia has no such strategy.

ICT Implementation for Sustainable Development

In EU documents, ICT is a novel and promising tool for economic development and the development of the overall society, which will enable the overcoming of 21st century challenges (ISTAG, 2006). It is expected that the development and the broadest implementation of ICT will enable prosperity in a manner that will be more equal, that it will influence upgrading of the general quality of life, and will enable development that will not have to be at the expense of degradation of natural resources. For this reason ICT development is directed by state and regional policies and initiatives.

Basic areas for ICT implementation are: administration, healthcare, and social welfare, education, and economic activity (trade, services, manufacturing, transport of goods). Its role is growing in local and global transfer of information, as well as in employment, development of information and leisure media, culture, sport, and recreation, but also in the domain of social contacts and organization of NGOs.

ICT development and implementation can support the development of an environmentally friendly economy, can improve the economy of transport, reduce energy consumption, reduce environmental pollution, improve efficiency of energy systems, improve population mobility by adding ''virtual mobility'', expand the potentials of the education system (distance learning), contribute to the independence and comfort of senior citizens and of individuals requiring some sort of assistance.

Adopted EU strategic documents permit a conclusion relative to the problems anticipated in the development of the technological society, for which a satisfactory solution is sought in advance:

- Dehumanization of relations – development of new social ties is expected at all levels;
- Loss of local cultural specificities – insisting on the preservation of the national language as the vehicle of culture;
- Fear that regardless of broad potentials for all, development will really benefit only certain groups – transparency and accessibility is expected to minimize this effect;
- Perception that development is too intensive and that the essential ''plunge'' will ensue before it is expected, and will be dramatic – development will have to be controlled to a certain extent.

Areas that Could Benefit from ICT and its Integral Implementation

ICT creates the environment for economic development, and underdeveloped rural areas in Serbia would in fact enjoy the highest benefits.

In case if ICT is applied for the development of rural areas of Serbia, the main goal in the first phase would primarily be directed toward the economic and the social aspect. The new economy is more oriented toward the production and distribution of information and services, and less toward the production of other types of goods (Friedich, Schoaafsma, 1999). In addition to services that ICT must provide – access to required information and business contacts, jointly forming potentials to develop adequate activities, they would also have to open the space for communication within the community in order to reestablish social ties which had been the basis of the vitality of these local communities, and that are in the present day context of social relations in economically developed countries and urban environments also a comparative advantage. Positive effects would be reflected also in the economic aspect – better possibilities for employment and choice of jobs, the quality of no privileged layers of the society would improve (ICT would be used as a means for social integration, for securing access and participation for handicapped citizens), inclusion in public life would be easier.

State strategies for the development of the ICT basis also form good foundations to take a step further – to integrate technologies into economic, cultural, social processes in order to especially assist specific communities.

ICT implementation and development could help to accelerate the development of the country and to ''skipping several steps'' that would otherwise be indispensable if the usual methods of urban-economic development, which demand more time for implementation and require more funds, were applied. This does not mean that the only goal is to electronically connect underdeveloped regions and to thus fulfill their basic needs without investments in the development of physical structures – roads, communal, educational, social and healthcare infrastructures. These two approaches must be simultaneous and support each other. It should be added that a higher level of democracy would also be achieved – due to data accessibility and transparency, and that the efficiency of public services for the citizens would be upgraded (Strrack, 1995).

Revitalization/regeneration of smaller settlements and villages would be based on interaction of tradition and modern technologies, i.e. on the development of authentic and autochthon values by applying ICT technology, because this would enable an additional "step forward". This would require an integrated approach, with the segment aimed at reestablishing social ties and the identity of the local community as the most sensitive area of development and implementation for such a project.

INITIATION AND ORGANIZATION OF A PROJECT FOR ICT IMPLEMENTATION FOR THE DEVELOPMENT OF RURAL AREAS

The project of assistance to the development of rural, underdeveloped areas in Serbia could be the first of the major, integrated projects of ICT development.

The Government of the Republic of Serbia has initiated strategic investments in the development of these regions. In 2007- 2008, 10 million euro were invested for construction of road, communal, and skiing infrastructure in the region of Stara planina, and considerable additional investments are expected, with a projection for public investments at a level of approximately 100 million euro, including the participation of foreign investors, and with the total value of the project by 2010 reaching approximately 550 million euro.

This is an investment in the underdeveloped area of East Serbia where all analyzed problems are very pronounced, but which is at the same time an area with exceptional natural characteristics, proclaimed a Nature Park and a protected natural resource with endemic species and rich in paleontological, speleological, and archeological sites.

Local governments have accepted these plans as the only possibility for the development of their municipalities, with parallel negative reactions of NGOs working on activities aimed at protecting Stara Planina as a preserved natural resource.

Local communities in this area, in an organized manner, and due to personal initiatives of individuals, are making an effort to present, make more accessible and develop own tourist offer using the Internet. Presently, these sites are primarily targeting the domestic market and the diaspora with its pronounced demand for domestic foods. The Tourist Organization of Serbia and local tourist organizations have raised the level of access to information, which has certainly contributed to the development of tourism evident in recent years.

What is lacking is in integrally conceived and organized project which would also encompass aspects that are presently not included, aspects of communication and organization for the direct producers, their education, access to information about state and local projects, and their mutual communication and organization, but also other fields that must be developed within local communities – social welfare, healthcare, culture, etc.

Due to local specificities, the communication network should also include the offer of goods, services, and information, for following target groups:

- Local population, young people without employment or with inadequate employment from urban milieus, with high school and higher education, with a significant level of awareness relevant to ecological ''healthy living'', etc.,
- Owners of housing facilities – population temporarily employed abroad and owners of weekend homes (in Serbia, especially in the 1970s and 1980s, there was a pronounced trend of building houses for recreation – weekend homes, which was to a certain degree compensation for the lack of possibility to own a house in the city where construction of apartments was organized),
- NGOs active in environmental protection,
- Associations of applied and other artists (organization of art colonies),
- Sports associations, etc.

The state has already created funds to offer favorable loans or once only assistance to small enterprises and individual development projects. However part of such funds could be designated and directed toward development projects that would unify all required aspects of development for rural areas. For example, within such projects, the state should assist the ''branding'' of the offer, the providing of protection for certain authentic and high quality foods, the promotion of climate, mountain, and eco tourism, and should use market analysis to channel the local offer.

As an example, there is an interesting and useful inventive Serbian project for implementation of ICT relevant to available resources and needs, which was presented in the finale of a World Bank competition entitled ''Sustainable Agriculture for Development'', with 2,000 projects from all over the world. It was developed by the company ''GM konsalting'' from Kragujevac, with the idea to use mobile phones possessed by over 80% of the agricultural population, and SMS to facilitate for agricultural producers the access to information on market prices of products, as well as communication with potential buyers.

Problems in Realization and Expected Results

One of the probably major problems is that the state must be prepared to initiate a project that would require a much higher level of communication and harmonization, i.e. more political coherence.

The basis for initiating such a project exists (readiness of local communities to support and implement development projects, development of the information base, investments in scientific research work, constant growth of ICT utilization).

There is also the issue of acceptance of ICT projects by the local population, their readiness to accept a new form of communication. For this reason, as already mentioned, it is necessary to use development projects to find frameworks for communication that would be supported by technical potentials, but also rooted in tradition and habits of such communities, and that would at the same time prompt the reestablishing of old ties and the creation of new ties. Internal connections, i.e. an internal ICT network should afford everyone his personal identity and personal space for creativity, but also a clear motive for the formation of a community that works together and offers mutual assistance.

Figure 9. Comparative presentation of GDP and the number of Internet users for countries in the region (2006)

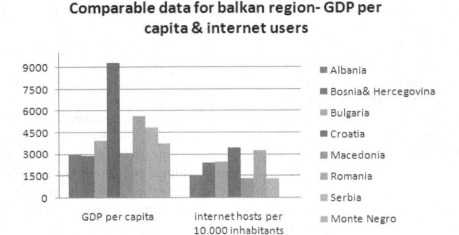

Stopping the process of depopulation of smaller settlements and villages would be the first and the most important indicator of success of such a project. The period required to note its effects would be a minimum of 10 years. The best indicator would be a higher percentage of the next generation that would decide to stay and to accept a location and a way of life.

Economic strengthening of local communities and of entire areas would increase investments in better transport communications and social, healthcare and communal infrastructure, which would in turn influence economic development.

Similar Problems in the Region

In the region, ICT development has similar trends, with constant growth in recent years, and direct ties to economic development. For example, the relative number of Internet users in Serbia is double compared to Bosnia and Herzegovina, but one half compared to Croatia which has almost in the same ratio higher Per Capita GDP. Romania has approximately 50% higher Per capita GDP than Serbia, and a similarly higher percent of Internet users (Figure 9).

The status of countries in the broader region varies, from EU member states (Hungary, Greece, Slovenia), candidates (Croatia, Macedonia, Turkey, Romania and Bulgaria in certain of its components), to potential candidates (Serbia, Montenegro, Albania, B&H), which also implies different levels of political and economic stability. The problem of underdeveloped rural areas is also present in Montenegro, Albania, B&H, Croatia, Macedonia, Turkey, Romania and Bulgaria, and this is sure to be a topic of future regional cooperation.

Ex-Yugoslav countries and countries of the Balkan Peninsula have similar cultural and historic heritage, and similar economic development problems. Balkan countries have strong patriarchal family relationships and similar family structures, especially pronounced in rural areas. Their ethnic tradition is also similar: especially in the domain of building, ethno music, traditional dress, folk dances, local foods. During the second half of the 20th century, most of these countries developed their social economic systems based on a doctrine of socialism or communism.

The most important comparative advantage of smaller rural communities in the Balkan region, within the context of the globalization process, may well be the preserved cultural heritage and the local tradition, natural resources, and autochthonous environment. The fact that during the period of economic stagnation these regions were mostly protected from excessive urbanization is also important.

Today, there are also differences and problems in cooperation between countries of the Balkan peninsula, seemingly insurmountable, however with good signals that this may not be so (in addition to the signed strategic documents, there are important concrete results: the establishing of a free trade zone for SEE countries in 2007, and the signing of the Memorandum for a Common Electricity Market on 2008).

It can be presumed with certainty that local projects and projects organized at the level of one state based on ICT, will, both in accordance with general trends and policies, and due to the very nature of ICT, over time become part of, and even maybe the key to regional cooperation. Basic preconditions will be project vitality and the fact if they have within their concept a sufficient number of common denominators that can serve as a focus for the interests of users and participants also outside a particular local community, i.e. state.

CONCLUSION

At this point in time it is very important for Serbia to set development priorities. The development and implementation of ICT via directional projects can be the key to overcoming:

- Discontinuity of development in the last two decades,
- Unequal regional development,
- Negative trends of depopulation of certain regions.

Certain underdeveloped parts of Central Serbia (rural communities in hilly regions, difficult to access rural areas, zones of National parks and border zones) are the most vulnerable.

Today, numerous countries state following goals as the strategic commitment for the development of rural settlements: the upgrading of the quality of life, economic development, development of the global network (connecting settlements locally and globally). The most important and ever more efficient tool for achieving these goals is the development of telecommunication infrastructure which would encompass the most important aspects of urbo-economic development – the development of the economy, of the education system, and of social infrastructure, with the potential to more efficiently apply principles of sustainable development.

Economic development must rely on a strong local community, supported by an educated and labor active population, motivated to remain in their environment and contribute to its development.

Relative to the level of development of ICT basics in the initial phases such technical solutions could be sought which would rely on existing capacities and technology (networking via SMS and iDVT).

Sustainable development and a knowledge-based economy require an intensive role of ICT. The Republic of Serbia still lacks a sufficiently broad level of IT literacy. Data indicates that ICT use is very low and inefficient, and if this is not the case, ICT is used passively rather than creatively. ICT development in Serbia should be aimed at improving the efficiency and competitiveness of the national economy by upgrading information exchange and information accessibility, and especially e-business, as well as economic-technological communication in general. In addition, the population, especially the young generation needs to be empowered for the broadest and creative to utilization of ICT, in order to enable them to equally compete on the international scene.

However, at this time, ICT development is not a priority in Serbia, even though it has a significant place in all strategic documents. In view of the complexity of local socioeconomic problems and the interrelationship of processes in progress there is an actual space for giving a significant role to ICT development and the development of neglected rural areas.

ICT development can provide underdeveloped rural areas with better access to information required for the development of agriculture, tourism and accompanying services, via a direct communication with potential markets as well as with local networks within the local community, with institutions and with other entrepreneurs, to enable them to unite and offer a product and a service at a high level of competitiveness.

Networking of rural settlements should become a strategic program of the state. Such a strategy should however contain aspects on how to renew the population and revitalize the almost abandoned and economically underdeveloped parts of the territory by relying on their comparative advantages. Virtual linking with cities, even metropolises, would considerably reduce both the disadvantages of rural life and the advantages city life, and would enable villages to compete on a global level. Electronic networking of rural settlements would create two spatial structures – the real and the virtual – while their intertwining would form a unified entity fully able to compete with larger cities and metropolises.

REFERENCES

Antonijevic, R. (2007). *Usage of computers and calculators and students achievement: results from TIMSS 2003*. ERIC, ED497737, retrieved from http://eric.ed.gov/ERICWebPortal/recordDetail?accno=ED497737

Books of Census (2002). Belgrade, Serbia: The Statistical Office of the Republic of Serbia.

Cabinet Office. UK (2000). *E-government: a strategic framework for public services in the Information Age*. Retrieved from http://www.e-envoy.gov.uk/ukonline/st rategy.html

Castels, M. (1996). *The Rise of the Network Society*. Oxford, UK: Blackwell Publishers.

Commission, E. U. (2003b). *Global standards for the Global Information Society, DN IP/03/1374*. Retrieved from http://europa.eu.int/documents/index_en.htm

Djukic, A. (2004). Internet kao podrska razvoju sela. In M. Ralevic (Ed.), *Planiranje i uredjenje sela i ruralnih podrucja*, (pp. 219- 231). Srbija, Banja Vrujici: Udruzenje urbanista Srbije, *eS-EEurope Agenda for the Development of the Information Society* (n.d.). Retrieved from www.eseeuropeconference.org/agenda.pdf

Djukic, A., & Colic, R. (2001). Moguce transformacije razvoja seoskih naselja. In M. Ralevic, R. Malobabic & R. Bogdanovic (Ed.), *Selo u Promenama*, (pp. 171-177). Beograd, Srbija: Udruzenje urbanista Srbije.

Doyle, S., & Batty, M. (1998). *Vitrual Regeneration*. London, UK: Centre for Advanced Spatial Analysis, University College London.

European Comission. (2002). *eWORK 2002-Status Report on New Ways to Work in the Knowledge Economy*. Retrieved from http://europa.eu.int/information_society/topics/ework

Friedich, S., & Schoaafsma, M. (1999). *Cyberspace and the Loss of the Concentracion and Centrifugation*. Paper presented in TAN 3 Conference report. Berlin, Germany.

Friedman, Y. (1980). *A better life in towns*. Brussels: EU, Council of Europe.

Goleman, D. (1995). *Emotional Intelligence*. New York: Bantam books.

Graham, S., & Marvin, S. (1996). *Telecommunications and the city: Electronic spaces, urban places*. New York: Routledge.

Imagawa, N. (n.d.). *Metamorphosis of Space: Long-life space connecting time-thoughts on materials and structures-difference between possible and impossible*. Retrieved from http://www.um.u-tokyo.ac.jp/dm2k-umdb/publish_db/books/va/english/virtual/08.html

ISTAG. (2006). *Report from the Information Society Technologies Advisory Group*. Retrieved from http://www.cordis.lu/ist/istag.htm

Ivić, I., Marojević, S., Chinapah, V., Uvalić Trumbić, S., Ivanović, S., Damjanović, R., et al. (2001). *Sveobuhvatna analiza sistema obrazovanja u SRJ*. Beograd, Srbija: UNICEF.

Kahn, H., Bronjn, W., & Martel, L. (1976). *The next 200 years*. New York: Hudson Institute.

Kolarevic, B. (1996). Space, Place, and the Infobahn: Architecture, Urbanism and the Electronic Infromation Age. In *Architecture& Urbanism at the Turn of the III Millennium* []. Beograd, Srbija: Faculty of Architecture University of Belgrade.]. *Proceedings*, *1*, 61–69.

Kostov, Z. (2006). *Global tendecies and local implications: Cyber exslusion and within Western Balkan countries*. Discussion paper 40, Proceedings of the Informing Science & IT Education Conference (InSITE), Centre for the Study of Global Governance, London School of Economics and Political Science, London. Retrieved from http://www.lse.ac.uk/Depts/global/Publications/DiscussionPapers/DP40.pdf

Milovanović, D. (2001). Interaktivni urbanizam: novi oblici saradnje podrzani internetom i novim kompjuterskim tehnologijama. In N. Randjelović, & M. Ralevic (Ed.), *Urbani menadzment, urbani marketing i preduzetnistvo*, (pp. 63-71). Beograd, Srbija: Udruzenje urbanista Srbije.

Mitchell, W. (1995). *City of Bits: Space, Place and the Infobahn*. Cambridge, MA: MIT Press.

Mitchell, W. (1999). *E-topia: Urban Life, Jim-But Not as We Know It*. Cambridge, MA: MIT Press.

Narushige, S. (2000, August). Urban Planning, Information Technology, and Cyberspace. *Journal of Urban Technology*, *7*(2), 105. doi:10.1080/713684111

Osnovni pravci tehnoloskog razvoja Autonomne pokrajine Vojvodine (2007). Novi Sad, Srbija: Izvrsno vece Autonomne pokrajine Vojvodina.

Penev, G. (2006). *Stanovnistvo i domacinstva Srbije prema popisu 2002*. Belgrade, Serbia: Statistical office of the Republic of Serbia, Institute of Social Sciences and Association of Demographers of Serbia. SCORE-045384 in FP6 (2007). The ICT Research environment in Serbia. *Strengthening the Strategic Cooperation Between the EU and Western Balkan Region in the field of ICT Research*. Retrieved from http://consultations.score-project.eu/attach/ictcr_rs_en.pdf

Segre, A., Vittuari, M., & Ricci, R. (2005). ICT and rurality, the role of information in the development process of the rural areas of the Western Balkans. *Rural development 2005 - Development of knowledge and information society in rural areas*. Retrieved from http://www.lzuu.lt/rural_development/archive/2005

Sieridis, A. B. (2006). *New ICT Concepts and Projects for the Development of Rural Areas: The project Bio@gro*. Retrieved from http://bioagro.aua.gr/modules/wfsection/html/sideridis_2006.pdf

Simonovic, D. (1976). *Sistem seoskih naselja u uzoj Srbiji*. Belgrade, Serbia: IAUS.

Statistical Office of the Republic of Serbia. (1991). *Statistical Yearbook of Serbia 2007*. Belgrade, Republic of Serbia: Author.

Stevanovic, R. (2006). Migrantsko stanovnistvo Srbije. In G. Penev (Ed.), *Stanovnistvo i domacinstva Srbije prema popisu 2002* (pp. 71- 106). Belgrade, Serbia: Statistical office of the Republic of Serbia, Institute of Social Sciences and Association of Demographers of Serbia.

Strack, C. (1995). *Managing cities with the help of telecomunications.* Retrieved from http://www.kpnqwest.at. /give/gv95/straclec.html

Stupar, A. (2003). Informacione tehnologije i razvoj ruralnih podrucja- mogucnosti i ogranicenja. In R. Bogdanovic, & M. Ralevic (Eds.), *Selo u novim razvojnim uslovima.* Beograd, Srbija: Udruzenje urbanista Srbije.

Tofler, A. (1980). *The third way.* New York: Bantam books.

Virilio, P. (2000). *Informaticka bomba.* Novi Sad, Srbija: Svetovi.

Vukmirovic, D., Pavlovic, K., & Sutic, V. (Eds.). (2008). *Upotreba informaciono- komunikacionih tehnologija u Republici Srbiji, 2008.* Beograd, Republika Srbija: Republicki zavod za statistiku Srbije.

Chapter 3
Green Urban Planning and Design for Smarter Communities

Ozge Yalciner Ercoskun
Gazi University, Turkey

ABSTRACT

Information and Communication Technology (ICT) changes the concept of place and social life. Researchers should find some solutions about how to combine ICT with sustainable construction to revitalize an existing neighborhood and to create a new model for growing areas especially in small cities. The objectives of this study are to search for new ways to create sustainable communities with the sustainable use of ICTs, to discuss the advantages and disadvantages and the use of ICTs in cities, to put a new approach as 'eco-tech' city, and to explore the potential ways of creating sustainability in practice. The study summarizes the advantages and disadvantages of the use of ICTs in cities and describes smart city and eco-tech city concepts. The following part, which is consisted of a discussion of urban planning and design, incorporating ICT for the construction of sustainable communities, explores the prospect that dehumanized communication can be ameliorated through progressive, innovative and green urban planning and design strategies.

INTRODUCTION

"We are convinced that sustainable human life on this globe cannot be achieved without sustainable local communities. Cities are key players in the process of changing lifestyles, production, consumption and spatial patterns" (The Aalborg Charter, 1994). The big question is how to meet the needs of urban systems. Is there any way to incorporate ICT in urban planning and design to construct sustainable communities? Can ICTs be employed to develop a prototype for a smart or ecological and technological (eco-tech) city? This chapter attempts to find some solutions to such questions.

ICT is a tool only however if it is not taken seriously and dealt with professionally, it can be a 'bastion to the denial of reality' in urbanism. ICT causes spatial changes in an urban area. Basically, it

DOI: 10.4018/978-1-60566-822-2.ch003

transforms some facilities into telespaces, such as bookstores to bitstores, galleries to virtual museums, schools to virtual campuses, banking chambers to ATMs, department stores to e-shopping and work in offices to telework (Drewe, 2000). The remarkable power of ICTs in supporting new types of information flow, communication, transaction and cultural experience can be mobilized and shaped in various ways, which can have positive impact on cities. The challenge is to design local ICTs, which are equitable and supportive of a genuine community and civic dialogue (Arifoglu, 2004). New models of social innovation are needed to bridge urban digital divides and to improve skills in different groups of community (Graham, 2002). Harvey points out social divide. For him, community often means enhancing privilege on the already privileged and leaving the underprivileged to their own devices. Since the 1950s, the nature of planning and zoning laws have fostered the separation of economic classes, destroyed open space, and eroded the sense of community and care for the common good. In this climate, public discourse degenerates into competitive clashes over resources pitting the suburbs against downtowns and the rich against the poor. Harvey argues that the direct effects of this polarization of rich and poor are: Division and fragmentation of the metropolitan space, loss of sociality across diversity, and localized defensive posture towards the rest of the city. He notes that global income inequalities are causing large-scale environmental devastation, cultural destruction, and the undermining of social cohesion. If policy created the situation, perhaps policy can alter it. He advocates the renewal of utopian dreaming as a hope. "As we collectively produce our cities, so we collectively produce ourselves. We need projects concerning what we want our cities to be are, therefore, projects concerning human possibilities, who we want, or, perhaps even more pertinently, who we do not want to become" (Harvey, 2000:200). Once again Harvey encourages us to engage in imagining utopias of urban space where the role of designer are assigned.

Urban designers should use new technical tools offered by new technological instruments. There should be balance between real spaces and digital spaces. Urban designers play a prominent role as a weaver between different groups and organizer of public places (Velibeyoglu, Gencel, 2001). Additionally, a new urban design approach should be generated for the cities of the future.

The symbolic importance of labeling and branding cities with 'cyber', 'intelligent', 'digital' or 'smart' prefixes is stressed around the world (Graham & Marvin, 1999). The solution proposed here is an 'eco-tech' (ecological and technological) city model to contribute to the better sustainability of small cities supporting localities in the globalized world. Such urban strategies shape face-to-face interactions in place in parallel with electronically mediated ones in eco-tech cities. Some kinds of technology can be useful in eco-tech cities (Bogunovich, 2002): Environmental technologies, which encompass technologies of energy, water and waste; ICTs, which include computer based hardware and software that enable the transfer of data; the environmental sensing technologies in wired or wireless environments, and finally, GIS, where geo-referenced data is stored, transformed, visualized, queried and reported (Bandyopadhyay, 2001).

The objectives of this study are 1) to examine the question of how to create sustainable communities with the sustainable use of ICTs 2) to discuss the advantages and disadvantages and the use of ICTs in cities 3) to put a new approach as 'eco-tech' city, and 4) to explore the potential ways of creating sustainability in practice.

The first part of this chapter states the advantages and disadvantages of the use of ICTs in cities and makes a description of smart city and eco-tech city concepts. The following part discusses urban planning and design approaches that incorporate ICT into the construction of sustainable communities. Developing new approaches and techniques for appropriate design outcomes is the main challenge to be explicated about how the changing urban community can continue to express an ongoing positive relationship with the natural environment by the sustainable use of ICTs.

ADVANTAGES AND DISADVANTAGES OF THE USE OF ICTS IN CITIES, SMART CITY AND ECO-TECH CITY CONCEPTS

The new ICTs are advantageous to many sectors. Most businesses, governments and schools have now moved from manual methods to the use of ICT while processing data. People can talk to each other when they have access to the right technology. Video conferencing and email have reduced the need for business travel, which has allowed people to have more time at home with their families than being stuck in an airport. Less travel generates less pollution, as fewer cars and aircraft is used. Video conferencing and remote control of another computer has allowed teachers and trainers to run lessons at distant locations. The 24-hour news networks bring events from around the world live. These facts point to the fact that a society can react almost immediately.

Being able to access the company network from anywhere means that people are no longer tied to the office, they could just as easily work from home. Because of this, teleworking is becoming more common. Additionally, international corporations' employees can travel from country to country on business and yet settle down to a fully networked local office desk and work as if they are at their home office.

Many developed country citizens in the use Internet while looking for a job, career advice and a new house. It shows that the Internet has become a milestone in searching for necessary information.

Having all these methods of communicating has a tendency to make people lazy. They may no longer bother to talk face to face; instead, they send an email to a work colleague only a few meters away. Some organizations have even introduced 'email free days' to encourage people to actually talk to one another. Furthermore, family members, each playing or working on their own computers may actually send instant messages to each other in the same house rather than talk to one another.

Technology can have a negative effect on family relationships. With this much entertainment availability, there is less need to actually sit around the table and talk to one another at home. Text messaging during lessons is a distraction and so this has a bad effect on learning at school. Being able to communicate with colleagues from a desk means people just do not walk around enough to keep fit. Eventually, a growing population of unfit people may have an impact on their health.

Electronic items, such as mobile phones are very expensive items; therefore, they encourage theft and other crime. As with most technologies, there is always a blend of good and bad effects on society. But for any technological development to succeed, it must have an overall benefit to the end-user (Akca, Sayili & Esengun, 2007). There should be always a balance in smart cities.

Smart cities can be accepted as the demonstration areas of e-government applications. Smart city concept is integrated with the information-based economy. Research and the use of new technologies accounted for the development in science, industry and commerce in a smart city. The impacts of ICTs can be observed in smart cities. The e-governance concept links the administrative institutions to these technologies. Public bodies using ICTs in management, commerce and communication across offer e-governance with multi-participation.

The financial services, information technologies and communication industry in a smart city bring economic development. Smart spaces are integrated with infrastructure in a smart city. Local governments should share their decisions, plans and projects with developing their internet networks for effective city management, should present some guidelines, make interactive talks with the community in the e-democracy process and virtual libraries should be created (Odendaal, 2003).

A study conducted in January 2005 in MIT explained smart cities, and stated that new century urban projects are located at the intersection of technology, urban design, social policies and real estate development. These projects vary in size, organization and management. As mixed use projects, they are home to technology enterprises, including enterprises that leverage information technology, and to creative workers who both live and work in development zones. The case studies are on Arabianranta-Helsinki, Seoul Digital Media City, Crossroads-Copenhagen, One north-Singapore etc. The televillage of Helsinki, Arabianranta has been developing since 1999 and it will be completed in 2010. The land supplies began in 2002 in Seoul Media City and are almost completed. Copenhagen was inaugurated in 2002 and works efficiently with universities and ministries today. One north- Singapore is in the second phase of construction, many developers started to construct a Fusionopolis for multifunctional facilities today. What new century cities have in common are (MIT Center For Real Estate, 2005, p.4):

1. They promote innovation to achieve significant social and economic value for their host cities. These projects lead to development of highly creative, cutting edge, value-added production in the global high technology fields, thereby building substantial social and economic capital for the geographic regions in which they are located.

2. They are livable. These developments are designed for a high degree of livability. The result is the creation of spaces and places that attract the younger generation of creative workers to these live/work/play environments that melt the old boundaries in space and time between residential, office, and retail/entertainment real estate.

3. The public and private sectors are collaborated. These developments are characterized by partnerships among governments, real estate developers, educational or research institutions, and technology companies.

4. Information and media technologies are woven into the design of these cities. These developments are pioneering integration of advanced communication and media technologies into the physical form and fabric of new century cities, and into the enterprises, institutions, retail and entertainment establishments, and residences that make them up. ICTs, which are applied to residential, work and recreational functions make life easier. They are used for the development of water, electricity, and cleaning and security systems. ICTs are tools for management of traffic, logistics, and car parking and public transport systems. The information on date, timetable and location can be found easily with these technologies. The communication is held between individuals, groups and business partners. ICTs with media technologies perform art; show and other experiences give the feeling of space in the smart cities.

Furthermore, eco-tech city proposed in this study, is an ecological friendly smart city and is seen as the city of tomorrow. Eco-tech is defined as technological equipment and tool that works with alternative energy resources in the world. In the architectural field, Slessor (1997) defines eco-tech architecture, and gives some world examples of sustainable architecture, high technology and eco-tech at the building scale. Marras (1999) discusses the philosophy of eco-tech architecture as well. These major studies explain the eco-tech concept explicitly. The topic is quite new; there is only a plenty of research and city planning literature on the application of the concept to city planning. The research of Bogunovich (2002) is the source of inspiration of this study. Moreover, Amborski and Lister give some clues on eco-tech settlement structure in their project report of Milton's development area in Canada. Therefore, this study refers to the researchers above and creates unique ideas for settlements.

Eco-tech is the transformation of one way of ecology (oykos-logos[1]) to technology (tekne-logos[2]) by smart tools appropriate to the physical rules of nature. Eco-tech, in-between ecology and technology, is a paradigm based on natural elements and processes that meets the requirements of sustainable planning by fitting it into the new century by using technology (Marras, 1999).

Today, garden cities with a lot of preserved natural open space, energy efficient cities that use alternative energy and reduce commuting, and other urban models that promote urban sustainability remain only as green or compact but also as smart in the 21st century. Eco-tech city planning contributes to better sustainability of cities. This subject is a utopia or techno-ecotopia[3] (Bogunovich, 2002).

Historically, eco-villages evolved from intentional, often self-sufficient communities that have their roots in the 1960s commune movement, as a reaction against urban decay. (For example, "The Farm" in Tennessee is one of the original commune-style, activist-oriented eco-villages. See http://gen.ecovillage.org/ for other examples of eco-villages around the world). Today, the eco-village concept has a broader appeal and may share many of the same features as other sustainable community developments. In particular, the eco-tech city concept is based on innovations in high technology resulting in more sustainable building designs that facilitate flexibility of space and advanced telecommunication. For context, the eco-tech city concept can be considered within a spectrum of sustainable or "green" developments that ranges from the more radical alternative communities to progressive New Urbanist and "smart-wired" communities (Amborski & Lister, 2002).

By means of technology, four kinds of technology can be useful in eco-tech cities: "Environmental Technologies (ET)" which encompass a broad range of technologies of energy, water and waste; "Information Technologies (IT)" which include the well known range of computer based hardware and software and the environmental sensing technologies to gather environmental data; "Geographic Information Technologies (GIS)" where geo-referenced data is stored, transformed, manipulated, managed, visualized, updated, queried and reported related with databases as tabular data (Bandyopadhyay, 2001). Urban information system which is a part of GIS include land use analysis, preparing development plans, environmental plans, monitoring and control of eco-zones, transportation etc. and sharing these on internet (Yalciner, 2002). The fourth one is the "Communication Technologies (CT)" which enables the transfer of environmental data, information, knowledge, and decisions; in wired or wireless environments. Their overall purpose is to overcome spatial distance and enable the flow and availability of urban and environmental information in real time to gain time.

Eco-tech city is a local solution- locally shaped model in a small scale, for raising awareness by design with nature, created by economic planning with energy saving, implemented in a short time with a plan promoting local climate, local culture and landscape, supported by eco-technologies which bring adaptation, flexibility, multi-use and reduce distance. It is designed by proactive planning approach, which is participatory, sharing and considering local information (Van der Ryn, 1999).

The principles of eco-tech city can be explained as the following (Karaaslan & Ercoskun, 2006):

Eco-tech city aims to reduce waste by technology and promotes renewable energy. It improves the quality of life. Eco-tech city changes the current planning understanding by sustaining environmental values and natural resources with the use of nature friendly technologies. It is self-sufficient because it produces its own energy and food. A settlement planned with the eco-tech approach, will be developed economically as well.

It promotes sustainable transport and reduces emissions for urban health by using environmental technologies. Eco-tech city is planned in a natural habitat for human comfort by selecting convenient locations for specific urban functions by using geographic information technologies. In an eco-tech city, location selections for living, working and leisure facilities in proximity facilitate fuel saving and increases social integration. Mixed-use decisions in this city create more alive, safe and equal urban environment. Finally, eco-tech city, which is planned nature-friendly, is disaster-resistant.

The eco-tech development pattern in new growth areas should be designed on the principles of New Urbanism. There exists a strong emphasis on the creation of a road system for vehicles and pedestrians to create connectivity, viewscapes, and accessibility to community resources. Each neighborhood will be centered on a neighborhood centre that includes a range of uses, including schools, daycare and religious facilities, convenience commercial and a park to provide a focus and gathering place for residents like Seaside Florida, the first New Urbanist community (Logan, 2001, Gauzin-Müller, 2002).

Eco-tech city which has a mixed use and compact planning/design; and when planned in collaboration with local investor, local management and technical team, can decrease the ecological footprint of that area by using high performance ecological buildings and city technologies. Flexible, adaptable living and working spaces are created by the state of the art telecommunication infrastructure. By using distance learning, interactive education and real time teleconferencing technologies; the social and environmental transportation costs will decrease (Mahizhnan, 1999). Three basic principles will be integrated: "the public", "well operated economy" and "clean and healthy environment" (Amborski & Lister, 2002).

The planning and design of the residential neighborhoods of a community are related to human and environmental aspects with a physical character that reflects the life of the community (Saleh, 2004). Eco-tech design, which offers this possibility is the combination of ecological, sustainable, high performance, green city and smart wired, techno-cities with high-tech living and working spaces. Many eco-cities and techno-cities exist in the world today but the settlements, which are based on both ecology and technology, are rather few.

The worldwide examples for such developments include an eco-tech village project, which was built for the development area of City of Milton in Canada (BGD, 2002). A campaign is held in Waitakere, New Zealand called eco-tech action, aims to transform the technological city to eco-tech city with public participation (WETA, 2004). Another example, Eco-Viikki, in the periphery of Helsinki, Finland is a techno-city with ecological principles (Viikki, 2004). Arcosanti is a famous and old eco-settlement in the middle of a desert with upgraded technology (Luke, 1994, Arcosanti, 2005). Another Scandinavian example is Bo01, an urban fragment in Malmö, Sweden, one of the most sustainable settlements in Europe, has an award in Housing Expo in 2001 and can compete with the Milton project by being closer to the eco-tech concept (Singh, 2004, Ekostaden, 2004). The other example is the referred Integer project in UK, which is more flexible project package and can be built in anywhere (Clark, 2001). The brand of "eco-tech" is only used in Milton and Waitakere, however, not resembled in the examples of Eco-Viikki, Arcosanti, Bo01 and Integer. But it can be stated that these settlements resemble the eco-tech concept. These cases are the best practices, which can be sources of inspiration for the cities of tomorrow in both developed and developing countries.

The idea of eco-tech design for small cities is derived from a doctorate dissertation (Ercoskun, 2007). The dissertation includes a performance guide that is consisted of 6 major themes. This guide aims to create a tool for eco-tech urban design techniques for small town development for their sustainability. It is useful to planners, developers and other decision-makers. Eco-tech design concept can be better understood with an operational design guide and eco-tech concept strategies and performance targets can determine sustainable urban design components.

While summarizing the concept of an eco-tech settlement and giving the main ideas that pioneer in the field (Ercoskun, 2007), the dissertation offers the design of a new development area next to a small town. The area is about 20-30 ha similar to the examples in the world. 1/3 of the built-up area is a low-rise residential area, and 2/3 of it is a mixed-use area. Residential areas are designe d on the silent part of the area, approximately 500-600 m away to the current settlement. Computer programs with shade cones measure height of the buildings and the distances between the buildings and their energy performances are simulated. The mixed-use area is oriented close to the current center with an appropriate distance. The area is walkable and close to the public transit stops. The amenities serve this new population close of about 3000-5000 inhabitants. The sense of neighborhood should be improved.

Low density and medium density residential areas are recommended for eco-tech settlement. Low-density areas have large permaculture gardens. Medium density areas are closer to the mixed-use area. In the area, life- and work units are designed for freelance workers with flexible interior design components. An eco-tech community center is of 8000 m² with a large green roof. A supermarket serving organic products and hardware department exist in the area.

New facilities such as a theater, a cinema, day-care center, a multifunctional hall, youth clubs and an ecological education center are recommended to improve socio-cultural life. Swimming pools and tennis courts will be built for enhancing the sense of community and healthy public. All amenities are within the walking distance. All of the designs should protect or restore at least 75% of the biodiversity and ecology in the area (Ercoskun, 2007).

A green street is designed in an eco-tech settlement. A ring road with traffic, bicycle and pedestrian lanes shaded by large trees connects live/work areas. Land uses are clustered in walking distances to promote accessibility and reduce transportation demands. The residential area includes a car-free section surrounded by the ring road and supported by public transport vehicles and bicycles. Performance targets are defined to increase the number of kilometers walked and to develop green roads. A bicycle network is proposed. A car-pooling system can be built in the eco-tech site in order to offer access to the environment. Additionally, green buses running by biogas circulate in the ring road.

Photovoltaic (PV) systems are proposed on the roof of commercial and administrative buildings of the eco-tech site, as well as on the parapets of live & work units and other detached houses. PV systems are used for street lighting. Moreover, collective solar gardens are proposed for the mixed-use area and residential area for heating of water in the units. Integrated systems with wind turbine and solar energy can be used in autumn and winter for effective use of energy. A geo-exchange pump is proposed in every detached house in the eco-tech site, and a biogas plant is proposed to produce energy from solid waste (Ercoskun, 2007).

Rainwater is collected by roof leaders of detached houses in the eco-tech site and by rain barrels that collects water to use in landscaping and toilet flushing; additionally, a biotope pond is built. Gray water coming from kitchen and bathroom are collected from residences and commercial buildings of the eco-tech site, treated and reused for irrigation and toilet flushing.

All buildings are constructed from local or recycled material and measured in the eco-tech site. Live-work units in mixed-use area of the eco-tech site have flexible housing design including mobile walls. Detached houses can be of timber; row houses can be of stone, timber, adobe and straw bale. These techniques are applied and measured by LEEDS etc.

An open and green system is proposed for the eco-tech community and is composed of arterial open space which connects and integrates eco-tech community to adjacent neighborhoods, collector open space which links eco-tech site to old town and nearby recreational areas and local open space which gives opportunity to access collector and arterial open spaces, established in conjunction with local. Every resident has an access to the open space with a 3-minute walk and fruit trees are planted in all parks. Green roofs are applied to the eco-tech center and supermarket in the mixed-use area. The south facades of the buildings, roads and pedestrian lanes and large parking areas are planted with appropriate shade trees in the eco-tech site. Eco-forest can be built close to the residential area to prevail the winter wind; the depth of the forest is to be determined by the wind intensity (Ercoskun, 2007).

In this context, eco-technologies are considered as solutions for environmental protection in technological societies. The information and communication technologies are used to share information, to strengthen communication, to decrease energy consumption and to raise awareness of the consumer on energy use by ICT such as 'WIMAX technology', 'life safety systems', 'automated energy control systems', 'smart metering' 'telecommunication systems' and 'car pooling'. The aim is to build international communities, smart cities/regions and to create flexible and easily adaptable spaces by integrating 21st century information and communication infrastructure in the eco-tech city.

Geographic Information Systems (GIS) such as 'GIS in urban planning and design' and 'kiosks' provide GIS applications in urban planning and urban design in the municipalities. OpenGIS supports community for public participation in planning studies. All urban activities and information on public buildings put into geographical information stations-kiosks, which can be located in public buildings for sharing information in streets. OpenGIS brings success and accuracy in spatial applications with better presentation, and enhances public participation in these applications.

ECO-TECH URBAN DESIGN FOR SOCIAL SUSTAINABILITY

Social sustainability is one of the three legs of the sustainability stool (the other two are environmental and economic): each leg needs the support of the other two. For example, to have a strong economy, we need a skilled and educated workforce, and the more people are able to participate in the economy, the stronger the economy is. It is environmentally beneficial when people afford to live in a community where they work and there is an efficient public transportation system because it reduces their reliance on fossil fuels and car emissions.

Furthermore, a community means much more than a pure physical form. A community is composed of people as well as the places they live; it is as much a social environment as a physical environment. Thus, communities must not only be environmentally sustainable, they must also be socially sustainable. Social sustainability cannot be created through physical design of a community but physical design prepares an environment and spaces for environmentally sustainable lifestyles, and it can help to make such environmentally sustainable choices easier.

Integration the physical and social design of communities is particularly necessary if we are to create communities that are both environmentally and socially sustainable. The soft infrastructure includes formal human services (health, education, social services, recreation and culture, etc.) as well as the community's informal structure, the web of voluntary organizations and social relationships that comprise a community. Urban design should integrate these elements, giving as much weight to the soft infrastructure as to the hard infrastructure. In designing the built environment, urban designers need to address issues of basic needs such as urban food production and availability; equitable access to work and education; urban design that enhances social interaction and participation; methods of reducing living costs etc. (Hancock, 1993). The physical design of communities to promote social sustainability serves as an eco-tech community.

In this framework, eco-tech urban design offers some opportunities to build a sustainable community that enhances social sustainability. Eco-tech site is a neighborhood design for households with various incomes coming together for a new lifestyle. Every small city offers the advantage of a homey, close-knit, family-oriented environment. However, with ever-changing and mobile populations, it is a challenge to welcome new residents into the communities and to inform them quickly on the quality of life. The current and new residents of the small town participate all ecological and social events/campaigns in the eco-tech site for environmental protection and energy conservation.

Mixed used area is designed as a 24-hour lively and safe environment. All soft infrastructures are located in walking distance to enhance the sense of community. The various housing types are supplied for a wide range of population groups by contemporary eco-tech housing techniques for cities of tomorrow. The residents of the eco-tech site make gardening to reach self-sufficiency in food. Tele-working is generally seen as one of the most important contributions to social sustainability providing a higher quality of life in the eco-tech site: less stress, better health, more flexible working hours and more time for family and leisure. It changes the relationship between individuals, work and communities, and, therefore, it has an impact on the social capital. The residents of live and work units can work from home and change the interior of their flats with movable walls according to their needs, seasons or their moods. They can buy organic food from the supermarket in the eco-tech center. The theater, cinema, youth clubs, daycare center, multifunctional hall, festival area and sports facilities will enhance social and cultural life of the eco-tech community and lead to healthy people. Internet, GIS café and ecological education center with lifelong learning raise awareness on sustainability and green technology issues. Understanding that face-to-face communication is the best way of integrating new neighbors into the city, a square in the eco-tech center with an odeon can bring the community together for various open-air activities (Ercoskun, 2007).

Pedestrians and bicycle users are encouraged for healthy lifestyles. The residents can save money by eco-tech appliances of renewable energy and smart metering. Moreover, the community will be self sufficient in energy against global warming. The waste can be collected by underground vacuum systems and human resource is saved by eco-technologies. Permaculture gardening, orchards, vineyards, pilot community gardens and other agricultural activities provide community spirit, taste of organic production and self-reliance.

Todd states that "it is possible to design living technologies that have the same capabilities as natural systems do —self design, self-repair, reproduction and self organization in relation to changes —functions that now take technological society inordinate amount of chemicals, materials, and energy, often with harmful environmental consequences" (Todd, 1993, p.41).

The next section discusses the changing meaning of urban space, public space and virtual space and investigates new ways of sustainable use of ICTs to establish sustainable communities.

DISCUSSION

Today urbanism goes beyond the post-fordist industrial metropolis, which is accepted as the new territorial division of labor and spatial organization of flexible production (Soja, 2000). The digital revolution dominates us, and the world cannot be thought without computers. Words such as cyberspace, netropolis, telecosmos have been enhancing this phenomenon. As new citizens of the digital domain, netizens feel the ideas of person and identity compete with virtual data, information and computerized knowledge for control of realm without being able to see anything except the components of technology (Welsh, 1996). The rise of the informational mode of development changed the world. Information as a qualitative element turned into an input and 'knowledge intervenes upon knowledge itself in order to generate higher productivity' (Castells, 1989, p.10). Castells (1989) introduces the concept of space of flows, where the space is the continuum of the knowledge dissemination requisite to the task wherever the task may be physically located. Therefore, the flow of information provides global networks of communications technology, and flexible production facility is the key component redefining space in the information age. However, he indicates the difficulty for the reconstruction of social meaning in the space of flows. So, local governments can mobilize local societies (in this case eco-tech communities) to support a collective strategy toward locality with dynamic control of universities, corporations, NGOs. Eco-tech communities can use the infrastructure of information technologies with other small eco-tech communities in the world to reconstruct the social meaning and to transfer best green strategies and practices. Then, space of flows can be reduced to space of *places* by those technologies disaggregating the large networks into small community networks.

Graham and Marvin's (1999) comparison of urban *places* and electronic spaces is also useful. The attributes of urban places are: Territory, material, visible, actual, tangible, embedded, fixity and social space, where the attributes of electronic spaces are: Network, immaterial, invisible, virtual, intangible, disembedded, motion and logical space. The main difference between them is about the level of materiality where every component can be explained in physical terms in urban places. Electronic spaces as post-industrial spaces primarily contain spaces for consumption-oriented activities.

Today, individuals spend their leisure time at home, office or at other consumption spaces. Thus, other urban public spaces are deprived and have become lifeless. Urban spaces have rapidly decreased in number and size where different groups came from different places and discussed their special problems on the public platform, made face-to face contact, met by coincidence, talked and discussed or reached a consensus on their ideas (Bauman, 1998). Urban public spaces as one of the main concern of urban design have been transformed. Today many researchers call this negative transformation by these keywords: Privatization, commodification (Madinipour, 1996, Sorkin, 1992), militarization (Davis, 1992), social polarization (Zukin, 1995) and the fall of public man (Sennett, 1992). Traditional urban public spaces are replaced by non-places refer to places of transience that do not hold enough significance to be regarded as places (Auge & Howe, 1995). Examples of a non-place would be a motorway, a hotel room, an airport or a supermarket. Public spaces have become traffic nodes due to lack of civic uses. Public spaces had become apolitical. They turned into places of private emotions. Speed has changed the spatial sensations. The main reasons and changes can be summarized as follows: Privatization of public spaces, rising control on design and uses of public spaces, increase in racism and social conflicts, dual city scene, simulated environments that breaks its ties with localities and emphasize on consumption and entertainment (Velibeyoglu & Gencel, 2006). Today, vital urban activities such as working, recreation and entertainment are incorporating whilst the boundaries delineating these areas are blurring. Ritzer explains the process of mixing of urban activities in the case of consumption activities. Now a single building complex can be able to house a number of urban activities such as walking, shopping, recreation in its structure (Ritzer, 2004).

Another dimension is the problem of "scale" in the electronic communication paradigm. With the time-space compression (Harvey 1990), urban spaces have begun to be reshaped by distant effects. People connecting virtual cities are able to shape their lives and relations with global communication networks. The discussion on the emerging realm of the virtual cities introduces a different viewpoint on the current understanding of public spaces in the information age. City's public spaces must be accessible to all groups of people. The problematic construction of access for both real and virtual spaces needs to be scrutinized. In the seamless integration of real and virtual public spaces the problem of ownership and the blurring boundary between private and public realm should be underlined. In high-tech world of the individualistic self, technology enables a territorialization of private and semi-public spaces.

According to Lynch (1981) public spaces should be welcoming to the members of the community that they serve. The friendliness in a virtual public space, on the other hand, resembles an issue of interface design. In recent decades, the substitution effect of new technologies has been concerned by urban planners and designers and is considered as a serious threat to most of the conventional urban patterns and functions in urban public spaces. For example, online delivery of many urban services has been blamed to disrupt the liveliness the streets. New public spaces capture people as consumers. Similarly, technological initiatives identify people as clients or end-users. The new semi-public spaces, such as shopping malls, or the Internet as a virtual public space have raised new questions on the users of public spaces. These new semi-public spaces are mostly in private hands that bring high security and control. Segregation and the trend of privatization gain significance. This is a threat

to the traditional public space that is empty and that looses much of its functions (Velibeyoglu & Gencel, 2006 p.6).

If public spaces are considered as active urban void areas and are allowed to construct their identity by their users, an opportunity will arise for the sustainability of these spaces in the future. The combination of real and virtual spaces that results as an augmented space, has redefined the way urban planners conceive, plan and control space in cities. This augmentation is linked to the development of the ability to communicate and to be present in multiple spaces with the help of the ICTs. The city which is a consequence of many role-players and forces operate both in global to local dimensions, utilizing tools which are invisible and strategic. They are knitted together through both physical and virtual networks of connection, telecommunication, social and political relationships (Firmino et al., 2008). However, urban studies and policies still discard ICT issues. This study intends to fill this gap. The complexity of the amalgamation of virtual and real spaces (Graham and Marvin, 1999) in the settings of urban public spaces needs a holistic approach of urban planning, management and design, which is referred to as the eco-tech approach in this study. The temporal changes in community interactions change the spatial pattern. There are different spaces and different spatial relations. The built environment designed in a particular manner will promote certain kind of social behavior (Gregory & Urry, 1985). A new type of urban design process should be configured in a locally sensitive way and should take into account various users and demands. As Harvey points out that there is a strong relationship between technological changes in economic production and structural changes in quality and production of urban spaces. In this context, urban design is an effective tool that advances the quality of the urban environment.

Eco-tech city, which is a product of a sustainable urban design, is a place where all citizens are able to harness the full potential of ICT in pursuit of equitable and sustainable development. The residents, businesses and communities in the eco-tech city have access to a broadband connection. To use ICT effectively, they have literate information and access to relevant and appropriate training to improve their skills. The eco-tech city is influenced by the declaration of principles from the World 1st Summit on the Information Society (http://www.wsis.org). ICT underpins much of the social, economic, environmental and cultural future of the eco-tech city. This strategy provides a future roadmap for the community, business, and government partnerships. New communication networks point to opportunities for more flexible living, working and learning. ICT is embedded in the children's futures through their schooling and future employment opportunities. A digital future is a reality. Delivering eco-tech strategy involves many stakeholders, such as central and local government institutions, business, community agencies and groups, education sector, and individual citizens. These stakeholders provide ideas and resources; project skills, support services, and funding. Each community is different than the other and for this reason, has different needs. Each project is uniquely molded to the community it serves and ideally it is designed by its stakeholders. So, eco-tech city approach seeks support from the key stakeholders to recognize itself and its synergies with their individual strategies, frameworks and action plans, such as in the City of Waitakere (WETA, 2004).

Sustainable development depends on human capital, good governance, an effective use of natural resources and the protection of the environment for future generations. ICTs can contribute to all these factors. If ICT is applied effectively, the rewards can be enormous.

It can help to enhance creativity and innovation, build communities, give more people access to goods and services, and use natural resources more efficiently.

We have the capacity to secure significant social and economic benefits with our decisions on how we produce, buy, use and apply ICT. These decisions include energy savings through monitoring and managing energy use, creating more efficient transport systems, reducing travel needs through electronic commerce, video links and other forms of electronic transactions, producing fewer physical products that consume finite resources and increasing interaction between people and organizations. The questions to be answered are as follow (Madden & Weißbrod, 2008): Do we minimize the resources used in manufacturing the hardware and maximize the social benefits for communities in the supply chain? Do we remarkably improve the energy efficiency by increasing the use of renewable energy? Do we ensure re-use, recycling and responsible disposal? Do we create wealth and satisfy needs with a lower environmental impact? Do we reduce the need for people and things to move and transport things more efficiently? Do we enable people to connect, interact and strengthen their communities? Do we innovate to solve the problems of how we live together sustainably, locally and across the world?

One of the innovations presented in this study as eco-tech community is to reach sustainability. ICT can be used in attaining eco-tech city's main goal, which is to reduce the ecological footprint. It can facilitate networks, partnerships and actions to work things out in a complex and connected world regardless of location, age, disability or income. Can ICT help to build a more inclusive society? Television, for instance, is long argued to be a prototype in the discourse of social decline, and is accused of isolating people, eroding social consciousness through a process of becoming apolitical. Hence, it is normal to hesitate when socio-political functions of new communication technologies, or namely the virtual environment, are of concern (Barlas & Caliskan, 2006). Despite the fears that e-revolution will contribute to the erosion of social relationships and undermine local communities, there are plenty of examples on the contrary. Many people have established online relationships in addition to, rather than instead of, existing social networks. Sometimes this occurs via new forms of virtual community, more often through strengthening the existing patterns of social interaction. Online communities can influence how people work and socialize. These are new technical substructures enabling new modes of socialization. Examples of such communities include MySpace, Facebook etc. They keep online diaries- blogs and comment on them. In this sense, it can be referred to text-based socialization, which leaves out normal forms of perception and cognition. These networks plug into the net to share information and to give technical or emotional support to the others. On the other hand, online communities tend to communicate in only one language: English. This means that some of the potential for cultural exchange and learning is not being realized and language diversity is being undermined.

Online interaction often encourages interaction off-line, and this may help to re-establish local communities rather than obliterate them. Sometimes, after online meetings, physical meetings can take place in a café or a restaurant or an urban square to talk face-to-face. The social role of ICTs has so far focused on the Internet but mobile phones play a significant role in social networks as well. Promoted access devices include mobile phones, information kiosks and resource centers are among the means used to broaden the ICT access.

How ICT can be a central mediator for a more sustainable living in cities? The ICT industry plays a compelling role in delivering a low carbon, sustainable future. For this reason, the industry must move from a model based on ever increasing consumption of natural resources to a service-led future that is more efficient and less reliant on hard-wired solutions.

By looking at the bigger picture, the opportunities for greening the ICT actually lie, not in the production and use of ICT, but in its application. Some key areas exist where ICT has the poten-

tial to deliver real improvements to people and the planet (Madden & Weißbrod, 2008): Energy, shopping, work and meeting.

ICT brings benefits in various sectors, which have impacts on the urban and rural space. In agriculture, ICT is being used to help to minimize waste in a water-intensive industry. The ICT firms can produce a wireless sensor network to help farmers optimizing irrigation. Each sensor monitors soil moisture, leaf temperature and evaporation. Some projects look at how embedding technology in industrial greenhouses might lead to the reduction of water, energy and chemical use to grow food.

Furthermore, ICT has a high potential impact on the rational use of heating energy. Heating has a higher share in total energy consumption, and the most effective conservation measures using physical materials tend only to be applied to a relatively small number of buildings that are renovated or newly built each year.

ICT can also spawn new business models. Some home-delivery services for organic food are mainly based on online ordering. Online shopping provides an opportunity to reduce the environmental impact of retailing, as well as increasing choice, information and targeting. Urban designers should find some solutions to keep the shopping streets alive.

Altering the work environments can also deliver productivity and environmental gains. For example, virtual meetings can save travel time and environmental costs of passenger transport. Until recently, video conferencing facilities often produced poor sound and visual quality. However, today, high-definition video conferencing system networks offer better results.

ICT is particularly important for current urban planning issues. Municipalities can benefit from the use of ICT to facilitate specific planning activities. Use of geographical information systems, for example, simplifies complex planning data the analysis and contributes to more accurate information. Additionally, Internet is a source of information for planning. ICT facilitates scenario development, which is useful for forecasting outcomes of alternate planning policies among which planners are able to choose the most sustainable development option. Visualizing planning issues with the help of 3D modeling contributes to a reliable forecast of planning outcomes, such as visual impact, noise and wind analyses. ICT is used to disseminate planning information via Internet and to promote the transparency of activities and public awareness of planning and sustainability issues. Planning participation is supported to achieve a better collaboration between public administration and civil society. Citizens are asked to comment on local and strategic urban planning projects. Finally, ICT is used for international communication because communication becomes easier and faster.

Currently ICT is mostly used for information retrieving. Additionally, some municipalities actively use the internet to support sustainable urban development, for example, by providing a database for vacant inner-city building lots and promoting an infill development and energy use in buildings with maps, such as in Haringey Municipality, London (Nisancioglu, 2008).

ICT will facilitate future work in urban planning and promote sustainability. Creating and calculating models, simulations and scenarios will contribute to improved planning information systems and simplify the forecast in process of the impact of different various alternatives on urban sustainability. Simulation, multimedia and interaction can even be substituted in traditional plans containing maps and texts and encourage communication of planning issuesby increasing participation in planning the social acceptance of plans. Additionally, ICT can lead to efficient infrastructure planning, a better management of services, and help spreading the information on best practices of urban sustainability.

The impact of ICT on urban planning will depend on technological innovations, regulations and the adaptation of ICT by planners and planning institutions. Negative impacts of a further ICT use for urban planning such as limited creativity, standardization, simplification and unification are put forward as well.

ICT will only be able to support sustainable urban development when certain conditions are met (INTELCITY, 2003): High accessibility of ICT needs to be guaranteed by low cost of equipment. ICT knowledge and awareness have to be encouraged by offering ICT training to city administrations and public. ICT development should be based on local skills and knowledge but not on foreign experts. The legislative frame should stimulate ICT development. A well-organized system of data collection and processing regarding sustainable urban development is required.

CONCLUSION

ICT is a tool that constitutes a new infrastructure, changing the way our societies function, while its technical applications will give us totally new opportunities to both preserve the best elements of our society, and develop new and better solutions to our existing problems. ICT is global, crosscutting, low-cost and fosters the dissemination of knowledge. In general, ICT is best viewed as a catalyst that can speed up current negative trends, or alternatively contribute to a shift towards sustainable development in cities.

This chapter attempted to synthesize knowledge from sustainable community development topics, eco-tech urban design and ICTs in order to identify how three concepts interact and overlap. The aim is to create visionary energy-saving infrastructure solutions for establishing long term, stable and dynamic societies. We must extend the definitions of urban planning and design to encompass virtual spaces as well as physical ones. We should reconsider the vital bonds that hold cities together and to reinvent urban design and development while adapting desirable, feasible, possible technologies, and maintaining social bonds.

This study will contribute to an extended understanding of urban restructuring in new century cities and the utilization of new ICTs as a means to urban development by the eco-tech concept. If ICTs seem to threaten the social and cultural stable society and is against social sustainability, there is a vital need to organize a hybrid of real spaces and digital spaces. The concept that was drawn in this chapter embraces the possibilities of sustainable ICTs and proposes green options towards the implementation of ICTs as communication tools in an eco-tech environment that fulfills local values.

Sustainability points to the reduction of the ecological footprint such as resource inputs and waste outputs, whilst simultaneously the improvement of the quality of life in health, housing, accessibility, community etc., within the capacity limits of a city. ICT systems can play a valuable role in reducing organizations' wider carbon footprints, for example, by reducing the need for travel through videoconferencing. Use of ICT leads to lower resource consumption, additionally; it leads to lower transport use of means of thus, decreasing the use of fuel and pollution. ICT also fosters inclusion in information societies in eco-tech settlements.

Collaboration and quality of life increase in small eco-tech settlements. Solution is grounded in place. When the size of the settlement enlarges, the problems escalate. Small, compact eco-tech settlements connected to the metropolitan cities by rail systems will solve the problems of metropolitan life and the heavy pressure on people created by stress, traffic, pollution etc. The feeling of alienation in a residence, sitting in front of the computer and meeting people only in virtual environments will be prevented by eco-tech settlements and their wide applications around metropolitan cities. In an eco-tech city, ICT helps to equalize and promote participation in society at all levels (i.e. social relationships, work, culture, political participation, etc.). Eco-tech city model will be a template for development elsewhere to encourage

planning and design of sustainable communities. It should be used as an educational project to foster environmental stewardship and lifelong learning opportunities for members of the wider community.

The eco-tech city model fully exploits the potential of ICT and leverages it for greater participation, efficiency and transparency in functioning of the local government as well as in time and cost savings in decision-making. ICTs encourage and facilitate effective public participation in planning by providing the necessary skills to planners and public to communicate with each other, and by developing the appropriate tools that would make such communication meaningful. The eco-tech city addresses all participants in the planning process, improves communication skills, and acquires an understanding of the built environment and spatial representations. ICT provides an opportunity to broaden public participation in government by crossing geographical boundaries. Web-based tools and workspaces help interaction on service design and delivery; they facilitate access to local government information, and enable access to information and consultation. They build engagement with governmental agencies and exchange information. Kiosks provide access to government information and transact to receive a governmental service.

The key of green future in urban planning and design is in the hands of technology supporting local applications. ICT-enabled developments of mixed-use, walkable, and sustainable neighborhoods can improve the environmental performance of cities significantly. Realizing these benefits on a broader scale, however, requires major changes in the process of financing, designing, and managing the built environment. This study, hopefully, enlightens the target group of practitioners and policy makers in decision-making. Authorities should put out their own efforts to build up demand for new configurations of real estate, ICT infrastructure in newly developed spaces, and all the associated technological hardware and services embedded in them. Public subsidies, discounted land deals, infrastructural assistance, tax discount, credibility and the sheer marketing weight of public policy makers can be advantageous to raise the profile of new eco-tech settlements by public and private partnerships. With proper focus, planning and policies, eco-tech cities can become the centers of ICT-enabled innovation for sustainable growth. The future urban society will be happier, less lonely, more prosperous, healthier and more involved in decision-making.

Finally, science, which created technology, is referred to bring the end of the world; however, it is again the science, which will save the world and ensure more livable places for human beings.

REFERENCES

Akca, H., Sayili, M., & Esengun, K. (2007). Challenge of rural people to reduce digital divide in the globalized world: Theory and practice. *Government Information Quarterly, 24,* 404–413. doi:10.1016/j.giq.2006.04.012

Amborski, D., & Lister, N. M. (2002). *An Eco-Tech Village for Milton: Considerations for Policy.* Commissioned by the Town of Milton, Toronto.

Arapkirlioglu, K. (2003). Ekoloji ve Planlama. *Planlama,* 4-.

Arifoglu, A. (2004). *E-Dönüşüm, Yol Haritası, Dünya, Türkiye.* Ankara: Yıldız Yayınları.

Atabek, U. (2003). *Iletisim Teknolojileri ve Yerel Medya için Olanaklar.* Istanbul: IPS.

Auge, M., & Howe, J. (1995). *Non-Places: Introduction to Anthropology of Supermodernity.* London: Verso.

Bandyopadhyay, P. (2001). Application of Information Technology and Impact of Cyber Eco Cities in New Millennium. In *ISOCARP Prooceedings,* Utrecht, (pp. 68-77).

Barlas, M. A., & Caliskan, O. (2006). Virtual Space As a Public Sphere: Rethinking The Political and Professional Agenda of Spatial Planning And Design. *METU Journal of Faculty of Architecture, 23*(2), 1–20.

Bauman, Z. (1998). *Globalization: The Human Consequences.* New York: Columbia University Press

B.G.D. Consulting Inc. (2002). *Implementation Options Report 2002.* Retrieved July 28, 2004 from http://www.milton.ca/execserv/ecotech_implementation.pdf

Bld, A. (n.d.). *The features of the settlement.* Retrieved May 5, 2005 from http://www.arcosanti.orghttp://www.arcosanti.org/project/project/future/arcosanti5000/main.html

Bogunovich, D. (2002). Eco-tech cities: Smart metabolism for a green urbanism. In C.A. Brebbia, Martin-Duque and L.C. Wasdhwa (Ed.), *The Sustainable City II,* (pp.75-84). London: Witpress.

Callenbach, E. (1994). *Ekotopya.* Istanbul: Ayrinti Yayinlari.

Castells, M. (1989). *The Informational City.* Cambridge, UK: Blackwell Publishers.

Clark, M. (2001). Domestic futures and sustainable residential development. *Futures, 33,* 817–836. doi:10.1016/S0016-3287(01)00021-0

Davis, M. (1992). Fortress Los Angeles: the Militarization of Urban Space. In M.Sorkin, (Ed.), *Variations on a Theme Park* (pp.154-180). New York: Noonday Press.

Drewe, P. (2000). *ICT and Urban Form Urban Planning and Design- Off The Beaten Track,* Design Studio Study, Faculty of Architecture, Delft University of Technology, Delft.

Ekostaden web site (n.d.). City of Malmö, Sweden. Retrieved September 14, 2004 from http://www.ekostaden.com/pdf/en_hallbar_stad_eng.pdf http://www.ekostaden.com/pdf/det_grona_bo01_eng.pdf http://www.ekostaden.com/pdf/vectura_eng.pdf

Ercoskun, O. Y. (2007). *Ecological and Technological (Eco-Tech) Design for A Sustainable City: A Case Study on Gudul, Ankara.* Unpublished doctoral dissertation, Gazi University, Ankara, Turkey.

Firmino, R. J., Duarte, F., & Moreira, T. (2008). Pervasive Technologies and Urban Planning in the Augmented City . *Journal of Urban Technology*, *15*(2), 77–93. doi:10.1080/10630730802401983

Gauzin-Müller, D. (2002). *Sustainable Architecture And Urbanism*. Berlin: Birkhäuser.

Graham, S. (2002). Bridging Urban Digital Divides? Urban Polarisation and Information and Communications Technologies (ICTs). *Urban Studies (Edinburgh, Scotland)*, *39*(1), 33–56. doi:10.1080/00420980220099050

Graham, S., & Marvin, S. (1999). Planning Cyber-Cities? Integrating Telecommunications into Urban Planning. *The Town Planning Review*, *70*(1), 89–114.

Gregory, D., & Urry, J. (Eds.). (1985). *Social Relations and Spatial Structures*. London: Macmillan.

Hancock, T. (1993). Strategic Directions for Community Sustainability", publication of the B.C. Roundtable on the Environment and the Economy, Canada.

Harvey, D. (1990) *The Condition Of Postmodernity*. Cambridge, MA: Blackwell.

Harvey, D. (2000). *Spaces of Hope*. Berkley, CA: U of California Press.

htpp://gen.ecovillage.org

htpp://wsis.org

http://www.integerproject.co.uk/maidenhead.html (05/05/2005).

http://www.integerproject.co.uk/project.html

http://www.integerproject.co.uk/wolverhampton.html

http://www.workraft.org.nz/WETA%20action%20plan.pdf

Integer web site "Intelligent and Green Projects"

INTELCITY. (2003). EU Final Report, VTT Finland.

Karaaslan, S., & Ercoskun, O. Y. (2006). *Eco-Tech Planning for Turkish Cities*. Paper presented at 12th Annual Sustainable Development Research Conference, Hong Kong.

Logan, K. (2001). Seaside Turns 20. *Architecture Week, 0919*, 1–2.

Luke, T. (1994). The Politics of Arcological Utopia: Soleri on Ecology, Architecture and Society. *Telos, 101*(55).

Lynch, K. (1981). *Good City Form*. Cambridge, MA: The MIT Press

Madden, P., & Weißbrod, I. (2008). *Connected ICT and sustainable development, Forum for the Future*. Menlo Park, CA: Sun Microsystems Publication.

Madinipour, A. (1996). *Design of Urban Space*. New York: John Wiley & Sons.

Mahizhnan, A. (1999). Smart Cities the Singapore Case. *Cities (London, England)*, *16*(1), 13–18. doi:10.1016/S0264-2751(98)00050-X

Marras, A. (1999). *ECO-TEC Architecture of the In-Between*. New York: Princeton Architectural Press.

MIT (Massachusetts Institute of Technology) Center For Real Estate. (2005). *New Century Cities: Real Estate Value in a Digital World.* Symposium Case Studies Report, 1-24.

Nisancioglu, S. (2008). *Climate Change and environmental urban planning: Implementations of Haringey Municipality.* Paper Presented at the International Conference on Ecological and Technological Cities, Gazi Uni. Ankara, Turkey.

Odendaal, N. (2003). Information and Communication Technology and local governance: understanding the difference between cities in developed and emerging economies. *Computers, Environment and Urban Systems, 6*(27), 585–607. doi:10.1016/S0198-9715(03)00016-4

Ritzer, G. (2004). *Enchanting a Disenchanted World,* (2nd Ed.). New York: SAGE Publishers.

Saleh, M. A. E. (2004). Learning from tradition: the planning of residential neighborhoods in a changing world. *Habitat International, 28*(4), 625–639. doi:10.1016/S0197-3975(03)00031-6

Sennett, R. (1992). *The Fall of Public Man.* New York: W.W. Norton & Company.

Singh, K. A. (2004). Bo01, A New Ecological Urban District in Malmö, Sweden, A Post-Occupancy Assessment of The Area", Unpublished Masters thesis, IHS-HDM, Rotterdam, Lund.

Slessor, C. (1997). *Eco-tech: Sustainable Architecture and High Technology.* London: Thames & Hudson.

Soja, E. (2000). *Postmetropolis: Critical Studies of Cities and Regions.* Oxford: Blackwell.

Sorkin, M. (Ed.). (1992). *Variations on a Theme Park: The New American City and the End of Public Space.* New York: Hill and Wang.

The Aalborg Charter. (1994). *Charter of European Cities and Towns Towards Sustainability.* Copenhagen: Denmark.

Todd, N. J., & Todd, J. (1993). *From Eco-Cities to Living Machines; principles for ecological design.* Berkeley, CA: North Atlantic Books.

Van der Ryn, S., & Cowan, S. (1999). *Ecological Design.* Washington DC: Island Press.

Velibeyoglu, K., & Gencel, Z. (2001). *Urban Design in Changing Public Spaces of Information Age.* Paper Presented at 1st International Urban Design Meeting, rendez-vous Istanbul.

Velibeyoglu, K., & Gencel, Z. (2006). *Reconsidering the Planning and Design of Urban Public Spaces in the Information Age: Opportunities & Challenges, Public Spaces in the Information Age.* Paper Presented at 42nd ISoCaRP Congress, Istanbul.

Viikki- Science Park & Latokartano Guide. (2004). City of Helsinki Planning Department, Town Planning Division, (pp. 1-10).

Welsh, G. (1996). *A review of Manuel Castells' The Informational City.* Department of Computer Science and Information Systems, American University, Washington, DC.

WETA. (2004). *Waitakere Municipality web site, Action Plan.* Retrieved October 13, 2004 from http://www.workraft.org.nz/WETA.htm (13/10/2004)

Yalciner, O. (2002). Depreme Dayanikli Kentler icin Cografi Bilgi Sistemleri (Geographic Information Systems for Earthquake-Resistant Cities). *Journal of Gazi University . Engineering and Architecture Faculty, 17*(3), 153–165.

Zukin, S. (1995). *Culture of Cities.* Oxford, MA: Blackwell Publishers.

ENDNOTES

[1]   *Oykos*-living environment, *logos*-science (Arapkirlioğlu, 2003)

2   *Tekne*-production, skill, *logos*-science
     (Atabek, 2003)

3   Techno-ecotopia, is a term introduced by
     Bogunovich. He combines technology which
     is abbreviated as techno with the term of
     Callenbach's ecotopia (ecology+utopia)
     (Callenbach, 1994).

Chapter 4
ECORadar–Shakti:
An Interactive Knowledge Base Contributing to the Greening of an Indian Megacity

Martin Kreeb
Potsdam University of Management and Communication, Germany

Georg Dold
Potsdam University of Management and Communication, Germany

Hans-Dietrich Haasis
Bremen University, Institute for Production and Logistics, ISL, Germany

ABSTRACT

This chapter describes concept, design and future implementation of a knowledge based Internet portal - ECORadar Shakti India - aimed at small and medium sized enterprises of the Indian megacity Hyderabad. The portal sets out to use the simplest and most persuasive means to motivate and enable sustainability management in those enterprises that have so far taken little or no interest in this aspect of management. Hyderabad, a prime example of an emerging mega city, is a laboratory where the goal of becoming a sustainable mega city faces of difficult challenges. The intention to work towards a sustainable future will be difficult to achieve without adequate data, tools and implementation strategies. The research idea of this approach in Hyderabad was set up in a research program funded by the German Federal Ministry of Education and Research (BMBF).

INTRODUCTION

The trend towards urbanization and the increasing number and size of metropolitan areas and megacities in all parts of the world but especially in the developing and newly industrializing countries is a striking example of global change. This restructuring and urban condensation of humankind is happening at an enormous speed that challenges innovativeness and strategic agendas of politics, economics and civil societies. Metropolitan regions and megacities are focal points of sustainable development because they give rise to massive problems in all three dimensions of sustainability. At the same time, however, opportunities arise for innovation strategies and

DOI: 10.4018/978-1-60566-822-2.ch004

for the support of efficient, compact and sustainable economic systems and lifestyles. Viewed from this perspective, such cities are more and more becoming arenas of decision about global sustainable development. Today's megacities are of particular political interest because they offer the chance for precautionary intervention and targeted urban development in order to prevent economic, social and ecological crises and to preserve or create scope for action.

Hyderabad, India's fifth largest city is one of these "megacities". The SHAKTI[1]-project, funded by the German Federal Ministry of Education and Research aims to develop collaborative learning and planning processes to design and implement sustainable solutions for urban infrastructure (Schwaiger, Wall & Gotsch, 2007). Among other SHAKTI-initiatves, which aim directly at the improvement of the urban infrastructure e.g. mobility or housing, the project "ECORadar-Shakti" is aimed at small and medium sized companies (SME) of the Hyderabad metropolis. It sets out to use the simplest and most persuasive means to motivate and enable sustainability management in those enterprises that have so far taken little or no interest in this aspect of management.

The concept and prototypical implementation of ECORadar was originally developed in Germany. It was especially designed to help SMEs in Germany to enhance their corporate sustainability management systems. The purpose of this chapter is to describe the process of transferring ECORadar from a highly industrialized country - for whose needs it was originally developed - to an area with very high rates of growth in all terms. The two geographical areas could not be more different from each other: Germany with its very high standards in terms of environmental and social protection and advanced managerial knowledge base on the one side. An Indian megacity counting 6.8 million inhabitants[2], a population growth rate of more than 3% per year, environmental and social standards comparatively poorly developed.

In the second chapter the original concept and scope of ECORadar-Shakti as an interactive, internet-based knowledge base to support corporate sustainability management is shown. The third part describes the results of the authors research work on site in Hyderabad and derives design concepts to be applied to an ECORadar prototype which is planned to be implemented in the city of Hyderabad. The last part evaluates the project status and describes further steps of development.

THE WEB-BASED ECORADAR-TOOL

A large variety of research has been published in the field of environmental management during the last 20 years. The problem is the conversion of this knowledge into enterprise practice. Development-target of the ECORadar-portal is to reduce the information costs of those SME enterprises, which are interested in environmental management. In order to achieve this target, a strategic Community concept of the third generation has been developed in order to build a knowledge-community in the SME sector (Kreeb 2002).

The main emphasis of the ECORadar-community is on the knowledge field and the service and project-areas. The community started as a project-community. In the beginning, ECORadar, as a classical research project, is measuring the success by certain criteria focusing on timeframe and milestones (Bullinger 2002). An additional feature is the use of a virtual project team (scientists, consultants, entrepreneurs). A virtual cooperation has been realized by establishing a specific editorship- and tele-cooperation system. These project-communities represent the preliminary stage on the way to a knowledge-community. ECORadar is a knowledge network stretched beyond the limits of individual universities and enterprises.

Wenger & Snyder (2000]) describes the knowledge-community as a "flexible organizational unit, beyond official organizational resp. informal units. The community is animated by the common interest of the members in the field of knowledge. The participation is voluntary. The motivation to participate is a positive cost/benefit relation". The collective benefit is categorized by Rheingold (1994, 2002) using the following three dimensions:

- Social use, identification by a common goal
- Knowledge capital, use of knowledge from various sources
- Community feeling, system of real contacts and experience backgrounds

The ECORadar-community understands itself as community of interests, with the following features defined by Hagel & Armstrong (1997):

- Focus and emphasis on a specific interest
- The ability to integrate contents and communication (Reisch/Bietz/Kreeb 2007)
- The use of information, supplied by the members
- The access to competing providers

The major task of the community-developers is the professional relations management between the individual community-members. The goal of the ECORadar-relation management is to integrate over 100 participants in the community process. This means that anonymous co-worker will be transformed into active community-members. The socio-economic-group-dynamic processes together with technological-organizational processes have absolute priority. It could be summarized as: Who makes what with whom for which purpose? The German content development of ECORadar was generated by several workshops with the users (esp. small and medium sized companies) and content developers (e.g. consultants and environmental scientists and environmental administration) and ECORadar users, which give information and knowledge, back via virtual communication by using email.

The original concept of portals was focused on the private, individual Internet user. The idea of the portal is now increasingly focusing on individual companies. This is called an "Enterprise Information Portal" (EIP). An EIP is focused both on internal users (employees and management) and external parties (customers, suppliers and other stakeholders of the company). The internal focus of the portal has increasingly been on knowledge-management and the supply of software applications (i.e. inventory management, PPS, sales).

The external focus has in addition also functions for transactions like e-procurement, e-logistics and supply-chain-management. The internal interface is sometimes referred to as "Workplace", while the external side is called "Marketplace". The themes of a portal, like applications, content and services can be designed to suit the needs of a specific geographical like the Hyderabad-region or enterprise and the themes can also be selected to cover the requirements of a specific task or problem. It is also possible to mix a focus of a specific subject and a specific enterprise. The basic idea of ECO-Radar is the combination of "Enterprise Radar" and "Surrounding Field Radar". This is the ideal basis to create a theme-related portal with a public/external side ("Marketplace") to supply content and services for all companies and individuals that are interested in "Sustainable Management" and an internal side ("Workplace") to supply the enterprise with functions for "Environmental-Management" with both strategic and operational tasks (Kuhre 1998).

Analytical Framework of the ECORadar Knowledge-Community

Modeling complex software like Community-Portals is a challenging task. Standard design and analysis patterns can be helpful but don't usually show how to apply techniques or demonstrate working examples that are similar to the problem at hand. Lieberman (2007) pointed out that "Fortunately, you can use analytical frameworks

Table 1. Business analysis framework of ECORadar (see Lieberman, 2007)

Element	Description	ECORadar Activity
Tools	Word processing, modeling software, document version control	Using a CMS (Imperia) and MS Visio to collect content
Patterns	Industry-specific patterns, business systems patterns, business organization structures	Best practice of sustainability business leaders, scientists and NGO
Model-forms	Zachman Framework	• What (Environmental Data) • How (Function) Providing Tools & Information • Where (Network): ECORadar-Virtual-Network (User Generated Content) • Who (People): Important Sustainability Organizations • When (Time): List of ECORadar Workshop Series/Events • Why (Motivation): Business Goals/Strategies like Supporting Sustainability Management
Techniques	Observation, interviewing, document study	Observation, interviewing the ECORadar Network Members during the workshops
Skills	Note-taking, active listening, meeting facilitation, team leadership, critical thinking, reasoning by analogy	Dto.
Categorization	Business process framework, department hierarchy, business use cases, business-functional dependency graph	Improving ECORadar Business analysis framework by ECORadar business use cases like Benchmarking tools, Transportation Indicator Tool etc.

to collect and organize analysis patterns, tools, skills, organization techniques, examples, and the expertise of others who have solved similar modeling problems". Table 1 describes the Business analysis framework of ECORadar based on the Zachmann Framework concept (Inmon, Zachman & Geiger, 1997).

ECORadar as a workable internet-tool creates interactive, creative opportunities for the user (examples: automatic generation of indexes on the basis of a personal database; form-filling assistance; checklist programs). The concept of the web portal ECORadar has proven to be useful to handle the overwhelming data available on the Internet. A portal can structure the information and is able to display the content in a user-friendly layout. This is the basis for an effective research by the business community. A portal is a universal and comfortable system to access applications, content and services that are focused on a specific topic.

- Task-oriented: adaptable regarding the tasks of users or customers

- Categorized: content and services structured by categories
- Personalized: individually designed to achieve 1:1 relationships with users/customers.

The users of ECORadar identify several demands how they can improve their environmental performance. The ECORadar project community developed IT Tools, to cover the information demands of the user, which is interested in sustainable management issues (Lehmann-Waffenschmidt 2007). The demand was located in the areas of decision support to sustain decision processes. The decision and information demand was matched to the specific ECORadar screens like data, policy, organization, costs and technology. One example: the user identifies a demand in his transport management system, how to improve the environmental performance of the transport fleet respectively .So the ECORadar expert group (consultants & scientists) begin to program a software-tool, which can describe the environmental influence of the transport activity of companies. The tool needs the basic data of transport like vehicle type, tonne kilometer, specific fuel consumption and fuel sort etc. of the users. This tool is able to generate individual transport indicators for the environmental corporate balance and gives information how corporate transport management system is improved.

Knowledge Management in the ECORadar-Community

For the joint-project an expert set of 21 different research institutions is involved. The expert set has the function to edit the relevant knowledge of the "community-environment" so that enterprises can transfer this expert knowledge into the practical environment-oriented management. The knowledge management model of ECORadar supports the creation of knowledge within the enterprise on the basis of the external source of knowledge in the sense of the ontological knowledge spiral. The expert knowledge helps to support the acquisition of external knowledge and the development of own knowledge. The actual knowledge

distribution is supported, both by a specifically designed tele-cooperation system as well as by the portal itself (Riedl, Böhmann, Rosemann & Krcmar, 2008). That tele-cooperation model and the portal are regularly updated by the experts and are supporting the knowledge preservation in the enterprise (Haasis & Kriwald 2001). In the later course of the project it has to be assessed by the experts whether an ontology-based knowledge evaluation can be realized. The evaluation research in co-operation with enterprise practice and with the help of empirical methods has to ensure that the quality criteria that are pursued by ECORadar such as environmental discharge, target group orientation and in particular practice fitness are actually respected and realized. The evaluation of enterprise practice will be performed by the practice-community.

The development team of ECORadar confirms the experience of Davenport & Prusak (1998), that knowledge can exclusively be created in the brains of the knowledge carriers. The knowledge carriers of ECORadar are scientific experts and entrepreneurs, who cooperate within the

Table 2. Knowledge warehouse vs ECORadar knowledge network approach based on (Wallert 2002)

Criteria	Knowledge Warehouse	Knowledge Network
Philosophy	Externalization of knowledge	Direct communication, Reference to human experts
Range of application	• Structured problem areas • Given goal • Known relevance of information • Consequences of the decision foreseeable • Re-usable solutions	• Unstructured problem areas • Goal not given • Unknown interdependencies • Consequences of the decision unforeseeable • Limited reusability of solutions
Artificial Intelligence	High	Low
Knowledge requirements	Rules and methods	Not exactly specifiable
Moment of knowledge division	At the beginning of the knowledge process	On demand
Method to display knowledge	Structured knowledge	Reference to knowledge carriers as well as presentations of expert's assessment
Knowledge transfer	Knowledge conveyed by knowledge carrier (experts)	Bilateral negotiating of the modalities for the sharing of knowledge
Role of IT	Storage and processing of knowledge	Support of the information process and communication process
Access to knowledge	Information Retrieval & Data Mining	Creating of contact and communication with knowledge carrier

community-process. The primary focus is on the externalization of the expert's knowledge. The know-how is transferred in an external information system (Knowledge Warehouse, CMS). Externalization of knowledge (Nonaka & Takeuchi 1995) is especially suitable for standardizable knowledge (standards, laws, etc.). The recent experience of the ECORadar research project has shown that direct communication in a Knowledge Network is the best way to convey the expert's knowledge and experience.

The ECORadar Practice-Community

Representatives of the joint project's target group, enterprises in Germany, have already given it broad approval in its start-up phase. Some 40 enterprises employing an estimated one million members of staff have made the decision to support production and development of the prototype. The development of so-called 'ECORadar' screens is to be carried out in eighteen workshops, hand in hand with business representatives and numerous experts. The organization of the high-caliber working groups has been taken on by Europe's largest business-led environmental initiative, the German Environmental Management Association (BAUM e. V.), Hamburg. In addition, in summer 2001 a representative written survey was conducted in around 9,000 enterprises. The survey results reflect the state of the art in the field of sustainable management in German enterprises. These results are integrated in the ECORadar development process in order to enable enterprises to identify relevant technical, political and economic risks – but also market opportunities – in the field of sustainability and environment much earlier than their competitors (Bhattacharya, Sen & Korschun, 2008).

Content-Model

The ECORadar system portal consists of eight screens, which can be used as an ensemble – or

individually if preferred – to scan a company profile (Company Radar – 'micro-level') or the wider economic setting (Macro Radar – 'macro-level'). The Company Radar is a system component that can be accessed from any ECORadar screen, enabling users to systematically record and evaluate their company Environmental Data, Policy and Goals. The Macro Radar, a similar system component that can be accessed from any ECORadar screen, enables users to record and evaluate the 'macro-level' on the basis of the latest research – like global, national and regional Environmental Data and Environmental Goals.

Within the project ECORadar the internet-portal is being created as environmental service. First, it is essential to embed information, references and checklists that have been already part of the ECORadar-framework and former designs. In addition to these functions, the final version will be able to support all interested by providing a virtual community. Further, it will also identify possibilities for cooperation between all participants. Finally, it is created to enable the integration of Environmental Management in business processes. The first step is the creation of a user-friendly layout of the portal's websites. The essentials are a clear graphical structure, easy handling and the direct access to the services that are available within short download times.

Portal Structure

Reflecting the development of a micro-macro-link respectively a link between company and its surrounding the following eight screens has been selected each as theme-oriented platform for supporting services and information to business and industry. The Company and the Macro Radar represent the micro-macro-link in each screen. The data are:

Figure 1. ECORadar-portal-screenshot

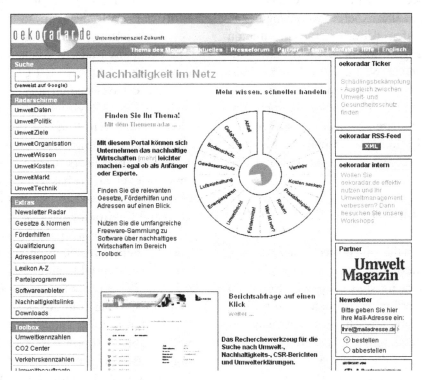

Environmental Data

Environmental data are generally regarded as the 'oxygen' of environmental policy and environmental administration (Haastrup & Wurtz, 2007). The regional, national and global environmental data provide a key basis on which companies can take action. Wherever the environmental situation is monitored and observed, wherever citizens are surveyed on their subjective experience of environmental problems, this can provide the impetus for action in environmental policy. Elementary company environmental data, for example, might be figures relating to energy, water, wastewater, waste, emissions and hazardous substances. Carbon dioxide emissions would be one example of key global environmental data.

Environmental Policy

The future environmental standards imposed on enterprises are molded partly by their own environmental policies but especially by national governments and party programs. For example, national environmental policy approaches for action form an important basis for the future use of 'command-and-control' instruments. In Germany, for instance, the ideas of the coalition parties, the opposition and the separate parties at national, federal state and municipal level are not the only matters of importance. A considerable influence is exerted on future environmental policy by the policy-making bodies of the European Union and numerous other international organizations.

Environmental Goals

While environmental data represent a significant basis on which to take environmental policy action, environmental goals provide principles for action, which, for their part, form the basis for the future application of environment policy instruments. Society should come together and use environment quality objectives to define core elements of environment policy action, working towards sustainable management in years to come. A company's own environmental targets, in contrast, are an element of the internal early detection system. Basically these should be geared to continuous improvement of environmental performance.

Environmental Organization

An effective environmental early-detection system can only be incorporated successfully within the enterprise once an efficient organization is in place for the structure and processes of environmental performance. Because then, and only then, it is possible to perform the target-performance comparisons which are necessary for early detection. Another important factor is to work closely with the public environmental authorities and associations: environmental authorities are the pivotal interface between the letter of the law and its enforcement. Enterprises that maintain good contacts with environmental authorities have swift access to information on new requirements according to environmental legislation. Associations are seen as powerful environmental policy actors and can pass on to their corporate members targeted advance information on environmental performance, picked up during the course of their lobbying.

Environmental Knowledge Management

Environmental know-how, both inside and outside a company, is a central element of environmental early-detection. A cornerstone for knowledge

transfer in the environmental sphere is formed by institutions such as the German Federal Environmental Agency, the Federal Agency for Nature Conservation, the Federal German Foundation for the Environment, and the International Transfer Centre for Environmental Technology. Likewise the media, as environment policy opinion-formers, play an important role in early detection.

Environmental Costs

Monitoring and assessment of environmental costs in the widest sense (calculation of a company's pollution control costs, anticipation of external costs and the costs of neglecting environmental aspects, identification of potential cost reductions) is a permanent task within early detection. In particular, deducting – at least mentally – the costs of environmental degradation (today's external costs – tomorrow's operating costs) is a strategic element of eco-controlling.

Environmental Market

Environmental protection has developed into a significant economic factor over the past 30 years. In the year 2005 only, German private and public sector spending on environmental protection was around € 34,000 million. Studies predict that the market for environmental technology and environmentally friendly products will continue to grow internationally in the coming years. Admittedly Germany still has a high market share in this area. However, other industrial nations – notably the USA, Canada and Great Britain – have developed strategies for gaining targeted access to new markets and supporting exports of environmental technology by their suppliers.

Environmental Technology

Technical indicators play an important role in the early detection process. In particular, specialist trade fairs and exhibitions not only create new contacts and stabilize business relationships but also provide advance information on technical innovations. Delphi surveys are increasingly conducted as part of this technology foresight process, and these can serve to guide future strategic orientation.

DESIGNING ECORADAR FOR THE CITY OF HYDERABAD

This chapter deals with requirements analysis and design of ECORadar for the city of Hyderabad ("ECORadar-Shakti"). First we summarize the results of our preliminary research work in Hyderabad. In the first section we briefly describe our methodic approach. The second section summarizes the results of our research work pertaining the requirements of Indian SMEs. The third section presents our design principles for an ECORadar-Shakti Prototype.

Methodology

Whilst our visit to Hyderabad (7 Days), representatives of relevant stakeholder groups, including NGOs like the local Chamber of Commerce & Industry or the Federation of Andhra Pradesh Chambers of Commerce & Industry (FAPCCI), the local city administration and selected managers and owners of SMEs of the industrial and commerce sector were interviewed. The following topics were subject of these interviews:

- **Environmental and Sustainability Management**
  Strategic role of EMS in domestic and export business, Implementation of Management Tools, Technical and Organizational Knowledge-basis, Information- Demand and Supply on various topics e.g. environmental legislation etc.
- **Information & Communication-Infrastructure and -Usage**

- **Habits, Techniques and Content of Cooperation among Stakeholders in the Area of Environmental Management**
  A preliminary prototype, showing basic functionalities and content of today's ECORadar was presented to selected interview partners.

Summary of Research Results

On the basis of our research on site in Hyderabad, three areas are of special interest were identified:

1. The Role of Corporate Environmental Management Systems

Benefits of corporate Environmental Management Systems (EMS) like EMAS or ISO 14001 in Germany are commonly seen in several categories. The subsequent table shows a brief summary of areas of interest based on intensive research executed in Germany for the past years (Kreeb, 2005; Braun, Russ, Schulz, Krcmar & Kreeb, 2005).

Internally German SME benefit from implementing EMS in terms of achieved improvements in ecological as well as financial performance (Orlitzky, Schmidt & Rynes, 2003). This is mainly due to short- and long-term enhancement of material- and energy efficiency of production processes. In times of rising prices of globally sourced raw materials, ecological and financial benefits of improved efficiency come hand in hand.

Green product innovations in terms of lowered ecological cost of carry for consumer of "green" products and services are not seen to be much influenced by mainstream EMS. Marketing- and innovation departments of SME in most cases are not linked to EMS in any way. General management issues in terms of analysis and control of business-processes can benefit from EMS in a limited way. But still the material- and quality-oriented views of EMS have some side effects on these issues.

Table 3. Benefits of corporate environmental management systems

Category	Sub-Category	Description	Importance indicator (empirical)
Internal	Ecological Performance	Improving material- & energy-efficiency of internal processes and products	High
	Financial Performance	Reducing monetary cost of material and energy input	High
	Product Innovation	Creation and marketing of eco-friendly products	Low
	General Management Objectives	Enhancement of analysis and control of administrative- and production-processes	Medium
External	Supply Chain Communication	Certified Environmental Management Systems like EMAS or ISO 14.001 ff	Medium, depending on branch
	Deregulation of Environmental Legislation	Replacement of legislative restrictions by voluntary implementation of certified EMS	Low, not as effective as expected

Externally the supply-chain communication is of some importance for EMS, depending on the branches. In automotive and other consumer-oriented branches, EMS certificates like EMAS or ISO 14.001 play an important role in establishing business relations. In other branches, more distant to end-consumers, EMS certificates are of lesser importance and not seen as a prerequisite for business relations. The chance for substantial deregulation in the area of environmental legislation, meaning that legal authorities would replace specific legal restrictions for EMS certificates, are not as profoundly realized as SMEs originally hoped for.

In the Hyderabad area as well as in all of India (1250 EMS), 2004 the diffusion of EMS is not very high, compared to Germany (6400 EMS) or the USA (3890 EMS). But stakeholder interviews showed a clear interest of SMEs in this area. The managers and owners of companies had a very pragmatic view on EMS and showed a special interest in the two areas "environmental and financial performance" and "supply chain communication". Product innovation and deregulation were of no special interest. Technical or organizational know-how in the areas of interest were quite low and help in any form would be more than welcomed by SMEs.

2. Information and Knowledge Demand and Supply

SMEs as well as all other stakeholders have a substantial demand for specific information in terms of theoretical knowledge as well as hands-on experience. This includes all areas of expertise without exceptions (Kytle & Ruggie, 2005).

3. Cooperation among Stakeholders

Cooperation among the stakeholders in the area of EMS is not very pronounced. Neither the chambers of industry & commerce nor the city authorities are able to cover today's information demand from SMEs. Local or state authorities are not very much accepted as potentially trusted sources of information.

Interpretation and Evaluation

Looking at the situation in the above mentioned three areas of special interest we conclude that ECORadar-Shakti has some potential to be a valuable tool for SMEs as well as for supporting organizations e.g. relevant NGOs in the Hyderabad area. But the success of ECORadar will be strongly depending on some prerequisites:

- *Subject-specific content*: Due to a very pragmatic approach of SMEs to Environmental Management the subject-specific knowledge content offered on the platform is key to its success. It must be aligned closely to effective needs of the individual users and their entrepreneurial contexts.
- *Cooperation among SMEs*: Besides the technical content provided by the platform, the cooperation of users is critical to its success. Due to the fact that Environmental Management for SMEs is not a critical issue in a strategic sense, cooperation is basically helpful and economically sound.
- *Cooperation with NGOs and local state authorities*: As expressed above, cooperation between SMEs and local state authorities is not very much developed or fruitful up-to-date. Is a difficult question whether ECORadar can positively influence this situation at all. Cooperation with NGOs is much more likely to be beneficial for the stakeholders involved. Some efforts should be made to support this type of cooperation.
- *Cooperation along the supply-chain*: Supply-Chain collaboration is a new topic so far not emphasized in the German ECORadar project. Interviews with SMEs have shown that transnational cooperation along the value chain is of some interest. The potential benefit still has to be evaluated.

Extending the Scope of ECORadar

Proceeding from these findings, the following section will discuss three major areas of development of the ECORadar-Shakti project. The scope extension must take into account the specific situation found on-site. A 1:1 transfer of content and methods applied in the German project is not feasible.

Define the Role of Stakeholders

For a successful and beneficial implementation of ECORadar five groups of stakeholders will be relevant as knowledge suppliers and demanders. All of them are potential users and beneficiaries of ECORadar. The subsequent table summarizes purposes and relevant aspects of each role-group.

Above the aspects of role-groups are not exhaustively outlined. The German ECORadar-project has shown that knowledge-supply and –demand of stakeholders and thereby individual users cannot be determined beforehand.

Extend the Scope of Knowledge-Content to Social Sustainability

Actual information content on ECORadar is partially subject to supplier and demander's interests and therefore cannot be fully controlled by its operator. The German project had a clear focus on environmental issues aiming to improve the efficiency and effectiveness of corporate EMS in terms of enhancing economical and environmental performance. While social and health issues are strongly regulated and therefore are playing a minor role in mature markets like Germany, in India the situation is seen different. Considering the strive for a sustainable development, the social part within the sustainability triangle (economical, social and ecological criteria in balance) has to make up some ground. This will have to shift the current knowledge contents focus from environmental to social criteria.

The adequate selection and motivation of suitable participants in the role-group of experts could help to build an appropriate knowledge base in this area of expertise. Recipients of this specialized content are SMEs as well as NGOs and local administration authorities. Above all, those stakeholders must be motivated to adopt a new field of expertise so far fairly untapped.

Table 4. Role-groups and their relevant aspects on ECORadar

Role Group	Main purpose of participation	Knowledge supplied	Knowledge demanded
SMEs	Efficient implementation and running of own EMS, thus gaining competitive advantage	• Best practice guidelines (with support of NGOs)	• Rich knowledge-base, covering all relevant technical and economical aspects of EMS
Local Government Authorities	Efficient communication with subordinated SMEs	• Environmental Data & Regulations	• Process-Know How of implementation esp. regulations
NGOs[3]	Active support of member organizations in terms of competitiveness & sustainability performance	• Know-How of implementation, Best-Practice Guidelines • Aggregate demand of Stakeholders • Practical Tools	• Set-up of Cooperation • Aggregate Performance Measurement • Benchmarking (Branch-specific)
Local Technical Experts[4]	Participation in highly specialized information market	• Know How of implementation • Market-Data, Tools, etc.	• Set-up of Cooperation • Access to customers
Potential or actual buyers of components (overseas)	"Greening" of own transnational supply-chain, thus reduction of environmental risk in supply chain	• Know-How of implementation • Best-practice guidelines	• Access to pioneering Indian suppliers • Performance data • Environmental Reports

Extend Collaborative Functionalities

As shown above, collaboration among stakeholders, especially among local government authorities and SMEs is much more difficult than in Germany. But besides content, collaborative functionalities will be key to ECORadar-Shakti´s success. Several different scenarios of collaboration are taken into consideration. The subsequent table shows and summarizes three exemplary scenarios of collaboration that are likely to support the portals success.

CONCLUSION

The chapter outlined the basic concept of ECO-Radar as a web-based knowledge base aimed to support and promote SME´s Environmental Management Systems in Germany. An extension

Table 5. Exemplary scenarios of collaboration in ECORadar-Shakti

Exemplary Scenario of Collaboration	Partners of collaboration	Content & Benefits	Tools
Enforcement of specific environmental policies (water, air, waste etc.)	Responsible local & state authorities ⇔ SMEs (eventually facilitated by NGOs)	• Publication and subscription of (temporary) media- or branch specific restrictions imposed by authority • Success control and aggregation reports • Facilitation and acceleration of law enforcement process	• Server Push-Technology, SMEs as "Channel Subscriber"
Benchmarking of EMS performance	SMEs ⇔ SMEs, (facilitated by NGOs)	• Interchange and aggregation of standardized[5] Key Performance Indicators (KPI) • Support of success control and Gap-Analysis	• Structured, form-based information exchange on Web-Platform
Supply-chain collaboration	SMEs ⇔ other domestic SMEs or buyers overseas	• Support of research process in terms of proven environmental or social performance standards • Publication of environmental reports / KPI	• Catalog- or search engine-based research tools • Publication portal • RFP[6]- Marketplace • E-mail communication

of scope was proposed and roughly specified to deploy it as a tool to contribute to the greening of an Indian megacity. It is obvious that prior to an effective implementation of ECORadar-Shakti as an offering for Indian SMEs (as primary addressees) and other stakeholders, major investments in scientific research, but also in (political) marketing and technology development would be necessary. Since the success of such a platform is strongly depending on the amount of participants and the market share covered, a deepened cooperation with political stakeholders is essential – all the more because a purely privately run system, depending on monetary contributions of its users, is expected to be difficult if not close to impossible to be realized. But a commercial implementation was not the author's aspiration. The objective was rather to outline the fundamental possibilities of the tool, may it be a system fully backed by politics or by a Public Private Partnership. Once implemented with a sufficient amount of users, the tool could be a valuable building block to push on the sustainability strategy of the Hyderabad Megacity. The proposed content and collaborative functionalities surpass its German role model in some of its key aspects. While emerging market countries like India are less developed than western countries in many domains, the utilization of innovative new technologies is sometimes stunning, often surpassing the western level. This could also be true for the implementation of sustainability strategies on a business or societal level. China markets a full Plug-In Hybrid Electric Vehicle (PHEV) in Europe[7], whereas leading German car manufacturers are still in the mode of making announcements. Against this background ECORadar-Shakti has some potential, not only to improve the environmental quality of the Hyderabad Megacity, but also to create a competitive advantage for the region and its resident companies. The regional expansion across India or other emerging market countries or the vertical diversification to private consumers is another possibility to be considered.

REFERENCES

Bhattacharya, C. B., Sen, S., & Korschun, D. (2008). Using Corporate Social Responsibility to Win the War for Talent. *MIT Sloan Management Review, 49*(2), 37–44.

Bleischwitz, R., & Hennicke, P. (2004). *Eco-efficiency, regulation, and sustainable business: towards a governance structure for sustainable development*. Cheltenham, UK: Edward Elgar Publishing.

Braun, R., Russ, M., Krcmar, H., Schulz, W. F., & Kreeb, M. (2003). An Open-Source Community for Building Ecological Tools. In Gnauck, A. & Heinrich, R. (Eds.) *Umweltinformatik Aktuell, 17th International Conference Informatics for Environmental Protection Cottbus 2003. Part 1: Concepts and Methods*, (pp. 165-170), Marburg.

Braun, R., Russ, M., Schulz, W. F., Krcmar, H., & Kreeb, M. (2004). Good-Practice-Examples and Indicators: Internet-based solutions for the Sustainable Management. In CERN (Eds.), *EnviroInfo 2004, 18th International Conference Informatics for Environmental Protection Genf 2004. Part 1*, (pp. 24-32). Genf.

Bullinger, H. J., Warnecke, H. J., & Westkämper, E. (2003). *Neue Organisationsformen im Unternehmen: Ein Handbuch für das moderne Management*. Berlin: Springer.

Davenport, Th. H., & Prusak, L. (1998). *Working Knowledge: How Organizations Manage What They Know*. Boston: Harvard Business School Press.

Haasis, H. D., & Kriwald, T. (2001). *Wissensmanagement in Produktion und Umweltschutz*. Berlin: Springer.

Haastrup, P., & Wurtz, J. (2007). *Environmental Data Exchange Network for Inland Water*. The Amsterdam: Elsevier Science & Technology.

Hagel, J., & Armstrong, A. (1997). *Net gain - expanding markets through virtual communities.* Boston: Harvard Business School Press.

Inmon, W. H., Zachman, J. A., & Geiger, J. G. (1997). *Data stores, data warehousing, and the Zachman framework, Managing enterprise knowledge.* New York: McGraw Hill.

Krcmar, H. (2003). *Informationsmanagement. 3.* Aufl. Berlin: Springer.

Kreeb, M., et al. (2005). Web Portals: A Tool for Environmental Management. In L. Hilty, E. K. Seifert, & R. Treibert, (Eds.), *Information Systems for Sustainable Development* (pp. 213-228). Hershey, PA: IGI Global.

Kuhre, W. L. (1998). *ISO 14031- Environmental Performance Evaluation (EPE): Practical Tools for Conducting an Environmental Performance Evaluation.* Upper Saddle River, NJ: Prentice Hall.

Kytle, B., & Ruggie, J. (2005). *Corporate Social Responsibility as Risk Management: A Model for Multinationals*, Social Responsibility Initiative Working Paper No. 10. John F. Kennedy School of Government. Boston: Harvard University.

Lehmann-Waffenschmidt, M. (2007). *Innovations Towards Sustainability: Conditions and Consequenses.* Berlin: Springer.

Lieberman, B. (2007). *Applying an analytical framework - Organize and reuse valuable techniques, tools, and examples.* BioLogic Software Consulting, S. Houstoun.

Nonaka, I., & Takeuchi, H. (1995). *The Knowledge-creating company.* New York: Oxford University Press.

Orlitzky, M., Schmidt, F., & Rynes, S. (2003). Corporate Social and Financial Performance: A Meta-analysis. *Organization Studies, 24*(3), 403–441. doi:10.1177/0170840603024003910

Reisch, L., Bietz, S., & Kreeb, M. (2006). How to communicate sustainable lifestyles to hard-to-reach consumers? A report on the large scale experiment "balance-f". In M. Charter & A. Tucker (Eds.), *Proceedings of the SCORE! Launch Conference "Sustainable Consumption and Production: Opportunities and Threats"*, (pp. 39-52). Wuppertal, Germany: Wuppertal Institute for Climate, Energy, and Environment, in cooperation with the UNEP Centre for Sustainable Consumption and Production (CSCP).

Reisch, L., Bietz, S., & Kreeb, M. (2007). An alternative to "preaching to the choir" - Communicating sustainable lifestyle options to a low interest target group. In *Proceedings of the International Society of Marketing and Development and the Macromarketing Society Joint Conference "Macromarketing and Development: Building Bridges and Forging Alliances"*, (pp. 187-193), June 2-5, 2007, Washington DC.

Rheingold, H. (1994). *Virtual Community: Homesteading on the Electronic Frontier.* Boston: Addison-Wesley.

Rheingold, H. (2002). *Smart Mobs: The Next Social Revolution.* Cambridge, UK: Perseus Publishing.

Riedl, C., Böhmann, T., Rosemann, M., & Krcmar, H. (2008). Quality Management in Service Ecosystems. *Information Systems And eBusiness Management,* (accepted for publication) [Ranking WKWI: B]

Schulz, W. F., & Kreeb, M. (2005). Cooperate Social Responsibility. In *Umweltmagazin, 35,* Jg., Heft 1, Januar, 70.

Schwaiger, B., Wall, A., & Gotsch, P. (2007). Sustainable Holistic Approach and Know-how Tailored to India, The SHAKTI-Project. *Trialog, 92/2007,* 16–21.

Wenger, E., & Snyder, W. (2000). Communities of practice: the organizational frontier. *Harvard Business Review*, (January-February): 139–145.

ENDNOTES

[1]   Sustainable Holistic Approach & Know-how Tailored to India

[2]   http://en.wikipedia.org/wiki/Hyderabad,_Andhra_Pradesh

[3]   Local Chamber of Commerce & Industry & the Federation of Andhra Pradesh Chambers of Commerce & Industry (FAPCCI)

[4]   Specialized Commercial or Academic Consultants

[5]   NGOs are needed as facilitators

[6]   = Request for Proposal

[7]   Http://en.wikipedia.org/wiki/BYD_Auto, http://www.byd.com.cn

Section 2
Communicating Sustainability

Chapter 5
Philanthropy, CSR and Sustainability

Arun Sahay
Strategic Management, Management Development Institute, Gurgaon, India

ABSTRACT

Despite business's business being business, the business owners have been doing acts of benevolence depending upon the owner's religion, faith, values and beliefs. Establishment of temples, mosques, churches, schools, hospitals etc. has been usual practice through which firms have shown their concern about the society and made contribution to the social cause. However, of late, it is observed that progressive businesses, after understanding the nuances of sustainable development and its reporting, have moved from philanthropic mode of contributing to society to the concept of Corporate Social Responsibity (CSR). Some of them have gone beyond CSR and have entered the domain of Strategic CSR. In the process, a new concept of Corporate Sustainability, which is based on Triple Bottom-line concept, has emerged in strategic management literature. Thus, today CSR activities are being aligned with the business strategy of the firm. In the developed countries, firms are increasingly integrating CSR with the core business activities e.g. innovation, marketing, finance etc. This article attempts to look into firm's CSR and corporate sustainability with special reference to a developing country - India.

STRUCTURE OF THE TEXT

The chapter, after the introduction of the subject, digs into the roots of sustainability and describes the processes through which sustainability, that we know today, has undergone. After dealing with industrial philanthropy, it moves to corporate social responsibility (CSR) and finally to the concept of strategic CSR that was propounded and communicated before Brundtland's definition of sustainability appeared on the horizon and became known to the whole world. I have discussed the issues of national and international framework of CSR before moving to sustainability, which is more communicated rather than acted upon, by nations or firms. Notwithstanding, after dealing with the

DOI: 10.4018/978-1-60566-822-2.ch005

general concept of sustainability, it delves into the issue of corporate sustainability and its reporting, especially by Indian industries. The author believes "Action speaks louder than words" and has therefore, concentrated on capturing CSR and sustainability actions of the firm rather than their strategy and process of communication.

INTRODUCTION

There was a time when religion preached for the welfare of the society and entrusted state with this pious responsibility. Now the time has come when business joins hands with government in adding value to the society right from "from cradle to grave". In earlier times religion had very crucial and dominant role to play in human life. Religion expresses itself both in an individual practices related to communal faith and in group sacraments and communication budding from collective commitment. The noble ideas of symbiosis, co-existence, harmony, giving back to the society, responsibility towards wellness of the environment, sensitization of human beings towards protection and preservation of natural resources and innumerable other good ideas stemmed from almost all the religions. These ideas seem to have universal acceptance despite all spreaded differences in beliefs and faiths across the religions around the globe. As a highly influential system, religion rules over the minds of people giving the thought direction and act prescription.

Business, being a part of the society, has always been influenced by it and its philosophies. From ancient times, business had been bearing cumulative social costs incurred by its own activities. Business adopted more philosophical way to be socially responsible following the value and belief system established by any religion or philosophy. It trusted more on making temples, mosques, churches; funding or running orphanages and educational institutes and donating for social cause.

However, there was hardly any well-established linkage between those ethical or moral acts and the business objectives. Further, they believed in "doing" rather than "telling" it.

With the advent of "industrial revolution" business expanded its horizons connecting suppliers and buyers; sometimes across the national boundary. Cost & Benefit Analysis of every activity performed by business became essential. In the ruthless race where industrialized nations jostled to get ahead and overlooked the hidden as well as visible socio-environmental costs acquired by it. In this era values lost sincere and serious implementation and were not counted in a powerful way by the firms.

It is interesting to note that at the same time tangible reflection of embedded ethical values were seen, when Indian industry was being set up by the great business visionaries and entrepreneurs. It would be relevant to quote Jamsetji Tata who was more than merely an entrepreneur; who helped India take her place in the league of industrialized nations. He was a patriot and a humanist whose ideals and vision shaped an exceptional business conglomerate. The brick-and-mortar endeavors that Jamsetji planned and executed were but one part of grand ideas. How much of a man of the future he was can be gauged from his views about his workers and their welfare. Jamsetji offered his people shorter working hours, well-ventilated workplaces, and provident fund and gratuity long before they became statutory in the west. He spelled out his concept of a township for the workers at the steel plant in a letter he wrote to his son, Dorab Tata, in 1902, five years before even a site for the enterprise had been decided;

Be sure to lay wide streets planted with shady trees, every other of a quick-growing variety, be sure that there is plenty of space for lawns and gardens, and reserve large areas for football, hockey and parks. Earmark areas for Hindu temples, Mohammedan mosques and Christian churches.

He, then, would have hardly thought of corporate social responsibility or sustainability. It was, then, a cry of his heart rather than a hard-core business strategy that is driven by not only economic issues but sustainability issues as well. Be it as it may, there was never a formal communication about the same to the masses. They knew it only through the deeds of the firm and it went on doing corporate philanthropy.

PHILANTHROPY

Philanthropy is the act of donating money, goods, time, or effort to support a charitable cause, usually over an extended period of time and in regard to a defined objective. In a more fundamental sense, philanthropy may encompass any altruistic activity, which is intended to promote good or improve human quality of life. Someone who is well known for practicing philanthropy may sometimes be called a *philanthropist*. Although such individuals are often very wealthy, people may nevertheless perform philanthropic acts without possessing great wealth (Wikipedia, December 7, 2008). As the society grew and organized businesses came into being, some of them, too, started acts of philanthropy.

Philanthropy has been seen by the society through different lenses. Some equate it with benevolence and charity for the poor and needy while others hold that philanthropy can be any altruistic giving towards any kind of social need that is not served, underserved, or perceived as unserved or underserved by the market. Some believe that philanthropy can be a means to build community by growing community funds and creating vehicles for service to society. When communities see themselves as being resource rich instead of asset poor, the community is in a better position to solve community problems.

By the conventional definition of philanthropy, donations are dedicated to a narrowly defined cause and the donation is targeted to make a recognizable change in social conditions. This often necessitates large donations and financial support sustained over time. The need for a large financial commitment creates a distinction between philanthropy and *charitable giving*, which typically plays a supporting role in a charitable organization initiated by someone else. Thus, the conventional usage of *philanthropy* applies mainly to wealthy persons, and sometimes to a trust created by a wealthy person with a particular cause or objective targeted. Business, too, does acts of philanthropy, mainly through trust or society and at times directly in response to their CSR/Sustainability activity.

Philanthropy responds to either present or future needs.(Joseph and Matthew, 2005, Payton Philanthropic Studies Library). The charitable response to an impending disaster is an essential function of philanthropy. It offers immediate honor for the philanthropist, yet requires no foresight. Responding to future needs, however, draws on the donor's foresight and wisdom, but seldom recognizes the donor. Prevention of future needs will often avert far more hardship than a response after the fact. For example, the charities responding to starvation from overpopulation in Africa are afforded swift recognition (www.indiamond6.ulib.iupui.edu, December 7, 2008). Meanwhile, philanthropists behind the U.S. population movement of the 1960s and 1970s were never recognized, and are lost in history. People are often supportive of philanthropic efforts. In many countries, those who donate money to a charity are given a title of good or one of great (Catherine the Great, Alexander the Great). Some governments are suspicious of philanthropic activities as possible grabs for favor, yet they allow for special interest groups (and votes/power in democracies) of portions of the population by non-governmental organizations. Philanthropists desire a government by the people who need them most and who have the least say.

Philanthropy attracts press and media coverage as big names are involved viz. rock star Bono's campaign to alleviate Third World debt to developed nations; the Gates Foundation's massive resources and ambitions, such as its campaigns to eradicate malaria and river blindness; and billionaire investor and Berkshire Hathaway Chairman Buffet's donation in 2006 of $30 billion to the Gates Foundation. Socially conscious entrepreneurs such as eBay founder Pierre Omidyar and Google co-founders Larry Page and Sergey Brin are trying to change philanthropy through unique networks and new forms of giving. Google's efforts are largely considered "for-profit," meaning it will not be constrained in how it spends by the 501(c)(3) section of the Internal Revenue Service code. The feeling is also that it will not restrict itself to conventional giving or old-line foundations when it comes to social investments. Back home, the family of Tatas has created various foundations to do the acts of philanthropy.

Jamsetji's philanthropic principles were rooted in the belief that for India to climb out of poverty, its finest minds would have to be harnessed. Charity and handouts were not his way, so he established the JN Tata Endowment in 1892. This enabled Indian students, regardless of caste or creed, to pursue higher studies in England. This beginning flowered into the Tata scholarships, which flourished to the extent that by 1924 two out of every five Indians coming into the elite Indian Civil Service were Tata scholars. The objective of creating the Indian Institute of Science came from the same source, Jamsetji pledged Rs. 30 lakh (Rs. 3 million) from his personal fortune towards setting up the institute, drew up a blueprint of the shape it ought to take, and solicited the support of everyone from the Viceroy Curzon, to Swami Vivekananda to turn it into reality. Recalls Jamsetji:

We do not claim to be more unselfish, more generous or more philanthropic than other people. But we think we started on sound and straightforward business principles, considering the interests of the shareholders our own, and the health and welfare of the employees, the sure foundation of our success.

Swami Vivekananda, who was the greatest religious and social leader of the time, supported this philosophy of Jamsetji. Backing the idea he wrote in 1899:

I am not aware if any project at once so opportune and so far reaching in its beneficent effects has ever been mooted in India. The scheme grasps the vital point of weakness in our national well-being with a clearness of vision and tightness of grip, the mastery of which is only equaled by the munificence of the gift that is being ushered to the public.

But the case has not been the same for every business endeavourer worldwide and there have been severely negative consequences representing darker side of industrial revolution such as; famine, health problems, noise, air, water pollution, poor nutrition, dangerous machinery, impersonal work, isolation, poverty, homelessness, and substance abuse. Business, because of having a major hold over people's wealth, had to act in response to the emerging problems.

THE PARADIGM SHIFT

The advocacy to make business responsible and responsive compounded with the dawn of "Globalization". The ICT revolution converted the world into a 'global village' and the wave of globalization did not leave any portion of the globe untouched. Along with this, problems such as pollution, poverty etc., earlier having limited geographical existence, started obtaining global character. These conditions led to a specific set of socially responsible practices, which are called 'reactive practices'. But the missing link with the business goals and objectives pressurized business to adapt 'proactive strategies' in place of reactive strategies. Commenting on corporate philanthropical acts, Carly Fiorina, CEO of Hewlett- Packard (Business for Social Responsibility Annual Conference, Nov. 12, 2003), said:

For many years, community development goals were philanthropic activities that were seen as separate from business objectives, not fundamental to them, doing well and doing good were seen as separate pursuits. But I think that is changing what many of organizations that are represented here today are learning is that cutting- edge innovation and competitive advantage can result from weaving social and environmental considerations into business strategy from the beginning.

Smaller organizations, too, have joined the bandwagon. The concept of measurable life change, with direct investments and follow-up to track results, is gaining more recognition through small and medium Enterprises (SMEs) as well. Philanthropy, now, is not always viewed as a universal good. Notable thinkers such as Friedrich Nietzsche opposed philanthropy on philosophical grounds, connecting it with the idea of the weak sponging off the strong, a view sometimes endorsed by those who oppose government welfare programs (Wicks, 2007). Mother Teresa made a big impact and changed the thinking for doing social good through her famous message, "Give the poor the fishing rod not the fish". This started a debate on the purpose and process of philanthropy and the firms started thinking in terms of their responsibilities to the society and how to discharge them.

CORPORATE SOCIAL RESPONSIBILITY

Corporate Social Responsibility is a component of sustainability of the firm, which has to be economically viable. Of course, it can operate its business only when it meets all environmental and social norms. CSR is not just meeting the norms but going beyond; bettering the quality of life and contributing to social and environmental agenda not only of the nation but whole world. There is no universally accepted definition of CSR. Selected definitions by CSR organizations and actors include:

- "Corporate Social Responsibility is the continuing commitment by business to behave ethically and contribute to economic development while improving the quality of life of the workforce and their families as well as of the local community and society at large" World Business Council for Sustainable Development [WBCSD, 2000]
- "CSR is about how companies manage the business processes to produce an overall positive impact on society." (Mallen Baker, 2007)
- "Corporate social responsibility is undertaking the role of "corporate citizenship" and ensuring the business values and behavior is aligned to balance between improving and developing the wealth of the business, with the intention to improve society, people and the planet" (Van Buren, 2006 and Business Respect – Oct 28, 2007)
- "CSR is a company's commitment to operating in an economically, socially and environmentally sustainable manner whilst balancing the interests of diverse stakeholders." (CSR Asia, December 5, 2007)
- "Corporate social responsibility is the commitment of businesses to contribute to sustainable economic development by working with employees, their families, the local community and society at large to improve their lives in ways that are good for business and for development." International Finance Corporation [www.ifc.org]

- "A concept whereby companies integrate social and environmental concerns in their business operations and in their interaction with their stakeholders on a voluntary basis." European Commission[www.ec.europa.eu]
- "There is one and only one social responsibility of business -to use its resources and engage in activities designed to increase its profits so long as it stays within the rules of the game, which is to say, engages in open and free competition without deception or fraud." (Milton Friedman, 1962)
- "Corporate Responsibility is about ensuring that organizations manage their businesses to make a positive impact on society and the environment whilst maximizing value for their shareholders." Institute of Chartered Accountants in England & Wales [www.icaew.com]

Thus, it will be seen that the concept of CSR has raised more dust than it has settled. There have been wide spread confusion regarding what is the nature and the extent of social responsibility of business. Presently, there is a growing literature attempting to define what it means for a company to be socially responsible. The problem with figuring out an exact definition of CSR has been a subject of contest and has been an evolving debate over the last four decades amongst various researchers (Meehan et al., 2006; McWilliams et al., 2006; Windsor, 2006 Leisinger, 2005; Valor, 2005; Acutt et al., 2004; Greenfield, 2004; Munshi, 2004; Young 2004; BSR, 2003; Hills et al., 2003; Ka¨rna et al., 2003; Frankental, 2001; Shrivastava and Venkateswaran, 2000; Willums, 1998; Waddock, 2004). Till date, there is no single definition available on CSR. Surprisingly Greenfield (2004) wrote that we don't know what CSR stands for. McWilliams *et al.,* 2006 wrote that the lack of clarity in the theoretical and definitional aspects of CSR is impeding further theoretical development and measurement difficult.

According to Indian authors, Shrivastava and Venkateswaran (2000), if a business works obeying the legal framework of the land and pays due taxes (Friedman, 1970) then the social responsibility is fulfilled for the firm. But they also pointed out that there are other views, like a socially responsible company is one that proactively takes up social issues and does well to the society and environment on its own. Ingram (1978) observed that the nature of CSR activities undertaken by firms' vary over time and are dependent on the type of the firm's business activities. Business and Society fields have many concepts and terms present, of which CSR is one of the most prominent one. A researcher or scholar new to the Business and Society field could get amazed by the number of terms present in this field (Valor, 2005).

The first big impact, seminal conceptualization of CSR came in 1979 from A. B.Carroll. He conceptualized CSR as "The Pyramid of Corporate Social Responsibility". This popular conceptualization of CSR, viewed CSR, as basically, businesses fulfilling four main responsibilities: economic, legal, ethical, and philanthropic. Business firms have to provide society (made up of customers as well) with goods and services it is meant to produce and be profitable to create wealth for the shareholders. Businesses are expected to carry out the production and delivery of goods and services while complying with the rules, regulations and laws of the land (Carroll, 1979). This is the Legal responsibility of business. Above legal compliance, business should do its business while respecting and being accommodative and sensitive to the values and norms of the society. This is the ethical responsibility of business. The fourth and final responsibility is the philanthropic responsibility of business. This is the discretionary set of activities businesses undertake to address the social ills and problems, so that the world becomes a better place to live (Schwartz and Carroll 2003). Sethi (1979) had also conceptualized CSR around the same themes. The conceptualization of CSR by Carroll (1979) and

Sethi (1979) were foundational and all the CSR explanations which came later were just variants of these (Karna et al., 2003).

Unlike philanthropy which is characterized by a one-way, top-down (corporate-community) relationship approach, CSR has been increasingly seen as a continuous collaboration between the corporate house and the stakeholders community (Osborn and Hagedoorn, 1997; Boatright, 2000; Altman, 1998; Waddock, 2004). Thus firm CSR activities are generally meant to be long-term longitudinal initiative unlike one time philanthropy like doing charity or providing donations. CSR has also been expected to benefit both the society as well as the corporation (Boatright, 2000; Pava and Krausz, 1997; Garone, 1999; Steiner and Steiner, 1991). This is quite logical because business exists and resides in society. A healthy society will be better able to house a business.

With the increased use of stakeholders rather than shareholders in management literature, the conception of larger society got lodged. Though CSR is on agenda of most major corporations, corporate executives still largely support the view that corporation should maximize the returns to their shareholders. In past Friedmanian view "The social responsibility of business is to increase its profits (Friedman 1970)" was largely accepted and admired by the business. However, from the last few years another position voiced by many executives, that CSR and profits go together has become firmer. But it has been realized that this position is not well supported by empirical evidences. Notwithstanding, Berle-Dodd debate on the concept of the corporation (Macintosh, 1999) has settled the issue that the companies work not only for shareholders but also for all stakeholders.

The inductive concept of Corporate Social Performance (CSP) receives its foundational inputs from CSR program's performance. For fulfilling the criteria of CSP, business goes for Corporate Social Reporting. Corporate Social Reporting is a CSR activity communication output mechanism-

keeping stakeholders in mind. Here it becomes necessary to clear that; CSR proponents never give undue importance to social responsibility of the business over its indispensable economic responsibility. Further, socially responsible firms can be as much or more profitable as compared to less socially responsible firms. However, the prerequisite of cost benefit analysis for undertaking CSR initiatives is very obvious and significant.

The way businesses engage/involve the shareholders, employees, customers, suppliers, governments, non-governmental organizations, international organizations, and at large society is usually a key feature of the concept. As such, CSR closely resembles the business pursuit of *sustainable development* and the *triple bottom line*. In addition to integration into corporate structures and processes, CSR also frequently involves creating innovative and proactive solutions to societal and environmental challenges, as well as collaborating with both internal and external stakeholders to improve CSR performance.

Companies interested in advancing corporate social responsibility and in improving their social and environmental performance as part of their business have a wide range of tools available for application. Tools can vary widely in terms of objectives, scope, costs, and levels of formality, partnerships, extent of stakeholder involvement, and many other characteristics. These tools can be applied to one or more of the planning, implementation, checking, and improvement facets of corporate operations. The tools reflect activity at the domestic and international levels as well as initiatives by both the private and public sectors. In some cases the tools may be focused on one element of CSR such as Environmental Protection and in others may be more comprehensive such as the Global Reporting Initiative. For the exhaustive study purpose in proposed project CSR tools can be clustered into the four following groups:

Ellkington (1994) championed the concept of Triple Bottom Line (TBL), which meant that corporations should focus not just on the economic value that it adds but also to the environmental and social value it destroys or adds. Henriques and Richardson, (2004) believe that it is all about 3P (People, Planet and Profits). 3P or TBL encompasses Win- Win -Win business strategies for business - society – environment. New terms also reflect this philosophy like Corporate Social Opportunity (CSO). CSO is seen as "commercially viable activities, which also advance environmental and social sustainability" (Grayson and Hodges, 2004). This concept of TBL, 3 P and CSO hammered in an important point that there are corporate benefits that can be achieved form managing CSR affairs.

STRATEGIC CSR

Securing business benefits from CSR became an emergent theme in the CSR knowledge and practice domains. CSR activities which provided business and strategic benefits is termed as Strategic CSR (Porter and Kramer, 2006 and 2002; Crawford and Scaletta, 2005; Salzmann *et al.,* 2005; Meehan *et al.,* 2006; Friedman, 1970; Kotler and Lee; 2005,Windsor, 2006; Altman, 1998; Waddock, 2000; Ricks, 2005; Perrini, 2005; Stead, and Stead, 2000; Jones *et al.,* 2005; Lewis, 2003; Bhattacharya *et al.,* 2004; Carroll, 2001; Burke and Logsdon, 1996; Marsden, 2000; Lantos, 2001; Quester and Thompson, 2001; Ricks, 2005; McAlister and Ferrell, 2002).

Conventional wisdom suggests that there is a conflict between the goals of environmental protection, CSR and economic competitiveness. But proactive industry leaders argue that this is not true as long as state policy creates a level playing field (Sahay, 2004). In fact, business is becoming more and more responsible in present scenario as CSR policies are knotted with all the three strategies (Corporate, Business and Executive) of a number of global conglomerates as well as national enterprises. Due to the increased level of awareness in society, environment friendly practices are becoming prerequisites for any business to be successful. A primary goal of CSR is to add value and achieve a reasonable and equitably distributed level of economic well being that can be perpetuated among all the stakeholders. Combined with this, pressure is mounting on business to respond strategically for 'doing well for being good' rather 'doing well for looking good'.

In a seminal article in the Harvard Business Review, Craig Smith (1994) identified "The New Corporate Philanthropy" describing it as a shift to making long term commitment to the specific social issues and initiatives; providing more than cash contributions, sourcing funds from business units as well as philanthropic budgets; forming strategic alliances; and doing all of this in a way that also advances business goals.

Earlier to 1990s generally corporations were more into allocating funds to a number of organizations as their gesture towards embedded core ethical values and act of philanthropic efforts. But there have been few pitfalls allied with the philanthropic approach as Kotler et al. (2005) recognizes them;

- Short term basis,
- Avoidance of those issues which might be associated with core business products,
- Steering clear of major and often controversial social issues such as AIDS, judging that these were best handled by governmental or non profit organizations,
- Decisions regarding issues to support and organizations to sponsor were heavily influenced by preferences or wishes of senior management than by need to support strategic business goals and objectives,
- 'Do good as easily as possible' as a rule of thumb was followed while developing and implementing specific initiatives resulting in a tendency to often give donations,
- Donors were satisfied with being one of the many corporate sponsors although those acts were not linked their business goals,

- Strategic CSR practices were perhaps also overlooked or were rarely developed because it would have required extra efforts to integrate and coordinate giving programs with other corporate strategies and business units such as marketing, human resources and operations,
- 'Trust' was simple approach followed to evaluate the outcomes of philanthropic CSR efforts; generally it was assumed that good happened.

To answer effectively to the above mentioned shortcomings it became necessary economic growth and social development go hand in hand. It requires the development of an innovative vision of the world leading to the incorporation of externalities and a positive contribution to the social context. If CSR is embedded in an organization, it can be at the heart of the business, linked to every business propositions and added value in the value chains of various stakeholders.

In present business scenario, a number of firms identify CSR practices with the core strategy and policy of the company based on the importance given to (Bryan W. et al. 2007):

1. Defining a plan for social action,
2. Intensity of investment in social programs,
3. Commitment of employees,
4. Perceived impact of social action on competitive position, and
5. Measuring outcomes of programs.

The business and society interact continuously. In fact society has much greater effect on the business than the business on society. A schematic diagram of interaction is shown in Figure 1.

Recent research efforts seek to recuperate the utility of planning in complex, dynamic environments (Grant, 2002). Companies need to answer to two aspects of their operations. These are:

Figure 1. Source www.mallenbaker.net

1. The quality of their management - both in terms of people and processes (the inner circle)
2. The nature and quantity of their impact on society in the various areas

To be economically triumphant and to be socially accountable have become dual purposes of a firm since early 1970s as argued by researchers in the field of business and society. However, in the 1980s this view was critically examined with the wave of corporate downsizing and reengineering. In the middle to late 1990s a new business model emerged; one that blends economics and social responsibility in a sophisticated fashion. In the second half of 1990s discussion of the concept of "corporate citizenship" thrived in the corporate sector. The corporate citizenship concept evokes many meanings, among corporations acting ethically, socially responsibly and proactively to jointly further the interests of external constituencies or stakeholders. In recent years corporations have begun programs promoting citizenship goals, both domestically and internationally. Many corporations are noting an association between these programs and their strategic goals.

CSR IN NATIONAL & INTERNATIONAL FRAMEWORK

Environmental Management (part of CSR) in India is as old as its history, its social and cultural milieu. Our forefathers used to worship the mountains, the rivers, the forests and even the animals. Himalayan Mountains, Ganga River, Pipal tree etc. have been worshipped since times immemorial. Elephants and cows are worshipped even today. The concept of bio-diversity and the green cover are age old in India. The social and religious fabric was woven around the concept of Environment Protection and Promotion. It was somewhere on the way to economic development that we went astray and have started looking to the west for

environmental management – the management of natural resources i.e. air, water, land, flora and fauna (Sahay 2006 a).

The present day increased awareness of CSR has also come about as a result of the United Nations Millennium Development Goals, in which a major goal is the increased contribution of assistance from large organizations, especially Multi-National Corporations, to help alleviate poverty and hunger, and for businesses to be more aware of their impact on society. There is a lot of potential for CSR to help with development in poor countries, especially community-based initiatives. Along with the corporations nations across the world have also recognized that a national sustainable development strategy (NSDS) can be an effective tool to allow countries to achieve their sustainable development goals.

Consequently, many countries are implementing their NSDSs as recommended in Agenda 21, the action program adopted at the United Nations Conference on Environment and Development in Rio de Janeiro (1992). In doing so, countries are also fulfilling their commitment made in 2002 in the Johannesburg Plan of Implementation, adopted at the World Summit on Sustainable Development, to take immediate steps to make progress in the formulation and elaboration of national strategies for sustainable development as well as to begin their implementation by 2005. Splendidly, in some European countries a separate ministry/department has been launched for CSR. These strategies, which are being followed by nations, give tremendous support and impetus to the CSR policies to be strategically embedded by the firms.

Corporate social responsibility (CSR) is the commitment of businesses to contribute to sustainable economic development by working with employees, their families, the local community and society at large to improve their lives in ways that are good for business and for development.

International Finance Corporation

Corporate CSR activities raise many questions for a firm, such as; whether doing CSR do well to the firm financial performance? Do firms engaging in CSR outperform firms not doing it? What is the nature and direction of CSR literature available discussing CSR with firm financial function? This article first attempt to look into these questions based upon the extant literature available from the developed countries. India is one of the fastest growing economies of the world. At the same time India is a country, which needs widespread socio- economic development, as it is home to the one of the worlds most poor and illiterate population. Firm CSR initiatives can be a medium of progress in developing countries like India (Shekhar and Sahay, 2007).

SUSTAINABLE DEVELOPMENT

The harmony between man and nature and mankind has been disturbed. In number of uses the mankind has inflicted irreversible loss on nature in its greed to make rapid economic development. With change in concept and definition of economic development, the growth of GNP Per capita income is not a single index of development of a country (Pandey and Sahay, 2008). Since the Second World War, nations are engaged in development but till recently development meant economic development. However, development does not mean only increase in per capita income but also the wellness of people, which can be achieved through both qualitative and quantitative transformation of whole society. This is a shift from traditional thinking and relates to new methods of production and distribution. Quality of life includes happiness and satisfaction and can be termed as subjective well being of society but there is additionally in quality of life such as nutrition, a non-hazardous environment and a long and healthy life (Philips, 2006). In fact, Bhutan, a small nation, has suggested a method to make development human and nature-centered. This country uses the concept of Gross National Happiness (GNH), instead of Gross National Product (GNP), to measure the achievements and impact of development. GNH includes all the regular indicators of economic development, ecological security, cultural promotion and spiritual values. GNH also includes good governance as additional parameter to measure whether development enhances human happiness or increases human misery (GNH Report, July 1999).

Sustainable development is a pattern of resource use that aims to meet human needs while preserving the environment so that these needs can be met not only in the present, but also in the indefinite future. It ties together concern for the carrying capacity of natural systems with the social challenges facing humanity. As early as the 1970s "sustainability" was employed to describe an economy "in equilibrium with basic ecological support systems" (Stivers, 1976). Ecologists have pointed to the "limits of growth" (Meadows, 1971) and presented the alternative of a "steady state economy" (Daly, 1973) in order to address environmental concerns.

Although the concept of sustainability has been around for a long time, it became more widely used in the 1980s. Back in 1983, the Secretary-General of the UN established a commission called the World Commission on the Environment and Development. This commission is frequently referred to as the Brundtland Commission, after Gro Harlem Brundtland, the head of the commission and formerly the Prime Minister of Norway. The commission was asked to look at the world's environmental problems and propose a global agenda for addressing them. She put together a team that went around the world and talked to people in all walks of life: fishermen, farmers, homemakers, loggers, school teachers, indigenous people and industry leaders. They asked what peoples' environmental concerns were and how they should be addressed. The commission came out with a definition of sustainable development as under:

Figure 2.

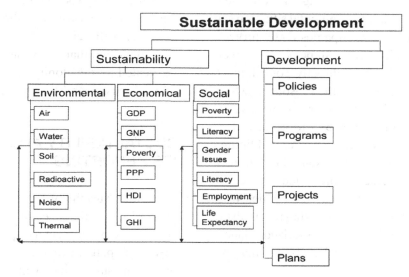

Sustainable Development: A diagrammatic view

..Development that meets the needs of the present without compromising the ability of future generations to meet their own needs (United Nations. 1987).

The schematic diagram of sustainable development concept is given below.

The field of sustainable development can be conceptually broken into three constituent parts:

- Environmental sustainability
- Economic sustainability
- Sociopolitical sustainability

CORPORATE SUSTAINABILITY

Sustainability is pervasive and is practiced at all levels; global, national, municipal and even at firm level. Corporate sustainability encompasses strategies and practices that aim to meet the needs of stakeholders today while seeking to protect, support and enhance the human and natural resources that will be needed in the future. Business and industry have a crucial role to play in helping not only the company but also the nation as a whole to become more sustainable and competitive. As a result, firms world over, are responding by reducing their environmental impacts and risks through improved environmental management practices and efficient use of natural resources.

Though the definition of sustainable development was in the context of "Earth", it automatically got extended to the nations. The nations found that the earth cannot be saved for future generation to meet their needs just by creating laws, rules and procedures but the citizen, including corporate citizen, have to actively participate. The business world found in this concept not only a contribution to the national efforts but a strategic element for their own sustainability and competitive advantage. Thus, some of the companies created a set up for sustainability management and some even started publishing sustainability report. The concept of sustainable development given below is equally applicable to the business houses where the word "development" means "growth". To ward of risks against growth, firms even started taking environmental insurance. However, environmental situation can improve if Insurance Companies come forward with products which deal with poverty in developing countries and also directly contribute to poverty alleviation through their resources which would help them discharge their corporate social responsibility (Sahay, 2006 b). Problems such as pollution, poverty etc., which earlier had limited geographical existence, have started obtaining a global character. These conditions led to a specific set of socially responsible practices, which were reactive in character. But the missing link with the business goals and objectives pressurized business to adapt 'proactive strategies' in place of reactive strategies (Sahay, 2009).

Even in developing country like India, Bombay Stock Exchange is planning to evolve a corporate sustainability index on the lines of Dow Jones Sustainability Index (DJSI), which performs better than Dow Jones Index (DJI). Such an index exists in Brazil also. BSE Managing Director and CEO, Rajnikant Patel stated this view during a panel discussion on "Are corporate sustainability and social sustainability interdependent," held under the aegis of the Institute of Company Secretaries of India (ICSI). However, the process of assessment was complicated and a robust framework would have to be evolved. It required co-operation from the companies and they would have to volunteer information. Mr. Patel's announcement came on the back of a remark made by Mr. Deveshwar, Chairman, ITC Ltd., that markets have failed to reward companies that were looking at sustainability issues. This comment found its resonance in the observation by speakers like Harshavardhan Neotia, Chairman, Ambuja Realty Development, who said that there was need to evolve a mechanism by which stock markets recognized companies that laid emphasis on the triple bottom line concept. Emphasizing on the need for convergence of societal sustainability and business sustainability, Mr. Deveshwar said that it would be

difficult for business to thrive in isolation in the face of growing social inequity. ITC had created business models whereby there was enmeshing of social well-being and shareholder value. He also suggested that a new stock exchange could be created for developing `trust' marks to denote a Firm's sustainability achievements.

SUSTAINABILITY AND ITS REPORTING

Corporate Sustainability is the capacity of an enterprise to maintain economic prosperity in the context of environmental responsibility and social stewardship. It is a business approach that creates long-term stakeholder value by embracing opportunities and managing risks deriving from economic, social and environmental developments. Corporate sustainability leaders (Knoepfel, 2001) achieve long-term stakeholder value by gearing their strategies to harness the market's potential for sustainability products and services as well as reducing and avoiding sustainability costs and risks. Leading sustainability companies display high levels of competence in addressing global and industry challenges in variety of areas. Their strategy is to integrate long-term economic, social and environmental aspects in their business while maintaining global competitiveness (Cornelius, 2003) and green brand equity (Davis, 1991).

The sustainability reporting varies from organization to organization, making it difficult for the stakeholders to evaluate the company for their investment and other decisions. Various reporting methods have been propounded from time to time by different agencies. Important among them are Responsible Care (1988), Coalition for Environmentally Responsible Economies (1989), ICC Business Charter (1990), Global Environmental Management Initiative (1990), CBI Environment Business Forum (1992), Rio Business and Industry Agenda (1992), Eco-Management and Audit Scheme (1992), European Chemical Industry

Council (1993), Global Environmental Charter (1993), Public Environmental Reporting Initiative (1993), World Business Council for Sustainable Development (1995), ACBE Guide (1997), Guide to Environmental and Energy Reporting and Accounting (1997), ISO 14031 (1999) and Global Reporting Initiative (GRI 2000, 2002, 2005). Of various approaches, GRI recommendations revised from time to time, the GRI – III has become popular among the business firms.

GRI REPORTING FRAMEWORK

The Guidelines contain principles and guidance, protocols, standard disclosures as well as sector supplements including indicators to outline a disclosure framework that organizations can voluntarily, flexibly, and incrementally adopt. At the outset, it defines what to report and how to report that. The broad Global Reporting Initiative Sustainability Guidelines are depicted in the figure below.

The following is the framework provided in GRI Reporting Initiative Sustainability Guidelines.

• Identify the topics and related Indicators that are relevant, and therefore might be appropriate to report, by undergoing an iterative process using the principles of materiality, stakeholder inclusiveness, sustainability context, and guidance on setting the Report Boundary.

• When identifying topics, consider the relevance of all Indicator Aspects identified in the GRI Guidelines and applicable Sector Supplements. Also consider other topics, if any that are relevant to report.

• From the set of relevant topics and Indicators identified, use the tests listed for each principle to assess which topics and Indicators are material, and therefore, should be reported.

GLOBAL REPORTING INITIATIVE SUSTAINABILITY GUIDELINES

Use the Principles to prioritize selected topics and decide which will be emphasized.

The specific methods or processes used for assessing materiality should:

a.   Differ for, and can be defined by, each organization;
b.   Always take into account the guidance and tests found in the GRI Reporting Principles; and
c.   Be disclosed.

In applying this approach:

a.   Differentiate between Core and Additional Indicators. All Indicators have been developed through GRI's multi-stakeholder processes, and those designated as Core are generally applicable Indicators and are assumed to be material for most organizations. An organization should report on these unless they are deemed not material on the

Figure 3. Source GRI Framework

G3 Reporting Framework

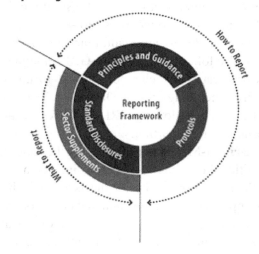

basis of the Reporting Principles. Additional Indicators may also be determined to be material.

b.   The Indicators in final versions of Sector Supplements are considered to be Core Indicators, and should be applied using the same approach as the Core Indicators found in the Guidelines.

c.   All other information (e.g., company specific Indicators) included in the report should be subject to the same Reporting Principles and have the same technical rigor as GRI Standard Disclosures.

d.   Confirm that the information to be reported and the Report Boundary are appropriate by applying the Principle of completeness.

GLOBAL EXAMPLES OF SUSTAINABILITY REPORTING

The Global Reporting Initiative (GRI) is a multi-stakeholder collaboration among the Coalition of Environmentally Responsible Economies (CERES) and numerous organizations, united to develop a common framework for global sustainability reporting. Issues reported using these guidelines are not limited to environmental performance, but also include social and economic indicators. As a member of the GRI Steering Committee, General Motors is pilot testing the draft GRI guidelines in its report. Bristol-Myers Squibb, Electrolux, Proctor and Gamble and Norsk Hydro have also followed some of the GRI guidelines in the preparation of their reports. In India, a number of firms including Jubilant Organosys, Tata Steel, ITC, etc. are following GRI guidelines for their sustainability reporting.

Bristol-Myers Squibb goes beyond the traditional one-line statement to include a comprehensive look at the all the issues that have an impact on operations and stakeholders (both local and global). BMS' overview of sustainability includes policy statements on external evaluation of EHS policies and procedures, supplier compliance, technology transfer, charitable contributions, transportation impacts, local noise and odor issues, new acquisition and divestiture processes, animal testing, pharmaceutical residuals in the environment, genomics, bio-safety, and bio-prospecting.

DuPont, Canada demonstrates a commitment to employee health, not only by reporting on injuries and illnesses resulting in lost time, but also by reporting on employee physical fitness levels. In its 1998 EHS report, DuPont provides data on rates of smoking, cholesterol levels, blood pressure and obesity among its employees. Benefits claims costs (as a percentage of payroll costs) are included as an EHS performance indicator. In addition, DuPont reports on the availability of on-site fitness facilities, on-site nutritional and health counseling, and health information seminars, to demonstrate the link between its policy and actions with regard to employee health.

Electrolux has also reported on the life cycle analysis of a number of their products. A strong impetus for the appliance industry to offer products with reduced environmental impact is the fact that the main environmental impact is usually greater in product use than during production, and furthermore is closely connected to the individual household economy. A life cycle assessment of a washing machine, for example, shows that about 80 percent of the total environmental impact during the life of the machine consists of water, energy and detergent consumption. A similar analysis of the total cost of the entire life cycle of the machine shows that the cost of water, energy and detergent consumption exceeds the initial purchase price.

Norsk Hydro has applied life cycle assessment (LCA) to the workings of the entire company. The aggregated data allows for a striking overview of company's consumption of natural resources and pollutant emissions in light of annual profits. LCA has also been completed for each major company division.

Ontario Power Generation, in its Towards Sustainable Development report, includes a description of the benchmarking study conducted by a consultant to compare OPG's corporate environmental management practices and processes to those of best-in-class organizations. The consultant's report affords OPG a third-party evaluation of both strengths and weaknesses in its corporate environmental practices and processes, and an essential baseline for measuring its progress. A synopsis of the findings is provided and OPG also outlines its response.

Procter and Gamble builds credibility and uses resources most effectively by providing detailed data on areas of greatest concern to the company. In their Sustainability Report emphasis was placed on water quality and use and on health and hygiene. Other more general indicators of progress were also reported upon but the detailed assessment in two areas gives the impression that the company is looking for triggers of improvement in areas where they are needed the most.

Rio Tinto includes an excellent graphic to illustrate responsibilities and information flow relating to the preparation of the company's Social and Environment Report. The reporting structure makes it apparent that Rio Tinto understands the importance of bringing corporate policy makers together with operational managers to produce a report that has meaning inside and outside of organization.

INDIAN CONTEXT

Environmental and social Management in India is as old as its history, its natural, social and cultural milieu. Our forefathers used to worship the mountains, the rivers, the forests and even the animals. Himalayan Mountains, Ganga River, Pipal tree etc. have been worshipped since times immemorial. Elephants and cows are worshipped even today. The concept of bio-diversity and the green cover are age old in India. The social and religious fabric was woven around the concept of Environment Protection and Promotion. Hindu religion followed by the majority preached for sacrifice for others. The age-old businesses were based on social equity and service to the mother earth. There are a number of shlokas (verses) in Vedas and Epics. Dhana (wealth) was meant for Dharma (religion) leading to Sukha (happiness). It was somewhere on the way to economic development that we went astray and have started looking to the west for sustainable development and corporate social responsibility – the essence of contributing to the upliftment of society and enhancement of natural resources i.e. air, water, land, flora and fauna.

SUSTAINABILITY REPORTING

In India, Jubilant Organosys Ltd became the first company to be the registered organizational Stakeholder of Global Reporting Initiative. This is both a recognition and acknowledgement of

Figure 4. Source Rio Tinto

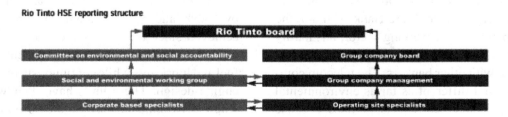

Rio Tinto HSE reporting structure

adherence to providing a safe working environment to employees and the communities around areas of operation. Jubilant Organosys Limited is a composite pharmaceuticals industry player, offering products and services to pharmaceuticals and life sciences industry. This is one of the country's leading Contract Research and Manufacturing Services *(CRAMS)* & Active Pharmaceutical Ingredients *(API)* companies, having business interests in Pharmaceuticals & Life Science Products, Performance Polymers and Industrial Products, and believe in sustainability of growth. Its approach to sustainable development focuses on the triple bottom lines of Economics, Environment and People.

The author had conducted a survey of leading companies belonging to automobile, banking, cement, chemical & fertilizer, engineering, FMCG, IT, mining & metallurgy, pulp & paper, pharmaceutical, power, and telecom sectors with regard to their annual reporting, especially environmental, social and sustainability reporting. The survey was based on secondary data, published reports, a questionnaire and personal interview of the executive looking after CSR/ Environmental management in the company. It revealed that conservation of energy finds place in the Directors report, presumably because of the provisions of Indian Company Law. Some companies have reported their social and environmental performance but sustainability report is scarce. The Environmental/Social/Sustainability reports, if provided, were mostly unsystematic and varied in content & character, the emphasis varying from sector to sector.

Some of Banking, Telecom and IT sector units belong to billion-dollar club but none of them have reported their sustainability, environmental or social performance. State Bank of India, the biggest player in the banking sector, has hardly reported its environmental responsibility and so is the case with other bankers. The telecom companies are not different as far as environmental reporting is concerned. This is, perhaps, because

they think that economics and technology are their only concern. IT sector in India has got three main sub-sectors namely hardware, software and IT enabled services. While hardware facilities seem to be environmentally aware, their report is scarce. Software and IT enabled services sectors do not consider environment to be an aspect of their business. Contrary to this, Paharpur Business Center (2003), a software technology infrastructure provider, has reported its Environmental Performance based on triple bottom line and is planning next report in GRI format. The leading software units like TCS (2003), INFOSYS (2003) and WIPRO (2003) have been reporting their performance more on social than environmental counts. The findings of some other sectors, where Environment has been considered as a business concern, are given below.

Automobile

With the liberalization policy of Indian government, almost all multinational automobile companies have entered this market. However, the top slot, both in 4wheeler as well as 2wheeler, is occupied by joint venture companies and the second position by the Indian companies. Automobile units are having ISO 14001 certification and are, thus, having a defined environmental management system. The exhaust emission (regulated since 1965 in developed countries but since 1991 in India) is their major environmental concern. Aggressive steps initiated towards introduction of cleaner fuels, Inspection and Maintenance, Stringent Emission Standards, Traffic Management and Good governance in Air Quality issues have yielded good environmental results. Reduction of CO by 68.5%, hydrocarbon by 68.5% and No_x by 55.5% has already been achieved since then. They are working closely with oil and gas industry for development of better fuel and lubricants while continuously improving engine design. These units have their web site where environmental performance is reported but more on product performance rather than on over all business performance. Their manufacturing plants are meeting legislative requirement and the same is being extended across the supply chain and service organizations. A study conducted by Centre for Science and Environment (CSE, 2001) on Environmental practices in automobile sector clearly shows that they have still to drive long way in green direction as the over all rating of automobile sector was 2 leaves (score 31.4%) only against 5 leaves for the best possible performance.

Chemicals and Fertilizer

The chemicals & fertilizer sector is environmentally very sensitive. The industry is of a peculiar nature in that pollution at plant level is minimal but peaks the moment the products leave the plant. They have no control over the products they manufacture. The life cycle assessment also becomes difficult because it undergoes continuous change from one form to another. They come under red category and, therefore, are closely monitored by pollution control boards. Bhopal unit producing methyl isocynide belonged to this category of industry. The environmental disaster took a toll of more than 4,000 lives and crippled the whole surrounding. The gas leak constituted the first International environmental case pursued in numerous courts in India and U.S.A. The compensation was settled in an Indian court at $495 million but thousands are still suffering and the poison effects will spill over to generations. The incidence exposed the environmental credibility of multinational companies especially with respect to their plants in developing countries. Green Rating for Caustic-Chlorine Sector (CSE, 2002) found that the environmentally best performing company had scored 46.6% in green rating. The study reported that the performance swings from as good as the global best to as bad as it could be. No company, however, qualified for the five leaves award - the highest rating.

Mining & Metallurgy

Both mining and metallurgical industries are considered dirty. They are energy intensive and environment damaging. Iron and Steel forms the backbone of this Sector. Primary steel producers have shown concern for environment and have reported their environmental performance in different ways. The leading steel producer, SAIL (2003), has reported reduction in particulate matter emission by 60%, water consumption by 47%, effluent discharge quantity by 32%, and energy consumption by 9% and an increase in solid waste utilization by 14%. TISCO (2003), the most cost effective Steel Company has reported its environmental performance in GRI format, which has been duly verified by Pricewaterhouse Coopers (PWC). The company has exceeded regulatory compliance standards. It has achieved a reduction in Greenhouse Gas (GHG) emissions by 9.0% (against a target of 5%), specific energy consumption by 1.8% (against a target of 4%), raw material consumption by 10.8% (against a target of 5%), water consumption by 10.2% (against a target of 5%) and has increased waste reuse and recycling from 70.2% to 72.6% (against a target of 72%) during the year. The Company has also undertaken a CDM project. In the mining sector, NALCO's (2003) bauxite mine has won environmental award but its reporting looks more a publicity matter rather than data based for continual improvement.

Oil & Gas Sector

The players in this sector rank high in Economic Times survey and carry great environmental risk even though the oil refineries have been merrily producing diesel with such high levels of sulphur in it as are unacceptable in any developed country (Sahay, 2007). Most of their facilities are ISO 14001 certified. In fact Koyali-Ahmedabad pipeline of Indian Oil Corporation (2003) was the first pipeline in the world to get ISO 14001 certification.

They have generally reported their Environmental Policy and environmental performance over the years. Environmental aspects in their processes and products have been recognized and revealed. This sector has done and reported laudable work in forestation, development of ecological parks and protection of heritage. Social aspect like ten point program for Taj trapezium (a world heritage) has been over emphasized by the companies working in that area. The environmental aspects of process (exploration, production, refining and blending) like levels of liquid effluents, gaseous emissions and hazardous wastes have been reported and compared with standards rather than target set under continual improvement clause of EMS. As far as products are concerned, low sulfur diesel, lead free petrol and development of bio-degradable lubricants find special mention though not evaluated against target. The sector, despite good work, has yet to report their environmental performance in globally recognized format.

Power

Indian power sector (2003) is dominated by thermal power having a share of 71.94% followed by hydel (25.09%), nuclear (2.59%) and wind (1.44%). The other non-conventional sources of energy like solar, geothermal, tidal etc. are non significant. National Thermal Power Corporation (Sahay, 2008), a central Public Sector Enterprise, is the biggest player in thermal power sector. Power plants of State Electricity Boards are other major players. Companies like Tata Power (2003) and Bombay Suburban Electric Supply (2003), Private Sector Units, are also significant players. Besides these, there are captive power plants of energy intensive industries. Thermal Power plants are the biggest greenhouse gas emitter. They (other than those of State Electricity Boards) have been reporting their environmental performance but it is in non-standard format suiting their own requirements. The reports include the trend in emission of particulate matters, SO_2,

NO_x, discharge of effluents and their hydrogen ion concentration, free chlorine, COD & BOD levels, coal consumption, ash generation, specific oil consumption etc. They also have reported plantation of tree saplings, pisciculture in their water ponds (hydro stations), pollution control equipments, electrostatic precipitators, height of chimneys, trial solar energy plants and wind power projects. Bombay Suburban Electric Supply has even appointed a committee of Directors on Environment. They have created facility for online analysis and monitoring of SO_x, NO_x and SPM in the flue gas duct, automatic weather monitoring station for monitoring weather conditions, ambient air quality monitoring stations and mobile environment monitoring van to monitor the emission parameters in nearby area. Nuclear power plants are of different species having very strict safety requirement. They are reporting more on safety than on environmental aspects. Hydel power plants were observed to be reporting more on social aspects.

Pharmaceutical

Pharmaceutical sector, of late, is gaining importance worldwide because of the new intellectual property rights regime under WTO. The two Indian players Ranbaxy (2003) and Dr. Reddy's Laboratories (2003) in this sector have taken great initiatives. Multinationals operating in India and Indian units in this sector are environmentally conscious. At Ranbaxy, regulatory consents, compliance with consent conditions, adequate resources, environment-impact assessment and EMS form the five absolutes for achieving corporate objectives defined by their EH&S policy. Environment Impact Assessment Studies are carried out periodically to assess the effect on local environmental conditions affected by various plants. Dr. Reddy's Lab has a two-pronged investment strategy. One in pollution control devices & safety equipment and the other in the management systems. They have reported that their operations can be sustainable only if safety, health & environment (SH&E) management is integrated into production processes and manufacturing practices. Learning to do more with less, their focus has shifted to process improvements for yield improvement from a traditional "end-of-pipe" approach of waste treatment. The reports, however, are unsystematic and haphazard.

Pulp & Paper

The pulp & paper sector is an expanding sector at the cost of denudation of forests. It uses many hazardous chemicals and also releases hazardous waste. Green Rating Project (CSE, 1999) in India was launched in this sector only. A life cycle approach beginning from raw material procurement to product recycling was adopted. It was observed that paper and pulp industry is a big consumer of natural resources like water, wood fiber and energy. During production and disposal stages, a large portion of these resources comes out as waste. The best Environmental performer in the sector had a score of 42.75 out of 100. There is a big difference in environmental performance between Indian Pulp & Paper industry and those in the developed world mainly on account of technology level and the size of the plant. This sector is not conscious about environmental reporting and has been more or less dwelling upon the minimum levels of environmental performance. The recycling is increasing but mainly under the pressure of user industries, which want to reduce their waste level.

Among the sustainability reporting systems Global Reporting Initiative (GRI) is becoming popular. GRI is a multi-stakeholder process, which, of late, is gaining acceptability worldwide. It is an independent institution whose mission is to develop and disseminate globally applicable Sustainability Reporting Guidelines. These Guidelines are voluntary in nature but getting popular among organizations for reporting on the economic, social, and environmental dimen-

sions of their activities (processes), products, and services. The GRI incorporates the active participation of representatives from business, accountancy, investment, environmental, human rights, research and labor organizations from all over the world. Started in 1997 by the Coalition for Environmentally Responsible Economies (CERES), the GRI became independent in 2002. It is an official collaborating center of the United Nations Environment Program (UNEP) and works in cooperation with Global Compact (UNIDO et al, 1999). The latest reporting system, known as GRI 3, was issued in 2007.

CSR AND SUSTAINABILITY CONNECTION

Gone are the days when accusations of socio-economic and environmental non-friendly practices used to be the key driver for the business to be philanthropic or to set apart in budget a portion of profit for CSR activities. Now they recognize paramount value of embedding CSR in the core strategy of the company.

The responsibilities are being converted by aggressive strategies of corporate warriors. This trend may better be expressed through seven steps process prescribed by David Grayson and Adrian Hodges (2004).

This model provides a methodology to show how to generate revised or potentially new business strategies to capitalize on spot business opportunities. Entrepreneurs are increasingly framing company's strategy in which CSR is a major component. Along with it, they do report annually about their corporate sustainability initiatives linking these with fundamental principles, goal and objectives of the business organization.

Triumph of this need reflects in the consciousness and commitment coming from the world community. Recently The World Business Council for Sustainable Development (WBCSD) and the International Chamber of Commerce (ICC) has

Figure 5. From CSR to Corporate Social Opportunity: 7 Steps, Grayson et al. (2004)

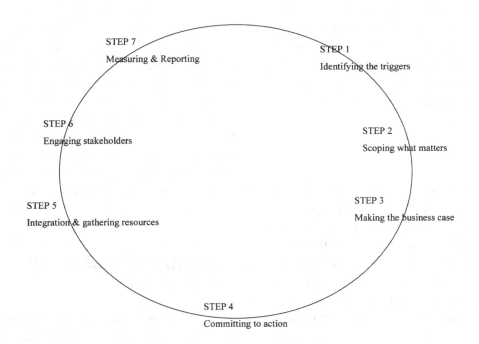

jointly organized a *Global Business Day* during the 13th Conference of the Parties (COP) to the United Nations Framework Convention on Climate Change (UNFCCC) in Bali. The name of the event, 'Tri Hita Karana', is derived from the Balinese philosophy of life. Tri Hita Karana emphasizes that happiness can only be attained if the Creator, people and nature live in harmony with each other. It reflects the objectives of responsible business, balancing people, the planet and profit as the basis for sustainable development. The Bali Global Business Day (10 December 2007) brought together 200-300 decision makers from companies, governments, and inter-governmental and non-governmental organizations. It demonstrated the capacities and commitments of leading companies and business sectors to provide solutions to the sustainability issue. Let us wait and watch how the business houses world over get tuned to sustainability and how firmly they embed CSR in their corporate/business strategy!

CONCLUSION

From the instances stated above, it will be clear that corporate philanthropy existed for centuries. However, the movement of majority of the firms from philanthropy to Corporate Social Responsibility is a phenomenon of 20th century. It was generally not voluntary. In many cases, the firms were forced to adapt good CSR practices either because of regulatory requirements or social pressure or in their own business interest. Cases like Nike, which faced extensive consumer boycott because of abusive labor practices by its suppliers, or Shell Oil, which had to swallow a bitter pill as the Greenpeace protests brought their sales drastically down forcing them to change their decision to dump Brent Spar oil rigs in north sea despite approval from the British Government, or Coca-Cola, which was facing injunction in India because of poor water extraction and utilization are glaring examples of such involuntary CSR. Worse was Union Carbide, which had poor safety practices that resulted in the death of many workers and people residing in the vicinity resulting in the closure of the plant; putting a question mark on its own sustainability. Later, the parent company itself had to be sold in distress.

Smarter global companies like Bristol-Myers Squibb, DuPont, Canada, Electrolux, Norsk Hydro, Ontario Power Generation, Procter and Gamble, Rio Tinto etc. took early steps in this direction and started sustainability reporting thus, communicating their actions not only to their shareholders but public at large. They quickly ingrained good CSR practice in their core business and strived to become a good corporate citizen. They understood the issues of their reputation, moral obligation, social approval to operate, need to protect and enhance natural environment and above all the issue of their own sustainability. In India Jubilent Organosys, Tatas, ITC, etc. are such examples. CSR has been part of their corporate/business strategy and forms a prominent part of the Board Agenda. They scout for the CSR activities required by the society in which they operate and align it with their core business activities. Some of them identify the strategic CSR activities those become part of their strategy to be pursued to create value for both the company as well as the society. Though their CSR/sustainability acts speak for themselves, their communication of the same in GRI format, both in hard and soft versions, adds further value to the firms.

REFERENCES

Altman, B. W. (1998). Transformed Corporate Community Relations: A Management Tool for Achieving Corporate Citizenship. *Business and Society Review.*

Cohen, D. V., & Altman, B. W. (2000). Corporate Citizenship in the New Millennium: Foundation for an Architecture of Excellence. *Business and Society Review, 105*(1), 145–168. doi:10.1111/0045-3609.00069

Cornelius, P. & Kogut, B. (2003). Creating the Responsible Firm: In Search for a New Corporate Governance Paradigm. *German Law Review, 4* (1).

Daly, H. E. (1973). *Towards a Steady State Economy*. San Francisco: Freeman.

Daly, H. E. (1991). *Steady-State Economics* (2nd ed.). Washington, DC: Island Press

Friedman (1962). Capitalism and Freedom. University of Chicago Press.

Grayson, D., & Hodges, A. (2004). *Corporate social opportunity!: 7 steps to make corporate social responsibility work for your business Greenleaf Pub.* Sheffield

Gross National Happiness (1999). Report of the Centre for Bhutan Studies, Thimphu, Bhutan.

Izza, M. (2007). *An overview of Corporate Responsibility - Institute of Chartered Accountants in England & Wales*, July, 2007

Jonker, J., & Witte, M. (Eds.). (2006). *Management models for corporate social responsibility.* Heidelberg: Springer Publication.

Kotler, P., & Lee, N. (2005). *Corporate social responsibility: doing the most good for your company and your cause.* Hoboken, NJ: John Wiley Publication.

Macintosh J.C.C (1999). The issues, effects and consequences of the Berle-Dodd debate. *Accounting, Organizations and Society,* 24(2), 139-153(15).

Marlin, A. & Tepper, J. (2003).

McWilliams, A., Siegel, D. S., & Wright, P. M. (2006). Corporate social responsibility: strategic implications. *Journal of Management Studies*, *43*(1), 1–18. doi:10.1111/j.1467-6486.2006.00580.x

Meadows, D., Meadows, D. L., Randers, J., & Behrens, W. (1971). *The Limits to Growth.* New York: Universe Books.

Munshi, K. (2004). Social Learning in a Heterogeneous Population: Technology Diffusion in the Indian Green Revolution. *Journal of Development Economics, LXXIII*, 185–215. doi:10.1016/j.jdeveco.2003.03.003

Pandey, N. & Sahay, A. (2008). Towards a New Paradigm of Sustainable Development. *International Journal of Environment and Development*, June, 2008.

Pava, M. L., & Krausz, J. (1997). Criteria for evaluating the legitimacy of corporate social responsibility. *Journal of Business Ethics*, *17*, 337–347. doi:10.1023/A:1017920217290

Philips, D. (2006). *Quality of Life: Concept, Policy and Practice.* New York: Routledge

Sahay, A. (2004). Indian Corporate Environmental and Financial Performance: Empirical Relationship between them.

Sahay, A. (2006 a). Environmental Management in India: Its Social, Economic and Legal Aspects. *Journal of the Social Sciences*, *1*(2).

Sahay, A. (2006 b). Environmental Insurance: The Need of the Hour, Pravartak. *Journal of National Insurance Academy*, *2*(Jan).

Sahay, A. (2007). Euro IV Norms in India: Social Historical and Legal Background. *Vikramshila Journal of Social Sciences, 4*(1), January – June.

Sahay, A. (2008). Perception of Pollution and Exprctation from NTPC's Talcher Sper Thermal Plant. In *Progress in Industrial Ecology*, (inderscience, UK), *5*(5/6), 536-554.

Sahay, A. (2009). Organization: Structures, Frameworks. *Reporting Business Management and Environmental Stewardship* (pp. 138 – 154). London: Palgrave Macmillan.

Shekhar, S., & Sahay, A. (2007). Firm financial management and Corporate Social Responsibility: A literature review of and perspectives for India. *Journal of Social and Environment Policy*, *4*(2).

Shrivastava, H., & Venkateswaran, S. (2000). *The Business of Social Responsibility: The Why, What and How of Corporate Social Responsibility in India, Partners in Change*, New Delhi, India.

Smith, C. (1994). The New Corporate Philanthropy. *Harvard Business Review*, *72*(3), 105–116.

Steiner, G., & Steiner, J. (1991). *Business, Government and Society: A Managerial Perspective* (6th Ed.). New York: McGraw Hill.

Stivers, R. (1976). *The Sustainable Society: Ethics and Economic Growth.* Philadelphia: Westminster Press.

Sustainable Development Strategies New York, (2007, November).

UNDSD. "Addressing climate change in national sustainable development strategies –common practices" Background Paper, Expert Group Meeting on Integrating Climate Change into National University of New Mexico Management Presentation, Van Buren, 2006

United Nations (1987). *Report of the World Commission on Environment and Development.* General Assembly Resolution 42/187. Retrieved December 16, 2008.

Valor, C. (2005). Corporate Social Responsibility and Corporate Citizenship: Towards Corporate Accountability. *Business and Society Review, 110*(2), 191–212. doi:10.1111/j.0045-3609.2005.00011.x

Waddock, S. (2004). Parallel universes: companies, academics and the progress of corporate citizenship. *Business and Society Review, 109*(1), 5–42. doi:10.1111/j.0045-3609.2004.00002.x

WBCSD. (2000). *Corporate Social Responsibility: Making good business sense.* World Business Council for Sustainable Development.

Windsor, D. (2006). Corporate social responsibility: three key approaches. *Journal of Management Studies, 43*(1), 93–114. doi:10.1111/j.1467-6486.2006.00584.x

Young, P. (2004). *Understanding NLP Principles and Practice.* Carmarthen, UK: Crown House Publishing Ltd.

WEB-LINKS

http://arno.unimaas.nl/, December 7, 2008

http://www.ec.europa.eu/, December 10, 2008

http://www.emeraldinsight.com/, December 9, 2008

http://www.environment.gov.au/, December 9 2008

http://www.globalreporting.org/, December 7, 2008

http://www.icaew.com/, December 10, 2008

http://www.ic.gc.ca/, December 7, 2008

http://www.ifc.org/, December 10, 2008

http://www.jstor.org/, December 10, 2008

http://www.mallenbaker.net/l, December 7, 2008

http://www.tata.com/, December 7, 2008

http://www.thesullivanfoundation.org/, December 7, 2008

http://www.wbcsd.org/, December 9, 2008

http://www.wikipedia.org/, December 7, 2008

www.unglobalcompact.org/, December 10, 2008

Chapter 6
Tools for Corporate Assessment of Sustainable Development

Cecilia Mark-Herbert
Department of Economics, The Swedish University of Agriculture Sciences, Uppsala, Sweden

Jonas Rorarius
Department of Economics, The Swedish University of Agriculture Sciences, Uppsala, Sweden

ABSTRACT

Corporate needs to assess, evaluate and communicate sustainability efforts are evident in the increasing use of management tools. A selected set of commonly used sustainability management tools are compared in this study with a key question in mind: how well does each of them provide grounds for assessing and communicating corporate sustainability ambitions? Each of the tools reflects different aspects of responsible conduct; expressed in economic, environmental, social and temporal & spatial terms. They represent a partial foundation for ex ante assessment and ex post evaluation and, as such, grounds for providing information and communicating. Selecting suitable tools for making sustainability management assessments presupposes an awareness of a need to integrate the perspectives on sustainability as well as finding a suitable marketing tool mix.

SUSTAINABILITY NEEDS

The current interest in environmental, social and economic problems of the world is a shared challenge for scholars, businesses, and politicians - humans in every day life all over the world. Examples of problems we all face include global climate change, population growth, loss of biodiversity, and social inequalities. These problems are not necessarily new phenomena – but embracing all of these changes

with an ambition of responsibility, in a long-term perspective refers to operationalizing the term "sustainability". It implies re-thinking old models, finding new methods in production and distribution, new ways of living – and, perhaps most importantly, a new way of evaluating and communicating all of the above.

Sustainable development issues are increasingly given attention and publicity, not just by governments, but also in the private sector and especially multi-national companies. Sustainability matters have become central parts of into consideration

DOI: 10.4018/978-1-60566-822-2.ch006

in corporate decision-making processes (Bell & Morse, 1999). Reasons for this development are seen in, for example, tightened environmental laws imposed by governments (Dobers, 1997) and pressure from conscious consumers (Welford, 1998) pushing for corporate responsible conduct. However, actions, taken in the name of corporate responsibility, communicated by companies are *not* always as good as their intentions appear on paper (Schwartz, 2004). One of the reasons for the shortcomings is that management tools are limited in what support they may provide and which stakeholders access the channel through which the information is provided. Management system tools, such as ISO 14001 provide a structure for addressing environmental aspects of corporate conduct in a continuous improvement framework – but they do not set any objectives or provide guidance in assessing strategic corporate options.

Yet, another root for the problems of lacking sustainability communication stems from ideological connections that determine not only which issues that are raised, but also the vocabulary for verbalizing possible views. Fiske (1990) refers to these limitations as "codes". In the prevailing market-economy paradigm, profit-maximization criteria, with a short-term perspective, dominates at the expense of non-monetary values and long-term perspectives (Rikhardsson & Welford, 1997; Söderbaum, 2000; Gillespie, 2001). Additional challenges relate to sustainable development aspects in decision-making and communication processes as it proves difficult due to a large information flow (Alvesson & Willmott, 1996) and lack of explicit tools for evaluating impacts of communicated corporate policies and strategies.

This chapter presents a critical view of how corporations currently use management assessment tools aimed at sustainability for communicating policies, plans and programs, which are assessed prior to their implementation (*ex-ante*). It questions neo-classical models and it focuses on the basis for sustainability communication – the

grounds for a message, which in this case is the result of a sustainability assessment. Selected, commonly used, tools for making such assessments are being compared in this chapter. The presented tools may be used as a part of a larger "tool kit", for example an ISO 14001 management system. Each tool may also be used separately, for example when alternatives for a large investment are being assessed.

Tools that allow for an *ex ante* assessment as opposed to an *ex post* evaluation, are desirable for many reasons; the primary reason being that of costs and challenges in changing procedures once a direction is taken. Ultimately, the ambition of *ex ante* assessment indicates a corporate willingness to take responsibility above and beyond what is required currently by law. These tools provide grounds for *internal* communication as well as a dialogue with *external* stakeholders. The ambition is to present a comparison of corporate forecasting tools for predicting long term consequences and particularly possible effects on different aspects of sustainable development.

The chapter starts with a brief presentation of different perspectives on corporate practices for addressing and communicating sustainability. These perspectives are implicit is the subsequent parts of the chapter where a comparison of a few commonly used management tools for assessing corporate sustainable development are presented. It is assumed that tools that are successfully used will make way for a wider application and they may even become a standardized way of estimating and communicating sustainable development. Each of the tools is analyzed and presented in a modified triple bottom line framework for analysis. Finally, we conclude by returning to our starting point: The established tools, before they get too far in a legitimization process, "how well do these tools cover our needs for communicating sustainability measures"?

Figure 1. Sustainability objectives refer to finding solutions that encompasses economic, environmental, social, cultural, spatial and temporal objectives

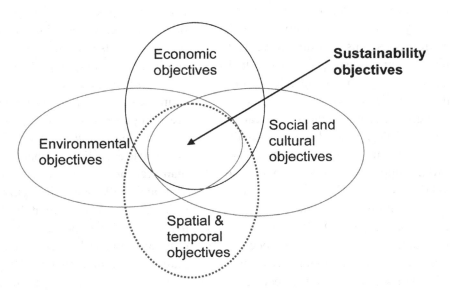

DIVERGENT PERSPECTIVES ON SUSTAINABLE DEVELOPMENT

There is no generally accepted specific scientific definition of what sustainable development encompasses. In fact, there are vast numbers of different interpretations and terminologies (Hardi, 2007). Some dominant perspectives and terminologies have gained a lot of attention and gradually made their way to become parts of a standardized vocabulary (Jacobsson, 2000) for capturing values in economy in general – including values for the complex phenomena sustainable development. This vocabulary refers to classical economics and business economics as disciplines, based on neo-classical economics. A brief discourse analysis is presented in *Appendix 1*.

A need for a broadened vocabulary above and beyond economic values is expressed by a number of scholars, for example, Elkington, (2004) in his "triple bottom line" framework.

Rotmans (2006) support this notion, of a growing awareness and need to include various disciplines as building blocks for developing sus-tainability assessment and communication tools (Figure 1). He argues that human behaviour, for example, should be addressed from microeconomics and sociology perspectives.

In order to capture a complex phenomenon, such as sustainable development, there is a need for a number of disciplinary perspectives to be represented in the values, vocabularies, models and tools used for evaluation and communication. Assuming that communication is regarded as an exchange of information between two or more parties (Fiske, 1990), the *dialogue* builds on words and symbols where meaning is created (Figure 2).

The meaning (Figure 2) is expressed in diverge vocabularies and perspectives offering a vast number of possible starting points for finding a tool that resolves a current corporate problem. Each of the tools that are presented in this chapter started as s solution to a local problem of making an assessment, which gradually has grown into a more commonly known tool that we now know by name, such as Environmental Impact Assessment, EIA. A shared *meaning* of the interpretation of what

Figure 2. Messages and meaning in a dialogue (Fiske, 1990, 14)

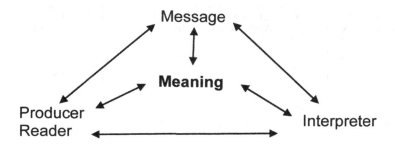

an EIA refers to is possible thanks to a dialogue (Fiske, 1990). The process of developing a commonly accepted tool to assess an environmental problem and even "*the* way of doing something" may be seen as a standardization process (Brunson & Jacobsson, 2002). Assuming that the set of tools we have for assessing sustainability in a corporate setting are starting points for such a standardization process – do they suffice? Do they provide grounds for communicating sustainability efforts?

TOOLS FOR ASSESSMENT AND COMMUNICATION

There are several assessment tools for evaluating different aspects of sustainability. A broad overview over currently used tools is provided in *Appendix 2*. In this presentation, corporate tools that are well established and frequently used are given priority (Vanclay, 2004). These tools are for example Cost Benefit Analysis, CBA, Environmental Impact Assessment, EIA, and Social Impact Assessment, sIA.

The main reason for omitting some of the currently used tools are that we want to compare tools that will provide a basis for an *ex ante* evaluation; in other words forecast the value, as opposed to a follow up analysis once the investment, transaction or action has been made. Product-related assessment tools, such as Life-Cycle Analysis (LCA), were not included in the study as these

are more straightforward scientific assessment tools; they do not involve stakeholder participation and are thus value judgement free. Sector and country-related assessment tools, such as Strategic Environmental Assessment (SEA), were excluded due a limited corporate use. Moreover, different kind of indicators and indices, such as Ecological Footprint (EF), are also excluded since they are not *ex-ante* assessment tools. They are, however, important in the follow-up assessment process.

Recent development of new tools for assessing sustainability has given rise to two tools that are included in this comparison, Sustainability Impact Assessment, SIA and Integrated Sustainability Assessment, ISA. So far work on these sustainability assessment tools has been targeted towards a government and EU policy level, yet they are included in the study, as we believe they provide valuable insights for corporate level sustainability assessments in the future. Also, multi national corporations operating in many places and cultures; influencing various people, communities and even governments - their role could very well be compared to action taken at a governmental policy level. The use of ISA and SIA, however, vary quite a bit. There is not a uniform standardized way of using and interpreting SIA. Instead, various EU countries have developed their own versions of procedures and interpretative grounds. ISA, on the other hand, has a more standardized procedure, largely based on European Commission funded study called Methods and Tools for

Table 1. Selected assessment tools* and dimensions of sustainable development

ASPECTS & CONCEPTS OF SUSTAINABLE DEVELOPMENT	SELECTED EXISTING CORPORATE ASSESSMENT TOOLS (CBA, EIA, sIA)	NEWER SUSTAINABILITY ASSESS-MENT TOOLS (SIA, ISA)
Economic		
Environmental		
Social and cultural		
Temporal and spatial		

* Each of these tools is presented and discussed more in detail in Rorarius (2007, 2008).

Integrated Sustainability Assessment (MATISSE) but has not yet become institutionalized as a part of a commonly used corporate tool box. In part, this is explained by the fact that they are not adapted to corporate needs.

The selected tools are analyzed in a comparison where four aspects of sustainable development are taken into account (Table 1) and are based on social sciences sustainable development discourses. The three aspects (economic, environmental and social) are the most well known framework of sustainable development, as identified in the Brundtland Report (WCED, 1987) and reaffirmed in Agenda 21 (www, UN, Agenda 21, 2004). Temporal and spatial aspects were included to provide intra- and intergenerational dimensions as identified by the Brundtland Report.

Sustainability assessment, in general, can be understood as a combination of impact assessment process tools. It refers to a combining evaluation tools to cover different aspects of sustainable development (CBA, EIA & sIA). The newer tools, sustainability assessment tools (SIA & ISA) differ from the established assessment tools as they do not separate economic, environmental and social aspects but rather treats them as a whole. The present development of these tools is primarily aimed at governmental needs for forecasting development with sustainability as a primary target. They emphasize interconnection and interdependence of these different aspects of sustainable development (Pope *et al.*, 2004).

HOW SUSTAINABLE ARE THE SUSTAINABILITY TOOLS?

The term sustainability implies an indefinite time frame. It is clear that our understanding of sustainability by *no* means is complete, so we will simply have to assume that there is a need to develop tools to meet the needs of a more complex understanding than the previous generation of models was based on. Keeping this in mind, we may look more closely at the commonly used assessment tools and the newer sustainability tools that are under development. Each of the tools is considered from a social science discourse point of view with a stand in a triple bottom line framework aiming at sustainable development (Table Z). Ethical dimensions in each of these aspects of sustainability are integrated, but they could very well be regarded as aspects of their own, using a whole set of ethical terms and models (Bonnedahl *et al.*, 2007; Donaldson & Werhane, 2008; Ketola, 2007; Mackie, 1977).

The first aspect, *economy*, seems obvious, but the different perceptions even within one subject call for some clarifications. With regard to *economic* aspects, social scientists emphasize long-term economic growth rather than short-term profit maximization. Preserving resource availability and at least efficiency, preferably sufficiency, are also stressed. In this sense, minimum consumption of resources, a so-called "lean production" is prioritized among many of them.

In terms of *environmental* aspects, social scientists stress the complexity and interconnectedness of ecosystems. Thus, ecological biodiversity and prevention is given priority as a part of the objectives to achieve the functions of ecosystems.

When considering *social and cultural aspects*, social scientists highlight the importance of cherishing socio-cultural diversity and human well being in general. In this sense, a multi-stakeholder approach and understanding ideological as well as cultural orientation of individuals is essential. Other key concepts stressed include justice, equity and transparency.

Temporal and spatial aspects, emphasized by the social scientists, include intra-generational and also inter-generational concepts. Moreover, it should be understand that sustainable development is a continuous process, which is shaped along the way.

In overall, social scientists stress the importance of considering all of the aspects mentioned above, as parts of a whole (Table 2). Focusing on one aspect at the time would not imply recognizing trade-offs (see e.g. Welford, 1998; Paehlke, 1999; Henriques & Richardson, 2004) between different aspects of sustainability. Focusing on one aspect at the time one would increase the risk of sub-optimization by missing out on objectives from other aspects of sustainability.

The comparison of the selected sustainability tools, presented in Table Z shows that each tool covers different aspects of sustainability, which in turn creates a basis for decision-making and communication. The grounds for assessment and communication, in using these tools are further discussed in the following sections.

Communicating Economic Aspects of Sustainable Development

CBA, Cost Benefit Analysis can arguably be said to be useful for evaluating policies, plans and programs in monetary terms. This assessment becomes also valid for corporation as CBA could rather easily predict financial cost and more precisely cost and benefits of, for example, a proposed project. Moreover it is a useful tool for assessing the efficient way of allocating resources (Hanley & Shoran, 2005). Thus, in principle, CBA aims for efficiency rather than sufficiency. The main problem of CBA is that it simply monetize all present human values (Boardman *et al.*, 2001), which does not give weight to values of general interest, that of the ecosystems, and societal interests in terms of democracy and freedom (Söderbaum, 2000). CBA is based on neoclassical economic perspectives and since neoclassical thinking is the prevailing market paradigm it is easy to see why it has been such a popular tool. In fact, CBA is probably the most standardized assessment method available.

In the turn of 1970s, when environmental problems were given more attention, it became rather evident that CBA was not sufficient enough for addressing environmental aspects. EIA, Environmental Impact Assessment, was believed to fill the gaps. Generally speaking EIA focuses on biophysical impacts. It does also include socio-economic aspects (Stolp, 2003) but not to same extent as CBA. In fact, EIA is more concerned with aspects such as fiscal policy, employment and wealth of the community. Nevertheless, EIA can show alternative ways of achieving the same objectives with better environmental ends and socio-economical impacts (Wathern, 1995).

Similarly, it can be said that sIA, Social Impact Assessment, also considers socio-economic aspects in the assessment but again it does not try to simply monetize impacts. Emphasizes is laid on wellbeing of individuals as well as wealth and prosperity of the community as a whole (van Schooten, *et al.*, 2003).

Communicating Environmental Aspects of Sustainable Development

In the CBA, Cost Benefit Analysis, there is no consensus of how to "value negative environmental impacts as a part of the attempt to find an optimal level of pollution control through

Table 2. Comparison of assessment tools and their sustainability aspects

ASPECTS & CONCEPTS OF SUSTAINABLE DEVELOPMENT	SELECTED CORPORATE ASSESSMENT TOOLS (CBA, EIA, sIA)	NEWER SUSTAINABILITY ASSESS-MENT TOOLS (SIA, ISA)
Economic		
-Long-term growth -Resource availability -Efficiency/sufficiency -Minimum consumption	**CBA**: resource allocation and efficiency main concern **EIA**: socio-economic (employment, fiscal policy) included into some extend **sIA**: economic impacts related to well-being of individuals/ community	**SIA**: proposal effectiveness to economic aspect, resource availability, **ISA**: considering overall effects from long-term perspective
Environmental		
-Ecological diversity and prevention -Maintaining ecosystems	**CBA**: basically just environmental optimaliza-tion **EIA**: environment quality and diversity included **sIA**: environmental impacts related to human health/well-being	**SIA**: impacts to ecological diversity **ISA**: considering overall impacts from long-term perspective
Social and cultural		
-Socio-cultural diversity -Multi-stakeholder approach/dialogue -Ideological and cultural orientation -Justice, equity and transparency -Human well-being	**CBA**: basically just social optimalization **EIA**: includes measurable aspects **sIA**: all well covered in terms of individuals, community thinking lacking	**SIA**: stakeholder participation included **ISA**: strong stakeholder participation, defin-ing sustainability together
Temporal and spatial		
-Intergenerational thinking -Intragenerational thinking -Continuing process	**CBA**: static assumptions, temporal aspects questionable **EIA**: intragenerational aspects, weak long term thinking **sIA**: intra- and intergenerational aspect consid-ered, ongoing process	**SIA**: short-term focus, general spatial dimen-sions, single project **ISA**: long-term vision, overall spatial dimen-sions, cyclical process

marginal analysis" (Söderbaum, 2000:12). CBA is therefore not sufficient as a sole tool for assessing environmental sustainability or creating grounds for environmental commu-nication. In addition, pollutant sinks such as the atmosphere and watercourses are regarded as external costs and thus are not included in the analysis (Wathern, 1995). This tool clearly does not consider the environmental aspects of sustainability sufficiently.

Environmental sustainability in the sIA, Social Impact Assessment, process is concerned with environmental impacts and their effects on social aspects, such as human health and well-being, as well as on cultural aspects, such as archaeologi-cal and community dimensions. Thus, it is not directed to biophysical aspects of the environment but rather possible environmental impacts linked

to humans. This can be seen due to the nature of sIA, which is mostly people-oriented.

Communicating Social and Cultural Aspects of Sustainable Development

CBA, Cost Benefit Analysis, is supposed to bring solutions that are optimal form a societal point of view. It aims for finding best alternative in terms of net benefits. In other words, optimal choice would be the one in which potential 'losers' would be compensated by the 'gainers' and they both would still be better off (Boardman *et al.*, 2001). Moreover, these are determined in monetary terms based on willingness to pay concept. In reality, however, there are different ideological orientations among stakeholders and these might be difficult to measure in money (Söderbaum,

2000). In general, CBA is not appropriate tool for assessing social and cultural impacts as it fails to capture their intangible connection to each other (Srinivasan & Mehta, 2003). More particularly, cultural differences are not necessarily accounted for, especially in cases in which no data/survey of willingness to pay concept has not been carried out. In fact, CBA disregards different views posed by stakeholders (Boardman *et al.*, 2001)

EIA, Environmental Impact Assessment, on the other hand is supposed to include social and cultural aspects in the assessment. Examples of these include aesthetical and health-related aspects. It is, however, argued that EIA actually fails to address them properly (Vanclay, 2004). Reasons for this can be seen due to its technocratic-orientation in which aspects that are measurable such as employment are only accounted (Stolp, 2003). In terms of public participation in the assessment process, such participation involvement is included in the EIA and thus indicating that interests and opinions of various stakeholders are heard (Glasson *et al.*, 2005). However, in general, stakeholder participation is left to few meetings at most.

Socio-cultural impacts are the main concern in the sIA, Social Impact Assessment, process (Stolp, 2003). However, even with sIA there has been criticism that cultural aspects are not well included. Reasons for this can be seen due to emphasize laid on the impacts of individuals while impacts on society as a whole have been given lesser attention (Vanclay, 2004). Nevertheless, stakeholder participation is argued to be well included in sIA process (Baines *et al.* 2003).

Temporal and Spatial Aspects of Sustainable Development

In the CBA, Cost Benefit Analysis, there are some problems of including temporal and spatial aspects with regards to sustainable development. The problems stem primarily from the difficulty of estimating unborn future generation's willingness to pay. Similarly, measuring the willingness to pay for large number of stakeholders, including non-human stakeholders is difficult to carry out (Boardman *et al.*, 2001). Such arguments indicate that inter- and intra-generational thinking is hard to implement. CBA also makes an assumption that future impacts are applied at one point in time, as opposed to gradual or unevenly distributed changes and effects over time (Söderbaum, 2000). In reality, uncertainty and complexity of ecosystems for example, makes it hard to make such basic assumptions as they presuppose a static context. At the end, CBA is more a once-off project meaning that continuance of the assessment process is ignored.

Spatial and temporal aspects in EIA, Environmental Impact Assessment, depend of the nature of the assessment (Glasson *et al.*, 2005). In general, it can be done at a local, regional or national level and even at global level (e.g. measuring CO_2 emissions). Thus, it can be stated that intra-generational thinking is included. In terms of time scale of impacts EIA is normally taken to consider current impacts, up to 10-20 years. This time scale might not be appropriate enough to include and consider future generations. Newer EIAs does, however, have follow-up assessments and thus it can be said that they have a continuing process with a feedback system.

Intra-generational –and intergenerational equity principles are seen being part of the sIA, Social Impact Assessment (Vanclay, 2003). These can be seen in terms of wide collaboration with stakeholders and concerns of future impacts to people. It is also an ongoing process allowing feedback from different stakeholders (Baines *et al.*, 2003).

In summary, the concept of sustainable development involves not only a great number of dimensions. Each of these dimensions can be estimated in a number of ways – and it is when these estimates are aggregated in a complex analysis that the true challenges arise. How do we compare present values and needs in comparison to future, forecasted, ditto? How can we account for values

Figure 3. Each of the tools, marked in bold inside the illustration, provide grounds for partial sustainability communication, but none of them give satisfactory grounds for sustainability communication. The tools, SIA and ISA, outside the illustration, if adapted to corporate needs may serve as tools for communicating sustainability objectives.

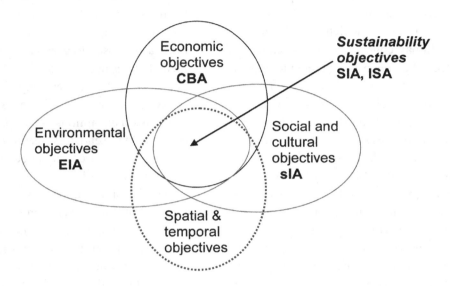

that are not a part of a traditional anthropocentric worldview? Temporal and spatial aspects further emphasize the needs to include cultural and political dimensions in the ongoing dialogues aimed at sustainable development (Attfield, 1999).

COMMUNICATIONAL CHALLENGES AND SOLUTIONS

A corporate need to communicate sustainability objectives, measures and results is a fact. The challenges associated with an assessment as well as reporting and communicating are verified by academia (for example by Cerin, 2002; Gray & Milke, 2002; Weeler & Elkington, 2001) as well as by corporate representatives from various industries.

Complex issues and questions require somewhat complex answers. The different assessment tools and their potentials for including these aspects should be treated as possible implications of their assessment processes (Figure 3).

Having discussed the need for integrating objectives in order to make a sustainability assessment, the illustration above gives us a visual answer to the question of communication needs. This comparison points at a need for developing new tools or adapting the current SIA & ISA-tools.

- *None* of the established tools alone (CBA, EIA & sIA) would fulfill the requirements for assessing and communicating sustainability efforts sufficiently. They give indications of environmental, economic or social aspects – but they do not offer guidance in finding solutions that take all of the above into account.
- Corporate needs are sustainability-oriented. Emphasizes in the assessment process should be then laid on meeting the sustainability aspects by integrating these different assessment tools. In general this means considering economic, environmental,

socio-cultural, spatial and temporal aspects of sustainability in their assessment processes as well as in communicational efforts. Integrating the assessment in a shared understanding (strategies, policies and plans) of corporate objectives requires a transparent communication system.

- The tools aimed at sustainability, Sustainability Impact Assessment (SIA) and Integrated Sustainability Assessment (ISA), are at a stage of development where they are of limited corporate use, primarily explained by resource requirements and complexity. When these tools have been used and modified at an industrial or national level, a second generation of sustainability tools may offer grounds for large corporations and at a later stage yet for medium size and small businesses.

- Most tools lack indicators that ensure spatial and temporal dimensions of sustainability, which may lead to over all suboptimization since the outcome at different times and in different geographical locations are not given weight in the analysis.

Corporate needs to find uniform tools for *ex ante* assessment as well as for *ex post* evaluations, geared towards sustainability, are expressed in search of tools as well as in participation in third party standardization programs. These tools are intended to simplify a complex reality, which enables various stakeholders to participate in the dialogue of sustainable development. The lack of apparent sustainability indicators (see Appendix 2) opens up for new initiatives. Successful use of a tool may lead the way for a shared meaning (Fiske, 1990) in a dialogue that leads to further development, establishing consistency in use of one specific tool; a standardized way of making an assessment. Early adaptors of a new tool are caught in a double responsibility, that of being critical of the tool it self and that of communicating the use of the particular tool in order to achieve a

general acceptance. As clarified by Schwartz in her study of corporate environmental strategies: "Organizations whose patterns of behavior become institutionalized gain increased legitimacy, which can then be pursued both internally and externally in future control attempts" (2006, 14).

The change process from using *ad hoc* assessment tools to an established method and estimate can be seen as a standardization process. It creates grounds for comparison and it simplifies communication. But, as argued by Brunson & Jacobson (2002, 130- 133) it also enhances the risk of adverse effects as the consequences of an inappropriate use of a standard is more severe. This further emphasize the needs for a transparent dialogue regarding aspects, indicators and ways of making measurements in using various tools geared towards *ex ante* assessment of dialogue regarding corporate sustainable development.

REFERENCES

Alvesson, M., & Willmott, H. (1996). *Making Sense of Management.* London, UK: Sage Publications Limited.

Attfield, R. (1999). *The Ethics of the Global Environment.* Edinburgh, UK: Edinburgh University Press.

Baines, J., McClintock, W., Taylor, N., & Buckenham, B. (2003). Using local knowledge. In H. Becker, & F. Vanclay, (Eds.) *The International Handbook of social Impact Assessment* (pp. 26-41). Cheltenham, UK: Edward Elgar Publishing.

Bell, S., & Morse, S. (1999). *Sustainability Indicators.* London: Earthscan Publications Ltd.

Bisset, R., & Tomlinson, P. (1995). Monitoring and auditing of impacts. In P. Wathern, (ed). *Environmental Impact Assessment: Theory and Practice.* (pp. 117-128). London, UK: Routledge.

Boardman, A., Greenberg, D., Vining, A., & Weimer, D. (2001). *Cost-Benefit Analysis: concepts and practice* (2nd ed). Upper Saddle River, NJ: Prentice Hall.

Bonnedahl, K. J., Jensen, T., & Sandström, J. (2007). *Ekonomi och moral – vägar mot ökat ansvarstagande.* Liber, Malmö.

Boulding, K. (1966). *The Economics of the Coming Spaceship Earth.,* Reprinted from H. Jarrett, Environmental Quality in a Growing Economy. Baltimore, MD: Johns Hopkins Press.

Brunson, N., & Jacobson, B. (2002). Standardization and Uniformity. In N. Brunson, B. Jacobson, et al (Eds.) *A World of Standards* (pp. 127 137). Oxford, UK: Oxford University Press.

Cerin, P. (2002). Communication in Corporate Environmental Reports. *Corporate Social Responsibility and Environmental Management, 9,* 46–66. doi:10.1002/csr.6

Dobers, P. (1997). *Organising Strategies of Environmental Control: towards a decentralisation of the Swedish environmental control repertoire.* Stockholm, Sweden: Nerenius & Santérus Förlag.

Donaldson, T., & Eerhane, P. (2008). *Ethical Issues in Business, A philosophical approach,* (8th ed.). Upper Saddle River, NJ: Pearson Prentice Hall.

Dryzek, J. (2005). *The Politics of the Earth: Environmental Discourses* (2nd ed). Oxford, UK: Oxford University Press.

Elkington, J. (1999). *Cannibals with Forks: The Triple Bottom Line of 21st Century Business.* Oxford, UK: Capstone Publishing Limited.

Elkinton, J. (2004). Enter the triple bottom line. In A. Henriques & J. Richardson, (Eds.) *The triple bottom line Does it all add up? Assessing the sustainability of business and CSR* (pp.1-17). Earthscan: London.

Epstein, M. (2008). *Making Sustainability Work: Best Practices in Managing and Measuring Corporate Social, Environmental and Economic Impacts.* Sheffield, UK: Greenleaf Publishing Limited.

Fiske, J. (1990). *Kommunikationsteorier. En introduction.* Wahlström & Widstrand, Stockholm.

Friedman, M. (1970, September 13). The social responsibility of business is to increase its profits. *New York Times Magazine.*

Gillespie, A. (2001). *The Illusion of Progress: Unsustainable Development in International Law and Policy.* London, UK: Earthscan Publications Ltd.

Glasson, J., Therivel, R., & Chadwick, A. (2005). *Introduction to Environmental Impact Assessment* (3rd ed.). London, UK: Routledge.

Gray, R., & Milke, M. J. (2002). Sustainability Reporting: Who's kidding whom? *Chartered Accountants Journal of New Zealand., 81*(6), 66–70.

Hardi, P. (2007). The long and winding road of sustainable development evaluation In C. George, & C. Kirkpatrick, (Eds). *Impact Assessment and Sustainable Development – European Practice and Experience* (pp.15-30). Cheltenham, UK: Edward Elgar Publishing Limited.

Hardin, G. (1967). The Tragedy of Commons. In D. VanDeVeer, & C. Pierce, (Eds.) *The Environmental Ethics & Policy Book* (2nd ed.). London, UK: Wadsworth Publishing Company.

Henriques, A., & Richardson, J. (Eds.). (2004). *The triple bottom line: does it all add up?* Earthscan: London, UK.

Jacobsson, B. (2006). Standardization and Expert Knowledge. In N. Brunsson, & B. Jacobsson, et al (Eds) *A World of Standards* (pp. 40-49). Oxford, UK: Oxford University Press.

Ketola, T. (Ed.). (2007). *Paradigms of corporate Sustainability.* Vaasan Yliopisoto. Report 146. Proceedings of Track 16, International Development Research Conference 2007.

Luke, T. (2005). Neither Sustainable nor Development: Reconsidering Sustainability in Development. *Journal of Sustainable Development, 13,* 228–238. doi:10.1002/sd.284

Mackie, J. L. (1977). *Ethics. Inventing right and wrong.* Penguin Group: London, UK.

Paehlke, R. (1999). Towards Defining, Measuring and Achieving Sustainability: Tools and Strategies for Environmental Valuation. In E. Becker, & T. Jahn, (Eds.) *Sustainability and the Social Sciences. A Cross-Disciplinary Approach to Integrating Environmental Considerations into Theoretical Reorientation* (pp 243-263). London, UK: Zed Books.

Pearce, D., & Turner, R. (1990). *Economics of Natural Resources and the Environment.* Baltimore, MD: John Hopkins University Press.

Pearce, D., & Warford, J. (1993). *World without End: Economics, environment and sustainable development.* New York: Oxford University Press.

Pope, J., Annandale, D., & Morrison-Saunders, A. (2004). Conceptualising sustainability assessment. *Environmental Impact Assessment Review, 24,* 595–616. doi:10.1016/j.eiar.2004.03.001

Prugh, T., Costanza, R., & Daly, H. (2000). *The Local Politics of Global Sustainability.* Washington DC: Island Press.

Rikhardsson, P., & Welford, R. (1997). Clouding the Crisis: the Construction of Corporate Environmental Management. In R. Welford, (Eds.) *Hijacking Environmentalism. Corporate Response to Sustainable Development* (pp. 40-62). London, UK: Earthscan Publications Limited.

Rorarius, J. (2007). *Existing Assessment Tools and Indicators: Building up Sustainability Assessment (Some Perspectives and Future Applications for Finland).* Helsinki, Finland, Project paper for Finland's Ministry of the Environment. Retrieved from http://www.ymparisto.fi/download.asp?contentid=73204&lan=en

Rorarius, J. (2008). *Assessing Sustainability from the Corporate Perspective: An interdisciplinary approach.* Uppsala, Sweden: Department of Economics, SLU, thesis vol. 530.

Rotmans, J. (2006). Tools for Integrated Sustainability Assessment: A two-track approach. *The Integrated Assessment Journal, 6,* 35–57.

Sachs, W. (1999). *Planet Dialectics: Explorations in Environment and Development.* London, UK: Zed Books.

Schwartz, B. (2006). Environmental Strategies as Automorphic patterns of Behaviour. *Business Strategy and the Environment . Retrieved from, 2006.* doi:.doi:10.1002/bse.567

Söderbaum, P. (2000). *Ecological Economics: A Political Economics Approach to Environment and Development.* London, UK: Earthscan Publications Limited.

Srinivasan, B., & Mehta, L. (2003). Assessing gender impacts. In H. Becker, & F. Vanclay, (Eds). *The International Handbook of Social Impact Assessment* (161-178). Cheltenham, UK: Edward Elgar Publishing.

Stolp, A. (2003). Citizen values assessment. In H. Becker, & F. Vanclay, (Eds). *The International Handbook of Social Impact Assessment: Conceptual and Methodological Advances* (pp. 231-257). Cheltenham, UK: Edward Elgar Publishing.

Thin, N. (2002). *Social Progress and Sustainable Development.* London, UK: ITDG Publishing.

UN, (n.d.). *Agenda 21: Chapter 8, Integrating environment and development in decision-making.* Retrieved April 4, 2008 from http://www.un.org/esa/sustdev/documents/agenda21/english/agenda21chapter8.htm

van Schooten, M., Vanclay, F., & Slootweg, R. (2003). Conceptualizing social change processes and social impacts. In H. Becker, & F. Vanclay, (Eds), *The International Handbook of Social Impact Assessment: Conceptual and Methodological Advances* (pp. 74-91). Cheltenham, UK: Edward Elgar Publishing.

Vanclay, F. (2003). Conceptual and methodological advances in social impact assessment. In H. Becker, & F. Vanclay, (Eds), *The International Handbook of Social Impact Assessment: Conceptual and Methodological Advances* (pp. 1-9). Cheltenham, UK: Edward Elgar Publishing.

Vanclay, F. (2004). The Triple Bottom Line and Impact Assessment: How do TBL, EIA, SEA and EMS relate to each other? *Journal of Environmental Assessment Policy and Management, 6*(3), 265–288. doi:10.1142/S1464333204001729

Wathern, P. (1995). An introductory guide to EIA. In P. Wathern, (Ed.), *Environmental Impact Assessment: Theory and Practice* (pp. 3-30). London, UK: Routledge.

Weeler, D., & Elkington, J. (2001). The end of the corporate environmental report? *Business Strategy and the Environment, 10*(1), 1–14. doi:10.1002/1099-0836(200101/02)10:1<1::AID-BSE274>3.0.CO;2-0

Welford, R. (Ed.). (1998). *Corporate Environmental Management Systems and Strategies,* (2nd ed.). London, UK: Earthscan Publications Limited.

World Commission on Environment and Development. (1987). *Our Common Future.* Oxford, UK: Oxford University Press.

APPENDIX 1

Development of Sustainability Perspectives from Different Disciplines

Newer vocabularies, such as ecological and institutional economics have emerged in response to criticism towards mainstream (classical-based) economics. Other social sciences offer vocabularies and models for including additional non-monetary values. Political- and socio-sciences represent such broadened perspectives. An overview of social science disciplines and examples of authors are presented in the table below.

Table 3. Disciplines and examples of social scholars representing different perspectives

DISCIPLINE	AUTHOR/S
Economics	
• neo-classical economics	- Boulding (1966); Friedman, (1970)
• environmental economics	- Pearce & Turner (1990); Pearce & Warford, (1993)
• business economics	- Elkington (1999); Epstein; (2008), Rikhardsson & Welford (1997); Welford, (1998)
• ecological/institutional economics	- Prugh, Costanza & Daly (2000); Söderbaum (2000)
Social sciences (other than economics)	
• social anthropology	- Thin (2002)
• sociology	- Sachs (1999)
• political sciences	- Dryzek, (1997); Luke, (2005); Paehlke. (1999)
• international law	- Gillespie (2001)
• environmental philosophy/ethics	- Attfield (1999)

Each of these scholars may address issues that tie to sustainable development, with very different vocabularies and underlying assumptions about human behaviour. They serve as examples from each discipline as the list of scholars in each discipline can be made quite extensive.

APPENDIX 2

Table 4. Different assessment tools* and their dimensions (modified from Rorarius, 2007:12)

DIMENSION	ASSESSMENT TOOLS			
	Indicators/Indices	*Product-Related Assessment*	*Project-Related Assessment*	*Sector and Country-Related Assessment*
Environmental	Environmental Pressure Indicators (EPIs) Ecological Footprint (EF) Environmental Sustainability Index (ESI)	Life Cycle Assessment (LCA) Material Input per Service (MIPS) Unit Substance Flow Analysis (SFA)	Environmental impact assessment (EIA) Environmental Risk Analysis (ERA)	Environmental Extended Input-Output (EEIO) Analysis Strategic Environmental Assessment (SEA)
Economic	Gross National Production (GNP)	Life Cycle Costing (LCC)	Cost-Benefit Analysis **(CBA)** Full Cost Accounting (FCA)	Economy-Wide Material Flow Analysis (EW-MFA) Economic Input-Output (EIO) analysis
Social	Human Development Index (HDI)		Social Impact Assessment **(sIA)**	Social Input-Output (SIO) analysis
Sustainable Development (all three dimensions considered)	Sustainable Development Indicators (SDI)			Sustainability Impact Assessment **(SIA)** Integrated Sustainability Assessment **(ISA)**

Chapter 7

Communicating Environmental Information on a Company and Inter-Organizational Level

Elke Perl-Vorbach
Institute of Systems Sciences, Innovation and Sustainability Research, Karl Franzens University Graz, Austria

ABSTRACT

The collection, managing and communication of environmental information are nowadays seen as an essential prerequisite for sustainable development. However, ways of generating and exchanging environmental information differ within and between companies. Moreover, the use of highly sophisticated environmental information systems can still be seen at in its infancy. The aim of this chapter is thus to assess ways of the application of environmental information systems for sustainable development, both within and between organizations, can be supported. An empirical analysis of those barriers and obstacles, which inhibit the implementation of environmental information systems, is also carried out. Additionally, we also pay attention to forms of industry wide environmental protection, and take existing cooperation and relationships, sustainable supply chains, and recycling networks into account. For this purpose, basic conditions for the inter-organizational exchange of environmental information are investigated. This provides the basis for identifying means to strengthen the position of environmental protection in connection with inter-organizational exchange of environmental information. Improved methods of implementing environmental information systems within and between companies are developed, thus promoting greater cooperation for sustainable development.

INTRODUCTION

In the present time, it is obvious that information and communication technologies have great potential in supporting sustainable development. Environmental information now plays a vital role in environmental protection, for example via production and processing techniques, pollution control, waste management etc. In former times, internal company activities were the main object of focus in the search for overall sustainable development. Nowadays however, environmental protection and sustainable development

DOI: 10.4018/978-1-60566-822-2.ch007

reach well beyond company borders, although it has to be admitted that these concepts are still not yet widely spread and companies are currently not as aware of the environmental advantages of interorganisational cooperation as they should be. Such cooperation demands that companies include business partners and stakeholders in environmentally related activities. For example, close cooperation with suppliers, customers and public authorities provides for far more effective environmental protection. Here, environmental information has become an indispensable factor, especially in the design and conception phases of inter-organizational cooperation. Furthermore, this specific kind of information is also important for communication with customers. Developing accessible information is thus a key priority, not only for the companies themselves, but also for their partners along the supply chain, and for all customers and business partners in general. However, to date, the potential available remains largely unexploited (see also Hilty et al., 2006).

On looking more closely at the managing and communication of environmental information, it becomes apparent that theory and science in the field of information systems are currently highly sophisticated activities. The same is true concerning the supporting communication systems of environmental information. Matters become ever more complicated when implementation involves more than one company or organisation since the collection, handling and communication of environmental information on such an overarching level are still in their early stages. Therefore, conscious action has to be taken to promote the usage of environmental information systems in order to support environmental protection. The present chapter thus deals with the rather new scientific field concerning the exchange of environmental information on a company-wide and inter-organizational level with a view to facilitating close relationships in sustainable development. Thus, this chapter is dedicated to the topic of supporting the communication of environmental

information systems within companies and in inter-organizational cooperation, in order to enhance industrial environmental protection.

Aims of the Chapter

The aim of this chapter is to identify the barriers and obstacles inhibiting the implementation of operational environmental information systems in companies – both technical and organizational. Based on an empirical survey of Austrian industry, the demands for and the use of specific systems of operational environmental information systems are identified. Possible inconsistencies between theoretical approaches and scientific knowledge and practical applications are thus investigated. Furthermore, the questions of how the exchange of environmental information now takes place and of how appropriate current company systems are is also discussed.

The second overall goal of the chapter is the extension of the implementation concept for operational environmental information systems to include the inter-organizational level. Here, the necessity of company awareness regarding the potential of cooperation in overall inter-organizational sustainability is investigated. For this purpose, the basic conditions, and the needs and demands with respect to the inter-organizational exchange of environmental information are investigated. Finally, the question of the extent to which companies already use environmental information to support their sustainable activities is also considered.

Methodology

An extensive literature review concerning the characteristics of environmental information and information systems and how they can contribute to sustainable development provided the starting point for this chapter. The results were then analysed with respect to their suitability for inter-organizational communication of environmental information. In addition, an extensive review of information systems in cooperative activity forms the foundation for the investigation of environmental information exchange in chapter 3.

We thus arrive at a research approach that is a combination of case analysis and descriptive study. The literature review forms the basis for the research hypothesis on environmental information and environmental information systems, and in particular, on the exchange of environmental information in inter-organizational cooperation. Technical and organizational aspects of implementation are also considered, particularly with a view to overcoming implementation barriers.

Such a descriptive analysis of inter-organizational cooperation and information exchange can then be used to conduct action research and to identify the opportunities and potential barriers of environmental information exchange in order to finally support the establishment of sustainable inter-organizational cooperation. Since the set of independent observations within the survey is relatively small, data analysis remains largely descriptive.

Inconsistencies between theoretical approaches and their practical applications are also investigated. This, together with the identification of barriers and demands in the implementation of environmental information systems on an operational and inter-organizational level, subsequently can form the basis for further research on the implementation of environmental information systems for sustainable development.

By analyzing initial forms of partnerships and emphasizing promising ways of dealing with the obstacles to information exchange, it is to be hoped that this approach may add to better understanding of management in sustainable cooperation. This may help motivate other companies to reorganize co-operative activity on a more sustainable level.

ENVIRONMENTAL INFORMATION AND INFORMATION SYSTEMS

General Aspects of Environmental Information

Communicating information and environmental information in and between companies is becoming an important and necessary factor in everyday business. Taking rational behavior in the business environment (at least to some extent), as given, the existence of appropriate information forms the basis for sound management and reasonable decisions. Moreover, Ansett also emphasizes the importance of collecting and analyzing key information outside and inside the organization in order to enable the business to make informed decisions (Ansett, 2007, p. 300).

When now dealing with specific issues of information for industrial ecology and the pursuit of environmental goals, the term environmental information has to be defined exactly, so as to avoid confusion. The exchange of information between companies can be more complex with respect to environmental information since it covers a huge spectrum. Environmental data for example provide information about the current state of soil, water, air, emissions etc. Not until they are linked together in a technical context and related to space and time can they be considered as true environmental information (Rautenstrauch, 1999, p. 8). In the chapter at hand, environmental information includes all available information that is decision-relevant, that applies to individual economic units, and that provides deeper information on biological and spatial environments (Behrendt, 2000).

In the industrial context, additional environmentally related information is needed. Although this kind of information is not directly linked to the environment, it can indicate after-effects, deviations, reciprocal effects etc. Due to the fact that environmental data, environmental information and environmentally related information are vital, and considering that the managing of the different types of information does not differ widely, they are all subsumed here under the term 'environmental information'. Additionally, when talking about sustainability, social effects also have to be considered. It is thus of importance to add information on aspects of social sustainability to environmental information.

The question now arises why such specific tools and instruments are needed when dealing with environmental information in order to improve the efficiency of communication. This will be clearer when looking at the characteristics of environmental information (Müller-Christ, 2001; Behrendt, 2000).

Mulidisciplinarity: environmental information is mostly related to many different disciplines such as chemistry, biology, sociology, law, business administration etc. It is thus impossible to assign environmental information to only one discipline.

Weak structuring: direct connections in the cause and effect chain are often not obvious.

Different aggregation levels: For the communication of environmental information, different levels of aggregation are needed, e.g. very detailed data for public authorities or more general information for strategic decisions concerning, for example, the selection of suppliers.

High level of complexity: Environmental information, especially that relating to cause and effect chains is very often complex. As a consequence, simple instructions and guidelines for managing environmental problems cannot be easily generated.

Different forms of presentation: Environmental information can be presented in many different forms, as legal text, in numerical and statistical form, or in cartographical and graphical form. Hence, it is difficult to merge the different forms of information.

Exact allocation of environmental information: Environmental information often exists in different information systems, in different departments, and is thus very decentralized.

Monetary assessment: Since an aggregation of the information is often not possible, generalized monetary assessment of environmental information can be highly problematic. Furthermore, a comparison of different data can be complicated, and monetary valuation of environmental information can lead to a distorted picture of reality.

For a company, environmental information has to serve a wide variety of recipients (Rautenstrauch, 1999, p.8). Internally, while the management board as well as the owners needs environmental information for strategic decisions, departments of companies need environmental information for their daily business. In this connection, environmental information is needed for example for the planning, development and control of environmentally relevant activities. In procurement for example, environmental information is needed to help purchase raw material with the least environmental impact. In research and development, environmental information is needed for environmental product and process design. And in addition, employees will need environmental information, especially in terms of occupational health and safety decisions (Müller, 1995, p.63; Schulz, 1989). On an external level, customers for example need environmental information in order to purchase environmentally sound products. In recent studies for example, the correlation between the existence of environmental information and personal consumption has been investigated. Although there are also many other different factors that can have an influence, it is clear that environmental information can have a positive impact on the consumption patterns (Bartiaux, 2008). Furthermore, industrial customers require environmental information if they need it for their own environment management system. Environmental supply chains as an example cannot be established without the relevant data on materials, energy etc.

What is also of importance to mention is that inter-organizational environmental communication is not obligatory, it nevertheless remains a vital factor in implementing transactions, and the exchange of environmental information within such bilateral cooperation can often be fairly standardized. This is particularly true for very long-term transactions where communication between companies is more highly regulated (Zillig, 2001). These aspects are even more important when taking the managing of environmental information in environmental information systems into account.

Environmental Information Systems

In this section we investigate ways how environmental information can efficiently be collected, stored and converted. Here, several types can be identified: operational environmental information systems, municipal environmental information systems and geographical information systems (Behrendt, 2000). Furthermore, metadata systems and semantic web can also be used for the handling of environmental information (Pillmann et al. 2006, p.1523). However, within this chapter, we concentrate on operational environmental information systems.

Operational environmental information systems are organizational and technical systems that are used for managing environmental information in an operational context. This covers the collection of operational environmental impacts and supporting for the planning and implementation of environmental measures (Hilty & Rautenstrauch, 1995). These environmental information systems may or may not be supported by electronic systems. Within the processes and departments of a company, the operational environmental information system serves to link eco-controlling with the processes of environmental management. Furthermore, it has to be noted that environmental information systems can employ specific methods and tools such as environmental checklists, material and energy balances, environmental performance measurement systems, product line analysis and assessment tools. Further advantages

are that such systems allow for cost reductions in identifying operational potential within the company, in storage, documentation and publication of environmental information, and in aiding better control of environmentally related activities (Haasis 1997; Harmsen et al., 1998).

Consequently, we focus here on systems using electronic media. While paper systems for environmental information can be as efficient as other systems, research of such systems is quite complex and complicated due to lack of data.

What is also important to notice is the fact that although the concept of environmental information systems has existed since the mid 1990s, practical application is still in its infancy (see Perl 2006). A boom in such software systems was seen at the beginning of this century. For example, in the German-speaking world, more than one hundred such software systems existed (see for example Perl, 2006 and the literature and websites mentioned there). Additionally, it has to be noted this vast amount of software comprises many systems for data exchange of legal requirements as well as very small software systems with only one pilot implementation. This leaves about 20 information systems for companies to use in handling environmental information. On the whole, user-oriented and self-structured systems based on common software such as Microsoft Excel are very common in the collection, storage and handling of environmental information. However, it has to be stated that the market for environmental software systems is rapidly changing, and studies of existing systems provide nothing but snapshots.

Inter-Organizational Environmental Information Systems

Before we discuss environmental information system on an inter-organizational level, we first have to describe how such cooperation between companies for sustainable development can look like. In the chapter at hand, we concentrate here on typical forms of cooperation for sustainable development,

For overall sustainable development, Korhonen (2002) distinguishes two different types of inter-organizational sustainable development. First, regional activities can be taken into account. Within this more or less geographical approach, networks of local companies aiming to reduce environmental impact such as eco-industrial parks (Lowe 1997) and recycling networks (Schwarz and Steininger 1997; Schwarz 1994; Strebel 1995) may be mentioned. Second, a more life-cycle oriented approach exists, which also integrates products and services from production of raw material up to consumption and reuse or recycling. This product oriented approach leads to the question of how primarily economically oriented supply chains may contribute to inter-organizational sustainable development (Seuring & Müller, 2008; Seuring, 2004) Furthermore, in literature other concepts such as sustainability networks where the goal of the cooperation is an overall sustainability can be identified (Posch, 2006). Last but not least networks for environmentally sound design (Ryan, 1999; Zwan & Bhamra, 2003) have to be mentioned, as these networks are appropriate means for sustainable product and process development as well. These forms of cooperation have all been described intensively in the literature. However, while informational aspects are an important requirement for successful cooperation for sustainability, thorough discussion of their contribution remains lacking and environmental information systems in particular have received relatively scant attention. However, it is exactly in the complex field of sustainability-oriented cooperation that the benefits of environmental information systems are greatest. (Childerhouse et al., 2003, p.500; Yu et al., 2001, p.115 Gattorna & Walters, 1996, pp.148ff, pp.269ff; Sahay & Gupta, 2003, p.106).

Moreover, a lack of integration and information sharing is seen as one of the major causes of unsuccessful cooperation (Weiling & Kwok-Kee, 2008, p.224). A structured and systematic exchange of information in the form of information systems hence enables the integration of separate operations into a unified system capable of responding to customer needs, to changes in market conditions and to the needs of an overarching corporate direction (Lin, Tseng 2006; Schary & Skjøtt-Larsen, 2001, pp.291ff). Advances in information and communication technologies also promote new possibilities for managing cooperation (Fredendall & Hill 2001, p.215). However, it has to be mentioned that information, information exchange, and information technologies, are merely enablers with respect to conscious exploitation of cooperation for sustainable development.

Another important aspect for the inter-organizational exchange of environmental information is that partners may fear that information be leaked to competitors or used to exploit them in future. In the context of information sharing, as elsewhere, trust is found to increase the amount of information exchanged (Childerhouse et al., 2003, 493; Weiling & Kwok-Kee, 2008, p.227). Partner reliability is also important, since sharing and exchanging information along the supply chain introduces new risks of vulnerability (Andaleeb, 1995; Weiling & Kwok-Kee 2008, p.229). It is thus important to discern exactly how such information exchange takes place.

Considering now the exchange of information in cooperation, it is important to note that such systems cover both the hardware and software system (Sahay & Gupta, 2003, p.98). Furthermore, how and how much information is to be exchanged in such an inter-organizational information system is a matter of values and perspective. The matter cannot be seen in a narrow technical sense since it transforms business operations. Numerous barriers exist, cultural, financial, organizational (question of teamwork, change, management, plans and vision, business process management and development, project management, monitoring and review) that may hinder the installation of effective information exchange in cooperation for sustainable development (on various barriers see Childerhouse et al. 2003, p.493). As Andraski

(1994) has already stated, 80% of the problems in information exchange arise due to people, not technology. This also applies to the exchange of environmental information. As a consequence, technological barriers, software development and testing, and hardware issues are only relatively minor considerations. Complex organizational change cannot be overcome by using technical solutions alone (McAdam & Galloway 2005, p.283). And new technology is not needed for its own sake, yet IT solutions often remain on a purely technological level. There is clearly an urgent need for careful management of organizational change issues (Mason-Jones & Towill 1997, p.140; McAdam & Galloway 2005, p.288).

Consequently, on an inter-organizational level, no specific environmental information systems can be identified for the exchange of environmental information. However, well-established systems for inter-organizational communication in networks, supply chains, clusters etc. can be utilized for the communication of environmental information. One example is electronic data interchange, EDI, where communication of common business data between companies is largely standardized. However, for the communication of environmental information some flexibility is needed, especially when the information is very weakly structured. Groupware systems can be an alternative for the exchange of environmental information, although these tend to be more suitable for communication between employees than for standardized communication of environmental information. On a process level, workflow management systems can help to support the exchange of environmental information, especially for processing and material data. Nonetheless, these systems are mostly used internally; an inter-organizational application is not very common. Furthermore, supply chain software systems can to some extent also be appropriate for the exchange of environmental information, but are obviously limited to environmental measures along the supply chain (see for example Helo & Szekely, 2005; Sahay & Gupta, 2003; Lyons et al., 2004, p.665; Gulledge, 2006, p.8).

However, beside all these more or less sophisticated systems for the communication of environmental information, Olhager & Selldin (2004, p.360) found out in their surveys that telephone, fax and e-mail were all prevalent means of communication in cooperation (especially in supply chains). More advanced means of communication such as EDI, internet-based extranets etc. are still in their infancy. In the near future there will be a trend towards more sophisticated tools, which will replace the classic forms of communication such as letter, phone and fax. However, both the common use of such systems and the utilization for environmental means is not very widespread.

To sum up, despite its advantages, exchange of information in inter-organizational cooperation remains an enormous challenge. Sufficient knowledge, access to information, and the ability to manage the information are vital factors in dealing with environmental issues and in enabling cooperative sustainable development (Hall, 2000; Lamming & Hampson, 1996; Walley & Whitehead, 1994).

EMPIRICAL ANALYSES OF SUSTAINABILITY ISSUES AND INTER-ORGANIZATIONAL INFORMATION EXCHANGE

Research Design

The goals of these research studies are to examine the status quo of operational environmental information systems in Austrian industry and the extent to which they are supported. Barriers in implementing such systems are also identified. An additional aim of this investigation is identification of essential conditions for successful implementation of environmental information systems in cooperation for sustainable development and to analyze the general suitability of such networks for intensive inter-organizational environmental communication.

In detail, the research aims at answering the following research questions.

- Research question 1: Do the companies see the importance of cooperative activities in meeting the needs and demands of sustainability (see for example Korhonen 2002 and 2004, Lowe 1997; Posch 2006, Schwarz and Steininger 1997, Seuring, S. 2004)
- Research question 2: How is the communication of environmental information in companies organized (see Perl 2006 and above)?
- Research question 3: Is the exchange of environmental information in cooperation based on less sophisticated means such as mail, telephone, email (as found in Olhager & Selldin 2004, p.360)?
- Research question 4: Do companies use environmental information to support their sustainable activities (according to Young, 2000)?

To collect appropriate data, we surveyed manufacturing companies in Austria. The Austrian Federal Ministry supported the empirical analysis for Traffic, Innovation and Technology. An 8-page questionnaire was used. Three experts and business managers examined the suitability of the survey questions. The questionnaire was sent out in Spring 2004 to 1,480 companies of more than 100 employees (representing all companies of this size and branches). 138 companies answered the survey, representing 9.8% of the manufacturing industry. The respondents were asked to evaluate the items on a 5-point Likert scale. For reasons of cost and time the questionnaire was only sent to the environmental managers, even though this might result in informant biases. However, the environmental manager seems to be the most

appropriate source concerning these issues. Since the response distribution regarding the number of employees and sales volume, is nearly equal to that of the whole population, the sample can be seen as representative, even though the response rate is not that high.

Importance of Inter-Organizational Cooperation for Sustainable Development

To analyze general attitudes towards sustainability and close cooperation, the companies were asked for their opinion on specific aspects of sustainability in such cooperative activity. Table 1 gives an overview of their answers based on a Likert scale from 1 – very unimportant – to 5 – very important. As can be seen, the grouped median is between 3 and 5, the companies thus rate the issues as rather important. Aspects such as employee safety and quality are rated as very important. However, aspects specific to sustainable supply chains such as environmental protection at supplier sites are rated as not very important. Overall, companies consider sustainability as quite important, but individual perceptions vary considerably.

Another important aspect in this respect is the question whether companies are aware of any inter-organizational cooperation for sustainability issues. It is thus important to know companies' attitudes towards cooperation and the aspects mentioned above. Companies were asked for their perceptions regarding the advantages of inter-organizational cooperation for sustainability. The answers, on a Likert scale from 1 – very unimportant to 5 – very important can be seen in Table 3. In contrast to the companies' perception about the importance of these issues, the correlation of these issues with cooperation and inter-organizational activities is not really clear for the companies. Hence, they do not rate these issues for cooperation as highly as sustainability issues in general (see Table 2). For example, cooperation for environmental protection in product use

Table 1. Importance of sustainability

	N	Grouped Median	Me-dian	Mini-mum	Maxi-mum	Range	25% Per-centile	75% Per-centile
Environmental protection at supplier site	136	3.48	3.00	1.00	5.00	4.00	3.00	4.00
Respecting human rights throughout the value chain	134	3.81	4.00	1.00	5.00	4.00	3.00	5.00
Comprehensive environmental protection in your production units	136	4.30	4.00	2.00	5.00	3.00	4.00	5.00
Support of disadvantaged groups (the elderly, handi-capped persons etc.)	136	3.40	3.00	1.00	5.00	4.00	3.00	4.00
Employee safety/security	136	4.57	5.00	2.00	5.00	3.00	4.00	5.00
Regional responsibility as an employer	136	4.10	4.00	1.00	5.00	4.00	4.00	5.00
Ensuring high quality and safety of your products	135	4.82	5.00	3.00	5.00	2.00	5.00	5.00
Environmental protection in the use and disposal of your product	136	4.07	4.00	1.00	5.00	4.00	3.00	5.00
Statistical significance (Friedman test)								
N	133							
Chi-Square	326.69							
df	7.00							
Significance	0.0000							

and disposal, or high quality and safety, are rated considerably lower than their importance indicated in Table 1. Hence, the investigation reveals that significant potential remains, especially in the field of sustainability, in realizing the benefits of cooperation.

A close correlation between the results of Table 1 and Table 2 can also be seen in Figure 1 (respec-

Table 2. Sustainable activities in cooperation

	N	Grouped Median	Median	Mini-mum	Max-imum	Range	25% Per-centile	75% Per-centile
Environmental protection at supplier site	129	3.19	3.00	1.00	5.00	4.00	2.00	4.00
Respecting human rights throughout the value chain	130	2.88	3.00	1.00	5.00	4.00	2.00	4.00
Comprehensive environmental protection in your production units	130	3.55	4.00	1.00	5.00	4.00	3.00	4.00
Support of disadvantaged groups (the elderly, handicapped persons etc.)	128	2.69	3.00	1.00	5.00	4.00	2.00	3.00
Employee safety/security	130	3.64	4.00	1.00	5.00	4.00	3.00	4.25
Regional responsibility as an employer	129	3.20	3.00	1.00	5.00	4.00	2.00	4.00
Ensuring high quality and safety of your products	130	3.61	4.00	1.00	5.00	4.00	3.00	4.00
Environmental protection in the use and disposal of your product	130	3.65	4.00	1.00	5.00	4.00	3.00	4.00
Statistical significance (Friedman test)								
N	127							
Chi-Square	159.09							
df	7.00							
Significance	0.0000							

Table 3. Factors against an organizational environmental information system

	N	Grouped Median	Median	Mini-mum	Maxi-mum	Range	25% Per-centile	75% Per-centile
Software too expensive	75	3.92	4.00	1.00	5.00	4.00	3.00	5.00
Software too detailed	79	3.52	4.00	1.00	5.00	4.00	3.00	4.00
Software not common for branches	62	3.03	3.00	1.00	5.00	4.00	1.00	4.00
Software cannot be integrated	60	2.59	3.00	1.00	5.00	4.00	1.00	4.00
Software does not provide additional help	78	2.84	3.00	1.00	5.00	4.00	2.00	4.00
Software provides no cost savings	83	3.78	4.00	1.00	5.00	4.00	3.00	4.00
Implementation too time-consuming	76	3.65	4.00	1.00	5.00	4.00	3.00	4.00
Employee resistance	89	2.10	2.00	1.00	5.00	4.00	1.00	3.00
Environmental information already integrated	94	2.77	3.00	1.00	5.00	4.00	1.00	4.00
Statistical significance (Friedman test)								
N	42							
Chi-Square	36.63							
df	8.00							
Significance	0.0000							

tive medians are represented by the crossed lines). The vertical axis represents whether the companies see the advantages of inter-organizational cooperation. On the horizontal axis the importance for sustainability issues is pictured.

Further, the dots illustrate the correlation between the importance of sustainability issues and the advantages of inter-organizational cooperation for specific aspects of sustainability in cooperation. Namely, these are the environmental protection in the production of raw materials, the human rights along the supply chain, the environmental protection at the production plant, the promotion of deprived groups, the responsibility as regional entrepreneurs, the product quality, occupational health and safety and the environmental protection in the use and disposal phase. All these activities represent means to realize sustainability on both a company and inter-organizational level as described above.

As a result of this investigation, it can be seen that both the relative importance of sustainability issues (n=137, χ^2=335.04, p<0.001) and the advantages of inter-organizational cooperation (n=131,

χ^2=155.70, p<0.001) are found to be statistically significant (see also Posch, 2007, p.87). It is no surprise that companies rate economic aspects such as high product quality (g) and occupational health and safety (e) as very high. Furthermore, environmental protection at own production plant (c), as well as environmental protection in product usage and disposal (h), are also of great importance. Companies can thus clearly see the relevance of close cooperation in sustainable supply chains. Surprisingly, environmental protection in the production of raw materials (a) is seen as being of low or medium importance. While this should be a clearly dominant issue in sustainable supply chains, the advantages of inter-organizational cooperation in this area are not seen as very important. The same holds true for issues relating to compliance with human rights throughout the whole supply chain (b) (Posch, 2007). So here, once again, there is need for appropriate persuasion in order to achieve overall sustainable development in inter-organizational cooperation.

Figure 1. Sustainable issues and advantages of inter-organizational cooperation (Posch 2007, 88)

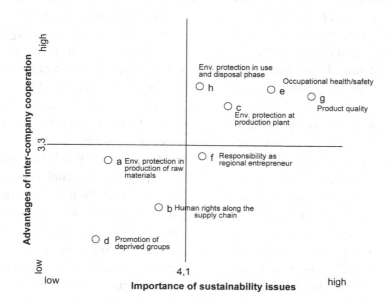

Organisation of environmental communication within companies

Organization of Environmental Communication within Companies

Empirical research revealed the following data concerning research question 2; i.e. the form of environmental communication within companies. A major noticeable finding is that only 12 companies indicated having a specific, internal environmental information system. Furthermore, databases are neither very well known nor much used in the companies. Only programs for spreadsheet analysis such as MS Excel are popular and used by more than 70% of the companies to handle environmental information. Nevertheless, those companies that admitted using specified environmental information systems also indicated that they predominantly use systems, which are integrated in other company wide software, thus isolated environmental software systems hardly exist. What is also noticeable is the fact that the companies already using environmental information systems are highly conscious of the numerous possibilities and functionalities the software pro-

grams offer. Companies also utilize the functions, mostly for the drawing of reports, monitoring legal compliance and analyzing material flows, but also for analyzing environmental indicators and risk analysis. Moreover, companies also see the economic advantages in using these systems.

The question now arises as to why the application of environmental information systems in companies is still in its infancy. Those companies not using environmental information systems were thus asked their reasons for not making use of environmental information systems in their company-wide communication. Most noticeable here, is the fact a great number of companies indicated that they cannot answer the questions. For example, 52 companies could not answer the question concerning the possibilities of integrating such software in existing software solutions. Most companies (only 20 companies answered "do not know") were able to answer whether environmental information was already integrated. An overview of responses on factors inhibiting implementation of operational environmental information systems can be seen in Table 3. Most of the companies see the software as too expensive and too complex. Furthermore, they see no correlation to cost savings and the work entailed in implementing the software is too excessive. Employee opposition does not appear to be a significant barrier.

Additionally, companies were questioned concerning those factors, which are seen to support the implementation of environmental information systems. All companies that could not answer the earlier question concerning barriers to environmental information could not answer this question either. Factors favoring application of environmental information systems are the expected decline in parallel workload in the handling of the information, and the possibility of integrating environmental information systems in the operational information systems used in the companies. Moreover, if the environmental law will be become more complex or the customers demand it the companies will install such an

environmental information system. Companies also expressed their willingness to install such systems if the environmental regulations become more complex or if customer demands for such information increase. Detailed responses to this question can be seen in Table 4.

Summing up, it can be seen that costs are the primary factor leading to the neglect of environmental information systems. This is strange considering the fact that those companies that have already implemented such systems nearly always emphasize their ability to generate cost savings. Many companies also assume that the software as too sophisticated and detailed for their own needs. While employee attitudes appear to exert no great influence one way or another regarding system selection, they are relevant for successful implementation of the software system (see also Childerhouse et al., 2003).

Table 4. Changing aspects for an improved implementation of organizational environmental information systems

	N	Grouped Median	Me-dian	Mini-mum	Maxi-mum	Range	25% Per-centile	75% Per-centile
Costs for environmental protection rise	93	3.09	3.00	1.00	5.00	4.00	2.00	4.00
Environmental protections becomes more important	102	3.23	3.00	1.00	5.00	4.00	2.00	4.00
Systems can be fully integrated in IT system	91	3.80	4.00	1.00	5.00	4.00	3.00	5.00
Parallel workload in data generation avoidable	95	4.05	4.00	1.00	5.00	4.00	3.00	5.00
Operational sequences get more complex	94	3.57	4.00	1.00	5.00	4.00	3.00	5.00
Implementation of EMS	99	3.25	3.00	1.00	5.00	4.00	1.00	5.00
Legal compliance gets more complex	102	3.69	4.00	1.00	5.00	4.00	3.00	4.00
Positive attitude of employees	94	2.41	2.00	1.00	5.00	4.00	1.00	4.00
Customers demands the system	100	3.37	3.00	1.00	5.00	4.00	2.00	3.00
Statistical significance (Friedman test)								
N	44							
Chi-Square	46.74							
df	8							
Significance	0.0000							

Table 5. Means of communication of environmental information

Communication with suppliers	N	Positive answer	Percentage
Oral	88	13	14.8
Telephone	88	35	39.8
Mail	88	42	47.7
Email	88	47	53.4
Specific programs	88	4	4.6
Communication with waste recipients			
Oral		42	31.3
Telephone		107	79.9
Mail		13	9.7
Email		47	35.1
Specific programs		0	0.0

Means of Environmental Information in Inter-Organizational Cooperation

First of all, the question concerning the core conditions needed for information exchange has to be dealt with. The exchange of environmental information between companies and their suppliers is particularly important. According to the empirical investigation, most of the companies which exchange their environmental information (88 companies) do this by email (see Table 5). Many of the companies, 47%, communicate in written form. Also worthy of note is the fact that only 5% of the companies communicate via specific programs, e.g. specific supply chain programs, EDI or specific ERP programs. Unsurprisingly, programs such as Microsoft Excel are used predominantly for intra-company communication (instead of specific environmental information systems such as Umberto®, GaBi® or SimaPro®). Analysis of communication with waste recipients reveals a similar picture; telephone and emailing are the dominant means of communication. This is also relevant concerning further enlargement of supply chains and the establishment of recycling networks, since the application of sophisticated communication systems for environmental information does not seem to enhance the probability of sustainable cooperation.

Regarding the reasons for and against the implementation of environmental information systems on an inter-organizational level, responses are similar to those for company-wide communication of environmental information. Many companies could not answer the question. The remaining companies answered that if suppliers and customers do not have corresponding systems, then they will not implement such a system at their own company site. As in company-wide communication of environmental information, the software appears to be too expensive for inter-organizational exchange of environmental information.

To conclude, on the inter-organizational level, the influence of suppliers and recipients is rather high. If suppliers and recipients do not have appropriate software standards, the companies see no point in implementing environmental information systems in their own company[1]. This brings us to the question how all these problems can be overcome when implementing environmental information systems both within and between companies. Thus this chapter addresses these issues and presents an implementation concept for environmental information systems.

Table 6. Use of environmental information for sustainable activities

	N	Grouped Median	Median	Mini-mum	Maxi-mum	Range	25% Per-centile	75% Per-centile
Environmentally friendly product design	125	2.82	3.00	1.00	5.00	4.00	1.00	4.00
Environmentally friendly process design	125	3.16	3.00	1.00	5.00	4.00	2.00	4.00
Recycling activities	126	3.14	3.00	1.00	5.00	4.00	2.00	4.00
Sustainable waste management	126	3.73	4.00	1.00	5.00	4.00	3.00	4.00
Selection of sustainable input materials	126	3.67	4.00	1.00	5.00	4.00	2.75	4.00
Life cycle assessment	124	1.69	1.00	1.00	5.00	4.00	1.00	3.00
Statistical significance (Friedman test)								
N	121							
Chi-Square	139.71							
df	5.0000							
Significance	0.0000							

The Usage of Environmental Information for Sustainability Issues

Another interesting question concerns the use of environmental information for activities in cooperation for sustainability. Table 6 illustrates responses in terms of the grouped medians. The most important aspect for the companies surveyed is sustainable waste management. This produced a median around a value of 4. In addition, the use of environmental information for the selection of sustainable input material is also of importance. This is a typical issue for sustainable supply chains. According to the results, the use of environmental information for other activities is negligible. The low consideration of environmental information for life cycle assessment, a typical activity that can be done in sustainable supply chains, is particularly noticeable. Additionally, the use of environmental information for recycling activities is also not that common. Here, adequate clarification on the significance of inter-organizational sustainable cooperation is highly necessary.

The correlation between the importance of measures for sustainable development and the usage of environmental information for the activities can be seen in table 6. Taking the Kendall Tau b as a measure for the depth of the relation between these two aspects, the value of 0.4 was only reached once, indicating slight correspondence. The companies that rated environmental activities as very important do not automatically use appropriate environmental information for executing related policies in their companies.

Here, once again, appropriate enlightenment is needed to convince the companies of both the

Table 7. Relation between sustainable activities and the use of environmental information

	Information from suppliers and customers on sustainable activities	
		Kendall Tau b
Activities concerning sustainable development	Environmentally friendly product design	0.389
	Environmentally friendly process design	0.271
	Recycling activities	0.351
	Sustainable waste management	0.205

necessity of measures for sustainable development and of the usefulness of information, especially environmental information, for the execution of these measures.

DISCUSSION

The empirical analysis reveals that companies in the Austrian production industry are largely unaware of the advantages of cooperation in implementing sustainable development. An ongoing process of awareness building will thus be necessary to motivate companies to undertake inter-organizational activities for sustainable development. However, it is exactly these aspects, which are essential for the generation of sustainable development in cooperation.

The results illustrated above, lend support to the research statement that at the time the survey was carried out more sophisticated means of exchanging information were still in their infancy, both at an intra- and inter-organizational level (as is also claimed by Olhager & Selldin, 2004). Although knowledge concerning the existence of highly sophisticated software systems for the communication of environmental information is clearly available (see for example Helo & Szekely, 2005; Hilty, 2007; Sahay & Gupt, a 2003), practical application remains wanting.

According to Young (2000), information in general and environmental information in particular, is both vital enablers for sustainable cooperation. In other words, it is normally taken for granted that companies are aware of this informational necessity. To some extent, the survey reveals a quite different picture. Although, to a certain degree, companies see the importance of sustainable activities in inter-organizational relationship, they do not use environmental information at all well. The argument that companies use environmental information to support their sustainable activities is thus weakened. Moreover, on the inter-organizational level the influence of suppliers and recipients is rather large, as

can be seen in the empirical investigation. If their suppliers and customers do not have appropriate software standards as well, the companies see no point in implementing environmental information systems in their own company.

CONCLUDING REMARKS

The results of this chapter have theoretical as well as practical implications.

The exchange of environmental information is an important prerequisite in initiating a change in thinking and acting towards more sustainable development and in the configuration of sustainable cooperation. Nonetheless, a clear lack of research concerning the exchange of environmental information in inter-organizational cooperation still prevails. A structured and systematic process for the gathering, preparation and storage of information is required. However, companies hardly utilize these systems although specialized environmental software systems exist. Unfortunately, systemic constraints in the survey samples preclude the possibility of generalizing the results described here.

On a more practical side, further awareness concerning the contribution of inter-organizational cooperation to overall sustainable development is needed. Companies are currently not aware of the advantages of sustainable development, nor of inter-organizational cooperation in reaching sustainability. As the survey reveals, both the integration of sustainable activities and the exchange of adequate environmental information are in their infancy. Inter-organizational relationships can go a long way towards improving and integrating economic, ecological, and social considerations.

To sum up, the chapter reveals the need for further research in answering the question of how sustainable development in company and increasing and intensifying the exchange of appropriate environmental information can support inter-organizational cooperation.

REFERENCES

Andaleeb, S. (1995). Dependence relations and the moderating role of trust: implications for behavioral intentions in marketing channels. *International Journal of Research in Marketing, 12*(2), 157–172. doi:10.1016/0167-8116(94)00020-O

Andraski, J. (1994). Foundations for successful continuous replenishment programs. *International Journal of Logistics Management, 5*(1), 1–8. doi:10.1108/09574099410805036

Ansett, S. (2007). Mind the Gap: A Journey to Sustainable Supply Chains. *Employ Response Rights Journal, 19*(4), 295–303. doi:10.1007/s10672-007-9055-x

Bartiaux, F. (2008). Does environmental information overcome practice compartmentalisation and change consumers' behaviours? *Journal of Cleaner Production, 16*, 1170–1190. doi:10.1016/j.jclepro.2007.08.013

Behrendt, I. (2000). Umweltinformationssysteme als informelle Basis strategischer Planungen: Eine Gestaltungsempfehlung zur Architektur von strategischen Umweltinformations¬systemen, Gießen.

Buxmann (2002). Strategien von Standardsoftwareanbietern: Eine Analyse auf der Basis von Netzeffekten, *zfbf* Nr. 54, August 2002, 442-457.

Childerhouse, P., Hermiz, R., Mason-Jones, R., Popp, A., & Towill, D. (2003). 'Information flow in automotive supply chains – identifying and learning to overcome barriers to change'. *Industrial Management & Data Systems, 103*(7), 491–502. doi:10.1108/02635570310489197

Fredendall, L., & Hill, E. (2001). *Basics in Supply Chain Management*. Boca Raton, FL: St. Lucie Press.

Gattorna, J. & Walters, D. (1996). *Managing the Supply Chain: A Strategic Perspective*. Hampshire.

Gulledge, T. (2006). What is integration . *Industrial Management & Data Systems, 106*(1), 5–20. doi:10.1108/02635570610640979

Haasis, H.-D. (1997). Ein Überblick über Betriebliche Umweltinformationssysteme. *uwf* 3/97, 4-6.

Hall, J. (2000). Supply Chain Dynamics. *Journal of Cleaner Production, 8*(6), 455–471. doi:10.1016/S0959-6526(00)00013-5

Hall, J. (2006). Environmental supply chain innovation, In J. Sarkis (Ed.). *Greening the supply chain*, (pp. 233-249).

Harmsen, D.-M., Hiessl, H., Lang, J., Matuschewski, A., & Zoche, P. (1998). *Betriebliche Umweltinformationssysteme: Entwicklungstrends und Anwenderbedarf zur Unterstützung des betrieblichen Umweltmanagements*, unpublished research report, Karlsruhe.

Helo, P., & Szekely, B. (2005). Logistics information systems – An analysis of software solutions for supply chain co-ordination. *Industrial Management & Data Systems, 105*(1), 5–18. doi:10.1108/02635570510575153

Hilty, L. (2007). Nachhaltige Informationsgesellschaft: Einfluss moderner Informations- und Kommunikationstechnologien. In R. Isenmann, M. v. Hauff (Ed.), *Industrial Ecology: Mit Ökologie zukunftsorientiert wirtschaften*, (pp. 189-208). München.

Hilty, L. (2006). The relevance of information and communication technologies for environmental sustainability – A prospective simulation study. *Environmental Modelling & Software, 21*, 1618–1629. doi:10.1016/j.envsoft.2006.05.007

Hilty, L. M., & Rautenstrauch, C. (1995). Betriebliche Umweltinformatik, In B. Page, L. Hilty, M. Lorenz (Ed.), *Umweltinformatik: Informatikmethoden für den Umweltschutz und Umweltforschung*, (2nd Ed., pp. 295-312). Handbuch der Informatik Band 13.3, München, Wien, Oldenbourg.

Hsu, L. (2005). Supply chain management effects on performance for interaction between suppliers and buyers. *Industrial Management & Data Systems, 105*(7), 857–875. doi:10.1108/02635570510616085

Korhonen, J. (2002). Two paths of industrial ecology: applying the product-based and geographical approaches. *Journal of Environmental Planning and Management, 45*(1), 39–57. doi:10.1080/09640560120100187

Kulp, S., Ofek, E., & Whitaker, J. (2004). Supply-Chain Coordination: How Companies Leverage Information Flows to Generate Value. In T. Harrison, H. Lee, & J. Neale (Ed.), *The Practice of Supply Chain Management: Where Theory and Application Converge*, (Part 2, pp. 91-107). New York.

Lamming, R., & Hampson, J. (1996). The environment as a supply chain management issue. *British Journal of Management, 7*, 45–62. doi:10.1111/j.1467-8551.1996.tb00147.x

Lang, C. (2000). Betriebliche Umweltinformationssysteme auf dem Prüfstand – ein Forschungskonzept. In L. Hilty & R. Schulthess (Ed.), *Strategische und betriebsübergreifende Anwendungen betrieblicher Umweltinformationssysteme*, Marburg, (pp. 47-58).

Letmathe, P., Schwarz, E., & Steven, M. (1996). Grundlagen der Umweltberichterstattung. *UE, 4*, 415-443.

Lin, C., & Tseng, H. (2006). Identifying the pivotal role of participation strategies and information technology application for supply chain excellence. *Industrial Management & Data Systems, 106*(5), 739–756. doi:10.1108/02635570610666476

Lowe, E. (1997). Creating by-product resource exchanges: strategies for eco-industrial parks. *Journal of Cleaner Production, 5*(1-2), 57–65. doi:10.1016/S0959-6526(97)00017-6

Lyons, A., Coleman, J., Kehoe, D., & Coronado, A. (2004). Performance observation and analysis of an information re-engineered supply chain: a case study of an automotive firm. *Industrial Management & Data Systems, 104*(8), 658–666. doi:10.1108/02635570410561645

Mason-Jones, R. & Towill, D. (1997). Information enrichment: designing the supply chain for competitive advantage. *Supply chain management, 2*(4), 137-148.

McAdam, R., & Galloway, A. (2005). Enterprise resource planning and organisational innovation: a management perspective. *Industrial Management & Data Systems, 105*(3), 280–290. doi:10.1108/02635570510590110

Müller, A. (1995). *Umweltorientiertes betriebliches Rechnungswesen*, (2nd rev. ed.). Munich, Vienna.

Müller-Christ, G. (2001). *Umweltmanagement: Umweltschutz und nachhaltige Entwicklung*, Munich.

Nissinen, A. (2007). Developing benchmarks for consumer-oriented life cycle assessment-based environmental information on products, services and consumption patterns. *Journal of Cleaner Production, 15*, 538–549. doi:10.1016/j.jclepro.2006.05.016

Olhager, J., & Selldin, E. (2004). Supply chain management survey of Swedish manufacturing firms. *International Journal of Production Economics*, *89*, 353–361. doi:10.1016/S0925-5273(03)00029-X

Perl, E. *(2006)*. Implementierung von Umweltinformationssystemen: Industrieller Umweltschutz und die Kommunikation von Umweltinformationen in Unternehmen und in Netzwerken, *Graz*.

Picot, A., Reichwald, R., & Wigand, R. T. (2003). *Die grenzenlose Unternehmung – Information, Organisation und Management: Lehrbuch zur Unternehmensführung im Informationszeitalter*, (5 rev. ed.), Wiesbaden.

Pillmann, W., Geiger, W., & Voigt, K. (2006). Survey of environmental informatics in Europe. *Environmental Modelling & Software, 21*, 1519–1527. doi:10.1016/j.envsoft.2006.05.008

Posch, A. *(2006)*. Zwischenbetriebliche Rückstandsverwertung: Kooperationen für eine nachhaltige Entwicklung am Beispiel industrieller Verwertungsnetze, *Wiesbaden*.

Posch, A. (2007). Nachhaltigkeitsorientierte Supply Chains – Voraussetzungen und potentielle Maßnahmenbereiche. In M. Tschandl, & S. Bäck (Ed.) *Einkauf optimieren: Effizienz und Effektivitäten in Einkauf und Logistik*, Kapfenberg, (pp. 84-90).

Rautenstrauch, C. (1999). *Betriebliche Umweltinformationssysteme: Grundlagen, Konzepte und Systeme*. Berlin Heidelberg.

Ryan, C. (1999). Information Technology and DfE: From Support Tool to Design Principle. *Journal of Industrial Ecology, 3*(1), 5–8. doi:10.1162/108819899569359

Sahay, B., & Gupta, A. (2003). Development of software selection criteria for supply chain solutions. *Industrial Management & Data Systems, 103*(2), 97–110. doi:10.1108/02635570310463429

Schary, P. & Skjøtt-Larsen T. (2001). *Managing the Global Supply Chain*. Copenhagen.

Schreyögg, G. (2001). Wissen, Wissenschaftstheorie und Wissensmanagement. In G. Schreyögg (Ed.), *Wissen in Unternehmen: Konzepte, Maßnahmen, Methoden*, Berlin, (pp. 3-20).

Schulz, W. (1989)... *Betriebliche Umweltinformationssysteme. UE, 6*, 33–99.

Schwarz, E., & Steininger, K. (1997). Implementing nature's lessons: the industrial recycling network enhancing regional development. *Journal of Cleaner Production, 5*(1-2), 47–56. doi:10.1016/S0959-6526(97)00009-7

Seuring, S. (2004b). Industrial ecology, life cycles, supply chains: differences and interrelations. *Business Strategy and the Environment, 13*(5), 306–319. doi:10.1002/bse.418

Seuring, S., & Müller, M. (2004). Beschaffungsmanagement und Nachhaltigkeit – eine Literaturübersicht. In M. Hülsmann, G. Müller-Christ, & H. Haasis (Ed.), *Betriebswirtschaftslehre und Nachhaltigkeit – Bestandsaufnahme und Forschungs¬programmatik*, Wiesbaden, 117-170.

Seuring, S., & Müller, M. (2008). From a literature review to a conceptual framework for sustainable supply chain management. *Journal of Cleaner Production, 16*, 1699–1710. doi:10.1016/j.jclepro.2008.04.020

Steinle, C., & Reiter, F. (2002). Mitarbeitereinstellungen als Gestaltungsgrundlage eines ökologieorientierten Anreizsystems. *uwf, 10*(1), 66-70.

Sterr. T. (1998). *Aufbau eines zwischenbetrieblichen Stoffverwertungsnetzwerks im Heidelberger Industriegebiet Pfaffengrund*, Heidelberg.

Strebel, H. (1995). Regionale Stoffverwertungsnetze am Beispiel der Steiermark. *Umweltwirtschaftsforum UWF, 3*(4), 48–55.

van der Zwan, F., & Bhamra, T. (2003). Alternative function fulfilment: incorporating environmental considerations into increased design space. *Journal of Cleaner Production*, *11*, 897–903. doi:10.1016/S0959-6526(02)00161-0

Walley, N., & Whitehead, B. (1994). It's not easy to be green. *Harvard Business Review*, (May-June): 46–53.

Weiling, K., & Kwok-Kee, W. (2008). Trust and Power Influences in Supply Chain Collaboration. *Operations Research & Management Sciences*, *119*(1), 223–239.

Wiegand, M. (1996). *Prozesse organisationalen Lernens*, Wiesbaden.

Young, R. (2000). Managing residual disposition: Achieving economy, environmental responsibility, and competitive advantage using the supply chain framework. *Journal of Supply Chain Management*, *36*(1), 57–66. doi:10.1111/j.1745-493X.2000.tb00070.x

Yu, Z., Yan, H., & Cheng, T. (2001). Benefits of information sharing with supply chain partnerships. *Industrial Management & Data Systems*, *101*(3), 114–119. doi:10.1108/02635570110386625

Zillig, U. *(2001)*. Integratives Logistikmanagement in Unternehmensnetzwerken: Gestaltung interorganisatorischer Logistiksysteme für die Zulieferindustrie, *Wiesbaden*.

ENDNOTE

[1]   Regarding the implementation of software systems this is also known as "pinguin effect" (see Buxmann 2002).

Section 3
Sustainable Communication

Chapter 8
Communicating in Multicultural Firms:
Boundary Creation, Fragmentation and the Social Use of ICT

Jakob Lauring
Department of Management, Aarhus School of Business, Aarhus University, Denmark

Anders Klitmøller
Department of Management, Aarhus School of Business, Aarhus University, Denmark

ABSTRACT

Based on a qualitative study of 14 knowledge intensive companies, this chapter suggests that multi-cultural and multilingual firms are faced with certain challenges in the attempt to fruitfully utilize the diverse background of their workforce. Firstly, through informal settings, the employees to create social boundaries within the firm use native languages strategically. Secondly, even though the introduction of English as cooperate language might solve some communication issues, it tends to render the communication less nuanced, thereby reducing the use of human resources within the firm. Thirdly, ICT does not necessarily solve communication problems within a given company. It can even be used as a social 'tool' to uphold social boundaries or social fragmentation. It is suggested that in order to address these challenges, the management should seek to reward not only individual employees, but also expand the notion of performance to include the collectivity of the workplace.

INTRODUCTION

ICT, or Information Communication Technology, has come to play a larger role in contemporary business communities due to the increased internationalization of companies worldwide (Griffith, 2002; Palmer-Silveira, Ruiz-Garrido, & Fortanet-Gómes, 2006).

Much like all other human interaction, communication is at the center of ICT. And communication is what seems to be one of the major managerial tasks that companies working in globalized markets are faced with. Therefore, managing interaction across national and linguistic boundaries has become a daily issue for a growing number of managers (Maznevski & Chudoba, 2000; Welch, Welch & Marschan-Piekkari, 2001).

DOI: 10.4018/978-1-60566-822-2.ch008

In the management of multicultural groups, the varied nature of the group has often been described as a competitive advantage in the creation of information and other human resources (Adler, 1997; Miller, Fields, Kumar, & Ortiz, 2000; Paulus, 2000). Nonetheless, the success of the diverse groups is not given, and managerial challenges should not be taken lightly (Leonard & Swap, 1999). A number of studies indicate that communication management is especially important (Distefano & Maznevski, 2000; Loosemore & Lee, 2002; Maznevski, 1994). And since ICT is the basis of much internal and inter-unit communication in multicultural firms, the relation between diversity management, communication and ICT is an important topic in the understanding of international business.

Communication is central to management since, in one way or another, challenges to communication have an effect on all managerial processes (Cheney, Thøger, Zorn & Ganesh, 2004). Furthermore, communication is the basis of all employee collaboration. In a multinational context, linguistic and cultural differences make communication even more of a concern (Beamer & Varner, 2005; Loosemore et al., 2002). In relation to this, the main managerial challenge of the diverse group is that efficient communication actually occurs (McDonough, Kahn & Barczak, 2001). If group members do not communicate well, cultural and linguistic diversity will most likely become unfavorable (Distefano et al., 2000; Hambrick, Davison, Snell & Snow, 1998). Therefore, the arguments presented in this chapter rely on the fundamental premise that communication is necessary in all coordination and organization of human resources. Accordingly, fostering a rich communication flow within a multicultural organization is an important source of competitive advantage, thus nurturing social and cultural sustainability within the company and society as a whole.

Language diversity is a theme that has received very little scholarly attention (Henderson, 2005).

At the theoretical level, the impact of multilingualism has been examined mainly in relation to language management, which conceives of language as a facilitator providing for the acquisition and transmission of information through social interaction (Dhir & Góké-Paríolá, 2002; Feely & Harzing, 2003; Vaara et al. 2003b). In comparison, empirical studies have focused on the manner in which language differences create a complicated managerial situation, with great implications for the practice of intercultural communication (Marschan-Piekkari, Welch, & Welch, 1999a; Marschan-Piekkari, Welch & Welch, 1999b; Vaara et al. 2003a). With specific reference to culturally diverse groups, Distefano and Maznevski (2000) have found language differences to have a negative impact on relationship building. Furthermore, research by Lagerström and Andersson (2003) indicates that a condition of multilingualism may challenge the socialization of team members. Henderson (2005) proposes an alternative approach to language diversity, by examining possible sources of communication failure within the global workplace. The research relies on a distinction between problems relating to the transmission and reception of messages, and to difficulties in the area of interpersonal perceptions and attitudes, which arise from interlocutors' encounters with the unfamiliar practices of alien speech communities. Thus, Henderson (2005) argues that communication failure should be read as a socio-cultural rather than a purely linguistic phenomenon.

In this Chapter, language use is considered to be the way the linguistic medium is used in communication. To further define the concept, it is the main argument of the chapter that language use should be understood as a dynamic and dialectical communicative process involving both relationship building and knowledge sharing between different groups and individuals (Cooren 2006, Vaara et al. 2005). In addition, language should be understood as socially and historically constituted in line with other human practices (Bourdieu 1977,

Bourdieu 1991). Language, then, is not only a means of understanding and communication, but also an object of action (e.g. Austin 1975, Taylor 2006). The communicative process is then to be understood, in a broader sense, as the transfer of information as well as the organization of social relationships thought patterns and actions (Robichaud 2006, Wittgenstein 1996). The focus of this chapter is on expressed discourses on verbal dialogue as it happens in face-to-face interaction or by the use of ICT.

Cultural diversity is here generally related to variance of national affiliation as it is done by most authors in this field (e.g. Adler 1997, Distefano & Maznevski 2000). However, differences in nationality as such do not create differences between individuals. It is the variety of identifications, behavioral patterns, linguistic skills and bodies of knowledge linked to growing up in different regions that provide the potential for human diversity (Roberson 2006). This chapter attempts to explore discourses on communication processes as individuals describe them in culturally diverse organizations. Furthermore, we wish to direct attention to social processes linked to face-to-face and ICT communication that may affect the utilization of human resources. Finally, it is the aim of the chapter to include the language theme in the discussion as a novel contribution to the understanding of culturally diverse groups, communication and ICT. This will be illustrated by data from 14 multicultural 'knowledge intensive' Danish organizations.

USING THE RESOURCES OF HUMAN DIVERSITY

Human differences are a challenge to the academic community, and for the last fifty years researchers have struggled to develop theories and methods to conceptualize and study those differences (Williams & O'Reilly, 1998). While results have been far from reaching any consistent conclusion

(Simons, Pelled & Smith, 1999), the interest in diversity has increased rapidly during recent years (van Knippenberg, De Dreu & Homan, 2004). Three dominating theoretical perspectives are relevant to the understanding of communication processes in organizations that consist of culturally diverse groups.

The Information and Decision Making Perspective

The literature on information and decision-making has a traditional functionalist view on cultural diversity - most often limited to static notions of national cultural differences. In this perspective it is argued that the potential advantage of diverse groups over homogeneous groups lies in the greater pool of distinct task-relevant information to which diverse groups may have access (Hambrick, Cho & Chen, 1996; Harrison & Klein, 2007; Page, 2007). Homogeneity, according to these authors, has been mentioned as being in danger of leading to 'groupthink', in which everyone assumes that since they all believe the same thing, it must be a good idea (Adler, 1997; Miller et al., 2000; Triandis, Hall & Ewen, 1965). As opposed to homogeneity, cultural differences are thus assumed to lead to differences with regard to information and perspectives (McLeod & Lobe, 1992; Watson, Kumar & Michaelsen, 1993). This, according to this research tradition, implies that multicultural groups, if managed correctly, should be more resourceful compared to more homogeneous groups (Distefano et al., 2000). In other words, the different cultural perspectives are believed to foster innovation and creativity through constructive conflicts of perspectives, heuristics and knowledge (Fiedler, 1966; Millikin & Martins, 1996; Paulus, 2000; Richard & Shelor, 2002; Simons et al., 1999).

While such ideas on information and decision-making are intriguing, diverse groups in organizations, regrettably, often fail to realize the potential (Stewart, 2006). According to Klein and Harrison

(2007), the weakness of the theory is related to the fact that the organizational reality of interpersonal and group processes is much more 'messy' than often accounted for in the literature (e.g. Page, 2007). In other words, social barriers may hinder the interaction processes.

The Social Categorization Perspective

Another theoretical perspective relevant to understanding communication in diverse organizations is more concerned with social categorization as a barrier that impedes cooperation and knowledge sharing in diverse groups (Tajfel, 1982; Tajfel & Turner, 1979; Williams et al., 1998). In this line of research, the difference of knowledge or perspective is not always enough to improve decision-making (Homan et al., In print; van Knippenberg et al., 2004). The distinct group member must also be able to win the approval of others with the new solution (Klein et al., 2007). It is argued that individuals tend to communicate mostly with those who are most similar to them (Zenger & Lawrence, 1989). Accordingly, Mor-Barak, Cherin, and Bergman (1998) maintain that dissimilarities are likely to be negatively related to group involvement because distinct individuals are in danger of being excluded from relevant information networks. In this way diversity can disturb communication processes, because the emergence of subgroups may hinder the use of available information (van Knippenberg et al., 2004).

In the literature of social categorization, the negative effects of diversity have often been explained as psychological processes of interpersonal attraction (Webber & Donahue, 2001). The similarity-attraction hypothesis asserts that similarity in attitudes is a major source of attraction between individuals (Byrne, Clore & Worchel, 1966). Consequences of high interpersonal attraction may include frequent communication, high social integration, and a desire to maintain group

affiliation (Tsui, Egan, & O'Reilly, 1992).

While the socio-psychological approach to diversity does include the 'messy' reality of group processes, there is a tendency to explain those aspects of diversity only by the psychological needs of the individual. By focusing heavily on the role of the individual in the group, the literature avoids looking into the continuous struggle to obtain resources and recognition among different groups (Bourdieu, 2004; Konrad, 2003; Liff, 1996; Struch & Schwartz, 1989). Consequently, the socio-psychological explanation for the lack of communication is limited to the extent that it does not adequately include inherent power relations between different groups.

The Inequality and Power Perspective

Most of the literature on inequality and power relations in diverse organizations takes a political stance against liberal notions of the management of diversity, as a neutral improvement of information processing and decision-making (e.g. Essed, 1996; Kelly & Dobbin, 1998; Liff & Wajcman, 1996). Litvin (2002) argues that these diversity management initiatives should be perceived as an 'iron cage' that prevents real changes in the power distribution within diverse organizations. Similarly, Foldy (2003) argues that diversity initiatives often ignore the identity formation among employees, thus assuming that useful individual knowledge and perspectives can be applied without interference from group domination. In a recent publication by Squires (2008) it is argued that diversity management which encourages employers to recognize cultural differences between employees may de-politicize social relations and contain equality objectives within a utilitarian market model. This, according to Squires, may bring only short-term benefits for some minority groups and entrench cultural stereotypes in the process by assuming, for instance, that nationality or ethnicity can be directly associated with certain characteristics. Authors working with organizational inequalities and power relations are concerned that the mainstream literature on diversity issues does little to give voice to or promote the problems of relatively powerless identity groups. They mainly conclude that differential rewards given to various groups form the material bases for group conflicts – which might prevent communication.

However, none of these studies are based on empirical evidence. Accordingly, this exploratory study provides an empirically based discussion of social obstacles to communication in culturally diverse organizations.

RESEARCH DESIGN

In Denmark, managing cultural diversity has become popular, especially after the arrival of a large number of immigrants and refugees during the 1990s (Hagedorn-Rasmussen & Kamp, 2003). These people now account for approximately seven percent of the Danish population. However, for the most part they have not been integrated into the knowledge intensive part of the labor market (e.g. Hedetoft, 2003; Hervik, 1999). As such, Denmark is still trying to create social and cultural sustainability for this group, and even though most of the immigrants and refugees living in Denmark are not integrated in knowledge intensive jobs, the rhetoric on the benefits of diversity management has been very positive, stating that *"the differences between people are an overlooked goldmine in Danish companies"* (Jacobs, Lûtzen & Plum, 2001: 5) (authors' translation). While the statements concerning the use of human resources through diversity management can be found in all types of organizations, large and small, public and private, the actual practices of using diversity constructively are more or less reserved to companies that employ foreign experts or expatriates from subsidiaries, as well as other individuals

with non-Danish backgrounds who are living in Denmark for other reasons.

This chapter is based on data generated in a qualitative study of 14 Danish multicultural companies. The selection of the companies was based on the percentage of employees with a national background other than Danish, and they represent some of the most culturally diverse organizations in Denmark (e.g. Lauring, 2005). The chosen organizations were all internationally knowledge intensive, aiming to achieve an innovative and creative environment by the use of diversity management. All organizations used English as their corporate language.

The study has set out to provide an overall picture of expressed discourses on communication issues in culturally diverse Danish companies, and so, rather than an in-depth study of one or two specific sites, a broad range of organizations have been chosen. This enables the researcher to develop a taxonomy of the challenges faced by managers in the chosen organizations, which adds to the understanding of intercultural communication as a social practice. The limitation is that even though the researcher will gain a broad picture of the informant's conception of intercultural communication, in practice the actual interaction will only be observed to a limited extent.

The data for this study was generated through semi-structured research interviews. In cooperation with organizational gatekeepers, key informants were identified on the basis of their experience with cultural diversity (Bernard, 1995). Out of a total of 82 interviews with managers and employees, 43 of the informants were Danish, while 39 represented other nationalities. Most non-Danish informants were living in Denmark on a more or less permanent basis. However, only five of them came from countries from which Denmark traditionally accepts refugees or immigrants. About 60 percent of the informants had managerial responsibilities. The interviews were performed in Danish as well as in English. With a single exception, all English interviews were conducted with non-native speakers. The native languages of these informants were Polish, Russian, Rumanian, Italian, Dutch, French, Mandarin, Hindi, and Arabic.

The interviews took the form of a dialogue between the researcher and the informants, in which questions were asked about the effects of cultural diversity on communication and knowledge sharing (see preliminary interview guide[1]). This way the main themes of the investigation were not selected before entering the setting. They slowly developed through the process of interacting with the informants. That also meant that the interview guide changed during the extent of the project. Some questions were added and others deleted (Alvesson, 2003; Fontana & Frey, 1994). At first, communication and language use were only two of a number of themes to be investigated. However, after a while it became apparent that especially language in one way or another seemed to be related to all other intercultural issues put forward by the informants. Initially, language use emerged from the data as a means to boundary creation. But in subsequent analyses and interviews, continuously the social fragmentation became more apparent. The study of ICT was not a part of the original research design. Nonetheless, ICT seemed to be important in the informants' conception of communication processes as they unfolded in the organization. In this way, the research project applied an iterative approach by processing incoming information in a circular fashion, allowing for the continuous integration of new questions in the interview guide (Kvale, 1996; Spradley, 1980). In this case, the perception of language used as the dominant obstacle to intercultural interaction and the role of ICT could not have been predicted from reviewing the literature on the subject of managing cultural diversity.

RESULTS

This section deals with communication issues linked to the social practices of the multicultural and multilingual organizations. Two kinds of social barriers can be described as formed by 1) boundary creation and 2) social fragmentation. Finally the use of ICT is related to the social practice of communication within the companies.

Boundary Creation

To most informants, the formation of social groups based on the national affiliation of the members constituted a central issue in the organizations. However, the introduction of an international environment and a common corporate language was, in all cases, implemented to counter the problems of communication between the different individuals and groups creating innovative knowledge sharing. Yet, sometimes the common language was not used consistently. As outlined by a French Canadian employee:

I was in a meeting and we were some English, some Canadians, and Swedes, and Danes, and within half an hour the Danes were speaking Danish and the Swedes were speaking Swedish. And after some time I said – I am leaving! And finally people started speaking English. After that, I actually found out that no one had actually understood each other before. The people from Aarhus didn't understand what the Swedes were saying and we didn't understand much of the Danish at all (Employee, North America).

Altogether, foreign informants frequently accused Danes of exercising exclusive behavior because of their tendency to stay together in a Danish-speaking group and thereby isolate members of other groups:

People get together and speak Danish. If you do not, then you will not be invited. You will not be put in the active discussion. It is the social things that are the problem. It is very hard to become part of it. If you start a conversation in English, people cut you short. (Employee, Southern Europe).

This kind of boundary creation is particularly important in relation to the employees' social integration into the workplace, because employees with limited Danish language skills find themselves unable to participate in social events.

I don't think the technical side is a big problem. But if you don't know the language, you get put in a box. Some of my colleagues are put in a box. If I say no to learning or speaking Danish, the effect would be that I would be isolated. (Employee, Northern Europe).

Exclusion from informal settings is an important problem felt by non-Danish informants. They might find themselves shut out from social interaction when it is carried out in Danish. This may prove damaging to the use of their resources. Sometimes informal gatherings can be important contributions to the innovative capacity, because different viewpoints are shared in an unconventional fashion. A Polish informant describes the situation as follows:

The small talk is always in Danish. And sometimes the small talk gives a lot of information. It gives you an idea of what is really happening. It is something I really miss, to be able to really feel part of the conversation. I don't think my knowledge is used properly because I don't know the small talk (Employee, Eastern Europe).

A Canadian employee describes a similar experience, underlining how a lack of Danish language skills might unintentionally isolate foreign employees from social exchanges with colleagues. Returning one afternoon from an informal gathering, a group of colleagues confronted her to ask why she had not joined them for a beer, and

she replied that she had not been invited. '*They said, but we were standing here speaking loudly and clearly about going... but it might not have been the right language*'. She concludes from this that non-Danish speakers risk developing weaker social ties to co-workers, thus limiting their involvement in knowledge sharing:

It is not just personal stuff you miss out on, but business relations too. If something is going on, if nobody directly tells you, you are not going to know. I would say yes, you could work here without speaking any Danish. You can do your job. But all the learning and what is going on around you, you would miss (Employee, North America).

As could be registered from interviews, more or less consciously, the dominating speech community limits the possibility of communication and, subsequently, acting and relating as well. Nonetheless, the Danish community may not be aware of the effect of their communicative practice. Often Danish organizations are represented as being much more tolerant and international than they actually are. This can sometimes lead to the disillusion of non-Danish organizational members:

When I came here I was so disappointed. We always heard talk about the Nordic countries and the expectations were very high. Like this company. I thought it was more international when I first came here. I asked them before – do I have to speak Danish and they said no, no, we are an international company and we speak English. But they cannot say that it is an international company and that English is the company language. It is just a Danish company with a lot of foreigners (Employee, Southern Europe).

Exclusion from the sharing of ideas due to language differences could be found in many places. Thus, the creation of social boundaries linked to categories that are strengthened by language can be identified as an important obstacle to the use of human resources in culturally diverse organizations. Furthermore, the lack of social commitment noted by several informants points to a second obstacle that impedes the constructive use of cultural diversity. This will be explored further below.

Social Fragmentation

As indicated by some studies, the lack of social coherence can sometimes be the undesired result of cultural diversity (Bassett-Jones, 2005). This may be the effect of individuals who feel more comfortable when associating with others who are similar to themselves, sharing the same beliefs, values, language, and other traits (Miller et al., 2000). Communication in culturally diverse organizations is, then, different from communication among national peers. As one of the Danish managers tells the researcher: '*Communication has to be much more clear than if we were all Danes. We now have to formulate the orders in more plain and precise words*'. In this way, daily communication in a second language has an influence on interaction. As one of the Danish informants mentioned '*then one keeps to oneself the little remarks that would otherwise be more natural - for good or bad*''. In many cases, this resulted in less dialogue and more focus on getting the job done. As outlined by a Danish Manager:

Because of the diversity, you focus more on the professional. You don't think about from where people come, but only whether they contribute their best no matter how they feel among themselves. You don't focus on people's mindset but on the result. Whether people get on socially or not is unimportant. In that respect, only being together with Danes probably gives you more strings to play (Manager, Denmark).

Another Danish informant describes the situation of a company that has done well in establish-

ing an internationalized environment by mainly using English for everyday communication. This manager has the impression that even though communication is conducted in English, it still results in the disappearance of some interaction:

There are a number of Danes who have actually left the organization because they find it is no longer the same place to work. There is no longer the same consensus. The culture has been shaken. I don't know if this is because of the market or because the company has grown or because of the foreigners. It may have something to do with the joking and the way we communicate (Manager, Denmark).

Other informants observe how foreigners conduct their everyday tasks without any knowledge of the Danish language and thus miss out on '*all the social stuff and all the small-talk across the lunch table*' (Employee, Northern Europe). Non-native employees often characterize their conversations as less detailed or 'deep', which may be due to the disappearance of humor from communication. As a result, communication becomes more formal and task-oriented. However, as a Canadian employee describes it, this does not necessarily improve communication:

One problem, though, is that if people tell you something, you often get a too neat version. You can't really function in this country without speaking and reading some Danish. We had a colleague from Canada who spoke only English, and I could hear that when people talked to her, it always came out in a too neat version (Employee, North America).

The formalization of communication endangers the social coherence and integration of the organization. As one Danish manager observed: '*Much of the informal interaction derives from a strong organizational culture that is valuable to us*'. When speaking to other nationalities, employees find that it becomes more difficult to uphold the same level of communication.

It is most often easier with only Danes. The meetings become more formal when conducted in English rather than Danish. There is less ping-pong across the table - less informal talking. That is a bit negative. It can be good to have the informal talk because it strengthens the group socially (Manager, Denmark).

The introduction of an international environment with a common language might prevent the kind of social categorization described in the previous section. In addition, according to the results of this study, communication tends to be more explicit, thus facilitating the integration of non-native employees in the working routines. Nonetheless, the internationalized environment does not solve all communication problems.

In this exploratory research project, two main obstacles to the use of human resources have been identified. On the one hand, cultural and social boundaries are created, which prevent communication between employees that are categorized as belonging to different groups. On the other hand, a social fragmentation may result in less effective communication with employees abstaining from informal interaction when speaking a second language. These obstacles to communication may have a vital impact on the possibility of using differences in human resources constructively. Furthermore, as will be elaborated in the following, the boundary creation and the social fragmentation that characterized the face-to-face contact of the informants was reinforced through the use of ICT in the companies.

ICT and the Construction of Group Boundaries and Social Fragmentation

As Welch et al. (2001) and Feely and Harzing (2003) propose, it could seem that ICT can minimize the impact of cultural barriers in the international business community, especially due to English as *lingua franca*. Many researchers closely link ICT to the rise of a knowledge-based economy and globalization (Roberts, 2000). As such, ICT has enabled data and information to cross great distances, thereby effecting a movement from organizations physically contained single-sited units to multi-sited global networks (Hängst & Sol 2001). This has made researchers argue that ICT, due to stronger cross-national coordination and communication, enhances homogenization (Gabberty & Thomas 2006). Even though this might be the case on an inter-organizational and global level, our research suggests that ICT may have social consequences also on the local organizational level. In this way ICT could enhance the creation of boundaries and social fragmentation in everyday face-to-face communication of the work force.

This, we believe, has to do with the double-sidedness of the globalization process, in which we include ICT. As it has long been promoted by social scientists, the expansion of the capitalist mode of production whereby all economies have been included in the global economy, has led to a homogenization in goods and services. Nonetheless, this process has also led to fragmentation and national boundary creation on the group and individual level (Friedman 1994). That is, what is taken as signs of globalization, such as ICT, is used strategically on the local level as a counter reaction to uphold identity markers such as nationality. In this study what we found was that ICT seemed to be used as a 'social tool' for creating these group boundaries and social fragmentation.

The companies in this research were all heavily dependent on the use of ICT in the everyday communication of the employees. Especially email seemed to have substituted a great part of what would formerly have been face-to-face interaction. As such, it was more common to send a joke via mail than to tell it face to face. Furthermore, some of the employees only referred to each other by their initials or 'user-names', and not by their real names:

Nobody has a name here, only initials [...] sometimes I feel not insulted but uneasy. It is a different style from what I am used to (Employee, Eastern Europe).

Our observations indicate that communication through the use of ICT did not remove existing barriers of communication. Rather, ICT - in this case the use of initials in face-to-face communication - was used strategically to uphold existing group boundaries, excluding the non-native Danes from participating in social interaction, and including the Danes. This way ICT further contributed to the creation of social boundaries in the multicultural companies. In addition, it is interesting to note how ICT affected the face-to-face interaction of the employees. The employment of 'user names' in everyday interaction created a feeling of uneasiness among certain non-Danish employees, which affected their willingness to participate and contribute to personal and professional discussions. As such, the strategic use of ICT by native Danes hindered the flow of information and communication between the culturally diverse groups within the workplace. When asked whether this was a deliberate strategy used to exclude non-Danes from the social group, an informant replied:

I have heard that some of them don't like it, but I really don't think about it. I just do it because I have gotten use to it and it's easier (Employee, Northern Europe).

As such, the study did not indicate that it was a deliberate and conscious strategy from the Danes; however, it seemed that this group was not willing to change their behavior in order to address the resentment experienced by the non-Danes.

In consequence, the national boundaries were upheld through an unwillingness to change behavior. Whether this led to an overall increase or decrease in communication, through the use of ICT and face-to-face communication, is not within the scope of this project to determine. Rather it should be noted that these perceptions of communication outline group boundaries in which the employees either feel included or excluded, and that these perceptions have an impact on workplace behavior.

ICT seemed also to create an environment in which there was less space to create personal relations and networks. As argued, this form of social fragmentation is especially problematic in knowledge intensive industries, since 'ping–ponging' seems crucial in the development of new ideas. The use of email and phone in the workplace seemed to create a certain perception of what was considered effective working time;

Even if you sit next to someone, you would send them an email. I even do it myself (Employee, Denmark.)

The employees would rather use their computer as the primary tool for communication, especially because sitting at the desk signalized that they were working, and they therefore seemed more effective. One could argue that the use of ICT created a work environment and a form of communication that was more fragmented and individualistic than would otherwise be the case. Such a perception of work might be suitable for traditional industrial firms, but it is less suitable for knowledge intensive corporations in which innovation is a hallmark for survival in a globalized economy. One of the problems with communicating through ICT has to do with knowledge transfer. Robert (2000) agues that communication through ICT favors knowledge, which can be codified and reduced to data. Tacit knowledge, which is crucial in creating an innovative workplace, might be problematic. Especially where face-to-face interaction is actually possible, since the employees are physically located together.

We found that even though ICT is crucial in multicultural firms, there may also be some problematic consequences. It can be used to uphold existing linguistic and national barriers, thereby reducing communication between these groups. Furthermore, it might individualize the workplace, thus reducing the transfer of tacit knowledge that is crucial to more knowledge intensive industries. In other words, ICT seems to enhance certain elements of social behavior as exercised in multicultural firms.

DISCUSSION

Cultural diversity has often been described as providing an important constructive potential to firms. This potential, however, cannot be activated without the mutual interaction of the different groups and individuals in the organizations. Accordingly, communication across cultural boundaries becomes one of the basic preconditions for the development of a resourceful environment. Unfortunately, communication in multicultural firms is often a complicated matter.

To handle daily collaboration, diverse groups need to have a good flow of communication. When describing obstacles to communication in multinational teams, most studies refer only to differences in language and national culture as leading to misunderstandings and group conflict (e.g. Beamer et al., 2005; Hambrick et al., 1998). However, in this study we suggest that communication practices may be a more complex matter than some studies of culture diversity and communication have indicated. We have argued that certain social elements in communicative behavior have great effect on the use of differences in human resources. And in addition to that, we argue that ICT can enhance some of the observed problems.

This research project has outlined how the perceptions of communication can affect two social processes, which, on the one hand, may create boundary formation, and, on the other hand, social fragmentation. Furthermore, ICT

may not solve these problems, but can instead be used as a social 'tool' that reinforces the dominant social categorization and fragmentation within the company, thereby upholding existing structures of social difference.

Three different theoretical perspectives have been mentioned to contribute to the understanding of communication in multicultural firms.

Firstly, the literature applying the information and decision-making perspective puts emphasis on the variety of differences in bodies of knowledge (Distefano & Maznevski, 2000; Page, 2007). However, as our case showed, information does not always flow undisturbed in organizations. Human resources may be embedded in particular social communities. Brown and Duguid (2000) argue that communities of practice enable people to communicate the more implicit elements of knowledge on how to act successfully in the organization. This implies that the membership of these communities can be essential to communication. The notion of communities of practice could provide further inspiration for researchers dealing with communication in multicultural firms from an information and decision-making perspective. This perspective is also highly relevant to understand the social use of ICT that allows communities to span physical settings.

Secondly, researchers operating in the social categorization paradigm put emphasis on boundaries between groups created along lines of similarity attraction. The argument is that similar individuals interact more with each other than with non-similar organization members (Tsui, Egan, & O'Reilly, 1992). However, the case material shows that focus should not only be put on group boundaries, but also on the socially fragmented internationalized environment where individuals have less in common and speak different natural languages. Turner (1987) argues that if the group membership is unsatisfactory, members will attempt to leave that group. And if that is not physically possible, individuals may engage in other forms of reduced attachment, such as psychologically withdrawing from the community. Such reduced group attachments are difficult to detect if much of the communication takes place by use of ICT. Social fragmentation should therefore be of particular concern for researchers and practitioners working with communication and ICT in multicultural firms.

Thirdly, the literature focusing of inequality and power relations stresses the importance of recognizing that some identity groups tend to dominate others. In our case it was obvious that the Danes were in a dominant position. This also affected communication when applying ICT. Here the dominating Danish styles seemed to exclude members of other nationals groups.

The argument of this chapter is that perceptions of communication and language use is intertwined with other social practices, and that cultural and linguistic diversity increases the complexity of interaction. The results of these processes are difficult to predict, and when ICT is added it becomes even more complicated. Consequently, managing communication in diverse environments by use of ICT should depart from a locally grounded notion of interaction patterns.

While practical implications for multicultural organizations wanting to improve the utilization of diverse human resources by means of improving communication may be somewhat premature due to the exploratory character of the study, some initial guideline can be provided.

To encourage communication in multinational organizations, managers not only need to reward measurable individual performance, they also need to expand the concept of performance to include contributions toward strengthening the collective human resources of the organization. One way of promoting communication is for management to make official the contribution to collective knowledge as dispersed by ICT or other means. Thereby, individuals will start to see communication as valuable and as a valued contribution to the organization's productivity. This has to be backed by unequivocal messages from the management regarding the value of interaction and teamwork. Furthermore, ICT can be used positively if it is not only seen as a simplified solution to the communication issues that are dominant in multi-cultural companies. While the use of ICT provides a different platform for communication compared to face-to-face interaction, this form is not detached from social processes. And some uses of ICT may create problems that can affect the social environment and subsequently the constructive use of differences in human resources. Hence, managers should make a clear statement about which forms of communication are suitable for ICT, and which should be handled on a face-to-face basis.

REFERENCES

Adler, N. J. (1997). *International dimensions of organizational behavior*. Cincinnati: South Western Publishing.

Alvesson, M. (2003). Beyond neopositivists, romantics, and localists: A reflexive approach to interviews in organizational research. *Academy of Management Review, 28*(1), 13–33.

Austin, J. L. (1975). *How to do things with words*. Oxford, UK: Oxford University Press.

Barth, F. (1971). *Ethnic Groups and Boundaries: The Social Organization of Cultural Difference*. Bergen: Universitetsforlaget.

Bassett-Jones, N. (2005). The paradox of diversity management, creativity and innovation. *Creativity and Innovation Management, 14*(2), 169–176. doi:10.1111/j.1467-8691.00337.x

Beamer, L. (1998). Bridging Business Cultures. *The China Business Review, 25*(3), 54–58.

Beamer, L., & Varner, I. (2001). *Intercultural Communication in the Global Workplace*. New York: McGraw-Hill Irvin.

Beamer, L., & Varner, I. (2005). *Intercultural Communication in the Global Workplace*. New York: McGraw-Hill/Irwin.

Bernard, R. H. (1995). *Research Methods in Anthropology: Qualitative and Quantitative Approaches*. Thousand Oaks, CA: Sage.

Bonache, J., & Brewster, C. (2001). Knowledge Transfer and the Management of Expatriation. *Thunderbird International Business Review*, *43*(1), 3–20. doi:10.1002/1520-6874(200101/02)43:1<3::AID-TIE2>3.0.CO;2-4

Bourdieu, P. (1977). *Outline of a Theory of Practice*. Cambridge, MA: Cambridge University Press.

Bourdieu, P. (1991). *Language and symbolic power*. Cambridge, UK: Polity Press.

Bourdieu, P. (2004). *Distinction: A Social Critique of the Judgment of Taste*. London: Routledge.

Byrne, D. E., Clore, G. L. J., & Worchel, P. (1966). The effect of economic similarity-dissimilarity as determinants of attraction. *Journal of Personality and Social Psychology Quarterly*, *4*, 220–224. doi:10.1037/h0023559

Cheney, G., Thøger, L. C., Zorn, T. E. J., & Ganesh, S. (2004). *Organizational Communication in an Age of Globalization*. Long Grove, IL: Waveland Press.

Cooren, F. (2006). The organizational world as a plenum of agencies. In F. Cooren, J. R. Taylor, & E. J. Van *Communication as Organizing*. (pp. 81-101). London: LEA.

Cronin, M. A., & Weingart, L. R. (2007). Representational gabs, information processing, and conflict in functionally diverse teams. *Academy of Management Review*, *32*(3).

Dhir, K. S., & Góké-Paríolá, A. (2002). The case for language policies in multinational corporations. *Corporate Communications: An International Journal*, *7*(4), 241–251. doi:10.1108/13563280210449822

Distefano, J. J., & Maznevski, M. L. (2000). Creating value with diverse teams in global management. *Organizational Dynamics*, *29*(1), 45–63. doi:10.1016/S0090-2616(00)00012-7

Essed, P. (1996). *Diversity, Color, and Culture*. Amherst: University of Massachusetts Press.

Feely, A. J., & Harzing, A.-W. (2003). Language management in multinational companies. *International Journal of Cross Cultural Management*, *10*(2), 37–53. doi:10.1108/13527600310797586

Fiedler, F. E. (1966). The effect of leadership and cultural heterogeneity on group performance: A test of the contingency model. *Journal of Experimental Social Psychology*, *2*, 237–264. doi:10.1016/0022-1031(66)90082-5

Foldy, E. G. (2003). Managing diversity: Power and identity in organizations. In I. Aaltio, & A. Mills (Eds.), *Gender, Identity and the Culture of Organizations*, (pp. 92-112). London: Routledge.

Fontana, A., & Frey, J. H. (1994). Interviewing: The art of the science. In N. Denzin, & Y. Lincoln (Eds.), *Handbook of qualitative research*, (pp. 361-376). London: Sage.

Friedman, J. 1994. *Cultural Identity and Global Process*. London: Sage Publications.

Gabberty, J. W., & Thomas, J. D. E. (2006). Modeling Creativity For The Multinational Firm. *International Business & Economics Research Journal*, *5*, 73–76.

Goodall, K., & Roberts, J. (2003). Only connect: teamwork in the multinational. *Journal of World Business*, *38*, 150–164. doi:10.1016/S1090-9516(03)00008-7

Griffith, D., A. (2002). The role of communication competencies in international business relationship development. *Journal of World Business, 37*, 256–265. doi:10.1016/S1090-9516(02)00092-5

Hagedorn-Rasmussen, P., & Kamp, A. (2003). *Mangfoldighedsledelse: mellem vision og ledelse.* København, Denmark: Socialforskningsinstituttet.

Hambrick, D. C., Cho, T. S., & Chen, C. C. (1996). The influence of top management team heterogeneity on firms' competitive moves. *Administrative Science Quarterly, 41*, 659–684. doi:10.2307/2393871

Hambrick, D. C., Davison, S. C., Snell, S. A., & Snow, C. C. (1998). When Groups Consist of Multiple Nationalities. *Organization Studies, 19*(2), 181–206. doi:10.1177/017084069801900202

Hängst, M., & Sol, H. G. (2001). The Impact of Information and Communication Technology on Interorganizational Level. *International Conference on System Sciences, Hawaii, 2001.*

Harrison, D. A., & Klein, K. J. (2007). What's the difference? Diversity constructs as separation, variety, or disparity in organizations. *Academy of Management Review, 32*(4).

Hedetoft, U. (2003). *The Global Turn - National encounters with the World.* Aalborg, Denmark: Aalborg University Press.

Henderson, J. K. (2005). Language diversity in international management teams. *International Studies of Management and Organization, 35*(1), 66–82.

Hervik, P. (1999). Forskellighedens logik: Fremstillingen, forestillingen og forskningen. In P. Hervik (Ed.), *Den generelle forskellighed: Danske svar på den stigende multikulturalisme,* (pp. 15-50). København, Denmark: Hans Reitzels Forlag.

Homan, A. C., Hollenbeck, J. R., Humphrey, S. E., van Knippenberg, D., Ilgen, D. R., & Van Kleef, G. A. (In print). Facing differences with an open mind: Openness to experience, salience of intra-group differences, and performance of diverse work groups. *Academy of Management Journal.*

Jacobs, B., Lûtzen, D. C., & Plum, E. (2001). *Mangfoldighed som virksomhedsstrategi - På vej mod den inkluderende organisation.* København, Denmark: Nordisk Forlag.

Janssens, M., Lambert, J., & Steyaert, C. (2004). Developing language strategies for international companies: The contribution of translation studies. *Journal of World Business, 39*, 414–430. doi:10.1016/j.jwb.2004.08.006

Jenkins, R. (1997). *Rethinking Ethnicity - Arguments and Explorations.* London: Sage Publications.

Kelly, E., & Dobbin, F. (1998). How Affirmative Action Became Diversity Management - Employer Response to Antidiscrimination Law, 1961 to 1996. *The American Behavioral Scientist, 41*(7), 960–984. doi:10.1177/0002764298041007008

Kim, Y. Y. (2005). Inquiry in intercultural and development communication. *The Journal of Communication,* (September): 554–577. doi:10.1111/j.1460-2466.2005.tb02685.x

Klein, K. J., & Harrison, D. A. (2007). On the Diversity of Diversity: Tidy Logic, Messier Realities. *Academy of Management Review, 32*(4), 26–34.

Konrad, A. M. (2003). Defining the domain of workplace diversity scholarship. *Group & Organization Management, 28*, 4–16. doi:10.1177/1059601102250013

Kvale, S. (1996). *Interviews - An Introduction to Qualitative Research Interviewing.* Thousand Oaks, CA: Sage.

Lagerström, K., & Andersson, M. (2003). Creating and sharing knowledge within a transnational team: The development of a global business system. *Journal of World Business, 38*, 84–95. doi:10.1016/S1090-9516(03)00003-8

Lauring, J. (2005). *Når organisationen bliver mangfoldig - om vidensdeling og interaktion i etnisk mangfoldige organisationer*. Århus, Denmark: Handelshøjskolen i Århus.

Lauring, J., & Ross, C. (2004). Cultural Diversity and Organisational Effiency. *New Zealand Journal of Employment Relations, 29*(1), 89–103.

Leonard, D., & Swap, W. (1999). *When Sparks Fly: Igniting Creativity in Groups*. Cambridge, MA: Harvard Business School Press.

Liff, S. (1996). Two routes to managing diversity: individual differences or social group characteristics. *Employee Relations, 19*(1), 11–26. doi:10.1108/01425459710163552

Liff, S., & Wajcman, J. (1996). 'Sameness' and 'Difference' revisited: Which Way Forward for Equal Opportunity Initiatives? *Journal of Management Studies, 33*(1), 79–94. doi:10.1111/j.1467-6486.1996.tb00799.x

Litvin, D. R. (2002). The business case for diversity and the iron cage. In B. Czarniawka, & H. Hopfl (Eds.), *Casting the Other: The Production and Maintenance of Inequalities in Work Organizations,* (pp. 20-39). London: Routledge.

Loosemore, M., & Lee, P. (2002). Communication problems with ethnic minorities in the construction industry. *International Journal of Project Management, 20*, 517–524. doi:10.1016/S0263-7863(01)00055-2

Marschan-Piekkari, R., Welch, D., & Welch, L. (1999a). In the shadow: the impact of language on structure, power and communication in the multinational. *International Business Review, 8*, 421–440. doi:10.1016/S0969-5931(99)00015-3

Marschan-Piekkari, R., Welch, D. E., & Welch, L. S. (1999b). Adopting a common corporate language: IHRM implications. *International Journal of Human Resource Management, 10*(3), 377–390. doi:10.1080/095851999340387

Maznevski, M. L. (1994). Understanding our differences: Performance in decision-making groups with diverse members. *Human Relations, 47*(5), 531–553. doi:10.1177/001872679404700504

Maznevski, M. L., & Chudoba, K. M. (2000). Bridging Space over Time: Global Virtual Team Dynamics and Effectiveness. *Organization Science, 11*(5), 473–492. doi:10.1287/orsc.11.5.473.15200

McDonough, E. F., Kahn, K. B., & Barczak, G. (2001). An investigation of the use of global, virtual, and colocated new product development teams. *Journal of Product Innovation Management, 18*(2), 110–121. doi:10.1016/S0737-6782(00)00073-4

McLeod, P. L., & Lobe, S. A. (1992). The effects of ethnic diversity on idea generation in small groups. *Academy of Management Executive, Best Papers Proceedings*, (pp. 227-231).

Miller, M., Fields, R., Kumar, A., & Ortiz, R. (2000). Leadership and organizational vision in managing a multiethnic and multicultural project team. *Journal of Management Engineering, 16*(6), 18–23. doi:10.1061/(ASCE)0742-597X(2000)16:6(18)

Millikin, F. J., & Martins, L. L. (1996). Searching for common threads: Understanding the multiple effects of diversity in organizational groups. *Academy of Management Review, 21*(2), 402–433. doi:10.2307/258667

Mor-Barak, M. E., Cherin, D. A., & Berkman, S. (1998). Organizational and personal dimensions in diversity climate. *The Journal of Applied Behavioral Science, 43*(1), 82–104. doi:10.1177/0021886398341006

Page, S. E. (2007). Making the difference: Applying a logic of diversity. *The Academy of Management Perspectives, 21*(4), 6–21.

Palmer-Silveira, J. C., Ruiz-Garrido, M. F., & Fortanet-Gómes, I. (2006). Facing the future of intercultural and international business communication. In J. C. Palmer-Silveira, M. F. Ruiz-Garrido, & I. Fortanet-Gómes, (Ed.), *Intercultural and International Business Communication.* Bern, Switzerland: Peter Lang.

Paulus, P. B. (2000). Groups, teams, and creativity: The creative potential of idea generating groups. *Applied Psychology: An International Review, 49*, 237–262. doi:10.1111/1464-0597.00013

Richard, O. C., & Shelor, M. (2002). Linking top management team heterogeneity to firm performance: Juxtaposing two midrange theories. *International Journal of Human Resource Management, 13*(6), 958–974. doi:10.1080/09585190210134309

Roberson, Q. M. (2006). Disentangling the meanings of diversity and inclusion in organizations. *Group & Organization Management, 31*, 212–236. doi:10.1177/1059601104273064

Roberts, J. (2000). From Know-how? Questioning the Role of Information and Communication Technologies in Knowledge Transfer. *Technology Analysis and Strategic Management, 12*(4), 429–429. doi:10.1080/713698499

Robichaud, D. (2006). Steps toward a relational view of agency. In F. Cooren, J. R. Taylor, & E. J. Van every (Eds.), *Communication as Organizing,* (pp. 101-115). London: LEA.

Robichaud, D. (2006). Steps toward a relational view of agency. in F. Cooren, J. R. Taylor, & E. J. Van every (ed.), *Communication as Organizing,* (pp. 101-115). London: LEA.

Roosens, E. E. (1989). *Creating ethnicity.* London: Sage.

Simons, T., Pelled, L. H., & Smith, K. A. (1999). Making use of difference: Diversity, debate, and decision comprehensiveness in top management teams. *Academy of Management Journal, 42*, 662–673. doi:10.2307/256987

Spradley, J. P. (1980). *Participant Observation.* New York: Holt Rinehart and Winston.

Squires, J. (2008). Intersecting Inequalities: Reflecting on the Subjects and Objects of Equality. *The Political Quarterly, 79*(1), 53–61. doi:10.1111/j.1467-923X.2008.00902.x

Stewart, G. L. (2006). A meta-analytic review of relationships between team design features and team performance. *Journal of Management, 32*, 29–54. doi:10.1177/0149206305277792

Struch, N., & Schwartz, S. H. (1989). Intergroup aggression: Its predictors and distinctness from in-group bias. *Journal of Personality and Social Psychology, 56*, 364–373. doi:10.1037/0022-3514.56.3.364

Tajfel, H. (1982). Social psychology of intergroup relations. *Annual Review of Psychology, 33*, 1–39. doi:10.1146/annurev.ps.33.020182.000245

Tajfel, H., & Turner, J. C. (1979). An integrative theory of intergroup conflict. In S. Worchel, & W. G. Austin (Eds.), *The social psychology of intergroup relations,* (pp. 33-47). Monterey, CA: Brooks/Cole Publ.

Taylor, F. (2006). Coorientation: a conceptual framework. In F. Cooren, J. R. Taylor, & E. J. Van Every (Eds.), *Communication as Organizing,* (pp. 141-157). London: LEA.

Thomas, D. A., & Ely, R. J. (1996). Making difference matter: A new paradigm for managing diversity. *Harvard Business Review,* (Sep-Oct): 79–90.

Triandis, N. C., Hall, E. R., & Ewen, R. B. (1965). Member homogeneity and dyadic creativity. *Human Relations*, *18*, 33–54. doi:10.1177/001872676501800104

Tsui, A., Egan, T., & O'Reilly, C. (1992). Being different: Relational Demography and Organizational Attachment. *Administrative Science Quarterly*, *37*, 549–579. doi:10.2307/2393472

Vaara, E., Risberg, A., Søderberg, A.-M., & Tienari, J. (2003a). Nation talk: The construction of national stereotypes in a merging multinational. In A. Søderberg & E. Vaara (ed.), *Merging across borders: People, cultures and politics*, (pp. 61-86).

Vaara, E., Tienari, J., Piekkari, R., & Säntti, R. (2005). Language and the circuits of power in a merging multinational corporation. *Journal of Management Studies*, *42*, 595–623. doi:10.1111/j.1467-6486.2005.00510.x

Vaara, E., Tienari, J., & Säntti, R. (2003b). The international match: Metaphors as vehicles of social identity-building in cross-border mergers. *Human Relations*, *56*, 419–451. doi:10.1177/0018726703056004002

van Knippenberg, D., De Dreu, C. K. W., & Homan, A. C. (2004). Work group diversity and group performance: An integrative model and research agenda. *The Journal of Applied Psychology*, *89*(6), 1008–1022. doi:10.1037/0021-9010.89.6.1008

Varey, R. J. (2006). Accounts in interactions: Implications of accounting practices for managing. In F. Cooren, J. R. Taylor, & E. J. Van every (Eds.), *Communication as Organizing*, (pp. 181-197).

Watson, W., Kumar, K., & Michaelsen, L. K. (1993). Cultural diversity's impact on interaction process and performance: Comparing homogeneous and diverse task groups. *Academy of Management Journal*, *36*, 560–602. doi:10.2307/256593

Webber, S. S., & Donahue, L. M. (2001). Impact of highly and less job-related diversity on work group cohesion and performance: A meta-analysis. *Journal of Management*, *27*, 141–162. doi:10.1016/S0149-2063(00)00093-3

Welch, D., Welch, L., & Marschan-Piekkari, R. (2001). The Persistent Impact of Language on Global Operations. *Prometheus*, *19*(3), 193–209. doi:10.1080/08109020110072180

Williams, K., & O'Reilly, C. A. (1998). Demography and diversity: A review of 40 years of research. In B. Staw, & R. Sutton (Eds.), *Research in organizational behavior*, (pp. 77-140). Greenwich, CT: JAI Press.

Wittgenstein, L. (1996). *Philosophical Investigations*. Oxford, UK: Basil Blackwell.

Zenger, T. R., & Lawrence, B. S. (1989). Organizational demography: The differential effects of age and tenure distributions on technical communication. *Academy of Management Journal*, *32*, 353–376. doi:10.2307/256366

¹SEMI-STRUCTURED INTERVIEW GUIDE, DIVERSITY MANAGEMENT IN DENMARK.

Subject	Time

1) Work background

Employed by	Years of employment

Position

2) Personal background — Prior cross-cultural experience

Language experience

3) What expectations did you have before entering the organisation?

4) What does cultural diversity mean to your everyday work assignments?

5) In which ways have you adapted to the situation?

6) Is there anything you would like to change?

7) What formal guideline does your organization have with regard to diversity?

8) Do other rules or guidelines affect the role of cultural diversity?

9) What effect does cultural diversity have on the social environment?

10) What characterizes a valuable employee?

11) In which ways are human differences employed in the organization?

12) What problems do human differences lead to in the organization?

13) How do human differences affect communication?

14) How do you feel when different languages are spoken in daily work situations/social situations?

Chapter 9
Communication in Global Development Projects:
Objectives, Mechanisms and Interpretations

Maria Adenfelt
Department of Business Studies, Uppsala University, Sweden

Katarina Lagerström
Department of Business Administration, School of Business, Economics and Law, University of Gothenburg, Sweden

ABSTRACT

Globalization trends make the task of revisiting the nature of the organization of global development projects (GDPs) within MNCs imperative. In this study, GDPs are viewed as contemporary ventures that seek scale economies in response to opportunities and threats posed by globalization trends. Our focus is to obtain a better understanding of how communication is managed and organized in GDPs. The study is of a GDP with the aim of developing a common global product to be used by all subsidiaries in an MNC, but with openings for local market adaptations. The empirical findings show that: (1) the management had two goals with the project, which were conveyed and understood differently depending on organizational level and organizational belonging, (2) the administrative heritage of the MNC influenced the use of information communication technology for sharing information and knowledge, and (3) the impact of frequency and structure of communication for information processing.

INTRODUCTION

Every era has a trend that captures popular imagination and, as the end of the second millennium drew to a close and the new one began, the overwhelming trend was globalization. It is suggested that the world is becoming a global village as the level of economic and social interdependencies among various countries is constantly increasing.

In this chapter, we refer to globalization as growing economic interdependencies among countries as reflected in increasing cross-border flows of three distinctive processes: goods and services, capital and knowledge (Govindarajan & Gupta, 2000). This implies that a multinational corporation's competitive position in one specific country is dependent

DOI: 10.4018/978-1-60566-822-2.ch009

on its competitive positions in other countries. Today, globalization has not only become increasingly feasible, but also more desirable, leading managers in multinational corporations (MNCs) to take actions for increased globalization by implementing different organizational tools and mechanisms for catering cross-border flows of knowledge in common product development agendas (Adenfelt & Lagerström, 2006; 2007; Atamer & Schweiger. 2003; Mazenevski & Chudoba, 2000; Snow, et al., 1996). In MNCs, global development projects (GDPs) are increasingly employed to develop global products for use in multiple markets around the globe. GDPs are viewed as contemporary ventures that seek scale economies in response to opportunities and threats posed by the globalization trends. This means that organizing in global development projects puts high demands on achieving efficient coordination and communication among the concerned members from different subsidiaries. Our main focus is to obtain a better understanding of how communication is managed and organized in GDPs for the development of global products.

Such an understanding is compelling for at least two reasons. First, globalization trends are, as mentioned, increasingly more critical for instilling a sense of urgency among MNC managers to take advantage of the knowledge potential among the dispersed subsidiaries in common development agendas (Foss & Pedersen, 2002; Mudambi, 2002). Second, management is under an increasing pressure to develop globally integrated products to achieve efficiency across geographically dispersed subsidiaries, by ensuring the use of the capabilities of all employees (Yamin & Otto, 2004). As such, we argue that the challenge for the MNC is not to obtain complete homogeneity across markets, but rather in finding a balance between local adaptations and global optimization (e.g. Bartlett and Ghoshal, 1989; Nohria & Ghoshal, 1997; Martinez and Jarillo, 1991). This often implies a need for management to formulate and implement coordinated processes across markets.

Such a strategy would require managing operations interdependently, exploiting scale economies, seeking coordination at the same time as giving leeway for local market adaptations (cf. Adenfelt & Lagerström, 2007; 2008). Studies have thus shown that this seemingly straightforward solution to establishing GDPs with members from dispersed subsidiaries working for a common global product solution is afflicted with a high level of complexity when it comes to organizing and managing these projects.

Consequently, we pursue two research objectives in this chapter. First, we delineate the dimensions of the GDPs in MNCs and link the discussions to how communication and coordination are means of global product development. Second, we use empirical data from a case study of a GDP in an MNC in the communication- and business intelligence industry to demonstrate the difficulties in organizing and managing a GDP for global product development, with the focus on coordination and communication within the GDP. In the following sections, we describe the theoretical framework and the relevant literature, as well as the research method followed by a presentation of the case and a discussion of the results.

THEORETICAL FRAMEWORK

In this section, we link what we have learnt about how the increased pressure of globalization on MNCs has lead to the development and implementation of different organizational mechanisms to take advantage of the dispersed subsidiaries' knowledge in global product development. Particular focus will be given to global development projects and the two elements: coordination and communication.

Multinational Corporations and Global Development Projects

Today, corporations throughout the world are challenged to not only be strategically competitive in their home market, or even in few distinct markets, but globally. Strategically competitive corporations have to learn to apply competitive insights gained locally on a global scale. But acting as if one solution fits all markets does not lead to any sustainable or viable development in the long run. Corporations that have successfully handled both the threats and opportunities, following the increased globalization, have realized that imposing homogenous solutions into a pluralistic world is not the solution to sustainable development. It is rather a question of nourishing both local and global knowledge development, encouraging cross-border flows of knowledge by establishing supporting organizational tools and mechanisms as well as realizing the need to allow for local market modifications when applying the knowledge in different countries. These new ways of organizing are often built on the notion of arranging events in broader cross-border structures with participants from the globally dispersed units in the MNC. They are used for various tasks and among the set of different organizational mechanisms, we have seen a constant increase in the use of global projects (Adenfelt & Lagerström 2006; Schweiger et al., 2003), and then not the least for global product development tasks. Global development projects (GDPs) are actually becoming one of the primary vehicles for coordinating joint efforts in global product development. Such projects have the potential of not only serving to accomplish the corporations' development agenda, but also as development forum for the participants. A study by Subramaniam and Venkatraman in 2001 concludes that the use of such development projects had a dramatic effect on the innovation capability of the entire organization.

A GDP is defined as a temporary, cross-border organizational mechanism composed of individuals of different nationalities, working in different units and functions, who are brought together for developing global products to meet demands in several markets (Gupta & Govindarajan 2001; Subramaniam & Venkatraman, 2001). Traditionally, headquarters appoint participants from different subsidiaries to take part in the project to ensure the use of specialized knowledge at the dispersed units. The knowledge of the participants can overlap or be complementary, thus giving rise to clearly recognized benefits of combining the knowledge of several subsidiaries (Zander, 1998). At the same time as GDPs offer the potentials of simultaneously tapping and combining the knowledge of several units, their performance is associated with problems due to the lack of shared knowledge among project participants (cf. Durnell Cramton, 2001; Hoopes & Postrel, 1990; Nelson & Cooprider, 1996) as well as problems arising from geographical distance, cultural differences, language and behavioral divergences among participants. All in all, these issues are destined to lead to difficulties in cooperation, coordination and communication. However, today there seems to be a common understanding that the advantages widely surpass the disadvantages of organizing global product development tasks in GDPs (e.g. Adenfelt & Lagerström, 2008; Atamer & Schweiger, 2003; Hambrick et al., 1998; Subramaniam & Venkatraman, 2001).

Coordination and Communication

Assuming that GDPs are good mechanisms for accomplishing global product development, successful coordination of activities across subsidiaries becomes an important organizational issue (Faraj & Sproull, 2000). While the GDP participants work together on the fundamental aspects of a common product, many activities are delegated to different sub-projects or even individual participants, based on existing knowledge and interests (Hoegl & Gemunden, 2001).

Coordination is usually a means of achieving an agreement of effort among different units within organizations (Lawrence & Lorsch, 1967, Martinez & Jarillo, 1991). GDPs typically use a variety of coordination mechanisms to manage temporal problems, such as scheduling, synchronization and allocation of resources (Montoya-Weiss, et al., 2001). Coordination usually concerns resolving resource and expertise dependencies (Ancona & Caldwell, 1992; Faraj & Sproull, 2000), since managing these dependencies is of significance for project performance (Hoegl & Weinkauf, 2005). While coordination occupies a great deal of the literature on project management, global product development requires a great deal more of the organization and the individuals involved, for example for solving a larger variety of problems and for ensuring that the components – often developed separately from each other – of the global product work properly together.

The linkage mechanism whereby participants of a GDP coordinate activities with one another is communication (e.g. Griffin & Hauser, 1992; Fulk & DeSanctis, 1995; Thompson, 1967). Communication is the process through which information flows (Mohr & Nevin, 1990; Mohr et al., 1996) and in a GDP, it needs to be handled despite geographical and cultural distances, differences in language as well as strategies, incentives and technical capabilities between members from MNC units (Bartlett & Ghoshal, 1989; Govindarajan & Gupta, 2001). Geographical distance reduces the amount of real time interactivity as well as opportunities for spontaneous intrateam communication (McDonough et al., 1999). Similarities in culture maximize communication efficiencies as the project participants are more familiar with each other's system of meaning and behavior (Gudykunst & Kim, 1997; Kim, 1991; Li, 1991). Variations in language skills and ways of communicating, often stemming from cultural and

professional differences, serve as other obstacles to communication (Chen, et al., 2006; Hambrick et al., 1998).

Research on cross-country communication has identified a variety of communication mechanisms such as information communication technologies (ICT), that is, e.g. e-mail, enterprise software applications, and company databases, face-to-face meetings, telephone and videoconferences (Jarvenpaa & Leidner, 1999; McDonough et al., 1999; McDonough & Kahn, 1996). Robb (2002) refers to e-mails and conference calls as first generation ICTs. Second generation ICTs are video tools, online tools and power point presentations whereas third generation technologies are web-enabled shared workspaces via the intranet and the Internet. Studies on the use of ICTs show that the use of advanced technologies is relatively uncommon in GDPs. First generation technologies such as e-mail seem to be the most common mechanism (Bell & Kozlowski, 2002; Gibson & Cohen, 2003).

Dimensions of the actual communication process are frequency, structure, and content (Gupta & Govindarajan, 1994; Hoegl & Gemuenden, 2001). Frequency refers to how often project participants communicate, whereas structure describes how informal versus formal communication within the GDP is. Informal communication is, for example, spontaneous e-mails or telephone calls. Formal communication requires a large amount of preparation or planning before it occurs, e.g. scheduled meetings and written reports. Content is simply what information and knowledge that flow and they can be of various degrees of richness, defined as the ability of information to change understanding within a time interval (Daft & Lengel, 1986).

Received theory suggests that organizations process information to reduce uncertainty and equivocality (cf. Galbraith, 1973; Weick, 1979). In a project setting, uncertainty reduction involves collecting information relevant to the GDP objective in order to attain an acceptable level of performance. Additional data is not the solution for reducing equivocality; it rather involves for the project participants to define and create a collective and common interpretation of information.

In response to the need to exchange information and knowledge within GDPs, the different communication mechanisms cater for the different dimensions of the communication process as the mechanisms vary in their capacity and degree to process rich information and manage uncertainty and equivocality. Face-to-face media, such as group meetings, facilitate equivocality reduction by making it possible for project participants to overcome different frames of reference and providing the capacity to process complex, subjective messages. Information that is well-understood and collective among project participants is, however, preferably shared using different types of documents since this is more efficient (Lengel & Daft, 1984). In GDPs, the most common communication mechanisms are ICTs and a common denominator for these is that they poorly handle information uncertainty and equivocality.

Summary

Globalization opens up for new possible ways in which to compete. Much has been written and a great deal of research has been done on the need for MNCs to meet the trends of globalization, but less is known about how global strategies are implemented and the obstacles related thereto. Global product development and launch are commonly organized in GDPs, which, in themselves, both serve as means for developing a global product but also to establish a global mindset. Commonly, the former is stressed in research at the expense of the latter. As global product development is contingent on combining knowledge of different subsidiaries within the MNC (Bartlett & Ghoshal, 1989; Subramaniam et al., 1998; Subramaniam & Venkatraman, 2001), we argue that the extent to which knowledge is simultaneously shared and understood consti-

tutes the basis for global product development (cf. Durnell Cramton, 2001; Hoopes & Postrel, 1999; Subramaniam & Venkatraman, 2001). Coordination of activities through the establishment of well functioning means for handling communication thus becomes a necessity for global product development.

METHOD

In order to study how global product development tasks are coordinated and communicated with in GDPs, a case study approach was chosen in order to capture perceptions and views by concerned employees in depth (cf. Yin, 1993). The use of GDPs is a recent, albeit important, phenomenon for the corporation studied as it is recognized as an efficient mode for organizing the product development of several corporate units and pursuing a global strategy. The GDP chosen was considered to be suitable based on a set of criteria. In order to be selected, the project had to encompass units and participants from several countries, and the outcome – a new product offering – was planned to be launched at multiple units. The GDP also had to have completed the initiation phase in order to study a project that had defined its objective and thereto-related activities (cf. Faraj & Sproull, 2000).

Case study research can make use of several means of data collection. In this study, we conducted semi-structured and open-ended interviews with members of the GDP. The interviews lasted from one hour to two hours and a half. A total of ten interviews were performed. For the analysis, the data collected was classified into two groups, based on role and responsibility in the GDP (see Table 1). The groups were project management and project members. The classification was made in order to detect differences within and between individuals in each group and enlighten the phenomena studied from different perspectives (Lincoln & Guba, 1985).

Table 1. Classification of interviews

	Project management	Project members
No. of interviews	4	6

In analyzing the data, the interviews were read, and information relevant for the purpose was extracted. Thereafter, the data was categorized according to the theoretical framework. The case study, although presented as a coherent whole, includes measures taken to enable discretion of views held by the two groups of interviewees or specific interviewees. Any view expressed by two individuals or more in a group is presented with the group name e.g., "project management". Any opinion of importance raised by a single individual is presented as "one of the project members" or "a member of project management" for example. Quotations are used to emphasize important points and issues that shed some light on the research question.

PRESENTATION OF THE CASE STUDY

Background: The Company Madenfield[1]

Madenfield – a company in the communication and business intelligence industry – was a multi-national company with operations in 13 countries. Over the last ten years, the company had witnessed a fast expansion through the acquisition of 22 companies, resulting in an increase in employees from 165 to about 2,600. The focus had for a long time been on building a market-leading position with international reach at the expense of integration. The subsidiaries were semi-autonomous within the corporation and local adaptations to individual markets were quite extensive. However, the relations between headquarters and subsid-

iaries varied a great deal, mainly depending on if they were greenfield or acquired units, which also influenced the subsidiaries' view on the role of headquarters.

The competitive strengths of Madenfield were the widespread geographic coverage, and the ability to offer products in different areas of communication and business intelligence. Recently, the need for increased integration between the different subsidiaries and products had been acknowledged as competitors were increasingly offering products that simultaneously target several markets. The differences between subsidiaries hampered the possibility of utilizing knowledge and products across countries. Different projects were conducted that were in line with the efforts of increasing integration, but the GDP studied – the *InfoGlobal* project – was the first project where Madenfield had decided to establish a project where several subsidiaries were to take part in the development of a product that was to be launched at multiple markets. In this project, members from five different subsidiaries as well as headquarters were appointed to participate. The benefits of organizing the development of the product in a GDP were, according to project management, the possibilities of involving employees who could convey their knowledge of the different customers' needs and requirements.

Overview of the InfoGlobal Project

In the fall of 2003, people from IT and business development at headquarters initiated discussions to develop the global product, based on two existing product offerings. Soon thereafter, five subsidiaries became involved, as their current product offerings did not meet the market demands or functionality requirements. The scope of *InfoGlobal* was to develop a global product that was to be launched on a global scale. A guiding principle in developing the product was to establish a common core that allowed for smaller adaptation to country-specific requirements, e.g. legislation and local customers' needs. The planned outcome of the GDP was perceived by corporate management as being of strategic importance for the company, which was reflected by involving top management in the steering committee of the project. By launching a product like *InfoGlobal*, the market position – vis-à-vis competitors – was anticipated to improve. There were actually four different factors driving the initiation of the *InfoGlobal* project. First, the changes in the market place with competitors introducing web-based and integrated products. Second, the current products were difficult to adapt to local market requirements and integrate with each other at the same time as they were developed on different technical platforms. Third, there was a need to improve the functionality and capacity of the product offerings in order to serve larger volumes of customers. Fourth, there was a need to meet the global customers in a more coherent way by means of offering global products, the *InfoGlobal* product being the first.

The GDP was planned to run for 18 months but was delayed for 12 months. Both existing and new customers welcomed the final launch of the new product. *InfoGlobal* turned out to be a success in terms of market performance. There was a consensus within the GDP that, by means of *InfoGlobal*, Madenfield reached a new group of customers with a subsequent increase in business volumes.

Managing and Coordinating the InfoGlobal Project

The GDP consisted of members from five countries. The project members had different functional backgrounds; information analysis, business development or information technology. Project management was located at headquarters and headed by a project manager who had extensive experience of working with business development. As the development of *InfoGlobal* was technically advanced, a technical project manager was assigned to specifically deal with these issues. The project members were appointed from subsidiaries that were to commercially launch the product as the first group of subsidiaries, while the remaining eight subsidiaries were planned to follow. The project management's point-of-view was that the manner in which the GDP was organized ensured that project members took responsibility for project activities at the local level. Project management went as far as stating that: *"Each unit has to be able to meet the local demands, therefore the project members have to make sure that it becomes possible to do so, but still the product has to have a common global platform and only the necessary adaptations are going to be allowed"*.

Project management was responsible for the overall architecture of *InfoGlobal* and the actual development activities were divided within the GDP on a subsidiary basis, each subsidiary being responsible for developing one specific part of *InfoGlobal*. The project was organized in such a way that most of the information passed by project management before it was communicated to the whole project. Project management also coordinated all development activities. According to project management, by strictly dividing the activities between subsidiaries, interdependencies were minimized and the development process was expected to become more efficient. A member of the project management described this as: *"The way the project activities are organized aims at minimizing interdependencies between the different subsidiaries. The worst thing you can ask of a subsidiary is to halt because another subsidiary needs to finish a module of the product."* However, this way of organizing the development work turned out to create problems later on in the project as not all subsidiaries managed to follow the time plan and did not communicate this to the rest of the project team. But the most problematic outcome of the decision to minimize coordination among participants might have been that it did not become known to the project management and the rest of the project group until very late that the project members from one of the participating subsidiaries lacked the necessary knowledge to solve the task they had been assigned. The project members neglected to inform the rest of the project of their problems and to ask for assistance. Instead, they continued to work on their own to solve their tasks: *"We felt that we had to deliver and tried to do so, but a better overview and more collaboration would probably have helped a lot"*.

A critical phase in the project was to compile the country-specific business requirement and agree on an overall design of the product. Project management headed this phase by gathering input from the different project members in the different countries. This procedure was new to many of the project members. One of the project members said: *"The manner in which the InfoGlobal-project is set up is new to us. In the past, headquarters developed the products for us whereas now we were asked to come up with a list of requirements. They said: "Tell us what you want and we will give it to you". The problem is that we do not have the skills or resources for doing so."* The skills in how to address business requirements differed between project members and the project management received business requirements mainly focusing on functionality. In most cases, the project management then had to complete the design and technical performance requirements.

The actual product development was performed in an iterative and incremental manner in order to ensure that the final solution would match the requirements of each subsidiary while, at the same time, having a common core. The project members reviewed and tested the delivered module of the product, which often resulted in additional requests or even the detection of "bugs".[2] Several aspects of the development process were highly technical and project members with a non-technical background had difficulties in interpreting and giving feedback during the development process. As stated by one of the project members: *"As I do not have the right background, it is difficult for me to discuss technical details of the product. I agree to certain things without knowing what the options are. Another problem is that I have a limited understanding of what costs are associated with the requests for the alterations or enhancements that I make."*

In the initial phase of the project, the project management and the project members agreed on a "sign-off" procedure to facilitate communication and coordination of activities within the GDP. The idea of the sign-off procedure was that project members should reach agreements on product specifications. Nevertheless, the sign-off procedure caused problems rather than facilitated the progress of the GDP. On many occasions, the project members did not approve or give feedback on the delivered specifications as they felt that they did not have the competencies required to do so, or they did not realize the implications of not approving of the specifications. It often resulted in the development activities proceeding without approval, which had repercussions on the deliveries of the actual product. Some of the project members expressed some concerns regarding the disparity in communicating within the GDP: *"We were given certain bits of information to work with and use for developing product specifications, which were then not signed off. We now have a situation where we are in discussions, putting it politely, concerning what should be in the system and what should not."* These concerns were also acknowledged by the project management as it lead to discrepancies in solutions delivered by the subsidiaries so they did not match which, in turn, lead to delays in the project.

It was actually not until the phase of commercial launch that project management realized the consequences of having organized and coordinated the activities in the manner chosen. Problems arose concerning how to integrate the deliveries into a final product, with the desired global base. In order not to delay the launch of the product too much, the first version of the product was a limited edition of the actual product stipulated in the original scope of the *InfoGlobal* project. One of the project managers remarked: *"It would have been better if we had worked together, instead of separately, in specifying the requirements and so forth. The outcome would have been a more competitive product for every party involved."* The need to coordinate the activities more was also recognized by the project members.

Conveying the Project Scope

The scope of the GDP was shared to various extents as well as in different ways in the MNC. At the corporate management level, there was a consensus that the goals of the GDP, and the possible outcomes, had to be in line with the larger strategic intent or objective of the corporation. The strategic intent was to develop this particular global product, but also to establish a common ground for future GDPs, to achieve economies of scale and not to re-invent the wheel in every market by exploiting generic needs, that is, needs that are common for several markets.

The agenda for developing a global product was to some extent known by the project participants, but they still believed that the product would, to a high degree, meet the specific demands of their local market customers, that is, that the product would be locally adapted to a high degree. Project management was less open to the project members concerning the agenda for instilling a global mindset regarding the future product offerings, implying that this GDP was seen as an exception to the regular working procedures where development projects were only started in response to specific customer requests. The dual goals of the GDP were affirmed by project management, as well as the decision not to share the strategic intent with project members *"...the global mindset goals are not directly communicated to the project members or to management at the units to which they belong. We speak with forked tongues and work to homogenize the products as much as possible at the same time as we know that the units don't want to homogenize at all, but want to have products that fit their customers in every detail. Here, we have decided that we at headquarters will strive to build a global solution. The reason for this is that we are convinced that it won't lead to any good telling everyone about our intentions as they will then automatically believe that the whole project will become bureaucratic."* It is thus interesting that even if the project members were not fully aware of the dual goals; a change towards increased global product offerings was recognized at the subsidiary level as important for the MNC. As one project member said: *"We need to meet our global customers in a more uniform manner world-wide"*. A similar view was also expressed by another project member, even if he/she acknowledged some of the problems linked to the GDP: *"This was a new way for us to work and we made a lot of mistakes as we did not know what headquarters wanted. We thus realize that we have to work to develop products that can serve customers globally"*.

The manner in which the scope of the project was shared within the GDP was by having kick-off meetings with the project members independently at each subsidiary, instead of one common kick-off meeting for all project participants. One member of the project management described the basic plan behind the decision as: *"It would have been impossible to have one kick-off meeting involving every project member. It would have been wrong to start with a kick-off meeting ... it would also be wrong to meet because of the project ... there must be such a tradition in place first. We do not have the practice of sharing knowledge or technical solu-*

tions". The views at the subsidiary level did thus diverge as several of the project members pointed out that a common meeting would certainly have been helpful, both for establishing a shared view of the project outcome and for getting to know each other. However, most project members still thought that they had successively got to know each other and had become united around the common goal even if, initially, it was rather difficult. Another outcome of how the different kick-off meetings serve as a means of providing information about the project scope was that the major part of the project members were not aware of the more strategic scope, and believed that the project was only about developing one common global product.

Many issues related to the coordination and integration problems in the GDP were also related to how information about the scope of the project had been shared by the project management. As expressed by the technical project leader: *"The scope of the project has been communicated with two voices. We, at headquarters, are used to handling the various expectations from the subsidiaries worldwide, and, on basis of that, to work homogeneously, which means working from the same platform whilst the subsidiaries do not harmonize a bit."* It is possible to conclude that the sharing of future intentions with the subsidiaries had been poorly handled by headquarters and project management since rather than stating uniformly: – "This is the future! This is how we will work in the future", the sharing of the overall strategic intent had been handled on a one-to-one basis. Not conveying the complete intent at an overall level during the project period resulted in a low degree of preparation and readiness from the subsidiaries to accept and own the final solution. Project management even admitted that most difficulties in the *InfoGlobal* project as well in the overall strategic intent derived from the neglect to share the intent: *There are lessons to be learnt from this project. Most of the problems with the InfoGlobal project are related to the open-ended scope of the project and the different understandings of the overall scope.*

Communication within the GDP

The means of communicating within the GDP were mainly e-mail and telephone. E-mail correspondence across subsidiaries was actually the main tool used for communicating and sharing information. In the subsidiaries, it was more or less standard that all project members were copied in on all communication, that is, on all e-mail correspondence among project members in their own subsidiary, with project management as well as with other project members.

The project manager and the project members had telephone conferences on a regular basis, in order to discuss the progress in developing the global product. All project members could access the project management database which covered a wide range of topics related to the project, such as memos from meetings of the steering committee, those of the project management and the whole project team, project plans and technical documentation. The project management database thus functioned as a means of sharing information. The project members mentioned the need for an updated database as a necessity in this project, especially as they worked internationally, a database into which all project members uploaded all relevant information for the rest of the team to access. They also mentioned the need for thorough reporting procedures as they found it important to document all important steps in the development of the global product. *"There are a lot of people involved from different countries; therefore we need to document everything we do on a detailed level. You cannot take anything for granted even if we are supposed to follow the overall plan. I think that we could have done this a little bit better, but it takes time and a lot of things you take for granted that everyone knows."* The need for better documentation as well as an increased sharing of information across subsidiaries were also mentioned by project management, but they saw this need for an increased flow of information and knowledge across subsidiaries in a longer perspective as the *InfoGlobal* project in their perspective was only the first GDP: *"As time passed in the project we realized that more direct communication across project members at the subsidiaries would probably have been needed. But since we had started off by saying the less dependence between the different parts of the project the better, we decided not to take the fight to increase communication and coordination in this GDP but instead bring that knowledge with us to future projects."*

Important to note is thus that the project group thought that the tools used for communication, that is, e-mail, telephone and the database, were quite well organized, even if they saw room for further improvements, not the least an increase in personal face-to-face meetings. One project member said: *"I tend to be copied on most of the e-mail communication, but direct communication is not that frequent."*

The problems and interruptions in the GDP were rather connected to how communication was carried out, the frequency in communication and how the activities were coordinated. As one project member said: *"Communication within the project has been complicated and time consuming as people are geographically dispersed and there are so many different people and units involved. You often got the feeling that information was lost somewhere along the line".* Another project member said on the issue of communication: *"At the beginning of the project we had regular teleconferences that worked well but for the past six months there have been less meetings ... everybody has been developing their own part of the product. Maybe this is the cause of the integration problems we now have."*

Geographical distance and differences in language skills, mainly stemming from cultural differences, were indicated as affecting communication. This can be exemplified by a statement by one of the project members who said: *"We have had a lot of communication issues. Within the global project group there is a lack of under-standing between subsidiaries of the different business needs and requirements, which is the local or global customer and his/her needs, and so forth. There are a lot of things in the grey area."* Cultural differences also became evident in what was considered to be most important when it came to delivering to project management as pointed out by one project manager: *"I can see a need for being clearer about what our priorities are when working in GDPs. One subsidiary for example always made sure to deliver on time even if they must have know that the quality was deficient, while another subsidiary just could not let anything through without checking it perhaps one time too many – in that country they are just thorough and quality aware."*

Several of the project members also mentioned misunderstandings directly related to lack of English language skills, English being the corporate language in Madenfield but, at the same time, they recognized that it was a problem that would successively decrease in importance. The geographical distance per se was also mentioned as a possible barrier to communication as it made it difficult for project members to meet in person, but both project managers and project members were cohesive in their view that it was not one of the major problems in this GDP due to the organization of the activities in this project.

It is important to note that how the development activities were coordinated within the GDP did neither encourage nor require communication. Only occasionally did the project members in different countries contact each other to discuss matters concerning *InfoGlobal*. According to one project member: *"Project members at the different subsidiaries tended to do what they were assigned to without giving much thought to the overall global project".* Another project member added that: *"The development process could have benefited from a continuous and shared dialogue, especially during the initial phase of the project".*

On the whole, the project members expressed frustration about poor communication and the lack of shared understanding within the GDP. The project members at the different subsidiaries did not understand how their part of the GDP contributed to achieving the overall project scope. A contributing factor to the poor communication was the manner in which project management coordinated the activities as it did not encourage communication or interaction directly between project members as all information was to go through project management. An additional factor also seemed to be that the project members did not know the common route mapped out by project management and headquarters, not only for this GDP, but also for the corporation as a whole, namely to try to instill a global attitude among all employees to become more competitive.

DISCUSSION AND CONCLUSION

This study shows how the use of a GDP served as a means for realizing global product development (cf. Subramaniam et al., 1998). The scope of the GDP was to develop a product with a common global core that allowed for only smaller but necessary adaptations to local market needs. The empirical study shows that there was also a second scope; to instill a global mindset in the corporation over time. Reaching the dual objectives of the GDP proved to be related to communication and coordination to a greater extent than project management acknowledged and thus acted upon, with clear implications for the progress of the development process.

Based on this case study, we have three main findings relating to communication and coordination within GDPs. The first issue concerns the extent to which the dual goals of the GDP were fully conveyed and understood within the MNC; communication processes that were clearly related to organizational level and belonging. The project was established and run by headquarters and at the corporate management level, the need for and the advantages of global products along with a global mindset were clearly understood and shared. At the subsidiary level, it was only the first mentioned goal that was actually shared, and that the project members from the subsidiaries worked towards accomplishing. The empirical findings also show that as the different subsidiaries even interpreted the first goal in different ways, they acted differently. As a consequence, when the project members entered the GDP, they only had the first goal in mind and there were then also variations across subsidiaries concerning the extent to which they viewed the global product as a common solution for all subsidiaries in the MNC. Since the project members were not aware of the other goal, no efforts were or even could be made towards achieving such a goal.

The main reason for not conveying both goals to subsidiary management and project members was that headquarters did not trust in the subsidiaries having the potential and interest to grasp the bigger picture relating to becoming a global corporation. Headquarters perceived that the subsidiaries would oppose the idea without knowing for a fact that they would. Interestingly, the information in the case does not support this preconception by headquarters; rather the opposite became evident during the study. This implies that if both goals had been conveyed, there would have been a reasonable possibility for both of them being accomplished, at least to some extent. Instead, the neglect to share the second goal of the GDP with all parties concerned lead to two major negative consequences for the MNC; the first being delays in the development of the global product *per se* since the project members became uncertain about what the goals of the GDP really were, and the second being that the strategic intent to build a foundation for instilling a global mindset among managers was not fulfilled.

The second issue concerns the capability of different communication mechanisms to process information and knowledge within the GDP. The dominating communication mechanisms were ICTs, which proved not to be suitable for processing complex and subjective information and knowledge within the GDP (Daft & Lengel, 1986). The project members perceived the channels of information as involving too many people and feared that information was lost somewhere along the way. In addition, the project members perceived that the information transmitted lacked contextual details; which is common for technology-mediated communication (e.g. Crampton & Hinds, 2004). This finding corroborates with received theory on the use of ICTs for knowledge integration and sharing (cf. Adenfelt & Lagerström, 2007, 2008; Durnell Crampton, 2001; Lagerström & Andersson, 2003). The common explanation for choosing ICTs as the dominating mechanisms for supporting and managing knowledge and information sharing is based on economic/financial considerations. In this study, the reliance on ICTs was founded upon the administrative heritage of the corporation (e.g. Bartlett & Ghoshal, 1989). The tradition within the corporation was not to encourage or support cooperation or sharing of knowledge and information across subsidiaries, which resulted in a project structure and coordination of activities that strived for independence between subsidiaries and project members and communication mechanisms that minimized interaction. As the knowledge of the GDP was highly complex and innovative, there was a mismatch between the communication mechanisms employed and the communication mechanisms needed for efficient and effective information and knowledge flows.

The third issue is tightly intertwined with the second issue addressed above, but pinpoints two other important aspects of communication, namely frequency and structure (cf. Hoegl & Gemuenden, 2001). In this particular GDP, it became apparent that neither the frequency nor the structure of the communication process were sufficiently developed to fill the need for information and knowledge sharing among project members, causing non complementarities in what was de-

livered and, naturally, delays in the development process. Project management did not realize the need for a high and continuous frequency in communication, trusting in both formal and informal communication directly among project members throughout the whole project process. Project management saw itself as the main and central hub for all information, not realizing that there is a need for all participants to define and create a collective and common interpretation of the information necessary for developing and agreeing upon a common solution to the task at hand (cf. Daft & Lengel, 1986). An unexpected empirical finding in relation to the frequency and structure of communication in the GDP is that it was only the scarcity in formal communication that was recognized as being a problem among project participants but, once more, we assume this to be the result of the administrative heritage in the MNC in terms of the subsidiaries not being used to communicating and sharing information and knowledge in between them.

The contribution of this study to received theory on the pursuit of a global strategy in MNCs is twofold. First, we found that the implementation of a global strategy – on an overall level – was influenced by two factors as they affected the actual rollout; i) the history and tradition of the, often diverse, subsidiaries, and ii) the subsidiaries' insights into and/or awareness of the need for change and adaptation. The history and tradition of the subsidiary partly determine the degree of autonomy enjoyed by a subsidiary and hence, the degree of integration with the rest of the MNC. Other factors influencing the degree of autonomy are the knowledge and the market position of the subsidiary. For example, the more embedded the subsidiary is in its local market, the better its access to knowledge about local customers' needs. A subsidiary with a strong market position is important from headquarters' point of view, not only in terms of being a revenue contributor but also in terms of its knowledge potentials. Thus, it becomes a delicate issue for headquarters to communicate the need for subsidiaries not only to adopt a global product concept but also to take on a global mindset. The adaptations relating to embracing a global mindset also require both an insight into the need to change as well as a willingness among subsidiaries to change and adapt to the new competitive arena, requiring increased integration in response to threats and opportunities following the globalization trend. The study discloses that the awareness is much more widespread among subsidiaries than what is perceived by headquarters. But, more importantly, the study indicates that too little time is devoted to communicating goals, strategies and expected outcomes in the MNC as a whole and therefore, no common position can be obtained for the overall strategy of the corporation.

The second contribution to received theory is the difficulties in communicating goals, which in itself is nothing new. However, we shed some new light on the issue by bringing some intriguing issues to light. Communication within MNC is a multi-level phenomenon, and it is a process occurring over time, as well as a process that needs to involve all parties concerned. Thus, all possible means for handling communication must be utilized to not only bridge the obvious problems connected with cross-border communication such as geographical, language and cultural barriers, but also the barriers between headquarters and subsidiaries.

As this study is set out as an attempt to explicitly capture and provide a deeper understanding of communication and coordination issues in GDPs, but also of the implementation of new strategic intents in corporations, we wish to inspire more research in at least two areas. First, with the rapid increase in the use of GDPs, there is still a gap in our knowledge of what factors affect the effectiveness of communication and coordination in GDPs. Second, how to implement a global mindset among employees by trusting in participation by all concerned parties in the whole process, instead of making it a top-down process controlled and run by headquarters. Throughout this study, we have tried to provide some additional understanding of these phenomena, but since this study is limited to the study of one GDP in one corporation, there is plenty of more work to be done in the field, especially since the use of such a project has outpaced our understanding of its dynamics.

REFERENCES

Adenfelt, M., & Lagerström, K. (2006). Enabling knowledge creation and sharing in transnational projects. *International Journal of Project Management, 24*(3), 191–198. doi:10.1016/j.ijproman.2005.09.003

Adenfelt, M., & Lagerström, K. (2007). Knowledge development and sharing: the case of a centre of excellence and a transnational team. *International Business Review, 15*(4), 381–400. doi:10.1016/j.ibusrev.2006.05.002

Adenfelt, M., & Lagerström, K. (2008). The development and sharing of knowledge by centres of excellence and transnational teams: a conceptual framework. *Management International Review, 48*(3), 319–338. doi:10.1007/s11575-008-0018-8

Ancona, D., & Caldwell, D. (1992). Bridging the boundary: external activity and performance in organizational teams. *Administrative Science Quarterly, 37*, 634–665. doi:10.2307/2393475

Atamer, T., & Schweiger, D. (2003). Transnational horizontal project teams. *Journal of World Business, 38*(2), 81–83. doi:10.1016/S1090-9516(03)00002-6

Bartlett, C. A., & Ghoshal, S. (1989). *Managing across borders*. Boston: Harvard Business School Press.

Bell, B. S., & Kozlowski, S. W. J. (2002). A typology of virtual teams: implications for effective leadership. *Group & Organization Management*, *27*(1), 14–36. doi:10.1177/1059601102027001003

Chen, S., Geluykens, R., & Choi, C. J. (2006). The importance of language in global teams: a linguistic perspective. *Management International Review*, *46*(6), 679–695. doi:10.1007/s11575-006-0122-6

Crampton, C. D., & Hinds, P. J. (2004). Subgroup dynamics in internationally distributed teams: ethnocentrism or cross-national learning? In B. Staw, & R. Kramer, (Eds.) *Research in Organizational Behavior* (pp. 213-263). Greenwich, CT: JAI Press.

Daft & Lengel. (1986). Organizational information requirements, media richness and structural design. *Management Science*, *32*(5), 554–571. doi:10.1287/mnsc.32.5.554

Durnell Cramton, C. (2001). The shared knowledge problem and its consequences for dispersed collaboration. *Organization Science*, *12*(39), 346–371. doi:10.1287/orsc.12.3.346.10098

Faraj, S., & Sproull, L. (2000). Coordinating expertise in software development teams. *Management Science*, *46*(12), 1554–1568. doi:10.1287/mnsc.46.12.1554.12072

Foss, N. J., & Pedersen, T. (2002). Transferring knowledge in MNCs: the role of sources of subsidiaries knowledge and organizational context. *Journal of International Management*, *8*, 49–67. doi:10.1016/S1075-4253(01)00054-0

Fulk, J., & DeSanctis, G. (1995). Electronic communication and changing organizational forms. *Organization Science*, *6*(4), 337–349. doi:10.1287/orsc.6.4.337

Galbraith, J. (1973). *Designing complex organizations*. Reading, MA: Addison-Wesley Publishing Company.

Griffin, A., & Hauser, J. R. (1992). Patterns of communication among marketing, engineering and manufacturing – a comparison between two new product teams. *Management Science*, *38*(3), 360–373. doi:10.1287/mnsc.38.3.360

Gudykunst, W. B., & Kim, Y. Y. (1997). *Communicating with strangers: an approach to intercultural communication* (3rd Ed). New York: McGraw-Hill.

Gupta, A., & Govindarajan, V. (2000). Knowledge flows within multinational corporations. *Strategic Management Journal*, *21*, 473–496. doi:10.1002/(SICI)1097-0266(200004)21:4<473::AID-SMJ84>3.0.CO;2-I

Gupta, A., & Govindarajan, V. (2001). Converting global presence into global competitive advantage. *The Academy of Management Executive*, *15*(2), 45–56.

Gupta, A., & Govindarajan, V. (2001). Building an effective global business team. *Sloan Management Review*, (Summer): 63–71.

Gupta, A., & Govindarajan, V. (2002). Cultivating a global mindset. *The Academy of Management Executive*, *16*(1), 116–126.

Hambrick, D., Davison, S., Snell, S., & Snow, C. (1998). When groups consist of multiple nationalities: towards a new understanding of the implications. *Organization Studies*, *19*(2), 181–205. doi:10.1177/017084069801900202

Hoegl, M., & Gemuenden, H. G. (2001). Teamwork quality and the success of innovative projects: a theoretical concept and empirical evidence. *Organization Science*, *12*(4), 435–449. doi:10.1287/orsc.12.4.435.10635

Hoegl, M., & Weinkauf, K. (2005). Managing task interdependencies in multi-team projects: a longitudinal study. *Journal of Management Studies*, *42*(6), 1287–1308. doi:10.1111/j.1467-6486.2005.00542.x

Hoopes, D. G., & Postrel, S. (1999). Shared knowledge, "glitches" and product development performance. *Strategic Management Journal, 20*, 837–865. doi:10.1002/(SICI)1097-0266(199909)20:9<837::AID-SMJ54>3.0.CO;2-I

Jarvenpaa, S. L., & Leidner, D. E. (1999). Communication and trust in global virtual teams. *Organization Science, 10*(6), 791–815. doi:10.1287/orsc.10.6.791

Kim, Y. Y. (1991). Intercultural communication competence: a systems-theoretic view. In T-S. Toomey & F. Korzenny (Eds.), *International and intercultural communications annual,* (pp. 259-275). Newbury Park, CA: Sage publications.

Lagerström, K. (2001). *Transnational projects within multinational corporations.* Uppsala, Sweden: Department of Business Studies, Uppsala University.

Lagerström, K., & Andersson, M. (2003). Creation and sharing knowledge within a transnational team – development of a global business system. *Journal of World Business, 38*(2), 84–95. doi:10.1016/S1090-9516(03)00003-8

Lawrence, P., & Lorsch, J. (1967). Organization and environment: managing differentiation and integration, Boston, MA: Graduate School of Business Administration.

Li, H. Z. (1991). Communicating information in conversations: A cross-cultural comparison. *International Journal of Intercultural Relations, 23*(3), 387–409. doi:10.1016/S0147-1767(99)00003-6

Lincoln, Y. S., & Guba, E. G. (1985). *Naturalistic inquiry.* London: Sage Publications.

Martinez, J. I., & Jarillo, J. C. (1991). Coordination Demands of International Strategies. *Journal of International Business Studies, 22*(3), 429–444. doi:10.1057/palgrave.jibs.8490309

Maznevski, M., & Chudoba, K. (2000). Bridging space over time: global virtual team dynamics and effectiveness. *Organization Science, 11*(5), 473–492. doi:10.1287/orsc.11.5.473.15200

McDonough, E. III, & Kahn, K. (1996). Using hard and soft technologies for global new product development. *R & D Management, 26*(2), 241–253. doi:10.1111/j.1467-9310.1996.tb00959.x

McDonough, E. III, Kahn, K., & Griffin, A. (1999). Managing communication in global product development teams. *IEEE Transactions on Engineering Management, 46*(4), 375–386. doi:10.1109/17.797960

Mohr, J., Fischer, R., & Nevin, J. (1996). Collaborative communication in interfirm relationships: moderating effects of integration and control. *Journal of Marketing, 50*, 103–115. doi:10.2307/1251844

Mohr, J., & Nevin, J. (1990). Communicating strategies in marketing channels: a theoretical perspective. *Journal of Marketing, 54*(4), 36–51. doi:10.2307/1251758

Montoya-Weiss, M. M., Massey, A. P., & Song, M. (2001). Getting it together: temporal coordination and conflict management in global virtual teams. *Academy of Management Journal, 44*(6), 1251–1262. doi:10.2307/3069399

Mudambi, R. (2002). Knowledge management in multinational firms. *Journal of International Management, 8*, 1–9. doi:10.1016/S1075-4253(02)00050-9

Nelson, K. M., & Cooprider, J. G. (1996). The Contribution of Shared Knowledge to IS group performance. *MIS Quarterly*, (December): 409–432. doi:10.2307/249562

Nohria, N., & Ghoshal, S. (1997). The differentiated network: organizing multinational corporations for value creation. San Francisco: Jossey-Bass Inc. Publishers.

Robb, D. (2002). Virtual workplace. *HRMagazine*, *47*(6), 105–110.

Schweiger, D., Atamer, T., & Calori, R. (2003). Transnational project teams and networks: making the multinational organization more effective. *Journal of World Business*, *38*(2), 127–140. doi:10.1016/S1090-9516(03)00006-3

Snow, C., Snell, S., Davison, S., & Hambrick, D. (1996). Use transnational teams to globalize your company. *Organizational Dynamics*, *32*(Spring), 30–32.

Subramaniam, M., Rosenthal, S., & Hatten, K. (1998). Global new product development processes: preliminary findings and research propositions. *Journal of Management Studies*, *35*(6), 773–796. doi:10.1111/1467-6486.00119

Subramaniam, M., & Venkatraman, N. (2001). Determinants of transnational new product development capability: Testing the influence of transferring and deploying tacit overseas knowledge. *Strategic Management Journal*, *22*, 359–378. doi:10.1002/smj.163

Thompson, J. D. (1967). *Organizations in Action*. New York: McGraw-Hill.

Weick, K. E. (1979). *The social psychology of organization*. Reading, MA: Addison-Wesley Publishing Company.

Yamin, M., & Otto, J. (2004). Patterns of knowledge flows and MNE innovation performance. *Journal of International Management*, *10*, 239–258. doi:10.1016/j.intman.2004.02.001

Yin, R. K. (1993). *Case study research: design and methods*. Beverly Hills, CA: Sage Publications.

Zander, I. (1998). The evolution of technological capabilities in the multinational corporation – dispersion, duplication and potential advantages from multinationality. *Research Policy*, *27*(1), 17–35. doi:10.1016/S0048-7333(97)00068-1

ENDNOTES

[1] Fictitious names are used in order to guarantee anonymity.

[2] A software bug (or just "bug") is an error, flaw, mistake, failure, or fault in a computer program that prevents it from behaving as intended (e.g., producing an incorrect result).

Chapter 10
The Relation Between ICT and Environmental Management Practice in a Construction Company

Mattias Jacobsson
Umeå School of Business, Umeå University, Sweden

Anneli Linde*
Umeå School of Business, Umeå University, Sweden

Henrik Linderoth
University of Skövde, Sweden

ABSTRACT

The aim of this chapter is to draw attention to the use of ICT in the building and construction industry with a special interest in the day-to-day activities of those companies that are working to develop more environmentally friendly and sustainable production processes. The chapter is based on a comprehensive survey of ICT use and attitudes to environmental related issues in middle and large sized construction companies in Sweden and two case studies: One of ICT use in a larger Swedish building and construction company and one of communication, coordination, and decision making processes in a construction project. Based on the empirical data we argue that in order to enhance a more environmentally friendly building and construction industry there is a need for a more genuine cooperation and knowledge sharing between different actors both in crossing project boundaries as well as overriding contractual limitations. Decisions in a construction project must be taken earlier in the process and construction companies need to focus more on those processes over which they actually do have power.

DOI: 10.4018/978-1-60566-822-2.ch010

INTRODUCTION

This chapter will address some important contemporary challenges facing the construction industry related to the demands on the industry to become more sustainable. The scope of the problem is immense, encompassing wide-ranging challenges - from those at the level of national strategy to those, which concern the practice of individual organizations. In this chapter we will narrow the scope and focus on environmental management insofar as it is related to communication and information practice in construction companies. The centre of attention is the day-to-day activities of actors at different levels in the companies, whose decisions, supported by ICT systems, set environmental and sustainability visions and strategies into action. Although this is only one small part of the sustainability challenge in the industry, it is however, a very important one and – as we argue – it is a part of the process that previously has been given little or no attention. Even taking account of both environmental management in the construction sector as well as the sector's use of modern ICT, little of this effort has been noted, explored or questioned.

Over the last decade the construction industry has often been criticized for being slow when it comes to "renewal" (Ekstedt et al. 1992), laggard in adoption of new information technology (Mitropoulos et al. 1999), and also uninterested in attending to issues of sustainability (Femenias, 2004; Gluch, 2006). However, although the acceptance and adoption rate of ICT has been slow, a major increase in both the scope and depth of usage has been identified (Samuelson, 2001, 2002, 2008). Today, the use of ICT among large building and construction companies is an essential part of the coordination and management of information flows as well as supply chain management, planning, control, and cost estimation (Dainty et al. 2006; Molnár et al. 2007; Samuelson, 2008; Cutting-Decelle et al. 2007). Nevertheless, the use of ICT in regard to

environmental management remains inadequate and also in need of further research.

According to Gluch (2000, 2006) environmental management systems in general are not used as an adequate support for environmental and "green" decisions. Moreover, it is claimed that there are large discrepancies between strategies and practice when it comes to sustainability and green decisions (Gluch, 2006). Hence, it appears there is a gap between the use of ICT for coordination, communication and management of "general" information flows, and the use of ICT for coordinating and managing issues related to sustainability.

The aim of this chapter is therefore to draw attention to the use of ICT in the building and construction industry with a special interest in the day-to-day activities of those companies that are working to develop more environmentally friendly and sustainable production processes. In the chapter we will scrutinize both the line- and the project organization in order to identify, describe, and analyze communication and information flows, how sustainable decisions are made, and how ICT is used in relation to these activities.

SOME EMPIRICAL EVIDENCE FROM THE SWEDISH CONSTRUCTION SECTOR

A vast variety of empirics from a comprehensive research project on *"ICT as a strategic resource for facilitating competitiveness and sustainability in the building and construction sector"* are used to support the discussion and analysis in this chapter. In this research project (executed from 2006 to early 2009) three main studies were conducted. The first study concerned ICT use and decision making related to sustainability. The data was collected via a survey in Swedish construction companies focusing on ICT use and formal decision-making structures. The aim of the study was to inquire how, where and by whom sustainability related decisions are made, and the possibilities for transferring the information and knowledge necessary for decision making among project actors via ICT solutions (see also Isaksson et al. 2009). The second study is a case study of a major Swedish construction company, which encompassed the entire organization, from top management to single projects, in order to understand how different ICT solutions are actually used in it. In the study an emphasis was put on the creation of an understanding of structures and processes in the company and how these affect ICT use and the management of sustainability issues (see also Linderoth & Jacobsson, 2008). The third study is a longitudinal case study, which scrutinized a specific construction project in depth. The aim of that study was to gain a deeper understanding of communication, coordination, and decision-making processes from an intra-project perspective (see also Jacobsson, 2008a, 2008b, 2009; Linderoth & Jacobsson, 2008).

THE CONSTRUCTION CONTEXT AND THE USE OF ICT

If an enhanced understanding is to be reached concerning ICT's potential to facilitate sustainability in the building and construction sectors, a more developed and nuanced picture of ICT-adoption must be provided. According to previous research on ICT's capacity to transform organizational structures, processes and trajectories, it is crucially important to take into consideration the context in which the ICT-induced transformation process is embedded (see Markus & Robey, 1988; Orlikowski & Robey, 1991; Orlikowski, 1992; Ciborra & Lanzara, 1994). Hence, first and foremost we need to take a look at the context and characteristics of the industry.

According to Harty (2005) there are a few central aspects that have to be kept in mind in order to grasp the challenges of the contemporary construction context. These are: the way power

is distributed; the centrality of communication to its performance; its organization around particular projects; the collaboration upon which construction work is based, including the importance of inter-organizational relations. From the perspective of the single company, activities are managed in a traditional (single firm) sense, acting in its own interest and sometimes at the expense of others (Harty, 2005). However, from the perspective of the building and construction process there is a big difference. Contrastingly, the construction process is fragmented, organized as projects, with its many different actors having different cultural backgrounds, tasks and responsibilities. In relation to ICT-adoption, this form of organizing, providing as it does a large degree of flexibility, is therefore a central contextual influence to take into consideration. The flexible and autonomous nature of projects and their significant discontinuities in the flow of personnel, material and information, have previously been shown to create difficulties when it comes to developing routines that will support the flow of information and knowledge between projects or to the permanent organization (see e.g. DeFilippi & Arthur, 1998; Gann & Salter, 2000). Moreover, the need to incorporate various interests from different professional groups has been identified as a hindrance in the adoption and use of ICT (Wikforss & Löfgren, 2007), which in turn also may lead to difficulties in co-operating (Söderholm, 2006).

Thus, when conducting research on ICT-related issues in the building and construction industry, it is important to make a distinction between the project-based organization, where operations are managed, and the line organization (see also Rowlinson, 2007). In the project based organization the use of ICT for intra- and inter-organizational coordination and information exchange in the planning, design and production processes has been limited even if it is claimed to be of recognized potential (see e.g. Wikforss & Löfgren, 2007). Linderoth and Jacobsson (2008) even claim that the organizing of operations as projects is one condition that has constrained the use of ICT in operations, and that the ICT used is mainly directed towards governance and control of projects. The use of ICT as a means for governance and control is however not unique for the building and construction sector. On the contrary, a common claim by scholars in the IS field is that one main idea behind the implementation of ICT is to increase to possibilities for governance and control of the organization (see Monteiro, 2003). Thus, contextual conditions like the organizing by project, the fragmentation of the industry, the lack of integration between design and production process (Dainty et al. 2006), along with informal communication and information flows (Wikforss & Löfgren, 2007) have had, and will have, a crucial impact on the deployment of ICT in the industry.

Taken together, the given contextual conditions are essential to bear in mind and to scrutinize further when we proceed with the analysis and discussion of whether, and how, ICT can contribute to more sustainable production processes in the building and construction industry. By focusing on the context, it will be possible to reveal issues concerning the management and decision making related to sustainability in production processes, and thereby show what role ICT and the prevailing environmental management system play in this process. However, before we continue to the empirical part of this chapter we need to address sustainability and environmental management within construction and its relation to ICT.

ENVIRONMENTAL MANAGEMENT IN THE CONSTRUCTION INDUSTRY

The overall principles and importance of environmental management and sustainable construction have been of substantial interest in previous research (Hill & Bowen, 1997; Ofori, 1998; Sjöström & Bakens, 1999; Bon & Hutchinson, 2000). New construction technologies including

life cycle costing approaches (Gluch & Baumann, 2004), alternative-building components, new design standards, and renewal-engineering methods are examples of contemporary research interests (see e.g. Kibert, 2007). Furthermore, it is well established that the construction of infrastructure and buildings brings about a substantial ecological load, both in terms of energy consumption and the materials used (Spence & Mulligan, 1995), an insight that is also recognized by the companies themselves. Companies in Sweden regard energy use, waste and air pollution as the most problematic aspects to manage. (Baumann et al. 2003). Hence, the importance of environmental management and the sustainable aspects of the work cannot be overestimated even if sustainable construction is claimed to be more expensive then traditional construction (Andrews, Rankin & Waugh, 2002).

Focusing on environmental management systems and the previously mentioned importance of distinguishing between the project organization and the line organization, consequences for sustainability and environmental management have also been identified. As mentioned, there is claimed to be a large discrepancy between strategies and practice regarding sustainability and environmental management (Gluch, 2006). There is seemingly also a gap between the use of ICT for coordination and management of "general" information flows, and the use of ICT for coordinating and managing issues related to sustainability. The discrepancy between strategy and practice has been described as a problem of alignment, *"projects are not aligned with centrally controlled and generic environmental practice"* (Gluch, 2005:57), and it is also argued that the temporary perspective of projects is out of alignment with the long-term principles of sustainable development and sustainable construction. That is, decisions in practice have an impact through all stages of the building process and beyond (Sobotka & Wyatt, 1998; Wenblad, 2001). This implies a complex chain of integrated decisions regarding production, resources, work environment, and standard/quality of living. Hence, there is a need for simultaneously integrated solutions and environmental consideration from both a process view and a resource view if high levels of quality of life, and social, economic, or cultural values are to be attained in such a fragmented contextual setting. It is therefore highly challenging for a single construction company or actor to control or even identify the important processes and activities, particularly if we also include the need for short as well as long-term forecasts of effects.

Consequently, there is a necessity for substantial and adequate environmental information to support the decisions taken in every part of the construction and building process. According to Gluch (2000, 2006), such decisions are not today adequately supported by the environmental management systems at hand.

THE FIELD STUDY: FROM A GENERAL PERCEPTION TO SPECIFIC ACTIVITIES

In this following section we will present some of the findings from our studies that can be linked to communication and decision-making about issues related to the environment. As described earlier, the material analyzed and discussed originates from three different but interrelated studies. The questionnaire – presented first – gives the broad picture of the area whilst the case studies give details and depth. The analysis and presentation of the findings are organized as follows.

The first part focuses exclusively on the results from the questionnaire where we analyze statistics based on information gathered from middle and large sized construction companies all over Sweden. The questions to which we were seeking an answer are related. They can be summarized as: "In general, to what extent and how are ICT solutions used and what are companies' general perceptions of those systems?" We es-

pecially wanted to identify how environmental systems were perceived and used in relation to other management systems. In addition, we were seeking knowledge about the level of decision-making influence and power people in different roles perceived as available to them during a project. That is, we were concerned with how they perceived their own as well as other actors' possibilities for influencing and taking decisions about matters related to the environment. These types of decisions concern production processes, material, and suppliers.

This knowledge gave us a base and a framework for exploring the "practice in action", that is, the different actors' day-to-day activities. The results from this next step of the study, when the questionnaire results were contextualized, are presented in two stages: 1) looking at the context from the line managers' point of view; and 2) taking the managers' point of view in the project settings. Both perspectives are provided in order to give some illustration of the reality manager's face in the project and how that reality influences environmental decisions.

Empirical Findings from the Questionnaire

The questionnaire was distributed as a web questionnaire to decision makers at different levels of construction companies around Sweden. The identified decision makers consisted of superintendents, head managers at the regional offices, division managers, site managers, foremen, purchasers, estimators, and project managers. This is, all managers who, according to their job descriptions, are able and also likely, to take decisions related to environmental issues. Some respondents were identified from an Internet search of Swedish construction companies, while somewhere identified with the help of regional offices from one of the major construction companies. In the latter case the work of identifying respondents and the specific company handled sending out

Table 1. Respondents by position

Position	%
Superintendent (at the office)	12%
Purchaser, estimator etc	27%
Site manager	31%
Asst. Site manager (foreman)	28%
Other	3%
Sum	100%

the surveys. Because of the structure of the data collection method it is not possible to assess a precise response rate of our sample. However, from the Internet search we were able to identify a total of 215 managers and received a response from 89 of them (giving in that case a response rate of 41 percent). The internal loss was quite high, since some respondents did not answer all the questions. In total 733 persons responded, at least in part, to our questionnaire and 466 persons completed the questionnaire in full. Out of the total respondents, 86 percent were male and 14 percent were female. In total 36 percent had a university degree and approximately 45 percent were technical college graduates. In table 1 the respondents are illustrated by (management) position in the company, in actual numbers and by percentage:'

Perception and Use of Internal ICT Systems and Applications

The initial part of the questionnaire focused on identifying the frequency of ICT use in general, both at work and at home. More specifically, it focused on what precise *communications technology* was used and what *ICT based systems* were implemented in the organization as well as the *frequencies of use* of different management systems, and the *attitudes* towards and *perceptions* of those systems.

One conclusion that can be drawn from this section of the survey is that neither lack of experi-

ence nor hostility to technology seems to be the cause of any problems associated with the use of strategic information and communication systems. ICT is used on a daily basis at all levels in the organizations, a trend that is very much in line with what previous studies have shown (se e.g. Samuelson, 2008). Close to 100 percent (98-97 percent) of the respondents used their own (not shared) computer with Internet access, email and a mobile phone (supported by their employer). A total of 37 percent also used a hand held PDA or smart phone in their job. Frequent ICT use was however not limited to the boundaries of their firm. A vast majority of the managers also used computers and Internet at home. Almost 80 percent of the respondents said that they very frequently (4 or 5 on a scale from 1 to 5) used Internet connected computers at home. Notable also is that 23 percent of the respondents claimed that they never used their home computer for work tasks while 10 percent said that they used their home computer every day for such tasks.

One further thing the results emphasized was a lack of technology hostility or any problems with ICT management in the companies. The managers in general were very satisfied with their companies' ICT strategies and policies. We can also conclude that the number of different systems and ICT applications that are implemented in construction companies in Sweden today (see Figure 1) is the same, as you would expect to find in any industry. However, there are huge differences related to these applications and systems insofar as frequency of use, perceived usefulness, and efficiency are concerned, as well as in attitudes towards the different systems or applications.

In the figure above we can see, among other things, that environmental management systems are the ICT systems that are used least frequently by the decision-makers. Only 13 percent of our respondents indicated that they used environmental management systems often or very often. The results from this question can be linked to other questions and are discussed below. Environmental

Figure 1. The use of ICT-applications in construction companies. The figure illustrates the ICT-systems/applications that are used most frequently by managers in construction companies.

Frequency (%) who say they use the system often or very often
4 or 5 on a scale from 1 = never to 5 = very often (daily)

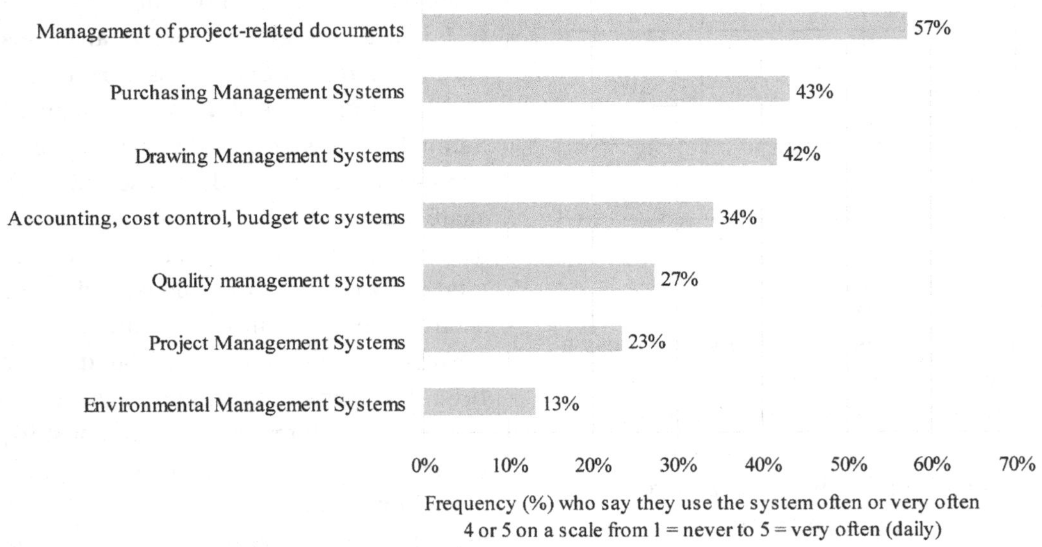

management systems are probably tailored to the obvious environmental decisions (for example, handling chemicals/hazardous substances) and such decisions are much more uncommon than the day-to-day decisions that the other ICT systems support.

The Power to Influence — Decision Making and Attitudes Towards Specific ICT Applications

In the following section we analyze those results from the questionnaire that concern perceptions of the possibility of influencing or taking decisions that are part of environmental management or otherwise affect it. Managers at all levels in the construction companies were asked if they had taken any decisions concerning a spectrum of areas ranging from production methods to handling chemicals (results in Figure 2). Further on we explore their perception of their own as well as their colleagues' power over these decisions. That is, we consider to what extent they thought they could affect them. The results from this

section of the questionnaire will be related in the discussion to the next questionnaire section which concerns how managers perceive the usefulness of different available ICT applications - that is, whether the systems/applications help them in their decision making.

The obvious, as well as logical, implication identifiable from the figure above is that the frequency of decision-making is very high. The most common decision is related to the choice of production methods (69 percent of the respondents indicated that they have made such decisions during the last week). The lowest in the decision intensity list, it can be noted, are decisions related to energy consumption (9 percent), and the selection or handling of chemicals/hazardous substances (9 percent). Even though this list is by no means an exhaustive one, it shows that the kinds of decisions that have immediate and clear sustainability implications (hazardous substances, for example) are rather limited compared with everyday decisions (such as selecting materials). This discrepancy can potentially explain why many individuals do not always recognize that

Figure 2. Environment-related decisions made by the respondents during the past week of answering the questionnaire. The number is percentage of respondents that said that they made such a decision. This question is further used for the index about the intensity of decision making.

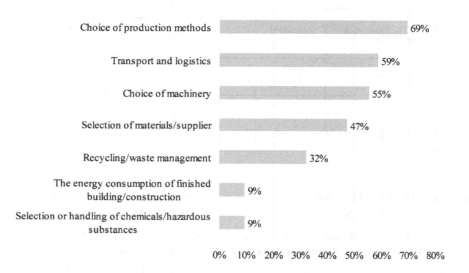

Percentage of respondents that said they made such a decision

they are involved in decisions that could have an environmental impact. The problems with this became even clearer when looking into managers' perceived power to influence.

In examining this issue, we explored both the managers' own perception of power as well as that of their colleagues. That is, we tested the extent to which they thought that they could influence choice of materials, production processes, etc. (see Tables 2 and 3). A surprisingly large number of actors perceive themselves to have a high influence on some decisions. The decisions that

Table 2. Managers' own perceptions of power to influence the decision to choose materials, suppliers, or production processes. On a scale from 1 (practically none) to 6 (to a very high degree). Hence, the score is the average on this scale. The ranking illustrates, in descending order, which actors are perceived to have the highest influence.

Decision-maker	Materials		Suppliers		Production methods		Total	
	Rank	*Score*	*Rank*	*Score*	*Rank*	*Score*	*Rank*	*Score*
Site manager	3	4,28	1	4,70	1	5,26	1	4,75
Customer	1	5,26	4	3,97	6	3,24	2	4,17
Superintendent	5	3,52	3	4,15	3	3,95	3	3,87
Purchaser	4	3,81	2	4,63	7	2,99	4	3,82
Architect	2	4,95	7	2,99	5	3,25	5	3,74
Ass. Site manager	6	3,27	5	3,40	2	4,50	6	3,73
Estimator	7	3,12	6	3,19	4	3,33	7	3,21
Average		4,03		3,86		3,79		3,90

Table 3. Summary of respondents' own perception of their power to influence decision and respondents' perception of other groups' power to influence. Averages on a scale from 1 (practically none) to 6 (to a very high degree).

Position	Own Perception	Super-intendent	Estimator	Purchaser	Site manager	Ass. Site manager
Superintendent	4,9	4,6	3,5	4,1	3,8	4,9
Estimator	3,9	4,0	3,6	3,9	3,5	4,6
Purchaser	3,9	4,1	3,1	4,3	3,5	4,8
Site manager	4,7	3,7	3,1	3,7	3,9	5,0
Ass. Site manager	3,6	3,7	3,1	3,6	3,9	4,6
All	4,0	3,9	3,2	3,8	3,7	4,8

they especially felt they could influence were the choice of suppliers and the production processes. The choice of material seems to be perceived as a decision made by a person outside the construction company, however only to a slightly higher degree than a person inside the company.

In the ranking above the scale was from 1 (practically not at all), to 6 (to a very high degree). In general it seems like the entire collective of actors believe that they have the highest degree of influence regarding the choice of materials (on average 4,2) and lowest influence on the choice of production processes (3,6). It is also interesting to note the difference between the individual groups of actors. Site managers, on the one hand, receive the overall highest influence ranking (5,2) and this group is also perceived to have the highest influence on production processes. The architects, on the other hand, are perceived to have the highest influence on choice of materials. The interesting results here though concern the degree to which other managers are also perceived to have significant influence over those aspects.

Respondents were in the first instance asked to judge *their own* power to influence the decision to select a) materials, b) suppliers and c) production methods. In a second set of questions, respondents were asked to judge *other* decision makers' power to influence decisions regarding a) materials, b) suppliers and c) production methods. The average

of these answers is illustrated in the five columns in Table 3. This can be compared to the results presented in Table 2, (where the average of the perceptions related to material production method and suppliers is illustrated in the column "own perception"). Hence, Superintendents had the highest perception of their own influence (4,9), while foremen had the lowest (3,6). The bottom line gives a summary of all respondents' perception of the others' power to influence decisions.

The results show clearly that managers at all levels of the organization perceive that they have a great deal of power and that they all take a large number of decisions concerning choice of material, production processes, and choice of suppliers. This means that they all clearly have the capacity to affect environmental decisions and choices. Furthermore, it can be noted that the companies have implemented a broad range of management systems and applications to support managers and to control production. It should therefore be of major importance that these systems are perceived as useful and helpful in the decision making process.

Attitudes Towards the Functionality of the Systems

Table 4 gives a comprehensive picture of attitudes towards the functionality of the com-

Table 4. Attitudes on the companies' environmental management system (EMS), quality management system (QMS), and project management system (PMS). Likert scale from 1 (totally disagree) to 5 (totally agree). In the table 1 and 2 is categorized as "do not agree"; 3 as "uncertain" and 4 or 5 as "agree". Cells with grey filling indicate the system within each statement that received the lowest "agree" score and the highest "do not agree" score. N = 390.

Statement	System	Do not agree (1-2)	Uncertain (3)	Agree (4-5)
Is well suited to the construction industry's conditions.	EMS	10%	34%	55%
	QMS	10%	32%	57%
	PMS	7%	31%	62%
Works generally very well.	EMS	13%	33%	54%
	QMS	10%	33%	57%
	PMS	6%	32%	63%
Gives me often relevant information when I need it.	EMS	16%	36%	49%
	QMS	11%	36%	53%
	PMS	8%	34%	58%
Is well integrated with the company's other IT systems.	EMS	19%	40%	41%
	QMS	14%	37%	49%
	PMS	12%	36%	51%
Often helps me in my decision making.	EMS	29%	39%	33%
	QMS	22%	40%	38%
	PMS	16%	40%	44%
Contains too little information.	EMS	35%	44%	21%
	QMS	48%	37%	15%
	PMS	42%	43%	15%
Lacks a lot of important functions.	EMS	39%	44%	16%
	QMS	45%	37%	18%
	PMS	47%	37%	16%

pany's quality system, project management system and environmental management system. In the first five statements a rank of 4 or 5 indicates a positive attitude towards the system (for example, that "the system helps me"). The last two statements have a reversed scale. That is, a high score reveals a negative attitude or functionality of the system.

In summary, the primary conclusion from these results is that all systems and applications have huge potential for improvement. There is an obvious uncertainty about the efficiency and usefulness of the systems, and in particular, the environmental management systems do not seem to help managers with their decisions. Moreover, nearly 60 percent of the respondents do not perceive the systems as well integrated.

In the following section we will continue by analyzing our respondents' perception of the effects of the increased environmental considerations to which the building and construction industry is exposed. We gave the respondents a scale of 1-5 and asked them to react to a number of statements measuring how increased environmental considerations will affect various aspects of the firm's operations. The statements and the answers are illustrated in Table 5.

Table 5. Answers to statements about how the requirements for increased environmental considerations (sustainable buildings) generally affect the projects. Numbers indicate the percentage of responses to a scale from 1 (strongly disagree) to 5 (strongly agree).

Statement	Do not agree (1-2)	Uncertain (3)	Agree (4-5)
Increased environmental considerations lead to higher costs	21%	31%	48%
Increased environmental considerations lead to reduced costs	53%	37%	10%
Increased environmental considerations lead to lower quality	62%	24%	14%
Increased environmental considerations lead to longer production times	30%	36%	34%
Environment-friendly production creates goodwill for the company	3%	9%	87%
Environment-friendly production is beneficial for the end user	6%	22%	72%
We often lack the knowledge to make environmentally friendly choices	39%	30%	31%

The most important effect of increased environmental friendliness that our respondents perceive is that it creates goodwill for the company: 87 percent agreed (4-5) with that statement. There also seems to be quite a large consensus that while increased environmental considerations are costly and potentially time-consuming, they do not lead to lower quality and are beneficial for the end-user.

The significant results from the survey can be summarized as follows:

. A large number of decisions are made on lower levels in the hierarchy;
. Many ICT-systems have a high frequency of use;
. The environmental management system has a low frequency of use;
. Decisions are made with the same frequency on site as at the office.

Moving on from the more static presentation of the questioner and the broad picture of the attitudes and opinions of the construction companies, we now present some standpoints and some more in-depth episodes from selected construction companies. These standpoints and episodes are based on the case studies and will strengthen the questionnaire results, in some cases explaining

them and highlighting some important aspects that have been identified.

THE CONTEXT FOR DECISION MAKING AND SYSTEM USE

As argued in the beginning of the chapter the contextual elements are of major importance. This section therefore describes the context in which decisions are made at the studied company Alfa, along with the systems and applications used there. As a point of departure the description will start with issues that are on line managers' agenda - that is, issues that are dealt with by managers who are not directly involved in the daily operations at the project level. Thereafter the project setting is described, using a few episodes from a construction site in order to create a deeper understanding of decision-making and system usage. Finally, we describe the work of trying to take decisions before, or earlier, in the production process.

A Cost Driven Business

As showed in the results from the survey, cost and quality considerations were the highest ranked factors when decisions are made about material purchase and production methods. This is not surprising since operations are organized by projects with set budgets and timelines. Furthermore, costs and the reduction of costs have come into closer focus in the industry during recent years. Alfa's CEO stated in an interview that cost control and cost reductions are one of his major concerns for several reasons. The major problem in the industry, he said, is the increase in building costs, cannot more be pushed to the customers. He argues that a continuous increase of costs in the industry will mean that potential investors - private, corporate and public - will choose to spend their resources on other products and services where they perceive higher value for invested money. Therefore a goal to reduce costs annually by 5 percent per year until 2012 has a high priority. In order to reach this goal a number of activities are mentioned in interviews with managers on different levels and in public material presenting Alfa's strategies for reducing costs. For example, the head of a region and head of business district discussed how the supply chain, operations and planning of operations can be re-organized in order to decrease costs. Furthermore, attention is paid to purchases, and especially purchases abroad of products and services, an activity which is undertaken at all managerial levels. The contractor's focus on reducing costs for purchases is self-evident. A rule of thumb in the industry is that approximately 70 percent of a contractor's cost is purchases of material and sub-contractors in cases where the contractor is responsible for purchases and accomplishment of the whole project. The focus on purchases abroad is actually visualized in one of Alfa's regional news magazines by a chart, which publicizes cost data as the standings in a "competition" between business district managers. The chart shows the percentage of the total value of purchases originating from abroad. This extreme focus on costs could be in direct conflict with efforts to increase the focus on sustainability since it is clear from our study that managers at all levels in those organization perceived an increased environmental consideration as something that will cost both money and time.

However, the topic is not forgotten. When it comes to aspects of sustainability the CEO stated that the industry is just at the beginning of this process and these issues will probably climb higher on the agenda quite soon. The manager referred to a published article in the *Harvard Business Review* (Lockwood, 2006) and reflected that when a well-known business magazine publishes an article on this topic, it will probably receive higher attention in the near future. Other managers interviewed stated that the industry tries to work proactively with regard to materials and chemicals that can cause damage to the health and environment. For example, the industry has developed the so-called "Basta list" that contains materials and chemicals that not should be used. Furthermore, the energy consumption in accomplished buildings has come into increased focus. This is primarily due to new state regulation, but as one manager claimed, the contractual form also plays a significant role regarding the attention paid to a building's energy consumption. We did moreover not find anything in our interviews that contradict the results from the questionnaire concerning the managers' perception of the companies' environmental management policies. Respondents are seldom critical of them. However, they do admit that with the exception of chemicals, they do not have specific knowledge to choose the most sustainable production process or material. Information about chemical products is often to be found in the company's EMS.

An Action-Centered Context

Visitors to construction sites soon realize that this is a context focused on immediate action on several levels and that consequently a huge amount of decision-making occurs at a high frequency and in a hurry by all managers. A manager explains the essence of life at a construction site:

If three or four construction workers and an excavator working together run into a problem, they want an immediate solution to it. The managers concerned try to solve the problem immediately, even if on many occasions it would have been better to stop the activity and communicate the problem with other disciplines and even actors involved in that stage of the project.

Another manager stated that his work is "structured unstructured". In one sense it can be claimed that managers' work is unstructured in order to facilitate a smooth structured process for the construction workers. The following episode illustrates this point. At a weekly Monday morning production meeting, a carpenter came suddenly into the room, furious because there were no scissor lifts available and the demanding the deputy site manager find one IMMEDIATELY. The manager called the local outlet of the machinery and equipment rental firm and 45 minutes later the lift was delivered. After the incident the manager said that he thought that it is good that people are engaged in their work and always want the process to move forward. However, when directly after the delivery we discovered another lift on the floor below where it was needed, he added that people sometimes needed to spend some extra minutes and communicate with each other in order to find out if the missing equipment is somewhere else at the site. This episode can on one hand be seen as an expression of engagement in the project's progression, but on the other hand, as an expression of how the structure of wages shapes the sense making of events and reinforces certain behavior. In the Swedish construction sector, piece wages dominate, with the effect that all occurrences and activities not included in the piecework can be regarded as real or potential threats to the achievement of higher wages.

It can be claimed that piece wages based on the accomplishment of tasks on time, or faster, can be problematic if environmental and sustainability considerations need to be incorporated into the construction process. In the studied building project, quality controls are accomplished by self-assessment where the contractors and sub-

contractors have to follow established checklists. If a subcontractor has not made the self assessments agreed upon at a certain point in time, 15 percent of the invoiced value will be subtracted until all necessary controls are accomplished. For the contractor this procedure caused some problems. While the construction workers wanted to do the self-assessment with regard to the established checklist, their representatives did not want to take this responsibility. Instead they reported a detected error to a manager who then had the responsibility for taking action and correcting it. However, the manager responsible for quality control stated that self-control is the normal quality control procedure in other industries. Thus, incentives for expanding quality control into a more comprehensive regime for encompassing environmental impacts are really weak.

The demand for immediate action is, however, not only a concern for construction workers and something that is only connected to quality controls. In an interview, a development manager stated that more time should be spent on planning in general before the production starts, but in practice this is often not be the case. Instead the focus is usually on immediate action, which the manager illustrated with the following example. A client could see no excavators on site, concluded that production had not yet started, and called the business area manager to ask why. The business area manager asked the site manager why they have not yet have started to excavate. The site manager took action for action's sake, by ordering an excavator to dig a hole, even though the hole may not have been correctly excavated. Such a habit of taking immediate action in practice could account for the results in the questionnaire showing that decisions on all kind of aspects were taken with the same frequency, whether it was at the office during the planning stage, or during the production stage at the construction sites.

However, even if the layout of the construction and its components has been decided upon, problems can arise, since actors sometimes lack the capability to take the whole picture and the consequences of changes into consideration. One manager described an incident with a sprinkler tube that was moved half a meter because the installation engineer thought that the new direction made his work easier. This resulted in three to four other professional categories becoming involved in order to work out how make alternative placements of components. The manager concerned stated that the new direction of a sprinkler tube caused at least 30 hours of extra work to be spent on this compensatory activity. This is yet another example of the flow on effects of the habit of wanting immediate solutions to problems.

Transforming Decision Making in Practice?

A head of a business district mentioned the commonly used expression "to be solved at construction site", which is used as a consequence of the fact that all details are not solved during the design stage and that the practical solutions are delegated to the actors at the construction site. The manager also claimed that a generally tighter time schedule in the design stage implied that more tasks are delegated to the construction site to be solved there. A site manager mentioned windows as one example among hundreds of a lack of standards. He stated that on every construction site there is always a search for special solutions for making windows and other components watertight. An R & D manager, working on standardization issues linked to the introduction and use of 3D-based building information models, stated that more than 3000 types of windows exist on the Swedish market, when 300 would be enough to satisfy the need. Adding another element for consideration - environmental and sustainability criteria - to the large number of different materials and components, from which choices must be made, would complicate the decision-making process even further. This is probably one explanation for why environmental aspects do not achieve higher attention in everyday

decision-making. However, consciousness of the problem is high among managers as is awareness that standardization is one solution.

In order to increase the degree of standardization, Alfa is currently working on a project aimed at standardizing production methods for different kinds of buildings. Undertaking such work implies that production methods and materials should be evaluated and decisions made earlier in the process. A wide variety of issues come into focus when considering standardization of processes. For example, standardization of ceiling height when apartments are built under own management, standardization of design stages for certain kinds of building, predefinition of design and equipment of office buildings. Furthermore, is it decided that selected production methods; materials etc. should be tested in order to guarantee their quality and sustainability. Furthermore, in interviews it was emphasized that standards should not be fixed at the outset; rather experiences and knowledge gained should be incorporated when methods and materials are selected. Moreover, it can be argued that scandals related to inappropriate choices of methods and materials originate from an insufficient validation of those methods and materials. In an interview with the CEO, we claimed that the building and construction sector is the antipode to the health care sector when it comes to validation of methods and materials. In the health care sector new treatment methods and drugs need to undergo a rigorous scientific validation before either methods or drugs can be used in practice. The CEO admitted that the building and construction sector will never come close to the health care sector in terms of validation of methods used, but steps are needed in that direction and at least a few should be taken. This change is especially necessary to achieve the visions described in the industry's environmental polices. Thus, theoretically, standardizing production methods and choices of material implies that environmental and sustainability aspects could be factors that would be systematically taken into consideration and not be delegated to managers at the construction site to decide upon with limited available information.

Intertwined with the process of standardization is the launch of 3D-based building information models, which is also an example of how new ICT continues to develop and be adapted to the industry. The managers concerned with the development and use of these models state that there is a heavy workload of inscribing standardized components and work methods into these models. However, some of the sub-contractors' consultants, in the project studied, already work with 3D-based tools. For example, the ventilation consultant stated that he draws everything in 3D, and about 90% of components needed are available in 3D and supplied by material suppliers. Thus, the emergence of 3D-based building and information models and attempts to standardize work processes and choices of materials, can also be aligned with environmental and sustainability issues. First, the amount of rework and number of errors detected after a building has been accomplished can be decreased. Decisions regarding choices of materials and production methods are made earlier and will not be dependent on the information that single actors have at hand when decisions are made.

To summarize, site observations make it possible to claim that the complexity of the interrelations between activities and components at a construction site put demands on the information flow and the forward planning for all parties involved. Participation in meetings of the different groups revealed that after a certain point of time there is no space for changes. At the design stage there is still space for discussions and negotiations about how different solutions should be accomplished. However, many interviewees and participants in meetings declared that a contemporary problem in the industry is the short time span between design/preparation and production. It is not unusual that a part of the construction that is discussed in a design meeting is produced a few days later. Circumstances like these place extraordinary demands on the both the decision-making and the information flows at the construction site and among other actors involved.

THE RELATION BETWEEN ICT AND ENVIRONMENTAL-MANAGEMENT PRACTICE

The aim of this chapter has been to draw attention to the construction company, and in particular, how ICT is, or could be, related to their day-to-day efforts to develop more environmentally friendly and sustainable production processes.

A well functioning and efficient information and communication flow is the heart of a construction company. Construction projects are complex and involve a very large number of actors both within the company as well as outside it. All these actors are related to one other in a multifaceted system of information flows and decision-making processes in what appear on paper to be a strict and clear power hierarchy. However, the picture is much more blurred when it comes to managers' own perceptions of power and their actual influence on the process. When it comes to decisions related to managing the environment, it is evident that this ambiguity can be a problem.

In these companies and projects, technology is an essential part of the information and communication flow. All managers, at all levels in the offices as well as on the construction sites, use computers on a daily basis. In addition, a surprisingly large number of different ICT applications are implemented and used although different groups use different systems. We can also observe a clear relation between the frequency of decision-making and the frequency of using ICT. The ICT systems used are mainly for controlling projects, or facilitating the control of project processes. 3D-systems created to coordinate different stages in the project and different actors are still not fully integrated, especially not over project and company boundaries. What is noteworthy and somewhat worrisome is that we can observe a tendency for the environmental management systems to be the least used and the ones perceived as least useful and effective. On the other hand, most managers do not miss them. However, we can also conclude that managers at all levels in Swedish construction companies are fairly satisfied with their company's ICT strategies and also with their company's environmental management strategies and policies.

The same study made it clear that in day-to-day practice in a fragmented working situation environmental decisions do not come high on the agenda. However, the problem in a construction project concerning decisions related to the environment is not, as previous claimed, directly related to inefficient ICT, even though the potential for improvement is large. We have observed that managers on a level, that should not be forced to do it, often take decisions that affect environmental issues at all levels in the organization. This situation is caused by circumstances such as deviations from original plans and/or inadequate project-related documents and contracts and it almost always occurs under time pressure. How these decisions are taken care of in such situations is closely related to the attitudes of single actors. Notable is the site manager's role, which seems to deviate from the official one. Ideally, many of those decisions that are made at the site by the site managers should have been made earlier. Moreover, we argue that there are some clear problems with the knowledge and information that is available for those managers at the time the decisions have to be made.

The implemented ICT application seldom supported such a decision process due to the simple fact that information is often missing but also since the dimension of co-coordinating and supporting complex information flows might have come to the foreground in the ICT systems used. Consequently, they do not support knowledge creation of complex communication patterns to a sufficient degree, especially not when it comes to environmentally related decisions at the construction site.

However, the main problem is still not the ICT, rather we should focus on factors such as unclear power structures, blurred responsibilities, and a general lack of knowledge and real awareness concerning environmental issues in the sector. In a money and time focused business with vague demands from customer and society as a whole, the incentives on a project level for taking sustainability issues into consideration, beyond current legal requirements, are not strong enough. Single managers are torn between private efforts to be "environmentally friendly" and a work situation where they do not know how to achieve that in that practice. It is especially clear in our cases that they lack information or feel powerless. However, as has been noted, some of the contemporary trends in the sector, such as the introduction of building information models, standardization and focus on quality issues, can also be viewed as vehicles for raising issues of sustainability higher on the agenda. In any event, environmental topics should not merely be regarded as "window dressing".

We strongly believe that in order to enhance a more environmentally friendly building and construction industry there is a need for a more genuine cooperation and knowledge sharing between different actors both in crossing project boundaries as well as overriding contractual limitations. Decisions in a construction project must be taken earlier in the process and construction companies need to focus more on those processes over which they actually do have power. To be able to do that, common ICT solutions, standardized platforms for information and knowledge sharing among all actors in a construction project, including across company borders is a necessity and a challenge for the sector as a whole.

ACKNOWLEDGMENT

This research project is funded by the Swedish research fund for environment, agricultural sciences, and spatial planning (Formas). The authors also wish to acknowledge Dr Anders Isaksson and Vladimir Vanyushyn for their extensive contribution to the survey study and for their contribution to this chapter.

REFERENCES

Andrews, A., Rankin, J. H., & Waugh, L. M. (2006). A framework to identify opportunities for ICT support when implementing sustainable design standards. *ITcon - . Electronic Journal of Information Technology in Construction, 11*, 17–33.

Baumann, H., Brunklaus, B., Gluch, P., Kadefors, A., Stenberg, A.-C., & Thuvander, L. (2003). *Byggsektorns Miljöbarometer 2002*. Sweden: Chalmers University of technology . *ESA Report, 2003*, 2.

Bon, R., & Hutchinson, K. (2000). Sustainable construction: some economic challenges. *Building Research and Information, 28*(5-6), 310–314. doi:10.1080/096132100418465

Ciborra, C. U., & Lanzara, G., F. (1994). Formative contexts and information technology, *Accounting . Management and Information Technology, 4*(2), 61–86. doi:10.1016/0959-8022(94)90005-1

Cutting-Decelle, A.-F., Young, B. I., Das, B. P., Case, K., Rahimifard, S., Anumba, C. J., & Bouchlaghem, D. M. (2007). A review of approaches to supply chain communications: from manufacturing to construction. *ITcon - . Electronic Journal of Information Technology in Construction*, (12): 73–102.

Dainty, A., Moore, D., & Murray, M. (2006). *Communication in construction: Theory and practice*. Oxon: Taylor & Francis.

DeFilippi, R. J., & Arthur, M. (1998). Paradox in project-based enterprises: the case of film making. *California Management Review, 40*(2), 125–140.

Ekstedt, E., Lundin, R. A., & Wirdenius, H. (1992). Conceptions and renewal in Swedish construction companies . *European Management Journal, 10*(2), 202–209. doi:10.1016/0263-2373(92)90070-K

Femenías, P. (2004). *Demonstration projects for Sustainable Building: Towards a strategy for Sustainable Development in the building sector based on Swedish and Dutch experience*. Dissertation thesis, Chalmers University of technology, Sweden.

Gann, D. M., & Salter, A. (2000). Innovation in project-based, service-enhanced firms: the construction of complex products and systems. *Research Policy, 29*(7-8), 955–972. doi:10.1016/S0048-7333(00)00114-1

Gluch, P. (2000). *Managerial Environmental Accounting in Construction Projects - Discussions on its Usability and Role in Decision Making*. Göteborg, Sweden: Chalmers University of Technology.

Gluch, P. (2005). *Building green – Perspectives on environmental management in construction*. Dissertation thesis, Chalmers University of technology, Sweden.

Gluch, P. (2006). *Effektivare miljöinformation i byggprojekt – Illustrationer från ett tunnelprojekt*. Göteborg, Sweden: Chalmers Repro.

Gluch, P., & Baumann, H. (2004). The life cycle costing (LCC) approach: a conceptual discussion of its usefulness for environmental decision-making. *Building and Environment, 39*(5), 571–580. doi:10.1016/j.buildenv.2003.10.008

Harty, C. (2005). Innovation in construction: a sociology of technology approach. *Building Research and Information, 33*(6), 512–522. doi:10.1080/09613210500288605

Hill, R. C., & Bowen, P. A. (1997). Sustainable construction: principles and a framework for attainment. *Construction Management and Economics, 15*(3), 223–239. doi:10.1080/014461997372971

Isaksson, A., Linde, A., & Vanyushyn, V. (2009). Environmental management in construction companies: Decisions, technologies and effects. *Proceeding of 5ᵗʰ Nordic Conference on Construction Economics and Organisation, 1, Reykjavík, Iceland* (pp. 193-204)

Jacobsson, M. (2008a). *Samordning och kommunikation i ett anläggningsprojekt – Mellan en laminerad A3-karta och ett dike*. Sweden . *BA-Publications, 2008*, 201.

Jacobsson, M. (2008b). Liaison devices in an information reduction process - Observations from a Swedish case stud, *EDEN seminar and Summer Workshop in Project Management*. Lille, France, 18-22 Aug. 2008

Jacobsson, M. (2009). Understanding project communication in a construction process: The importance of project liaisons, *Proceeding of 5ᵗʰ Nordic Conference on Construction Economics and Organisation, 1, Reykjavík, Iceland*, (pp. 155-166).

Kibert, C. J. (2007). The next generation of sustainable construction. *Building Research and Information, 35*(6), 595–601. doi:10.1080/09613210701467040

Linderoth, C. J. H., & Jacobsson, M. (2008). Understanding adoption and use of ICT in construction projects through the lens of context, actors and technology. In L. Rischmoller, (Ed.), *Proceeding of CIB W78, Improving the management of construction projects through IT adoption. Talca, Chile,* (pp. 203-212).

Lockwood, C. (2006). Building the green way. *Harvard Business Review, 84*(6), 129–137.

Markus, M. L., & Robey, D. (1988). Information technology and organizational change: Causal structure in theory and research. *Management Science, 34*(5), 583–598. doi:10.1287/mnsc.34.5.583

Mitropoulos, P., & Tatum, C. B. (1999). Technology adoption decisions in construction organizations. *Journal of Construction Engineering and Management, 125*(5), 330–339. doi:10.1061/(ASCE)0733-9364(1999)125:5(330)

Molnár, M., Anderson, R., & Ekholm, A. (2007). Benefits of ICT in the construction industry – Characterization of the present situation the house building processes. In D. Rebolj, (Ed.) *Proceeding of CIB 24th W78 Conference Maribor - Bringing ITC knowledge to work. Maribor, Slovenia,* (pp. 423-428).

Monteiro, E. (2003). Integrating health information systems: A critical appraisal. *Methods of Information in Medicine, 42*, 428–432.

Ofori, G. (1998). Sustainable construction: principles and a framework for attainment - comment. *Construction Management and Economics, 16*(2), 141–145. doi:10.1080/014461998372448

Orlikowski, W. J. (1992). The duality of technology: Rethinking the concept of technology in organizations. *Organization Science, 3*(3), 398–427. doi:10.1287/orsc.3.3.398

Orlikowski, W. J., & Robey, D. (1991). Information technology and structuring of organizations. *Information Systems Research, 2*(2), 143–169. doi:10.1287/isre.2.2.143

Rowlinson, S. (2007). The temporal nature of forces acting on innovative IT in major construction projects. *Construction Management and Economics, 25*(3), 227–238. doi:10.1080/01446190600953698

Samuelson, O. (2001). *IT-Barometern 2000 – En undersökning om IT-användning i bygg- och Fastighetsbranschen, IT Bygg och Fastighet 2002.* Sundbyberg, Sweden: BodoniTryck AB.

Samuelson, O. (2002). IT-Barometer 2000 - The use of IT in the Nordic construction industry. *ITcon - . Electronic Journal of Information Technology in Construction, 7,* 1–26.

Samuelson, O. (2008). The IT-barometer - a decade's development of IT use in the Swedish construction sector. *ITcon - . Electronic Journal of Information Technology in Construction, 13,* 1–19.

Sjöström, C., & Bakens, W. (1999). CIB Agenda 21 for sustainable construction: why, how and what. *Building Research and Information, 27*(6), 347–353. doi:10.1080/096132199369174

Sobotka, A., & Wyatt, D. P. (1998). Sustainable development in the practice of building resources renovation. *Facilities, 16*(11), 319–325. doi:10.1108/02632779810233584

Söderholm, A. (2006). Kampen om kommunikationen. In Ö. Wikforss (Ed.), *Kampen om kommunikationen - Om projektledningens Informationsteknologi.* Sweden: Research report, Royal Institute of Technology.

Spence, R., & Mulligan, H. (1995). Sustainable Development and the Construction Industry. *Habitat International, 19*(3), 279–292. doi:10.1016/0197-3975(94)00071-9

Wenblad, A. (2001). Sustainability in the Construction Business - A Case Study. *Corporate Environmental Strategy, 8*(2), 157–164. doi:10.1016/S1066-7938(01)00096-3

Wikforss, Ö. (Ed.). (2006). *Kampen om kommunikationen: Om projektledningens Informationsteknologi.* Sweden: Research report, Royal Institute of Technology.

Wikforss, Ö., & Löfgren, A. (2007). Rethinking communication in construction. *ITcon - . Electronic Journal of Information Technology in Construction, 12,* 337–345.

ENDNOTE

[*] Corresponding author

Chapter 11
The Need for Accounting in Dialects:
Making the Special Competitive Culture in Family–Run Companies Sustainable

Per Forsberg
University of Borås, Sweden

Mikael Lind
University of Borås, Sweden

ABSTRACT

This chapter deals with the challenge of ensuring and sustaining cultural competitiveness in a globalised world where control and management tend to be made at a distance. The authors illustrate this by arguing that family-run businesses have a special culture that makes them good at creating and taking part in innovative networks. Today this culture is however threatened. Implementation of technologies for controlling and governing at a distance destroy this special family-run business culture. As a solution to this problem the authors suggest that new technologies of communication have the potential to strengthen the ability to create innovative networks. New technologies of communication do this when they give rise to alternative forms of communication and thus complement management based on "controlling and acting at a distance".

THE CHALLENGE OF ENSURING AND SUSTAINING CULTURAL COMPETITIVENESS

Family firms have a special culture that makes them good at creating and taking part in networks. But, there is a risk that this culture is destroyed when technologies for controlling and acting at a distance are implemented, as often is the case when alliances with bigger firms are created or when a family-run company itself becomes larger. Such technologies, as for example standardized accounting systems, often tend to leave out the informal accounting that is important for the special family firm culture. The question then is how this special culture can be made sustainable? Questions like these have been discussed in accounting research before, see for example Bebbington et al. (2007); Boyce (2000); Brown (2008); Forsberg (2009); Gray (2002): Gray

DOI: 10.4018/978-1-60566-822-2.ch011

et al. (1997); Macintosh and Baker (2002); Morgan (1988); O'Dwyer (2005) and Towley et al. (2003). In these studies an alternative accounting form that stimulates democracy and deliberation are discussed. Therefore, accounting that is more informal, dialogical and include oral accounts have been suggested.

It is against this background that we in this chapter explore how different "communication technologies" affect the competitiveness of family-run business. As stated above, smaller family-run companies have a special culture that gives them a special competitiveness. This culture is especially beneficial for creating networks. Below we describe three conditions that are required for the successful joining and creating of such networks under three different headlines:

1. Informal ways of decision-making and a non-hierarchical organization,
2. Being an agent of a community, family and place,
3. Mutual interest and sympathy

Our argument that informal ways of decision-making and less hierarchy are prerequisites for innovative networks is based on theories about industrial networks (Gadde, et al. 2003) together with theories on the strategies of development companies and what might happen to small companies that are incorporated into big companies (Jönsson 1973). But we also discuss negative effects that companies may experience when they to an increasing degree are managed and controlled from a distance (Robson 1992, Latour 1987, Preston 2006) and when financial incentives create "agents of economy".

The ability to join and create networks also depends on the actions of the management. Networking is facilitated if the management in the words of Wendell Berry (2005) acts as an agent "of a place, a family and a community" rather than as an "agent of an economy". In communities virtues and qualities are developed that en-

able people to cooperate. Moreover, the fact that a person belongs to a family, a community and a place directs his/her actions towards what is good in the long run, which in turn entails that others know "where they have you".

Mutual interest and sympathy (sympathy that explains actions that are based on empathy and what are considered to be good actions in the eyes of others) instead of individual interest and individual rationality increase the company's capability to create and take part in networks. Our presentation of sympathy builds on Adam Smith's theory of moral sentiment (Smith 1759, Otteson 2002).

However, problems arise when these rather small family-run companies expand by themselves or if they are bought and incorporated into a larger group of companies. When this happens it is common that new technologies for governance are implemented and an external decision center starts to manage and control the local company from distance. People at these decision centers often face problems that have to do with access to good information about what actually is going on. The local communities (in the family company) that work close to the costumer make use of informal accounts that hardly can travel to the external center. Another problem occurs when an external center is governing from a distance - it might crowd-out the informal ways of decision-making together with the informal way of organizing, the connection to a place, community and family together with the role of sympathy.

It is against this background that new technologies of communication must be explored. Can such technologies give rise to, not one standardized language developed in order to make controlling and acting from a distance possible - but accounting in dialects in order to make cooperation and networking possible, and thereby strengthen the competitiveness of family-run business?

To summarize our argument:

1. Family-run businesses have a special culture that makes them good at creating and taking part in networks.
2. This culture is threatened when technologies for controlling and governing at a distance are implemented or when the informal decision making is formalized, as often is the case when the companies become bigger or when they are merged into other companies.
3. The special family firm culture can be made sustainable with new communication technologies if they allow accounts in dialects, which stimulate democratic deliberations.

FAMILY-RUN FIRMS AND THEIR COMPETITIVENESS

Family-run business can be found in many different countries and different industries. In Sweden they are most frequent in the agriculture and forest industry, but they are also dominating in industries as retailing, manufacturing, building, and transport (Emling, 2000). They are an important part of the Swedish national economy, 54.5% of the companies in Sweden are family-run business (defined as at least one succession has occurred). This importance of family-run business can also be found in the rest of Europe (Emling, 2000).

Previous studies (Miller & Le Breton Miller, 2005) of family-run companies have shown that this type of business has certain competitive advantages that have to do with:

1. The management being independent and enjoying a high degree of ability to act on its own,
2. The management striving towards survival of the business in a long-term perspective,
3. A strong feeling among the employees of belonging to a community (inside the company), which makes them focused on fulfilling the mission of the company. Incentives or bureaucracy does not create this attitude.

4. A desire for good relations with neighbors, clients, suppliers and the broader community.

Miller and Le Breton-Miller have studied rather large family companies. But, the competitive factors mentioned above certainly hold true also for smaller family-run businesses. However, they do not capture the specific advantage that small companies have when it comes to joining and creating networks.

According to Wincent (2006), companies can increase their competitiveness by joining networks. The companies that succeed best in networks are the ones that share their ideas and have time to be engaged in the network. Beside this, management needs to have a great deal of self-confidence and tolerance for uncertainty. The reason that family-run companies do better then those who are not is that they have more and better networks and thereby manage to get good information (Gudmunson et. al., 1999)

What we know from research on family-owned companies and competitiveness in family-run business is that community-based innovative networks play an important role. This can be exemplified with a common attitude in the Swedish shipping industry. In the shipping trade there are those who consider goals and control - that comes from the stock market – to be a hamper on the entrepreneurial spirit. Torsten Rinman (1999), former editor for Svensk Sjöfarts Tidning (Swedish Shipping Gazette), has written about the characteristics of successful archipelago shipping companies. He writes that these companies do not fit the stock market and refers to the fact that ship-owners belong to an entrepreneurial type who often feels hampered by the respect they have to pay to stockowners, stock-exchange quotations and rules. Rinman writes that ship-owners of companies noted on the stock exchange often need to invest a lot of time in "talking up" the stock price. Stockowners are often ignorant of the shipping trade and merely take the general market trends into consideration. During periods when the price of the stock is low, a shipping company on the stock market risks being purchased by its competitors. The consideration a shipping company listed on the stock market has to take often conflicts with the operational economics that characterizes most archipelago shipping companies (Rinman 1999).

From a Swedish perspective it seems as if shipping companies that do better over time are all anchored in the local shipping trade cultures and have a management that is very well defined in terms of a family that is engaged in its everyday operation. The Scandinavian Shipping Gazette has published a special issue on the theme of "Shipping communities"[1]. Here are a number of local shipping trade cultures that have been significant for the emergence of shipping companies emphasized. One example of this is Donsö, an island in the southern Göteborg archipelago. An additional example is that of Skärhamn, where 50% of the Swedish commercial fleet is run. There are also the Norwegian regions of Haugesund and Vestfold. In Denmark there is Marstal, and in Finland there is Åland. In these regions there is a strong shipping tradition and its practice is said to be more than a business. The particular lifestyle that the people of these cultures maintain, together with their experiences at sea, has to them a value of its own. People who have grown up in shipping trade cultures do often not contend themselves with being employed but would like to have their own boat to run. Usually these companies have chosen to finance their operation in other ways than being noted on the stock market. In the few cases, at least in Sweden, when companies from such regions are listed on the stock exchange, the family usually has a clear majority of the shares and is actively running the business (Rinman 1999).

Since way back, several constellations of collaboration are developed in these shipping trade cultures – and it seems as if it is the very ability to join and create innovative networks that form the basis for the good development of the businesses in these regions.

The importance of the special culture in family-run business can be found in different industries and countries. Below we will give some examples of empirical studies to clarify this.

Elmhester (2008) studied the difference between larger and smaller firms (in Sweden) when it comes to what networks mean to companies in the wood product-manufacturing sector. Her conclusion is that it might be easier for smaller companies to establish social networks, but also, that an active manager seems to be more important for successful networking than a highly developed formal organization.

Based on a case studies of three wine firms and one firm in the spirits industry (two from Italy and two from Switzerland), Salvato & Melin (2008) argue that there is a strong relationship between value creation and social capital and that family companies are especially successful when it comes to create social and professional networks. Furthermore, mutual trust between the family members together with the firms' reputation and external networks makes it easier to adapt to a changing environment and transfer knowledge inside the firm and between different firms.

Research about family-run business in Middle East (Kuwait and Lebanon) has confirmed the view that family-run business is not a phenomenon that only can be found in western countries. There are a lot of similarities in how retail managers and salespersons in Middle East and Western family-run business behave (Welsh and Raven, 2006). Moreover, "Being smaller and more flexible, family-run retailers should be able to understand their customers and fulfill their needs much more efficiently than can global retailers. Their competitive advantage cannot be found in the huge buying power and extensive research capabilities, but in their ability to intimately know their customers and their needs. Price competition is unlikely to be their advantage, but service can be …" (Welsh & Raven, 2006, p. 44).

In a study of family-run business in China the importance of families when it comes to 'collective values, centralized authority, conformity and the importance of reputation achieved through hard work' (Pistrui, 2006, et. al., p. 483) are emphasized. But it is not only the families that influence these Chinese firms but also traditions of Confucianism and Guanxi (a Chinese term for personal network that is based on mutual trust and understanding). The family business seems to dominate the entrepreneurship in China.

Thus, research of family-run business in Europe and Middle East and Asia highlight the importance of family business for the national economies but also indicate that family controlled business gives better performance.

However, a different picture of the importance of family-run business for the national economy can be found in studies from the Balkan countries. Poutziouris et al. (1997) argue that the relative few small and mid-size companies in post-soviet countries as Bulgaria and Romania "inhibits the development of industrial capacity, creating employment, generating innovations, and drawing companies into the marketing process." (Poutziouris et al. 1997, pp. 239-240). It is therefore important to facilitate the institutional infrastructure that facilitates entrepreneurships and family-run business in order to make the economy growing.

In Pistrui et al. (1997) the Romanian society is said to rely on family and personal networks. The authors claim, "the family has developed networks based on kinship and friendship, which banded together to offer socioeconomic support" (p. 236).

In a study of entrepreneurship and the role of the family-run business in East and West Germany some important differences could be identified (Pistrui et. al. 2000). The owners of small firms in East Germany are more engaged and involved and find more enjoyment in their work and are more inclined to support the surrounding community. The most important to the company owners in West Germany seem to be more about supporting the family welfare. However, even if the entrepreneurial spirit is not that strong in West Germany as in East Germany, West Germany has an environment that is more supportive for small companies.

But, it is important to note that there are also studies in where it is argued that smaller companies are more affected by the industrial sector and their geographical location compared to bigger companies (Wiklund, 1998).

To conclude, there are cultural differences and differences between family-run companies in the same culture. But what has been called the "family ownership logic" are claimed to be valid for the major part of family-run business. Big family-run businesses at the global market or small ones that operate at a small and local market share a common set of values. (Brundin, et al., 2008)

However, while a lot of research about family competitiveness has been about identifying strengths and how the environment can be made more supportive for family business we will in this chapter concentrate on how communication technologies can hinder but also facilitate the competiveness of family firms.

THE ABILITY TO JOIN AND CREATE NETWORKS

Parallel to the belief that control and management from a distance creates added value is the belief that participating in a network does the same. Networks are significant, for example when it comes to development and innovations, which often requires collaboration and dialogues between several actors. For small businesses, networks can lead to cooperation and generate access to large-scale benefits and other coordination profits that they would not have been able to achieve on their own. Even the relations to the customers can be described in terms of a network. A long-term customer relation is not characterized by exploitation and short-term profit maximum, but is about mutual gain. (For a discussion about hostile take over of family firms and what consequences it has on the family firm's network see Steen & Welch, 1998)

Below, we will introduce theories, divided into three aspects, which help explain why small family companies' competitive advantages work in networks. By illustrating these it is possible to increase knowledge about what the competitive force of small companies consist of and what potential they have to grow without loosing it.

First, we will look closer at the strength of the non-hierarchical structure of the family-firm organization and at informal and fast decision-making procedures. Second, we will look into the advantages of acting as an agent of a community, family and place. Third, we will focus on the fact that the management that gets involved in networks and various collaborative constellations and act as an agent of the family, community and place, ground their decision on sympathy and mutual interest rather than calculations of individual benefits.

Un-Hierarchical Forms of Organizing as Advantages in Networking

Networks can make it easier for businesses to come up with or generate innovations and improvements (c.f. e.g. Albinsson et al, 2007). But it is important that the networks are dynamic. Gadde, et al. (2003) claim that the dynamics of a network is kept alive when different members of the network "constantly interacting and [trying] to influence each other" (Gadde, et al. 2003).

Each individual company, which is involved in the network, must be focused on mutual interests instead of individualistic goals. In a well working network the companies constantly interacting with each other and continuously search for new possibilities. Furthermore, companies in an industrial network strive to cooperate - therefore mutual trust is important. Both economic and social dimensions are important in networks. (Gadde, et al. 2003)

Gadde, et al. (2003) states that: "The company must analyze its situation in terms of its relationships and their connections. It is crucial that a company relates its activities to those of other firms in order to enhance its performance, and it is through the continuous combining and recombining in business relationships that new resource dimensions are identified and further developed." (p. 363).

This speaks for small un-hierarchical (family-) businesses having competitive advantages that might disappear if strong hierarchies together with control and management from external centers are introduced.

In a network, no company should have a dominant position; there should be no company that acts as the center of the network. In such cases the network will become less innovative. Gadde, et al. writes:

A centrally controlled system is based on a limited view of the entire network, which makes a 'pluralistic' network better able to respond to changing conditions. The greater the influence exercised by a company on its relationships, the more restricted will be the responses from the network. (Gadde, et al., p. 361)

Gadde, et al. (2003) emphasize that companies often should take part in several value-creating chains at the same time. But, a company that has its strategy determined by an external center (focused on single value-chains) may lose the dynamics required of business in industrial networks. The strategy needs to be influenced by a variety of collaborating partners.

In an unstable environment, it is beneficial with an "organic system of management" (Jönsson, 1973). This type of management is characterized by "sounding out" instead of instructing. In an organic system, people are uncertain of what is expected from them, and, consequently, they continuously search for their role. However, uncertainty and inadequate specification regarding positions also give room for maneuvering. This leads to increased commitment and dependence on others. External pressure (crises) generates a tendency to strive away from an organic form towards a mechanical one (Jönsson, 1973).

The potential and efficiency that comes with the inherent uncertainty of organic forms of organization may thus be a pre-condition for a functioning network, which might be threatened by clear hierarchies and formal ways of decision-making.

...the more successful a company is in its control ambitions, the less innovative the network becomes. If one actor totally directs the development processes, the network runs the risk of becoming a hierarchy, with reduced potential for innovation. (Gadde, et al. p. 358)

Acting as an Agent of Community, Family and Place

In this section we argue that well working network depends on if the people in a company acts as agents of a community, family and place. The ability to be accepted in a network also depends on the importance of having a reputation that pictures the company as a serious enterprise. Another factor is collective experiences and values and learning to nurture things one has in common.

As an agent of community you share a culture with others (Berry 2005). This culture contains collected experience and knowledge manifested in collections of agents' worldviews. Such a culture arises where people stay at the same place over a long period of time. In this way agents engaged in the community continuously refine their worldviews.

Belonging to a culture makes it possible to find "... guidance from the knowledge we most authentically possess, from experience, from

tradition, and from the inward promptings of affection, conscience, decency, compassion and even inspiration." (Berry 2005, p. 63)

Local and personal loyalty is involved in business (Berry 2005). The business is created in a context where work is a link in a bigger chain that secures the existence of the family, the community and the place. Berry contrasts this community mind with the corporate mind:

The corporate mind at work overthrows all the virtues of the personal mind, or it throws them out of account. The corporate mind knows no affection, no desire that is not greedy, no local or personal loyalty, no sympathy or reverence or gratitude, no temperance or thrift or self-restraint. It does not observe the first responsibility of intelligence, which is to know when you don't know or when you are being unintelligent. (Berry 2005, p. 60)

In the following section, we will go further into "the community mind"; specifically the role sympathy has for the network.

Sympathy and Cooperation

As mentioned above, people that argue for external centers and incentive systems often refer to *Wealth of Nations* (Smith 1776). Here we will argue for another line of reasoning, that which begins with Adam Smith's theory of moral sentiments. For this purpose we have made use of Otteson's book: *Adam Smith's Market Place of Life*, from 2002. The theory of moral sentiments can help us explain the competitiveness in companies embedded in communities. Because it is only in the community that the special virtues that make cooperation possible are created.

Instead of individual rationality it is sympathy that makes cooperation possible and guides the agent of a family, community and place. Life in a community prepares people for exchange with others outside the community. The abilities that the community provides its members with become pre-conditions for exchanges on a market, since such exchanges build on mutual interest. (Otteson 2002)

There is a mechanism/ability/passion that affects us which Smith calls sympathy. Human beings are naturally prone to sharing joy. They feel sympathetic towards that which keeps a group together and makes things sustainable.

Otteson summarizes the Adam Smith idea about sympathy and cooperation:

...the fortunes and happiness of others are necessary to each person. Without the help of and associations with other people, we cannot physically survive or psychologically flourish, and we cannot engage the help or associations of others without taking a sincere interest in their situations. Nature, again thankfully, has constituted us so that before any philosophy or deliberation we are inclined to be interested in others. This inclination makes possible the mutual concern that ultimately, Smith thinks, forms the basis of civil society. (Otteson, 2002, p. 91)

and...

...the development of personal moral stands, of a conscience and the impartial spectator procedure, and of the accepted moral standards of a community all depend on the regular associations people make with one another. It is in these associations, in the daily intercourse people have with one another, that they encourage each other to discover and adopt rules of behavior and judgment that will lead to mutual sympathy. (Otteson p. 123)

Therefore sympathy can be seen as "a powerful social bond that enables us to form communities and that provides strong incentives toward social stability." (Otteson 2002, p. 293)

Beside our desire for sympathy, humans also have a desire to improve their condition of life. This gives rise to markets that make it possible for people that do not know each other to meet and make exchanges. What is interesting with Otteson's interpretation of Smith is that the desire for sympathy and the desire of humans to make their condition better are not necessarily decoupled.

...people cannot succeed in markets unless they take an interest in others, which requires that they spend time getting to know others' needs and wants... this mutual familiarity will lead to mutual natural affection and hence benevolence. (Otteson, p. 304)

On the other hand, one feels stronger sympathy for that which is close: first the family, then the firm, and then the community. The sympathy also grows stronger as meetings are repeated. It is therefore possible to imagine that pure calculation dominates where people make decisions from a distance and on markets where the seller and the buyer are unknown to one another.

INFORMAL INFORMATION PROCESSES IN THE LOCAL CULTURE

In previous sections we have described what characterizes local cultures that are good at participating in networks. Now we turn our attention to mechanisms and information processes that underlie the informal information process.

Two different forms of information processes can be derived from the distinction between occupational community and organization.

In theory, occupational community is defined as "a group of people who consider themselves to be engaged in the same sort of work; whose identity is drawn from their work; who share with one another a set of values, norms and perspectives that apply to but extend beyond work related matters; and whose social relationships meld work and leisure" (van Maanen & Barley 1984, p. 287). This informal way of organizing is competing with the more formal and hierarchical one that van Maanen & Barley call "organization". This organization is pictured as a vertical hierarchy and control mechanisms have a central role. In an organization, the people are talking about formal matters such as status, power, money and other rewards. In an occupational community, people talk about if they are getting better or worse at cooperate, if they actually help their costumers to maintain their abilities to fulfil their mission etc. Furthermore, in an organization the employees often have detailed work descriptions and fragmented functions. Members in an occupational community are bound together through common values, tradition and solidarity. This kind of community stands in sharp contrast with the organization that often put up individualistic goals like profit making and rational calculations. Members in an occupational community strive to present a socially acceptable image to the other members. According to Forsberg & Westerdahl (2007) the ideal occupational community also strife to present a good image to other shareholders, for example the costumers.

In the article "For the sake of serving the broader community: comparing auditors and sea-pilots" by Forsberg & Westerdahl (2007) the sea-piloting practice is described as depending on a strong occupational community. In this community a special culture has been developed that forms the identity and what the work is about. The knowledge of sea-pilots is basically based on experience, transferred and reflected upon in informal meetings. This knowledge is stored in an oral based culture. Their special culture makes them equipped to meet unique situations and focus on creating the ability to make it possible for the shipping companies to fulfill their transports.

However, this special culture and giving account for what a good service is, is difficult to give account for to people outside the culture, for example politicians, central management and other shareholders. What is important to them are expressed in oral stories, which are hard to grasp for decision makers that work at distance.

STANDARDIZED ACCOUNTING VS. ACCOUNTING IN DIALECTS

To simplify, there are two positions in the discussion about agency costs in family owned companies (Bartholomeusz & Tanewski 2006). According to one of these positions firms with family control have good mechanisms for reducing agency costs. Family owners are often active in preventing free riders and in creating efficient management. The wealth of the family depends on how the business turns out in the long run, and therefore family firms strive to maximize the wealth of the firm in the long run.

According to the other position family control in fact creates "agency costs". The family can increase its own wealth at the cost of other shareholders. Thanks to the powerful position of the family, there is a risk that the family maximizes the value of the family instead of the value of the firm. Family firms have another corporate structure than non-family firms, and this structure is not always in consistence with the goal of maximizing the value of the firm. (Bartholomeusz & Tanewski 2006)

Advocates of external management and control (e.g. Bartholomeusz & Tanewski, 2006) think that incentives are needed that encourage, above all the management, but also the employees, to work for the owners or the value of the company when necessary. Such advocates often lean on Smith's *Wealth of Nations* (1776) and emphasize that s/he who is not an owner of the company is not willing to make the same kind of sacrifices as s/he who is – and not with the same dedication. The tools used for managing are quantitative and shaped to enable control and management from a distance. Besides that, they often apply incentive programs (Jensen & Meckling, 1994) with the aim of directing the focus of the manager and the employees on short-term profits.

We hold it for true that these ideas about the importance that family-run firms need to be governed from distance is put into focus in bigger family firms, especially in cases when the family is not the only owner and there are many different stakeholders included.

When companies become larger, new tools for control and management are adopted: detailed rule-based work descriptions, strong hierarchies and accounting with the aim of controlling from a distance are said to add value to companies (Gold & Campbell, 1987). Acting and controlling from a distance is there to enable action without knowledge of the context (Robson 1992; Latour 1987). This kind of control may have non-intended negative effects (Preston 2006). These tools may have consequences that make people start acting like "agents of economy".

Thus, formal accounting and mechanisms for communication are in theory claimed to solve different kind of problems within family-run companies. However, we will put the focus on the negative effects of controlling from a distance. But, when we argue for the important role of informal accounts it does not necessarily mean that we will abandon all kinds of new forms of technologies for communication. But it is important that the mechanisms of formal and informal ways of communication are arranged in ways that complement each other. We will return to this discussion later in the chapter.

Towley et al. (2003) argue that technologies as accountability reports, business plans and performance measurements can give rise to a domination of instrumental rationalization over "reasoned justification and communicative action" (p. 1065). However, it could also be the other way around. These processes should be complementary.

People's voices can also be excluded when technical information is used with a monologic approach. In order to invite more people in debates or decisions dialogic accounting has been suggested (Brown, 2008). Dialogic tools can facilitate critical reflection and discussion. Such tools make it possible to create a space for communication without reducing or exclude different opinions.

HOW COMMUNICATION TECHNOLOGIES CAN GIVE RISE TO ACCOUNTING IN DIALECTS AND FACILITATE NETWORKING

As clarified in earlier sections, new forms of "technologies of communication" can both prevent and facilitate networks. When smaller family-run businesses are incorporated into larger organization they run the risk to lose the ability to take part in innovative networks. One reason for this is the implementation of formal communication systems, designed to make it possible to control and manage from distance. Such systems might hinder face-to-face meetings. As indicated earlier do network often consist of informal personal meetings and therefore do formalizations of information processes affect networks in a negative way. Technology can also destroy the relationships to the neighborhood if it for example creates isolated entities.

In the same way the focus on maximizing profit may hinder networks from being sustainable, accounting systems or other information system may influence individuals to maximize their own profit instead of seeking mutual benefits. In other words new communication technologies may create agents of economics instead of agents of families and agents of communities – depending on whose voices are included and excluded. It is thus a call for communication technologies that encourage participation of several voices to be included in content-generation processes.

Implementation of information system that brings in hierarchies may crowd-out the special culture that is the core in many family-run businesses. For example a more organically organization that have the ability to have good relations to the surrounding might turn to a more mechanical organization and start optimize what is good for it self instead of develop relations.

We will now turn the attention to how new technologies of communication can facilitate social networks and co-exist with an organic form of organization and thereby make it possible for the special culture that can be found in family-run business sustainable.

We suggest that controlling and acting based on co-design and with technologies as web 2.0 is an alternative to traditional systems made with the intention to control and act from a distance. Below we will outline this idea.

CO-DESIGN AS AN ENABLER FOR SUSTAINABLE LOCAL CULTURES

One possible approach for enhancing co-operation in local cultures is co-design. As seen above information sharing becomes crucial for preserving, or at least base change and innovation on the legacy bound to the local culture. It is thus a call for an approach building upon interactivity, collaboration and co-design.

Co-design is to a high degree inspired by Churchman and his late postmodern writings (Churchman, 1979). The basic fundament can be described as a social constructive pragmatism where it is possible to design an infinite numbers of views of reality. They may differ in their granularity (level of detail), their level of abstraction, and so on. Every such view opens for actions and possibilities in specific directions. This necessity to agree upon some common design for a system has also been put attention on by other scholars (Liu et al, 2002). This collective, or individual, process of challenging existing views, designing new views and choosing the best one for re-implementation is called co-design. It has shaped the way we look at knowledge in general and at information systems in particular (Ackoff, 1981; Checkland, 1988; Mitroff & Mason, 1981). People affected by such actions are regarded as stakeholders. A view of a retail chain focusing the role of different stakeholders, including the role that the consumer has in inspiring service development, opens for possibilities for an efficient sales and distribution of desired products. In that way all

views are corresponding to values and interests of different groups of people.

A core idea in the co-design, which is both a scientific approach as well as a development approach, is that there is a close relation between innovative product/service development and knowledge creation (Forsgren, 1995; Lind et al, 2007). Businesses and organizations constantly try to capture knowledge about ideal situations for customers or clients, which they match with knowledge about resources they have or can create. Successful businesses/organizations are able to constantly developing their knowledge about customer ideals and their own matching resources. Customers or clients on the other hand constantly try to imagine and find out knowledge about their own ideal situations and look for affordable resources, which can make it possible for them to come closer to ideal situations. In this view, different intermediaries ideally collaborate with businesses and organizations as well as customers in discovering the lack of knowledge. These intermediaries, who many times act as facilitators, place themselves in between the organization(s) and the customers trying to manage the design in order to come to agreements among the different stakeholders. The dynamic interplay between these actors and processes constitutes the core of the co-design knowledge creation process (Grönlund, 2000). All the way through this process there is also a constantly ongoing inspiration communication flow. The involved actors try to get inspiration from the knowledge creation in other relevant projects as well as they try to get others inspired by their work.

One of the strongest trends in the ICT-field of today is e-empowerment of different kinds of clients, such as citizens, customers, and consumers. This means that more emphasis is put upon the possibility for clients to manage and contribute to the information galaxy (Albinsson et al, 2006) – both in terms of the use and supply of content as well as services. A common concept in relation to this trend is Web 2.0. O'Reilley (2007), one of the people who coined the term, claims that

Web 2.0 is the network as platform, spanning all connected devices; Web 2.0 applications are those that make the most of the intrinsic advantages of that platform: delivering software as a continually-updated service that gets better the more people use it, consuming and remixing data from multiple sources, including individual users, while providing their own data and services in a form that allows remixing by others, creating network effects through an "architecture of participation," and going beyond the page metaphor of Web 1.0 to deliver rich user experiences.

Web 2.0 is a concept that puts emphasis on participation and co-production of data and services that is in strong resonance with the notion of co-design (Lind & Forsgren, 2008). O'Reilley (2007) contrasts, among other things, Britannica Online (as Web 1.0) with Wikipedia (as Web 2.0). Wikipedia is a technology for creating collaborative websites by letting people from several different contexts contributing to common knowledge. In this way traditional borders dissolve. People start in this way to exist in a collaborative world without any real borders. In this way borders are continuously defined and re-defined by the participators' performance of communicative actions (c.f. e.g. Allwood & Lind, 2008).

As can be identified there are some key factors for adopting successful co-design in family-run business in order to facilitate innovative networks. There is a need for:

1) Let the worldviews of the agents engaged in the community be shared and collided with other world views represented by other stakeholders engaged in the same community

2) One (or several) facilitator(s) acting as intermediary between different stakeholders and their world views

3) Arenas or forums, often enhanced by technology, for sharing information and experiences (Lind & Rittgen, 2009)

4) Techniques and models for communication to engage participation of several stakeholders in the knowledge creation (Albinsson et al, 2006)

Given the fact that businesses are constantly changing there is a need to let people in communities to become engaged in the formation of the future. We strongly believe that a co-design like-approach that builds on admitting peoples' experiences, beliefs and worldviews is a necessity in such processes of change.

In contemporary research adopting a co-design approach has showed to be important when it comes to the identification of a common focus to the involved participants. In the process where the participants indentify a common focus "scenario techniques" (Albinsson et al, 2006) have proven to be successful for sharing ideas and desires between diverse stakeholders. A scenario technique is a way for the participants in a network to test and change each other's scenarios. In this testing process it is important with many different voices.

SUMMARY AND DISCUSSION

In this chapter a number of challenges that point towards the necessity for enhancing the sustainability of the culture of family firms have been highlighted. The demand of constant development requires people to become engaged in diverse networks, inside and outside the firm, and in that way get their own worldviews to become collided with others. This must however to be done in a structured way. In this chapter we have explored the possibility of co-design as an approach and technique to be one solution to these challenges. Below we are commenting on some key challenges identified and put them in relation to co-design.

Non-Hierarchical Organizing and Informal Decision-Making

A company that is rather small has the possibility to maintain a relatively small non-hierarchical organization and informal ways of decision-making. But these may be hard to keep as the company grows bigger and the work becomes more specialized. It becomes thus essential to establish procedural knowledge in the company of how to continuously share and foster a culture of letting people be involved in decision-making. To be able to successfully join and create networks with people outside the organization "openness", "good ability to change" and a "holistic perspective" are needed. Certain unpredictability as regards the work tasks is therefore required, which encourages the employees and management to actively seek their tasks in a continuous dialogue within and without the company.

Increased work specialization might separate the management from the operative activities. This gives rise to problems since people generally want to be sure that decisions are carried out quickly, and this is easier to assume if the same people you have been in touch with are also the ones who will carry out what has been decided. It is therefore important to ensure that diverse co-design inspired procedures include diverse people in purposeful actions in where they share information and thereby bridge the gap between management and operation. The ultimate solution would be a non-hierarchical transparency between reflections over diverse actions by operative personnel taking place on operative level as a basis for a joint discussion between operation and management for making the firm become controlled as efficient as possible.

Being an Agent of a Family, Community and a Place

Belonging to a family, community and place, to have the goal to be successful in the long run and

to be predictable make it easier to find cooperation partners. Organizational devices that create agents of economy may prohibit cooperation and decrease the possibility of participating in networks.

Co-design, on the other hand, would make it possible to make people at a distance aware of diverse happenings at the local site and thereby make decisions that take the "local" culture into consideration. Another essential component in such setting would also be the facilitation of structures that improve the information sharing between the people in the local operation and the people at the distance better. In the spirit of Web 2.0 (O'Reilley, 2007) some parts of this structuring would preferably be done by the involved agents, but on a higher level there will always be a need for a facilitator.

Sympathy

Sympathy often arises as a spontaneous reaction to whatever is present: other people, things, or nature. But sympathy can also arise through people's imagination. Sympathy is a capacity which people have that makes them herd animals. Sympathy guides actions towards communal activity and care for what is close and local, rather than for what is distant.

The localization in a specific place thus plays a meaningful role together with personal and informal meetings with people within and outside the company. The role of sympathy therefore decreases the greater and more hierarchical the company becomes. On the other hand, an adaptation of co-design makes the role of sympathy more important. It does this because it makes informal ways of accounting possible, which is the prerequisite for accounting in dialects

FINAL WORDS

In this chapter we have theoretically explored the potential of a co-design approach for meeting the challenges of making the family-run business culture sustainable. The next step in this research endeavor is to take these theoretically generated ideas for solution and put them into application for the purpose of contributing to a better practice.

REFERENCES

Ackoff, R. L. (1981). *Creating the corporate future*. New York: Wiley.

Albinsson, L., Forsgren, O., & Lind, M. (2006). *e-Me Stories & Scenarios - The Ideal Electronic Galaxy of the Student*. School of Business and Informatics, University College of Borås, Sweden

Albinsson, L., Lind, M., & Forsgren, O. (2007). Co-Design: An approach to border crossing, Network Innovation. In P. Cunningham, & M. Cunningham, (Eds), *Expanding the Knowledge Economy: Issues, Applications, Case Studies* (Vol. 4, Part 2, pp. 977-983). Amsterdam: IOS Press.

Allwood, J., & Lind, M. (2008). *Making the Web more Pragmatic - Exploring the Potential of some Pragmatic Concepts for IS Research and Development*. The Inaugural meeting of The AIS Special Interest Group on Pragmatist IS Research (SIGPrag 2008) at International Conference on Information Systems (ICIS2008), France

Bartholomeusz, S., & Tanewski, G. (2006). The relationship between Family Firms and Corporate Governance. *Journal of Small Business Management*, *44*(2), 245–267. doi:10.1111/j.1540-627X.2006.00166.x

Bebbington, J., Brown, J., Frame, B., & Thomson, I. (2007). Theorizing engagement: the potential of a critical dialogic approach. *Accounting, Auditing & Accountability Journal*, *20*(3). doi:10.1108/09513570710748544

Berry, W. (2005). *The way of ignorance*. New York: Shoemaker & Hoard.

Boyce, G. (2000). Public discourse and decision making: exploring possibilities for financial, social and environmental accounting. *Accounting, Auditing & Accountability Journal*, *13*(1). doi:10.1108/09513570010316135

Brown, J. (in press). Democracy, sustainability and dialogic accounting technologies: Taking pluralism seriously. *Critical Perspectives on Accounting*.

Brundin, E., Florin, E., & Melin, L. (2008). *The Family Ownership Logic: Core Characteristics of Family-Controlled Business*. CeFEO Working Paper, 2008:1.

Checkland, P. B. (1988). Soft systems methodology: An overview. *J. of Applied Systems Analysis*, *15*, 27–30.

Churchman, C. W. (1979). *The systems approach and its enemies*. New York: Basic Books.

Elmhester, K. (2008). *Småföretag i strategiska nätverk*. Linköping Studies in Science and Technology Dissertations, No.1217

Emling, E. (2000). *Svenskt familjeföretagande*. Stockholm: EFI.

Forsberg, P. (2001). *Berättelser och omdömen i en redares vardag* (Judging and storytelling in the everyday life of a ship owner). Gothenburg, Sweden: BAS.

Forsberg, P. (2009). Crowding-in and crowding-out of the community principle. *International Journal of Critical Accounting*, *1*(3).

Forsberg, P., & Westerdahl, S. (2007). For the sake of serving the broader community: sea piloting compared with auditing. *Critical Perspectives on Accounting*, *8*, 7.

Forsgren, O. (2005). C West Churchman and the new world of co-design. In J.P. van Gigch & J. (Eds.), *McIntyre Rescuing the Enlightenment from Itself*, (Vol. 1 in *Churchman's Legacy and Related Works)*. Amsterdam: Springer/Kluwer.

Gadde, L.-E., Huemer, L., & Håkansson, H. (2003). Strategizing in industrial networks. *Industrial Marketing Management, 32*, 357–364. doi:10.1016/S0019-8501(03)00009-9

Goold, M., & Campbell, A. (1987). *Strategies and Styles. The role of centers in managing diversified corporations.* Oxford, UK: Blackwell.

Gray, R. (2002). The social accounting project and privileging engagement, imaginings, new accountings and pragmatism over critique? *Accounting, Organizations and Society, 27*(7). doi:10.1016/S0361-3682(00)00003-9

Gray, R., Dey, C., Owen, D., Evans, R., & Zadek, D. (1997). Struggling with the praxis of social accounting: stakeholders, accountability, audits and procedures. *Accounting, Auditing & Accountability Journal, 10*(3). doi:10.1108/09513579710178106

Grönlund, Å. (2000). *Managing electronic services: A Public Service Perspective.* London: Springer.

Gudmunson, D., Hartman, E. A., & Tower, C. B. (1999). Strategic Orientation: Differences between Family and Nonfamily Firms. *Family Business Review, 12*(1).

Jensen, M., & Meckling, W. (1994). The nature of man. *Journal of Applied Corporate Finance,* (Summer).

Jönsson, S. (1973). *Decentralisering och utveckling.* Gothenburg, Sweden: BAS.

Latour, B. (1987). *Science in action.* Cambrigde, MA: Harvard University Press.

Lind, M., Albinsson, L., Forsgren, O., & Hedman, J. (2007). *Integrated Development, Use and Learning in a Co-design Setting: Experiences from the Incremental Deployment of e-Me, eChallenges e-2007,* The Hague, The Netherlands.

Lind, M., & Forsgren, O. (2008). Co-design and Web 2.0: Theoretical foundations and application. In Cunningham P., Cunningham M. (Eds*.) Collaboration and the Knowledge Economy: Issues, Applications, Case Studies* (pp. 1105-1112). IOS Press, Amsterdam.

Lind, M., & Rittgen, P. (2009). Challenges of Co-Design: The Case of e-Me. In B. Whitworth & A. de Moor (eds.), *Handbook of Research on Socio-Technical Design and Social Networking Systems.* Hershey, PA: IGI Global

Liu, K., Sun, L., & Bennett, K. (2002). Co-Design of Business and IT Systems. *Information Systems Frontiers, 4*(3), 251–256. doi:10.1023/A:1019942501848

Macintosh, N. B., & Baker, C. R. (2002). A literary theory perspective on accounting: towards heteroglossic accounting reports. *Accounting, Auditing & Accountability Journal, 15*(2). doi:10.1108/09513570210425600

Miller, D., & Le Breton-Miller, I. (2005). *Managing for the long run: lessons in competitive advantage from great family business.* Boston: Harvard business school press.

Mitroff, I. I., & Mason, R. O. (1981). *Creating a dialectical social science.* Dordrecht, The Netherlands: Reidel.

Morgan, G. (1988). Accounting as reality construction: towards a new epistemology for accounting practice. *Accounting, Organizations and Society, 13*(5). doi:10.1016/0361-3682(88)90018-9

O'Dwyer, B. (2005). The construction of a social account: a case study in an overseas aid agency. *Accounting, Organizations and Society, 30*(3).

Oreilly, T. (2007). What is Web 2.0: Design Patterns and Business Models for the Next Generation of Software. *Communications & Strategies,* (1), *17.*

Otteson (2002). *Adam Smith's marketplace of life*. Cambridge, UK: Cambridge university press.

Pistrui, D., Huang, W. V., Welsch, H. P., & Jing, Z. (2006). Family and Cultural Forces: Shaping Entrepreneurship and SME Development in China. In P. Z. Poutziouris, K. X. Smyrnios, & S. B. Klein (Eds.), *Handbook of Research on Family Business*. Cheltenham, UK: Edgar Elgar.

Pistrui, D., Welsch, H., & Roberts, J. (1997). The [Re] – Emergence of Family Business in the Transforming Soviet Bloc: Family Contribution to Entrepreneurship Development in Romania. *Family Business Review*, *10*(3). doi:10.1111/j.1741-6248.1997.00221.x

Pistrui, D., Welsch, H., Wintermantel, O., Liao, J., & Pohl, H. J. (2000). Entrepreneurial Orientation and Family Forces in the New Germany: Similarities and Differences Between East and West German Entrepreneurs. *Family Business Review*, *13*(3). doi:10.1111/j.1741-6248.2000.00251.x

Poutziouris, P., O'Sullivan, K., & Nicolescu, L. (1997). The [Re] – Generation of Family-Business Entrepreneurship in the Balkans. *Family Business Review*, *10*(3). doi:10.1111/j.1741-6248.1997.00239.x

Preston, A. (2006). Enabling, enacting and maintaining action at a distance: An historical case study of the role of accounts in the reduction of the Navajo herds. *Accounting, Organizations and Society*, *31*, 559–578. doi:10.1016/j.aos.2005.03.003

Robson, K. (1992). Accounting numbers as "Inscriptions": Action at a distance and the development of Accounting. *Accounting, Organizations and Society*, 685–708. doi:10.1016/0361-3682(92)90019-O

Salvato, C., & Melin, L. (2008). Creating Value Across Generations in Family-Controlled Business: The Role of Family Social Capital. *Family Business Review*, *21*(3).

Steen, A., & Welch, L. (1998). Dancing With Giants; Acquisation and Survival of the Family Firm. *Family Business Review*, *19*(4).

Svensk Sjöfarts Tidning. (1998). Nr 37.

Svensk Sjöfarts Tidning. (2001). Nr 17.

Towley, B., Cooper, D., & Oakes, L. (2003). Performance Measures and the Rationalization of Organizations. *Critical Perspectives on Accounting*, *24*(7).

Welsh, D. H. B., & Raven, P. (2006). Family Business in the Middle East: An Exploratory Study of Retail Management in Kuwait and Lebanon. *Family Business Review*, *19*(1). doi:10.1111/j.1741-6248.2006.00058.x

Wiklund, J. (1998), *Small firm growth and performance*. Jönköping, Sweden: Jönköpings Internationella Handelshögskola.

Wincent, J. (2006). *On building Competitiveness in strategic SME Networks: Empirical analysis of 54 firms in two networks*. Luleå, Sweden: Luleå tekniska Universitet. [1] Scandinavian Shipping Gazette (2001) nr 17

Chapter 12
Workplace Location and ICTs Substituting Travel

Greger Henriksson
The Royal Institute of Technology, Stockholm, Sweden

Minna Räsänen
The Royal Institute of Technology, Stockholm, Sweden

ABSTRACT

This chapter is based on the assumption that keeping the number and length of business and commuting trips at reasonable levels could contribute to reaching targets of environmental sustainability. The authors highlight a couple of options for reducing or avoiding business trips and commuting through workplace location or improved use of communications. They present case studies concerning travel and communications, carried out by using diaries and interviews. They also present relevant literature on social practices and sustainability goals in relation to use of ICT. The aim is to shed light on variation in the use of travel and communications on an individual level in work life. The case studies illustrate that such variation is mainly due to the concrete practices involved in execution of professional duties and roles. Duties that involve a clearly defined end result or product being delivered regularly by the member of staff are correlated to clearly defined needs for communications. Less clearly defined end results of the work duties seem to make it harder for the individual to plan and perform communication and travel in a more energy saving way. The difference in professional duties can thus be expressed in terms of clarity and maturity. Another factor that affect who can replace travel with ICTs is relations of power, e.g., when a purchaser dictates the terms for a subcontractor concerning how and where to "deliver" his working time, service or product. The importance of clarity, maturity and power aspects means that professional practices need to be studied at a detailed level to find out who could substitute ICTs for travel and how this could be done.

DOI: 10.4018/978-1-60566-822-2.ch012

INTRODUCTION

Today a widely recognized goal related to sustainable development is to restrict the energy use and (greenhouse gas) emissions that companies and households cause through their production and use of premises, goods, services and transport. Controlling such factors requires well informed choices based on methods like life cycle assessments, since there are risks of sub-optimizing, for instance when an energy-saving choice concerning one factor (e.g., transport) may lead to worsened environmental consequences in another area (e.g., use of premises). However, the aim of this chapter is not to go into detail regarding such effects on the system level but rather to keep them in mind as a background to the study of human practices and choices on the local and individual level. Among the activities that cause environmental consequences we will focus on transport in office work life.

ICT is frequently discussed as a means of changing, and in some instances cutting down on, travel in work life. The starting point of this discussion is the potential of ICT to make work less tied to location (less location-dependent). In order to cut down on travel, this potential has to be realized in terms of "staying where you are for longer intervals." This means, e.g., to stay at home and work or to have a meeting with someone outside your office without leaving it. When reasoning this way the existence of different alternatives for performing a certain amount of work ("a work day," "a meeting") must be presumed. One of the alternatives includes a journey while the other does not.

This means that the location and use of workplaces become important aspects. In the light of this, the chapter is based on qualitative interviews with civil servants concerning their use of ICT for meetings and business contacts and also their choice and use of workplaces.

We will present the interviews under two different headings, "Business as usual" and "Unusual use." Under the first we consider how the interviewees travel and communicate (with customers and colleagues) on a regular basis. Under the second we focus on instances of unusual or pioneering use of ICT or workplace location in which some of the interviewees are involved.

As a background we will present a handful of research lines that we find theoretically and methodologically relevant. More specifically we want to create an overview of research suitable for answering the question: How could the use of ICT and social practices be studied in relation to issues of environmental and social sustainability?

BACKGROUND

Studies of ICT Use

Everyday life consists of repetitive practices through time-space.[1] An understanding of day-to-day life is therefore essential to the analysis of reproduction of institutionalized practices. As we engage in everyday practices and attend, e.g., to the working life, we also recreate and maintain them as part of the culture and society to which we belong.

The intersection between use of ICT and social practices refers to analyses on how ICT supports and changes practices in various situations, both at work and during leisure time. Social practices may transform the use of ICT as well as ICT affords possibilities to modify existing and create new practices. Analyses of ICT use are of interest for various multidisciplinary approaches within social science traditions such as Science and Technology Studies (STS). STS address the social and cultural significance of scientific and technological change, how science and technology function in different societies and how social forces attempt to shape and control these forces to serve certain objectives. Research traditions such as Computer Supported Cooperative Work (CSCW) and Human-computer interaction (HCI) on the other hand approach social practices from the development perspective in order to design and develop technology to support various practices, e.g., at the workplace.

Within the multidisciplinary research areas of HCI and CSCW, perspectives from social science disciplines such as anthropology and sociology are sometimes brought in for analyses of social practices. Within the HCI research tradition, an influential analysis of this kind is Schuman's (1987/1990) study of a photocopier. The study was based on ethnomethodology, an analytic approach to social analysis developed by Garfinkel (1967/2002). Suchman focused on the practical, everyday achievements and actions in a particular context. She showed that people's interaction with the technology did not follow a formal model, but rather exhibited a moment-by-moment, improvised character. The study highlighted the situated actions among the actors, but also what occurred between the actors and the technology as well as between the actors and their immediate environments.

The socially oriented perspective of HCI thus focuses on groups of people and their interaction and/or cooperation with each other. Various workplace studies combine an interest in technology use and work practices in various fields and work settings covering cooperative work, organizational roles as well as the uses and consequences of information and communication technology in the organizations (see, e.g. Bentley, Hughes, Randall, Rodden, Sawyer, Shapiro & Sommerville, 1992; Heath & Luff, 1992; Heath, Hindmarsh & Luff, 1999; Rouncefield, Viller, Hughes & Rodden, 1995; and Pycock & Bowers, 1996).

Social Practices

When Suchman and others, brought the activities and moment-by-moment actions of each lay actor into the HCI tradition, it was a considerable achievement. However, it has later been argued that the influence of other important elements in social life, not directly related to the studied technology or situation, often has been neglected or underestimated (Chalmers, 2004; Nardi, 1996). When the focus of the analysis is on the particularities of the immediate situation it often misses the larger picture of what is going on. It is also argued that studies, as they have been carried out within HCI, deemphasize the study of more stable and elemental phenomena (Nardi, 1996). These studies tend to be less concerned with society's "[...] reproduction as a series of structures" (Chalmers, 2004, p. 230). In conclusion, the study of moment-by-moment actions of the use of technology can give us only a partial understanding of the social context. Analysis of the immediate use context and moment-by-moment actions can be useful for certain purposes. But this does not exhaust the possible ways in which social context can be understood (see also Räsänen 2007; Räsänen & Nyce 2008).

This brings us to a central problem in the social sciences, how can we connect all the various elements, the "layers" such as individual and social perspectives in analysis? What is the significance (conditions, forces, motives, causes, consequences, etc.) of the relationships between the individuals and society? According to Giddens, perhaps the most important contribution social sciences can make to intellectual discourse is to rework conceptions of human action, i.e., social reproduction and social transformation (Giddens, 1984/2004). Concerning analysis of the reproduction of institutionalized practices, the point of departure for Giddens is the actions of knowledgeable individuals. In other words, "structure" should not in be objectified and explained. Rather, human action has to be explained to bring understanding to its social production. However, everyday activities should not be treated as the "foundation" of social life, but rather "connections should be understood in terms of an interpretation of social and system integration" (op. cit. 282). In this chapter, we analyze human action and practices in organizational situations and make connections to the structures and norms of the workplaces.

The lesson learnt from our review is that there is abundant empirically grounded research on how people use ICTs in specific contexts, but not much literature dealing with this in a broader context of socio-cultural stability and change. However, we believe that actor-network-theory (ANT) is useful for such an approach. This is because ANT focus on specific constellations of actors, actions and objects that together create power relations, stability respectively options for change (Brembeck, Ekström, & Mörck, 2007).

In actor-network-theory the materiality in courses of events and in power relations is emphasized by regarding human actors, as well as material objects, as *actants* (Latour, 1998a). Decisive for a project or for the spread of a technology in a certain context is, according to ANT, how actants become linked to the actor-network of the project or technology during its development (Hagman, 2005). Formal decisions or rules are not seen as decisive. But the fate of a certain decision or aim could be tracked in terms of *translations*.

A translation is a spread in time and space that takes place through moving about, displacement, recreation and mediation (Brembeck et al., 2007). Individuals as well as organizations stage their projects in those contexts where they act. A task for the researcher is to clarify what lines different actants take to a project or how they become linked to it.

Below we will use ANT in relation to our fieldwork. But first we conclude the review by exemplifying how environmental sustainability has been brought into the study of social practices and technology use.

Sustainability

Social practices and human choices are often cited as obstacles to change, when discussed in an environmental context (Rayner & Malone, 1998).

This is particularly the case when problems and trends are identified from technical or statistical perspectives. The study object (e.g., a transport system) is often defined in functional terms and assessed with category-specified value judgments (Hansson, 2007). From such a viewpoint, the social practice (habit, lifestyle, etc.) of, e.g., travelling by car to a larger extent than by public transport is identified as an obstacle to a sustainable transport system. The question arising is how preferences and behavior can be changed.

But this may not be the best way of framing the problem since qualitative change is continuously ongoing in the technology-supported practices (and underlying motives, social norms etc.) of everyday life. To understand such change it is necessary to provide analyses of people's conditions and choices. Solutions to societal problems are not generally found by viewing individual behaviors as parts of systems that can be optimized. Such views must be considered as too static and shortsighted, founded as they are on an "asocial model of the social world" (Shove, Lutzenhiser, Guy, Hacket, & Wilhite, 1998). Still, social practices are important for creating opportunities and conditions for long-term solutions to environmental and social problems. It is important to review main and subsidiary motives for actions in a certain context and to suggest more socially beneficial and environmentally friendly patterns. Sustainable development should not mainly be seen as a question of breaking practices and habits, but rather of collectively and gradually affecting the maintaining and replacement of them (Henriksson, 2008). In the short term, an important goal (for this kind of, and indeed our, research) is to show why measures designed to make certain practices more sustainable are working or not, depending on people's conditions of life, as citizens, consumers and professionals.

We have found a good starting point in the works of British sociologist Elisabeth Shove. Together with other researchers she has stated that it is important to reconsider a widespread individualistic view of action (common, e.g., in psychology and market research) concerning energy intense consumption in everyday life. Research on why people choose more or less energy demanding alternatives should to a higher extent focus on historic, social and cultural explanations and understanding (Shove et al., 1998). Her purpose has been to develop sociological theory in relation to consumption, technology and social change through an analysis of 'invisible' everyday habits. Focus is put on the collective elements in the restructuring of routines and expectations. Shove has especially looked upon resource-intensive, home-based consumption and writes that mundane fields of consumption like thermal comfort and cleanliness have been neglected in most theoretical approaches to consumption.

Shove argues that questions of the following kind must be asked: How are habits and expectations naturalized and possibly spread on a global level? She uses the concept of escalation to put questions about whether resource-intensity is increasing or not for different kinds of routinized consumption. The concepts convergence and standardizing are used concerning the direction of change. Shove wants to ask whether expectations and practices are converging 'around the world' (Shove, 2003b). This means that it is important to ask whether the process of change that the researcher has identified is part of a widespread pattern.

The term standardizing implies asking if technologies include organization and ways of use that means a lock in of the level of resource intensity. Shove maintains that this is the case with indoor thermal comfort. A temperature of around 20° C has become a global norm which is gradually diminishing the importance of localized and culturally rooted ways of creating thermal comfort by building traditions, clothing or management of periods of the day used for work or rest. Shove assigns much of this international convergence to the successful work with establishing an international organization for defining thermal comfort in terms of technical standards.

Except for thermal comfort Shove has studied the activities of bathing/showering and washing clothes (ibid.). For the analysis she uses literature on cultural and technical history in combination with statistics and interviews about these habits in present times. By comparing the three fields of consumption, she has been able to show that they have different patterns of change, e.g., that when indoor temperature is changing in a path-dependant way, changes in bathing and showering are less locked in and resources devoted to these activities can alternately increase or decrease, at least on the local level.

Many of the concepts and analytical elements Shove uses seem to be applicable concerning use of ICT, since they take the interplay between habits, social conventions and technology development in consideration. But Shove has not yet put them to use within the ICT field to any substantial extent. So at the end of this exposition of relevant research lines, we have still not presented literature that deal with ICT from an environmental and qualitative social science perspective. We have found very little research explicitly using an environmental sociology perspective on ICTs (admitting that our search of international literature, especially of journal articles, has not yet been exhaustive).

However, we have found a relevant, recent anthology in Swedish (Palm & Ellegård, 2008). The book definitely concerns social practices and cultural patterns in relation to issues of environmental sustainability. However, most of its contributions do not directly concern individual use of ICTs in everyday life. Rather themes of the following kinds are brought up: investing in IT during the "bubble" around year 2000, the consumption stimulating messages in "make-over" series on television. The most relevant contribution in relation to our criteria concerns tenants' reactions to ICT-based individual measurement of energy use for heating in apartment buildings (Glad, 2008). Glad makes the conclusion that individual measurements implemented by real estate managers leads to certain balances between 'imposed control and self discipline.' These balances are different in different cases depending on how the reform is presented and what the level of participation is among the tenants during the introduction. In a particularly successful case the reform was primarily presented as a means for the households to gain control over their heating costs and only secondly as a way for the real estate manager to achieve certain environmental goals.

Finally, there is relevant literature on virtual mobility, although sociological approaches are still rare. An interdisciplinary approach including a few sociological elements is used in a thesis on telework, 'virtual mobility and pollution prevention' by Peter Arnfalk (2002).

To sum up, our review indicates that research on evolving social practices and patterns that include (widespread) use of ICTs have until now, to any substantial extent, not been coupled with research on environmentally significant social practices. In the analysis of our fieldwork we intend to strive for such a coupling.

BUSINESS AS USUAL

Authorities and companies are becoming increasingly involved in using technological possibilities to reduce travel and improve efficiency among their staff. Achieving environmental sustainability, or at least *carbon neutrality*, is one of the most important motives behind this today, at least in theory. We want to shed light on what can happen if such plans or ambitions are put into practice. How do they fit in with everyday work-life realities? When and for whom is it possible to substitute communications for travel?

The idea behind our empirical analysis is to go into detail with the work life conditions among a few individuals to find out how they use, relate and adapt to different means of communications, meetings and work place locations. One of our procedures is to compare interviewees in pairs. From the individual cases we generalize in terms

of important aspects behind the readiness to substitute and/or reduce work trips.

How do staff travel and communicate when performing office work? In this section we focus on how they employ established (rather than more experimental or groundbreaking) technologies, business premises or practices. Telephone and e-mail are established forms of ICT that can be used to keep in touch, replace meetings and thereby to "stay where you are" for a longer period of time. Use of e-mail and telephone in relation to meetings and trips will work as a first point of departure, and statements and reasoning about choice of workplace location as a second.

Established ICTs as Travel-Saving or Not

Bonnie is editor-in-chief of a lifestyle magazine published by a major, Swedish publishing company. Erica is marketing director for global product development at a major, Swedish telecommunications company. In the following we will compare their use of meetings, e-mail and telephone.

Bonnie claimed that she seldom goes to meetings outside the office. She said that a very important part of her work is to keep in contact with co-workers and freelance staff that produce the pictures, text and design for the magazine. Some co-workers and all freelancers have their workplaces outside the magazine's office. Bonnie does not normally need to see them in person since ideas and lines of approach are discussed via telephone, while draft and finished materials are sent via e-mail. Therefore she and the freelance staff do not need to travel much in order to cooperate.[2]

Erica on the other hand travels extensively in her work, both for meetings and to perform work in other cities and countries. Her work tasks relate to development and promotion of new products and business solutions. In the interview she mentioned being responsible for an upcoming marketing event in India. She also reported a recent three-week stay with colleagues at the research & development office in Montreal, Canada. But more frequent than her stays abroad is travel for meetings and seminars in the Stockholm region. Included are frequent internal meetings at the company. Erica claimed that much of her time is spent in seeking knowledge and in embedding ideas and decisions internally.

This brief comparison shows that Erica seems to travel more and have more meetings than Bonnie. It also seems that this is related to different kind of work tasks. When asked about their options for avoiding travel and substituting telecommunications for meetings, Bonnie consequently estimated her options in more optimistic terms than Erica. Erica cannot use e-mail and telephone in the same way as Bonnie in order to 'be efficient' and keep travel to a minimum level.[3]

But we noticed that their reports on meetings and possible work in different locations did not fully account for the nature of work tasks and networking behind their different practices. Therefore we continue by presenting their views on handling e-mail, which we think add to the picture.

The Use of E-Mail

In regards to e-mail, editor-in-chief Bonnie reported that she manages her inbox systematically and actually writes replies to all e-mails where the sender could expect a reply. Marketing director Erica on the other hand said that she is quite passive in her e-mail handling. She does not have time to deal with all her e-mails and therefore counts on the sender getting in contact again, possibly in another way, if she fails to respond to something important.

The difference between Erica and Bennie's e-mail handling presumably reflects a range that exists among the working population as a whole. Some want to and can be consistent, while others more or less abandon full checks of their inbox. These differences could be linked to personal disposition, but it appears that the work role is significant.

An interesting fact is that Bonnie expressed strong dissatisfaction with certain types of e-mail. Bonnie claims that she can receive repeated e-mails advertising a certain consumer product. She welcomes such advertising for products to a certain degree, since the magazine carries a lot of editorial material on fashion, food, etc. However, Bennie's concrete example concerned a product on which she had recently received too much information, in far too many e-mail messages. The fact that Bonnie can draw these boundaries between interesting, acceptable and unwelcome or excessive in what can be assumed to be rather similar types of e-mail indicates that her criteria are well defined. She appears to apply a criterion linked to potential material for a future edition of the magazine regarding what is important e-mail. This method of dealing with her e-mails appears in turn to be linked to a relatively structured and cyclical work schedule. This includes e.g., keeping in contact with co-workers and freelance staff, discussing ideas and commissioning the material that will make up a new issue of the magazine every fortnight.

Erica also raised concrete e-mail messages as an example. One of these contained an invitation to a seminar that appeared to be of interest to her, so she attended. However, it proved to be of minor interest and Erica felt that she had wasted her time. The mistake of attending the seminar can be linked to Erica having to continuously assess and reassess what is, or could be, useful information. This uncertainty regarding what is more or less relevant affects her way of dealing with her e-mail. Erica does not have criteria for sorting her e-mail as clear as Bennie's. Nevertheless, Erica reported to have at least one way of prioritizing, a function in her e-mail program that diverts mail addressed to her alone to a particular folder to which she pays more attention.

In Bonnie's and Erica's approaches, we see a pattern as regards the relationship between the work role and use of communication. This pattern was repeated in our other interviews with professional people. To some extent all the interviewees had concrete end-goals for their work, something that they supply, so to speak. An auditor supplied audited end-of-year accounts to companies. Two experts at an authority produced documents that provide decision support for politicians. Sales agents had sales contracts with customers as the end-goal for their activities, and so on.

However, there were degrees of difference between the amounts of work that was actually devoted to completion of the end product. These degrees of difference can be said to cover a range between two poles. At one pole, workers devote the majority of their time to creating and maintaining contacts and to seeking knowledge that is only occasionally of direct benefit to something that they supply (although it may prove valuable in the long term). At the other pole are those that we believe devote the majority of their time to the concrete creation of products that they regularly deliver.

In the case of editor-in-chief Bonnie, we would tend to place her quite close to the latter, the concrete delivery pole, while Erica at the telecommunications company would be placed near the pole at which most time goes to information handling and contact creation rather than the execution and completion of well-defined work duties.

The differing work roles and communication strategies of Bonnie and Erica as we have outlined them can also be expressed in actor-network-theory (ANT) terms. Bonnie is involved in the running of a mature, commercial project, namely the publication of a magazine. Erica's role can be viewed more as involvement in the design of new projects (e.g., business ideas) and driving them toward the kind of maturity that the magazine project already has. Erica needs to *enroll* other actants (both human and non-human) within and outside the company. She also gets drawn into other people's projects, in ANT terminology this means that there is a process of translation when projects spread in space and time and new links are created between people, ideas and technolo-

gies (Brembeck et al., 2007). In this network of project creation, different forms of communication are used for different purposes.

The handling of communication (in this case e-mail) can also be considered on the basis of, the by de Certeau (1984) paired concepts of *strategy* and *tactics*. De Certeau uses strategy to denote the formalized and accepted, while tactics deal with the incidental (c.f. Högdahl, 2003). Strategies are applied from the basis of a platform constructed by, e.g., an authority or a company, from which they can define the surrounding environment (de Certeau, 1984). However a tactic is based on a calculation or reckoning by someone who cannot rely on a spatial or institutional location of their own. The tactic has no given base and thus has to seize the moment.

It can therefore be concluded on the basis of the comparative examples above that Bonnie relies on the strategy of using a lot of e-mailing and telephoning and few meetings in her contact with her co-workers. The classification as strategy works here since, according to Bonnie, it involves ways of communication that have been built up together with the actual magazine, by its founders. This strategy is adapted to the work task, particularly in view of the fortnightly production of new issues of the magazine.

The fact that Erica seems rather passive in her handling of her e-mail inbox can be regarded as a tactic she uses to manage communications at work. Erica also tries to tactically choose which meetings she attends and which trips she makes to maintain contact with her co-workers. Work duties of a knowledge- and contact-creating character and the company's organization and internal culture both appear to lie behind the need Erica and her colleagues have for face-to-face meetings. The meeting culture at the company and the need for internal embedding should thus be viewed as somewhat strategic, but at the same time problematic from certain aspects such as cost-effectiveness, since a lot of trips and working time for meetings quite simply amount to a lot of expenses.

We can see that these two persons have very different opportunities for controlling their amount of travel, if they want to do this for personal, social or environmental reasons. And actually Erica travels much more on duty than Bonnie does. This seems to be very much due to the nature of the difference in their work duties. We chose the two persons as examples to illustrate a span in compatibility between demands or wishes for limited travel and the real life conditions for actually achieving such goals.

This means that we have exemplified how established ICTs like e-mail can be used to balance the use of business trips for meetings. We will now in parallel look at how workplace locations can be used to balance the use of business trips for meetings. We will then use some of our other interviews (that we found more fit to illustrate this specific theme).

Choice of Workplace Location

Above we have exemplified choices between going to meetings and telecommunicating in different work roles and situations. The choice of workplace location arises more seldom than the choice of means of communication. Whether workplace location becomes a choice or not seems to be a matter of the individual's position and work tasks. Let us exemplify by comparing the situation of three other interviewees.

Niklas is a consultant and managing director of a small company that he runs with two partners. He says his work consists of helping other organizations function well and efficiently, and that this is partly concerned with computers. The systems and applications that the companies use must operate in a satisfactory way for their businesses.

Niklas lives in a suburb of Stockholm and travels into the city almost every day in order to meet and work with his clients. His situation was similar when he was employed, just before he started the company. Then he and his two partners considered options of having their offices at home

or renting premises. After a couple of months Niklas decided to rent a room in an office hotel close to where he lives. He says that an important reason for this was that he wanted to break up his daily commuter trips. By travelling to the hotel first and start his working day there, he avoids the rush hour traffic into the city. He therefore also books all his meetings in town for ten o'clock or later and drives his car into the city when the rush hour has passed. Through the choice of the local office hotel, Niklas achieves a sort of flexibility and convenience in the organization of his travel-dependent work.

Two other interviewees, Zachary and Jonathan, work with the hardware side of the IT sector, i.e., for companies trading in components for, e.g., computers and mobile phones. Zachary's task is to arrange annual contracts, e.g., for a new phone model. His company produces new components or modifies old. He says that he travels a lot with his work. The year before the interview he had 110 travel days and was in the USA, England, Germany, Denmark and Norway. Where he travels depends on where the customers (and subcontractors) are located.

Jonathan works with 'marketing and major customer sales' and says that his employer is a world leader in its niche, sales of hard discs for computers. This means that his work duties are similar to Zachary's. Their total number of flights and travel days are also approximately the same.

The companies Zachary and Jonathan work for have no headquarters in Scandinavia (but in other parts of the world, where they have many employees). According to Zachary most of the company's employees, with work duties similar to his, work from home. But when Zachary started his job he requested an office hotel place close to his home, which was granted by his new employer.

Jonathan and one or two colleagues first manned an office in Kista (a suburb north of Stockholm where most of the ICT and telecom companies in the region have clustered). When he got new work tasks (described above) he was asked by his employer to move to the company's headquarters in Munich. But Jonathan instead suggested that he should work from home, which is a detached house in a suburb northeast of Stockholm, and this request was granted.

Like Niklas, both Zachary and Jonathan therefore seem to compensate for numerous business journeys through the choice of close-to-home locations for their respective base offices. Their close-to-home offices they use telephone (sometimes teleconferences) and e-mail to communicate with colleagues and business contacts.

This shows that professionals who can choose workplace location are, e.g., sales agents, consultants or other self-employed persons (from other interviews auditors, journalists, publishers, innovators, forestry traders and others were noted). Among those not self-employed, sales agents were in majority, the only deviating example being a person who was a maintenance person within the IT sector.

However it is interesting to note that within a given sector only certain work roles seem to admit choosing workplace location. For instance, other people than sales agents within the IT sector may not so easily choose to work on their own, although the sector is relatively young and to some extent groundbreaking as regards working conditions. Time, space and boundaries between private and professional can take on partly new forms, as shown by Willim (2002) and Ó'Riain (2004). In a study of a group of software providers in Ireland, the latter showed that physical presence on the local shared workplace and work time are very important, despite the fact that managers, co-workers and sub-contractors, in the studied actual case, are on the other side of the Atlantic. According to Ó'Riain, another distinguishing feature is the pressures from the global economy in which the work groups are involved:

However, these pressures actually make local space and social context all the more important. The speed-up of time and the extension of social space across physical distance in the global economy do not destroy space but in fact intensify the impact of space in constituting successful global workplaces (Ó'Riain, 2004:17).

Ó'Riain refers to some extent to the individual, but mainly to the work group. The group, or at least parts of it, needs to be physically gathered to do a good job, and they presumably also need a rewarding social environment around them. In Zachary's and Jonathan's cases it is clear that the formal work group is seldom gathered. It is rather the individuals who have chosen and requires the local roots. Arranging large contracts for the supply of hard discs or circuit boards is naturally a completely different role from creating programs and applications. Sales staff, agents or distributors seem to be able to work alone to a large extent. However Jonathan reported that the company regularly has a type of computer-based telephone conference, where departments in different parts of the world report on their respective operations.

The motives these three professionals expressed behind their choices of workplace location were both social and practical. Zachary's motives behind the choice of the office hotel were mainly related to his family situation. The same actually goes for Niklas and Jonathan, although the latter chose to have his office at home. The types of factors that swung the decision were of the same type. They all mentioned:

- Family situation (small children)
- Form of residence (detached house or apartment)
- Extensive travel with work, leading to a wish to avoid daily commuter trips completely (as a kind of compensation)
- Attitude to social interaction at work.

The second point seems to have differed between them, since Zachary explicitly claimed living in an apartment with small children as a reason for not wanting to work from home. Niklas on the other hand started by working from home, but after a couple of months he "felt he needed a workplace to go to." Niklas did not explicitly mention whether his small child and the work situation of his wife affected this decision. Jonathan, finally, said that since he was travelling a lot he felt comfortable with being close to the children and their kindergarten when being in Stockholm.

Concerning the fourth point above Jonathan also differed from the other two, which can be illustrated by a quote from the interview.

Jonathan: "This thing about the social side of work, I get so much of that when I travel. I am not used to going to an office that is full of workmates chatting. Instead I travel to Munich or London or wherever and go into our offices there. I have a few workmates who I chat to there, but otherwise there is a lot that goes on by telephone in any case."

Just like balancing "staying in one place" with "frequent work related trips," balancing "social stimulation" with "being on one's own" seemed important for their socially grounded choices.

We have seen how professionals like the sales agents, a consultant, an editor-in-chief and a marketing director have higher or lower demands on mobility in their work life. Some of them handle these demands, e.g., by choosing workplace location (if they have the opportunity) and all of them by choosing different means of communication for different kinds of business contacts. In short, they maintain and modify social practices while carrying on business as usual. However, two elements, in the individual work-life cases presented above we consider as unusual. This is the use of an office hotel close to home and the extensive use of video mediated communication.

UNUSUAL USE

Suburban Office Hotels

Visions of local, cooperative or commercial workplaces for office work, named, e.g., telecottages, have been discussed for a couple of decades. The ideas behind these have been to give collaborative, economical and practical prerequisites for small companies and to support businesses in non-urban regions. The commercial form of such shared office premises is often called office hotel and exists in some suburbs of Stockholm.

We selected a couple of our interviewees that had their main working places in office hotels. Among these interviewees were Niklas and Zachary that have already been presented. The unusualness or particularity in their use of suburban office hotels seemed to lie in the following aspects:

- Independent work roles – working on one's own responsibility
- An individual aspiration to keep the daily commuting distance short
- The suburban office hotel as an alternative/complement to working from home, offering advantages in terms of social, administrative and technological resources
- The joint location and pooling of resources for businesses/individuals that are of different nature and independent from each other

Niklas and especially Zachary clearly stated that the social aspects were important; they liked having other people working around them. They also mentioned positive features like being able to express ideas in a mixed group and not just meet one's 'own people.' Another advantage with the office hotel they saw in the access to a work address. A home address is not so imposing – 'people can think that you only have half an eye on the job,' said Zachary. His employer has also recognized that the office hotel is a good base for colleagues and managers on visits to Scandinavia.

Historically the attraction of working in an office has been associated with the office environment and its visible prestige, although office work in itself has not always been perceived as glamorous (Conradsson, 1988). For many, working in the big city has been an important attraction. Traditionally, one of the perceived advantages of offices has been that they have been located in the big city and have offered proximity to, e.g., business, commerce and entertainment. The value of the central position of offices was probably devalued somewhat in line with expansion of suburban living. On the other hand, the daily movement behavior of many suburban-dwelling office workers can fulfill a need for change, providing both mobility and permanence (Vilhelmson, 2002).

The dream of the office has probably become weaker with the construction of increasing numbers of offices on the outskirts of cities in recent decades. However, there are surely expectations of access to commerce, lunch restaurants and entertainment, in which case these should be significant for the location and attractiveness of the office hotel.

The ethnologist Conradsson writes that historically, the choice of workplace often have appeared to be random, with many ending up in a specific firm because it 'was closest' (Conradsson, 1988:73). There is a parallel to the office hotel here, as the majority of those we interviewed had chosen a particular office hotel because it was closest to them.

Another perspective on the choice of the office hotel is Elisabeth Shove's (2003a) discussions on *convenience* and *time shifting*. The concept of convenience includes, e.g., that the advent of e-mail has provided certain opportunities to shift time.

What the workers in the three cases elected do when they chose to work in an office hotel or home was to tinker a little with the spatio-temporal structure of their work life. They use services and technologies that offer ease and convenience – e.g., e-mail, car and telephone – in order to increase their individual free scope.

One could imagine that if the strategy employed by consultant Niklas (of avoiding rush hour traffic by having a workplace half-way in to

the city centre) were to become common, it would contribute toward altering use of time and space in the business sector. This involves (yet) another mechanism of change, according to Shove. She refers to it as a *creep* (sliding) concerning the feeling for what is proper, normal and necessary. This hardly visible process of change arises from many individuals' management of time pressures.

Shove believes that the convenience spiral often leads to fragmentation and individualization, resulting in increased use of resources, but that it can go both ways. In the case of telecommuting and working from home/office hotel, we believe that it can also involve positive developments from a resource viewpoint.

Commuter travel deals with presence at work, with arriving at work, with the transition between leisure and work. It is a question of a transformation service, of going from absence to presence. Commuter trips are the transition – one 'travels' from one social context to another, even if one stays at home and goes down to an office in the basement, or simply removes the breakfast dishes from the kitchen table and puts a laptop there instead. We are socialized into this interplay, but at the same time the conditions for it are changing. New sectors and changes in production relations can give rise to new conditions for work and also for the social interaction between work and leisure.

The point that can be considered as regards commuter trips is that it is the structure rather than the actors that primarily determines when, where and how they are carried out. Being at work is determined by formal structures that we perhaps do not think about in daily life. However, they can become apparent when conflicts or crisis points arise. The Swedish teaching body can be seen as an example. Teaching is a category of profession with a long tradition of working from home. The attractive power of the profession consists partly of the distinction between bound time (teaching) and free time (school holidays and planning/marking). This degree of freedom was questioned and altered in 1994 when the teachers' trade union agreed a contract with the employers on having 'workplace-located time,' which in fact meant that they were provided office desks in the schools and were obliged to do a certain amount of their preparatory work there. The amount of time that teachers could still work from home was quantified to nine hours per week and labeled 'trust time,' i.e., the time that the teachers have their employer's trust to carry out traditional work on their own.

Within most other organizations that have wished to keep up with the times the development has gone in the opposite direction, toward a higher proportion of distance working and 'trust time' (time that is not workplace-located and that is often the subject of contracts).

In relation to our material, it can be discussed how the social control on sales personnel, consultants and staff of various authorities doing their job is exerted. At the office hotel there were one-man companies where people were self-determining, but at the same time they were dependent on, or had undertakings in relation to, suppliers, customers etc. Travel opportunities and forms of communication can both be regarded as services that are used to adopt different positions in relation to interacting actors.

When the consultant Niklas, e.g., received a call one morning via the office hotel's receptionist, then both forms of communication, the first commuter trip of the day and the premises, transformed Niklas into a consultant in his office. The structural side of this means, e.g., that individual responsibility and a certain freedom is associated with company form. Niklas was able to create his own organization in space and time as long as he had the confidence of his clients. However, in practice his timetable is also controlled by the fact that he spends a lot of time at his clients' premises.

If one looks at the other categories of profession, then, e.g., sales personnel are not self-employed, but their spatio-temporal freedom within responsibilities is a result of the mobile nature of their work duties. Among the interviewees were also civil servants employed by authorities. For them other kind of patterns showed. Meeting cultures within the authorities seemed crucial, as did formal regulations and job descriptions. These factors affected how much they needed to or could be in their main place of work, travel or work from home. However, those employed by authorities also had freedom frameworks within this structure. They could choose to travel on work trips or not to a certain extent, while even in position at their desk they could control their use of the available forms of communication as they wished. An illustrative example was that one of them reported that even for communication with colleagues working in the same building, the telephone was a common choice.

Returning to the office hotel, one motive for choosing this was to avoid rush hour traffic, congestion and time-consuming travel to work. This is interesting in relation to the fact that the main alternative to working in an office hotel was to work from home. It is thus not clear how the motive of avoiding rush hour traffic is involved. In this case the concept of transition services can offer an explanatory perspective. Transforming oneself into a professional at work is made easier by the facilities and the social structure that the office hotel provides. The actual trip is also important as a transformation from a private to a work mode. Even a short trip can fulfill such a need, particularly if one can self-justify one's choice by pointing out the problems with other alternatives (commuting in to the city in rush hour traffic).

The question of the approach to the trip between home and the workplace also encompasses an interesting complexity since extensive work travel, in Europe, appears to be linked to the attitude that one wishes to avoid unnecessary travel. This means that work trips are not disengaged from private trips (as commuter trips are formally classified). If someone thinks that they travel a lot in one way, they can choose to try to compensate for this by travelling less in the other.

Figure 1. Distance meeting place (DMP) for the Public Employment Service. © 2006 Photograph: Charlie Gullström. Used with permission.

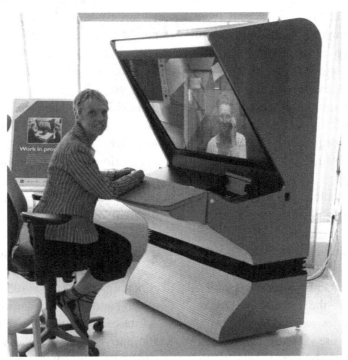

Distance Meeting Places as Substitutes for Travel

In the debate on sustainable development, video conferencing and other concepts for virtual meetings are seen as possible ways to create connections and offer communicative surfaces between co-workers at a distance. The same underlying technology may be used for different purposes. Similar technology may be used for short-term, focused activities, but also for long-term, less focused activities in order to provide and support casual, informal interaction between work groups and allow peripheral background awareness to remote sites and the situation of others (e.g. Dourish & Bly, 1992; Gaver et al., 1992) as well as to establish and maintain long-term working relationships and collaboration between geographically scattered groups of people (e.g. Gaver, 1992; Mantei et al., 1991).

Some years ago, the Swedish Public Employment Service was requested to provide equal access to all clients and offer service in the most efficient way possible. However, it was not economically possible to man all the offices on equal terms. The employment agency in Dalarna needed a new solution for sparsely populated areas in northern parts of the county and gradually decided to run the development project 'Service, Development and Communication Dalarna.' This led to so-called distance meeting places, a solution to accessibility that is now used in eight office environments at the Public Employment Services in Idre, Orsa, Sälen, Särna, Vansbro and Älvdalen (connected to the main offices in Malung and Mora).

It is regulated that each new jobseeker needs to register in person at the employment agency. People living in the sparsely populated areas have had an exemption, a possibility to make the initial contact with the employment agency via telephone. However, this had to be followed up with a scheduled meeting in person within two weeks. But since the introduction of the new solution, people at all six locations can make new declarations of unemployment on every weekday through registering themselves as jobseekers via the distance meeting place (hereafter referred to as the DMP). The DMP consists of a small room or an enclosed space. In the prototype used in the project, image and data transfer technology is available, brought together in a unit (see illustration). This unit has been designed together with users as a part of the development project mentioned above. The unit holds a semi-opaque, one square meter-sized mirror, behind which is a TV screen. Underneath there is a camera, which creates an image of the user via the mirror. The result is that people can communicate via something that can be described as a two-way, large-screen TV with the possibility of direct eye contact.[4]

The demonstration in Dalarna had different consequences in different places. While an employment office provided service only a few hours per week (e.g., one afternoon), the service via DMPs is now available daily, e.g., 9.00-15.00 on Mondays and 9.00-12.00 on Tuesdays-Fridays. In the town Särna, for example, the DMP was perceived as an improvement, compared with travelling 120 kilometers to Mora or managing to register during one of the few hours the office was previously manned by a visiting employment agent.

However, residents in Orsa perceived the service via DMP in more negative terms. The employment office in Orsa was previously a manned office where people could make drop-in visits at certain times to declare themselves unemployed. Now it is not longer possible to make unemployment declarations in person. However, this is still possible in what many regard as the favored central location of Mora, 17 kilometers from Orsa (Räsänen, 2006).

The DMPs have now been used for a few years. According to the Public Employment Services in Dalarna, around 20 000 conversations between the employment agency and jobseekers have taken place via the DMP during the past two years. These have been relatively good times on the employment market and many of those temporarily unemployed in Dalarna have returned to work. The employment agency and jobseekers both appear to have generally accepted the new way of arranging unemployment declarations.

The personnel at the Public Employment Service and their directors are happy with the change since they have been able to cut down on travel (Moberg, Hedberg, Henriksson, Räsänen, & Westermark, 2008). They mainly save on expenses, but also on travel time and fuel, and have thus decreased the environmental impact of their operations. Jobseekers mainly save on expenses and travel time (if they would otherwise have travelled to a central location) and have also acquired an increased flexibility in time as regards access to the services of the employment agency.

Of more general interest with the example from Dalarna are the power and time/space aspects. One can assume that an introduction into other companies and for other types of meetings this will also be dependent on such aspects. It will probably seldom be a question of simply 'replacing trips.' The use of technology is involved in and dependent on social and institutional relations. It is also dependent on the opportunities and demands people experience in relation to reorganizing their daily presence in time and space.

Whenever technology is introduced the issue of technical capacity and quality is often raised. Low user-friendliness, access to information and resources, data transfer capacity, image and sound quality, etc. are pointed out as obstacles to increased use of communication solutions to replace travel. One way to test the actual importance of technical obstacles is to monitor projects in which attempts are being made to overcome some of these obstacles. Was there a technical obstacle here, and if so, how was it overcome? The obstacle was not only, perhaps not even primarily, technical. Rather it was formal, since telephone and other means of communication are not suitable for new declarations of unemployment. Declaring one's presence via telephone or the Internet would present (too) many opportunities to bend the formal regulations. With the site-specific and unique link-ups and the DMPs, this risk is decreased. In ANT terms, a detour or a new path is created past the compulsory point of passage of the jobseeker having to be present. This shows that the obstacle to distance declarations of unemployment was formal or institutional, while the solution consisted of a decision on principle linked with a certain technology. It is thus not the quality of the communication that should be regarded as the launching point but the possibility to observe the regulations through a type of check of presence in time and space (although the mediated meeting must maintain a certain quality in order to be 'approved').

However, this does not mean that the quality is uninteresting. In the area in question, companies, societies and other operators in the public sector have shown an interest in the DMPs. Different activities perceive different opportunities with the technology and therefore the quality is significant.

At the same time, there are currently economic and organizational obstacles to its use being spread to new areas. The technology and its use are not generally distributed. The DMPs can be hanging by a slender thread, since it is not the ordinary Internet that is used but technology with a higher capacity for data transfer. However, the problem is not a lack of free capacity in the network of optic and electronic fibers, but rather that the way of using this fiber network is pioneering. It is not an established product and there is no specified market price for it. Since the distance employment agency has been a special development project from the outset, the actors involved have succeeded in creating a route bypassing this organizational (economically, legally and collaboratively) obstacle.[5] According to ANT terminol-

ogy, the transition to commercial operation can be referred to as a compulsory point of passage for the employment agency's distance service. However, it is not a choice between a distance employment agency and none, but a choice between various methods of handling communications. This transition should probably occur via a solution to the problem of obtaining more permanent access to the fiber network at a reasonable price. This is also necessary in order to allow more users and use on a larger scale.

The factor that decreases the significance of quality, or at least the possibility to evaluate it, is thus the specific regulations that apply for the employment agency and unemployment benefits. Therefore any comparison between the traditional and the groundbreaking alternative should deal with something beyond the difference between an actual and a mediated meeting, particularly since neither the staff nor the jobseeker has been able to choose between these alternatives but has had to respond to a given change.

The changes that have occurred can thus be discussed with the help of Shove's concepts of convenience and time shifting. As well as communication technologies in general, this specialist technology for a specialist area of application provides opportunities to work with presence in relation to other activities, demands and possibilities in daily life. The reports from the use of the DMP at the job agencies also reveal that a number of factors are different since its introduction. For example, the time used per new application/meeting has decreased. We will not discuss this in any further detail except to say that this should be related to the fact that mediated meetings and electronic presence are always qualitatively different from physical presence in real life.

CONCLUSION

The different examples discussed in this chapter can be regarded as projects in the ANT sense of the concept. Publication of a magazine is a project, administering new declarations of unemployment is another, etc. The use of an office at a certain location or of certain communication technology is included as one of many elements in each such project. It has become apparent from the case studies that the issues of place and form of communication involve power aspects. For example, the editor-in-chief and the employment agents could avoid trips by either having others travel to them or by using a certain form of communication.

Bruno Latour (1998b) claims that technology renders society sustainable. However, when using the concept of sustainability, Latour refers to stability from the viewpoint of power relations. Sustainable as in sustainable development is something different. For example, one can say that the employment agency in Dalarna has become more ecologically sustainable (as in sustainable development) with the help of the DMPs, since the environmentally damaging trips for new declarations have decreased. At the same time, the employment agency, as it appears at present, has also become more sustainable in Latour's meaning, since the formal regulation that jobseekers must be present in person to declare their unemployment can now be circumvented with the help of technology. On the other hand, it is not known how stable this relationship is. For example, technology can prove to be vulnerable and lose its power to fulfill the legal requirements.

The double meaning of the concept of sustainability indicates that sustainable development is linked to power. Use of technology can, and probably should in certain cases, be controlled by various means of power in order to achieve social and environmental sustainability. At the same time, technology in itself acts as a power factor. It may be necessary to dismantle or phase out a technology that proves to counteract sustainable development. There can also be a conflict between a social dimension of sustainability, e.g., the right to participate and influence, and an environmental dimension, which would mean restricting certain travel.

In the study of the office hotel, it became apparent that the location of the office hotel was based on individual desires and decisions. One can therefore refer to individual projects.

Locating one's self at an office hotel proved to be one way, at least for some, of optimizing their individual daily life project. Here the power perspective is different. It deals with people whose work roles provide an opportunity to choose that which most people cannot choose – where their workplace is based. Organizations and companies have different reasons for exerting power over where their employees should be while they are working. In order to create sustainable travel in Stockholm, working from home or a local office hotel on a large scale would be an excellent possibility with which to experiment. However just now this does not appear to be of interest to employers to any great extent. In relation to the need of individual life projects for spatial proximity, the role that central localization of the workforce plays in company projects is therefore an obstacle.

In conclusion, it also transpired that ICT use played a limited role in the interviewees' choice of locating themselves at an office hotel. Instead, it was specialist work roles and career possibilities in combination with family circumstances, social needs and 'travel fatigue' that lay behind their choice. As regards the scope of commuter travel, for those interviewed it proved to be dependent on the extent of other types of trips. It appeared to involve a type of balancing act whereby, e.g., extensive business travel was compensated for by reduced commuter travel. The interviewees belonged to categories of profession that provided the potential to alter their commuter travel through their choice of workplace.

Variations in the need and motive for communications and work trips from this contrasting example thus appear to be linked to the concrete practices involved in work tasks and work roles.

Work tasks that involve a certain product being regularly supplied by the employee are associated with clearly defined needs and motives. The clarity is due partly to the product being well delineated and defined, and partly to the work tasks being traditional and forming part of projects, companies or sectors that have achieved a high degree of maturity.

When the work task is to achieve 'something new,' it can be less clear what the employee should deliver as a result of their work. The lower degree of maturity can mean that the clarity decreases and the complexity increases. This affects how the individual travels and communicates in order to complete the task. Work tasks with a high component of creativity, knowledge seeking and/ or collaboration can in general be expected to give great variation in how trips, meetings and electronic communication are used. It can simply be the case that these types of tasks give rise to extensive travelling that is rather difficult to convert to other forms of communication.

The examples of differences between various types of work tasks or work roles outlined above do not necessarily correspond to the differences between much and little, or between difficult and easily rectified. However the correlation between the concrete practice of the work role and choice of communication method is clear. The maturity aspect is one of several aspects that are influential. Another is the power aspect. In both the private and the public sector, there are many examples of how power relations control who is expected to travel or communicate in a certain way. Not having to travel or being able to restrict how accessible one is via telephone and computer communication can, e.g., be an expression of an influential and stable position.

In order to evaluate the possibility of replacing work trips with mediated communication, working practices need to be studied on a detailed level. It is not sufficient to simply base such studies on the traditional subdivisions into different branches, jobs and functions. Such subdivisions were not created for dealing with issues concerning what determines the balance between being physically present at a site, travelling and communicating across space and time. Two people with different jobs in different branches can probably have ways of working that are practically identical from a communications perspective. At the same time, two people with precisely the same job can have completely different communication patterns. It is also not possible to simply base suppositions or strategies for reducing travel on the formal job description. This seldom coincides completely with the type of results people are trying to achieve in the execution of their work or the concrete ways of working and methods that they use in practice. One challenge is therefore to define in a relevant way work tasks in relation to forms of communication.

In addition, by looking beyond the use of ICT and ICT itself we can start seeing the relationship between agency and structure (cf. Giddens 1984/2004). The individuals participate in establishing and reproducing the practices that may become part of everyday life and of institutionalized practices. We have pointed out a direction in which analyses could move to bridge the gap between individual (but not any particular individual) and societal (structural) points of views. We believe that different analytical methods for understanding the individual's actions are necessary to understand how the technology is (or is not) used and embedded in everyday practices. Frameworks for the purpose of studying environmental and social sustainability need to be developed further. Then they can provide us with an analytic terminology for linking individual practices to the context in which they occur. That will help us to discuss not solely the practices of workplaces, but also to ask questions about what kind of "fundamental" processes the employees participate in and contribute to.

REFERENCES

Arnfalk, P. (2002). *Virtual Mobility and Pollution Prevention*. Lund, Sweden: The International Institute for Industrial Environmental Economics, Lund University.

Bentley, R., Hughes, J. A., Randall, D., Rodden, T., Sawyer, P., Shapiro, D., & Sommerville, I. (1992). Ethnographically-Informed System Design for Air Traffic Control. In *Proceedings of the 1992 ACM Conference on Computer-supported Cooperative Work* (pp. 123-129).

Brembeck, H., Ekström, K. M., & Mörck, M. (2007). Shopping with Humans and Non-humans. In H. Brembeck, K. M. Ekström & M. Mörck (Eds.), *Little monsters: (de)coupling assemblages of consumption*. Berlin: Lit Verlag.

Chalmers, M. (2004). A Historical View of Context. *Journal of Computer Supported Cooperative Work*, *13*(3), 223–247. doi:10.1007/s10606-004-2802-8

Conradsson, B. (1988). *Kontorsfolket. Etnologiska bilder av livet på kontor*. Stockholm, Sweden: Nordiska museet. Etnologiska institutionen, Stockholms universitet.

de Certeau, M. (1984). *The practice of everyday life*. Los Angeles: University of California Press.

Dourish, P., & Bly, S. (1992). Portholes: Supporting Awareness in a Distributed Work Group. In *Proceedings of the SIGCHI conference on Human factors in computing systems* (pp. 541-547).

Garfinkel, H. (1967/2002). *Studies in Ethnomethodology*. Cambridge, UK: Polity Press.

Gaver, W., Moran, T., MacLean, A., Lövstrand, L., Dourish, P., Carter, K., & Buxton, W. (1992). Realizing a Video Environment: Europarc's Rave System. In *Proceedings of the SIGCHI Conference on Human Factors in Computing Systems*, (pp. 27-35).

Gaver, W. W. (1992). The Affordances of Media Spaces for Collaboration. In *Proceedings of the 1992 ACM conference on Computer-supported Cooperative Work* (pp. 17-24).

Giddens, A. (1984/2004). *The Constitution of Society*. Cambridge, UK: Polity Press.

Glad, W. (2008). Individuell mätning - mjuk reglering för minskad energianvändning i hyreslägenheter. In *Vardagsteknik: energi och IT: forskning om hållbar användning av samhällets IT- och energisystem*. Stockholm: Carlsson.

Grübler, A. (1990). *The Rise and Fall of Infrastructures*. Heidelberg, Germany: Physica-Verlag.

Hansson, S. O. (2007). What is technological science? *Studies in History and Philosophy of Science*, *38*, 523–527. doi:10.1016/j.shpsa.2007.06.003

Heath, C., Hindmarsh, J., & Luff, P. (1999). Interaction in Isolation: The Dislocated World of the London Underground Train Driver. *Sociology*, *33*(3), 555–575.

Heath, C., & Luff, P. (1992). Collaboration and Control: Crisis Management and Multimedia Technology in London Underground Line Control Rooms. *Journal of Computer Supported Cooperative Works*, *1*(1), 24–48.

Henriksson, G. (2008). *Stockholmarnas resvanor - mellan trängselskatt och klimatdebatt*. Stockholm: Avdelningen för miljöstrategisk analys – fms, KTH Royal Institute of Technology. *TRITA-INFRA-FMS No., 2008, 5*.

Högdahl, E. (2003). *Göra gata. Om gränser och kryphål på Möllevången och i Kapstaden*. Gidlunds förlag. Etnologiska institutionen, Lunds universitet.

Latour, B. (1998a). *Artefaktens återkomst. Ett möte mellan organisationsteori och tingens sociologi*. Stockholm: Nerenius & Santérus förlag.

Latour, B. (1998b). Teknik är samhället som gjorts hållbart. In *Artefaktens återkomst. Ett möte mellan organisationsteori och tingens sociologi.* Stockholm: Nerenius & Santérus förlag.

Mantei, M. M., Baecker, R. M., Sellen, A. J., Buxton, W. A. S., Milligan, T., & Wellman, B. (1991). Experiences in the Use of a Media Space. In *Proceedings of the SIGCHI Conference on Human Factors in Computing Systems* (pp. 203-208).

Moberg, Å., Hedberg, L., Henriksson, G., Räsänen, M., & Westermark, M. (2008). *Hållbarhetsbedömning av en medierad tjänst - en pilotstudie* (Report from the KTH Centre for Sustainable Communications. No. []. KTH Centre for Sustainable Communications.]. *TRITA-SUS, 2008,* 1.

Nardi, B. A. (1996). Studying Context: A Comparison of Activity Theory, Situated Action Models, and Distributed Cognition. In B. A. Nardi (Ed.), *Context and consciousness: Activity Theory and Human-Computer Interaction.* Cambridge, MA: MIT Press.

Ó'Riain. S. (2004). Networking for a Living. In A. Amin & N. Thrift (Eds.), *The Blackwell Cultural Economy Reader.* London: Blackwell Publishing.

Palm, J., & Ellegård, K. (Eds.). (2008). *Vardagsteknik: energi och IT: forskning om hållbar användning av samhällets IT- och energisystem.* Stockholm: Carlsson.

Pycock, J., & Bowers, J. (1996). Getting Others To Get It Right. An Ethnography of Design Work in the Fashion Industry. In *Proceedings of the 1996 ACM Conference on Computer Supported Cooperative Work* (pp. 219-228).

Räsänen, M. (2006). *Om möten i Distansen: Uppfattningar om möten på distans mellan arbetssökande och handläggare* (Technical report, HCI-report series, No. HCI-42). Stockholm: Avdelningen för Människa-Datorinteraktion. KTH Royal Institute of Technology

Räsänen, M. (2007). *Islands of Togetherness: Rewriting Context Analysis.* Stockholm: Royal Institute of technology, KTH.

Räsänen, M., & Nyce, J. M. (2008). Rewriting Context and Analysis: Bringing Anthropology into HCI Research. In S. Pinder (Ed.), *Advances in Human Computer Interaction* (pp. 397-414). Vienna: InTech Education and Publishing.

Rayner, S., & Malone, E. L. (1998). Why study human choice and climate change? In S. Rayner & E. L. Malone, (Eds.), *Human Coice and Climate Change. Volume two. Resources and Technology* (pp. xiii-xlii). Columbus, Ohio: Batelle Press.

Rouncefield, M., Viller, S., Hughes, J. A., & Rodden, T. (1995). Working with "Constant Interruption": CSCW and the Small Office. *The Information Society, 11,* 173–188.

Shove, E. (2003a). *Comfort, cleanliness and convenience: the social organization of normality.* Oxford, UK: Berg.

Shove, E. (2003b). Converging Conventions of Comfort, Cleanliness and Convenience. *Journal of Consumer Policy,* (26): 395–418. doi:10.1023/A:1026362829781

Shove, E., Lutzenhiser, L., Guy, S., Hacket, B., & Wilhite, H. (1998). Energy and social systems. In E. L. M. Steve Rayner (Ed.), *Human Coice and Climate Change. Volume two.* Resources and Technology. Columbus, Ohio: Batelle Press.

Suchman, L. A. (1987/1990). *Plans and Situated Actions: The Problem of Human Machine Communication.* Cambridge, UK: Cambridge University Press.

Vilhelmson, B. (2002). *Rörlighet och förankring - Geografiska aspekter på människors välfärd* ([]. Göteborg, Sweden: Department of Human and Economic Geography.]. *Choros, No., 2002,* 1.

Willim, R. (2002). *Framtid.nu: flyt och friktion i ett snabbt företag.* Stockholm/Stehag: Symposion. Etnologiska institutionen, Lunds universitet.

ENDNOTES

[1] The background description in this section has been elaborated previously for other purposes in Räsänen (2007) and Räsänen and Nyce (2008).

[2] Judging by Bonnie's communication diary, she has a number of brief meetings with colleagues at the office. She had only made entries for one working day. This included the following two meetings:
13.00-13.20 Quick meeting with the controller.
13.20-13.30 Quick meeting with the marketing department.

[3] In a wider perspective, e-mailing and telephoning, such as Erica's and Bonnie's, can lead to contacts and knowledge that create a need to visit people and places. This has been the subject of much discussion on recent decades in various contexts. See e.g. Grübler (1990: 258) who writes "Although a number of (e.g. business) trips may be substituted by new communication technologies, /- - -/ [these] may in turn also *induce* additional travel".

[4] The space has been designed with lighting, furnishings and textiles in order to create a good environment for meetings. Data transfer occurs over existing infrastructure of optic or electronic fibres, but communication takes place not via the internet and personal computer but as an uncompromised video signal via a separate media network. This gives more of a TV, or perhaps home cinema, picture quality compared with what can be obtained through web cameras and image transfer services via the internet.

[5] The transition from project status to ongoing operation means that one has to choose between alternative paths. According to the engineers at KTH who installed the technology, data transmission can occur in various ways, either as at the time of the study (and agreement is reached on what it would cost to have acces to the network) or though the use of an ordinary computer and good software. The software needs to be obtained and the staff need training in using it, but otherwise operations can continue as usual.

Section 4
Critical Perspectives

Chapter 13
Communication, Information and Sustainability:
A Geographical Perspective on Regional Communication Policies

Marco Tortora
Political Science School, University of Florence, Italy

ABSTRACT

This chapter, recognizing that the main communication concepts are deeply geographical in their inner nature, has the intent of introducing an analysis of the connection there should be between geography, communication, organization and sustainability. The author will use the geography of information as the main framework to detect these links and to present the analysis of a regional communication infrastructure to understand how the Internet can be pivotal to communication and local development strategies. The analysis will present regional communication policies, projects and practices to understand if these are positive or negative forces for a regional sustainable development.

INTRODUCTION

The traditional world of information has been completely transformed since the new information and communication technologies (ICTs) have pervaded the whole society. This 'revolution' has produced adjustments and changes in political, economic, financial and social terms, from the local to the global scale of analysis, changing the way information itself is considered and used in society.

There is neither a linear nor a causal correlation between development, technological dissemination, and social changes, but there is rather a multitude of complex connections between each element of the analysis.

The territorial and spatial effects produced by new technologies have also been studied by geographical sciences. Beyond the cultural tradition in which each work can be filed, and the different theoretical perspectives and methodologies adopted by each researcher, there should be a research for the identification of a common thread, language, structure, framework or paradigm that will link together various works. In general, a common thread should be the recognition of the analyzed reality's complexity that makes it difficult to simplify differ-

DOI: 10.4018/978-1-60566-822-2.ch013

ent and various concepts in a very extreme way and leads to inter- and multi-discipline. Since communication issues present many geographical aspects and concepts (space/place, distance/proximity, inclusion/exclusion, local/global), the main aim of the chapter is to introduce a different theoretical structure which develops in a new light the dialectical interpretations of previous concepts with the intention of proposing a different point of view to scholars of many fields, first of all to organizational communication researchers.

In the following paragraphs, I will try to introduce and trace the recent development in the field of geography of information (or Information Society) and its multi-discipline aspects. Using the main concepts, theories, approaches of this field of research, it should be possible to make different social sciences 'communicate' to have a more complete view of the analyzed reality, especially from the perspective of sustainable communication and development.

In the second section I will define what geography of information is, and how it can be useful in studying communication processes and phenomena. I will introduce the main framework of analysis and present three spatial concepts used in the following example (networks, flows, and information).

In the third section I will introduce the analysis of a regional communication system. The focus is on the organization based on the Internet and the main applications used to develop the basic infrastructure of future communication and information projects. Then I will analyze the communication policies and initiatives of the regional government to understand: how they use the network (the Internet) to mould regional and local organizational structures; how and if regional communicational policies are coordinated with local ones; what kind of communication means local places have to boost their local development. I finally highlight the existing difficulties in coordinating different scales of governance, especially if investments are driven from the top to develop only new technological infrastructures, without any initiative to spread the knowledge and culture of communication and information processes to local stages of government.

A GEOGRAPHICAL FRAMEWORK OF ANALYSIS

The main idea of this chapter is to present and use the geography of information as the main framework to link together and read in a different perspective the three main concepts of the book: sustainable development (sustainability), communication (organization) and flows (mobility of people, information, etc.).

In fact, the topic is strictly connected to the objectives of geography of information, which is related to the analysis of relationships between receivers and senders, flows, infrastructures, technology and networks (Bakis & Vidal 2007; Graham & Marvin, 1996; Kellerman, 1993, 2000, 2002; Kellerman & Paradiso, 2007; Paradiso, 2003a, 2003b; Paradiso & Wilson, 2006; Zook, 2000a, 200b, 2001). Since communication is today more than ever central to the social, economic and political developments of a community at different scales (local, regional, national, meso, international and global), geography should be of interest for other disciplines to read similar events from a different point of view.

Communication is strictly connected to geography, even if it refers to the most immaterial network we know – the Internet, since it is embedded in territories and involves people from different cultures and places, who use the same technologies starting from and depending on different levels of economic growth (Castells, 2000). This means that communication depends on the territories where senders, receivers and technical equipments are located and on how the actors connect and use the technology to communicate and create new paths of local development.

According to the general literature in the field, geography of information explores and studies spatial dynamics and dimensions of the Information Society, including the aspects of global communication and its spatial effects, contributions to the globalization of territories and the role of ICT in the territorial development and how places interact with the production, transmission and consumption of information, showing to what extent concepts such as the death of distance and dissolution of cities in the information era are misleading (Paradiso, 2006).

In this chapter I first introduce what I assume for information geography. Then I analyze a regional communication organization following the methodological framework provided below, to focus on an empirical example: how a region of the so-called modern (or post-modern) and rich world, here defined by its political and administrative boundaries (Tuscany, Italy), uses the new communication technologies, and especially the Internet, to give a chance to local actors and agents to develop in a sustainable way. I will try to answer the following questions: what kind of measures and projects has this developed region planned to reach its goals? What kind of idea of sustainability do they have in mind? Are they using the Internet to help local communities to develop in a sustainable manner? At this point it is important to clarify one point: I will present a brief introduction of the geography of information, especially referring to the geography of media since they are the major producers and transmitters of information, and I will pay special attention to the Internet as the main media to be analyzed.

COMMUNICATION, INFORMATION AND GEOGRAPHY

Since we live in an Information Society, we should assume the point of view of Sheppard (2000), who proposes three different definitions for geography of the Information Society, and consequently of the geography of information. He defines the 'actual geography' as the study of the actual effects produced by the diffusion of the ICT; the 'virtual geography' as the study of the geographical aspects of nods, hubs, networks of ICTs; and the 'conceptual geography' as the study of the images produced in the mind of the receiver or observer. Mainardi (1996) has a similar point of view, but more coherent to our goal. For him, one of the paths of research in the field of the geography of information/communication is the geography of media. Geography of media studies the distribution of production and message transmission centers over the space and place, which means that it identifies the centers and peripheries of the communication world and the characteristics and shapes of the transmission and distribution networks.

Under this point of view, the geography of media (or of information) focuses on the three phases or moments of the communication process: the production, the distribution and the consumption of information. Each phase correlates to a specific geography: the geography of production, of the network and of the content. The geography of production identifies the centers of production, the level of their activities and the power of their relationships. The geography of the network looks at how messages (information) move around in a definite space (among different places), detecting relationships of hegemony/dependence and proximity/distance between various knots of the net. The geography of contents highlights all kinds of inclusion/exclusion relations in communication networks, that is it focus on the different relevance given by the media to single identities, communities and places. It also analyzes what is communicated: the content – the discourse, such as political programs and values, ideas or philosophies, communicated by a specific agent to a targeted audience.

This scheme is just an extreme simplification and a model given to demonstrate the importance of geography in an analysis of communication, and to trace a useful path of study. Researchers can focus on just a single part or use more than one according to different approaches, paradigms and fields of study. But since reality is complex, the more the research tries to focus on each aspect at the same time, and on their relationships, the closer the eye of the observer is to reality.

Recognizing the complexity of reality brings the researcher to focus also on the main product of communication processes, that means what is produced, transmitted and consumed. Information is the main resource and product of communication networks, but during the last years it has not received the right attention.

In this chapter the network is not a predominant element of analysis, because I consider it only a technical and technological tool of communication. This is possible, if I refuse the deterministic approach, and recognize that information "exists" (it assumes a material characteristic) only in the moment in which it is de-codified and "consumed" by the receiver. A complete and more complex definition of what is transmitted through communication networks can be given only if we consider the whole process of communication, and not just one phase of it (centers of production and consumption, networks). What is produced, transmitted and consumed is a relevant aspect of the communication process, so it is important to give it the right emphasis. This approach also includes the fact that if I accept to analyze the consumption moment, I give relevance to the de-codification phase, that means to the culture and know-how of the receiver, involving in the analysis the sender and the production/codification phase (and the opposite is worth at the same time). Regardless of any academic attempt of classification, what one should keep in mind is that the relevance given to network and information issues started during the Nineties with the development of the Internet and the boom of the New Economy (Kellerman, 2002). Initially, the geographical analysis was about the technological infrastructure of the so-called Information Society and Economy, rather than about information itself. For example, there are researches on ICT networks and infrastructures (Bakis, Abler & Roche, 1993; Graham & Marvin, 1996; Hepworth, 1990; Kellerman, 1993).

With the dissemination of the Internet among nations and different classes of population, with the reappraisal of the New Economy phenomenon and the acknowledgement of information as a resource and a final product, many studies focused on the production of a new space produced by the new ICTs – the cyberspace (Aurigi & Graham, 2000; Aurigi, 2005; Dodge, 1999; Dodge & Kitchin, 2001; Graham & Marvin, 1999). Cyberspace or the virtual space has been defined in many ways. It is an organizational structure and a medium to manage information (Kellerman, 2002), or a world created by flows and the digital accumulation of knowledge, fed by communication networks and computers. This world is a space of places, generated by the accumulation of information and the given structure (Mainardi, 1996). According to the previous definition, cyberspace has been studied as the main tool for territorial governance and urban planning (Aurigi & Graham 2000, Graham & Marvin 1996; Paradiso, 2003b). Other authors shed light on the new centers and peripheries inside the urban areas, on the role of ICT as development tools for places, and on the specialization of cities in two phases: the management of information in the phases of production, distribution, consumption, and the kinds of information produced such as information, knowledge or innovation (Graham & Marvin, 1996; Lorentzon 2000, 2003, 2004; Arai & Sugizaki, 2003). Other research interests of the field are strictly connected to the role of communication processes and infrastructures in regional and local development strategies (Corey & Wilson, 2006; Graham & Marvin, 2001; Paradiso & Wilson 2006a, 2006b).

From Information Networks to Flows of Information

How many times have we heard about information networks, flows of information, networks of flows and so on? Many of these concepts have spread transversally among many disciplines because of the soaring importance of new ICTs and their infrastructure in many aspects of social life. Since every aspect of the communication field, from organizational structures to processes and flows, is strictly and inherently geographical in many ways, there are numerous concepts and models used to describe the spatial effects of ICTs. Networks, flows and information are necessary spatial concepts to comprehend how ICTs are changing communication processes in organizations and places.

Networks are models that describe in a very simple way organizations and processes of any given social system (a community, a company, a bureau, a corporation). They consist in hubs, knots and lines, but what is really important is the content of their segments, the material or immaterial flows of people, goods, capital and information. Concerning our field of analysis, the main content of immaterial networks like the ICTs is information. Even if the content is immaterial, ICT networks have territorial effects that derive from their widespread over the space, but these effects are difficult to describe because they are characterized by two parallel and, at the same time, opposite forces: on one side there are tendencies of centralization, globalization and inter-dependency, since these networks developed in the same paths of the previous technologies (i.e. telegraphs), that is in the same areas (metropolitan and urban areas); on the other side, there are effects of access, flexibility and adaptability to new opportunities that ICT networks offer to companies, public powers and communities. These two forces actually realize the concept of the glocalization process that means how localities can connect and influence the global. Globalization

is no longer a one-way process, but it is a complex and multi-directional group of forces, which act together, in different directions. An example of how the new technologies have changed the shape of organizations is the so-called network company. Business cycles are decomposed and the re-territorialization of production phases and processes is a common strategy to reduce production costs. Public bureaus are changing too, even if at a different pace. Nevertheless, public administrations are investing to structure themselves like organized system units connected to different networks, where the knots and centers are the different communities inside a space defined by administrative and bureaucratic boundaries. The application of the subsidiary principle is the right example to show and confirm that it is not easy to realize any idea, until the technical and knowledge opportunities are achieved.

Castells (1996, 2000) defines our society as the Network Society. This model of society is composed of three levels. The first is the cyberspace, a space constituted by electronic interchanges and technological network. The technological infrastructure is an important element since it defines the new space and its architecture and contents are determined by the powers that rule the world. The second level is constituted by the network's material structure (hubs, nods, lines), the single nods correspond to real places, points of access and transmission with different degree of power depending on their functions. The third level is about the spatial organization of the power elites and their spatial localization (global cities).

So the world we live in can be represented like a space of flows of which direction and intensity are given by the powerful elites of the world, which correspond to the main urban areas.

If we totally accept this representation of the world, we fail to describe the importance of places for the production and consumption processes. The space of flows cannot contrast the space of places, imagined as a poorer level of the former. Places determine the direction, intensity and contents of flows, so places (spaces, networks of, or systems of) and not spaces should be the main goal of the analysis. In these terms, spaces of places and flows between them can be imagined as an archipelago of regions (Scott, 2001), composed mainly of metropolitan areas.

So flows depend on the places of transmission and reception, the culture in locus (know-how, know-what) and the content. In the case of ICT networks, the main content has a digital shape – information.

Information has been variously defined over the years, generating confusion and misunderstanding. For some authors, the reason is the lack of an organic approach in social sciences and their tendency to use a terminology derived from statistics or to consider information only where there is technical equipment; for others, the problem is that information is described only in economic terms or as units of measurement according to the cybernetics theory. In 1949 C.E. Shannon presented a mathematical theory of information where he defined information in physical, quantitative and statistic terms, with the aim of detecting the most efficient way to send and de-codify a message (Mattelart, 1999). During these years the quantitative analysis has been favored instead of other approaches. In 1948 Wiener, the father of the cybernetic theory and of the theory of messages, defined information as a group of communication tools. During the sixties, the theorists of the Information Society defined information as a transmitted message-content or a transmitted content that creates knowledge in the receiver once the message is de-codified (Machlup, 1984).

According to the economics of information and physical studies, information is also the main force against the entropic forces of nature. This representation is possible because information is the opposite of the entropy that is present in any given system, and they must be open systems for hypothesis (if the system is closed, according to the second law of thermodynamics, it risks exhaus-

tion). Since it helps to measure the informational content of a system, the lower the content of information in a system, the higher the level of chaos and disorder in a system (maximum level of entropy) (Ziliotti, 2001).

On the opposite side, from a qualitative point of view, Kellerman (2002) defines information as a wide family of communicative codified materials. The communicative material is composed of four elements put in a linear sequence: data, information, knowledge and innovation. In this case it is important to focus on the context of the communication process, like Castells (1996) does, defining information as a group of organized and communicated data. If we refer to a specific context, like the economic one (or to society), it is possible to identify four kinds of information (Kellerman, 2002): a 'pure' information; an 'incorporated' information in business processes; an information like a 'final product'; and 'transformed services' (i.e. capital). An example of the two latter definitions can be the wired services offered by news agencies like Reuters: information like news and financial information.

Shapiro and Varian (1999) define information as something that can be transformed into the digital format and sent by the new kinds of communication technologies.

Whatever the definition preferred, it is important to highlight the polysemic nature of this concept and the complexity and ambiguity related to it. It is also important to remember that in each case of study at the empirical level, whether observing the real world of affairs and business or the whole society, there are multiple and multi-dimensional linkages between the different aspects put under the lens of the research. So it is honest to recognize the limits of the observation, especially at the empirical level of the analysis, and to be conscious that what is described is just a part of the reality's complexity, and much of the description depends on what kind of position we assume during the analysis.

COMMUNICATION AND SUSTAINABILITY, A POSSIBLE NEXUS?

It is possible to use the framework presented above (the geographies of production, of transmission and of content) to analyze and study social issues, if we consider the sustainability of social development like a goal of political programs by local communities embedded in specific places. This means that sustainable development values are the content (implicit or explicit) of what is communicated between all the agents involved in the communication process with reference to the development project and at any scales of analysis.

If sustainability is the main goal for communities and their governments, communication is the process that assumes the feature of being 'sustainable' (sustainable communication) only if it has the purpose to reach a sustainable goal. Since sustainability is the right of present generations to meet their needs without compromising the right of future generations to meet their own needs (Brundtland Commission, 1987), it follows that the sustainability of a communication process, in terms of social and economic development, can be reached only if there is a perfect control and management of communication processes and its content (information, the main resource and output of the process) at different scales of analysis and intervention. The following example presents the role and usage of the Internet by a regional government to reach, among others, the goal of sustainable development. I use the geographical framework introduced above to express under a different light the organization of a communication process: the geography of production (the organization of communication processes), the geography of the network (the technical infrastructure) and the geography of the content (the main policies and programs that should underline any decision taken by public and private bodies or individuals), calling back the main key words of analysis (places, networks, flows and information). In doing so, I use a qualitative approach, based on the analysis of academic literature (most of it geographical) of official statistical and economic data, of discourses and documents (official documents, regional laws, news and texts found on the Internet and produced by official and public offices or bureaus), of interviews to professionals employed in the communication field of the Tuscany region, and of observations and informal and formal meetings with professionals and politicians.

Communication in Tuscany

Before presenting how and if communication could help improve a regional sustainable development,[1] we need to describe the regional communication system and how it is organized (geography of production), the degree of development of the technological equipment – the Internet (geography of the network) and then the policies used to implement the infrastructure to help local communities to grow in a path of sustainability (geography of content).

Tuscany

Tuscany is one of the richest regions in Italy. With a population of almost 7% of the total, it has a GDP that covers 6.8% of the national one. Traditionally, Tuscany is one of the most open regions in Italy in terms of import-export balance of flows. It exports almost 8% of the Italian total exports. The Tuscan economic system bases itself specifically on the service sector (47%). Communication systems[2] and ICTs are a very important area for public investments and a decisive factor to boost productivity, that is why since 2004 the goal of the Tuscan government has been to invest new resources in communication processes and strategies, above all the Internet.

The Geography of Production

The two main channels of the Tuscany region Web institutional communication are: the main website (www.regione.toscana.it) and the portal website (www.intoscana.it). The institutional communication is a necessary activity to have a direct and correct relation with media and citizens. Informational and communicational activities of public administrations are ruled by national laws. Tuscany has also its own regional law about information and communication (Law N.22/2002) that applies the principles of the national law. The regional law's main goal is to inform Tuscan citizens about laws, programs, activities, initiatives of regional organisms and bodies, and opportunities and services of the regional administrations. There is a particular distinction between the two main communicative activities: information and communication. Each activity has its own structures and requires specific professional profiles. The informational activities are about relations with media and the realization of news or other journalistic products, while communicational activities are about direct relations with citizens and local communities. The regional law also regulates the regional news agency that works for the regional government (Tuscany News). Started in April 2007, Tuscany News is the regional news agency that exploits all the opportunities offered by multimedia tools. Visiting the main website of Tuscany, it is possible to find news about all the activities of the regional ministries and much more, press releases and conferences, newsletters, radio and TV products.

Tuscany has also its own official web portal. A web portal is a site that provides several functions, being a point of access to information from diverse sources and about different themes. The regional web portal is a virtual place or 'agora' where people can find all the information and services they need about different themes. It is described as a privileged window and point of observation of the regional life. This description comes from its structure. It is thought as the eye and the voice of all the activities that happen daily in Tuscany, from the production activities to the social, cultural and religious ones. It is organized to be visited and useful not only for regional communities, but also for foreign visitors, whether companies or institutions. It is a useful news attractor and producer of news about many aspects of the Tuscan life, from environment and innovation, to the political and economic activities. It uses the most up-to-date web applications, the Web 2.0 social networking applications like Second Life, FaceBook, Linkedin, Youtube, Flickr and others, to share information and ideas and to make people participate actively in the social life at different levels, from the local to the global.

This structure and its relative channels need a technical infrastructure to work. This one is represented by a regional digital network, the technological and hardware heart of the regional system of public communication.

The Geography of the Network: The Digital Network of the Tuscany Region

The Digital Network is the main technical infrastructure of the region and the driving force of all the investments in the development field. It can be described as an organic intervention for the development of the Information Society promoted by the regional government. It was created with the idea of being managed and developed primarily by the Tuscany Region, but also by all those public corporations and bodies that believe in the project.

So, first of all, it is a network composed of different local agents. The actors of the network are the Tuscany Region, the regional agencies and authorities, the public health agencies and corporations, the municipalities, the provincial administrations, the metropolitan areas, the mountain villages. There are also universities, research institutes and public bodies, the peripheral administration bodies of the National State, the local public services companies, the chambers of commerce, economic categories and other public and private associations.

This network was designed to be an organizational model and a technological infrastructure. It is an organizational model because it is structured to be capable of producing and sustaining innovation processes. It is based on the relationships between the involved actors and on the concepts of sharing goals and cooperating among members. It is also a technological infrastructure, spread all over the regional territory and interconnected to the Internet. It has been developed to meet the standards promoted by the National Agency for the Use of Informatics in the Public Administration sector (CNIPA) and by the project called Public System of Connectivity (a sort of unique network which connects all the public administrations of the national state).

Whether an organizational model or a 'simple' technical infrastructure, the shape of it – the network - is what characterizes its organizational processes and informational activities. It is considered by the regional government as a unique opportunity for local development, since it establishes new relationships between the public administrations, the latter and the citizens, companies and society. It also should boost technological and organizational innovation promoted by all the involved actors, promote the resources of Tuscany (territory, culture, production activities) on the Net and help ICT small and medium enterprises, thanks to the possible new investments in the IT sector.

Each single agent can actively use this infrastructure to create, distribute, receive, consume, and share information, at least to reach the collective goal of a sustainable development. Before any attempt to analyze the information process (creation and distribution of information – the content) it is important, from the point of view followed in this analysis (the public and institutional side of the communication process), to present the main directives that inform all the policies, programs, decisions and practices produced in communication activities at the regional level.

The Geography of the Content: The Use of the Internet in Regional Communication Processes

Today we live in an Information Society or post-industrial society, indicating a society in which information is the main resource and product of many human activities, a strategic resource that must be managed by local communities to help and drive their local development. The latest development and innovations related to the Internet have lead many observers and futurologists to describe our age as the Web 2.0 era, the time of the sharing of ideas, values and knowledge, starting from the bottom of society, the interconnection ideology at the nth power.

Information is a resource and a product also for public agents, for governments that must manage every day an increasingly differentiated quantity of information. So it is important for them to invest in the sector, trying to be connected in an active way, that means to know, control, and manage the new forms of communication and information, like those of the Internet and the so-called Web 2.0. It becomes ever more strategic to help local communities to get connected to the Net to give them a chance of development and growth. That is why the Tuscany region has programmed to invest 209 millions euro within 2010 through the Regional Program for the Development of the Information Society[3]

The Regional Program for the Promotion and Development of a Digital Public Administration and of the Information Society was approved in 2007 by the regional parliament with the aim to ease the process of organizational and technological innovation of the Tuscan Public Administration, the digital inclusion of all communities, and the development of a regional competitiveness. The main object of the Regional Program for the Development of the Information Society is to develop a process to approach the issues of the informational and knowledge field in a planned and systemic way. The regional program has, among its objectives, to develop a digital platform to allow citizens to participate to the digital public life. More in detail, it means that 85% of all the citizens of all the municipalities could access the digital services[4]. Today 34 projects have been activated: from the realization of a technological infrastructure to safely access all the public services, the reduction of the use of paper, the intra-communication processes inside the public administration and the management of public e-health services.

The regional program is articulated in four thematic areas under the umbrella of the e-government policy (e-community, e-services, e-competitiveness, quality infrastructures), which is the main framework and defines goals, actions, and specific results to be reached.

These four areas are all included in the E-democracy project, which stands for a digital democracy, a democracy online, that helps all communities to participate actively to the public life and transform the original space of public life, where people used to confront themselves with the public authorities. It means to involve citizens and communities of citizens to the life and activities of the public administration at different levels of organization (online votes, polls, electronic town meeting, forums, labs, etc.) The government of Tuscany has recently approved a law about the participation of citizens: it allows to share public documents and acts related to important development programs, in order to create the opportunity of launching and observing online debates to check the sensitivity of population about certain 'hot' and 'updated' issues. The main goals of a participative democracy are to inform, discuss, and decide 'together': are all these goals really realizable or are they just new ideological visions of the power of technical means and hypothetical and irrational illusions?

Going back to the main four areas, 'E-community' stands for the policies developed for the access and the participation of local agents (access to the network, services of networks, fields of knowledge). 'E-services' stand for regional policies developed for the delivery of digital services to local communities according to the rules of efficiency, transparency, and integrity; to improve organizational innovation through the use and dissemination of the main tools of the Net. 'E-competitiveness' stands for a sustainable economic development: the main aim of the regional government is to increase the value and the competitiveness of local companies through the use of ICTs in the production chain of the business cycle production-marketing-sales. 'Quality infrastructures' are all the actions used to build and complete the technological infrastructure of the Regional Digital Network. Examples of these actions are the dissemination of digital networks, the sharing of services, the creation of interconnected systems.

All these areas are realized under the umbrella of an E-government policy, which stands for public programs that use digital technologies to apply governance activities and maintain political relationships. Tuscany wants to offer most of the services to citizens online through the creation of a digital network, the so-called Regional Digital Network. According to recent statistical reports and data (CORECOM, 2006), only 5% of Tuscan municipalities allow citizens to pay online for some services, and a little more than 10% of them have experienced the so-called e-procurement (procedures of buying online). Since there is the idea that investments in new technology are a decisive factor to boost productivity, since 2004 the goal is to develop online services for all local administrative bureaus at different levels and in different sectors, and to invest in infrastructures and communications (public system transportations, digital divide, Wi-Fi systems). The material and technical network through which local administrative bureaus can connect to the digital world and put online their services is the Regional Digital Network. The Regional Program is the main element of comparison that local public agents have to consider and follow if they want to use the Internet in an efficient way according to the regional directives. But does this organization of regional communication processes really help local agents to develop efficient strategies to boost local development?

CAN COMMUNICATION POLICIES HELP TO REALIZE A REGIONAL SUSTAINABILITY?

Before answering the previous questions, it is necessary to define the two main key words: sustainable communication and development. A sustainable communication is possible only when all communication processes tend to reach the goal of sustainability or sustainable development of any given organization, in any given place and at any level. Communication strategies, infrastructures, and technologies (like the Internet) can be useful (and sustainable) only if used for this very specific goal. In this chapter sustainable development has been generally defined as a development that meets the needs of the present generations without compromising the ability of future generations to meet their own needs (Brundtland Commission, 1987). In more specific terms, it seems that a sustainable approach recognizes the complexity of reality, searches for alternatives, and takes into account the three areas or systems (natural, social, and economic) that compose the context of every analysis. In our analysis, a social organization can be sustainable if it considers at the same time different areas (the social, ecological, and economic one) and structures itself (in organizational terms) to reach the goal of sustainability. At the same time the sustainable development becomes a means used to resolve all those problems related to the future of natural environments, the consumption of resources, the development of present and future local communities. So it can be said the sustainable development is not only a paradigm or a generic goal, but it is also a process and an approach for the development of communicational processes and organizations.

In the following lines I try to answer the question I used to close the previous paragraph and open this one. I present a very brief and limited example of an application of a geographical discourse and thought about how local agents can meet their local sustainable goals of growth using communication means like the Internet. In doing this, I stress the analysis on the content of communication processes, that means on how local agents can produce information and use it in a specific context (an economic sector like tourism) through web strategies. In doing so, I summarize and put into practice the concepts presented in the previous paragraph.

Tuscany and the Tourism Sector

As presented above, Tuscany is one of the richest regions in Italy, and one of the favorite tourist destinations in Italy. One of the reasons for this result is the correct and unique mix of art, culture and environments. There are a lot of opportunities to develop new forms of environmental and cultural tourism, since Tuscany is characterized by a good equilibrium between the use of land for urban areas and green areas. The diversity of land use and the variety of physical and morphological environments creates different resources for tourist attractions and activities, different production activities and strategies.

The tourism sector is primarily based on the environmental quality, which stands for the protection of green areas. Today more than 8% of the land is a protected area (i.e. regional park). This policy is a very important phase of the sustainable development strategy because it allows a redistribution of income to less developed sectors and local areas (IRPET, 2008).

But it is not enough. It is important to help local communities to have the chance and formulate the right policies to grow in a sustainable manner. Tuscany gives such an importance to sustainable development that it recognizes it as the main paradigm for the economic growth of local communities (Agenda 21). Since tourism is related first of all to flows of people (mobility) and it is considered an opportunity of growth and sustainable development for the regional government, it could be interesting to understand how communication tools like the Internet can boost local developments.

An Example of a Sustainable Opportunity of Growth at the Regional Level: The Ecotourism Market

One of the main resources of Tuscany is tourism. Tuscany is the second region in Italy for flows of tourism (IRPET, 2008). Since this sector is so important for the economic growth of the region, it is interesting to understand in what measure and if communication technologies are used to boost the local development of places in the tourist sector.

Tuscany has passed away the period of the mass-tourism (it is not ended, but regional policies are trying to transform it, creating new niches in the market), and thanks to a unique mix of art, culture, and socio-natural environments, it is possible to find new niches of the market to diversify and enrich the supply side. The ecotourism market[5] is a niche market since it offers a specific and restricted group of services for a specific target. It is important for our purpose because it links together the paradigm of social sustainability (the sustainable development of local communities), mobility (since tourist activities are strictly correlated with flows of people, money, information, etc.), and communication tools for development. Through the analysis of the communication network, in our case the Internet, it should be possible to understand if what has been done by the regional government is enough for local places to attract the right flows of people to sustain their local economic growths.

The presence of tourists in a place is a source of impact under different aspects, since the use of urban and green areas can overcome the upper limit of sustainable growth. Tourists impact local places in many ways, having many negative effects on the environments (externalities), like pollution. Since local places such as villages, towns, communities have a limited carrying capacity and the efficiency of scale are far from those of metropolitan areas, they require a different management approach. Local governments have the priority to limit and control these impacts if they want to grow in a sustainable manner. On One way is to reposition themselves in different niches of the market through investments in communication strategies to create or differ their images. Strategic communication becomes very important, especially through the Internet where it becomes necessary to be present and active part and nod of specialized networks (i.e. green tourist networks).

In a globalized world, where all markets and segments are intertwined and interconnected because of the spread and use of new information and communication technologies, the Internet assumes the role of a strategic communication tool to be implemented for competitive organizational strategies in different fields (local development, public institutions, private companies) and at various levels (local, regional, national). The Internet is a media that can be used by local managers in many phases of the tourist consumption process (from the search for new information about benchmarking competitors' products and services to marketing strategies, from online advertising campaigns to the sharing of experiences and knowledge on blogs and online forums) because it allows new techniques for producing, managing and sending information, amplifying marketing and communication opportunities.

It is important to communicate and inform the different subjects involved in the consumption process about the right opportunities, choices, values, programs, projects they can find in a given place or area. Tourists have to be informed about the different policies and rules they have to follow once arrived in the place of destination. Local officers have to be prepared to welcome and inform tourists in the right manner, and at the same time they have to receive the instructions to manage and rule local services networks.

It can be said that one efficient way to create the right connections and inter-changes between the supply side (local communities) and the demand side (tourists) is to communicate in both directions the principles, ideas, rules, acts that inform a specific topic, in this case ecological tourism. The Internet makes this rule valuable. A possible and efficient way to do that is to create the right organizational infrastructure, like a consortium of local actors, with a strong presence both on the territory and on the Web. Local networks of communities try to associate to create a sub-regional actor capable to pool resources and offer a unique supply system. There are many consortia of micro companies that work together to achieve a greater role in the regional productive process. Communication is the pivotal element to create and use these networks of local actors to manage the local development. One advantage of these organizations lies in an integrated system of communication, that means the usage of the same brand and logo, the same advertising message, the same chart of principles and values, in a few words the same supplied system of services through different media.

In the case of the ecological tourism in Tuscany, and despite many investments in the communication and tourism sectors, there could be the risk of a lack of coordination between productive areas and government levels. Because of a high percentage of investments was given to material infrastructures and networks, and to professionals of the communicational field, the program of investments would risk to miss an important aspect of the supply side: to educate and train all involved agents to create a common culture and a sharing knowledge about the content of communication (in the given example about ecotourism). For instance, it seems[6] there is no common culture and knowledge of ecological values, ideas, and procedures of ecotourism among regional players.

It seems there is no culture of information at different levels of the regional system; local communities do not have the knowledge to use communication tools in a proper and efficient way, like the Internet, least of all to grow in a sustainable manner. In the specific case of ecotourism, if we compare the institutional websites of regional and sub-regional public bodies and private websites of micro companies and local communities involved in the tourist sector and in the ecotourism niche, there is the contradiction that local places should take out on the sustainable path of ecotourism, but with different strategies and meanings (the problem of language and misleading concepts) and without any regional coordination (in terms of communication strategies) from the regional government. If the two levels do not proceed at the same pace, there should be difficulties to reach the planned goal.

This fact brings the role of communication to our attention in cultural terms, the importance of investing not only in infrastructure but also in educational and training systems, to prepare local managers to use communication like principal means of sustainable development, and in information – the creation of the right content and output for communication channels. If there is no culture of sustainability, the same technical tools become inefficient. So the goal of sustainable development can be realized through sustainable communication processes only in the presence of a disseminated and shared knowledge and culture of sustainability.

What Next?

As presented above, whatever the political program and its scale of applications, it is not so easy to describe why programs and activities fail at a certain point to reach their planned goals. Nevertheless, it is necessary to try to understand the limits and the disadvantages of each policy because in doing so researchers can help public and private actors in efficiently managing their plans and initiatives. But it is also important that researchers of different disciplines start communicating between themselves to make any analysis richer and closer to the observed reality. One of the aims of this chapter is to present the main topics of the book under a different light to give a different image of a known reality, and to give a relative contribution to the analysis of complex realities such as organizational communication systems.

CONCLUSION

In the previous paragraphs, I have introduced the main concepts, theories and approaches of the geography of information to use its multi-discipline aspects to present communication and organization facts in a new light, to make different social sciences 'communicate' to have a more complete view of the analyzed reality, especially from the perspective of organizational communication and sustainable development.

I have used the main framework of analysis to "read" the organization of a regional public communication system. The focus has been put on the organization based on the Internet, its main communication channels and its role in the development of communication and information projects and programs. The analysis of the organization and the evidence of the discrepancies there are between the regional government's communication policies and initiatives and local agent's opportunities and resources, have shown the existing difficulties to coordinate different scales of governance, especially if investments are driven from the top to develop only new technological infrastructures, without any initiative to spread the knowledge and culture of com-

munication and information processes to bottom and local stages of government. In fact, communication and information could be one of the main drivers of a local sustainable development, only if local managers were prepared to manage those two forces in a proper manner. Most of the times regional governments invest huge amounts of money in infrastructural investments to build technological networks and give local agents the chance to use the new information and communication technologies, and to be connected to different networks, first of all the Internet. But it happens that there is a lack of interest in investing in training the main actors of a communication process: the knowledge and capacity of producing, controlling and managing information cannot be related to bottom-up or upper-down processes, but it should be the right mix of the two processes. The example of Tuscany and its investments in technological networks is clear: if the main goal of social and economic development of a region is sustainable development, communication can help local communities to reach this goal only if there is a coherent and systemic plan of investments in the knowledge of communication and information tools. Since information depends on places where it is produced and consumed, the role of culture is essential. Places and local communities are the main informational fields to invest in to guarantee a sustainable future.

REFERENCES

Antonelli, C. (2002). The Digital Divide: Understanding the Economics of New Information and Communication Technology in the Global Economy. Information Economics and Policy, 15(2), 173–199. doi:10.1016/S0167-6245(02)00093-8doi:10.1016/S0167-6245(02)00093-8

Aray, Y., & Sugizaki, K. (2003). Concentration of Call Centers in Peripheral Areas: Cases in Japan. NETCOM, 17, 187–202.

Aurigi, A. (2005). Making the Digital City. Aldershot, UK: Ashgate

Aurigi, A., & Graham, S. (2000). Cyberspace and the City: the Virtual City in Europe. In Bridge, G., & Watson, S. (Eds.), A Companion to the City (pp. 489-502). Oxford, UK: Blackwell.

Bakis, H., Abler, R., & Roche, E. M. (1993). Corporate Networks, International Telecommunications and Interdependence. Perspectives from Geography and Information Systems. London: Belhaven.

Bakis, H., & Roche, E. M. (1997) Cyberspace: The Emerging Nervous System of Global Society and Its Spatial Functions. In E. M. Roche, & H. Bakis, (Eds.) Developments in Telecommunications: Between Global and Local (pp.1-12). Aldershot, UK: Ashgate.

Bakis, H., & Vidal, P. (2007) De la Négation du Territoire au Géocyberespace: Vers une Approche Intégrée de la Relation entre Espace et TIC. In C. Brossaud, & B. Reber, (Eds.) Humanités Numériques, 1, 101-117.

Brundtland Commission. (1987). Our Common Future: From One Earth to One World. World Commission on Environment and Development. Oxford, UK: Oxford University Press.

Castells, M. (1996). The Rise of the Network Society. The Information Age: Economy, Society and Culture (Vol.1). Oxford, UK: Blackwell Publishing.

Castells, M. (2000). The Internet Galaxy: Reflections on the Internet, Business, and Society. Oxford, UK: Oxford University Press.

CORECOM. Law N.22/2002. Retrieved July 2008, from http://www.consiglio.regione.toscana.it/corecom/normativa_doc/leg_22_2002.htm

CORECOM. (2005). Guida alla comunicazione in Toscana. Retrieved July 2008, from http://www.consiglio.regione.toscana.it/corecom /GuidaTv/index.asp

CORECOM. (2006). La Toscana nel Sistema delle Comunicazioni. Situazioni e Tendenze. I quaderni del Corecom. Regione Toscana. Retrieved July 2008, form http://www.consiglio.regione.toscana.it/corecom/att_studio/ricerche.htm

CORECOM. (2006). Ecologia della mente. Ambienti sostenibili per contesti comunicativi, sociali e produttivi. I quaderni del Corecom. Retrieved September 2008, from http://www.consiglio.regione.toscana.it/corecom/att_studio/ricerche.htm

CORECOM. (2006). Analisi delle trasmissioni istituzionali del Consiglio Regionale della Toscana 2004-2005. I quaderni del Corecom. Retrieved September 2008, from http://www.consiglio.regione.toscana.it/corecom/att_studio/ricerche.htm

CORECOM. (2007). Come comunica l'Assemblea Toscana. I quaderni del Corecom. Retrieved September 2008, from http://www.consiglio.regione.toscana.it/corecom/att_studio/ricerche.htm

CORECOM. Statistical data. Retrieved July 2008, from http://www.consiglio.regione.toscana.it/corecom/

CORECOM, & Nielsen. (2005). Il consumo della rete in Toscana. Retrieved July 2008, from http://www.consiglio.regione.toscana.it/corecom/att_studio/ricerche.htm

CORECOM, & Nielsen/Net-Ratings (2005). La Toscana in rete, 2002-2005. Retrieved July 2008, from http://www.consiglio.regione.toscana.it/corecom/att_studio/ricerche.htm

Corey, K. E., & Wilson, M. I. (2006). Urban and regional technology planning. New York: Routledge.

Cottle, S. (Ed.). (2003). Media Organization and Production. London: Sage Publications.

Dodge, M. (1999). Measuring and mapping the geographies of Cyberspace: a research note. NETCOM, 1(2), 53–66.

Dodge, M., & Kitchin, R. (2001). Mapping Cyberspace. London: Routledge.

Fennell, D. A. (2002). Ecotourism Program Planning. Oxford, UK: Cabi Publishing.

Fennell, D. A. (2003). Ecotourism Policy Planning. Oxford, UK: Cabi Publishing.

Fennell, D. A. (2007). Ecotourism. London: Routledge Publishing.

Graham, S. (Ed.). (2004) The Cybercities Reader. London: Routledge.

Graham, S., & Marvin, S. (1996). Telecommunications and the City: Electronic Spaces, Urban Place. New York: Routledge.

Graham, S., & Marvin, S. (2001) Splintering Urbanism: Networked Infrastructures, Technological Mobilities, and the Urban Condition. London: Routledge.

Hepworth, M. E. (1990). Geography of the Information Economy. New York: Guilford.

IRPET. (2008). Tuscany Info and Databases. Retrieved June 2008, from http://www.irpet.it

ISTAT. (2007). Le Tecnologie dell'Informazione e della Comunicazione: Disponibilita' delle Famiglie e Utilizzo degli Individui. Retrieved June 2008, from http://www.istat.it

Kellerman, A. (1993). Telecommunication and Geography. London: Belhaven.

Kellerman, A. (1999). Leading Nations in the Adoption of Communications Media 1975-1995. Urban Geography, 20, 377–389.

Kellerman, A. (2000). Where does it happen? The Location of the Production and Consumption of Web Information. Journal of Urban Technology, 7, 45–61. doi:10.1080/713684101doi:10.1080/713684101

Kellerman, A. (2002). The Internet on Earth. A Geography of information. San Francisco: John Wiley & Sons.

Kellerman, A., & Paradiso, M. (2007). The Geographical Location in the Information Age: from Destiny to Opportunity? GeoJournal, 70, 195–211. doi:10.1007/s10708-008-9131-2doi:10.1007/s10708-008-9131-2

Kotler, P., Bowen, R. J., & Makens, C. J. (2006). Marketing for Hospitality and Tourism. Upper Saddle River, NJ: Pearson Education Inc.

Kotler, P., Haider, D. H., & Rein, I. (2008). Marketing Places: Attracting Investment, Industry, and Tourism to Cities, States, and Nations. New York: The Free Press.

Kumar, K. (2004). From Post-industrial to Postmodern Societies. New Theories of the Contemporary World. Oxford, UK: Wiley Blackwell.

Lanza, A. (1999). Lo Sviluppo Sostenibile. Bologna, IT: Il Mulino.

Loretzon, S. (1998). The Role of ICT as a Locational Factor in Peripheral Regions: Examples from 'IT-active' Local Authority Areas in Sweden. NETCOM, 1(2), 303–333.

Loretzon, S. (Ed.). (2000). The Use of ICT in a Geographical Context: Research at Gotheborg University, Sweden. NETCOM, 14.

Loretzon, S. (2003). The Role of ICT as a Locational Factor in Peripheral Regions. NETCOM, 17, 159–186.

Loretzon, S. (2004). Call Centres – a Swedish Geographical Perspective Exemplified by Conditions in the West of Sweden. NETCOM, 18, 203–223.

Machlup, F. (1984). The Economics of Information and Human Capital. Princeton, NJ: Princeton University Press.

Mainardi, (1996). Geografia delle Comunicazioni. Turin, IT: NIS.

Mattelart, A. (1999). Histoire de l'Utopie Planétaire: de la Cité Prophétique à la Société Globale. Paris, FR: La découverte.

Paradiso, M. (2003a). Geography, Planning and the Internet: Introductionary Remarks. NETCOM, 3-4, 129–138.

Paradiso, M. (Ed.). (2003b). Geocyberspaces Dynamics in an Interconnected World. NETCOM, 3-4.

Paradiso, M. (2003c). Geografia e Pianificazione Territoriale della Società dell'informazione. Milano, IT: FrancoAngeli.

Paradiso, M. (2006). Le Logiche della Globalizzazione: gli Studi in Tema di Geografia della Società dell'Informazione. Paper presented at the meeting of Societa' Geografica Italiana, Florence, Italy.

Paradiso, M., & Wilson, M. (Eds.). (2006a). The Role of Place in the Information Age: ICT Use and Knowledge Creation. NETCOM, 1-2.

Paradiso, M., & Wilson, M. (Eds.). (2006b). Technology, Knowledge and Place. Journal of Urban Technology, 3.

Robins, K. (Ed.). (1992). Understanding Information. Business, Technology and Geography. London: Belhavenpress.

Robins, K., & Gillespie, A. (1992). Communication, Organization, and Territory. In K. Robins, (Ed.), Understanding information. Business, Technology and Geography (pp.145-164). London: Belhavenpress.

Scott, A. J. (2001). The Cultural Economies of Cities. London: Sage Publications.

Scott, A. J. (2004). Cultural Product Industries and Urban Economic Development. Prospects for Growth and Market Contestation in Global Context. Urban Affairs Review, 39(4), 461–490. doi:10.1177/1078087403261256doi:10.1177/1078087403261256

Shapiro, C., & Varian, H. R. (1999). Information Rules. Boston: Harvard Business School Press.

Sheppard, E. (2002). The Space and Time of Globalization: Place, Scale, Networks, and Positionality. Economic Geography, 78(3), 307–330. doi:10.2307/4140812doi:10.2307/4140812

Thrift, N. (2000). Communications Geography. In R.J. Johnston, D. Gregory, G. Pratt, & M. Watts, (Eds.), The Dictionary of Human Geography (pp.98-100). Oxford, UK: Blackwell Publishing.

Vidal, P. (Ed.). (2007). European ICT Spatial Policies. Does a political European Information Society Model Exist? NETCOM, 1-2.

Ziliotti, M. (2001). L'economia dell'informazione. Bologna, IT: Il Mulino.

Zook, M. A. (2000a). The Web of Production: the Economic Geography of Commercial Internet Content Production in the United States. Environment & Planning A, (32): 411–426. doi:10.1068/a32124doi:10.1068/a32124

Zook, M. A. (2000b). Internet Metrics: Using Hosts and Domain Counts to Map the Internet Globally. Telecommunications Policy, 24, 6–7. doi:10.1016/S0308-5961(00)00039-2doi:10.1016/S0308-5961(00)00039-2

Zook, M. A. (2001). Connected is a Matter of Geography. Networker, 5, 13–17. doi:10.1145/383719.383724doi:10.1145/383719.383724

ENDNOTES

[1] Referring to the following note local development or local sustainable development is thought as the main goal for the economic and social development of local communities, here thought like social systems.

[2] I define a system (according to biological theories) a group of elements in a relationship, facing a common goal, and character-

ized by dynamics. From this perspective, a system is an organization defined by relational, systemic and dynamic levels of relations. Each system has its own internal rules that manage the life and growth of the system. In these terms, any social organization can be considered as a system (i.e. the communication department of a company, a local government, an administrative region). Internal rules are very important inputs for the life of the system since they are and belong to the genetic code of the social system. At the same time, the external world is fundamental for the survival of the system, because of external inputs but also because of the necessity for the system to be open (the second law of thermodynamics). In these terms, an administrative region can be defined as an open system composed of sub- or local systems, each one interconnected with the others and turned towards the same goal that should be the goal of a sustainable development. Since external forces can be positive but also negative for the single system, it is important that there is the presence of a fundamental law of each system that is the resilience (the capacity of each system to have a structural stability, that means to be capable to manage external flows of information and to adapt and change them to local needs and wants).

3   It is important to note here that, according to the last statistical data (ISTAT, 2007), only 50% of Tuscan families can connect to the Internet from home, and of these only 50% have a high speed digital connection. These data, read together with the data of the spread and use of mobile phones among Tuscan individuals (circa 90%) and without any detail about the distribution of these technologies over the administrative territory, can lead us to think that maybe political top-down actions and decisions should read in more detail the diffusion and use of technology among locals, or leave to local governments the last decision in terms of investment in technologies.

4   These data were found on the official website of the Tuscany Region. www.regione.toscana.it (August–October 2008)

5   Ecotourism or ecological tourism can be considered a niche of the tourist market. It comprehends a segment of the many and vast forms that tourism can have. It can be defined as a form of sustainable tourism based on the use of natural resources, that highlight the phases of experiment and learning from nature, and that is ethically managed to have a low level of impact, to be non consumptive, and to be oriented to the micro and local scale. It is characterized by and based on the natural history of a region, the cultural component but only if it is linked to the natural history of the place, the respect for ecology and local human agents, the education of agents (Fennell, 2002).

6   In the period August-November 2008 a web research has been conducted on the most used research engines by national and international internauts (google.com and google.it, yahoo.com and yahoo.it), using different key words such as ecotourism, ecological tourism, ethical tourism, etc. and three languages (English, French, and Italian). The main goal was to detect and discover the "state of the art" of the diffusion of ecological values, practices, activities, programs, and projects among local communities and governments.

Chapter 14
African Families Faced with NICT:
Stakes and Effect on Inter–Individual and Intergenerational Relation

Honoré Mimche
IFORD-University of Yaounde II, Cameroon

Norbert Tohnain Lengha
CNE-Ministry of Scientific Research and Innovation, Yaounde, Cameroon

ABSTRACT

In Africa, family structures are today committed or involved in the dynamics of social transformation which jeopardize their mode of constitution their future, the sustenance of intergenerational and individual relationships as well as the traditional systems of social relationships based on direct and personal communication. This chapter is a sociological analysis of the future of the family through its relationship with NICT notably the Internet and the cellular telephone. The analyses lay emphasizes on the consequences of NICTs on the modalities for the constitution of marriage covenants, family relationships and intergenerational transfers.

INTRODUCTION

In sub-Saharan Africa in general, the family is the lowest social institution, which has undergone several changes during the years (Scanzoni, 1971; Minas, 1987; Locoh, 1988a). Its structures are today caught up in the dynamics of social transformations which affect the modalities of its constitution, future, the equilibrium of intergenerational and inter-individual relationships (Locoh, 1988b) as well as the traditional systems of human relationships

sustained by direct and committed communication. Since technological development in matters concerning communication has been particularly very fast these last years, it is difficult not to mention the influence of information and communication technologies on the life of the family (Rieffer, 2001). However, the new changes affecting the family today are linked to the generalization or the availability of new communication technologies to almost all the societal actors.

Among the diverse factors of change being known today, new technologies of information and

DOI: 10.4018/978-1-60566-822-2.ch014

communication are playing a significant role and hence constituting a major stake for social and intra-family relationships. This explains why at the level of its modes of constitution and in its daily evolution, the family is in a process of being adapted to the new modes of social communication put in place by *«the technological revolution and the move towards the new information and communication technologies »*. This alone puts to question the sustainability of existing cultural values concerning the family. In the North as well as in the south, changes resulting from technological development are not in favor of traditional family ideologies. An unpublished field of study which is opened to researchers, that is the user's sociology and the appreciation of NICT, applied to the observation of practices put in place for the use of ICT in the society in general and in the families in particular (Rieffer, 2001:147). New information and communication technologies (NICTs) refer to information and communication channels such as the mobile telephone, the Internet and the net phone, which were formerly not used. This domain if developed could permits us to understand the impact of these technologies on the daily life of social actors

BACKGROUND

As a communication technique and a means of bringing social actors together, NICTs are progressively becoming preferred social actors for social communication hence, reducing the *« face to face »* social communication which for many years regulated the functioning of African families. The effects of these new trends in communication encourage intensified migratory movements, which in the long run result in multinational families and the breakdown of African traditional solidarity, which relied on effective co-presence of family actors. The main consequence is the destabilization of the latter. In the same way, the irruption of NICTs in social life is becoming a major way

to have a partner through electronic courtship. Further more, NICTs have an effect on the daily lives of individuals, and hence, constituting a major stake for the future of African families especially as they lead to a recomposition of intergenerational relationships through new communication mechanisms which sustain them.

This chapter is a sociological analysis of family changes and the future of this basic social institution from its relationship with NICTs as a package with the Internet and the mobile phone as examples. The analyses emphasize on the consequences of NICTs on the modes of constitution of marriage covenants by examining the increase of Internet marriages as a social phenomenon which has upsetted traditional marriage in favor of mediatized negotiations between future partners considered as an ideal type. In fact progress in technology is a threat to the sustainability of traditional family structures. Besides, the progress in the communication systems like the mobile phone and the generalization of these modes of communication among family actors is reducing *« communication based on face to face »* and hence bringing about solidarity crisis. This can be justified by the limitation of family visits and the distant management of family problems by *« social juniors »* who in most cases have immigrated to the cities to look for greener pastures or to improve upon their living conditions or for professional reasons. Equally in favor of an emergence of new financial agencies enhanced by the development of computer soft ware services, intergenerational transfers are becoming more and more mediatized or passed through NICT channels with family members using them more increasingly. The consequence is that interpersonal relationships are becoming more effective only through this NICT channels.

TECHNOLOGICAL INNOVATION AND SOCIAL CHANGE: A MOVE TOWARDS AN INFORMATION SOCIETY

A Technological Boom without Antecedent: the Example of the Internet and the Mobile Phone

Since, the last twenty years, it is incontestable to ascertain that progress in microelectronics, computer and telecommunications as a direct result of industrial revolution and other associated aspects like the advancement in information and communication technologies have revolutionalized the functioning of societies. Several studies done today by educationists have shown for example the impact of NICTs in the educational system (Hirsch Buhl and Bishop, 2000, Onguene Essono, 2006). As Onguene Essono (2006: 57) asserts, in most African cities, there is a very strong commitment to ICTs with the introduction of a global awareness about ICTs in many schools. To quote Petitgirard (2001), new technologies constitute at the same time an important factor of change but equally *"a big choice"* for the social actors faced with the challenges imposed by the modern society. In effect, the world seems to be found in a context where new illiterates will be those members of the society who are not yet adapted to new technologies. In the new edition of *Médias et sociétés*, the French sociologist Balle (1999) shows that it has become difficult to analyze the evolution of the changing society without taking into consideration the evolution that is taking place in the domain of communication especially with an irruption of NICTs.

This new technological progress which is almost an explosion (Breton and Proulx, 1989; Wolton, 1999) has enhanced or speeded up the rhythm of change (Flichy, 1995). At the same time we agree with Goode to talk about a *"family revolution"*, if we admit that these technologies are cultural industries and vehicles of ideologies.

These changes confirm the idea of Vitalis (1994) according to which technological instruments and communication means structure the forms of social organization and modes of knowledge. This argument could be justified when we see the way in which social actors use new technologies and the manner in which these usages affect the family's living condition.

Although the Internet as an aspect was developed in the 1970s, it has already touched the whole continent and is continuing its expansion in a lightning manner to urban and rural zones. In 1996, for example, only five African countries were equipped to have access to the Internet, but today almost all the countries are connected and endowed with the necessary capacities. The number of subscribers is galloping therefore, attracting more economic operators to the sector. This new era, which has several brand names such as computer age, virtual civilization, the Internet age, makes knowledge to be a consumable good to the point where countries, which are rich in information and knowledge, are equally rich according to other conventional criteria. This is reflected by a division, which seems to march with previous established boundaries between the rich and the poor societies, between the developed and the developing countries.

The landscape of ICTs on the continent has dramatically changed since 1980. During the last ten years, NICTs have practically possessed all African countries although at varying degrees. The continent has witnessed a boom in technological development particularly in the sector concerned with information and communication notably with the generalization of the computer software. At the world level, Africa is the core of change, which is sociologically very pertinent. However, in spite of the numerical cleavage observed between the South and the North, technological progress and the irruption of NICTs constitute a major aspect of change that has taken place during the last twenty years in the African continent. As Mvesso (2006:11) states, " *the out break of information and communication technologies is a spark and also accompanies modernity and the emergence of a society of knowledge*" For instance, service delivery markets are at their extreme growth to respond to increasing quantitative and qualitative solicitations thanks to the new information and communication technologies (NICT). Because of their interchangeable use at several domains of the human activity (health, education, training, trade, environment etc.), NICTs are touching all aspects of societal life as well as all the sectors of human life. Today, their advancement constitutes priority strategic axes for the development of Africa.

In the face of ongoing mutations, orchestrated by technological growth, most research carried out on the progress of NICTs confirms the idea that Africa is moving towards a generalization of the usage of ICTs in the households and in the management of daily life. We can affirm without delay with Miege (1997) that our society is being progressively conquered by NICTs. Despite the low level of infrastructure in this domain, the exposure of Africa to NICTs is making history for the continent. Concerning the Internet, UNDP (2001) in her human development report states that « *¾ of Internet subscribers live in high income countries which make up more than 14% of the world's population* ». As for the mobile telephone, several numbering changes and the passage to eight figures in several countries is an indication that there is increase in the demand of services in the domain of ICTs in Africa.

Generalization of the Use of Mobile Phone and the Internet

Although the domestic use of the telephone was up to a certain moment limited to a restricted urban elite, ownership and use has today known a remarkable quantitative and qualitative evolution. In 2001, there were about 350 000 public telephones in the continent, with 75 000 in sub-Saharan Africa (about one telephone for 85 00 persons), against one for 500 persons in average

in the world and one for two hundred persons averagely in high income countries. However, teledensity in most cases is still less than one telephone for one hundred inhabitants in several countries either in the urban or rural milieu. The number of mobile telephone subscribers is now higher than for the fix or standard phone subscribers in most countries. This number, which in 2001 totaled 24 million subscribers, is proof of the non-satisfied vocal service needs by operators of fixed networks managed by the state during the years of uncontested monopoly. Relative low cost and the portable nature of cellular phones have enabled several zones to be covered by the mobile telephone network. Some of them just capture telephone signals because of their altitudinal positions. This evolution as well as the number of new communication products has had as catalyser, the extension of satellite coverage for the whole continent. For the case of Internet, the number of users is becoming important for several countries of the African continent.

The influence of the media and more particularly NICTs in contemporary society is becoming a sensitive issue hence an object of argument and even of controversy. As Rieffel (2001), observes "*some boast of the merits of information and communication technologies in matters concern-*

Table 1. Percentage of Internet users in Africa in relation to the world population

Region of the World	1998	2000
United States	26,3	54,3
High income countries excluding USA	6,9	28,2
Latin America and the Caribbean	0,8	3,2
East Asia and the Pacific	0,5	2,3
East Europe	0,8	3,9
Arab States	0,2	0,6
Sub-Saharan Africa	0,1	0,4
South Asia	0,04	0,4
The Rest of the World	**2,4**	**6,7**

Source: UNDP *World Development Report 2001.*

ing cultural and social democratization; others denounce their negative effects by accusing them for encouraging manipulation and uniformisation of minds" Because the use of NICTs is touching the type of relationships in the family (Chambat, 1994, Vitalis, 1994), the organization of the daily life of the family actors, it is important to question their influence on family life (Bios, 2007). In effect, the move towards the methods of social communication brought about by technological development notably the mobile phone and the Internet, calls for a closer look on the functioning modalities of the contemporary family structures. Most studies carried out in this domain do not agree with the user's model as a simple passive consumer and hence, looks at the action of appropriation as a personalized construction form of the usage.

Development of Mobile Telephone and Distant Socio-Family Relationships

The Development of Multinational Families and Distant Family Relationships

In every human society, the family appears as the basic social institution. As the first agent of socialization, it is also a place for social control in essence. Its level of involvement in the lives of individuals confirms the structuro-functionalist arguments, which have shown that social actors are determined by normative systems. In a context of social mutations characterized by fluctuations in social control, the privatization of the means of production (land, cattle), schooling, labor migration, monetarisation of exchange, the development of NICTs, families are embedded in a kind of dynamism which questions the forms and traditional modes of family construction. The analysis of the use of NICTs by family actors enables one to have a glimpse of the influence of these new tools on the forms of sociability that is on the manner in which individuals built interpersonal relationships and redefine the modes of social interaction since they have an influence on the daily activities of the latter.

The Internet and the mobile phone seem to be a great innovation today since they are talked of as a virtual civilization to mean this technological and social revolution. However, the problem of a whole installation of a new social and family order linked to the information and communication between different components of social structures affecting the system of cohabitation is being left out. As observed at the end of the 20th century when talking about globalization to designate change projected by progress in information and technological revolution a resultant of the development of NICTs, a significant change in the nature of transactions and relationships between the different family members. More so, this has brought the later closer by easing non-visible contact through communication via the **net** or cellular phone in a context where migratory influx is intensifying. This is also facilitating decohabitation or imaginary cohabitation with these innovations contributing to prolong the latter hence, making people to feel « *living together/vient on reste* » as is commonly referred to in Cameroon in either French or English.

New Forms of Sociability

As a result of progress in NICT, family relationships are more and more being mediatized. Family actors who have migrated to the cities or to developed countries are using these tools to create new forms of sociability through microgroups of persons who themselves also have easy access to these technologies. Making a sort of social selection, NICTs create new togetherness in the families. This particular case was observed in France with the development of technologies of communication at the beginning of 1980. Some sociologist have therefore, shown that the advent of ICTs could be an identity folding. It is for this reason that Rieffer (2001) affirms that *"techno-logical sociability cannot replace traditional sociability, by substituting the art of conversation and dialogue without any media technology"*. Observation shows that these technologies are also registered in social relationships that go across the family such as, power struggle, relationships of inequality, sex relationship.

Does NICTs Facilitate Family and Intergenerational Decohabitation?

In order to understand the effects of information society on family structures, it suffices in priority to recall that in most African countries there is intense migratory influx between Africa and Europe, Africa and America and Africa and Asia. These migratory trends have led to family restructuring and to the development of multipollar/multinational or multiethnic families in which it is increasingly difficult for the younger generations to be in contact with all the other members of the lineage. This is one of the causes of eminent identity crisis in the society as a whole. With technological development, solidarity **risks** are becoming significant since the frequency of communication with distant members of the family gives the impression that there is cohabitation. There is in the face of all this another problem, which is that of a real lineage in the future generation.

The Telefamily Meeting: A New Stand for Meetings between Members of a Lineage

Jus as teleconferences that are increasingly common today, members of some families who have migrated to other continents or countries in Africa, use new modalities for family meetings. It is in this way that telefamily meetings or distant family meetings are developed. The over usage of telephone and the Internet has ruptured with the old traditional family patterns which in the

process of adaptation to the mutations imposed by colonization were consecrated to annual meetings as a strategy of social cohesion.

Development of NICTs and Intergenerational Transfers

In Africa, the system of rights and obligations involves economic transfers between the members of the family. This logic of solidarity is justified by high fertility, which seems to be a principle of intergenerational solidarity. Generational transfers participate in the social and cultural reproduction since it contributes in the perpetuation of networking among the members of a lineage. They are further intensified by low family revenue, the system of social security and more especially weaker saving systems. Economic transfers among the youths and social seniors are to be regulated in several traditions. In the post-migratory context, migrants often had difficulties to ensure transfers. On the other hand, the low level of communication between places of immigration and take off areas for the migrants does not facilitate their transfers or regularity. But with the development of financial agencies fostered by progress in computer sciences, the transfers are today becoming very significant between African and European countries.

In some countries like Mali, Senegal, Cameroon, Ivory Coast and Benin where migratory movements are significant, financial agencies such as Express Union, Western Union, and Money Gram play an important role for the migrants and their families. The birth of these structures does not only influence resource flow between migrant families and originating families but also contribute to improve upon the living conditions of the old generation left behind in the villages. Therefore, this intensification of transfers is moving hand in hand with the consolidation of the linkages within multipolar families established in two or more continents in favor of globalization. Concerning care giving, the whole family contributes irrespective of where its members are found due to the proximity created by NICTs. In this light, the hypothesis that old days are secured through economic transfers with the aid of NICTs is validated. But it should be remembered that the rush for **Internet** participates especially in a modification of the modalities for the constitution of unions.

The Rush for Internet and the New Modalities for the Constitution of African Families

Marriage as a Social Institution

Marriage is a traditional or customary, religious and civil institution, which confers to any form of conjugality its social validity. It is submitted to norms, which vary from one ethnic group to the other and from one society to the other. Culturally, matrimonial ceremonies require matrimonial charges and jokes. In most of our African societies, marriage is a condition of social fatherhood because it attributes to men their rights over the descendants. On the contrary, for women, it is more a factor of ascending social mobility because it permits them to move from the status of a girl to that of a woman in the full sense of the word. The woman is always perceived as a "*character in transit*" in her family of origin because she is "*destined to go*" and meet a man to constitute a family of alliance. It confers more social considerations to individuals who cease to be children or adolescents who are independent persons. It is a durable or sustainable union between a man and a woman or women, fulfilling the role of cooperation, solidarity and social or demographic reproduction. In African traditions, marriage is at the bases of a family and authentifies legitimacy to children in the community. Marriage is a social and cultural process, which is accomplished after six stages. In other words, traditional marriage arranged by the family does not recognize the personality of the individuals involved. Another

type puts aside all principles of social reciprocity. It is an individual contract preceded by a simplified ceremony borrowed from the ritual of traditional marriage where young girls are already promised for marriage. Like in other African communities, marriage is a value, a social "*obligation*". It is a factor of social mobility for men and women, even though more importance is attached to the marriage of women. It is through this practice that the individual is given the assurance of life and responsibility. From this therefore, celibacy appears as a form of pathology in social life. Zahan (1970), writes concerning this issue:

It is noted that in Africa, the single enjoys no value and that apart from ritual loneliness, and desperation, men and women chose marriage as an essential form of the human ideal in this world. This is true and deeply written in the minds of Africans that celibates (singles) if they exist except for particular cases mentioned have no excuse of reason for that. They are treated with contempt, chased away from the family and the society. Celibacy for Africans is a non understandable disorganization of social and religious order

In the same way as fertility is considered culturally, it is "*a factor of social success*". In this way, evolution in matrimonial practices is an expression of the evolution of family structures. In its frequency and the whole set of social and capital services mobilized for its effective existence or better still the diverse phases that it takes today, marriage is an essential element of the society, social belonging and community life since it constitute an important component of the society.

Today, several changes are affecting the matrimonial institution and the modes of constitution of the families. In a context of social mutations characterized by: urbanization, labor migration, the scholarisation of a greater number of persons, professionalization of women, economic crisis and the reduction of the population's purchase power, the frittering of social control of the seniors over the juniors, the monetarisation of the bride price, the development of information and communication technologies-with Internet notably, the traditional modalities of the family have evolved. This has facilitated the emergence of new forms of conjugality or new family patterns. In the matrimonial domain these modifications are characterized by progressive late entry of youths into active marital life. This is accounting for a sudden increase of celibacy especially among the men. The evolution of matrimonial charges and the bride price, the increase of free unions and of *"bureaugamy"*, the diversification of marriage forms, matrimonial regimes and modes of residence for the couple (marriage without co-residence or decohabitation due to labor migration) and preliminary changes before commitment in unions and their socio-cultural determinants are some of the consequences. Similarly the development of new matrimonial strategies, which started in the 1990s with the emergence of matrimonial agencies, is also witnessed.

The advent of the computer tool and more particularly the Internet has come just to modify the matrimonial habits of the young generation. It is in this way that electronic (e-marriages) or **Internet** marriages have come about and are establishing themselves in our societies. Consequently, cyber-cafés (Internet centers) are flooded at late hours by single women and even married women in search of matrimonial partners. Some even take pictures of some parts of their bodies with camera mobile telephones to be forwarded on line to the would-be matrimonial partners. This explains why the managers of Internet centers have been compelled to modify the boxes used in the cyber rooms to suit the demands of their clients. Not necessarily a phenomenon specific to women, e-marriages do not exempt any sex even if it has some specificities within the both sexes. As one Cameroonian artist states, *« Internet has come to save »* many youths that crisis has pushed

into uncertainty, poverty and the impossibility to be integrated into the matrimonial market. All these upheavals reflect a profound adjustment of family ideals, which were at a certain moment greatly valued in African societies. Are we moving towards a crisis in this social institution?

Electronic Marriages as a New Mode of Social Promotion

For more than a decade, the growth of the Internet has gradually become important. The number of cyber-cafés created in African cities and the feminization of the users of this new social communication framework justifies this growth. While most of our matrimonial traditions are termed as endogamic because the choice of a partner must be done inside the ethnic community, the development of e-marriages has come to push away these ideals and the traditional norms concerning marriage. This could be justified in several ways. But the most pertinent explanation seems to be that marriage is considered in the same way as crisis is considered in our societies. The ongoing changes in this domain are expressions of this crisis on the traditional values. In fact for many families today, the best channel for social success is not necessarily the quest to procure lucrative professional integration for the children at the local level. It is instead a hard struggle to see to it that a family member goes to Europe. It appears as if in the society every one is working by the « *myth of elsewhere* », « *every means to go is good provided it is efficient* ». The essential thing is to go or *"fall in the bush"* as it is commonly said in the English speaking part of Cameroon. Bush fallers as they are called are therefore, the pride of most African families. It is in this manner that parents encourage their children to search for partners in the Internet with the sole aim of having an *"ambassador or a bush faller"* across the Atlantic.

In the context of crisis that our country is going through there is a vast development of survival strategies and an irruption of youth in sectors in which they were formerly least represented. Under economic crisis, most of these youths are confronted with a situation of vulnerability since most of the institutions that were created to facilitate their transition to adult life are in difficulties and hence cannot bring in adequate solutions to their socio-professional integration even if their level of education is also a problem. In Cameroon, the creation of FOGAPE (support fund for small and medium size entreprises), NFE (national fund for employment) and many other private initiatives aim at promoting the integration (professional integration) of youths, has yielded little fruit as they are very unable to re-absorb these frustrated youth. Therefore, youths who are the immediate victims have developed survival strategies which even include illicite practices most of which are encriminating the state in general and the family in particular. Among these altenative strategies developed by youths as a mode of accumulation and especially of social control we could cite « *Feymania* ». But today, clandestine migration and Internet marriages are becoming more significant and are also considered as new modes of social control. So, in a society where one needs to struggle in order to succeed, every means is used to achieve this goal. This explains why the practice is gradually being generalized and hence becoming one of the main forms of Internet usages in cameroon.

A New Form of International Migration

Whatever thing is stated, the development of these new forms of unions is a phenomenon, which shows that there is crisis in the matrimonial institution in Africa as well as in the world at large. In a situation where emigration conditions to the European Eldorado have been reviewed by the host countries of the migrants, and especially with the emergence of more restrictive and selective migratory policies like the case of Europe where President Sarkosy talks of selective immigration, new immigration candidates are partners whose

marriage unions were constituted through the Internet. In Embassies in Africa for example, the new reason or motive for immigration is to meet one's family, which in reality is the concretization of electronic marriages.

A Factor of Cultural Mixage

Linked to the phenomenon of globalization, Internet marriages do not longer exempt African families. Youths in scholarly migration have made cyber-cafés their privilege place for distraction. Encouraged by parents in some cases, there is a real rupture with the traditional values. Members of the clan do not value the matrimonial institution again. « *Marriage, yes! But marriage with a white* », this we think is a new norm that regulate marriage practices in these cities. In reality, as these practices are developing, there is a cultural mix age in the families and since the consequences of these unions go beyond the descendants, the problem of cultural identity remains at stake. Hence, these marriages remodulate or reconstitute the pattern of functioning for our families.

What Stakes for Tomorrow's Family

The new forms of residence among family members or partners, the evolution of family structures and other indicators of family changes are being gradually perceived as a trajectory for the institutionalization of new forms of the family. This state of affairs leads us to argue, "*Family structures are now embedded in an economic, social, political and demographic dynamism which gives room for transformations and new rules*". The development of NICTs is a factor for family reconfiguration. Considering what precedes, family structures change as they adapt to political, economic, social and cultural transformations imposed by the context of technological shift.

The vulgarization of NICTs is influencing all aspects of family life. In the face of ongoing changes in the modes of technological appropriation, family actors want to adapt to the new circumstances imposed by today's society especially from the strategies that its members are adopting daily. Family structures change as well as social organizations in which they are found. They change, they move, but towards horizons that are yet to be defined. They are printed in the dynamics of transformations whose magnitude, brutality and speed could lead to the proclamation of the end of the family or of the traditional crisis (Minas, 1987). We are witnesses to the institutionalization of new patterns such as families without co-habitation, multipolar families, multinational families and the single parent families led especially by women; with men being the most affected by the new forms of labor migrations towards the cities. Therefore, the new factors of mobility and social success are leading to the destabilization of family structures. However, the forms of intergenerational transfers being developed between urban migrants and parents remaining in the village gives room for the consolidation of family links, even if the importance of transfers remain mitigated.

Some traditional functions of the family institution are undergoing change. This is particularly the case with socialization and demographic reproduction functions. Concerning socialization, there is an alternative educational form with the Internet. Equally, on socialization, Internet is becoming an important means of social mobility. An important aspect in the evolution of socialization function of the family lies in a specialization, which comes from the new stakes of the modern society. The family is tending to specialize in the transmission of moral and cultural values, while access conditions to a partner comes from the competence on Internet or ICTs.

CONCLUSION

Whenever questions are raised on the contemporary social change, the role of the family becomes primordial and justifies why social science actors always stop to observe the changing family. At the end of this analysis, it seems defining what a family is has become very difficult because of the transformations that are affecting this social institution since colonial times. With the advent of all the new forms of information technologies, all conditions are there through sociology of the family to study the modes of life and communication (Rieffer, 2001:148). In Africa, as in most western societies these mutations are profound. The development of NICTs is today characterized by moral individualism and the solidarity crisis since it limits the meeting between family members but facilitating communication or distant social relationships. Individual exigencies are continuously being affirmed at the detriment of the stability of the family institution. These analyses show that in the face of progress in new information technologies, there is a crisis of traditional affiliation and of the growth of new forms of sociability and togetherness, which leads to an individual emancipation.

Although not being dissolved, norms are being multiplied and redefined: there is an existence of different ways of « *making a family* », which are equally legitimate. This coexistence is the source of instability and also of inequality between social environments, sexes and generations. New forms of the family are developed with the emergence of new family patterns especially with the birth of transnational unions. The diffusion of electronic marriages commonly known as « e-marriages » indicates a step back of traditional modes of marriage. Could we in the face of such indicators proclaim the end of the family?

REFERENCES

Balle, F. (1999). *Médias et societies,* (9 ed.). Paris: Monchrétien

Bios, N. C. (2007). De la séduction médiatique à la mobilité transfrontalière: l'utilisation de l'Internet par la femme camerounaise. *Revue camerounaise de sociologie, 4*(1), 65-90.

Breton, P., & Proulx, S. (1989). *L'explosion de la communication*. Paris: La Découverte.

Flichy, P. (n.d.). *L'innovation technique. Récents développements en sciences sociales. Vers une nouvelle théorie de l'innovation.* Paris: La Découverte.

Goode, W. J. (1963). *World Revolution and Family Patterns*. New York: The Free Press.

Hirsh, B., & Bishop, D. (2000). (Ed.) *Computer in Education*. New York: Dushkin/McGraw-Hill.

Kayongo, M., & Onyango, P. (1984). *The Sociology of the African Family*. London: Longman.

Locoh, T. (1988). Structures familiales et changements sociaux. In D. Tabutin (Ed.), *Populations et sociétés en Afrique au sud du Sahara,* (pp. 441-478). Paris: L'Harmattan.

Locoh, T. (1988). L'évolution de la famille en Afrique. In E. Van De Walle, (ed.), *L'état de la démographie africaine,* (pp. 45-66). Liège, Belgium: UIESP.

Miege, B. (1997). *La société conquise par la communication*, tome 2. Grenoble, France: PUG.

Minas (1987). *Colloque sur la famille en Afrique noire*. Yaoundé, Cameroon: Imprimerie nationale.

Mvesso, A. (2006). Préface. In F. Pierre, *Intégration des TIC dans le processus enseignement-apprentissage au Cameroun*, éditions terroir, (pp. 11-12).

Onguene Essono, L. M., & Onguene Essono, C. (2006). TIC et Internet à l'école: analyse des nouvelles pratiques enseignantes dans les salles de classes d'Afrique noire. In F. Pierre, *Intégration des TIC dans le processus enseignement-apprentissage au Cameroun*, éditions terroir, (pp. 55-75).

Parsons, T. (1965). The ''normal''American Family'. In S. M. Faber (ed.), *Man and Civilization: The Family's Search for Survival,* (pp. 34-36). New York: McGraw-Hill.

Rieffer, R. (2001). *Sociologie des medias*. Paris: Ellipses.

Scanzoni, H. J. (1971). *The Black Family in Modern Society*. Chicago: The University of Chicago Press.

UNDP (2001). *World Development Report.*

Vitalis, A. (1944). *Médias et nouvelles technologies. Pour une sociopolitique des usages*. Rennes, France: Apogée.

Wolton, D. (1999). *Internet et après? Une théorie critique des nouveaux médias*. Paris: Flammarion.

Zahan, D. (1970). *Religion, spiritualité et pensée africaine*. Paris: Payot.

Chapter 15
Gender and Technology:
Mind the Gap!

Michela Cozza
Department of Sociology and Social Research, Faculty of Sociology, University of Trento, Italy

ABSTRACT

In this chapter the mutual shaping of the technology and gender is analyzed in relation to the phenomenon of gender digital divide. The discussion starts with the re-construction of the theoretical background, shedding light on different analytical approaches to technological development. The gender blind perspective of mainstream technology studies is uncovered; looking at theoretical contributes of feminist and gender studies. This positioning is aimed to consider the cultural and material aspects involved in the digital gender gap. The chapter leads to a general conclusion: it is of utmost importance that researchers, decision-makers and professionals in Information Technology field take into account that all spheres inhabited by human beings are inevitably gendered. The gender mainstreaming approach may inform the construction of a gender-aware research agenda and the identification of the following transformative actions. The synergy among researchers, practitioners and decision-makers at political and business level is crucial for a gender-sensitive and sustainable development.

INTRODUCTION

There is a large amount of writing that falls under the rubric of "technologies studies". In their reflections on the end of the twentieth century and the beginning of the twenty-first, many social scientists as well as popular commentators have given attention to tremendous power of technol-ogy to shape the identities, the public and private life, the social trends and transformations. Nevertheless, the sociological literature has failed for a long time to consider whether this technological revolution – that in this chapter will be associated to Information Communication Technology (ICT) and particularly to Internet – might be analyzed in a perspective of gender.

This "gender blindness" (Maddock & Parkin, 1993) arises from the myth of a neutral and pure

DOI: 10.4018/978-1-60566-822-2.ch015

technology, which is free from any sexual and gendered implication (and implications of race, class and so on, too). Nevertheless, if we take into account that technology evolves continually, involving new ways of doing, making and producing things (tools, appliances, machines), it becomes clear that technology is a fundamental part of social and everyday life. In this sense technology and the relations in which the social construction of a technology occurs are also inevitably gender relations. "Inevitably, because gender is one of the major structures of the social order and gender relations are found wherever people are found" (Cockburn & Ormrod, 1993, p. 155).

Feminist and gender studies have contributed to pinpoint the relation between gender and technology.[1] More precisely, within this growing stream of research it is useful to distinguish between gender *in* technology and gender *of* technology: in both cases the two-way mutual shaping relationship between gender and technology is emphasized.

In the former case, gender relations are both embodied in and constructed or reinforced by artifacts to yield a very material form of the mutual shaping of gender and technology. In the latter, the gendering of artifacts is more by association than by material embodiment. In practice, various forms of gendering can be identified between these two scenarios. (Faulkner, 2001, p. 83)

The idea of this mutual process benefits on one hand from the representation of gender as a relational play: gender identity is what people do, think and say about material and immaterial things *in relation to* other people conceived as sexed (Connell, 1987). On the other hand the reflections on this co-production arises from the concept of technology as relational too. As deployed in production, in everyday life, in the household, technological artifacts *entail* relations. They embody "some" (those that went into their making); they prefigure "others" (those implied in their use, abuse or neglect) (Cockburn, 1992).

This chapter is based on a fundamental statement: it is difficult, if not obtuse, to attempt an understanding of technology, technological contexts and social networks – mainly in post-modern society or rather in the digital age – without taking account of gender. Technology can tell us something we need to know about gender identity. Gender identity can tell us something we need to know about technology.

The increasing importance of gender and technology studies in the international scenario is a result of the sociological and feminist research carried out in the 20th century. Thanks to important analysis on co-construction of gender and technology in organizational contexts (for instance: Cockburn & Ormrod, 1993; Cockburn, 1985; Coombs, Knights & Willmot, 1992; Haraway, 1988; 1997; Henwood, 1993; Stone, 1995; Turkle, 1984; 1995; Wajcman, 1991; 2004) we now work from the basis that neither masculinity, femininity nor technology are fixed, unitary categories, but that they are situated, they contain multiple possibilities and they are constructed in relation to each other. There are many academic groups[2] that focus on gender science and technology studies, with a specific attention to women status. For instance there is the Center for Women & Information Technology (University of Maryland, Baltimore), the Massachusetts Institute of Technology (MIT) Society of Women Engineers, the WICS: Women in Computer Science (Stanford), the WICSE: Women in Computer Science & Electrical Engineering (U.C. Berkeley), the WISE: Women in Applied Science and Engineering (Arizona State), the Women@SCS - Carnegie Mellon School of Computer Science, the Centro di Studi Interdisciplinari di Genere (Italy, Trento), the Nordic Research School in Interdisciplinary Gender Studies[3]. Besides there are many international refereed journals, also online, that serve as forum for exploring the linkages among changing gender relations, technological development and organizations such as "*Gender, Technology and Development*", "*Gender, Work and Organization*",

"*Gender and Development*", "*Feminist Theory*" or the recently established "*International Journal of Feminist Technoscience*" (http://feministtechno-science.se). The last, using an open peer review process, may be considered an example of the feminist practice[4] in ICT.

This debate might be the framework of reference for many researchers for networking and developing new researches and programs, passing from a gender blind vision to a gender-aware vision (Wajcman, 2004). Making the gender dimension explicit in technology studies might affect the practices of "experts" in Information Technology (IT) field, the policy of decision-makers and the lives of individual men and women.

The rapid development of new information and communication technologies is changing the way that governments, private sector and civil society all conduct their daily business and activities. In particular Internet might be considered – as I try to highlight in this chapter – the symbol of technologies that are not an end in themselves, but rather an important tool and a key that can unlock many doors, for instance to parts of the labor market, to new information, to education, to the ability to connect and communicate with the entire world. Given this significance, it seems obvious that those shut out of this innovation have much to lose (UNCTAD, 2002). Moreover, without a balanced involvement of different "stakehold-ers" (by sex, race, class and so on) the potential of ITs and Internet, as tools promoting sustainable development in terms of human development and empowerment, might be wasted.

Practitioners and decision-makers should cooperate with researchers to learn more about gender dynamics in IT sector. The results of gender technology studies should feed back into policies that help to redress adverse gender effects. This virtuous circle responds more effectively to objectives of a sustainable development – that is the motif of this book.

Sustainable development is a process of change in which the exploitation of resources, the direction of investments, the orientation of technological development and institutional change are all in harmony and enhance both current and future potential to meet human needs and aspirations. (WCED, 1987, p. 57)

If the aim of this book is to shed light on the advantages as well as the disadvantages of the use of technologies in and for human interaction, I try to contribute to it adopting a pluralistic understanding by exploring, at the beginning, the tensions among and inside the different theoretical visions of gender and technology.

The first focus is to point at the different ways in which IT – in particular Internet and the virtual relations that it makes possible – is studied through gender-aware research. The synthesis of approaches is not exhaustive, but it copes with the intention to clarify ambiguity of technological development. Internet may be considered emblematic: it embeds the dream of a gender friendly cyberspace; yet, if technological development does not proceed in a balanced manner, it enhances new barriers or widens existing gender gaps. How does the two-way mutual shaping relationship between gender and technology make sense of the "digital gender gap"? Is this gap the same everywhere? What are the principal aspects of the gender gap on Internet as tool and symbol of technological potential? What are the strategic issues of a gender-aware research agenda and how might it weigh on technology sustainable development?

I will try to answer to these questions bearing in mind that gender and technology are not separated but co-constructed in every day life: gender is a fundamental way of organizing and classifying our social experience as well as technologies create new kinds of social relationships and a host of new activities and practices.

THE "EITHER/OR" TECHNOLOGY ON THE BACKGROUND

A deep division marks the scientific literature on technology: on one side the "optimists", on the other the "pessimists" (Kraft & Siegenthaler, 1989). By this traditional distinction, the technology is *either* "good" *or* "bad".

Communication technologies, in particular, either help us to stay informed or they overload us with too much information; they either connect us with like-minded people or they allow harassers to track us down; they either make us feel a part of something social or they alienate us. (Takayoshi, 2000, p. 132)

The blindly confident and enthusiastic attitude towards technology has been defined "rhetoric of technology" (Hawisher & Selfe, 1991). This positive tendency is typical of Eighties: "a period characterized by general optimism regarding the potential of the Internet to provide increased opportunities for traditionally subordinate groups" (Herring, 2000). In this perspective the medium (the computer, but also Internet) is considered intrinsically democratic, egalitarian, immune to gender stereotypes and discriminatory practices (Adam, 2002; Ahuja, 2002; Herring, 2000; Orlikowski & Baroudi, 1989; Panteli, Stack & Ramsay, 2001). As tools, new ICTs and particularly Internet offer many possibilities for making our lives more efficient and thus for increasing the prosperity of nation. People can make "productive" use of time spent in third spaces such as airports, cars, subways and cafes by phoning, sending text messages, and increasingly accessing their e-mail and information services. The easily available Internet makes the web a convenient place to find quick information and makes e-mail a handy way to share quick thoughts. It also makes it easier to work from home. Flexible working regimes and opportunities for "telecommuting" (working from home with the aid of electronic communications)

provide new possibilities for people to balance reproductive work with productive work. Gershuny (2003), on the basis of the United Kingdom time-diary panel study, investigates the impact of the Worldwide Web on time-use patterns and concludes that the Internet is positively associated with efficiency and effectiveness because it resets the "dead time". Likewise, Wellman (2001) takes into account the "social affordances" of technology[5] examining the opportunities of computerized communication networks. He states that "these ties have transformed cyber*space* into cyber*places*, as people connect online with kindred spirits, engage in supportive and sociable relationships with them, and imbue their activity online with meaning, belonging and identity" (Wellman, 2001, p. 229).

The apocalyptic scenario is quite different. The pessimistic vision of technology looks at the "Post-Market Era" as the epoch of "the end of work". The intelligent machines, taking the place of human beings in many working activities, produce an increasing rate of unemployment, a general aggravation of economic, political and cultural life, a segmentation of society and the weakening of relationships (Lash, 2002; Newman, 1988; Rifkin, 1995; Schor, 1992). Many researchers and policy makers have expressed concern that inequality in access to Internet technology increases the existing polarity between countries as well as between groups within a country. Without a cultural turn and – more concretely – in the absence of the access to market, skills and decision-making positions at the highest levels, the availability of infrastructures alone does not enhance participation of traditionally subordinated groups in digital economy, it does not reduce the digital gap. Besides, the cost of infrastructure is likely to remain a major issue for both women and men, particularly in the poorer countries. In Bangladesh, for example, the cost of a computer equals nearly two years' salary for a professional person, and a modem costs more than a cow (Mitter, 2001).

The mainstream researchers – as "apocalyptic" as "integrated" – not only has strengthened a dichotomic logic (*either/or*), that is typical of western thought, but they have also associated themselves to the image of an (apparently) gender-neutral techno science. The role recently – but not easily – gained by feminist and gender studies in the scientific community and the work done at the international level by women's advocacy groups and non-governmental organizations (NGOs) have addressed the question of gender construction into the debate on the digital divide and ICT policy making.

Nevertheless, if we turn our attention to feminist and gender studies on gender and technology, does the conflict between optimistic and pessimistic vision of technology disappear? How is this tension constructed around the gender? A significant debate is that concerning the gender of the Internet that I am going to map.

GENDERING THE INTERNET[6]

Internet is a contested medium as far as its social cultural meanings and significance are concerned. A core issue in the debate is the meaning of the Internet for gender: both are multidimensional concepts that are articulated in complex and contradictory ways. The analysis of different visions of this topic may be a good starting point for the following understanding of digital gender gap. In particular, it is interesting to discuss the common claims and interpretations of the Internet as masculine, Internet as feminine, Internet as the medium that enables new identities not limited by gender (De Ruggieri & Pugliese, 2006). In this section I consider only the first and second approach.

The first perspective expresses a negative vision of technology and Internet because they are perceived as deeply embedded in masculine codes which then spill over into digital culture and world of work; the second one is based on a positive view of the Web and IT because they appear gender-friendly in terms of opportunities and challenges in areas such as education and training, health, participation in public life and the productive sphere. Anyway, it is useful to go on step by step.

For some scholars the Web, as it came to life in the Sixties for defensive purposes from the collaboration between American universities and the Pentagon (Edwards, 1990; Naughton, 1999; Perry & Greber, 1990), is a medium being deep-seated in men's values (van Zoonen, 1992). According to this perspective the (material and discursive) construction of technology (Berner, 1997) represent "male hegemony" (Connell, 1987; Hearn, 2004) and include the values of patriarchal tradition (Wajcman, 1995; 2004) insomuch as Jane Caputi (1988) talks of "Phallotechnology".

Technology is more than a set of physical objects or artifacts. It also fundamentally embodies a culture or set of social relations made up of certain sorts of knowledge, beliefs, desires and practices. Treating technology as a culture has enabled us to see the way in which technology is expressive of masculinity and how, in turn, men characteristically view themselves in relation to these machines. (Wajcman, 1991, p. 149)

For instance, this perspective shares the opinion that the technological devices for home-based work instead of being a real chance for women have reinforced the traditional patterns regarding gender. The telework may foster overly the traditional division of labor at home (first of all the care giving), confirming the cultural norms that mandate different priorities for men and women in terms of public and private obligations, and management of time and space. Besides, the literature has focused the risks arising from female home-based work such as the deprivation of the status of working women and the restraint on their professional or business efficiency (Rodrigues Araújo, 2008; UNCAT, 2002). This perspective marks also some analysis about increasing globalization. Joan Acker states, "the new dominant growth sectors, information technology, biotech innovation, and global finance, are all heavily male-dominated" (2004, p. 31). As identified by Acker, much of the work on gender and globalization is actually research on women, work, and family under contemporary conditions of economic transformations. This gender research may include men as their actions and practices shape the worlds of women. Again, much feminist research on globalization is about women in the South, the Third World, or in "peripheral" or "developing" countries where certain IT-enabled services have grown exponentially employing a large number of low-paid female workers (Wajcman, 1995).

The advances in computer and communication technologies have made it possible to transfer digitized data online when there is an adequate supply of infrastructure and bandwidth. Through the use of networking technologies, large amounts of information can be transported at a very low cost from the companies' core offices to satellite or subcontracting units. This possibility has led companies to externalize and decentralize non-core sections of business operations to distant and often cheaper locations. The targeted sites are usually the ones that offer the promises of a cheap, skilled computer and English literate workforce. The United Nations Conference on Trade And Development's (UNCAT) Report on e-commerce and development explains the correlation of outsourcing, English proficiency and inclusion of women in digital economy.

Since the top two outsourcing markets – the United States and the United Kingdom – are both English-speaking, those developing countries that would want to tap those markets would have to learn English [...] This gives rise to some policy implications for improving the schooling and literacy of women where a second language – English – should be learned. (UNCAT, 2002, p. 78)

Some recent feminist studies have claimed the intrinsic *femininity of Internet* by repositioning its cultural meaning as opposed to the male logic of the American military-industrial-academic apparatus from which it originated. This positioning within the feminist debate leaves behind the adverse criticism towards men's technological hegemony and gives space to optimism as regards the potential of the Internet and the World Wide Web. Dale Spender (1995), for instance, made an early feminist claim on Internet as a medium especially relevant for individual and collective networking of women, and also for other traditionally subordinated groups, for that matter. Sherry Turkle, professor in the sociology of science at the MIT and author of an influential book on the construction of identities through Internet communication (Turkle, 1995), claims that one needs an ethic of community, consensus and communication on the Internet and this is what she thinks women in particular are good at.

Other authors have compared the experience of the Net, the immersion of its textual, visual and virtual realities, to that of the fetus in the womb. Internet experience is considered analogous to the secure and unconstrained experience of the maternal matrix that offers an escape from the constraints of the body (Smelik, 2000, as cited in van Zoonen, 2002). If we look at the developing countries, the UNCAT's Report (2002) offers numerous examples of attractive possibilities given to women entrepreneurs by ITs: the telecentres in Senegal and Marocco, phone shops in Ghana, Internet cafes or kiosks in Thailand and Malaysia. According to some scholars, the telework too is considered a good opportunity: with the computer and a modem, people can be connected to the office and can perform their professional work from a distant site such as a neighborhood centre or their own home. This new mode of working has received much attention, particularly in the context of women's career prospects and work-family balance.

Briefly, some feminist theories of the gender and technology relationship have long oscillated, in the same way as mainstream technology studies, between pessimism and optimism, "utopian" and "dystopian" visions. The (feminist) utopian view is that technology and Internet have an emancipatory potential because women – as traditionally subordinated group – can "transcend" their corporeal "limitations" to participate fully in the digital age. On the other extreme, dystopian visions of the future seen through the lens of various feminisms posit that technological advances will continue to subjugate women through the masculine project of dominating women and nature: for instance, life becomes further biomedicalized and commodified through genetic and reproductive engineering. Looking at the world of work, the demands of post-industrial capitalist society for cheap and flexible labor will continue, with women (their knowledge, skills and body), remaining the pool from which the "knowledge economy" draws to maintain and extend its capital gains (Moore et al., 2008).

According to Takayoshi (2000) this dualistic approach can be overcome by adopting a "balanced perspective" ascribing to the technology the possibility of being both oppressive and empowering. The figure of cyborg (Haraway, 1991) that has inspired the cyber feminism makes it possible to keep tensions and contradictions, possibilities and risks arising from gender and technology relationship.

THE "TRANSGENDER" IDENTITY OF INTERNET

In order to complete the review, I have to discuss the third claim about gender and Internet concerning the cyber feminist interpretation of it.

The proposal of cyber feminist authors is added to the previous ones: nevertheless their prevailing techno-enthusiasm flows into a different definition of Internet. The cyber feminists – and many other feminist authors (for instance: Butler, 1990; Knights & Kerfoot, 2004; Linstead & Brewis, 2004) – contend a transgression of the dichotomous categories of male and female defining Internet as "transgender" (Braidotti, 1996), "a gender laboratory, a playground for experimenting with gender symbols and identity, a space to escape from the dichotomy of gender and the boundaries produced by physical bodies" (van Zoonen, 2002, p. 12).

Cyber feminism is a term for a variety of academic and artistic practices that centre around and in Internet and other Information Communication Technologies. It is the interpreter of a new generation of feminism interested in the online world, named "cyberspace" by William Gibson. In a social context imbued with technology and with the imaginary world arising from it, the contemporary feminism has redefined itself, its own epistemology and political positioning. Donna Haraway's writing on cyborgs offers the almost canonical frame of reference here, the cyborg being "a cybernetic organism, a fusion of the organic and the technical forged in particular, historical, cultural practices" (Haraway, 1997, p. 51).

The cyborg might be used as a metaphor of the already mentioned technological ambivalence because, according to Donna Haraway (1991), it may suggest the increased control, command and communication in science and society, provided for instance by the connectivity or the "always on" capacity of wireless devices, but the metaphor of cyborg may suggest too the possibility to change the images of universality, modernity and progress in favor of the (re) construction and (re) constitution of gender, ethnicity, age and class as intertwined with networks of socio-technical relations (Jansson, Mörtberg, & Berg, 2007).

Cyber feminism on the Internet is found among others in the so-called Multi User Dungeons (MUDs). MUDs have attracted the attention of many feminist authors and seem to have become paradigmatic for the Internet as a laboratory for gender.

MUDs are text-based, virtual games, which may have the different purposes of seeking adventure and killing monsters, of socializing with others and building new communities. They also offer a tool for teaching by constructing virtual classrooms. One usually does not access a MUD through the World Wide Web, but links up through Telnet. When login on for the first time, one chooses a name for the character one wants to be and keeps that name for the duration of the game, which can – in fact – go on for years. It is precisely this choice of identity at the beginning of the game that the MUD reputation of being a laboratory for gender experiments comes from. Women play as men, men operate as women, others choose multiple identities [...] or try what it means to operate as an "it". (van Zoonen, 2002, p. 13).

There are many places in Internet for women and men to socialize, blurring (or maintaining) the gender identity. In Usenet, the largest public area of Internet, people get together in newsgroups to discuss diverse subjects. For people who want to role-play in another persona, or even another gender, there are not only MUD but also Multi-User Shared Hallucination (MUSH): it is a text-based online social medium to which multiple users are connected at the same time. MUSH is often used for online social intercourse and role-playing games, although the first forms of MUSH do not appear to be coded specifically to implement gaming activity. Besides there are mailing lists, chat, forum, blog and many other Internet services.

For cyber feminism, cyberspace represents the post-gendered world where the traditional ideas about gendered identities and roles are subverted empowering women (Plant, 1998). Internet is a democratic agora, an electronic meeting place where individuals throughout the world could interact as equals despite differences in nationality, race, social status, sex, and other status or physical attributes. However this transcendence of the body are very problematic because they concern a particularly masculine form of reasoning.

Several authors have noted that women's work often involves looking after bodies, cleaning and feeding the young, old and the sick [...] Looking after bodily needs is a process which sinks into invisibility and leaves men free to live the higher status life of the mind. Small wonder that transcending the body should have become associated with masculinist modes of reasoning and should be reflected, not only in the work of AI [Artificial Intelligence] robotics but also in the desire of cyber culture enthusiasts to leave the body behind in cyberspace. (Adam, 1997, p. 21)

Cyberspace has its own (gender) culture, morals, and expectations, but in just as many ways, it replicates the biases, contradictions, prejudices, stereotypes and gender social practices. "Cyberspace is no paradise on Earth. Quite the contrary!" (Neutopia, 1994).

The way in which Internet allows new kinds of social relationships by revolutionizing communication and access to information does not seem therefore to suffice to celebrate its democratic vocation. Most importantly, the techno-enthusiasm of cyber feminism does not substantiate its claim to make women's lives better. It shows little engagement with the growing body of empirical research on gender and technology. The apparent absence of a political agenda is reinforced by the alliance of cyber feminism to cyberpunk, science fiction versions of cyber culture which are deliberately alienated from politics.

In order to follow a more concrete reasoning about gender and technology that is about the way in which the gender studies can help professionals and decision-makers, in the next paragraph the digital divide and the gender gap will be analyzed – in relation to Internet – as principal obstacles to a sustainable technological development.

DIFFERENT ASPECTS OF DIGITAL GENDER GAP

Inclusion and openness are features, which have marked Internet since its birth and have fed the myth of a democratic and egalitarian network being able to fill geographical and social gaps among people. The democratic vocation of the Internet would seem confirmed also by its extraordinary development from 1994 on, without precedents in the history of media; but the possibility to access or not to ICT, and particularly to Internet, determines considerable differences among individuals, families and countries. These disparities impact on life quality and on job and cultural opportunities, overdrawing, on technological level, traditional mechanisms of social stratification.

Such a fracture is defined as "digital divide": this expression summarizes all kinds of inequality existing in relation with technology both inside and outside of a country. The expression "digital divide" generally refers to the gap dividing the minority of privileged people connected to Internet from the big majority of world population who cannot access to basic communication infrastructures yet. In reality researchers have also noticed in different social groups great disparities in the mastery of this medium and in the freedom of action. These differences can be interpreted in a gender perspective, by considering the cultural and material elements distinguishing the technological positioning of male users from that of female users. Mainly, the literature stresses the women's disadvantage so that the gender perspective, in many cases, focus on feminine situation.

In considering the gender gap on the Internet, Wasserman and Richmond-Abbott (2005) define three aspects: (1) access to the Internet, (2) frequency of use of the Internet, and (3) scope of the use of the Internet.

Access refers to the opportunity for individuals to use the web because they can utilize a computer in a public or private setting and have connections to the Internet. The frequency of use refers to the amount of time that an individual devotes to the use of the Internet. The scope of use refers to the variety of websites [...] used by an individual. (Wasserman & Richmond-Abbott, 2005, p. 254)

The question of the access has been interpreted differently in relation to the period and analytical perspective. In the early stages of home computer, the new technology was popularly portrayed as a male domain; at that time, women were more likely to be "technophobic".

There is much talk about women and "computer phobia". My research suggests that women's phobic reactions to the machine are a transitional phenomenon. There is the legacy of women's traditional socialization into relationships with technical objects, for many of them best summed up by the admonishment: "Don't touch it, you'll get a shock". There is the legacy of a computer culture that has traditionally been dominated by images of competition, sports and violence. There are still computer operating systems that communicate to their users in terms of "killing" and "aborting" programs. These are things that have kept women fearful and far away from the machine. But these are things that are subject to change. (Turkle, 1988, p. 41)

The most recent studies have conflicting opinions about the numbers of women that today access to ICT and Internet (Huyer & Carr, 2002; Ono & Zavodny, 2003). Yet in literature and statistical overview, we found that there is a general increase in the number of women using ICTs, whereas there is not a corresponding increase in women working within the ICT professions and there is still a gender gap in terms of ownership of ICT products. If we consider the Europe "the overall picture is a contradictory one: optimistic with respect to what we call women *and* ICT (that is, women as users) and pessimistic with respect to women *in* ICT (that is, women within the ICT professions)" (Faulkner & Lie, 2007, p.158).

The transnational/(post) colonial feminism, leaving a logo centric point of view and giving attention to spaces and opportunities offered to the so called "third-world" by electronic networks and cyberspace (Calás & Smircich 2006), extends the discussion about the question of access to the Internet and ICTs, recognizing that even if Internet has its "headquarters" in the first world, this does not mean neither that it is contextually empowering all women in the Northern societies, nor that Internet is the panacea for the problems of Southern under-privileged women.

Whether located in the Northern hemisphere or the South, whether rich or poor, global structures or power (through their "invisible" control of the market, Internet service providers, software design, language and so on) clearly determine women's use of the Internet. If cyber feminists want to ensure that the Internet is empowering, it is not enough to "get connected" and set up websites and maintain e-mail-discussion lists. The latter tasks, while necessary, are only a minuscule part of the battle. (Gajjala & Mamidipudi, 1999, pp. 15-16)

"It is not enough to *get connected*": indeed, the gender gap is directly linked to social and cultural factors. For instance, the access to ITs and Internet is associated to different roles and positions of women and men in society and family. In developing countries – especially in low-income families – the parents tend to give priority to the education of boys rather than girls. Also, women often have less control over family income (in particular if men are the main income earners), which makes it more difficult for them to pursue (fee-based) training in IT-related fields or spend family income on ICT access and use (UNCAT, 2002). Again, in developing and developed countries too, the prevailing gender stereotypes sustain the male hegemony in the world of work and discourage girls from pursuing science, technology or engineering careers (Adya & Kaiser, 2005).

Following the analysis of Wasserman and Richmond-Abbott (2005), the second aspect of gender gap is the frequency of use of the Internet. It involves the amount of time an individual uses the web for social and/or professional activity. Many individuals use Internet for social entertainment, to play games, and for hobby interests. By contrast, other individuals use this ICT for business and commercial activities (i.e., banking, stock transactions). Nevertheless the frequency of use can be analyzed, apart from the consideration of the time one dedicates to Internet, also in relation with the level of socializing and familiarity with technology. As regards the process of socializing with technology we know that it begins during childhood and that toys have an important role of "facilitators" in this phase.

Children enter a world that is heavily reliant on technology in both a physical and culture sense [...] Often the first social commentary on technology that children encounter is mediated through the toys they are given which are not only technologically based themselves but also carry messages about the social relations in which technology, gender, class, and much more are embedded. The impact of these first cultural utensils cannot be overlooked [...] Successes in strong gender demarcation by toy manufactures who have firm ideas as to what sells best to each gender reinforce for the industry notions that girls and boys are different, but they also promote that precise idea to children. (Varney, 2002, pp. 154-155).

Business strategies and manufacturing processes in the field of ICT can bear on digital gender gap in a way or in another. Women are poorly represented as information technology designers and experts and, as feminists have stressed, the women's absence from spheres of influence, among the principal actors in technological design and decision-making, is a key feature of gender power relation (Fountain, 2000; Wajcman, 2004). In the ICT sector, as well in many other techno scientist fields, the occupational segregation legitimizes the reproduction of gender stereotypes. At the productive level, we might consider the problem of scripting language[7]: into many professional communities prevails the use of "I-methodology" – that refers to a design practice in which designers consider themselves as representative of the users (Oudshoorn, Rommes & Stienstra, 2004) – gender identity and the stereotypical perceptions of designers about the users shape the gender of technological artifacts (Balka, 1997). The case study of Faulkner and Lie (2007), that is the designing of an electronics girlish game, is emblematic.

This case highlights the prevalence of the I-methodology in ICT design. This means that the designers, usually young or middle-aged men from Europe, USA or Japan, make what they themselves find interesting or attractive. When imagining other user groups, they tend to lean on their own imaginings of the group. (Faulkner & Lie, 2007, p. 171)

The gender imbalance in professional communities reflects the gender imbalance in decision-making structures, which may influence the technological innovation and its sustainability. For instance women are under-represented in organizations such as European Computer Manufacturers Association (ECMA), the Internet Engineering Task Force (IETF), the World Wide Web Consortium (W3C), International Telecommunications Union (ITU) and the Institute of Electronic and Electrical Engineers (IEEE). These international working groups have high influence on IT corporations because they undertake policy deliberations and propagate Internet standards, but they do not involve equally women and men professionals in their decisions. This situation clashes, at the base, with the definition of sustainable development as socially equal.

The third aspect of digital gender gap is that of the scope of the use of the Internet. There are very different websites. Some of these sites (i.e., sports, sexually explicit materials) are more likely to be male oriented; others (i.e. cooking, religious) are classified as female oriented, while a vast majority of them (i.e., health and fitness, games) might be classified as "androgynous" (Wasserman & Richmond-Abbott, 2005).

The variation in the scope and frequency of use of these various sites by gender may be caused first by socio-economic differences between men and women. These differences are generally related to the fact that men have higher income levels and, at this moment, a greater presence in science, engineering and technological areas starting from the educational context. On the contrary in the same area there is an "educational pipeline" for women (Cozza, 2008; Levenson, 1990; Schumacher & Morahan-Martin, 2001; Trauth, 2002). The different use of Internet between men and women may also be related to work and home activity by men and women that influence the availability of the web and of free time to navigate online systems. Secondly, as we have already said, the variation in frequency and scope of use may be caused by lifetime experience with technology. Generally speaking, men have been more familiar with computers and Internet than women and they are more involved in decision-making processes than feminine colleagues.

In this sense interest and competence in ICTs evolve within complex interactions between education, work and leisure (Faulkner & Lie, 2007). The phenomenon of digital gender gap needs to be raised again, systematically discussed and included in the research agenda: the results of gender technology studies should feed back into action-researches, empirical projects and co-operations between researchers, practitioners and decision-makers too, aimed to redress adverse gender effects.

WHAT TO DO?

Gender refers to the distinct roles that men and women are assigned in any society. As a result, women and men assume distinct socially and culturally defined responsibilities and tasks both within the household and in the wider community. The situated knowledge and experience gained from undertaking these tasks, as well as their requirements, lead women and men to have different needs and aspirations. This concept of gender differentiation underpins the conviction that "science and technology for development" must systematically and purposefully recognize the gender-specific nature of development and respond to the concerns, needs, and aspirations of both women and men appropriately and equitably (UN Commission on Science and Technology for Development, 1995).

The research and knowledge have an increased salience in the technological innovation and this role is worldwide recognized (Etzkowitz & Leydesdorff, 2000). According to Neimanis (2002), the research agenda (both in natural and in social sciences) should be constructed with reference to the "gender mainstreaming" (United Nations, 1997) strategy, that is an approach that does not look at women in isolation, but looks at women and men – both as actors in the development process, and as its beneficiaries.

The contribute of gender studies might be significant in this way, mainly in relation to some issues and related policy and program options for the consideration of national governments and science and technology bodies and agencies. With reference to the recommendations of UN Commission on Science and Technology for Development (1995), specific attention should be devoted to these topics:

- Gender equity in science and technology education. The transformative actions recommended might regard (1) the equity in gaining the access to formal education both from boys and girls; (2) the equality of opportunity within schools, for instance recognizing the importance of mentors and role models by women science teachers and provide rewards to those who devote substantial time to this activity; (3) the opportunity for distance education introducing new approaches to science and technology education, such as distance learning, making optimal use of both old (radio) and new (multimedia) technologies.

- Removing obstacles to women in scientific and technological careers. The transformative actions recommended might encompass initiatives in academia and the school system such as (1) establish networks of female professionals in science and engineering; (2) enhance mentoring, role-model, and career advisory programs; (3) provide flexible tenure criteria to accommodate family roles and responsibilities; (4) provide refresher courses and re-entry scholarships for women returning to careers in science.

- Making the science and technology decision-making process more "gender-aware". The transformative actions recommended should involve end users, men and women equally, in the determination of research priorities and in the design and implementation of technology and development programs. This will require explicit attention to the participation of women. Subject all development programs with a high science and technology component to "gender impact analysis" before initiation. Gender analysis should be included in the design and the subsequent monitoring and evaluation. Technology-assessment techniques and decision framework should incorporate a gender dimension. Governments should establish a focal point of expertise in gender, science and technology to be available to advise government departments, facilitate training sessions, and monitor and report on the implementation of government strategies in gender, science, and technology.

- Relating better with local knowledge systems. The transformative actions recommended involve development agencies that should give full consideration to the contributions of local knowledge systems, giving specific recognition to the gendered nature of these systems and the situated character of digital gender gap, too.

It is clear that the level of intervention, arising from a gender-aware research agenda, will depend on the specific needs and priorities revealed by a gender-sensitive situation assessment.

FUTURE TRENDS FOR GENDER STUDIES ON TECHNOLOGY

The discussion about the gender of the Internet arises from the feminist technology studies. This particular research trajectory provides a helpful framework for analyzing the "co-production" of gender and technology. In this perspective both are seen as performed and processual in character, rather than given and unchanging. In particular, there are two key foundations to remember: first, two-way mutually shaping relationship between gender and technology in which technology is both a source and a consequence of gender relations and vice versa; second, gender-technology relations are manifest not only in gender structures but also in gender symbols and identities (Cockburn, 1985; Faulkner, 2001; Wajcman, 1991). Thus, a useful way to approach the subject matter is to ask the question "how is technology gendered?" This issue is open to debate because it is referred to changeable practices (Poggio, 2006) and effects that are unpredictable (Eriksson-Zetterquist, 2007). The future of gender-technology studies depends on the ability of researchers to abandon

gender as a fixed binary, constructing other platforms that enable critique to gendered technology (Landström, 2007).

This methodological turn defies the kind of simplistic treatments in which technology is seen as *either* "good" *or* "bad", and Internet *either* deterministically patriarchal – a "toy for boys" – *or* empowering for women – an exciting tool and a means of gaining technical confidence.

There are some important implications of this challenge for feminist research and gender studies about technology.

First, if technology is considered – both materially and symbolically – a huge, often critical, element of hegemonic masculinity (Connell, 1987), the effort has to be going beyond the technology-masculinity equation. Further research has to be done on the diverse interactions between technolog*ies* and masculinit*ies* found in practice: there are many versions of gender, different masculinities (as well as femininities) lived differently in different times and places, but also varying within particular times and places (Acker, 2004). Internet offers many places or virtual spaces differently gendered.

Second, serious attention has to be given to the notion of the cyborg (Haraway, 1997), understanding its theoretical and "disturbing" potential. For Haraway the denaturalizing of cyborg bodies – at once organic and inorganic, machine and flesh – is an important response to the technophobia of a school of feminist analysis, which she sees as retrograde in its recourse to an organic, essential femininity grounded in the body (Currier, 2003). Despite critics to this transcendence of the body – that is accused to be a particularly masculine form of reasoning (Adam, 1997) – the cyber feminism gives new theoretical tools (in terms of representations and concepts) to understand and analyze the ongoing gendering practices in virtual settings as Internet.

In conclusion, there are a number of matters arising out of feminist and gender studies about technology, and the question for the future remains: "how is technology gendered?"

CONCLUSION

One noted dimension of inequality in Internet access and usage is gender. A number of studies have noted that women are less likely than men to use the Internet, particularly when the technology was first accessible to the general public in the mind-1990s. Gender differences in adoption rates may exit because men and women differ, on average, in socioeconomic status, which influences Internet access and use. Alternatively, men tend to be more interested in computers than women, on average, contributing – also in terms of design – to gender differences in Internet use. These gender differences in Internet are frequently examined with quantitative methods, using several measures, the cross-sectional data, report descriptive statistics and cross-tabulations (Ono & Zavodny, 2003).

Intentionally, this chapter is based on qualitative approach, positioning the discussion about Internet within gender and technology studies. The reasoning is aimed to shed light on the gender of the Internet sustaining that gender and technology are co-produced. This chapter may be considered, on one side, a contribute to view gender as an integral part of the social shaping of technology – which is neither unproblematic nor neutral – and, on the other side, an attempt to focus on gendered dimension of sustainable human and technological development, actually hampered by the digital gender gap.

In this sense, the chapter is aligned with the feminist theories that, as Marta Calás and Linda Smircich state, are "not in search of universal "knowledge" but as a way to continue critical engagement in a world that evolves in multiple directions maintaining, or even exacerbating, conditions of inequality" (2006, p. 328). Nevertheless, the conclusion does not want to be pessimistic because, in relation to gendering on the Internet, the gaze looks at the potential of the cyberspace: it may open new places and subject positions breaking the gendered boundaries.

REFERENCES

Acker, J. (2004). Gender, Capitalism and Globalization. *Critical Sociology*, *30*(1), 17–41. doi:10.1163/156916304322981668

Adam, A. (1997). What should we do with cyberfeminism? In R. Lander & A. Adam (Eds.), *Women in Computing* (pp. 17-27). Exeter, UK: Intellect Books.

Adam, A., Howcroft, D., & Richardson, H. (2004). A decade of neglect: reflecting on gender and IS. *New Technology, Work and Employment*, *19*(3), 222–240. doi:10.1111/j.1468-005X.2004.00139.x

Adya, M., & Kaiser, K. M. (2005). Early determinants of women in the IT workforce: a model of girls' career choices. *Information Technology & People*, *18*(3), 230–259. doi:10.1108/09593840510615860

Ahujia, M. K. (2002). Women in the information technology profession: a literature review, synthesis and research agenda. *European Journal of Information Systems*, *11*, 20–34. doi:10.1057/palgrave/ejis/3000417

Balka, E. (1997). Participatory Design in Women's Organizations: The Social World of Organizational Structure and the Gendered Nature of Expertise. *Gender, Work and Organization*, *4*(2), 99–115. doi:10.1111/1468-0432.00027

Berner, B. (Ed.). (1997). *Gendered Practices. Feminist Studies of Technology and Society*. Linköping, Sweden: Nova Print.

Braidotti, R. (1996, July 15). *Cyberfeminism with a Difference*. Retrieved from http://www.let.uu.nl/women's_studies/rosi/cyberfem.htm

Butler, J. (1990). *Gender Trouble: Feminism and the Subversion of Identity*. London: Routledge.

Calás, M. B., & Smircich, L. (2006). From the "Woman's Point of View Ten Years Later: Towards a Feminist Organization Studies. In S. Clegg, C. Hardy, T. Lawrence & W. R. Nord (Eds.), *The Sage handbook of organization studies* (pp. 284-346). London: Sage.

Caputi, J. (1988). Seeing Elephants: The Myths of Phallotechnology. *Feminist Studies, 14*(3), 487–524. doi:10.2307/3178062

Chesley, N. (2005). Blurring Boundaries? Linking Technology Use, Spillover, Individual Distress, and Family Satisfaction. *Journal of Marriage and the Family, 67*(5), 1237–1248. doi:10.1111/j.1741-3737.2005.00213.x

Cockburn, C. (1985). *Machinery of dominance: Women, men and technical know-how*. London: Pluto.

Cockburn, C., & Ormrod, S. (1993). *Gender & Technology in the Making*. London: Sage.

Connell, R. (1987). *Gender and Power*. Cambridge, UK: Polity Press.

Coombs, R., Knights, D., & Willmott, C. (1992). Culture, Control and Competition: Towards a Conceptual Framework for the Study of Information Technology in Organizations. *Organization Studies, 13*(1), 51–72. doi:10.1177/017084069201300106

Cozza, M. (2008). Narratives on platform: stories for women in computer science. *Int. J. Cont. Engineering Education and Life-Long Learning, 18*(2), 197–213. doi:10.1504/IJCEELL.2008.017376

Currier, D. (2003). Feminist Technological Futures: Deleuze and Body/Technology Assemblages. *Feminist Theory, 4*(3), 321–338. doi:10.1177/14647001030043005

De Ruggieri, F., & Pugliese, A. C. (Eds.). (2006). *Futura. Genere e tecnologia*. Roma: Meltemi.

Edwards, P. N. (1990). The army and the microworld: computers and the politics of gender identity. *Signs: Journal of Women in Culture and Society, 16*(1), 102–127. doi:10.1086/494647

Eriksson-Zetterquist, U. (2007). Editorial: Gender and New Technologies. *Gender, Work and Organization, 14*(4), 305–311. doi:10.1111/j.1468-0432.2007.00345.x

Etzkowitz, H., & Leydesdorff, L. (2000). The dynamics of innovation: from National Systems and "Mode 2" to a Triple Helix of university-industry-government relations. *Research Policy, 29*, 109–123. doi:10.1016/S0048-7333(99)00055-4

Faulkner, W. (2000). The Power and the Pleasure? A Research Agenda for "Making Gender Stick" to Engineers. *Science, Technology & Human Values, 25*(1), 87–119. doi:10.1177/016224390002500104

Faulkner, W., & Lie, M. (2007). Gender in the Information Society: Strategies of Inclusion. *Gender, Technology and Development, 11*(2), 157–177. doi:10.1177/097185240701100202

Fountain, J. E. (2000). Constructing the information society: women, information technology, and design. *Technology in Society, 22*, 45–62. doi:10.1016/S0160-791X(99)00036-6

Gajjala, R., & Mamidipudi, A. (1999). Cyberfeminism, technology, and international "development." . *Gender and Development, 7*(2), 8–16. doi:10.1080/741923122

Gherardi, S. (1995). *Gender, Symbolism and Organizational Cultures*. London: Sage.

Grey, S., & Healy, G. (2004). Women and IT contracting work – a testing process. *New Technology, Work and Employment, 19*(1), 30–42. doi:10.1111/j.1468-005X.2004.00126.x

Gustavsson, E. (2005). Virtual Servants: Stereotyping Female Front-Office Employees on the Internet. *Gender, Work and Organization, 12*(5), 400–419. doi:10.1111/j.1468-0432.2005.00281.x

Haraway, D. (1988). Situated Knowledges: The Science Question in Feminism and the Privilege of Partial Perspective. *Feminist Studies, 14*(3), 575–599. doi:10.2307/3178066

Hearn, J. (2004). From Hegemonic Masculinity to the Hegemony of Men. *Feminist Theory, 5*(49), 49–72. doi:10.1177/1464700104040813

Henwood, F. (1993). Establishing Gender Perspectives on Information Technology: Problems. Issues and Opportunities. In E. Green, J. Owen & D. Pain (Eds.), *Gendered by Design? Information Technology and Office Systems* (pp. 31-49).

Herring, S. C. (1994). *Gender differences in computer-mediated communication: bringing familiar baggage to the new frontier.* Paper presented at the American Library Association annual convention, Miami. ID (2001, May 23). Gender Differences in CMC: Findings and Implications. *CPSR Newsletter, 18*(1). Retrieved from http://cpsr.org/issues/womenintech/herring/

Huyer, S., & Carr, M. (2002). Information and Communication Technologies: A Priority for Women. *Gender, Technology and Development, 6*(1), 85–100. doi:10.1177/097185240200600105

ID. (1991). *Simians, Cyborgs, and Women: The Reinvention of Nature.* New York: Routledge.

ID. (1992). The circuit of technology. Gender, identity and power. In R. Silverstone & E. Hirsch (Eds.), *Consuming Technologies. Media and Information in Domestic Spaces* (pp. 32-47). London: Routledge.

ID. (1994). Feminist Theories of Technology. In S. Jasanoff, et al. (Eds.), *Handbook of science and technology studies* (pp. 189-204). Thousand Oaks, CA: Sage.

ID. (1995). *Life on the Screen: Identity in the Age of the Internet.* New York: Simon and Schuster.

ID. (1997). *Modest_Witness@Second_Millennium. Female Man Meets Onco Mouse.* London: Routledge.

ID. (2000). From the Woman Question in Technology to the Technology Question in Feminism. *European Journal of Women's Studies, 7*(2), 209–227. doi:10.1177/135050680000700209

ID. (2001). The technology question in feminism: a view from feminist technology studies. *Women's Studies International Forum, 24*(1), 79–95. doi:10.1016/S0277-5395(00)00166-7

ID. (2002). Exploring the gender question in critical information systems. *Journal of Information Technology, 17*, 59–67. doi:10.1080/02683960210145959

ID. (2002). Gendering the Internet: Claims, Controversies and Cultures. *European Journal of Communication, 17*(5), 5–23.

ID. (2004). *Techno Feminism.* Cambridge, UK: Polity Press.

ID. (2008). Life in the fast lane? Towards a sociology of technology and time. *The British Journal of Sociology, 59*(1), 59–77. doi:10.1111/j.1468-4446.2007.00182.x

Janson, M., Mörtberg, C., & Berg, E. (2007). Old Dreams, New Means: an Exploration of Visions and Situated Knowledge in Information Technology. *Gender, Work and Organization, 14*(4), 371–387. doi:10.1111/j.1468-0432.2007.00349.x

Knights, D., & Kerfoot, D. (2004). Between Representations and Subjectivity: Gender Binaries and the Politics of Organizational Transformation. *Gender, Work and Organization, 11*(4), 430–454. doi:10.1111/j.1468-0432.2004.00241.x

Kraft, J. F., & Siegenthaler, J. K. (1989). Office Automation, Gender, and Change: An Analysis of the Management Literature. *Science, Technology & Human Values*, *14*(2), 195–212. doi:10.1177/016224398901400204

Landström, C. (2007). Queering feminist technology studies. *Feminist Theory*, *8*(7), 7–26. doi:10.1177/1464700107074193

Lash, S. (2002). *Critique of Information*. London: Sage.

Levenson, N. G. (1990). *Educational Pipeline Issues for Women*. Paper presented at Computer Research Association Annual Meeting, Snowbird, UT.

Linstead, A., & Brewis, J. (2004). Editorial: Beyond Boundaries: Towards Fluidity in Theorizing and Practice. *Gender, Work and Organization*, *11*(4), 355–362. doi:10.1111/j.1468-0432.2004.00237.x

Mitter, S. (2001). *Asian Women in the Digital Economy: Policies for Participation*. Malaysia, UNDP.

Moore, K., Griffiths, M., Richardson, H., & Adam, A. (2008). Gendered Futures? Women, the ICT Workplace and Stories of the Future. *Gender, Work and Organization*, *15*(5), 523–542. doi:10.1111/j.1468-0432.2008.00416.x

Naughton, J. (1999). *A Brief History of the Future: The Origins of the Internet*. London: Weidenfeld and Nicolson.

Neimanis, A. (2002). *Gender mainstreaming in practice: a Handbook*. UNDP.

Neutopia, D. (1994, July 16). *The feminization of Cyberspace*. Retrieved from http://feminism.eserver.org/gender/cyberspace/feminization-of-cyberspace.txt

Newman, K. (1988). *Falling from Grace; the Experience of Downward Mobility in the American Middle Class*. New York: Vintage Books.

Ono, H., & Zavodny, M. (2003). Gender and the Internet. *Social Science Quarterly*, *84*(1), 111–121. doi:10.1111/1540-6237.t01-1-8401007

Orlikowski, W. J., & Baroudi, J. J. (1989). The Information systems profession: myth or reality? *Office: Technology & People*, *4*, 13–30. doi:10.1108/eb022652

Oudshoorn, N., Rommes, E., & Stienstra, M. (2004). Configuring the Users as Everybody: Gender and Design Cultures in Information and Communication Technologies. *Science, Technology & Human Values*, *29*(1), 30–63. doi:10.1177/0162243903259190

Panteli, N., Stack, J., & Ramsay, H. (2001). Gendered patterns in computing work in the late 1990s. *New Technology, Work and Employment*, *16*(1), 3–17. doi:10.1111/1468-005X.00073

Perry, R., & Greber, L. (1990). Women and Computers: an Introduction. *Signs: Journal of Women in Culture and Society*, *16*(1), 74–101. doi:10.1086/494646

Plant, S. (1998). *Zeros and Ones: Digital Women and the New Technoculture*. London: Fourth Estate.

Poggio, B. (2006). Editorial: Outline of a Theory of Gender Practices. *Gender, Work and Organization*, *13*(3), 225–233. doi:10.1111/j.1468-0432.2006.00305.x

Reinharz, S. (1992). *Feminist methods in Social Research*. New York: Oxford University Press.

Rifkin, J. (1995). *The end of work: the decline of the global labor force and the dawn of the post-market era*, New York: Putnam's Sons.

Rodrigues Araújo, E. (2008). Technology, Gender and Time: A Contribution to the Debate. *Gender, Work and Organization*, *15*(5), 477–503. doi:10.1111/j.1468-0432.2008.00414.x

Schor, J. (1992). *The Overworked American: the Unexpected Decline of Leisure*. New York: Basic Books.

Schumacher, P., & Morahan-Martin, J. (2001). Gender, Internet and computer attitudes and experiences. *Computers in Human Behavior*, *17*, 95–110. doi:10.1016/S0747-5632(00)00032-7

Smelik, A. (2000). Die virtuele matrix. Het lichaam in cyberpunkfilms. *Tijdschrift voor Genderstudies*, *3*(4), 4–13.

Spender, D. (1995). *Nattering on the net: Women, Power an Cyberspace*. North Melbourne, Australia: Spinifex Press.

Stone, A. R. (1995). *The War of Deside and Technology, at the Close of the Mechanical Age*. Cambridge, MA: MIT Press.

Takayoshi, P. (2000). Complicated Women: Examining Methodologies for Understanding the Uses of Technology. *Computers and Composition*, *17*, 123–138. doi:10.1016/S8755-4615(00)00025-6

Trauth, M. E. (2002). Odd girls out: an individual differences perspective on women in the IT profession. *Information Technology & People*, *15*(2), 98–118. doi:10.1108/09593840210430552

Turkle, S. (1984). *The second self: Computers and the Human Spirit*. London: Granada. ID. (1988). Computational reticence: why women fear the intimate machine. In C. Kramarae (Ed.), *Technology and women's voices* (pp. 41-61). New York: Routledge & Kegan Paul Inc.

UN Commission on Science and Technology for Development. (1995). *Missing Links: Gender Equity in Science and Technology for Development*, Canada, International Development Research Centre.

UNCAT-United Nations Conference on Trade and Development (2002). *E-Commerce and development report*. New York: United Nations.

United Nations. (1997). *The Report of the Economic and Social Council for 1997*. New York: United Nations, Department of Economic and Social Affairs, Division for the Advancement of Women.

Van Zoonen, L. (1991). Feminist theory and information technology. *Media Culture & Society*, *14*(1), 9–29. doi:10.1177/016344392014001002

Varney, W. (2002). Of Men and Machines: Images of Masculinities in Boys' Toys. *Feminist Studies*, *28*(1), 153–174. doi:10.2307/3178498

Wajcman, J. (1991). *Feminism confronts Technology*. Cambridge, UK: Polity Press.

Wasserman, I. M., & Richmond-Abbott, M. (2005). Gender and the Internet: Causes of Variation in Access, Level, and Scope. *Social Science Quarterly*, *86*(1), 252–270. doi:10.1111/j.0038-4941.2005.00301.x

WCDE-World Commission on Environment and Development. (1987). *Our Common Future*. Oxford, UK: Oxford University Press.

Wellman, B. (2001). Physical Place and Cyberspace: The Rise of Personalized Networking. *International Journal of Urban and Regional Research*, *25*(2), 227–252. doi:10.1111/1468-2427.00309

West, C., & Zimmerman, D. H. (1987). Doing Gender. *Gender & Society*, *1*(2), 125–151. doi:10.1177/0891243287001002002

ENDNOTES

[1]   Faulkner (2000) identifies four streams of work in this area: the first – women *in* technology – focuses on the agendas of govern-

ments and industry and their scant regard for discriminations towards women in the labour market (i.e., the occupational segregation, the women's career advancement compared with men's). The second stream – women *and* technology – reflects a desire to broaden the agenda beyond the equity issue, on the basis that the vast majority of women encounters technology as users rather than designers. The third stream – *gender* and technology – signal two different priorities: first, understanding relations between men as well as between women and men to make sense of the position of women; second, understanding technology as socially shaped and thus potentially reshapeable. Finally he identifies a fourth stream that is *men/masculinity* and technology: a new avenue for feminist technology studies.

2   There are also many professional organizations. For instance: the Alliance of Technology and Women (ATW) (http://www.atwinternational.org), the European Platform of Women Scientists (http://www.epws.org/index.php), the Committee on the Status of Women in Computing Research-CRA-W (http://www.cra.org/Activities/craw), Gender and Sciences (http://gssnet.fbk.eu/en/presentation). It might be useful to mention also the "miscellaneous" resources on gender and technology such as Women-Related Email Lists for Cyberculture or Internet Information (http://userpages.umbc.edu/~korenman/wmst/f_net.html), GenTech (http://educ.ubc.ca/faculty/bryson/gentech), Women Internet Researchers (http://www.nicola-doering.de/women.htm), Information and Communication Technologies and Gender Seminar Series (http://web.worldbank.org/WBSITE/EXTERNAL/TOPICS/EXTGENDER/0,,contentMDK:20207786~menuPK:489311~pagePK:148956~piPK:216618~theSitePK:336868,00.html).

3   The School is a joint venture among the Department for Gender Studies (Tema Genus), Linköping University, Sweden, NIKK (Nordic Institute for Women's Studies and Gender Research), Oslo, Norway, and 36 partner institutions at 33 universities and institutions for higher education in Denmark, Finland, Iceland, Norway, Sweden, Estonia, Latvia, Lithuania and North West Russia.

4   Shulamit Reinhatz (1992) says that "the feminist research practice must be recognized as a plurality"(p. 4), that is an open perspective aimed to give voice to different positions, rejecting the notion of a transcendent authority, one truth and a pure knowledge. The problems with the traditional peer review system are exactly linked to the question of how authority is created and distributed. I have to thank the anonymous reviewer for the interesting suggestion about this conceptual link.

5   Erin Bradner writing for computer scientists, has coined the term "social affordances" to emphasize the *social* as well as individual implications of the technological features of computer-supported communication networks and human-computer interfaces (Wellman, 2001).

6   The title of this section arises from the reading of Liesbet van Zoonen's article "Gendering the Internet: Claims, Controversies and Cultures" (2002). It is suitable for this section because it refers not only to the mutual shaping of the Internet *and* gender, but also it suggests the idea of gender as "do*ing*" (West & Zimmerman, 1987).

7   A scripting language, script language or extension language, is a programming language that allows some control of a single or many software application(s).

Compilation of References

Acker, J. (2004). Gender, Capitalism and Globalization. *Critical Sociology*, *30*(1), 17–41. doi:10.1163/156916304322981668

Ackoff, R. L. (1981). *Creating the corporate future*. New York: Wiley.

Adam, A. (1997). What should we do with cyberfeminism? In R. Lander & A. Adam (Eds.), *Women in Computing* (pp. 17-27). Exeter, UK: Intellect Books.

Adam, A., Howcroft, D., & Richardson, H. (2004). A decade of neglect: reflecting on gender and IS. *New Technology, Work and Employment*, *19*(3), 222–240. doi:10.1111/j.1468-005X.2004.00139.x

Adenfelt, M., & Lagerström, K. (2006). Enabling knowledge creation and sharing in transnational projects. *International Journal of Project Management*, *24*(3), 191–198. doi:10.1016/j.ijproman.2005.09.003

Adenfelt, M., & Lagerström, K. (2007). Knowledge development and sharing: the case of a centre of excellence and a transnational team. *International Business Review*, *15*(4), 381–400. doi:10.1016/j.ibusrev.2006.05.002

Adenfelt, M., & Lagerström, K. (2008). The development and sharing of knowledge by centres of excellence and transnational teams: a conceptual framework. *Management International Review*, *48*(3), 319–338. doi:10.1007/s11575-008-0018-8

Adler, N. J. (1997). *International dimensions of organizational behavior*. Cincinnati: South Western Publishing.

Adya, M., & Kaiser, K. M. (2005). Early determinants of women in the IT workforce: a model of girls' career choices. *Information Technology & People*, *18*(3), 230–259. doi:10.1108/09593840510615860

Ahujia, M. K. (2002). Women in the information technology profession: a literature review, synthesis and research agenda. *European Journal of Information Systems*, *11*, 20–34. doi:10.1057/palgrave/ejis/3000417

Akca, H., Sayili, M., & Esengun, K. (2007). Challenge of rural people to reduce digital divide in the globalized world: Theory and practice. *Government Information Quarterly*, *24*, 404–413. doi:10.1016/j.giq.2006.04.012

Albinsson, L., Forsgren, O., & Lind, M. (2006). *e-Me Stories & Scenarios - The Ideal Electronic Galaxy of the Student*. School of Business and Informatics, University College of Borås, Sweden

Albinsson, L., Lind, M., & Forsgren, O. (2007). Co-Design: An approach to border crossing, Network Innovation. In P. Cunningham, & M. Cunningham, (Eds), *Expanding the Knowledge Economy: Issues, Applications, Case Studies* (Vol. 4, Part 2, pp. 977-983). Amsterdam: IOS Press.

Allwood, J., & Lind, M. (2008). *Making the Web more Pragmatic - Exploring the Potential of some Pragmatic Concepts for IS Research and Development*. The Inaugural meeting of The AIS Special Interest Group on Pragmatist IS Research (SIGPrag 2008) at International Conference on Information Systems (ICIS2008), France

Altman, B. W. (1998). Transformed Corporate Community Relations: A Management Tool for Achieving Corporate Citizenship. *Business and Society Review.*

Alvesson, M. (2003). Beyond neopositivists, romantics, and localists: A reflexive approach to interviews in organizational research. *Academy of Management Review, 28*(1), 13–33.

Alvesson, M., & Willmott, H. (1996). *Making Sense of Management.* London, UK: Sage Publications Limited.

Amborski, D., & Lister, N. M. (2002). *An Eco-Tech Village for Milton: Considerations for Policy.* Commissioned by the Town of Milton, Toronto.

Ancona, D., & Caldwell, D. (1992). Bridging the boundary: external activity and performance in organizational teams. *Administrative Science Quarterly, 37,* 634–665. doi:10.2307/2393475

Andaleeb, S. (1995). Dependence relations and the moderating role of trust: implications for behavioral intentions in marketing channels. *International Journal of Research in Marketing, 12*(2), 157–172. doi:10.1016/0167-8116(94)00020-O

Andersson, P., Essler, U., & Thorngren, B. (2007). *Beyond Mobility.* Lund: Studentlitteratur

Andraski, J. (1994). Foundations for successful continuous replenishment programs. *International Journal of Logistics Management, 5*(1), 1–8. doi:10.1108/09574099410805036

Andrews, A., Rankin, J. H., & Waugh, L. M. (2006). A framework to identify opportunities for ICT support when implementing sustainable design standards. *ITcon - . Electronic Journal of Information Technology in Construction, 11,* 17–33.

Ansett, S. (2007). Mind the Gap: A Journey to Sustainable Supply Chains. *Employ Response Rights Journal, 19*(4), 295–303. doi:10.1007/s10672-007-9055-x

Antonelli, C. (2002). The Digital Divide: Understanding the Economics of New Information and Communication Technology in the Global Economy. Information Economics and Policy, 15(2), 173–199. doi:10.1016/S0167-6245(02)00093-8doi:10.1016/S0167-6245(02)00093-8

Antonijevic, R. (2007). *Usage of computers and calculators and students achievement: results from TIMSS 2003.* ERIC, ED497737, retrieved from http://eric.ed.gov/ERICWebPortal/recordDetail?accno=ED497737

Arapkirlioglu, K. (2003). Ekoloji ve Planlama. *Planlama,* 4-.

Aray, Y., & Sugizaki, K. (2003). Concentration of Call Centers in Peripheral Areas: Cases in Japan. NETCOM, 17, 187–202.

Arifoglu, A. (2004). *E-Dönüşüm, Yol Haritası, Dünya, Türkiye.* Ankara:Yıldız Yayınları.

Arnfalk, P. (2002). *Virtual Mobility and Pollution Prevention.* Lund, Sweden: The International Institute for Industrial Environmental Economics, Lund University.

Atabek, U. (2003). *Iletisim Teknolojileri ve Yerel Medya için Olanaklar.* Istanbul: IPS.

Atamer, T., & Schweiger, D. (2003). Transnational horizontal project teams. *Journal of World Business, 38*(2), 81–83. doi:10.1016/S1090-9516(03)00002-6

Attfield, R. (1999). *The Ethics of the Global Environment.* Edinburgh, UK: Edinburgh University Press.

Auge, M., & Howe, J. (1995). *Non-Places: Introduction to Anthropology of Supermodernity.* London: Verso.

Aurigi, A. (2005). Making the Digital City. Aldershot, UK: Ashgate

Aurigi, A., & Graham, S. (2000). Cyberspace and the City: the Virtual City in Europe. In Bridge, G., & Watson, S. (Eds.), A Companion to the City (pp. 489-502). Oxford, UK: Blackwell.

Austin, J. L. (1975). *How to do things with words.* Oxford, UK: Oxford University Press.

Axelsson, B., & Easton, G. (Eds.). (1992). *Industrial Networks - A New View of Reality.* London: Routledge.

B.G.D. Consulting Inc. (2002). *Implementation Options Report 2002.* Retrieved July 28, 2004 from http://www.milton.ca/execserv/ecotech_implementation.pdf

Baines, J., McClintock, W., Taylor, N., & Buckenham, B. (2003). Using local knowledge. In H. Becker, & F. Vanclay, (Eds.) *The International Handbook of social Impact Assessment* (pp. 26-41). Cheltenham, UK: Edward Elgar Publishing.

Bakis, H., & Roche, E. M. (1997) Cyberspace: The Emerging Nervous System of Global Society and Its Spatial Functions. In E. M. Roche, & H. Bakis, (Eds.) Developments in Telecommunications: Between Global and Local (pp.1-12). Aldershot, UK: Ashgate.

Bakis, H., & Vidal, P. (2007) De la Négation du Territoire au Géocyberespace: Vers une Approche Intégrée de la Relation entre Espace et TIC. In C. Brossaud, & B. Reber, (Eds.) Humanités Numériques, 1, 101-117.

Bakis, H., Abler, R., & Roche, E. M. (1993). Corporate Networks, International Telecommunications and Interdependence. Perspectives from Geography and Information Systems. London: Belhaven.

Balka, E. (1997). Participatory Design in Women's Organizations: The Social World of Organizational Structure and the Gendered Nature of Expertise. *Gender, Work and Organization, 4*(2), 99–115. doi:10.1111/1468-0432.00027

Balle, F. (1999). *Médias et societies,* (9 ed.). Paris: Monchrétien

Bandyopadhyay, P. (2001). Application of Information Technology and Impact of Cyber Eco Cities in New Millennium. In *ISOCARP Prooceedings,* Utrecht, (pp. 68-77).

Barlas, M. A., & Caliskan, O. (2006). Virtual Space As a Public Sphere: Rethinking The Political and Professional Agenda of Spatial Planning And Design. *METU Journal of Faculty of Architecture, 23*(2), 1–20.

Barth, F. (1971). *Ethnic Groups and Boundaries: The Social Organization of Cultural Difference.* Bergen: Universitetsforlaget.

Bartholomeusz, S., & Tanewski, G. (2006). The relationship between Family Firms and Corporate Governance. *Journal of Small Business Management, 44*(2), 245–267. doi:10.1111/j.1540-627X.2006.00166.x

Bartiaux, F. (2008). Does environmental information overcome practice compartmentalisation and change consumers' behaviours? *Journal of Cleaner Production, 16,* 1170–1190. doi:10.1016/j.jclepro.2007.08.013

Bartlett, C. A., & Ghoshal, S. (1989). *Managing across borders.* Boston: Harvard Business School Press.

Bassett-Jones, N. (2005). The paradox of diversity management, creativity and innovation. *Creativity and Innovation Management, 14*(2), 169–176. doi:10.1111/j.1467-8691.00337.x

Bauman, Z. (1998). *Globalization: The Human Consequences.* New York: Columbia University Press

Baumann, H., Brunklaus, B., Gluch, P., Kadefors, A., Stenberg, A.-C., & Thuvander, L. (2003). *Byggsektorns Miljöbarometer 2002.* Sweden: Chalmers University of technology . *ESA Report, 2003,* 2.

Beamer, L. (1998). Bridging Business Cultures. *The China Business Review, 25*(3), 54–58.

Beamer, L., & Varner, I. (2001). *Intercultural Communication in the Global Workplace.* New York: McGraw-Hill Irvin.

Bebbington, J., Brown, J., Frame, B., & Thomson, I. (2007). Theorizing engagement: the potential of a critical dialogic approach. *Accounting, Auditing & Accountability Journal, 20*(3). doi:10.1108/09513570710748544

Behrendt, I. (2000). Umweltinformationssysteme als informelle Basis strategischer Planungen: Eine Gestaltungsempfehlung zur Architektur von strategischen Umweltinformations¬systemen, Gießen.

Bell, B. S., & Kozlowski, S. W. J. (2002). A typology of virtual teams: implications for effective leadership. *Group & Organization Management, 27*(1), 14–36. doi:10.1177/1059601102027001003

Bell, S., & Morse, S. (1999). *Sustainability Indicators.* London: Earthscan Publications Ltd.

Bentley, R., Hughes, J. A., Randall, D., Rodden, T., Sawyer, P., Shapiro, D., & Sommerville, I. (1992). Ethnographically-Informed System Design for Air Traffic Control. In *Proceedings of the 1992 ACM Conference on Computer-supported Cooperative Work* (pp. 123-129).

Bernard, R. H. (1995). *Research Methods in Anthropology: Qualitative and Quantitative Approaches.* Thousand Oaks, CA: Sage.

Berner, B. (Ed.). (1997). *Gendered Practices. Feminist Studies of Technology and Society.* Linköping, Sweden: Nova Print.

Berry, W. (2005). *The way of ignorance.* New York: Shoemaker & Hoard.

Bhattacharya, C. B., Sen, S., & Korschun, D. (2008). Using Corporate Social Responsibility to Win the War for Talent. *MIT Sloan Management Review, 49*(2), 37–44.

Bios, N. C. (2007). De la séduction médiatique à la mobilité transfrontalière: l'utilisation de l'Internet par la femme camerounaise. *Revue camerounaise de sociologie, 4*(1), 65-90.

Bisset, R., & Tomlinson, P. (1995). Monitoring and auditing of impacts. In P. Wathern, (ed). *Environmental Impact Assessment: Theory and Practice.* (pp. 117-128). London, UK: Routledge.

Bld, A. (n.d.). *The features of the settlement.* Retrieved May 5, 2005 from http://www.arcosanti.orghttp://www.arcosanti.org/project/project/future/arcosanti5000/main.html

Bleischwitz, R., & Hennicke, P. (2004). *Eco-efficiency, regulation, and sustainable business: towards a governance structure for sustainable development.* Cheltenham, UK: Edward Elgar Publishing.

Boardman, A., Greenberg, D., Vining, A., & Weimer, D. (2001). *Cost-Benefit Analysis: concepts and practice* (2nd ed). Upper Saddle River, NJ: Prentice Hall.

Bogunovich, D. (2002). Eco-tech cities: Smart metabolism for a green urbanism. In C.A. Brebbia, Martin-Duque and L.C. Wasdhwa (Ed.), *The Sustainable City II,* (pp.75-84). London: Witpress.

Bon, R., & Hutchinson, K. (2000). Sustainable construction: some economic challenges. *Building Research and Information, 28*(5-6), 310–314. doi:10.1080/096132100418465

Bonache, J., & Brewster, C. (2001). Knowledge Transfer and the Management of Expatriation. *Thunderbird International Business Review, 43*(1), 3–20. doi:10.1002/1520-6874(200101/02)43:1<3::AID-TIE2>3.0.CO;2-4

Bonnedahl, K. J., Jensen, T., & Sandström, J. (2007). *Ekonomi och moral □ vägar mot ökat ansvarstagande.* Liber, Malmö.

Books of Census (2002). Belgrade, Serbia: The Statistical Office of the Republic of Serbia.

Boulding, K. (1966). *The Economics of the Coming Spaceship Earth.,* Reprinted from H. Jarrett, Environmental Quality in a Growing Economy. Baltimore, MD: Johns Hopkins Press.

Bourdieu, P. (1977). *Outline of a Theory of Practice.* Cambridge, MA: Cambridge University Press.

Bourdieu, P. (1991). *Language and symbolic power.* Cambridge, UK: Polity Press.

Bourdieu, P. (2004). *Distinction: A Social Critique of the Judgment of Taste.* London: Routledge.

Boyce, G. (2000). Public discourse and decision making: exploring possibilities for financial, social and environmental accounting. *Accounting, Auditing & Accountability Journal, 13*(1). doi:10.1108/09513570010316135

Braidotti, R. (1996, July 15). *Cyberfeminism with a Difference*. Retrieved from http://www.let.uu.nl/women's_studies/rosi/cyberfem.htm

Braun, R., Russ, M., Krcmar, H., Schulz, W. F., & Kreeb, M. (2003). An Open-Source Community for Building Ecological Tools. In Gnauck, A. & Heinrich, R. (Eds.) *Umweltinformatik Aktuell, 17th International Conference Informatics for Environmental Protection Cottbus 2003. Part 1: Concepts and Methods*, (pp. 165-170), Marburg.

Braun, R., Russ, M., Schulz, W. F., Krcmar, H., & Kreeb, M. (2004). Good-Practice-Examples and Indicators: Internet-based solutions for the Sustainable Management. In CERN (Eds.), *EnviroInfo 2004, 18th International Conference Informatics for Environmental Protection Genf 2004. Part 1*, (pp. 24-32). Genf.

Brembeck, H., Ekström, K. M., & Mörck, M. (2007). Shopping with Humans and Non-humans. In H. Brembeck, K. M. Ekström & M. Mörck (Eds.), *Little monsters: (de) coupling assemblages of consumption*. Berlin: Lit Verlag.

Breton, P., & Proulx, S. (1989). *L'explosion de la communication*. Paris: La Découverte.

Brown, J. (in press). Democracy, sustainability and dialogic accounting technologies: Taking pluralism seriously. *Critical Perspectives on Accounting*.

Brundin, E., Florin, E., & Melin, L. (2008). *The Family Ownership Logic: Core Characteristics of Family-Controlled Business*. CeFEO Working Paper, 2008:1.

Brundtland Commission. (1987). Our Common Future: From One Earth to One World. World Commission on Environment and Development. Oxford, UK: Oxford University Press.

Brunson, N., & Jacobson, B. (2002). Standardization and Uniformity. In N. Brunson, B. Jacobson, et al (Eds.) *A World of Standards* (pp. 127 137). Oxford, UK: Oxford University Press.

Bullinger, H. J., Warnecke, H. J., & Westkämper, E. (2003). *Neue Organisationsformen im Unternehmen: Ein Handbuch für das moderne Management*. Berlin: Springer.

Butler, J. (1990). *Gender Trouble: Feminism and the Subversion of Identity*. London: Routledge.

Buxmann (2002). Strategien von Standardsoftwareanbietern: Eine Analyse auf der Basis von Netzeffekten, *zfbf* Nr. 54, August 2002, 442-457.

Byrne, D. E., Clore, G. L. J., & Worchel, P. (1966). The effect of economic similarity-dissimilarity as determinants of attraction. *Journal of Personality and Social Psychology Quarterly, 4*, 220–224. doi:10.1037/h0023559

Cabinet Office. UK (2000). *E-government: a strategic framework for public services in the Information Age*. Retrieved from http://www.e-envoy.gov.uk/ukonline/st rategy.html

Calás, M. B., & Smircich, L. (2006). From the "Woman's Point of View Ten Years Later: Towards a Feminist Organization Studies. In S. Clegg, C. Hardy, T. Lawrence & W. R. Nord (Eds.), *The Sage handbook of organization studies* (pp. 284-346). London: Sage.

Callenbach, E. (1994). *Ekotopya*. Istanbul: Ayrinti Yayinlari.

Caputi, J. (1988). Seeing Elephants: The Myths of Phallotechnology. *Feminist Studies, 14*(3), 487–524. doi:10.2307/3178062

Casey, E. (1993). *Getting back into place: toward a renewed understanding of the place-world*. Bloomington, IN: Indiana University Press

Casey, E. (1997). *The fate of place: a philosophical history*. Berkeley, CA: University of California Press.

Castells, M. (1989). *The Informational City*. Cambridge, UK: Blackwell Publishers.

Castells, M. (1996). The Rise of the Network Society. The Information Age: Economy, Society and Culture (Vol.1). Oxford, UK: Blackwell Publishing.

Castells, M. (2000). The Internet Galaxy: Reflections on the Internet, Business, and Society. Oxford, UK: Oxford University Press.

Castels, M. (1996). *The Rise of the Network Society*. Oxford, UK: Blackwell Publishers.

Cerin, P. (2002). Communication in Corporate Environmental Reports. *Corporate Social Responsibility and Environmental Management, 9*, 46–66. doi:10.1002/csr.6

Chalmers, M. (2004). A Historical View of Context. *Journal of Computer Supported Cooperative Work, 13*(3), 223–247. doi:10.1007/s10606-004-2802-8

Checkland, P. B. (1988). Soft systems methodology: An overview. *J. of Applied Systems Analysis, 15*, 27–30.

Chen, L., & Nath, R. (2004). A framework for mobile business applications. *International Journal of Mobile Communications, 2*(4), 368–381. doi:10.1504/IJMC.2004.005857

Chen, S., Geluykens, R., & Choi, C. J. (2006). The importance of language in global teams: a linguistic perspective. *Management International Review, 46*(6), 679–695. doi:10.1007/s11575-006-0122-6

Cheney, G., Thøger, L. C., Zorn, T. E. J., & Ganesh, S. (2004). *Organizational Communication in an Age of Globalization*. Long Grove, IL: Waveland Press.

Chesley, N. (2005). Blurring Boundaries? Linking Technology Use, Spillover, Individual Distress, and Family Satisfaction. *Journal of Marriage and the Family, 67*(5), 1237–1248. doi:10.1111/j.1741-3737.2005.00213.x

Childerhouse, P., Hermiz, R., Mason-Jones, R., Popp, A., & Towill, D. (2003). 'Information flow in automotive supply chains – identifying and learning to overcome barriers to change'. *Industrial Management & Data Systems, 103*(7), 491–502. doi:10.1108/02635570310489197

Churchman, C. W. (1979). *The systems approach and its enemies*. New York: Basic Books.

Ciborra, C. U., & Lanzara, G., F. (1994). Formative contexts and information technology, *Accounting . Management and Information Technology, 4*(2), 61–86. doi:10.1016/0959-8022(94)90005-1

Clark, M. (2001). Domestic futures and sustainable residential development. *Futures, 33*, 817–836. doi:10.1016/S0016-3287(01)00021-0

Cockburn, C. (1985). *Machinery of dominance: Women, men and technical know-how*. London: Pluto.

Cockburn, C., & Ormrod, S. (1993). *Gender & Technology in the Making*. London: Sage.

Cohen, D. V., & Altman, B. W. (2000). Corporate Citizenship in the New Millennium: Foundation for an Architecture of Excellence. *Business and Society Review, 105*(1), 145–168. doi:10.1111/0045-3609.00069

Commission, E. U. (2003b). *Global standards for the Global Information Society, DN IP/03/1374*. Retrieved from http://europa.eu.int/documents/index_en.htm

Connell, R. (1987). *Gender and Power*. Cambridge, UK: Polity Press.

Conradsson, B. (1988). *Kontorsfolket. Etnologiska bilder av livet på kontor*. Stockholm, Sweden: Nordiska museet. Etnologiska institutionen, Stockholms universitet.

Coombs, R., Knights, D., & Willmott, C. (1992). Culture, Control and Competition: Towards a Conceptual Framework for the Study of Information Technology in Organizations. *Organization Studies, 13*(1), 51–72. doi:10.1177/017084069201300106

Cooren, F. (2006). The organizational world as a plenum of agencies. In F. Cooren, J. R. Taylor, & E. J. Van *Communication as Organizing*. (pp. 81-101). London: LEA.

CORECOM, & Nielsen. (2005). Il consumo della rete in Toscana. Retrieved July 2008, from http://www.consiglio.regione.toscana.it/corecom/att_studio/ricerche.htm

CORECOM, & Nielsen/Net-Ratings (2005). La Toscana in rete, 2002-2005. Retrieved July 2008, from http://www.consiglio.regione.toscana.it/corecom/att_studio/ricerche.htm

CORECOM. (2005). Guida alla comunicazione in Toscana. Retrieved July 2008, from http://www.consiglio.regione.toscana.it/corecom /GuidaTv/index.asp

CORECOM. (2006). Analisi delle trasmissioni istituzionali del Consiglio Regionale della Toscana 2004-2005. I quaderni del Corecom. Retrieved September 2008, from http://www.consiglio.regione.toscana.it/corecom/att_studio/ricerche.htm

CORECOM. (2006). Ecologia della mente. Ambienti sostenibili per contesti comunicativi, sociali e produttivi. I quaderni del Corecom. Retrieved September 2008, from http://www.consiglio.regione.toscana.it/corecom/att_studio/ricerche.htm

CORECOM. (2006). La Toscana nel Sistema delle Comunicazioni. Situazioni e Tendenze. I quaderni del Corecom. Regione Toscana. Retrieved July 2008, form http://www.consiglio.regione.toscana.it/corecom/att_studio/ricerche.htm

CORECOM. (2007). Come comunica l'Assemblea Toscana. I quaderni del Corecom. Retrieved September 2008, from http://www.consiglio.regione.toscana.it/corecom/att_studio/ricerche.htm

CORECOM. Law N.22/2002. Retrieved July 2008, from http://www.consiglio.regione.toscana.it/corecom/normativa_doc/leg_22_2002.htm

CORECOM. Statistical data. Retrieved July 2008, from http://www.consiglio.regione.toscana.it/corecom/

Corey, K. E., & Wilson, M. I. (2006). Urban and regional technology planning. New York: Routledge.

Cornelius, P. & Kogut, B. (2003). Creating the Responsible Firm: In Search for a New Corporate Governance Paradigm. *German Law Review, 4* (1).

Cottle, S. (Ed.). (2003). Media Organization and Production. London: Sage Publications.

Cozza, M. (2008). Narratives on platform: stories for women in computer science. *Int. J. Cont. Engineering Education and Life-Long Learning, 18*(2), 197–213. doi:10.1504/IJCEELL.2008.017376

Crampton, C. D., & Hinds, P. J. (2004). Subgroup dynamics in internationally distributed teams: ethnocentrism or cross-national learning? In B. Staw, & R. Kramer, (Eds.) *Research in Organizational Behavior* (pp. 213-263). Greenwich, CT: JAI Press.

Cronin, M. A., & Weingart, L. R. (2007). Representational gabs, information processing, and conflict in functionally diverse teams. *Academy of Management Review, 32*(3).

Currier, D. (2003). Feminist Technological Futures: Deleuze and Body/Technology Assemblages. *Feminist Theory, 4*(3), 321–338. doi:10.1177/14647001030043005

Cutting-Decelle, A.-F., Young, B. I., Das, B. P., Case, K., Rahimifard, S., Anumba, C. J., & Bouchlaghem, D. M. (2007). A review of approaches to supply chain communications: from manufacturing to construction. *ITcon - . Electronic Journal of Information Technology in Construction*, (12): 73–102.

Daft & Lengel. (1986). Organizational information requirements, media richness and structural design. *Management Science, 32*(5), 554–571. doi:10.1287/mnsc.32.5.554

Dainty, A., Moore, D., & Murray, M. (2006). *Communication in construction: Theory and practice.* Oxon: Taylor & Francis.

Daly, H. E. (1973). *Towards a Steady State Economy.* San Francisco: Freeman.

Daly, H. E. (1991). *Steady-State Economics* (2nd ed.). Washington, DC: Island Press

Davenport, Th. H., & Prusak, L. (1998). *Working Knowledge: How Organizations Manage What They Know.* Boston: Harvard Business School Press.

Davis, M. (1992). Fortress Los Angeles: the Militarization of Urban Space. In M. Sorkin, (Ed.), *Variations on a Theme Park* (pp.154-180). New York: Noonday Press.

de Certeau, M. (1984). *The practice of everyday life.* Los Angeles: University of California Press.

De Ruggieri, F., & Pugliese, A. C. (Eds.). (2006). *Futura. Genere e tecnologia.* Roma: Meltemi.

DeFilippi, R. J., & Arthur, M. (1998). Paradox in project-based enterprises: the case of film making. *California Management Review, 40*(2), 125–140.

Dhir, K. S., & Góké-Paríolá, A. (2002). The case for language policies in multinational corporations. *Corporate Communications: An International Journal, 7*(4), 241–251. doi:10.1108/13563280210449822

Distefano, J. J., & Maznevski, M. L. (2000). Creating value with diverse teams in global management. *Organizational Dynamics, 29*(1), 45–63. doi:10.1016/S0090-2616(00)00012-7

Djukic, A. (2004). Internet kao podrska razvoju sela. In M. Ralevic (Ed.), *Planiranje i uredjenje sela i ruralnih podrucja,* (pp. 219-231). Srbija, Banja Vrujici: Udruzenje urbanista Srbije, *eSEEurope Agenda for the Development of the Information Society* (n.d.). Retrieved from www.eseeuropeconference.org/agenda.pdf

Djukic, A., & Colic, R. (2001). Moguce transformacije razvoja seoskih naselja. In M. Ralevic, R. Malobabic & R. Bogdanovic (Ed.), *Selo u Promenama,* (pp. 171-177). Beograd, Srbija: Udruzenje urbanista Srbije.

Dobers, P. (1997). *Organising Strategies of Environmental Control: towards a decentralisation of the Swedish environmental control repertoire.* Stockholm, Sweden: Nerenius & Santérus Förlag.

Dodge, M. (1999). Measuring and mapping the geographies of Cyberspace: a research note. NETCOM, 1(2), 53–66.

Dodge, M., & Kitchin, R. (2001). Mapping Cyberspace. London: Routledge.

Donaldson, T., & Eerhane, P. (2008). *Ethical Issues in Business, A philosophical approach,* (8th ed.). Upper Saddle River, NJ: Pearson Prentice Hall.

Dourish, P., & Bly, S. (1992). Portholes: Supporting Awareness in a Distributed Work Group. In *Proceedings of the SIGCHI conference on Human factors in computing systems* (pp. 541-547).

Doyle, S., & Batty, M. (1998). *Vitrual Regeneration.* London, UK: Centre for Advanced Spatial Analysis, University College London.

Drewe, P. (2000). *ICT and Urban Form Urban Planning and Design- Off The Beaten Track,* Design Studio Study, Faculty of Architecture, Delft University of Technology, Delft.

Dryzek, J. (2005). *The Politics of the Earth: Environmental Discourses* (2nd ed). Oxford, UK: Oxford University Press.

Durnell Cramton, C. (2001). The shared knowledge problem and its consequences for dispersed collaboration. *Organization Science, 12*(39), 346–371. doi:10.1287/orsc.12.3.346.10098

Edwards, P. N. (1990). The army and the microworld: computers and the politics of gender identity. *Signs: Journal of Women in Culture and Society, 16*(1), 102–127. doi:10.1086/494647

Ekostaden web site (n.d.). City of Malmö, Sweden. Retrieved September 14, 2004 from http://www.ekostaden.com/pdf/en_hallbar_stad_eng.pdf http://www.ekostaden.com/pdf/det_grona_bo01_eng.pdf http://www.ekostaden.com/pdf/vectura_eng.pdf

Ekstedt, E., Lundin, R. A., & Wirdenius, H. (1992). Conceptions and renewal in Swedish construction companies . *European Management Journal, 10*(2), 202–209. doi:10.1016/0263-2373(92)90070-K

Elkington, J. (1999). *Cannibals with Forks: The Triple Bottom Line of 21st Century Business.* Oxford, UK: Capstone Publishing Limited.

Elkinton, J. (2004). Enter the triple bottom line. In A. Henriques & J. Richardson, (Eds.) *The triple bottom line Does it all add up? Assessing the sustainability of business and CSR* (pp.1-17). Earthscan: London.

Elmhester, K. (2008). *Småföretag i strategiska nätverk.* Linköping Studies in Science and Technology Dissertations, No.1217

Emling, E. (2000). *Svenskt familjeföretagande.* Stockholm: EFI.

Epstein, M. (2008). *Making Sustainability Work: Best Practices in Managing and Measuring Corporate Social, Environmental and Economic Impacts.* Sheffield, UK: Greenleaf Publishing Limited.

Ercoskun, O. Y. (2007). *Ecological and Technological (Eco-Tech) Design for A Sustainable City: A Case Study on Gudul, Ankara.* Unpublished doctoral dissertation, Gazi University, Ankara, Turkey.

Eriksson-Zetterquist, U. (2007). Editorial: Gender and New Technologies. *Gender, Work and Organization, 14*(4), 305–311. doi:10.1111/j.1468-0432.2007.00345.x

Essed, P. (1996). *Diversity, Color, and Culture*. Amherst: University of Massachusetts Press.

Etzkowitz, H., & Leydesdorff, L. (2000). The dynamics of innovation: from National Systems and "Mode 2" to a Triple Helix of university-industry-government relations. *Research Policy, 29*, 109–123. doi:10.1016/S0048-7333(99)00055-4

Faraj, S., & Sproull, L. (2000). Coordinating expertise in software development teams. *Management Science, 46*(12), 1554–1568. doi:10.1287/mnsc.46.12.1554.12072

Faulkner, W. (2000). The Power and the Pleasure? A Research Agenda for "Making Gender Stick" to Engineers. *Science, Technology & Human Values, 25*(1), 87–119. doi:10.1177/016224390002500104

Faulkner, W., & Lie, M. (2007). Gender in the Information Society: Strategies of Inclusion. *Gender, Technology and Development, 11*(2), 157–177. doi:10.1177/097185240701100202

Feely, A. J., & Harzing, A.-W. (2003). Language management in multinational companies. *International Journal of Cross Cultural Management, 10*(2), 37–53. doi:10.1108/13527600310797586

Femenías, P. (2004). *Demonstration projects for Sustainable Building: Towards a strategy for Sustainable Development in the building sector based on Swedish and Dutch experience*. Dissertation thesis, Chalmers University of technology, Sweden.

Fennell, D. A. (2007). Ecotourism. London: Routledge Publishing.

Fiedler, F. E. (1966). The effect of leadership and cultural heterogeneity on group performance: A test of the contingency model. *Journal of Experimental Social Psychology, 2*, 237–264. doi:10.1016/0022-1031(66)90082-5

Firmino, R. J., Duarte, F., & Moreira, T. (2008). Pervasive Technologies and Urban Planning in the Augmented City . *Journal of Urban Technology, 15*(2), 77–93. doi:10.1080/10630730802401983

Fiske, J. (1990). *Kommunikationsteorier. En introduction*. Wahlström & Widstrand, Stockholm.

Flichy, P. (n.d.). *Linnovation technique. Récents développements en sciences sociales. Vers une nouvelle théorie de linnovation*. Paris: La Découverte.

Foldy, E. G. (2003). Managing diversity: Power and identity in organizations. In I. Aaltio, & A. Mills (Eds.), *Gender, Identity and the Culture of Organizations*, (pp. 92-112). London: Routledge.

Fontana, A., & Frey, J. H. (1994). Interviewing: The art of the science. In N. Denzin, & Y. Lincoln (Eds.), *Handbook of qualitative research*, (pp. 361-376). London: Sage.

Forsberg, P. (2001). *Berättelser och omdömen i enredares vardag* (Judging and storytelling in the everyday life of a ship owner). Gothenburg, Sweden: BAS.

Forsberg, P. (2009). Crowding-in and crowding-out of the community principle. *International Journal of Critical Accounting, 1*(3).

Forsberg, P., & Westerdahl, S. (2007). For the sake of serving the broader community: sea piloting compared with auditing. *Critical Perspectives on Accounting, 8*, 7.

Forsgren, O. (2005). C West Churchman and the new world of co-design. In J.P. van Gigch & J. (Eds.), *McIntyre Rescuing the Enlightenment from Itself*, (Vol. 1 in *Churchman's Legacy and Related Works*). Amsterdam: Springer/Kluwer.

Foss, N. J., & Pedersen, T. (2002). Transferring knowledge in MNCs: the role of sources of subsidiaries knowledge and organizational context. *Journal of International Management, 8*, 49–67. doi:10.1016/S1075-4253(01)00054-0

Fountain, J. E. (2000). Constructing the information society: women, information technology, and design. *Technology in Society, 22*, 45–62. doi:10.1016/S0160-791X(99)00036-6

Fredendall, L., & Hill, E. (2001). *Basics in Supply Chain Management*. Boca Raton, FL: St. Lucie Press.

Friedich, S., & Schoaafsma, M. (1999). *Cyberspace and the Loss of the Concentracion and Centrifugation*. Paper presented in TAN 3 Conference report. Berlin, Germany.

Friedman (1962). Capitalism and Freedom. University of Chicago Press.

Friedman, J. 1994. *Cultural Identity and Global Process*. London: Sage Publications.

Friedman, M. (1970, September 13). The social responsibility of business is to increase its profits. *New York Times Magazine*.

Friedman, Y. (1980). *A better life in towns*. Brussels: EU, Council of Europe.

Fulk, J., & DeSanctis, G. (1995). Electronic communication and changing organizational forms. *Organization Science, 6*(4), 337–349. doi:10.1287/orsc.6.4.337

Gabberty, J. W., & Thomas, J. D. E. (2006). Modeling Creativity For The Multinational Firm. *International Business & Economics Research Journal, 5*, 73–76.

Gadde, L.-E., Huemer, L., & Håkansson, H. (2003). Strategizing in industrial networks. *Industrial Marketing Management, 32*, 357–364. doi:10.1016/S0019-8501(03)00009-9

Gajjala, R., & Mamidipudi, A. (1999). Cyberfeminism, technology, and international "development." . *Gender and Development, 7*(2), 8–16. doi:10.1080/741923122

Galbraith, J. (1973). *Designing complex organizations*. Reading, MA: Addison-Wesley Publishing Company.

Gann, D. M., & Salter, A. (2000). Innovation in project-based, service-enhanced firms: the construction of complex products and systems. *Research Policy, 29*(7-8), 955–972. doi:10.1016/S0048-7333(00)00114-1

Garfinkel, H. (1967/2002). *Studies in Ethnomethodology*. Cambridge, UK: Polity Press.

Gattorna, J. & Walters, D. (1996). *Managing the Supply Chain: A Strategic Perspective*. Hampshire.

Gauzin-Müller, D. (2002). *Sustainable Architecture And Urbanism*. Berlin: Birkhäuser.

Gaver, W. W. (1992). The Affordances of Media Spaces for Collaboration. In *Proceedings of the 1992 ACM conference on Computer-supported Cooperative Work* (pp. 17-24).

Gaver, W., Moran, T., MacLean, A., Lövstrand, L., Dourish, P., Carter, K., & Buxton, W. (1992). Realizing a Video Environment: Europarc's Rave System. In *Proceedings of the SIGCHI Conference on Human Factors in Computing Systems*, (pp. 27-35).

Gherardi, S. (1995). *Gender, Symbolism and Organizational Cultures*. London: Sage.

Giddens, A. (1984/2004). *The Constitution of Society*. Cambridge, UK: Polity Press.

Gillespie, A. (2001). *The Illusion of Progress: Unsustainable Development in International Law and Policy*. London, UK: Earthscan Publications Ltd.

Glad, W. (2008). Individuell mätning - mjuk reglering för minskad energianvändning i hyreslägenheter. In *Vardagsteknik: energi och IT: forskning om hållbar användning av samhällets IT- och energisystem*. Stockholm: Carlsson.

Glasson, J., Therivel, R., & Chadwick, A. (2005). *Introduction to Environmental Impact Assessment* (3rd ed.). London, UK: Routledge.

Gluch, P. (2000). *Managerial Environmental Accounting in Construction Projects - Discussions on its Usability and Role in Decision Making*. Göteborg, Sweden: Chalmers University of Technology.

Gluch, P. (2005). *Building green – Perspectives on environmental management in construction*. Dissertation thesis, Chalmers University of technology, Sweden.

Gluch, P. (2006). *Effektivare miljöinformation i byggprojekt Illustrationer från ett tunnelprojekt.* Göteborg, Sweden: Chalmers Repro.

Gluch, P., & Baumann, H. (2004). The life cycle costing (LCC) approach: a conceptual discussion of its usefulness for environmental decision-making. *Building and Environment, 39*(5), 571–580. doi:10.1016/j.buildenv.2003.10.008

Goleman, D. (1995). *Emotional Intelligence.* New York: Bantam books.

Goodall, K., & Roberts, J. (2003). Only connect: teamwork in the multinational. *Journal of World Business, 38,* 150–164. doi:10.1016/S1090-9516(03)00008-7

Goode, W. J. (1963). *World Revolution and Family Patterns.* New York: The Free Press.

Goold, M., & Campbell, A. (1987). *Strategies and Styles. The role of centers in managing diversified corporations.* Oxford, UK: Blackwell.

Graham, S. (2002). Bridging Urban Digital Divides? Urban Polarisation and Information and Communications Technologies (ICTs). *Urban Studies (Edinburgh, Scotland), 39*(1), 33–56. doi:10.1080/00420980220099050

Graham, S. (Ed.). (2004) The Cybercities Reader. London: Routledge.

Graham, S., & Marvin, S. (1996). Telecommunications and the City: Electronic Spaces, Urban Place. New York: Routledge.

Graham, S., & Marvin, S. (1999). Planning Cyber-Cities? Integrating Telecommunications into Urban Planning. *The Town Planning Review, 70*(1), 89–114.

Graham, S., & Marvin, S. (2001) Splintering Urbanism: Networked Infrastructures, Technological Mobilities, and the Urban Condition. London: Routledge.

Gray, R. (2002). The social accounting project and privileging engagement, imaginings, new accountings and pragmatism over critique? *Accounting, Organizations and Society, 27*(7). doi:10.1016/S0361-3682(00)00003-9

Gray, R., & Milke, M. J. (2002). Sustainability Reporting: Who's kidding whom? *Chartered Accountants Journal of New Zealand., 81*(6), 66–70.

Gray, R., Dey, C., Owen, D., Evans, R., & Zadek, D. (1997). Struggling with the praxis of social accounting: stakeholders, accountability, audits and procedures. *Accounting, Auditing & Accountability Journal, 10*(3). doi:10.1108/09513579710178106

Grayson, D., & Hodges, A. (2004). *Corporate social opportunity!: 7 steps to make corporate social responsibility work for your business Greenleaf Pub.* Sheffield

Gregory, D., & Urry, J. (Eds.). (1985). *Social Relations and Spatial Structures.* London: Macmillan.

Grey, S., & Healy, G. (2004). Women and IT contracting work – a testing process. *New Technology, Work and Employment, 19*(1), 30–42. doi:10.1111/j.1468-005X.2004.00126.x

Griffin, A., & Hauser, J. R. (1992). Patterns of communication among marketing, engineering and manufacturing – a comparison between two new product teams. *Management Science, 38*(3), 360–373. doi:10.1287/mnsc.38.3.360

Griffith, D., A. (2002). The role of communication competencies in international business relationship development. *Journal of World Business, 37,* 256–265. doi:10.1016/S1090-9516(02)00092-5

Grönlund, Å. (2000). *Managing electronic services: A Public Service Perspective.* London: Springer.

Gross National Happiness (1999). Report of the Centre for Bhutan Studies, Thimphu, Bhutan.

Grübler, A. (1990). *The Rise and Fall of Infrastructures.* Heidelberg, Germany: Physica-Verlag.

Gudmunson, D., Hartman, E. A., & Tower, C. B. (1999). Strategic Orientation: Differences between Family and Nonfamily Firms. *Family Business Review, 12*(1).

Gudykunst, W. B., & Kim, Y. Y. (1997). *Communicating with strangers: an approach to intercultural communication* (3rd Ed). New York: McGraw-Hill.

Gulledge, T. (2006). What is integration . *Industrial Management & Data Systems, 106*(1), 5–20. doi:10.1108/02635570610640979

Gupta, A., & Govindarajan, V. (2000). Knowledge flows within multinational corporations. *Strategic Management Journal, 21*, 473–496. doi:10.1002/(SICI)1097-0266(200004)21:4<473::AID-SMJ84>3.0.CO;2-I

Gupta, A., & Govindarajan, V. (2001). Building an effective global business team. *Sloan Management Review*, (Summer): 63–71.

Gupta, A., & Govindarajan, V. (2001). Converting global presence into global competitive advantage. *The Academy of Management Executive, 15*(2), 45–56.

Gupta, A., & Govindarajan, V. (2002). Cultivating a global mindset. *The Academy of Management Executive, 16*(1), 116–126.

Gustavsson, E. (2005). Virtual Servants: Stereotyping Female Front-Office Employees on the Internet. *Gender, Work and Organization, 12*(5), 400–419. doi:10.1111/j.1468-0432.2005.00281.x

Haasis, H. D., & Kriwald, T. (2001). *Wissensmanagement in Produktion und Umweltschutz*. Berlin: Springer.

Haasis, H.-D. (1997). Ein Überblick über Betriebliche Umweltinformationssysteme. *uwf* 3/97, 4-6.

Haastrup, P., & Wurtz, J. (2007). *Environmental Data Exchange Network for Inland Water*. The Amsterdam: Elsevier Science & Technology.

Hagedorn-Rasmussen, P., & Kamp, A. (2003). *Mangfoldighedsledelse: mellem vision og ledelse*. København, Denmark: Socialforskningsinstituttet.

Hagel, J., & Armstrong, A. (1997). *Net gain - expanding markets through virtual communities*. Boston: Harvard Business School Press.

Håkansson, H. (Ed.). (1982). *International Marketing and Purchasing of Industrial Goods - An Interaction Approach*. Chichester, UK: Wiley.

Håkansson, H., & Snehota, I. (1995). *Developing Relationships in Business Networks*. London: Routledge.

Hall, J. (2000). Supply Chain Dynamics. *Journal of Cleaner Production, 8*(6), 455–471. doi:10.1016/S0959-6526(00)00013-5

Hall, J. (2006). Environmental supply chain innovation, In J. Sarkis (Ed.). *Greening the supply chain*, (pp. 233-249).

Hambrick, D. C., Cho, T. S., & Chen, C. C. (1996). The influence of top management team heterogeneity on firms' competitive moves. *Administrative Science Quarterly, 41*, 659–684. doi:10.2307/2393871

Hambrick, D. C., Davison, S. C., Snell, S. A., & Snow, C. C. (1998). When Groups Consist of Multiple Nationalities. *Organization Studies, 19*(2), 181–206. doi:10.1177/017084069801900202

Hambrick, D., Davison, S., Snell, S., & Snow, C. (1998). When groups consist of multiple nationalities: towards a new understanding of the implications. *Organization Studies, 19*(2), 181–205. doi:10.1177/017084069801900202

Hancock, T. (1993). Strategic Directions for Community Sustainability", publication of the B.C. Roundtable on the Environment and the Economy, Canada.

Hängst, M., & Sol, H. G. (2001). The Impact of Information and Communication Technology on Interorganizational Level. *International Conference on System Sciences, Hawaii, 2001.*

Hansson, S. O. (2007). What is technological science? *Studies in History and Philosophy of Science, 38*, 523–527. doi:10.1016/j.shpsa.2007.06.003

Haraway, D. (1988). Situated Knowledges: The Science Question in Feminism and the Privilege of Partial Perspective. *Feminist Studies, 14*(3), 575–599. doi:10.2307/3178066

Hardi, P. (2007). The long and winding road of sustainable development evaluation In C. George, & C. Kirkpatrick, (Eds). *Impact Assessment and Sustainable Development – European Practice and Experience* (pp.15-30). Cheltenham, UK: Edward Elgar Publishing Limited.

Hardin, G. (1967). The Tragedy of Commons. In D. VanDeVeer, & C. Pierce, (Eds.) *The Environmental Ethics & Policy Book* (2nd ed.). London, UK: Wadsworth Publishing Company.

Harmsen, D.-M., Hiessl, H., Lang, J., Matuschewski, A., & Zoche, P. (1998). *Betriebliche Umweltinformationssysteme: Entwicklungstrends und Anwenderbedarf zur Unterstützung des betrieblichen Umweltmanagements*, unpublished research report, Karlsruhe.

Harrison, D. A., & Klein, K. J. (2007). What's the difference? Diversity constructs as separation, variety, or disparity in organizations. *Academy of Management Review, 32*(4).

Harty, C. (2005). Innovation in construction: a sociology of technology approach. *Building Research and Information, 33*(6), 512–522. doi:10.1080/09613210500288605

Harvey, D. (1990) *The Condition Of Postmodernity.* Cambridge, MA: Blackwell.

Harvey, D. (2000). *Spaces of Hope.* Berkley, CA: U of California Press.

Hearn, J. (2004). From Hegemonic Masculinity to the Hegemony of Men. *Feminist Theory, 5*(49), 49–72. doi:10.1177/1464700104040813

Heath, C., & Luff, P. (1992). Collaboration and Control: Crisis Management and Multimedia Technology in London Underground Line Control Rooms. *Journal of Computer Supported Cooperative Works, 1*(1), 24–48.

Heath, C., Hindmarsh, J., & Luff, P. (1999). Interaction in Isolation: The Dislocated World of the London Underground Train Driver. *Sociology, 33*(3), 555–575.

Hedetoft, U. (2003). *The Global Turn - National encounters with the World.* Aalborg, Denmark: Aalborg University Press.

Heinonen, K. (2004). Reconceptualizing customer perceived value – the value of time and place. *Managing Service Quality, 14*(2/3), 205–215. doi:10.1108/09604520410528626

Helo, P., & Szekely, B. (2005). Logistics information systems – An analysis of software solutions for supply chain co-ordination. *Industrial Management & Data Systems, 105*(1), 5–18. doi:10.1108/02635570510575153

Henderson, J. K. (2005). Language diversity in international management teams. *International Studies of Management and Organization, 35*(1), 66–82.

Henriksson, G. (2008). *Stockholmarnas resvanor - mellan trängselskatt och klimatdebatt.* Stockholm: Avdelningen för miljöstrategisk analys – fms, KTH Royal Institute of Technology. *TRITA-INFRA-FMS No., 2008,* 5.

Henriques, A., & Richardson, J. (Eds.). (2004). *The triple bottom line: does it all add up?* Earthscan: London, UK.

Henwood, F. (1993). Establishing Gender Perspectives on Information Technology: Problems. Issues and Opportunities. In E. Green, J. Owen & D. Pain (Eds.), *Gendered by Design? Information Technology and Office Systems* (pp. 31-49).

Hepworth, M. E. (1990). Geography of the Information Economy. New York: Guilford.

Herring, S. C. (1994). *Gender differences in computer-mediated communication: bringing familiar baggage to the new frontier.* Paper presented at the American Library Association annual convention, Miami. ID (2001, May 23). Gender Differences in CMC: Findings and Implications. *CPSR Newsletter, 18*(1). Retrivied from http://cpsr.org/issues/womenintech/herring/

Hervik, P. (1999). Forskellighedens logik: Fremstillingen, forestillingen og forskningen. In P. Hervik (Ed.), *Den generelle forskellighed: Danske svar på den stigende multikulturalisme,* (pp. 15-50). København, Denmark: Hans Reitzels Forlag.

Hill, R. C., & Bowen, P. A. (1997). Sustainable construction: principles and a framework for attainment. *Construction Management and Economics, 15*(3), 223–239. doi:10.1080/014461997372971

Hilty, L. (2006). The relevance of information and communication technologies for environmental sustainability – A prospective simulation study. *Environmental Modelling & Software, 21*, 1618–1629. doi:10.1016/j.envsoft.2006.05.007

Hilty, L. (2007). Nachhaltige Informationsgesellschaft: Einfluss moderner Informations- und Kommunikationstechnologien. In R. Isenmann, M. v. Hauff (Ed.), *Industrial Ecology: Mit Ökologie zukunftsorientiert wirtschaften*, (pp. 189-208). München.

Hilty, L. M., & Rautenstrauch, C. (1995). Betriebliche Umweltinformatik, In B. Page, L. Hilty, M. Lorenz (Ed.), *Umweltinformatik: Informatikmethoden für den Umweltschutz und Umweltforschung*, (2nd Ed., pp. 295-312). Handbuch der Informatik Band 13.3, München, Wien, Oldenbourg.

Hirsh, B., & Bishop, D. (2000). (Ed.) *Computer in Education*. New York: Dushkin/McGraw-Hill.

Hoegl, M., & Gemuenden, H. G. (2001). Teamwork quality and the success of innovative projects: a theoretical concept and empirical evidence. *Organization Science, 12*(4), 435–449. doi:10.1287/orsc.12.4.435.10635

Hoegl, M., & Weinkauf, K. (2005). Managing task interdependencies in multi-team projects: a longitudinal study. *Journal of Management Studies, 42*(6), 1287–1308. doi:10.1111/j.1467-6486.2005.00542.x

Högdahl, E. (2003). *Göra gata. Om gränser och kryphål på Möllevången och i Kapstaden*. Gidlunds förlag. Etnologiska institutionen, Lunds universitet.

Homan, A. C., Hollenbeck, J. R., Humphrey, S. E., van Knippenberg, D., Ilgen, D. R., & Van Kleef, G. A. (In print). Facing differences with an open mind: Openness to experience, salience of intra-group differences, and performance of diverse work groups. *Academy of Management Journal*.

Hoopes, D. G., & Postrel, S. (1999). Shared knowledge, "glitches" and product development performance. *Strategic Management Journal, 20*, 837–865. doi:10.1002/(SICI)1097-0266(199909)20:9<837::AID-SMJ54>3.0.CO;2-I

Hsu, L. (2005). Supply chain management effects on performance for interaction between suppliers and buyers. *Industrial Management & Data Systems, 105*(7), 857–875. doi:10.1108/02635570510616085

Huyer, S., & Carr, M. (2002). Information and Communication Technologies: A Priority for Women. *Gender, Technology and Development, 6*(1), 85–100. doi:10.1177/097185240200600105

ID. (1991). *Simians, Cyborgs, and Women: The Reinvention of Nature*. New York: Routledge.

ID. (1992). The circuit of technology. Gender, identity and power. In R. Silverstone & E. Hirsch (Eds.), *Consuming Technologies. Media and Information in Domestic Spaces* (pp. 32-47). London: Routledge.

ID. (1994). Feminist Theories of Technology. In S. Jasanoff, et al. (Eds.), *Handbook of science and technology studies* (pp. 189-204). Thousand Oaks, CA: Sage.

ID. (1995). *Life on the Screen: Identity in the Age of the Internet*. New York: Simon and Schuster.

ID. (1997). *Modest_Witness@Second_Millennium. Female Man Meets Onco Mouse*. London: Routledge.

ID. (2000). From the Woman Question in Technology to the Technology Question in Feminism. *European Journal of Women's Studies, 7*(2), 209–227. doi:10.1177/135050680000700209

ID. (2001). The technology question in feminism: a view from feminist technology studies. *Women's Studies International Forum, 24*(1), 79–95. doi:10.1016/S0277-5395(00)00166-7

ID. (2002). Exploring the gender question in critical information systems. *Journal of Information Technology, 17*, 59–67. doi:10.1080/02683960210145959

ID. (2002). Gendering the Internet: Claims, Controversies and Cultures. *European Journal of Communication, 17*(5), 5–23.

ID. (2004). *Techno Feminism.* Cambridge, UK: Polity Press.

ID. (2008). Life in the fast lane? Towards a sociology of technology and time. *The British Journal of Sociology, 59*(1), 59–77. doi:10.1111/j.1468-4446.2007.00182.x

Imagawa, N. (n.d.). *Metamorphosis of Space: Long-life space connecting time-thoughts on materials and structures-difference between possible and impossible.* Retrieved from http://www.um.u-tokyo.ac.jp/dm2k-umdb/publish_db/books/va/english/virtual/08.html

Inmon, W. H., Zachman, J. A., & Geiger, J. G. (1997). *Data stores, data warehousing, and the Zachman framework, Managing enterprise knowledge.* New York: McGraw Hill.

Integer web site "Intelligent and Green Projects"

INTELCITY. (2003). EU Final Report, VTT Finland.

IRPET. (2008). Tuscany Info and Databases. Retrieved June 2008, from http://www.irpet.it

Isaksson, A., Linde, A., & Vanyushyn, V. (2009). Environmental management in construction companies: Decisions, technologies and effects. *Proceeding of 5th Nordic Conference on Construction Economics and Organisation, 1, Reykjavík, Iceland* (pp. 193-204)

ISTAG. (2006). *Report from the Information Society Technologies Advisory Group.* Retrieved from http://www.cordis.lu/ist/istag.htm

ISTAT. (2007). Le Tecnologie dell'Informazione e della Comunicazione: Disponibilita' delle Famiglie e Utilizzo degli Individui. Retrieved June 2008, from http://www.istat.it

Ivić, I., Marojević, S., Chinapah, V., Uvalić Trumbić, S., Ivanović, S., Damjanović, R., et al. (2001). *Sveobuhvatna analiza sistema obrazovanja u SRJ.* Beograd, Srbija: UNICEF.

Izza, M. (2007). *An overview of Corporate Responsibility - Institute of Chartered Accountants in England & Wales,* July, 2007

Jacobs, B., Lûtzen, D. C., & Plum, E. (2001). *Mangfoldighed som virksomhedsstrategi - På vej mod den inkluderende organisation.* København, Denmark: Nordisk Forlag.

Jacobsson, B. (2006). Standardization and Expert Knowledge. In N. Brunsson, & B. Jacobsson, et al (Eds) *A World of Standards* (pp. 40-49). Oxford, UK: Oxford University Press.

Jacobsson, M. (2008a). *Samordning och kommunikation i ett anläggningsprojekt □ Mellan en laminerad A3-karta och ett dike.* Sweden . *BA-Publications, 2008,* 201.

Jacobsson, M. (2008b). Liaison devices in an information reduction process - Observations from a Swedish case stud, *EDEN seminar and Summer Workshop in Project Management.* Lille, France, 18-22 Aug. 2008

Jacobsson, M. (2009). Understanding project communication in a construction process: The importance of project liaisons, *Proceeding of 5th Nordic Conference on Construction Economics and Organisation, 1, Reykjavík, Iceland,* (pp. 155-166).

Janson, M., Mörtberg, C., & Berg, E. (2007). Old Dreams, New Means: an Exploration of Visions and Situated Knowledge in Information Technology. *Gender, Work and Organization, 14*(4), 371–387. doi:10.1111/j.1468-0432.2007.00349.x

Janssens, M., Lambert, J., & Steyaert, C. (2004). Developing language strategies for international companies: The contribution of translation studies. *Journal of World Business, 39,* 414–430. doi:10.1016/j.jwb.2004.08.006

Jarvenpaa, S. L., & Leidner, D. E. (1999). Communication and trust in global virtual teams. *Organization Science, 10*(6), 791–815. doi:10.1287/orsc.10.6.791

Jenkins, R. (1997). *Rethinking Ethnicity - Arguments and Explorations.* London: Sage Publications.

Jensen, M., & Meckling, W. (1994). The nature of man. *Journal of Applied Corporate Finance,* (Summer).

Jonker, J., & Witte, M. (Eds.). (2006). *Management models for corporate social responsibility.* Heidelberg: Springer Publication.

Jönsson, S. (1973). *Decentralisering och utveckling.* Gothenburg, Sweden: BAS.

Kahn, H., Bronjn, W., & Martel, L. (1976). *The next 200 years.* New York: Hudson Institute.

Kakihara, M., & Sörensen, C. (2004). Mobile Urban Professionals in Tokyo. *Info, 6.*

Kandachar, P., & Halme, M. (Eds.). (2008). *Sustainability Challenges and Solutions at the Base of the Pyramid. Business, Technology and the Poor.* London: Greenleaf Publishing Ltd.

Karaaslan, S., & Ercoskun, O. Y. (2006). *Eco-Tech Planning for Turkish Cities.* Paper presented at 12th Annual Sustainable Development Research Conference, Hong Kong.

Kayongo, M., & Onyango, P. (1984). *The Sociology of the African Family.* London: Longman.

Kellerman, A. (1993). Telecommunication and Geography. London: Belhaven.

Kellerman, A. (1999). Leading Nations in the Adoption of Communications Media 1975-1995. Urban Geography, 20, 377–389.

Kellerman, A. (2000). Where does it happen? The Location of the Production and Consumption of Web Information. Journal of Urban Technology, 7, 45–61. doi:10.1080/7136 84101doi:10.1080/713684101

Kellerman, A. (2002). The Internet on Earth. A Geography of information. San Francisco: John Wiley & Sons.

Kellerman, A., & Paradiso, M. (2007). The Geographical Location in the Information Age: from Destiny to Opportunity? GeoJournal, 70, 195–211. doi:10.1007/s10708-008-9131-2doi:10.1007/s10708-008-9131-2

Kelly, E., & Dobbin, F. (1998). How Affirmative Action Became Diversity Management - Employer Response to Antidiscrimination Law, 1961 to 1996. *The American Behavioral Scientist, 41*(7), 960–984. doi:10.1177/0002764298041007008

Ketola, T. (Ed.). (2007). *Paradigms of corporate Sustainability.* Vaasan Yliopisoto. Report 146. Proceedings of Track 16, International Development Research Conference 2007.

Kibert, C. J. (2007). The next generation of sustainable construction. *Building Research and Information, 35*(6), 595–601. doi:10.1080/09613210701467040

Kim, Y. Y. (1991). Intercultural communication competence: a systems-theoretic view. In T-S. Toomey & F. Korzenny (Eds.), *International and intercultural communications annual,* (pp. 259-275). Newbury Park, CA: Sage publications.

Kim, Y. Y. (2005). Inquiry in intercultural and development communication. *The Journal of Communication,* (September): 554–577. doi:10.1111/j.1460-2466.2005.tb02685.x

Klein, K. J., & Harrison, D. A. (2007). On the Diversity of Diversity: Tidy Logic, Messier Realities. *Academy of Management Review, 32*(4), 26–34.

Knights, D., & Kerfoot, D. (2004). Between Representations and Subjectivity: Gender Binaries and the Politics of Organizational Transformation. *Gender, Work and Organization, 11*(4), 430–454. doi:10.1111/j.1468-0432.2004.00241.x

Kolarevic, B. (1996). Space, Place, and the Infobahn: Architecture, Urbanism and the Electronic Infromation Age. In *Architecture& Urbanism at the Turn of the III Millennium* []. Beograd, Srbija: Faculty of Architecture University of Belgrade.]. *Proceedings, 1,* 61–69.

Konrad, A. M. (2003). Defining the domain of workplace diversity scholarship. *Group & Organization Management, 28,* 4–16. doi:10.1177/1059601102250013

Korhonen, J. (2002). Two paths of industrial ecology: applying the product-based and geographical approaches. *Journal of Environmental Planning and Management, 45*(1), 39–57. doi:10.1080/09640560120100187

Kostov, Z. (2006). *Global tendecies and local implications: Cyber exslusion and within Western Balkan countries.* Discussion paper 40, Proceedings of the Informing Science & IT Education Conference (InSITE), Centre for the Study of Global Governance, London School of Economics and Political Science, London. Retrieved from http://www.lse.ac.uk/Depts/global/Publications/DiscussionPapers/DP40.pdf

Kotler, P., & Lee, N. (2005). *Corporate social responsibility: doing the most good for your company and your cause.* Hoboken, NJ: John Wiley Publication.

Kotler, P., Bowen, R. J., & Makens, C. J. (2006). Marketing for Hospitality and Tourism. Upper Saddle River, NJ: Pearson Education Inc.

Kotler, P., Haider, D. H., & Rein, I. (2008). Marketing Places: Attracting Investment, Industry, and Tourism to Cities, States, and Nations. New York: The Free Press.

Kraft, J. F., & Siegenthaler, J. K. (1989). Office Automation, Gender, and Change: An Analysis of the Management Literature. *Science, Technology & Human Values, 14*(2), 195–212. doi:10.1177/016224398901400204

Krcmar, H. (2003). *Informationsmanagement. 3.* Aufl. Berlin: Springer.

Kreeb, M., et al. (2005). Web Portals: A Tool for Environmental Management. In L. Hilty, E. K. Seifert, & R. Treibert, (Eds.), *Information Systems for Sustainable Development* (pp. 213-228). Hershey, PA: IGI Global.

Kristoffersen, S., & Ljungberg, F. (1999). Mobile use of IT. In *Proceedings of the 22nd Information Systems Research Seminar in Scandinavia,* IRIS 22.

Kristoffersen, S., & Ljungberg, F. (2000). Mobility: From Stationary to Mobile Work. In K. Braa, C. Sorenssen, & B. Dahlbom (eds.) *Planet Internet.* Lund, Sweden: Studentlitteratur.

Kuhre, W. L. (1998). *ISO 14031- Environmental Performance Evaluation (EPE): Practical Tools for Conducting an Environmental Performance Evaluation.* Upper Saddle River, NJ: Prentice Hall.

Kulp, S., Ofek, E., & Whitaker, J. (2004). Supply-Chain Coordination: How Companies Leverage Information Flows to Generate Value. In T. Harrison, H. Lee, & J. Neale (Ed.), *The Practice of Supply Chain Management: Where Theory and Application Converge,* (Part 2, pp. 91-107). New York.

Kumar, K. (2004). From Post-industrial to Post-modern Societies. New Theories of the Contemporary World. Oxford, UK: Wiley Blackwell.

Kvale, S. (1996). *Interviews - An Introduction to Qualitative Research Interviewing.* Thousand Oaks, CA: Sage.

Kytle, B., & Ruggie, J. (2005). *Corporate Social Responsibility as Risk Management: A Model for Multinationals,* Social Responsibility Initiative Working Paper No. 10. John F. Kennedy School of Government. Boston: Harvard University.

Lagerström, K. (2001). *Transnational projects within multinational corporations.* Uppsala, Sweden: Department of Business Studies, Uppsala University.

Lagerström, K., & Andersson, M. (2003). Creating and sharing knowledge within a transnational team: The development of a global business system. *Journal of World Business, 38,* 84–95. doi:10.1016/S1090-9516(03)00003-8

Lagerström, K., & Andersson, M. (2003). Creation and sharing knowledge within a transnational team – development of a global business system. *Journal of World Business, 38*(2), 84–95. doi:10.1016/S1090-9516(03)00003-8

Lamming, R., & Hampson, J. (1996). The environment as a supply chain management issue. *British Journal of Management, 7,* 45–62. doi:10.1111/j.1467-8551.1996.tb00147.x

Landström, C. (2007). Queering feminist technology studies. *Feminist Theory*, *8*(7), 7–26. doi:10.1177/1464700107074193

Lang, C. (2000). Betriebliche Umweltinformationssysteme auf dem Prüfstand – ein Forschungskonzept. In L. Hilty & R. Schulthess (Ed.), *Strategische und betriebsübergreifende Anwendungen betrieblicher Umweltinformationssysteme*, Marburg, (pp. 47-58).

Lanza, A. (1999). Lo Sviluppo Sostenibile. Bologna, IT: Il Mulino.

Lash, S. (2002). *Critique of Information*. London: Sage.

Latour, B. (1987). *Science in action*. Cambrigde, MA: Harvard University Press.

Latour, B. (1998a). *Artefaktens återkomst. Ett möte mellan organisationsteori och tingens sociologi*. Stockholm: Nerenius & Santérus förlag.

Latour, B. (1998b). Teknik är samhället som gjorts hållbart. In *Artefaktens återkomst. Ett möte mellan organisationsteori och tingens sociologi*. Stockholm: Nerenius & Santérus förlag.

Lauring, J. (2005). *Når organisationen bliver mangfoldig - om vidensdeling og interaktion i etnisk mangfoldige organisationer*. Århus, Denmark: Handelshøjskolen i Århus.

Lauring, J., & Ross, C. (2004). Cultural Diversity and Organisational Effiency. *New Zealand Journal of Employment Relations*, *29*(1), 89–103.

Lawrence, P., & Lorsch, J. (1967). Organization and environment: managing differentiation and integration, Boston, MA: Graduate School of Business Administration.

Lehmann-Waffenschmidt, M. (2007). *Innovations Towards Sustainability: Conditions and Consequenses*. Berlin: Springer.

Leonard, D., & Swap, W. (1999). *When Sparks Fly: Igniting Creativity in Groups*. Cambridge, MA: Harvard Business School Press.

Letmathe, P., Schwarz, E., & Steven, M. (1996). Grundlagen der Umweltberichterstattung. *UE, 4*, 415-443.

Levenson, N. G. (1990). *Educational Pipeline Issues for Women*. Paper presented at Computer Research Association Annual Meeting, Snowbird, UT.

Li, H. Z. (1991). Communicating information in conversations: A cross-cultural comparison. *International Journal of Intercultural Relations*, *23*(3), 387–409. doi:10.1016/S0147-1767(99)00003-6

Lieberman, B. (2007). *Applying an analytical framework - Organize and reuse valuable techniques, tools, and examples*. BioLogic Software Consulting, S. Houstoun.

Liff, S. (1996). Two routes to managing diversity: individual differences or social group characteristics. *Employee Relations*, *19*(1), 11–26. doi:10.1108/01425459710163552

Liff, S., & Wajcman, J. (1996). 'Sameness' and 'Difference' revisited: Which Way Forward for Equal Opportunity Initiatives? *Journal of Management Studies*, *33*(1), 79–94. doi:10.1111/j.1467-6486.1996.tb00799.x

Lin, C., & Tseng, H. (2006). Identifying the pivotal role of participation strategies and information technology application for supply chain excellence. *Industrial Management & Data Systems*, *106*(5), 739–756. doi:10.1108/02635570610666476

Lincoln, Y. S., & Guba, E. G. (1985). *Naturalistic inquiry*. London: Sage Publications.

Lind, M., & Forsgren, O. (2008). Co-design and Web 2.0: Theoretical foundations and application. In Cunningham P., Cunningham M. (Eds.) *Collaboration and the Knowledge Economy: Issues, Applications, Case Studies* (pp. 1105-1112). IOS Press, Amsterdam.

Lind, M., & Rittgen, P. (2009). Challenges of Co-Design: The Case of e-Me. In B. Whitworth & A. de Moor (eds.), *Handbook of Research on Socio-Technical Design and Social Networking Systems*. Hershey, PA: IGI Global

Lind, M., Albinsson, L., Forsgren, O., & Hedman, J. (2007). *Integrated Development, Use and Learning in a Co-design Setting: Experiences from the Incremental Deployment of e-Me, eChallenges e-2007*, The Hague, The Netherlands.

Linderoth, C. J. H., & Jacobsson, M. (2008). Understanding adoption and use of ICT in construction projects through the lens of context, actors and technology. In L. Rischmoller, (Ed.), *Proceeding of CIB W78, Improving the management of construction projects through IT adoption. Talca, Chile,* (pp. 203-212).

Lindgreen, A., & Wynstra, F. (2005). Value in business markets: What do we know? Where are we going? *Industrial Marketing Management, 34*(7), 732–748. doi:10.1016/j.indmarman.2005.01.001

Linstead, A., & Brewis, J. (2004). Editorial: Beyond Boundaries: Towards Fluidity in Theorizing and Practice. *Gender, Work and Organization, 11*(4), 355–362. doi:10.1111/j.1468-0432.2004.00237.x

Litvin, D. R. (2002). The business case for diversity and the iron cage. In B. Czarniawka, & H. Hopfl (Eds.), *Casting the Other: The Production and Maintenance of Inequalities in Work Organizations,* (pp. 20-39). London: Routledge.

Liu, K., Sun, L., & Bennett, K. (2002). Co-Design of Business and IT Systems. *Information Systems Frontiers, 4*(3), 251–256. doi:10.1023/A:1019942501848

Lockwood, C. (2006). Building the green way. *Harvard Business Review, 84*(6), 129–137.

Locoh, T. (1988). L'évolution de la famille en Afrique. In E. Van De Walle, (ed.), *L☐état de la démographie africaine,* (pp. 45-66). Liège, Belgium: UIESP.

Locoh, T. (1988). Structures familiales et changements sociaux. In D. Tabutin (Ed.), *Populations et sociétés en Afrique au sud du Sahara,* (pp. 441-478). Paris: L'Harmattan.

Logan, K. (2001). Seaside Turns 20. *Architecture Week, 0919,* 1–2.

Loosemore, M., & Lee, P. (2002). Communication problems with ethnic minorities in the construction industry. *International Journal of Project Management, 20,* 517–524. doi:10.1016/S0263-7863(01)00055-2

Loretzon, S. (1998). The Role of ICT as a Locational Factor in Peripheral Regions: Examples from 'IT-active' Local Authority Areas in Sweden. NETCOM, 1(2), 303–333.

Loretzon, S. (2004). Call Centres – a Swedish Geographical Perspective Exemplified by Conditions in the West of Sweden. NETCOM, 18, 203–223.

Loretzon, S. (Ed.). (2000). The Use of ICT in a Geographical Context: Research at Gotheborg University, Sweden. NETCOM, 14.

Lowe, E. (1997). Creating by-product resource exchanges: strategies for eco-industrial parks. *Journal of Cleaner Production, 5*(1-2), 57–65. doi:10.1016/S0959-6526(97)00017-6

Luff, P., & Heath, C. (1998). Mobility in collaboration. In *Proceedings of the 1998 ACM conference on Computer supported cooperative work.* Seattle, Washington.

Luke, T. (1994). The Politics of Arcological Utopia: Soleri on Ecology, Architecture and Society. *Telos, 101*(55).

Luke, T. (2005). Neither Sustainable nor Development: Reconsidering Sustainability in Development. *Journal of Sustainable Development, 13,* 228–238. doi:10.1002/sd.284

Lynch, K. (1981). *Good City Form.* Cambridge, MA: The MIT Press

Lyons, A., Coleman, J., Kehoe, D., & Coronado, A. (2004). Performance observation and analysis of an information re-engineered supply chain: a case study of an automotive firm. *Industrial Management & Data Systems, 104*(8), 658–666. doi:10.1108/02635570410561645

Machlup, F. (1984). The Economics of Information and Human Capital. Princeton, NJ: Princeton University Press.

Macintosh J.C.C (1999). The issues, effects and consequences of the Berle-Dodd debate. *Accounting, Organizations and Society,* 24(2), 139-153(15).

Macintosh, N. B., & Baker, C. R. (2002). A literary theory perspective on accounting: towards heteroglossic accounting reports. *Accounting, Auditing & Accountability Journal,* 15(2). doi:10.1108/09513570210425600

Mackie, J. L. (1977). *Ethics. Inventing right and wrong.* Penguin Group: London, UK.

Madden, P., & Weißbrod, I. (2008). *Connected ICT and sustainable development, Forum for the Future.* Menlo Park, CA: Sun Microsystems Publication.

Madinipour, A. (1996). *Design of Urban Space.* New York: John Wiley & Sons.

Mahizhnan, A. (1999). Smart Cities the Singapore Case. *Cities (London, England),* 16(1), 13–18. doi:10.1016/S0264-2751(98)00050-X

Mainardi, (1996). Geografia delle Comunicazioni. Turin, IT: NIS.

Mantei, M. M., Baecker, R. M., Sellen, A. J., Buxton, W. A. S., Milligan, T., & Wellman, B. (1991). Experiences in the Use of a Media Space. In *Proceedings of the SIGCHI Conference on Human Factors in Computing Systems* (pp. 203-208).

Markus, M. L., & Robey, D. (1988). Information technology and organizational change: Causal structure in theory and research. *Management Science,* 34(5), 583–598. doi:10.1287/mnsc.34.5.583

Marlin, A. & Tepper, J. (2003).

Marras, A. (1999). *ECO-TEC Architecture of the In-Between.* New York: Princeton Architectural Press.

Marschan-Piekkari, R., Welch, D. E., & Welch, L. S. (1999b). Adopting a common corporate language: IHRM implications. *International Journal of Human Resource Management,* 10(3), 377–390. doi:10.1080/095851999340387

Marschan-Piekkari, R., Welch, D., & Welch, L. (1999a). In the shadow: the impact of language on structure, power and communication in the multinational. *International Business Review,* 8, 421–440. doi:10.1016/S0969-5931(99)00015-3

Martinez, J. I., & Jarillo, J. C. (1991). Coordination Demands of International Strategies. *Journal of International Business Studies,* 22(3), 429–444. doi:10.1057/palgrave.jibs.8490309

Mason-Jones, R. & Towill, D. (1997). Information enrichment: designing the supply chain for competitive advantage. *Supply chain management,* 2(4), 137-148.

Mattelart, A. (1999). Histoire de l'Utopie Planétaire: de la Cité Prophétique à la Société Globale. Paris, FR: La découverte.

Maznevski, M. L. (1994). Understanding our differences: Performance in decision-making groups with diverse members. *Human Relations,* 47(5), 531–553. doi:10.1177/001872679404700504

Maznevski, M. L., & Chudoba, K. M. (2000). Bridging Space over Time: Global Virtual Team Dynamics and Effectiveness. *Organization Science,* 11(5), 473–492. doi:10.1287/orsc.11.5.473.15200

McAdam, R., & Galloway, A. (2005). Enterprise resource planning and organisational innovation: a management perspective. *Industrial Management & Data Systems,* 105(3), 280–290. doi:10.1108/02635570510590110

McDonough, E. F., Kahn, K. B., & Barczak, G. (2001). An investigation of the use of global, virtual, and colocated new product development teams. *Journal of Product Innovation Management,* 18(2), 110–121. doi:10.1016/S0737-6782(00)00073-4

McDonough, E. III, & Kahn, K. (1996). Using hard and soft technologies for global new product development. *R & D Management,* 26(2), 241–253. doi:10.1111/j.1467-9310.1996.tb00959.x

McDonough, E. III, Kahn, K., & Griffin, A. (1999). Managing communication in global product development teams. *IEEE Transactions on Engineering Management, 46*(4), 375–386. doi:10.1109/17.797960

McLeod, P. L., & Lobe, S. A. (1992). The effects of ethnic diversity on idea generation in small groups. *Academy of Management Executive, Best Papers Proceedings,* (pp. 227-231).

McWilliams, A., Siegel, D. S., & Wright, P. M. (2006). Corporate social responsibility: strategic implications. *Journal of Management Studies, 43*(1), 1–18. doi:10.1111/j.1467-6486.2006.00580.x

Meadows, D., Meadows, D. L., Randers, J., & Behrens, W. (1971). *The Limits to Growth.* New York: Universe Books.

Miege, B. (1997). *La société conquise par la communication,* tome 2. Grenoble, France: PUG.

Miller, D., & Le Breton-Miller, I. (2005). *Managing for the long run: lessons in competitive advantage from great family business.* Boston: Harvard business school press.

Miller, M., Fields, R., Kumar, A., & Ortiz, R. (2000). Leadership and organizational vision in managing a multiethnic and multicultural project team. *Journal of Management Engineering, 16*(6), 18–23. doi:10.1061/(ASCE)0742-597X(2000)16:6(18)

Millikin, F. J., & Martins, L. L. (1996). Searching for common threads: Understanding the multiple effects of diversity in organizational groups. *Academy of Management Review, 21*(2), 402–433. doi:10.2307/258667

Milovanović, D. (2001). Interaktivni urbanizam: novi oblici saradnje podrzani internetom i novim kompjuterskim tehnologijama. In N. Randjelović, & M. Ralevic (Ed.), *Urbani menadzment, urbani marketing i preduzetnistvo,* (pp. 63-71). Beograd, Srbija: Udruzenje urbanista Srbije.

Minas (1987). *Colloque sur la famille en Afrique noire.* Yaoundé, Cameroon: Imprimerie nationale.

MIT (Massachusetts Institute of Technology) Center For Real Estate. (2005). *New Century Cities: Real Estate Value in a Digital World.* Symposium Case Studies Report, 1-24.

Mitchell, W. (1995). *City of Bits: Space, Place and the Infobahn.* Cambridge, MA: MIT Press.

Mitchell, W. (1999). *E-topia: Urban Life, Jim-But Not as We Know It.* Cambridge, MA: MIT Press.

Mitroff, I. I., & Mason, R. O. (1981). *Creating a dialectical social science.* Dordrecht, The Netherlands: Reidel.

Mitropoulos, P., & Tatum, C. B. (1999). Technology adoption decisions in construction organizations. *Journal of Construction Engineering and Management, 125*(5), 330–339. doi:10.1061/(ASCE)0733-9364(1999)125:5(330)

Mitter, S. (2001). *Asian Women in the Digital Economy: Policies for Participation.* Malaysia, UNDP.

Moberg, Å., Hedberg, L., Henriksson, G., Räsänen, M., & Westermark, M. (2008). *Hållbarhetsbedömning av en medieradtjänst-en pilotstudie* (Report from the KTH Centre for Sustainable Communications. No. []. KTH Centre for Sustainable Communications.]. *TRITA-SUS, 2008,* 1.

Mohr, J., & Nevin, J. (1990). Communicating strategies in marketing channels: a theoretical perspective. *Journal of Marketing, 54*(4), 36–51. doi:10.2307/1251758

Mohr, J., Fischer, R., & Nevin, J. (1996). Collaborative communication in interfirm relationships: moderating effects of integration and control. *Journal of Marketing, 50,* 103–115. doi:10.2307/1251844

Molnár, M., Anderson, R., & Ekholm, A. (2007). Benefits of ICT in the construction industry – Characterization of the present situation the house building processes. In D. Rebolj, (Ed.) *Proceeding of CIB 24th W78 Conference Maribor - Bringing ITC knowledge to work. Maribor, Slovenia,* (pp. 423-428).

Monteiro, E. (2003). Integrating health information systems: A critical appraisal. *Methods of Information in Medicine, 42,* 428–432.

Montoya-Weiss, M. M., Massey, A. P., & Song, M. (2001). Getting it together: temporal coordination and conflict management in global virtual teams. *Academy of Management Journal, 44*(6), 1251–1262. doi:10.2307/3069399

Moore, K., Griffiths, M., Richardson, H., & Adam, A. (2008). Gendered Futures? Women, the ICT Workplace and Stories of the Future. *Gender, Work and Organization, 15*(5), 523–542. doi:10.1111/j.1468-0432.2008.00416.x

Mor-Barak, M. E., Cherin, D. A., & Berkman, S. (1998). Organizational and personal dimensions in diversity climate. *The Journal of Applied Behavioral Science, 43*(1), 82–104. doi:10.1177/0021886398341006

Morgan, G. (1988). Accounting as reality construction: towards a new epistemology for accounting practice. *Accounting, Organizations and Society, 13*(5). doi:10.1016/0361-3682(88)90018-9

Mudambi, R. (2002). Knowledge management in multinational firms. *Journal of International Management, 8*, 1–9. doi:10.1016/S1075-4253(02)00050-9

Müller, A. (1995). *Umweltorientiertes betriebliches Rechnungswesen,* (2nd rev. ed.). Munich, Vienna.

Müller-Christ, G. (2001). *Umweltmanagement: Umweltschutz und nachhaltige Entwicklung,* Munich.

Munshi, K. (2004). Social Learning in a Heterogeneous Population: Technology Diffusion in the Indian Green Revolution. *Journal of Development Economics, LXXIII,* 185–215. doi:10.1016/j.jdeveco.2003.03.003

Mvesso, A. (2006). Préface. In F. Pierre, *Intégration des TIC dans le processus enseignement-apprentissage au Cameroun,* éditions terroir, (pp. 11-12).

Nardi, B. A. (1996). Studying Context: A Comparison of Activity Theory, Situated Action Models, and Distributed Cognition. In B. A. Nardi (Ed.), *Context and consciousness: Activity Theory and Human-Computer Interaction.* Cambridge, MA: MIT Press.

Narushige, S. (2000, August). Urban Planning, Information Technology, and Cyberspace. *Journal of Urban Technology, 7*(2), 105. doi:10.1080/713684111

Naughton, J. (1999). *A Brief History of the Future: The Origins of the Internet.* London: Weidenfeld and Nicolson.

Neimanis, A. (2002). *Gender mainstreaming in practice: a Handbook.* UNDP.

Nelson, K. M., & Cooprider, J. G. (1996). The Contribution of Shared Knowledge to IS group performance. *MIS Quarterly,* (December): 409–432. doi:10.2307/249562

Neutopia, D. (1994, July 16). *The feminization of Cyberspace.* Retrieved from http://feminism.eserver.org/gender/cyberspace/feminization-of-cyberspace.txt

Newman, K. (1988). *Falling from Grace; the Experience of Downward Mobility in the American Middle Class.* New York: Vintage Books.

Nisancioglu, S. (2008). *Climate Change and environmental urban planning: Implementations of Haringey Municipality.* Paper Presented at the International Conference on Ecological and Technological Cities, Gazi Uni. Ankara, Turkey.

Nissinen, A. (2007). Developing benchmarks for consumer-oriented life cycle assessment-based environmental information on products, services and consumption patterns. *Journal of Cleaner Production, 15*, 538–549. doi:10.1016/j.jclepro.2006.05.016

Nohria, N., & Ghoshal, S. (1997). The differentiated network: organizing multinational corporations for value creation. San Francisco: Jossey-Bass Inc. Publishers.

Nonaka, I., & Takeuchi, H. (1995). *The Knowledge-creating company.* New York: Oxford University Press.

Norman, R., & Ramirez, R. (1993). From Value Chain to Value Constellation: Designing Interactive Strategy. *Harvard Business Review,* 65–77.

O'Dwyer, B. (2005). The construction of a social account: a case study in an overseas aid agency. *Accounting, Organizations and Society, 30*(3).

Ó'Riain. S. (2004). Networking for a Living. In A. Amin & N. Thrift (Eds.), *The Blackwell Cultural Economy Reader*. London: Blackwell Publishing.

Odendaal, N. (2003). Information and Communication Technology and local governance: understanding the difference between cities in developed and emerging economies. *Computers, Environment and Urban Systems, 6*(27), 585–607. doi:10.1016/S0198-9715(03)00016-4

Ofori, G. (1998). Sustainable construction: principles and a framework for attainment - comment . *Construction Management and Economics, 16*(2), 141–145. doi:10.1080/014461998372448

Olhager, J., & Selldin, E. (2004). Supply chain management survey of Swedish manufacturing firms. *International Journal of Production Economics, 89*, 353–361. doi:10.1016/S0925-5273(03)00029-X

Onguene Essono, L. M., & Onguene Essono, C. (2006). TIC et Internet à l'école: analyse des nouvelles pratiques enseignantes dans les salles de classes d'Afrique noire. In F. Pierre, *Intégration des TIC dans le processus enseignement-apprentissage au Cameroun,* éditions terroir, (pp. 55-75).

Ono, H., & Zavodny, M. (2003). Gender and the Internet. *Social Science Quarterly, 84*(1), 111–121. doi:10.1111/1540-6237.t01-1-8401007

Oreilly, T. (2007). What is Web 2.0: Design Patterns and Business Models for the Next Generation of Software. *Communications & Strategies,* (1), *17*.

Orlikowski, W. J. (1992). The duality of technology: Rethinking the concept of technology in organizations. *Organization Science, 3*(3), 398–427. doi:10.1287/orsc.3.3.398

Orlikowski, W. J., & Baroudi, J. J. (1989). The Information systems profession: myth or reality? *Office: Technology & People, 4*, 13–30. doi:10.1108/eb022652

Orlikowski, W. J., & Robey, D. (1991). Information technology and structuring of organizations. *Information Systems Research, 2*(2), 143–169. doi:10.1287/isre.2.2.143

Orlitzky, M., Schmidt, F., & Rynes, S. (2003). Corporate Social and Financial Performance: A Meta-analysis. *Organization Studies, 24*(3), 403–441. doi:10.1177/0170840603024003910

Osnovni pravci tehnoloskog razvoja Autonomne pokrajine Vojvodine (2007). Novi Sad, Srbija: Izvrsno vece Autonomne pokrajine Vojvodina.

Otteson (2002). *Adam Smith's marketplace of life.* Cambridge, UK: Cambridge university press.

Oudshoorn, N., Rommes, E., & Stienstra, M. (2004). Configuring the Users as Everybody: Gender and Design Cultures in Information and Communication Technologies. *Science, Technology & Human Values, 29*(1), 30–63. doi:10.1177/0162243903259190

Paavilainen, J. (2001). Mobile Business Strategies. *Understanding the technologies and opportunities.* London: Addison-Wesley.

Paehlke, R. (1999). Towards Defining, Measuring and Achieving Sustainability: Tools and Strategies for Environmental Valuation. In E. Becker, & T. Jahn, (Eds.) *Sustainability and the Social Sciences. A Cross-Disciplinary Approach to Integrating Environmental Considerations into Theoretical Reorientation* (pp 243-263). London, UK: Zed Books.

Page, S. E. (2007). Making the difference: Applying a logic of diversity. *The Academy of Management Perspectives, 21*(4), 6–21.

Palm, J., & Ellegård, K. (Eds.). (2008). *Vardagsteknik: energi och IT: forskning om hållbar användning av samhällets IT- och energisystem.* Stockholm: Carlsson.

Palmer-Silveira, J. C., Ruiz-Garrido, M. F., & Fortanet-Gómes, I. (2006). Facing the future of intercultural and international business communication. In J. C. Palmer-Silveira, M. F. Ruiz-Garrido, & I. Fortanet-Gómes, (Ed.), *Intercultural and International Business Communication.* Bern, Switzerland: Peter Lang.

Pandey, N. & Sahay, A. (2008). Towards a New Paradigm of Sustainable Development. *International Journal of Environment and Development,* June, 2008.

Panteli, N., Stack, J., & Ramsay, H. (2001). Gendered patterns in computing work in the late 1990s. *New Technology, Work and Employment, 16*(1), 3–17. doi:10.1111/1468-005X.00073

Paradiso, M. (2003a). Geography, Planning and the Internet: Introductionary Remarks. NETCOM, 3-4, 129–138.

Paradiso, M. (2003c). Geografia e Pianificazione Territoriale della Società dell'informazione. Milano, IT: FrancoAngeli.

Paradiso, M. (2006). Le Logiche della Globalizzazione: gli Studi in Tema di Geografia della Società dell'Informazione. Paper presented at the meeting of Societa' Geografica Italiana, Florence, Italy.

Paradiso, M. (Ed.). (2003b). Geocyberspaces Dynamics in an Interconnected World. NETCOM, 3-4.

Paradiso, M., & Wilson, M. (Eds.). (2006a). The Role of Place in the Information Age: ICT Use and Knowledge Creation. NETCOM, 1-2.

Paradiso, M., & Wilson, M. (Eds.). (2006b). Technology, Knowledge and Place. Journal of Urban Technology, 3.

Parsons, T. (1965). The "normal" American Family'. In S. M. Faber (ed.), *Man and Civilization: The Family's Search for Survival,* (pp. 34-36). New York: McGraw-Hill.

Paulus, P. B. (2000). Groups, teams, and creativity: The creative potential of idea generating groups. *Applied Psychology: An International Review, 49,* 237–262. doi:10.1111/1464-0597.00013

Pava, M. L., & Krausz, J. (1997). Criteria for evaluating the legitimacy of corporate social responsibility. *Journal of Business Ethics, 17,* 337–347. doi:10.1023/A:1017920217290

Payne, A., & Holt, S. (2001). Diagnosing Customer Value: Integrating the Value Process and Relationship Marketing. *British Journal of Management, 12*(2), 159–182. doi:10.1111/1467-8551.00192

Pearce, D., & Turner, R. (1990). *Economics of Natural Resources and the Environment.* Baltimore, MD: John Hopkins University Press.

Pearce, D., & Warford, J. (1993). *World without End: Economics, environment and sustainable development.* New York: Oxford University Press.

Penev, G. (2006). *Stanovnistvo i domacinstva Srbije prema popisu 2002.* Belgrade, Serbia: Statistical office of the Republic of Serbia, Institute of Social Sciences and Association of Demographers of Serbia. SCORE-045384 in FP6 (2007). The ICT Research environment in Serbia. *Strengthening the Strategic Cooperation Between the EU and Western Balkan Region in the field of ICT Research.* Retrieved from http://consultations.score-project.eu/attach/ictcr_rs_en.pdf

Perl, E. *(2006).* Implementierung von Umweltinformationssystemen: Industrieller Umweltschutz und die Kommunikation von Umweltinformationen in Unternehmen und in Netzwerken, *Graz.*

Perry, R., & Greber, L. (1990). Women and Computers: an Introduction. *Signs: Journal of Women in Culture and Society, 16*(1), 74–101. doi:10.1086/494646

Philips, D. (2006). *Quality of Life: Concept, Policy and Practice.* New York: Routledge

Picot, A., Reichwald, R., & Wigand, R. T. (2003). *Die grenzenlose Unternehmung □ Information, Organisation und Management: Lehrbuch zur Unternehmensführung im Informationszeitalter,* (5 rev. ed.), Wiesbaden.

Pillmann, W., Geiger, W., & Voigt, K. (2006). Survey of environmental informatics in Europe. *Environmental Modelling & Software, 21,* 1519–1527. doi:10.1016/j.envsoft.2006.05.008

Pistrui, D., Huang, W. V., Welsch, H. P., & Jing, Z. (2006). Family and Cultural Forces: Shaping Entrepreneurship and SME Development in China. In P. Z. Poutziouris, K. X. Smyrnios, & S. B. Klein (Eds.), *Handbook of Research on Family Business.* Cheltenham, UK: Edgar Elgar.

Pistrui, D., Welsch, H., & Roberts, J. (1997). The [Re] – Emergence of Family Business in the Transforming Soviet Bloc: Family Contribution to Entrepreneurship Development in Romania. *Family Business Review, 10*(3). doi:10.1111/j.1741-6248.1997.00221.x

Pistrui, D., Welsch, H., Wintermantel, O., Liao, J., & Pohl, H. J. (2000). Entrepreneurial Orientation and Family Forces in the New Germany: Similarities and Differences Between East and West German Entrepreneurs. *Family Business Review, 13*(3). doi:10.1111/j.1741-6248.2000.00251.x

Plant, S. (1998). *Zeros and Ones: Digital Women and the New Technoculture.* London: Fourth Estate.

Poggio, B. (2006). Editorial: Outline of a Theory of Gender Practices. *Gender, Work and Organization, 13*(3), 225–233. doi:10.1111/j.1468-0432.2006.00305.x

Pope, J., Annandale, D., & Morrison-Saunders, A. (2004). Conceptualising sustainability assessment. *Environmental Impact Assessment Review, 24,* 595–616. doi:10.1016/j.eiar.2004.03.001

Posch, A. *(2006).* Zwischenbetriebliche Rückstandsverwertung: Kooperationen für eine nachhaltige Entwicklung am Beispiel industrieller Verwertungsnetze, *Wiesbaden.*

Posch, A. (2007). Nachhaltigkeitsorientierte Supply Chains – Voraussetzungen und potentielle Maßnahmenbereiche. In M. Tschandl, & S. Bäck (Ed.) *Einkauf optimieren: Effizienz und Effektivitäten in Einkauf und Logistik,* Kapfenberg, (pp. 84-90).

Poutziouris, P., O'Sullivan, K., & Nicolescu, L. (1997). The [Re] – Generation of Family-Business Entrepreneurship in the Balkans. *Family Business Review, 10*(3). doi:10.1111/j.1741-6248.1997.00239.x

Prahalad, C. K. (2005). *The Fortune at the Bottom of the Pyramid, eradicating poverty through profits.* Boston: Wharton School Publishing.

Prahalad, C.K. & Hart, S. (2002). The Fortune at the Bottom of the Pyramid. *Strategy + Business,* (January).

Preston, A. (2006). Enabling, enacting and maintaining action at a distance: An historical case study of the role of accounts in the reduction of the Navajo herds. *Accounting, Organizations and Society, 31,* 559–578. doi:10.1016/j.aos.2005.03.003

Prugh, T., Costanza, R., & Daly, H. (2000). *The Local Politics of Global Sustainability.* Washington DC: Island Press.

Pycock, J., & Bowers, J. (1996). Getting Others To Get It Right. An Ethnography of Design Work in the Fashion Industry. In *Proceedings of the 1996 ACM Conference on Computer Supported Cooperative Work* (pp. 219-228).

Räsänen, M. (2006). *Om möten i Distansen: Uppfattningar om möten på distans mellan arbetssökande och handläggare* (Technical report, HCI-report series, No. HCI-42). Stockholm: Avdelningen för Människa-Datorinteraktion. KTH Royal Institute of Technology

Räsänen, M. (2007). *Islands of Togetherness: Rewriting Context Analysis.* Stockholm: Royal Institute of technology, KTH.

Räsänen, M., & Nyce, J. M. (2008). Rewriting Context and Analysis: Bringing Anthropology into HCI Research. In S. Pinder (Ed.), *Advances in Human Computer Interaction* (pp. 397-414). Vienna: InTech Education and Publishing.

Rautenstrauch, C. (1999). *Betriebliche Umweltinformationssysteme: Grundlagen, Konzepte und Systeme.* Berlin Heidelberg.

Rayner, S., & Malone, E. L. (1998). Why study human choice and climate change? In S. Rayner & E. L. Malone, (Eds.), *Human Coice and Climate Change. Volume two. Resources and Technology* (pp. xiii-xlii). Columbus, Ohio: Batelle Press.

Reinharz, S. (1992). *Feminist methods in Social Research.* New York: Oxford University Press.

Reisch, L., Bietz, S., & Kreeb, M. (2006). How to communicate sustainable lifestyles to hard-to-reach consumers? A report on the large scale experiment "balance-f". In M. Charter & A. Tucker (Eds.), *Proceedings of the SCORE! Launch Conference "Sustainable Consumption and Production: Opportunities and Threats"*, (pp. 39-52). Wuppertal, Germany: Wuppertal Institute for Climate, Energy, and Environment, in cooperation with the UNEP Centre for Sustainable Consumption and Production (CSCP).

Reisch, L., Bietz, S., & Kreeb, M. (2007). An alternative to "preaching to the choir" - Communicating sustainable lifestyle options to a low interest target group. In *Proceedings of the International Society of Marketing and Development and the Macromarketing Society Joint Conference "Macromarketing and Development: Building Bridges and Forging Alliances"*, (pp. 187-193), June 2-5, 2007, Washington DC.

Rheingold, H. (1994). *Virtual Community: Homesteading on the Electronic Frontier*. Boston: Addison-Wesley.

Rheingold, H. (2002). *Smart Mobs: The Next Social Revolution*. Cambridge, UK: Perseus Publishing.

Richard, O. C., & Shelor, M. (2002). Linking top management team heterogeneity to firm performance: Juxtaposing two mid-range theories. *International Journal of Human Resource Management, 13*(6), 958–974. doi:10.1080/09585190210134309

Richardson, B., & Callegari, N. (2008). WIZZIT. Mobile banking for the poor in South Africa. In Kandachar, P. & M. Halme (Eds) *Sustainability Challenges and Solutions at the Base of the Pyramid: business, technology and the poor*. London: Greenleaf Publishing Ltd.

Riedl, C., Böhmann, T., Rosemann, M., & Krcmar, H. (2008). Quality Management in Service Ecosystems. *Information Systems And eBusiness Management*, (accepted for publication) [Ranking WKWI: B]

Rieffer, R. (2001). *Sociologie des medias*. Paris: Ellipses.

Rifkin, J. (1995). *The end of work: the decline of the global labor force and the dawn of the post-market era*, New York: Putnam's Sons.

Rikhardsson, P., & Welford, R. (1997). Clouding the Crisis: the Construction of Corporate Environmental Management. In R. Welford, (Eds.) *Hijacking Environmentalism. Corporate Response to Sustainable Development* (pp. 40-62). London, UK: Earthscan Publications Limited.

Ritzer, G. (2004). *Enchanting a Disenchanted World*, (2nd Ed.). New York: SAGE Publishers.

Robb, D. (2002). Virtual workplace. *HR Magazine, 47*(6), 105–110.

Roberson, Q. M. (2006). Disentangling the meanings of diversity and inclusion in organizations. *Group & Organization Management, 31*, 212–236. doi:10.1177/1059601104273064

Roberts, J. (2000). From Know-how? Questioning the Role of Information and Communication Technologies in Knowledge Transfer. *Technology Analysis and Strategic Management, 12*(4), 429–429. doi:10.1080/713698499

Robichaud, D. (2006). Steps toward a relational view of agency. In F. Cooren, J. R. Taylor, & E. J. Van every (Eds.), *Communication as Organizing*, (pp. 101-115). London: LEA.

Robins, K. (Ed.). (1992). Understanding Information. Business, Technology and Geography. London: Belhavenpress.

Robins, K., & Gillespie, A. (1992). Communication, Organization, and Territory. In K. Robins, (Ed.), Understanding information. Business, Technology and Geography (pp.145-164). London: Belhavenpress.

Robson, K. (1992). Accounting numbers as "Inscriptions": Action at a distance and the development of Accounting. *Accounting, Organizations and Society*, 685–708. doi:10.1016/0361-3682(92)90019-O

Rodrigues Araújo, E. (2008). Technology, Gender and Time: A Contribution to the Debate. *Gender, Work and Organization, 15*(5), 477–503. doi:10.1111/j.1468-0432.2008.00414.x

Roosens, E. E. (1989). *Creating ethnicity.* London: Sage.

Rorarius, J. (2007). *Existing Assessment Tools and Indicators: Building up Sustainability Assessment (Some Perspectives and Future Applications for Finland).* Helsinki, Finland, Project paper for Finland's Ministry of the Environment. Retrieved from http://www.ymparisto. fi/download.asp?contentid=73204&lan=en

Rorarius, J. (2008). *Assessing Sustainability from the Corporate Perspective: An interdisciplinary approach.* Uppsala, Sweden: Department of Economics, SLU, thesis vol. 530.

Rotmans, J. (2006). Tools for Integrated Sustainability Assessment: A two-track approach. *The Integrated Assessment Journal, 6,* 35–57.

Rouncefield, M., Viller, S., Hughes, J. A., & Rodden, T. (1995). Working with "Constant Interruption": CSCW and the Small Office. *The Information Society, 11,* 173–188.

Rowlinson, S. (2007). The temporal nature of forces acting on innovative IT in major construction projects. *Construction Management and Economics, 25*(3), 227–238. doi:10.1080/01446190600953698

Ryan, C. (1999). Information Technology and DfE: From Support Tool to Design Principle. *Journal of Industrial Ecology, 3*(1), 5–8. doi:10.1162/108819899569359

Sachs, W. (1999). *Planet Dialectics: Explorations in Environment and Development.* London, UK: Zed Books.

Sahay, A. (2006 a). Environmental Management in India: Its Social, Economic and Legal Aspects. *Journal of the Social Sciences, 1*(2).

Sahay, A. (2007). Euro IV Norms in India: Social Historical and Legal Background. *Vikramshila Journal of Social Sciences, 4*(1), January – June.

Sahay, A. (2008). Perception of Pollution and Exprctation from NTPC's Talcher Sper Thermal Plant. In *Progress in Industrial Ecology,* (inderscience, UK), *5*(5/6), 536-554.

Sahay, A. (2009). Organization: Structures, Frameworks. *Reporting Business Management and Environmental Stewardship* (pp. 138 – 154). London: Palgrave Macmillan.

Sahay, B., & Gupta, A. (2003). Development of software selection criteria for supply chain solutions. *Industrial Management & Data Systems, 103*(2), 97–110. doi:10.1108/02635570310463429

Sahay, A. (2004). Indian Corporate Environmental and Financial Performance: Empirical Relationship between them.

Saleh, M. A. E. (2004). Learning from tradition: the planning of residential neighborhoods in a changing world. *Habitat International, 28*(4), 625–639. doi:10.1016/S0197-3975(03)00031-6

Salvato, C., & Melin, L. (2008). Creating Value Across Generations in Family-Controlled Business: The Role of Family Social Capital. *Family Business Review, 21*(3).

Samuelson, O. (2002). IT-Barometer 2000 - The use of IT in the Nordic construction industry. *ITcon - . Electronic Journal of Information Technology in Construction, 7,* 1–26.

Scanzoni, H. J. (1971). *The Black Family in Modern Society.* Chicago: The University of Chicago Press.

Schary, P. & Skjøtt-Larsen T. (2001). *Managing the Global Supply Chain.* Copenhagen.

Schor, J. (1992). *The Overworked American: the Unexpected Decline of Leisure.* New York: Basic Books.

Schreyögg, G. (2001). Wissen, Wissenschaftstheorie und Wissensmanagement. In G. Schreyögg (Ed.), *Wissen in Unternehmen: Konzepte, Maßnahmen, Methoden,* Berlin, (pp. 3-20).

Schulz, W. F., & Kreeb, M. (2005). Cooperate Social Responsibility. In *Umweltmagazin, 35*, Jg., Heft 1, Januar, 70.

Schumacher, P., & Morahan-Martin, J. (2001). Gender, Internet and computer attitudes and experiences. *Computers in Human Behavior, 17*, 95–110. doi:10.1016/S0747-5632(00)00032-7

Schwaiger, B., Wall, A., & Gotsch, P. (2007). Sustainable Holistic Approach and Know-how Tailored to India, The SHAKTI-Project. *Trialog, 92/2007*, 16–21.

Schwartz, B. (2006). Environmental Strategies as Automorphic patterns of Behaviour. *Business Strategy and the Environment . Retrieved from, 2006*. doi:. doi:10.1002/bse.567

Schwarz, E., & Steininger, K. (1997). Implementing nature's lessons: the industrial recycling network enhancing regional development. *Journal of Cleaner Production, 5*(1-2), 47–56. doi:10.1016/S0959-6526(97)00009-7

Schweiger, D., Atamer, T., & Calori, R. (2003). Transnational project teams and networks: making the multinational organization more effective. *Journal of World Business, 38*(2), 127–140. doi:10.1016/S1090-9516(03)00006-3

Scott, A. J. (2001). The Cultural Economies of Cities. London: Sage Publications.

Scott, A. J. (2004). Cultural Product Industries and Urban Economic Development. Prospects for Growth and Market Contestation in Global Context. Urban Affairs Review, 39(4), 461–490. doi:10.1177/1078087403261256doi:10.1177/1078087403261256

Segre, A., Vittuari, M., & Ricci, R. (2005). ICT and rurality, the role of information in the development process of the rural areas of the Western Balkans. *Rural development 2005 - Development of knowledge and information society in rural areas*. Retrieved from http://www.lzuu.lt/rural_development/archive/2005

Sennett, R. (1992). *The Fall of Public Man*. New York: W.W. Norton & Company.

Seuring, S. (2004b). Industrial ecology, life cycles, supply chains: differences and interrelations. *Business Strategy and the Environment, 13*(5), 306–319. doi:10.1002/bse.418

Seuring, S., & Müller, M. (2004). Beschaffungsmanagement und Nachhaltigkeit – eine Literaturübersicht. In M. Hülsmann, G. Müller-Christ, & H. Haasis (Ed.), *Betriebswirtschaftslehre und Nachhaltigkeit Bestandsaufnahme und Forschungs¬programmatik*, Wiesbaden, 117-170.

Seuring, S., & Müller, M. (2008). From a literature review to a conceptual framework for sustainable supply chain management. *Journal of Cleaner Production, 16*, 1699–1710. doi:10.1016/j.jclepro.2008.04.020

Shapiro, C., & Varian, H. R. (1999). Information Rules. Boston: Harvard Business School Press.

Shekhar, S., & Sahay, A. (2007). Firm financial management and Corporate Social Responsibility: A literature review of and perspectives for India. *Journal of Social and Environment Policy, 4*(2).

Sheppard, E. (2002). The Space and Time of Globalization: Place, Scale, Networks, and Positionality. Economic Geography, 78(3), 307–330. doi:10.2307/4140812doi:10.2307/4140812

Shove, E. (2003a). *Comfort, cleanliness and convenience: the social organization of normality*. Oxford, UK: Berg.

Shove, E. (2003b). Converging Conventions of Comfort, Cleanliness and Convenience. *Journal of Consumer Policy*, (26): 395–418. doi:10.1023/A:1026362829781

Shove, E., Lutzenhiser, L., Guy, S., Hacket, B., & Wilhite, H. (1998). Energy and social systems. In E. L. M. Steve Rayner (Ed.), *Human Coice and Climate Change. Volume two*. Resources and Technology. Columbus, Ohio: Batelle Press.

Shrivastava, H., & Venkateswaran, S. (2000). *The Business of Social Responsibility: The Why, What and How of Corporate Social Responsibility in India, Partners in Change*, New Delhi, India.

Sieridis, A. B. (2006). *New ICT Concepts and Projects for the Development of Rural Areas: The project Bio@gro*. Retrieved from http://bioagro.aua.gr/modules/wfsection/html/sideridis_2006.pdf

Simonovic, D. (1976). *Sistem seoskih naselja u uzoj Srbiji*. Belgrade, Serbia: IAUS.

Simons, T., Pelled, L. H., & Smith, K. A. (1999). Making use of difference: Diversity, debate, and decision comprehensiveness in top management teams. *Academy of Management Journal, 42*, 662–673. doi:10.2307/256987

Singh, K. A. (2004). Bo01, A New Ecological Urban District in Malmö, Sweden, A Post-Occupancy Assessment of The Area", Unpublished Masters thesis, IHS-HDM, Rotterdam, Lund.

Sjöström, C., & Bakens, W. (1999). CIB Agenda 21 for sustainable construction: why, how and what. *Building Research and Information, 27*(6), 347–353. doi:10.1080/096132199369174

Slessor, C. (1997). *Eco-tech: Sustainable Architecture and High Technology*. London: Thames & Hudson.

Smelik, A. (2000). Die virtuele matrix. Het lichaam in cyberpunkfilms. *Tijdschrift voor Genderstudies, 3*(4), 4–13.

Smith, C. (1994). The New Corporate Philanthropy. *Harvard Business Review, 72*(3), 105–116.

Snow, C., Snell, S., Davison, S., & Hambrick, D. (1996). Use transnational teams to globalize your company. *Organizational Dynamics, 32*(Spring), 30–32.

Sobotka, A., & Wyatt, D. P. (1998). Sustainable development in the practice of building resources renovation. *Facilities, 16*(11), 319–325. doi:10.1108/02632779810233584

Söderbaum, P. (2000). *Ecological Economics: A Political Economics Approach to Environment and Development*. London, UK: Earthscan Publications Limited.

Söderholm, A. (2006). Kampen om kommunikationen. In Ö. Wikforss (Ed.), *Kampen om kommunikationen - Om projektledningens Informationsteknologi*. Sweden: Research report, Royal Institute of Technology.

Soja, E. (2000). *Postmetropolis: Critical Studies of Cities and Regions*. Oxford: Blackwell.

Sorkin, M. (Ed.). (1992). *Variations on a Theme Park: The New American City and the End of Public Space*. New York: Hill and Wang.

Spence, R., & Mulligan, H. (1995). Sustainable Development and the Construction Industry. *Habitat International, 19*(3), 279–292. doi:10.1016/0197-3975(94)00071-9

Spender, D. (1995). *Nattering on the net: Women, Power an Cyberspace*. North Melbourne, Australia: Spinifex Press.

Spradley, J. P. (1980). *Participant Observation*. New York: Holt Rinehart and Winston.

Squires, J. (2008). Intersecting Inequalities: Reflecting on the Subjects and Objects of Equality. *The Political Quarterly, 79*(1), 53–61. doi:10.1111/j.1467-923X.2008.00902.x

Srinivasan, B., & Mehta, L. (2003). Assessing gender impacts. In H. Becker, & F. Vanclay, (Eds). *The International Handbook of Social Impact Assessment* (161-178). Cheltenham, UK: Edward Elgar Publishing.

Statistical Office of the Republic of Serbia. (1991). *Statistical Yearbook of Serbia 2007*. Belgrade, Republic of Serbia: Author.

Steen, A., & Welch, L. (1998). Dancing With Giants; Acquisation and Survival of the Family Firm. *Family Business Review, 19*(4).

Steiner, G., & Steiner, J. (1991). *Business, Government and Society: A Managerial Perspective* (6th Ed.). New York: McGraw Hill.

Steinle, C., & Reiter, F. (2002). Mitarbeitereinstellungen als Gestaltungsgrundlage eines ökologieorientierten Anreizsystems. *uwf, 10*(1), 66-70.

Sterr. T. (1998). *Aufbau eines zwischenbetrieblichen Stoffverwertungsnetzwerks im Heidelberger Industriegebiet Pfaffengrund*, Heidelberg.

Stevanovic, R. (2006). Migrantsko stanovnistvo Srbije. In G. Penev (Ed.), *Stanovnistvo i domacinstva Srbije prema popisu 2002* (pp. 71- 106). Belgrade, Serbia: Statistical office of the Republic of Serbia, Institute of Social Sciences and Association of Demographers of Serbia.

Stewart, G. L. (2006). A meta-analytic review of relationships between team design features and team performance. *Journal of Management, 32*, 29–54. doi:10.1177/0149206305277792

Stivers, R. (1976). *The Sustainable Society: Ethics and Economic Growth*. Philadelphia: Westminster Press.

Stolp, A. (2003). Citizen values assessment. In H. Becker, & F. Vanclay, (Eds). *The International Handbook of Social Impact Assessment: Conceptual and Methodological Advances* (pp. 231-257). Cheltenham, UK: Edward Elgar Publishing.

Stone, A. R. (1995). *The War of Deside and Technology, at the Close of the Mechanical Age*. Cambridge, MA: MIT Press.

Strack, C. (1995). *Managing cities with the help of telecomunications*. Retrieved from http://www.kpnqwest.at. /give/gv95/straclec.html

Strebel, H. (1995). Regionale Stoffverwertungsnetze am Beispiel der Steiermark. *Umweltwirtschaftsforum UWF, 3*(4), 48–55.

Struch, N., & Schwartz, S. H. (1989). Intergroup aggression: Its predictors and distinctness from in-group bias. *Journal of Personality and Social Psychology, 56*, 364–373. doi:10.1037/0022-3514.56.3.364

Stupar, A. (2003). Informacione tehnologije i razvoj ruralnih podrucja- mogucnosti i ogranicenja. In R. Bogdanovic, & M. Ralevic (Eds.), *Selo u novim razvojnim uslovima*. Beograd, Srbija: Udruzenje urbanista Srbije.

Subramaniam, M., & Venkatraman, N. (2001). Determinants of transnational new product development capability: Testing the influence of transferring and deploying tacit overseas knowledge. *Strategic Management Journal, 22*, 359–378. doi:10.1002/smj.163

Subramaniam, M., Rosenthal, S., & Hatten, K. (1998). Global new product development processes: preliminary findings and research propositions. *Journal of Management Studies, 35*(6), 773–796. doi:10.1111/1467-6486.00119

Suchman, L. A. (1987/1990). *Plans and Situated Actions: The Problem of Human Machine Communication*. Cambridge, UK: Cambridge University Press.

Sustainable Development Strategies New York, (2007, November).

Tajfel, H. (1982). Social psychology of intergroup relations. *Annual Review of Psychology, 33*, 1–39. doi:10.1146/annurev.ps.33.020182.000245

Tajfel, H., & Turner, J. C. (1979). An integrative theory of intergroup conflict. In S. Worchel, & W. G. Austin (Eds.), *The social psychology of intergroup relations*, (pp. 33-47). Monterey, CA: Brooks/Cole Publ.

Takayoshi, P. (2000). Complicated Women: Examining Methodologies for Understanding the Uses of Technology. *Computers and Composition, 17*, 123–138. doi:10.1016/S8755-4615(00)00025-6

Taylor, F. (2006). Coorientation: a conceptual framework. In F. Cooren, J. R. Taylor, & E. J. Van Every (Eds.), *Communication as Organizing*, (pp. 141-157). London: LEA.

The Aalborg Charter. (1994). *Charter of European Cities and Towns Towards Sustainability*. Copenhagen: Denmark.

Thin, N. (2002). *Social Progress and Sustainable Development*. London, UK: ITDG Publishing. UN, (n.d.). *Agenda 21: Chapter 8, Integrating environment and development in decision-making*. Retrieved April 4, 2008 from http://www.un.org/esa/sustdev/documents/agenda21/english/agenda21chapter8.htm

Thomas, D. A., & Ely, R. J. (1996). Making difference matter: A new paradigm for managing diversity. *Harvard Business Review*, (Sep-Oct): 79–90.

Thompson, J. D. (1967). *Organizations in Action*. New York: McGraw-Hill.

Thrift, N. (2000). Communications Geography. In R.J. Johnston, D. Gregory, G. Pratt, & M. Watts, (Eds.), The Dictionary of Human Geography (pp.98-100). Oxford, UK: Blackwell Publishing.

Todd, N. J., & Todd, J. (1993). *From Eco-Cities to Living Machines; principles for ecological design*. Berkeley, CA: North Atlantic Books.

Tofler, A. (1980). *The third way*. New York: Bantam books.

Towley, B., Cooper, D., & Oakes, L. (2003). Performance Measures and the Rationalization of Organizations. *Critical Perspectives on Accounting, 24*(7).

Trauth, M. E. (2002). Odd girls out: an individual differences perspective on women in the IT profession. *Information Technology & People, 15*(2), 98–118. doi:10.1108/09593840210430552

Triandis, N. C., Hall, E. R., & Ewen, R. B. (1965). Member homogeneity and dyadic creativity. *Human Relations, 18*, 33–54. doi:10.1177/001872676501800104

Tsui, A., Egan, T., & O'Reilly, C. (1992). Being different: Relational Demography and Organizational Attachment. *Administrative Science Quarterly, 37*, 549–579. doi:10.2307/2393472

Tuan, Y.-F. (1977). *Space and place: the perspective of experience*. Minneapolis, MN: University of Minnesota Press.

Turkle, S. (1984). *The second self: Computers and the Human Spirit*. London: Granada. ID. (1988). Computational reticence: why women fear the intimate machine. In C. Kramarae (Ed.), *Technology and women's voices* (pp. 41-61). New York: Routledge & Kegan Paul Inc.

UN (1987). *Report of the World Commission on Environment and Development: Our Common Future*. Transmitted to the General Assembly as an Annex to document A/42/427 - Development and International Co-operation: Environment.

UN (2008). Overview of progress towards sustainable development: a review of the implementation of Agenda 21. *Programme for the Further Implementation of Agenda 21 and the Johannesburg Plan of Implementation*. Report of the Secretary-General E/CN.17/2008/2

UN Commission on Science and Technology for Development. (1995). *Missing Links: Gender Equity in Science and Technology for Development*, Canada, International Development Research Centre.

UNCAT-United Nations Conference on Trade and Development (2002). *E-Commerce and development report*. New York: United Nations.

UNDP (2001). *World Development Report*.

UNDSD. "Addressing climate change in national sustainable development strategies – common practices" Background Paper, Expert Group Meeting on Integrating Climate Change into National University of New Mexico Management Presentation, Van Buren, 2006

United Nations (1987). *Report of the World Commission on Environment and Development*. General Assembly Resolution 42/187. Retrieved December 16, 2008.

United Nations. (1997). *The Report of the Economic and Social Council for 1997*. New York: United Nations, Department of Economic and Social Affairs, Division for the Advancement of Women.

Vaara, E., Risberg, A., Søderberg, A.-M., & Tienari, J. (2003a). Nation talk: The construction of national stereotypes in a merging multinational. In A. Søderberg & E. Vaara (ed.), *Merging across borders: People, cultures and politics*, (pp. 61-86).

Vaara, E., Tienari, J., & Säntti, R. (2003b). The international match: Metaphors as vehicles of social identity-building in cross-border mergers. *Human Relations, 56*, 419–451. doi:10.1177/0018726703056004002

Vaara, E., Tienari, J., Piekkari, R., & Säntti, R. (2005). Language and the circuits of power in a merging multinational corporation. *Journal of Management Studies*, 42, 595–623. doi:10.1111/j.1467-6486.2005.00510.x

Valor, C. (2005). Corporate Social Responsibility and Corporate Citizenship: Towards Corporate Accountability. *Business and Society Review*, 110(2), 191–212. doi:10.1111/j.0045-3609.2005.00011.x

Van der Ryn, S., & Cowan, S. (1999). *Ecological Design*. Washington DC: Island Press.

van der Zwan, F., & Bhamra, T. (2003). Alternative function fulfilment: incorporating environmental considerations into increased design space. *Journal of Cleaner Production*, 11, 897–903. doi:10.1016/S0959-6526(02)00161-0

van Knippenberg, D., De Dreu, C. K. W., & Homan, A. C. (2004). Work group diversity and group performance: An integrative model and research agenda. *The Journal of Applied Psychology*, 89(6), 1008–1022. doi:10.1037/0021-9010.89.6.1008

van Schooten, M., Vanclay, F., & Slootweg, R. (2003). Conceptualizing social change processes and social impacts. In H. Becker, & F. Vanclay, (Eds), *The International Handbook of Social Impact Assessment: Conceptual and Methodological Advances* (pp. 74-91). Cheltenham, UK: Edward Elgar Publishing.

Van Zoonen, L. (1991). Feminist theory and information technology. *Media Culture & Society*, 14(1), 9–29. doi:10.1177/016344392014001002

Vanclay, F. (2003). Conceptual and methodological advances in social impact assessment. In H. Becker, & F. Vanclay, (Eds), *The International Handbook of Social Impact Assessment: Conceptual and Methodological Advances* (pp. 1-9). Cheltenham, UK: Edward Elgar Publishing.

Vanclay, F. (2004). The Triple Bottom Line and Impact Assessment: How do TBL, EIA, SEA and EMS relate to each other? *Journal of Environmental Assessment Policy and Management*, 6(3), 265–288. doi:10.1142/S1464333204001729

Varey, R. J. (2006). Accounts in interactions: Implications of accounting practices for managing. In F. Cooren, J. R. Taylor, & E. J. Van every (Eds.), *Communication as Organizing*, (pp. 181-197).

Varney, W. (2002). Of Men and Machines: Images of Masculinities in Boys' Toys. *Feminist Studies*, 28(1), 153–174. doi:10.2307/3178498

Velibeyoglu, K., & Gencel, Z. (2001). *Urban Design in Changing Public Spaces of Information Age*. Paper Presented at 1st International Urban Design Meeting, rendez-vous Istanbul.

Velibeyoglu, K., & Gencel, Z. (2006). *Reconsidering the Planning and Design of Urban Public Spaces in the Information Age: Opportunities & Challenges, Public Spaces in the Information Age*. Paper Presented at 42nd ISoCaRP Congress, Istanbul.

Vidal, P. (Ed.). (2007). European ICT Spatial Policies. Does a political European Information Society Model Exist? NETCOM, 1-2.

Viikki- Science Park & Latokartano Guide. (2004). City of Helsinki Planning Department, Town Planning Division, (pp. 1-10).

Vilhelmson, B. (2002). *Rörlighet och förankring - Geografiska aspekter på människors välfärd* ([]. Göteborg, Sweden: Department of Human and Economic Geography.]. *Choros, No.*, 2002, 1.

Virilio, P. (2000). *Informaticka bomba*. Novi Sad, Srbija: Svetovi.

Vitalis, A. (1944). *Médias et nouvelles technologies. Pour une sociopolitique des usages*. Rennes, France: Apogée.

Vukmirovic, D., Pavlovic, K., & Sutic, V. (Eds.). (2008). *Upotreba informaciono- komunikacionih tehnologija u Republici Srbiji, 2008.* Beograd, Republika Srbija: Republicki zavod za statistiku Srbije.

Waddock, S. (2004). Parallel universes: companies, academics and the progress of corporate citizenship. *Business and Society Review, 109*(1), 5–42. doi:10.1111/j.0045-3609.2004.00002.x

Wajcman, J. (1991). *Feminism confronts Technology.* Cambridge, UK: Polity Press.

Walley, N., & Whitehead, B. (1994). It's not easy to be green. *Harvard Business Review,* (May-June): 46–53.

Wasserman, I. M., & Richmond-Abbott, M. (2005). Gender and the Internet: Causes of Variation in Access, Level, and Scope. *Social Science Quarterly, 86*(1), 252–270. doi:10.1111/j.0038-4941.2005.00301.x

Wathern, P. (1995). An introductory guide to EIA. In P. Wathern, (Ed.), *Environmental Impact Assessment: Theory and Practice* (pp. 3-30). London, UK: Routledge.

Watson, W., Kumar, K., & Michaelsen, L. K. (1993). Cultural diversity's impact on interaction process and performance: Comparing homogeneous and diverse task groups. *Academy of Management Journal, 36,* 560–602. doi:10.2307/256593

WBCSD. (2000). *Corporate Social Responsibility: Making good business sense.* World Business Council for Sustainable Development.

WCDE-World Commission on Environment and Development. (1987). *Our Common Future.* Oxford, UK: Oxford University Press.

Webber, S. S., & Donahue, L. M. (2001). Impact of highly and less job-related diversity on work group cohesion and performance: A meta-analysis. *Journal of Management, 27,* 141–162. doi:10.1016/S0149-2063(00)00093-3

Weeler, D., & Elkington, J. (2001). The end of the corporate environmental report? *Business Strategy and the Environment, 10*(1), 1–14. doi:10.1002/1099-0836(200101/02)10:1<1::AID-BSE274>3.0.CO;2-0

Weick, K. E. (1979). *The social psychology of organization.* Reading, MA: Addison-Wesley Publishing Company.

Weilenmann, A. (2003). *Doing Mobility.* PhD Thesis, Gothenburg Studies in Informatics, Report 28, Gothenburg, Sweden: Gothenburg University.

Weiling, K., & Kwok-Kee, W. (2008). Trust and Power Influences in Supply Chain Collaboration. *Operations Research & Management Sciences, 119*(1), 223–239.

Welch, D., Welch, L., & Marschan-Piekkari, R. (2001). The Persistent Impact of Language on Global Operations. *Prometheus, 19*(3), 193–209. doi:10.1080/08109020110072180

Welford, R. (Ed.). (1998). *Corporate Environmental Management Systems and Strategies,* (2nd ed.). London, UK: Earthscan Publications Limited.

Wellman, B. (2001). Physical Place and Cyberspace: The Rise of Personalized Networking. *International Journal of Urban and Regional Research, 25*(2), 227–252. doi:10.1111/1468-2427.00309

Welsh, D. H. B., & Raven, P. (2006). Family Business in the Middle East: An Exploratory Study of Retail Management in Kuwait and Lebanon. *Family Business Review, 19*(1). doi:10.1111/j.1741-6248.2006.00058.x

Welsh, G. (1996). *A review of Manuel Castells' The Informational City.* Department of Computer Science and Information Systems, American University, Washington, DC.

Wenblad, A. (2001). Sustainability in the Construction Business - A Case Study. *Corporate Environmental Strategy, 8*(2), 157–164. doi:10.1016/S1066-7938(01)00096-3

Wenger, E., & Snyder, W. (2000). Communities of practice: the organizational frontier. *Harvard Business Review,* (January-February): 139–145.

West, C., & Zimmerman, D. H. (1987). Doing Gender. *Gender & Society, 1*(2), 125–151. doi:10.1177/0891243287001002002

WETA. (2004). *Waitakere Municipality web site, Action Plan*. Retrieved October 13, 2004 from http://www.workraft.org.nz/WETA.htm (13/10/2004)

Wiegand, M. (1996). *Prozesse organisationalen Lernens*, Wiesbaden.

Wikforss, Ö. (Ed.). (2006). *Kampen om kommunikationen: Om projektledningens Informationsteknologi*. Sweden: Research report, Royal Institute of Technology.

Wikforss, Ö., & Löfgren, A. (2007). Rethinking communication in construction. *ITcon - . Electronic Journal of Information Technology in Construction*, *12*, 337–345.

Wikipedia (2009). *Sustainable Development*. Retrieved April 30, 2009 from http://en.wikipedia.org/wiki/Sustainable_development

Wiklund, J. (1998), *Small firm growth and performance*. Jönköping, Sweden: Jönköpings Internationella Handelshögskola.

Williams, K., & O'Reilly, C. A. (1998). Demography and diversity: A review of 40 years of research. In B. Staw, & R. Sutton (Eds.), *Research in organizational behavior*, (pp. 77-140). Greenwich, CT: JAI Press.

Willim, R. (2002). *Framtid.nu: flyt och friktion i ett snabbt företag*. Stockholm/Stehag: Symposion. Etnologiska institutionen, Lunds universitet.

Wincent, J. (2006). *On building Competitiveness in strategic SME Networks: Empirical analysis of 54 firms in two networks*. Luleå, Sweden: Luleå tekniska Universitet.
[1] Scandinavian Shipping Gazette (2001) nr 17

Windsor, D. (2006). Corporate social responsibility: three key approaches. *Journal of Management Studies*, *43*(1), 93–114. doi:10.1111/j.1467-6486.2006.00584.x

Wittgenstein, L. (1996). *Philosophical Investigations*. Oxford, UK: Basil Blackwell.

Wolton, D. (1999). *Internet et après? Une théorie critique des nouveaux médias*. Paris: Flammarion.

Woodruff, R. B., & Gardial, S. F. (1996). *Know Your Customer: New Approaches to Understanding Customer Value and Satisfaction*. Cambridge, MA: Blackwell Publishers.

World Commission on Environment and Development. (1987). *Our Common Future*. Oxford, UK: Oxford University Press.

European Comission. (2002). *eWORK 2002-Status Report on New Ways to Work in the Knowledge Economy*. Retrieved from http://europa.eu.int/information_society/topics/ework

Yalciner, O. (2002). Depreme Dayanikli Kentler icin Cografi Bilgi Sistemleri (Geographic Information Systems for Earthquake-Resistant Cities). *Journal of Gazi University . Engineering and Architecture Faculty*, *17*(3), 153–165.

Yamin, M., & Otto, J. (2004). Patterns of knowledge flows and MNE innovation performance. *Journal of International Management*, *10*, 239–258. doi:10.1016/j.intman.2004.02.001

Yin, R. K. (1993). *Case study research: design and methods*. Beverly Hills, CA: Sage Publications.

Young, P. (2004). *Understanding NLP Principles and Practice*. Carmarthen, UK: Crown House Publishing Ltd.

Young, R. (2000). Managing residual disposition: Achieving economy, environmental responsibility, and competitive advantage using the supply chain framework. *Journal of Supply Chain Management*, *36*(1), 57–66. doi:10.1111/j.1745-493X.2000.tb00070.x

Yu, Z., Yan, H., & Cheng, T. (2001). Benefits of information sharing with supply chain partnerships. *Industrial Management & Data Systems*, *101*(3), 114–119. doi:10.1108/02635570110386625

Zahan, D. (1970). *Religion, spiritualité et pensée africaine*. Paris: Payot.

Zander, I. (1998). The evolution of technological capabilities in the multinational corporation – dispersion, duplication and potential advantages from multinationality. *Research Policy*, *27*(1), 17–35. doi:10.1016/S0048-7333(97)00068-1

Zenger, T. R., & Lawrence, B. S. (1989). Organizational demography: The differential effects of age and tenure distributions on technical communication.

Academy of Management Journal, 32, 353–376. doi:10.2307/256366

Ziliotti, M. (2001). L'economia dell'informazione. Bologna, IT: Il Mulino.

Zillig, U. *(2001).* Integratives Logistikmanagement in Unternehmensnetzwerken: Gestaltung interorganisatorischer Logistiksysteme für die Zulieferindustrie, *Wiesbaden.*

Zook, M. A. (2000a). The Web of Production: the Economic Geography of Commercial Internet Content Production in the United States. Environment & Planning A, (32): 411–426. doi:10.1068/a32124doi:10.1068/a32124

Zook, M. A. (2000b). Internet Metrics: Using Hosts and Domain Counts to Map the Internet Globally. Telecommunications Policy, 24, 6–7. doi:10.1016/S0308-5961(00)00039-2doi:10.1016/S0308-5961(00)00039-2

Zook, M. A. (2001). Connected is a Matter of Geography. Networker, 5, 13–17. doi:10.1145/383719.383724doi:10.1145/383719.383724

Zukin, S. (1995). *Culture of Cities.* Oxford, MA: Blackwell Publishers.

About the Contributors

Anette Hallin is a researcher at the Department of Industrial Economy and Management at the Royal Institute of Technology in Stockholm, Sweden where she also teaches. She takes a general interest in the creation of organizational images and the relationship between image making and organizing and has written on the matter, both in journals as well as in books (see for eg "Information Communication Technologies and City Marketing. Digital Opportunities for Cities Around the World", Eds. Mila Gascó-Hernández & Teresa Torres-Coronas). An example of a recent text relevant to the theme of this book is "Managing Death. Corporate Social Responsibility and Tragedy" in the Corporate Social Responsibility and Environmental Management, 16:4.

Dr. **Tina Karrbom-Gustavsson,** PhD, is currently working as Development Director of "Flemingsberg – From Brains to Business", a joint initiative by Stockholm County Council, Huddinge and Botkyrka municipalities, with support from Karolinska Institute, the Royal Institute of Technology and Södertörn University, to promote and coordinate the development of Flemingsberg, one of the most interesting areas in Europe and Stockholm – "the Capital of Scandinavia". Dr. Karrbom Gustavsson has previously worked as Ass. Professor at the Department of Industrial Management at the Royal Institute of Technology in Stockholm, Sweden. Her teaching and research concerns organization and management in general and the management of project organizations in particular.

* * *

Maria Adenfelt, PhD in International Business, is an associated researcher to the Department of Business Studies at Uppsala University and a Senior Management Consultant (e-mail: maria.adenfelt@ gmailcom). She received her PhD in International Business at the Department of Business Studies at Uppsala University in 2003 with a thesis titled "Creating and Sharing Subsidiary Knowledge within Multinational Corporations". In 2004-2005, she was a Visiting Scholar at Stanford University. Her research interests include knowledge creation and sharing in multinational corporations, the strategy role of excellence and the management of transnational projects in the MNC. Her research on transnational projects concerns IT, product development and business projects as well as different aspects of project management such as performance, knowledge management, communication and coordination.

Per Andersson is Professor at the Centre for Information and Communication Research (CIC), Stockholm School of Economics. Since 1993 he has participated in several research projects related to mobile communications, which have resulted in published articles in journals, conference proceedings, and books. In 1996 the focus of these projects changed to user organizations, particularly where related to the term "mobility" (including "mobile organizations"). A recently initiated project involves examining how firms and other organizations co-produce and create values from new mobile technologies and applications. His research projects involve analyzing processes of value creation in this emerging market, focusing on co-production processes in the context of mobility offerings provided by emerging constellations of firms.

Michela Cozza holds a PhD in Information Systems and Organizations from the University of Trento, Italy. She is a member of Research Unit on Communication, Organizational Learning and Aesthetics (www.unin.it/rucola). Her research interests centre on issues addressed by feminist/gender studies and feminist/gender technology studies: in particular, the construction of male and female careers in work settings. She teaches Public Policies-Gender Auditing at the University of Trento-Master in Gender policies in the labor world. Her current research concerns the storytelling and organizational change and the social construction of gender in organizations and scientific-technological sectors, with particular regard to the construction of gender through discursive practices.

Aleksandra Djukic, MSc in architecture and urban planning, is Ass. Professor at the Faculty of Architecture (Department of Urbanism), University of Belgrade. Besides lecturing on "Open Public Spaces- Composition", "Urban design studio" and "Urban Morphology" she has been a research fellow in several national and international research studies and projects. She is currently engaged in the research project, founded by the Ministry of Science of the Republic of Serbia and two COST actions. At the moment she is Vice chief of Department and the member of the Council of the Ministry of Environment and Spatial Planning. She studied at the Faculty of Architecture, University of Belgrade, participated in numerous international conferences, workshops and summer schools and her papers have been published in various national and international professional journals, magazines and monographs and two times won best paper rewards. She is also a project leader in a couple of Master plans and Urban Designs. She is a member of Serbian Town Planners Association. Her professional interests in research and teaching are urban design, urban morphology and transformations, sustainable development and development policies.

Dr. **Georg Dold** has studied economics, business administration and commercial information systems. He graduated from Hohenheim University in Stuttgart, Germany in 1991 and obtained a doctoral degree in 1996. He researched in the area of information management and its application in the area of corporate sustainability management. He developed environmental information systems in various contexts of corporate management. Together with Daimler-Benz Research he developed an IT system to support the holistic evaluation of products and processes in the automotive industry. He currently works in the design and development of IT banking applications and lectures at Potsdam University of Management and Communication and Hohenheim University.

Per Forsberg is a lecturer and researcher at University of Borås. His previous research consists of critical ethnographical studies and critical perspectives on accounting. His ongoing research projects concern the challenge how to make companies and organizations more connected to each other and to the wider community. The focus is mainly on what accounting and different accounting systems do to human relations and what relations they constitute.

Univ.-Prof. Dr. **Hans-Dietrich Haasis** studied industrial engineering, graduated in 1987 and promoted in 1993 to professor at the University of Karlsruhe. Since 1994 he is full professor for Business Administration, Production Management and Industrial Economics at the University of Bremen. From 1998 to 2001 he was Dean of the Department of Economics. Since December 2001 he is director of the ISL - Institute of Shipping Economics and Logistics, Bremen. He is member of the Council of Supply Chain Management Professionals as well as member of the Editorial and Review Boards of „Logistics Research", „OR Spektrum", „International Journal of Operations and Quantitative Management", and the "International Journal of Applied Logistics". He was invited to give guest lecturers amongst others at the St. Petersburg State University of Economics and Finance, and the Hunan University of Changsha, China. In 2003 he received the B.A.U.M.-Environment Award.

Greger Henriksson is a senior researcher at the Division of Environmental Strategies Research at KTH Royal Institute of technology, Stockholm. His research draws on habits and cultural patterns of travel and consumption in relation to environmental issues. He has been employed at the Stockholm University 1996-2001; at the Swedish Defense Research Agency 2002-2004; and at the Royal Institute of Technology (KTH), Stockholm 2004-current. At present he is conducting research on communications respectively waste handling. Earlier he has worked in research programmes on sustainable cities, sustainable consumption (EU-funded) and the introduction of congestion charges in Stockholm. Henriksson holds a MA (1994) and a Ph.D. (2008) in European Ethnology at Lund University. Henriksson has participated at a handful of national and international conferences on sustainability and has also been teaching students of planning at the Royal Institute of Technology in matters of cultural patterns and future study methodology. Earlier work-life experience includes educational tasks and museum work

Mattias Jacobsson is a Lecturer and a PhD candidate at Umeå School of Business, Umeå University. His current research mainly concerns projects, project communication, ICT and coordination issues -- with a present empirical focus on the construction industry. He moreover primarily teaches project management, organizational theory and leadership. Jacobsson has a Degree of Licentiate of Philosophy, a Master of Social Science with a major in Business Administration, a Degree of Master in Information Technology in Business Development and a University diploma in Law. His previous work experiences span from the ICT industry to the insurance and real estate business

Anders Klitmøller, Research Assistant at Aarhus School of Business, Aarhus University. He conducts research on cross-cultural management and innovation. He has published in several Danish journals, and is currently working with Lean Management in a cross-cultural and international perspective.

Prof. Dr. **Martin Kreeb** has studied economics, business administration and environmental management at Hohenheim University and St. Gallen University. He graduated from Witten/Herdecke University , Germany in 1999 and obtained a doctoral degree at Bremen University. Since 2009 he is professor for Sustainable Marketing at the Potsdam University of Management and Communication (UMC) for Applied Science. Kreeb´s research fields are corporate sustainability management, environmental information systems, environmental cost management, sustainable communication and media. Since 2003 he was management director of the research projects ecoradar and balance, financed by the German ministry of research and communication. He gives lectures at Potsdam University of Management and Communication (UMC), Hohenheim University and Tübingen University.

Katarina Lagerström is Associate Professor at the Department of Business Administration, School of Business, Economics, and Law, Göteborg University. She received her PhD at the Department of Business Studies, Uppsala University in 2001 with a thesis titled *Transnational Project in Multinational Corporations*. Thereafter, she worked at the Norwegian School of Economics and Business Administration in Bergen until 2005. Her primary research interests include knowledge development and knowledge sharing in MNCs, global projects as organizational mechanisms and there-to related aspects such as performance, communication, culture, and languages. In the last few years, Katarina has also been part of a research program aiming at increasing the understanding of how the internationalization process of firms unfolds, where her special interest has been in the internal change processes. Katarina mainly teaches within the fields of International Business and Project Management in the Bachelor and Master of Science Programs, as well as in the Executive MBA program.

Jakob Lauring, Associate Professor at Aarhus school of Business, Aarhus University. He conducts research on cross-cultural management and interaction, multicultural teams and diversity management. Specifically he has focused on intercultural communication, knowledge sharing and language use. He has published in international books and journals such as the International Journal of Cross Cultural Management, Journal of Business Communication and International Journal of Human Resource Management. He has received a number of research awards for his work on cross-cultural management and diversity management.

Associate professor **Mikael Lind** (http://www.adm.hb.se/~ML) is connected to the University of Borås, Viktoria Institute, and Linköping University, Sweden. He is the director of the informatics department and the founder of the InnovationLab at the School of Business and Informatics in Borås. He is also the co-founder of the Swedish GSI (Graduate School of Informatics). He is associated to the research network VITS in Sweden and is active in different international communities such as Language/action and Pragmatic Web. He is also part of the management board for the AIS special interest group SIGPrag (www.sigprag.org). His research focus is on Management, e-Service Innovation, Method Engineering, and Research Methods for Information Systems Development. His research is mainly characterized by empirically driven theory and method development, action research, design science, multi-grounded theory, and practical theory. He is also the project manager of the citizen-centric e-service project e-Me – turning the Internet around (www.e-me.se) as well as associate editor for the open journal Systems, Signs & Actions (www.sysiac.org).

Anneli Linde is a Lecturer at Umeå School of Business, Umeå University. Her research is interest in primarily on IT based management systems in multi-project organizations and she has several international publications in this area. Present research focuses on the relation between ICT and sustainability and environmental issues in the construction industry. Linde has a long experience of teaching management and leadership both at Chalmers University of Technology as well as at Umeå University. She has a Master's Degree in Civil Engineering (construction management) as well as several years of work experience from the construction industry.

Henrik Linderoth, PhD, assistant professor at Umeå School of Business, and University of Skövde. His research interest is primarily focused on ICT-triggered change processes and consequences of project based organizing. Linderoth has accomplished studies of ICT use in for example the health care sector and in the building and construction industry. His publications have appeared in for example International Journal of Project Management, Enterprise Information Systems, Journal of Telemedicine and Telecare and Journal of Change Management.

Cecilia Mark-Herbert is an associate professor at the Department of Economics at the Swedish University of Agricultural Sciences. She works as a researcher and lecturer in marketing. Her specialization is in sustainable marketing management and most of her research is related to economic, environmental, social and ethical aspects of agricultural production. In her scientific perspective of marketing management communication holds a central role – as a basis for building relationships in a long-term perspective. Much or her previous research is in the field of R&D Management with a focus on the development of health related food products (so called functional foods).

Holder of a PhD in Sociology from the University of Yaounde I (Cameroon), **Honoré Mimche** worked at the National Center of Education (Ministry of Scientific Research and Innovation) as Senior Researcher. He is currently teaching at the "Institut de Formation et de Recherche Démographiques" (IFORD) of the University of Yaoundé II, where he offers courses on qualititative approaches, Sociology of population, family and household demography as well as field surveys. Since 2006, he is country coordinator of the Network "Family and Schooling in Africa". He is the author of several articles in national and international journals and has been co-author in several scientific documents.

Tohnain Norbert Lengha, has a PhD in Rural Sociology from the University of Yaounde I, Cameroon. He is a researcher with the Cameroon Ministry of Scientific research and Innovation. He is also lecturer of Rural Sociology at the University of Yaounde I. He has published several articles in the domain of sociology in general and Rural Sociology in particular. He has been involved in many research projects funded by both the national and International research organizations. He is currently the coordinator of a project on: *Children living with disabilities and Education in Cameroon: Challenges and perspectives*, funded by the Educational Research network for West and Central Africa.

Elke Perl-Vorbach studied business administration and environmental systems sciences at the University of Graz, Austria, and Lund University, Sweden. Since 2005 she is a scientific assistant at the Institute of Systems Sciences, Innovation and Sustainability Research (former Institute of Innovation and Environmental Management) at the Karl-Franzens-University of Graz. In her dissertation on "Implementing environmental information systems – An analysis on an internal and inter-company level" she investigated informational aspects as enablers for sustainable development in an interorganisational perspective. Further research projects cover sustainable supply chains and recycling networks, sustainability networks, sustainable product service systems, sustainable systems innovation and innovation management for SME.

Jonas Rorarius has professional experience from both the public and the private sector related to sustainable development and corporate social responsibility. His academic background includes Bachelor Degree in International Politics and Economics from the University of Wales, Aberystwyth (UK). He has also a Master Degree in Ecological Economics from the Mälardalen University (Sweden) and a Master of Science Degree in Environmental Science from the Swedish University of Agricultural Sciences and Uppsala University (joint degree). Both master degrees had an interdisciplinary approach focusing on sustainability issues. Jonas Rorarius' current academic interest is related to corporate sustainability issues focusing on environmental communication aspects.

Christopher Rosenqvist is Assistant Professor at the Centre for Information and Communication Research (CIC), Stockholm School of Economics. Since 1996 he has participated in several research projects within the field of media product development. After completing his Ph.D. thesis at the Royal Institute of Technology he joined the Stenbeck Group (Metro, MTG, and Tele2). In 2003 he returned to academia to assume responsibility for media management education at the Stockholm School of Economics. His main research interest is customer-oriented product development, specifically in helping media corporations to react faster to market changes and to seize business opportunities.

Minna Räsänen is a senior researcher in the Human-Computer Interaction group at KTH Royal Institute of technology, Stockholm and a lecturer in Media Technology at Södertörn University. She has studied computer science, holds an M Sc with major in social anthropology (1998) and a Ph D in Human Computer Interaction (KTH, 2007). Räsänen's research draws primarily on investigation and analysis of social practices. She is interested in encounters between people and their acting with and through technology. She has worked in projects where communication environments with audio and video have been established to span and connect geographically distant workplaces (2002-2004, 2006) and in a project (EU-funded), in which communication with and among robots was in focus (2007). Her current research concern in part; social practices of ICT use with explicit objectives of sustainability and in part; work organization and work processes.

Dr. **Arun Sahay**, a hard-core business executive turned an academician has been a champion of both the corporate and academic world. Starting his career as an academician, he turned to the corporate world early in life and wading through both public and private sectors, he made to the top to become the Chairman and Managing Director of Scooters India Limited, a company that was declared a mortuary case only to be given a ceremonial burial. The turnaround of Scooters India Limited, under his leadership, is considered a management miracle both by the practicing managers as well as academicians. In recognition of this, he was made the founder President of the Strategic Management Forum of India. As a mastermind in strategy, he was invited to serve on many Corporate Boards as well as those of the technical and management Institutions. He has been conferred many corporate awards, has written three books, further two are in pipeline and has written several articles in the field of Environmental Management, Sustainability and CSR. He was awarded the Best Researcher of the year 2006 by Management Development Institute.

Susanne Sweet is Associate Professor at Stockholm School of Economics (SSE), with a specialization in sustainable market and marketing research. She is the founder and acting chair of Sustainability Research Group, SuRe, at SSE since 2003 (http://www.suregroup.se). Her research field includes Corporate Social Responsibility (CSR) and Social and Environmental Sustainable Business Development. Current research projects at SuRe includes sustainable business models at the base-of-the-pyramid; markets and marketing of ecological foods; micro finance and poverty alleviation; the role of the financial market in shaping CSR etcetera. She is also a board member of the international research network Greening of Industry Network, GIN (http://www.greeningofindustry.org), with offices in Europe, North America and

Asia. She is chairing the publishing group in GIN and part of the editorial board in the journal Business Strategy and the Environment. She is also acting and founding member of the Nordic research group, NCCR, Nordic Center of Corporate Responsibility (members are SSE, CBS, HSE, BI and Reykjavik University). Her research appears in journals and books, for example: *Scandinavian Journal of Management*; *Journal of Cleaner Production*; *Business Strategy and the Environment.*

Vesna Tomic, BSc in architecture and urban planning, worked in the Institute for Architecture and Urban Planning of Serbia, the Town Planning Institute of Belgrade, and presently working in Ski Resorts of Serbia. He was also a Board Member of Town Planner Association of Belgrade and Association of Architects of Belgrade. She was born in 1964, in Novi Sad, Serbia, and studied at the Faculty of Architecture, University of Belgrade. Worked as a project leader on several detailed town planning designs of housing settlements, town planning projects and studies, and was as a member of the synthesis team of the Master Plan of Belgrade 2021. Also received several awards for her professional accomplishments at the Urban Exhibition, organized by the Serbian Town Planners Association. Her professional interests are in the field of new urban planning ideas and practice, especially relevant to problems of methodology and implementation of new technologies.

Marco Tortora is Adjunct Professor in Economic Geography and Geopolitics at the University of Florence, and in International Business at Kent State University, Florence Program. He is also a faculty member of the Florentine School of Communication and collaborates with the Economics Department at University of Florence. His research interests are: international business and globalization, media and communication, information markets, sustainable development and energy. Current and recent research projects include: sustainable tourism and the marketing of places, new media and business organizations, global and international news agencies. Dr. Tortora also works as a consultant in the communication and marketing industry and has been member of National Committees and Board of Directors for not-for-profit associations in the Media and Education field.

Ozge Yalciner Ercoskun is a research assistant in the City and Regional Planning Department of the Gazi University, Ankara, Turkey. She graduated from the City and Regional Planning Department of the Istanbul Technical University in 1998. She completed her master's studies in the Geodetic and Geographic Information Technologies Department of the METU in 2002. She got her Ph.D. degree from the City and Regional Planning Department of the Gazi University in 2007. She has attended several national and international congresses; summer schools and workshops related to ecological urban planning and geographic information systems. She has written more than 35 papers on sustainable urban design and ecological and smart urban planning, geographic information systems and information technologies. She worked as a researcher in many national and institutional projects. She has awards about sustainability and urban growth, sustainable tourism and is the member of International Sustainable Development Research Society.

Index